NEW TESTAMENT THEOLOGY

Ethelbert Stauffer

NEW TESTAMENT THEOLOGY

Translated from the German by
JOHN MARSH
*Principal of Mansfield College, Oxford, and
sometime Professor of Christian Theology
in the University of Nottingham*

THE MACMILLAN COMPANY
NEW YORK

Translated from the fifth edition of
DIE THEOLOGIE DES
NEUEN TESTAMENTS
published by
W. Kohlhammer Verlag
Stuttgart
First published in English 1955

PRINTED IN THE UNITED STATES OF AMERICA
FIRST AMERICAN EDITION 1956

LIBRARY OF CONGRESS CATALOG CARD NUMBER: 56-11575

To
MY WIFE

PREFACE
to the First Edition

A THEOLOGY of the New Testament has to serve a twofold aim.
It must provide an introduction to the thought world of the New
Testament for everyone who looks to the Bible for an answer to
the ultimate problems of life, whether he be a theological student,
a minister of religion, or an ordinary layman. This is attempted in
the first part of this book, pages 1–257. But a theology of the New
Testament must also be a sort of workman's pass to admit the
student who is working for his college or university examinations
to the workshop of New Testament research. The second part of
this book, with its notes and appendices, is intended to fulfil this
aim.

The number of documents, discoveries and problems that ought
to be considered in a theology of the New Testament has grown so
much in the last thirty years that it would be easy enough to write
a textbook of a thousand pages. But the present work has been kept
down to a few hundred pages only. This is possible because the
reader can now consult Kittel's *Wörterbuch* and its preliminary
lexicographical work can be presupposed. This saves many pages.
In general the author has striven for the brevity of Tacitus in print,
and the precision of a mathematician in thought and has specially
tried to save space, wherever possible, in the references. Thus in
the literary surveys of Part I each work is mentioned once only;
new publications have been preferred to old, because older works
are mostly quoted in them; and details of publication have been
restricted to the date, which is all the student needs to identify a
work in a library catalogue. I have refrained from naming com-
mentaries and articles in Kittel in these literary surveys, since they
can be found without any further assistance. A number of standard
works in numismatics and archeology, together with their abbreviations, will be found on page 352.

I have received many kindnesses in the final editing and preparation of this book. I would like to express my very sincere thanks
to the authorities of the Berlin State Museum, the Directors of the

Vienna Museum of the History of Art, of the Coin Rooms in Berlin, Munich and Vienna, of the Provincial Library in Stuttgart and the University Library in Tübingen, and to their assistants. Also to my esteemed colleagues Hermann Wolfgang Beyer, Friedrich Gerke, Joachim Jeremias, Anton Jirku, Theodor Klauser, Ernst Kohlmeyer, Hans Lietzmann, Stephan Lösch, Wilhelm Neuss, Franz Joseph Peters, Martin Schlunk, Erich Seeberg and Oskar Thulin. But I owe special thanks to Richard Delbrueck and Carl Watzinger, who gave unstintingly of their expert advice. That this book could appear in this form in the middle of a war is due to the initiative of the publisher and the co-operation of his firm.

One of my sponsors I can mention only with sorrow. Franz Joseph Dölger was in his sick-room as he watched the conclusion of this work with his youthful sympathy and his paternal readiness to help. But I can no longer lay the finished book on his over-crowded desk. *Beati mortui, qui in Domino moriuntur. Amodo iam dicit Spiritus, ut requiescant a laboribus suis: opera enim illorum sequuntur illos.*

Bonn   ETHELBERT STAUFFER
  February 1941

PREFACE
to the Second and Third Editions

THE manuscript of this book was finished in the autumn of 1938. Government regulations delayed printing, so that it could not be published before the summer of 1941. The first edition was quickly sold out. At that time, in spite of ceaseless endeavours, it was not possible to obtain permission for a second edition. At the instigation of the 'Evangelisches Hilfswerk' and other Church organizations preparations were started in 1944 in Switzerland to produce a re-print as a second edition; this appeared at the end of 1945, and was distributed by the World Council of Churches.

New Testament scholarship in Germany has not made any recognizable advance since the beginning of the war, and certainly none since its close. So the third edition is confined to the most necessary formal and material amendments. The task of correction has been almost completely taken over from me by my esteemed colleague, Professor Dr Wladimir Szylkarski, and my young assistant, Dr Ernst Bammel, who has also prepared the much-wanted list of abbreviations. To both I would express my warmest thanks.

Bonn   ETHELBERT STAUFFER
October 1946

PREFACE
to the Fourth and Fifth Editions

FOR a long time I have wanted to make a number of amendments, particularly in the chapter on the sacraments, and this revision has given me the opportunity to effect them.

Bonn   ETHELBERT STAUFFER
April 1948

CONTENTS

Part Three
THE CREEDS OF THE PRIMITIVE CHURCH

PART ONE

The Development of Primitive Christian Theology

F. J. F. Jackson and K. Lake, *The Beginnings of Christianity,* I, *The Acts of the Apostles,* 1–5, 1920–33; E. Seeberg, 'Das Christentum', im: C. Clemen, *Die Religionen der Erde,* 1927; H. Lietzmann, *The Beginnings of the Christian Church,* 1949; J. Lebreton and J. Zeiler, *History of the Primitive Church,* 1951; A. Ehrhard, *Urkirche und Frühkatholizismus,* 1935; O. Kuss, *Theologie des NT,* 1937; E. C. Hoskyns and F. N. Davey, *The Riddle of the NT,* 1931; M. Werner, *Die Entstehung des chr. Dogmas,* 1941; A. N. Wilder, 'NT Theology in Transition' (Willoughby, *The Story of the Bible*) 1947; R. Bultmann, *Theology of the New Testament* (E.T.), vol. I, 1952, vol. II, 1955.

Chapter 1

ANTECEDENTS OF PRIMITIVE CHRISTIANITY

Ch. F. Jean, *Le milieu biblique avant Jésus-Christ*, I, 1922, II, 1923, III, 1936; G. F. Moore, *Judaism*, I, II, 1927, III, 1930; A. Schlatter, *Die Theologie des Judentums nach dem Bericht des Josefus*, 1932; J. J. Brierre-Narbonne, *Les Prophéties Messianiques de l'AT dans la Littérature Juive*, 1933; J. Bonsirven, *Le Judaïsme Palestinien au Temps de Jésus-Christ*, I, II, 1935; M. J. Rostovtzeff, 'The Excavations at Dura-Europos', Sixth Season (1932–3), 1936; J. J. Brierre-Narbonne, *Exégèse Apocryphe des Prophéties Messianiques*, 1937; E. L. Sukenik, *Megilloth Genuzoth*, I, 1948, II, 1950; M. Burrows, *The Dead Sea Scrolls*, I, 1950, II, 1951.

THE place that Christianity takes in the history of religions is a matter of continual controversy. Scholars like Deissmann and Reitzenstein have made an exhaustive study of the hellenistic world to discover the roots of original Christianity, while Dalman and Billerbeck have turned their attention to rabbinic literature. Yet both lines of research are hampered by the fact that to a very great extent they have to work with texts written decades and sometimes even centuries after the NT itself. But for the most part these two lines of enquiry provide only contrasts with the NT (Jesus against the Scribes, John against the Emperor cult), only seldom offering analogies with it, and almost never any real affinity.

But the NT itself shows us another way.

The first thing that is bound to strike us on opening a Greek NT is the immense number of OT quotations. Admittedly, there are some quotations from hellenistic literature (I Cor. 15.33; Titus 1.12; Acts 17.28), but they are insignificantly few, and serve only as adornments of style, not as foundation stones of thought. There are also some references to rabbinic traditions, to the Halacha, which was then in process of formation, and once there is a reference to ideas characteristic of the Alexandrian Jew Philo (I Cor. 15.46). But such references are polemic in character and harshly antithetic in substance and in form. By contrast the OT is quoted again and again, almost always as an authority of self-evident validity. Moreover, this appeal to the OT grows rather than diminishes in the primitive Church. So we are brought back to an old truth which, for all its age, cannot be too often repeated (especially in the present position of research): *the OT was the Bible of primitive Christianity*. What the writers of the NT read in the OT became the normal starting-point for their own formulation of ideas. What the OT has to say about God and man and history is presupposed in the NT as something already known and acknowledged. From this fact we have to draw the appropriate methodological consequences: wherever in the NT the presuppositions of primitive Christian theology are not sufficiently self-evident, we must turn in the first place to the OT to find their antecedents.

The OT was translated into Greek in the centuries just before the birth of Christ. Thus appeared the first comprehensive attempt to express biblical ideas in Greek concepts and formulae—the Septuagint (LXX). A certain amount of interpretation, and sometimes of deliberate reinterpretation, is inevitable in such a linguistic process. At the time that the translation was being made, new scriptures were being written or, in some instances, translated, and finally admitted to the traditional stock of holy scriptures. So there grew up the group of books constituting the Apocrypha, which appears in the Greek canon only. The writers of the NT were very deeply versed in the LXX, its language, its text, and its textual tradition. They wrote Greek, and so tended to favour the style of the LXX.[1] They quoted Greek, often in the words of the LXX (Matt. 21.16; 1.23; Justin Dial. 43, etc.; Acts 15.16 f.; Jas. 4.6). Even their freer references to scripture often presuppose the text of the Greek Bible (Acts 7.42, 53; Gal. 3.19; II Cor. 9.7; Heb. 8.2). They ranged exhaustively over the whole corpus of the LXX, including the Apocrypha (Matt. 1.11; Heb. 11.35; Herm.m 1.1.). This is adequate ground for us to take the LXX as our constant aid in understanding the NT, and in the main to use the Greek text for OT references.

Yet there are in the NT a considerable number of 'unidentified' quotations, for whose source we search the LXX in vain (Luke 11.49; John 7.38; Jas. 4.5; I Cl. 8.3). Whence do they come? We cannot often trace their origin accurately (Heb. 11.37; I Pet. 1.12; 3.19; Jdth. 9.14; Barn. 4.3; 12.1; 16.5). Sometimes the sources quoted have been lost since the early Church used them (Herm.v 2, 3, 4). But their form and content provide us with sufficient clues to recognize the native environment from which they must have come (John 8.56; I Cl. 17.6; 23.3 f.). It is the world of post-canonical Jewish national literature that sprang up so prolifically in the centuries round about the beginning of the Christian era (Eccl. 12.12!). From their literary form they are called pseudepigrapha, and from their content *e potiore* they may be classed as apocalypses, for most of them appeared under the authoritative name of some ancient man of God (Enoch, Moses, Elijah, Baruch, Ezra . . .) who is introduced as an apocalyptist to utter predictions relating to the present (*vaticinia ex eventu*) and the future of the actual author. These late apocalypses were not admitted to the OT canon, but in their own day, and demonstrably as late as the Judaism of the third century A.D. they were held in great esteem. The Synagogue of Dura on the Euphrates was excavated in 1933, and in the place of honour on the main wall there were found representations not only of Moses and Joshua, but also of Enoch and Ezra.[2] The effect of apocalyptic upon spiritual development has been decisive for the further advances of OT thought, and for the preparation for that of the NT and this not only in matters eschatological. For the pseudepigrapha are by no means confined to considerations about the end, showing, as they do, a partiality for revelations about the primeval era, about creation and the fall, and about the beginnings of salvation-history. But they think of man's destiny as determining universal destiny. Salvation-history is thus the clue to human history, and human history in turn the clue to cosmic history, embracing heaven and earth and beasts and stars—'universal history' as we might put it in a word. But universal history has all the marks of a conflict.[3] Its main theme is the dramatic conflict between the *civitas dei* and the *civitas diaboli*, from primeval times right through to the end. These are the main theological principles which dominate an otherwise quite diversified pseudepigraphic literature. Accordingly, we propose from now on to use the ambiguous term 'apocalyptic' in a strictly theological sense, and to mean by it that pre-Christian theology of history characterized by the four presuppositions we have mentioned above, viz. the principle of primordiality, of conflict, of eschatology and of universalism.

The most difficult quotations from scripture that we find in the NT are those which, though they cite specific passages from the OT, often with an express introductory formula, and which we can locate in our canon, yet neither say nor contain what the NT writers suppose. (I Cor. 2.9; 10.4; Heb. 11.4; II Tim. 3.8; John

12.41; cf. Luke 24.26 f.). How is this to be explained? The NT
writers used and interpreted these canonical texts in accordance
with a post-canonical tradition. We shall call such scripture references 'traditional'. A mural painting has been found recently in
Dura showing Job and his friends in royal garments. But though
the canonical book of Job tells us nothing of any such royal dignity,
the post-canonical tradition does.[4] Another fresco shows Moses
striking the rock, and the miraculous spring rises in the middle of
the Israelites' camp and immediately divides into twelve streams
flowing to the twelve tents of the tribal chieftains. There is nothing
of all that in Ex. 17.6 or Num. 20.11, though later tradition joined
those passages with Ex. 15.27 and Num. 21.16 to turn the short
miracle story into a long midrash.[5] The painter of the Dura mural
adopts this tradition[6]; he reads the canonical books with the
eyes of his contemporaries. In the same way Paul understands and
uses the OT in the light of contemporary exegesis in I Cor. 2.9; 10.4.
Indeed, there has recently been a discovery—or better a rediscovery
—of a post-canonical text which gives both these passages in a form
midway between the OT and the Pauline wording. This throws
a decisive light upon the contemporary traditions with which Paul
worked (Ch. 22; 58). Such considerations drive us to some fundamental methodological conclusions: In NT study we do not have to
ask how modern exegesis deals with an OT passage, but only how
it was understood by first-century exegesis (cf. Brierre-Narbonne).
But this exegesis is dominated by apocalyptic ideas as the traditional
quotations everywhere make plain.

But the deeper we go into the world of apocalyptic, the more
frequently we meet with reminders of the NT and we realize that
the number of apocalyptic allusions and suggestions in the NT is
much greater than the first indications would lead us to expect.
Indeed, the central ideas of the NT such as the Kingdom of God or
the Son of Man, turn out to be apocalyptic *termini technici*. Further,
the crucial problems of the NT such as the problem of theodicy, of
the world of demons, of original sin, of the Church, the martyrs
(App. I) and the resurrection of the dead have all been dealt with in a
preparatory way by apocalyptic. In fine, the NT writers are rooted,
so far as their exegetical and theological thought forms go, in a living
tradition which comes to them from the OT via the apocryphal literature down to the apocalyptic national writings of their own time. We
need some short term by which to refer to this many-sided theological
tradition, and we will call it, therefore, the 'old biblical tradition'.

These considerations have taken us into the actual spiritual environment which is chronologically and topographically nearest to primitive Christianity. They thus prescribe for us a certain historical concentration, which straightaway frees us from the anarchy so widely associated with the study of the history of religions. We shall have no need to collect 'NT parallels' from all sorts of times and religions, but persistently to enquire about the antecedents of primitive Christianity. It will only be in cases of need that we shall be required, or indeed allowed, to search for analogies in primitive magic, Indian mythology, the Inca religion, late Roman astrology, amoraic scholasticism or gnostic speculations. First and foremost we shall exhaust the old biblical tradition, and only if this source fails us shall we need to seek further, step by step.

The world of apocalyptic ideas is the one in which the NT writers were really at home. This proposition provides the required indication of the place of Christianity in the history of religion, so far as that can be indicated in this introduction, i.e. in the sense of a working hypothesis, which must be verified in the actual working out of our theme. We start with the same pattern of ideas that the NT writers used at the beginning of the gospel.

Chapter 2

JOHN THE BAPTIST

M. Goguel, *Jean Baptiste*, 1928; J. Jeremias, 'Der Ursprung der Johannestaufe', ZNW, 1929; E. Lohmeyer, *Das Urchristentum*, I, *Joh. der Taufer*, 1932; L. Finkelstein, 'The Institution of Baptism for Proselytes', JBL, 1933; J. Kosnetter, *Die Taufe Jesu*, 1936.

The portrait of John the Baptist has undergone a good deal of change in the course of time. Of our oldest sources the Gospels paint an apocalyptic figure, the Greek Josephus a moralist,[7] the Slavonic Josephus a political,[8] Byzantine art an ascetic,[9] and Mandaean speculation a mythological [10] figure. Modern research favours first this and then that element of these traditions. Where can we find the truth about the Baptist?

The thing that we can be most sure about is John's name of 'the Baptist'. This name is not only the subject of unanimous testimony from the synoptic sources (M and Q), but is preserved in both Josephus and the medieval Mandaean texts (Lidz Ginzar. 189). What does this name convey?

First and foremost the name 'Baptist' denotes the use of baptism, which John practised: he 'preached the baptism of repentance unto remission of sins' (Mark 1.4). Baptisms, lustrations, immersions and baptismal baths were quite frequent among the Jews because of their levitical purificatory rites, and at the time of John the Baptist they were widespread throughout Palestine in many forms.[11] Their significance derived from the OT. The man who carried out the purification that God had ordained, and so pleased him, stood in a new relation to the deity, by whom he was accounted purified, though he was not so substantially (cf. Ch. 34). The baptism which John preached was essentially of this thoroughly unhellenistic type—and the most reliable witness to that is the hellenist Josephus when he describes John's baptism as 'acceptable' to God. In the NT John's baptism is of one of repentance. This brings it very near to the baptismal use presupposed in a more or less contemporary writing of Jewish origin, and which would therefore be widespread in the apocalyptic circles where that writing circulated, VitAdEv 4 ff.: The penitent descended into the Jordan until the water reached his neck, and there he waited in silent penance before God's face until heaven showed him mercy.[12] Indeed, in Mark 1.5 we read of a spoken prayer of penitence, though even to that there is a parallel in Sib. 4.162 ff. This summons mankind to repent of their doings in view of the approach of an universal conflagration, and to bathe their whole bodies in streams that never dry up, with hands raised to heaven, praying for forgiveness of their sin. According to Mark 1.4; Luke 3.3 John's baptism is a baptism unto remission of sins. The baptismal message of the Sibylline Oracles likewise closes with an expectation of God's clemency.[13] This secures the original double significance of John's baptism, which is at once both an act of penitence and a promise of the forgiveness of sins.

But when John's fellow countrymen called him 'the Baptist' they meant to emphasize not only the connection with recognized ideas and customs, but also something quite new and unique. What is the peculiarity of John's baptismal sacrament? The name 'Baptist' really tells us. Here for the first time appeared somebody who baptized, who performs baptisms on others. The baptisms which were customary in Judaism at that time, whether traditional or new, were always done by individuals for and on themselves.[14] But here the act of baptism is bound up with an unique historical figure who finds his eschatological mission in the administration of baptism. Just as John was called 'the Baptist' so his baptism was named after him 'the baptism of John' (Mark 11.30; Luke 7.29; Acts 1.22; 18.25).

The Baptist was sent 'to make ready for the Lord a people prepared for him' (Luke 1.17). His baptism is the covenant sign of the new and true people of God. OT prophecy had already joined repentance and 'baptism' with the idea of the remnant (Isa. 4.3 ff.; Ezek. 36.25 ff.; Zech. 13.1 Mas). The Sibylline Oracles also summon both to repentance and to joining the people of God (3.716 ff.). And about this same time the Jewish community itself received new adherents from the Gentile world by baptism, the so-called proselyte baptism. But John's preaching of baptism means more than the sifting or, indeed, the expansion of the old people of God. For him the previous boundaries of the people of the covenant are absolutely of no consequence. To be a son of Abraham means nothing at all. Everyone who wants to belong to the true people of the covenant, even if he be a Jew, needs to accept the baptism of repentance. Moreover no one, not even the Gentile, is excluded from the new people of God (Luke 3.8).

The new people of the covenant which the Baptist prepares for the Lord is the people of the saints of the latter days. John's baptism is an eschatological covenant sign. For John is the herald of the imminent universal conflagration (Luke 3.7 ff.; cf. Sib. 4.171 ff.). According to Matt. 3.2 he is also the forerunner of the coming Kingdom of God. Both these expectations had been intimately connected in Jewish apocalyptic since the time of Daniel. In the same way the Sibylline Oracles pass beyond a threatened world conflagration to a promise of a coming kingdom where God will pour out his spirit upon the eschatological covenant people (4.187 ff.). And it is God himself who is to send both the mortal fire and the quickening spirit. But the Baptist speaks mystically of one mightier than himself who shall come after him with Spirit and with fire (Matt. 3.11 ff.). This is clearly not a reference to God himself,[15] but to a mysterious figure of a Saviour, who will bring the divinely-purposed end to pass (cp. Matt. 3.12 with 3.10). John is the one who prepares the way for the final deliverer (so also John 1 ff.).

Everywhere we find ourselves driven back to apocalyptic presuppositions. But it may be possible to indicate more precisely from which strand of apocalyptic tradition John the Baptist comes. His baptism was a development from the levitical lustrations and baths, and the Lukan report that John the Baptist was of pure levitical stock supports this (Luke 1.5). There is further support in John's account that the Sanhedrin sent priests and levites to him to discuss his person and his baptism with him (John 1.19 ff.). Again, there is support in everything that we know of Zebedee, who was at one time a disciple of John (Ch. 6). So the Baptist comes on the scene as an apocalyptist of levitical stamp. He derives from the priestly tradition, by which we mean that strand of tradition which runs through Deuteronomy, the priestly code, the book of Ezekiel, Ben Sira,[16] the Maccabean corpus,[17] the Testament of the Twelve Patriarchs, a large part of the Jericho scrolls discovered in 1947, the Zadokite Fragment, the Assumption of Moses, etc. According to Deut. 18.15; TestL. 8.12 ff.; TestB. 9.2 the 'prophet' who is to be the eschatological deliverer will be of levitical descent; and in John 1.21 the priestly deputation asks the levite John: 'Art thou the prophet?' In ZF 12.23; 19.10; 20.1 the eschatological deliverer is 'the Messiah from Aaron and Israel',[18] and in John 1.20 the levite John tells the levitical delegation: 'I am not the Messiah.' In the Zadokite Fragment we hear of a teacher who gathers the 'people of the new covenant' about him within a short distance of the desecrated soil of the Holy City,[19] and announces the coming of the Messiah from the house of Aaron, though he dies before the Messiah comes. It is possible that in this sense the Baptist expected a levitical Messiah, and meant to prepare for his coming.

John the Baptist became the herald of Jesus. Did he intend this? The Gospel sources have preserved a somewhat objectionable (and therefore presumably uninvented) story of the Baptist's puzzled question to Jesus: 'Art thou he that should come, or look we for another?' Then comes Jesus' pregnant reply: 'Blessed is he, whosoever shall find none occasion of stumbling in me' (Matt. 11.2 ff.). In light of this Jesus could not at that time have reckoned the Baptist as one of his followers without more ado. But Jesus draws the line of division even more unambiguously and sharply in the saying with which Matthew closes this incident: The Baptist is not the first of the New Age, but the last of the one that is passing, the greatest indeed of these, but nevertheless less than the least in the Kingdom of Heaven (Matt. 11.11). Here Jesus reckons the total number of his followers, but does not count the Baptist among them. The priestly tradition from which the Baptist emerges reckoned on a Messiah of the house of Aaron, out of the tribe of Levi. But Jesus came from the tribe of Judah and the house of David (Ch. 25).

Perhaps this is connected with the Baptist's reserve about Jesus, and with a good many of the tensions of which we read, or which we may deduce, between the disciples of Jesus and those of John (John 3.22 ff.). Down to the middle of the first century A.D. there were disciples in Ephesus who were aware of John's baptism only (Acts 18 f.).

Nevertheless, it is with historical and not only theological justification that the whole NT puts the Baptist at the beginning of the gospel (Acts 13.24), for the history of the baptist movement is the immediate antecedent of Christianity. The apocalyptic ideas of a theology of history achieved formative historical power in the figure of the Baptist, in his baptism and his baptismal message, in his proclamation of the remnant of the last days, and of the divine fire and the heavenly kingdom, and his announcement of the coming of the final deliverer. John 3.26 tells us that Jesus came from the Baptist circle. He certainly received John's baptism, and according to John 3.22; 4.2 f. administered it himself for a time. According to John 1.35 his first disciples came to him from the Baptist. Thus the Baptist is the historical link between pre-Christian apocalyptic and the primitive Church.

Chapter 3

THE WAY OF THE LORD

R. Bultmann, *Jesus and the Word*, 1935; K. L. Schmidt, 'Jesus Christus', RGG,[2] 1929; E. Hirsch, *Jesus Christus der Herr*,[2] 1929; J. Klausner, *Jesus of Nazareth*, 1929; P. Feine, *Jesus*, 1930; K. Adam, *Son of God*, 1934; M. Goguel, *Life of Jesus*, 1933; A. C. Headlam, *The Life and Teaching of Jesus*, 1936; E. Seeberg, *Wer ist Christus?*, 1937; M. Dibelius, *Jesus*, 1949; E. Stauffer, *Neue Wege der Lebenjesuforschung*, 1952.

The nineteenth-century quest for the historical Jesus led to the conclusion that a biography of Jesus is impossible. What remains? His preaching, says Bultmann: his words and works, says K. L. Schmidt. Feine says, his words and works and passion, and Dibelius his somewhat impressionist appearance.[20] The NT has another answer: the Way of Jesus!

The most reliable sayings of Jesus that we have, and also those which are most distinctive of him, are those about the Son of Man (Ch. 24). The Baptist had already spoken of the wrath of God, his kingdom, his people, and of the final deliverer. Jesus is the first to speak of the Son of Man. In doing so he adopts a terminology that goes back to Daniel and beyond into Persian traditions. But Jesus fills the concept with new meaning. He speaks of the Way of the Son of Man, and in doing so refers to his own. The apostles had a solemn respect for the concept of the Son of Man, but their primitive christological theme is identical. By their newly-formed conception of the Way of Jesus they mean in essentials nothing else than an explanation of the sayings about the Son of Man, or the self-inter-pretation which is contained in those sayings of Jesus. Thus the sayings about the Son of Man constitute the basic criterion for the originality of the sayings of Jesus that have come down to us, and for the legitimacy of apostolic christology.[21]

What do the sayings about the Son of Man, and other related traditions, have to say about the Way of the Lord? In the first place they point out, in a threefold fashion, that the Way of Christ is laid out for him. Thus it places a constraint upon him, the hour for it has struck, and its range is vast.

'The Son of Man indeed goeth, as it hath been determined' (Luke 22.22). The Gospels abound in sayings of Jesus which bear witness to this element of constraint, this mysterious 'must' (Mark 8.31). In God's all-embracing providence it is determined that Jesus must enter the home of Zacchaeus, whatever offence that might cause, for salvation had to come to that house that day (Luke 19.5, 9 f.). Jesus had to leave Capernaum because he had been sent to preach the good tidings in all the cities of Israel (Luke 4.42 f.). The 'must' of divine predestination covered every step that Jesus took (John 10.16). But the Way of the Lord, which God had ordained before-hand from the beginning, is foretold in scripture chiefly as a way of suffering (Luke 22.37). The Son of Man treads this way, 'even as it is written of him' (Mark 14.21). The scripture is a guarantee that along this road there are neither accidents nor chances. Like a star that shines in the night sky, Jesus pursues his prescribed path.

'The hour is come; behold, the Son of Man is betrayed into the hands of sinners' (Mark 14.41; cf. John 11.8 f.; Luke 18.31). In this saying we can recognize the secret monitor of the Lord's Way. There are other sayings of the same import: 'Behold, I cast out devils and perform cures today and tomorrow, and the third day I am perfected. Howbeit I must go on my way today and tomorrow and the day following: for it cannot be that a prophet perish out of Jerusalem' (Luke 13.31 ff.). From day to day, from hour to hour, Jesus listened to God's directions about the way to take and the course to follow (Matt. 26.18; John 9.4). In Gethsemane he prepared himself for the fateful hour of his own life, and indeed of all history (Mark 14.35 ff.; John 12.27). He met his captors with the words: 'When I was daily with you in the temple, ye stretched not forth your hands against me: but this is your hour, and the power of darkness' (Luke 22.53; cf. John 7.30). But it is the fourth evangelist who has most consistently worked out that unique freedom from men and freedom towards God in which Jesus listened to the secret promptings about the way he should go (John 4.33; 17.1 ff.): so long as there is need to do so, he speaks to the disciples in parables, but when the hour has come, he speaks openly (16.25, 29). He rejected his mother's suggestion at Cana and said: 'Woman, what have I to do with thee? Mine hour is not yet come.' His concern is entirely with God, and he awaits his prompting before performing the miracle (John 2.4 ff.). His brothers urged him to go up to Jerusalem, but he remained behind: 'My time is not yet come; but your time is alway ready . . . . Go ye up unto the feast: I go not up unto this feast; because my time is not yet fulfilled.' Yet when his brothers had gone, he followed (John 7.3 ff.). The Father had given the Sign!

The sayings about the range of Christ's Way are rooted in a basic conviction that the earthly road trodden by the Son of Man is only a part, albeit the decisive part, of a path that has its origin and termination in a world beyond this. It seems that Jesus supposed that the heavenly existence of the Son of Man reached back into primordial time (Mark 2.10; John 3.13; 6.62; cf. Ch. 24). At all events he spoke repeatedly about the eschatological future of the Son of Man, whom the peoples will see in the end coming with the clouds of heaven and sitting on the right hand of power (Mark 13.26; 14.62). In reality, then, the Way of the Son of Man stretches from the beginning to the end of time. It took some years before this christology of universal history permeated the thought of the primitive Church. The Petrine formulae, which represent the thought of the first generation of Christians, depict Christ's Way as from the baptism to the resurrection and ascension (Acts 10.37 ff.), and Mark gives it precisely the same span in his Gospel.[22] Both longer synoptics take the start farther back, and see the Way of the Lord beginning not at his baptism, but in his becoming man, which is considered the really decisive event (cf. Luke 2.34 ff.; Matt. 2.13 ff!). Indeed, they suggest that the story of Jesus has antecedents which go back to Abraham (Matt. 1.2) and, finally, to Adam (Luke 3.38). At the same time Luke carries the story of his Gospel past the death and exaltation into a second 'treatise', the *acta apostolorum*, which, in fact, are intended to be a report of the *acta domini*, the miracles of the exalted Christ.[23] Meanwhile, the Petrine formulae were developed considerably in the Pauline gospel, where the Way of the Lord comes to be understood in terms of universal history (Phil. 2.6 ff.; Col. 1.15 ff.). In John that understanding attains its fulfilment, for he sees the decisive starting-point no longer, as Mark did, in the baptism, nor yet, as Luke in the birth at Christmas, but in the beginning which preceded creation itself.[24] Similarly, it is no longer just to the passion that he carries the story of the Way of the Lord, neither does he stop with the story of the Church's development from Jerusalem to Rome. He puts Luke's Acts of the Apostles well in the shade with a second 'treatise' entirely his own, viz. the book of Revelation. In this work the same Christ, who appears in John 1.1 ff. at the beginning of all history, now comes as the consummation of all history. The revealing traces of the Way of the Lord illuminate the whole course of universal history.

Nevertheless, the sayings which tell of the preparedness of Christ's Way constitute already in the logia about the Son of Man only the formal presuppositions for the indications of its meaning, which is again summed up under three main heads: the doxological, the antagonistic, and the soteriological understanding of the Way of the Lord.

The doxological understanding looks to the relation between Christ and God. Jesus was sent to reveal and accomplish the *gloria dei* in the midst of a world that, intoxicated with its own self-glorification, hears, and wants to hear, nothing further about God's glory. But he can only fulfil his mission if his own glory means nothing to him, and God's glory all. Hence the Son of Man hath not where to lay his head (Luke 9.58). So he meets the disciples' confession that he is the Messiah with a saying about his passion. And so he goes from the mount of transfiguration on his way of self-renunciation to the cross on Golgotha (Mark 9.12; Luke 9.51). The life of Jesus is an acted doxology (Matt. 4.1 ff.). But God does not fail to answer this self-renunciation (Luke 11.30 ff.). The hour comes when the Son of Man is glorified through him for whose sole glory he lived and died (John 12.23; 13.31 f.). The day is coming when the Son of Man appears in glory and ascends the throne of his glory (Mark 8.38; Matt. 19.28). So the Way of the Son of Man is a road that goes *per crucem ad lucem*.

The antagonistic conception of the Way of Christ considers the relation between him and the devil. The life of the Son of Man is a continual fight with the demonic prince of this world and all who are in his service (Matt. 13.37 ff.; Luke 18.8; 22.48). Jesus 'goes under' in this fight (Matt. 26.53), and that has to be. For it is precisely in 'going under' that Jesus wins his final power over the demonic opponent, and after the premature triumph of the devil the Son of Man is exalted to a position of incomparable power (Matt. 13.41; 16.28). So the Way of the Lord is a road that goes through catastrophe to victory (Luke 12.49 f.; Mark 10.37 f.).

The soteriological interpretation of the Way of the Lord deals with the relation between Christ and the world. 'The Son of Man came to seek and to save that which was lost' (Luke 19.10; cf. Mark 2.10). His life is spent and fulfilled in this service to the world (John 12.23 f.). 'The Son of man came not to be ministered unto, but to minister, and to give his life a ransom for many' (Mark 10.45). He submits to the baptism of those who are burdened with sin, so as to fulfil his mission as the bearer of others' burdens, and so as to remove the sin that burdened many (Matt. 3.14 ff.; John 1.29 ff.). He submits to the death of sin-burdened man, though himself without sin, as the one who bears the burdens of men (John 3.16; 11.51 f.). In this way the sayings about the Son of Man, and the evangelists as they tell of Jesus' ministry to the troubles of the world, show the road that leads through the death of the one to the life of the many. Flesh and blood have not conceived this Way of the Lord, but to the writers of the NT there has been unfolded a purposeful will, which decrees what is divine, not what is human.

This is the threefold meaning of the Way of the Lord. It finds provisional expression in the sayings about the Son of Man. It is sustained throughout the Gospels. It is unfolded and perfected in the christology of the NT (Chs. 26–37).

Chapter 4

PETER AND THE PRIMITIVE CHURCH

P. Battifol, 'Princeps Apostolorum', *Rech. de science rel.*, 1928; B. H. Streeter, *The Primitive Church*, 1929; E. Caspar, *Geschichte des Papsttums*, I, 1930; E. Kohlmeyer, 'Zur Ideologie des ältesten Papsttums', ThStKr 1931; J. Haller, *Das Papsttum*, I, 1934; E. Seeberg, 'Wer war Petrus?', SKG, 1934; E. Lohmeyer, *Galiläa und Jerusalem*, 1936; M. Dibelius, *Rom und die Christen im 1 Jh.*, 1942; E. Stauffer, 'Zur Vor- und Frügeschichte des Primatus Petri', ZKG 62 (1944); H. J. Schoeps, *Theologie und Geschichte des Juden-Christentums*, 1949; H. J. Schoeps, *Aus Frühchristlicher Zeit*, 1950; E. Kohlmeyer, Charisma oder Recht? Vom Wesem des ältesten Kirchenrechts, ZRGK, 1952; E. Stauffer, 'Zum Kalifat des Jakobus', ZRGG, 1952.

Did Jesus intend to found the Church? Roman scholarship answers in the affirmative, and appeals especially to the saying about the rock in Matt. 16.18. Protestant criticism has opposed this position with an over-eager negative, and contested the genuineness of the Matthean passage. But the newer criticism of Kattenbusch and Kohlmeyer has started a counter-movement which is still undergoing development. The idea of the Church (and of the primacy and of the succession as well) are no invention of the early papacy, but in origin older than Christianity itself. That is the position that is becoming more and more recognized today, and which in its essentials is entirely independent of the genuineness or otherwise of the saying about the rock.

John the Baptist had himself gathered together the true sons of Abraham, sealed them with the covenant sign of baptism, and promised them the Messiah who would baptize them as an eschatological covenant community with Spirit and with fire. Jesus referred to the Baptist as his forerunner (Matt. 11.9 ff.), and took over his task of calling and gathering a community together (Mark 2.18 f.; Matt. 4.17; John 4.1 ff., 35 ff.). He took to himself the title of Son of Man, to which, since the days of Daniel and AEn, the concepts of the people and the kingdom of God were inseparably joined (Ch. 24). In this sense, at least, Jesus meant to found a Church: he gathered the new people of God about himself (Ch. 38).

Again like the Baptist, Jesus gathered a circle of disciples about himself, and in particular appointed the twelve apostles, who were in the first place to be messengers to the twelve tribes of Israel, but in the end were to be the beginning of the new people of God.[25] The twelve were the future bearers of responsibility and power in the people of the saints of the Most High, and also the bearers of the responsibilities and duties that this people had to exercise beyond their own borders (Matt. 18.18 ff.; Luke 22.24 ff.; John 20.21 ff.).

As the twelve took a central place inside the people of God, so Peter took a central place within the twelve. He is their spokesman, and in particular, according to the unanimous witness of all the evangelists, the one who utters the decisive messianic confession (Mark 8.29; John 6.68 f.). He is no prize specimen, either as thinker or as a character. He speaks only the 'things that be of men'. Satan himself can talk through him (Matt. 16.23). Our sources speak of these matters with relentless candour. Does that mean they were attacking Peter and his privileged position?[26] On the contrary, the Gospels intend to make clear the unimpeachable basis of Peter's privilege, try to show what kind of a man Peter is and what God has wrought in him—so that no man should glory in his presence:[27] 'Blessed art thou, Simon Bar-jonah: for flesh and blood hath not revealed it unto thee, but my Father which is in heaven' (Matt. 16.17).

The apostle who, by virtue of a divine appointment, already had a central position among the twelve was meant in the days to come to attain a *fundamental* significance for the building up of the people of God. This was promised him, according to unanimous testimony of all four Gospels, by Jesus himself when he gave him the name of Peter (cf. ZKG, 1944). And the risen Christ confirmed that to him by a special commissioning whose essential content is given in Luke 22.31 f. and Matt. 16.18 f., and whose original occasion is preserved for us in I Cor. 15.5 and John 21.15 ff.

We may begin with the saying of Jesus that research[28] has hitherto most neglected, Luke 22.31 f.: 'Simon, Simon, behold, Satan asked to have you, that he might sift you as wheat: but I have made supplication for thee, that thy faith fail not; and do thou, when once thou hast turned again, stablish thy brethren.'[29] What is the basis of Peter's unique position? Not upon any special qualification of the apostle, but upon the intercession of the Lord.[30] The adversary intends to destroy the people of God, and he will have much success. But Jesus appears as an advocate against the accuser.[31] But Jesus does not appear for his followers as a whole, but (and this is the surprising turn in the passage quoted above) for Peter. In praying specially for Peter, Jesus is protecting and delivering the young community as a whole. He prays for fallen Peter so that Peter up-lifted [32] might strengthen his brethren in the faith, and so all attain the goal reserved for them—the Kingdom. [33] So in this one saying it is made clear that the only possible ground of the Church's existence and the very basis of its life is the mediatorial office of Christ, and also that Peter's own mediatorial function is to be co-ordinated with and subordinated to this christological office of the mediator. But Peter's mediatorial office is the prototype of all ecclesiastical office and ministry. We meet here for the first time the basic conception of the divinely-chosen individual as the historical mediator between God and the many (Ch. 51). This is no mere men-tal construction, but the comprehension of a divine principle, which Jesus established at the very beginning of the history of the Church.

Luke 22.31 f. comes from Luke's special source, though it has a parallel, in which the same thing is spoken of in different terms, in Matthew's special source, in the saying about the rock (Matt. 16). Matthew, as Luke, talks of the appearance of the people of God and the destructive attacks of Satan. The difference in Matthew is that the title 'Church' is applied to the new messianic community that had hitherto been reserved to the people of the old covenant (cf. Ch. 38). In both passages the unique position of Peter is indicated, but the distinguishing thing in Matthew is that the traditional imagery of the rock foundation and the superstructure of the Church (cf. Ch. 38) is brought into use and linked with the name of Peter. Finally, the power of the keys, [34] which immediately afterwards is assigned to Peter, does not exclude, but rather includes, the body of the disciples (cf. Mark 13.34). The holder of the keys is the heavenly Christ (cf. Rev. 1.18; 3.7). The earthly administrator of the office of the keys is the Church (cf. Matt. 18.15 ff.; John 20.23). But the actual executor of this office is Peter, who exercises the power of the keys in the name of Christ and in full agreement with the apostolic college. [35]

It cannot escape notice that on any showing Mark, the Gospel of the Petrine circle, contains no report of such sayings. That is the more remarkable in that the primitive Church had two further and impartial witnesses to the special commissioning of Peter, viz. Paul and John. According to I Cor. 15.5 Peter was the first person to receive a *revelation of the risen Christ*. But, in that passage, to receive a revelation is to be given an appointment (cf. I Cor. 15.5, 8 f. with Gal. 1.16; 2.8). Therefore, the emphasis on Peter being the first to receive a revelation is certain to involve a special appointment and a special task. Possibly Mark wrote of this first revelation and commissioning of Peter in his last chapter, now lost (cf. Luke 24.34; EvPt. 14.60). In any case, memories of that special revelation may well have been worked into the narrative of John 21.15 ff., and from that passage we may form some picture of what Peter's special authority was. Just as Peter in Matt. 16.19 received the power of the keys, so here he receives from the hands of the chief shepherd (cf. John 10.11; Mark 14.27 f.; I Peter 5.4) the shepherd's staff, which he must carry till his death. And just as in Luke 22.32b he is made responsible for his fellow apostles, so here he is installed as *pastor pastorum* (cf. John 21.15). Luke and Matthew place the special authorization of Peter in the time before Easter, while Paul and John refer it to the days following the resurrection.[36] But the idea of all these special commissionings is the same: a special responsibility of Peter for the Church that is coming to be.

Did Jesus himself think of a successor to Peter? The idea is not impossible, for the notion of succession was widespread in the realm of biblical practice. God was Israel's heavenly shepherd, though Moses was his representative on earth; and after Moses' death the shepherd's staff was passed on from hand to hand throughout the generations.[37] The mediatorial office which Moses received from God's hand was quite unique. Nevertheless, he appointed Joshua to be his successor,[38] and the historical uniqueness of Moses remained unaffected.[39] But it was essential to have a successor in office, who could ascend his *cathedra*.[40] Consequently the raised chair on which the Ruler of the Synagogue sits is known as *Cathedra Mosis*.[41] Moses received the law from heaven, and handed it on to a long succession of bearers of the tradition that has persisted right down to our own times.[42] Thoughts such as these were very much alive and active in the time of Jesus. But Jesus did count on Peter dying before the history of the Church and of the world attained its goal (John 21.18). Should Peter also have a successor? The uniqueness of Peter's position in the history of the Church is not affected thereby. He is the rock, and he alone.[43] Must not someone take over his office, the shepherd's staff and the keys (cf. Isa. 22.22)? Perhaps Jesus had already talked about such future eventualities (John 21.22)? At all events the congregations in Ephesus [44] and Rome at that time drew these consequences [45] under the influence of pre-Christian concepts, and as early as the first century A.D. were fighting about Peter's legitimate successor.

In the years immediately following the crucifixion Peter was the authoritative spokesman of the primitive Church, and the executor of its first mission (Gal. 1.18; cf. 2.7 f.). There is a large number of fully-reported speeches by Peter in Acts 1–12, which doubtless betray the literary style and mannerisms of Luke. But they contain christological formulae which recur surprisingly often and in such uniformity that they can hardly derive from the author of Acts, but exhibit a quite distinctive literary as well as theological character, and may well go back to Peter himself (Ch. 63). We have referred to these in Ch. 3 as the Petrine formulae, and mentioned their later effects in the construction of Mark's Gospel. We may well, then, believe the tradition of the early Church that presents Mark as the disciple and interpreter of Peter, who has preserved for us in literary form the great apostle's preaching.[46] It is possible that the original form of the passion narrative derived from the Petrine circle. In I Pet., too, Petrine traditions have been incorporated. There is one leading thought which appears in all the texts, which we may trace back with some certainty to Peter or his agency: the knowledge that the story of Christ, that the great historical way of Providence itself, must be understood in relation to its end. It is only from the end that the premundane counsel of God, that God's word in the OT, begets light and meaning (Ch. 51). This is the tremendous intuition of Easter Day, and it points the way forward for the elaboration of primitive Christian theology.

The personal influence of Peter on the general course of things gradually grew less and less. James, the Lord's brother, carried the infant Church with him, filled as he was, fanatic as he was, with one great idea: Jerusalem, the OT *civitas dei* must become the holy city of the new and true people of God, the Christian centre of the growing Church, the headquarters for all questions of church order, mission and teaching, of Christian living and eternal salvation. The city of David had waited in vain to become the political capital of the world (Acts 1.6). But now it could rise to be the world's ecclesiastical capital. That was the audacious idea of this last Davidian and this first curialist.[47] James fought for his ideas with radical, perhaps with unscrupulous consistency. But this fearsome ecclesiastical politician was also passionate in his prayer. Day and night, the tradition has it, he was on his knees in the temple praying for the salvation of his people—till the Jews murdered him. Immediately catastrophe broke out over the holy city for which he had struggled and prayed.[48]

life he shows in his exegetical deductions and in his terminology the effects of his training as a scribe.[51] If then we want to have a true and living picture of the 'pre-Christian' Paul, of his inner and outer world, we shall not need to study Philo, and certainly not Epictetus or Seneca, but rather the men of the school of Hillel, Paul's contemporaries like Johanan ben Zakkai and, most of all, Rabbi Akiba ben Joseph, the most prominent representative of the Hillel school and of the Halacha, the master of scriptural exegesis, the messianic apostle and martyr, the great apocalyptist among the rabbis.[52]

The young scholar, like his father, his teacher and the majority of his companions, joined the order of strict observance of the law, the Pharisaic community, and according to his own evidence was 'as touching the righteousness which is in the law blameless'. But he also very early won the goodwill of the ruling Sadducees, and quite soon made himself useful to them in the struggle with Christianity (Phil. 3.5 f.; Gal. 1.13 f.). The finest evidence for the good testimony that his teacher Gamaliel bore to him, perhaps in the Sanhedrin itself (cf. Acts 5.34), and for the unusual trust which the High Court reposed in him, is the fact that he was sent to Damascus on a special inquisitorial mission (Acts 9.2b). The young Saul was the hope of all serious-minded people. But no teacher of the law of the stamp of Akiba was to be made out of him.

The incident on the road to Damascus made him alter his course. Indeed, he was thrown off his course, just as a vessel taking part in a chase might be swung on to a new course (Gal. 1.23; Phil. 3.7–12). Paul himself has compared his experience on the Damascus road with the calling of the prophets (Gal. 1.15 cf. Isa. 49.1; Jer. 1.5) and has placed it as one of a series with the calling of Peter and the other apostles (I Cor. 9.1; 15.8 ff.). So what took place on the Damascus road was, in fact, a calling, indeed Paul's call to become the apostle to the Gentiles (Gal. 1.16; 2.8 f.). Paul became a Christian and the apostle to the Gentiles at one and the same time. 'Immediately' (Gal. 1.16; cf. Acts 9.20) the Sanhedrin's ambassador enters upon his new service under the authority of God, and began his missionary work in Arabia to the east of Damascus, and thereby made so many enemies so soon that he was in the end hunted and persecuted by the authorities there (Gal. 1.17; II Cor. 11.32; Acts 9.25).[53]

The rabbinic disciple Paul became a Christian, not an hellenist, not even in Antioch, as Bousset maintains by special emphasis on the *kyrios* formula. On any showing the *kyrios* formula goes back to the primitive Palestinian tradition (Ch. 25). And Paul knew the

Churches in Jerusalem and Palestine long before he came to Antioch, and when he began his work in the hellenized capital of Syria, his gospel had long since reached its settled form. What is the essential content of the Pauline gospel?

In his ingenious little book on Paul, Wrede has given a double picture of the Pauline message: essentially Paul belongs to the hellenistic tradition with its teaching about a saviour, but in his discussions with legalism he develops his doctrine from the Jewish-anti-Jewish controversy. It is Wrede's great service to have used this formula to make the actual double-sidedness of Paul's message—which manifests itself in the puzzling variety of Thessalonians, Corinthians, Philipians and Colossians on the one side, and Galatians and Romans on the other—the starting-point of Pauline interpretation. Since his day Pauline research has been dominated by antitheses and alternatives. Christology and theology, Christ mysticism and faith, salvation or eschatology, mysticism or justification—first one and then the other side is emphasized, first there is a mere unrelated co-existence, then a paradoxical dialectic between the two sides. All this tends to confirm rather than to destroy Wrede's dual formula. A new start is needed, and we can find it by taking Galatians and Colossians, the two most differing letters, and putting them strictly in their original historical situations. Galatians is a dialectical controversy-document written at the height of Paul's activity, while Colossians is the most important witness to Paul's later years, his testament from prison, when he is overwhelmed by the multitude of apocalyptic visions. We can then understand the two letters as the two determinative points on the apostle's inner pilgrimage.[54] But beyond that we can think of them as two historically necessary steps towards the unfolding of the secret of Christ, steps that are valid examples for all time.

Is Christ alone sufficient for the saving of the nations, or is some specific form of Christianity necessary beyond that? Paul's answer is 'Christ alone'. James, the Lord's brother, required a special form of Christianity—the Jewish-Christian, even from the Gentiles. An apostolic council was to settle the question, or at any rate clarify the situation. A council of five, consisting of James, Peter and John, Paul and Barnabas, met in Jerusalem behind closed doors (Gal. 2.2). James fought for an unified world Church under the leadership of Jerusalem, while Paul contended for multiform national Churches under the guidance of the Lord,—and maintained his position without compromise (Gal. 2.3 ff.).[55] Yet after the apostolic council some of

James' supporters appeared in Antioch and canvassed their Jewish-Christian ideals, and not only won Peter over to their side, but even Barnabas for a while (Gal. 2.11 ff.). Paul attacked this position trenchantly and on principle: Anyone who proclaims the absoluteness of Christianity, any sort of Christianity, puts an end to the absoluteness of Christ (cf. Ch. 39). It may well be that Peter understood then something of the rightness and the range of the struggle for principles that Paul would have to wage. But James' supporters continued to undermine the work of the apostle to the Gentiles, and very soon came into the Churches of Galatia (Gal. 1.7; 4.17). It was then that Paul wrote his letter to the Galatians, and began the great story of his struggle, repeating his *ceterum censeo*: the cross is all—or nothing! If there be another way of salvation besides the *sola cruce*, then Christ has died in vain. Anybody who adds to the *sola cruce* something else necessary for salvation may seem to be extra pious; but in reality he has fallen to the piety of self-glorification, and invalidates the exclusiveness and sufficiency of God's grace. Our eternal destiny stands or falls with the cross of Jesus Christ alone (Gal. 2.16 ff.). That is the movement of theological concentration that Paul carries out in the letter to the Galatians.[56]

In the years during which the letter to the Galatians took shape, Paul was working in Ephesus, where a man from the town of Colossae in Asia Minor was converted to Christ. His name was Epaphras. He carried the gospel of Christ back to his home town, and there preached the *sola cruce*, so far as he was able and understood it, and he thereby laid the foundations of a Christian Church (Col. 1.7; 2.7). But there was one word which apparently did not appear in the gospel of Epaphras—the word 'cosmos'. So the Colossians readily believed on the Lord Jesus Christ and the redeeming work of the crucified (Col. 1.6; 2.6), but remained afterwards, as they had been before, in the grip of a view of life in which the fulness of God's power was dissipated among a vast number of cosmic powers, who had final authority over the salvation or otherwise of mankind.[57] They saw no connection between the gospel and this view of life, and so it could come about, that the new faith was engulfed by the old anxiety (cf. Ch. 36). In this dangerous situation Epaphras went to his master Paul for help. Paul was a prisoner (in Rome?) at the time (Col. 1.8; 4.1 f.; Philem., 23) and interested himself in his distant Church by incessant prayers and by letters, just as Luther in the fortress at Coburg was interested in the decisions of the distant Parliament at Augsburg (Col. 1.9; 4.16; Phil. 3.2 ff.).

Out of such wrestlings in prayer Paul now writes to the Colossians, and opposes the misleading human 'philosophy' of worldly elemental powers with a *christocentric 'philosophy'* (Col. 2.8). He never thought of coming to terms with the theories and phantasies of this view of life from Asia Minor. But he took the facts and problems of the ancient understanding of the world seriously, and built them into an inclusive theology of history with its centre in the cross. There are cosmic powers. Paul did not contest that, but Christ was before them (Col. 1.15 ff.). Christ bears in himself the whole fulness of the Godhead (Col. 1.19, 2.9), and his redemptive work embraces both heaven and earth (Col. 1.20). The crucified has disarmed the principalities and powers, and led them in his triumphal procession (Col. 2.15). Therefore, Christ is Lord not only of his Church, but of the whole cosmos, and all its powers (Col. 2.10). In this way Paul opened the Colossians' eyes to the world-wide range of the *sola cruce* which Epaphras had preached to them. So in the same spirit that produced the movement of concentration in Galatia Paul developed now an audacious and unheard of movement of expansion (Col. 1.9 ff.). The coming of Christ is either the centre of our conception of the world, or it has no place in it.

Paul had a multitude of important disciples.[58] But none of them really understood Galatians until Luther. The Colossian legacy for the theology of history no one has really entered upon yet. Another figure has appeared to do the work of Paul—John.

Chapter 6

JOHN

W. Larfeld, *Die Beiden Johannes von Ephesus*, 1921; W. Larfeld, *Ein verhängnisvoller Schreibfehler bei Euseb.*, *Byz.-Neugriech. Jahrbücher*, 1922; Ch. Picard, *Ephèse et Claros*, 1922; V. Schultze, *Kleinasien* I, II, 1922–6; W. v. Loewenich, *Das Johannesverständnis im 2 Jahrhundert*, 1932; W. v. Loewenich, 'Johanneisches Denken', ThBL, 1936; H. Preuss, *Johannes in den Jahrhunderten*, 1939; E. Percy, *Untersuchungen über den Ursprung der Johanneischen Theologie*, 1939; O. A. Piper, 'I John and the Didache of the Primitive Church', JBL, 1947.

'John' is the puzzle of the NT, both historically and literarily, in theology and in the history of religion. It is not necessary for us to go into all the many problems of the Johannine question, but we can sufficiently indicate our standpoint as a kind of simple working hypothesis.

In Mark 10.39 Jesus prophesies a martyr's death for the two sons of Zebedee; James and John. From Rev. 11,[59] alongside a reference from Philippus Sidetes and other texts,[60] the conclusion has been drawn that both the sons of Zebedee suffered a martyr's death together in Palestine sometime before 70 A.D. But the evidence is not convincing, and the opposite indications in our sources are overwhelming. Acts 12.2 reports the martyrdom of the apostle James in Judea before the apostolic council took place, whereas John survived that persecution. According to Gal. 2.9 he took part in the apostolic council, though afterwards he fell into the background behind James, the Lord's brother. In all probability he is to be identified with the beloved disciple of the fourth Gospel, who according to John 21.23 must have attained a remarkably great age. Indeed, the tradition of the early Church has it that he was the longest-lived of all the twelve.[61] We also hear of the aged apostle gathering disciples around him in Ephesus in Asia Minor, and that Papias was one of them.[62] It was in Ephesus that the apostle John ended his days as a martyr, 'slain by Jews'—for so a later writer informs us, according to Papias.[63] The striking absence of the article[64] suggests the conclusion that (contrary to Acts 12.2) the perpetrators of this martyrdom were anonymous Jews, not officials, and that it was not an execution, but an incident in a popular rising.[65] But all these observations and pieces of evidences point to the fact that John long outlived his brother James, and that he died a martyr's death in Ephesus as a very aged man.[66] Such a conclusion makes it a chronological possibility to ascribe the Johannine writings (which must all have been written after 70 A.D.) to the apostle John.

John was at one time a disciple of the Baptist (John 1.35) and quite at home in levitical circles and traditions.[67] Early tradition described him as 'the priest wearing the sacerdotal plate' and called him 'John the theologian',[68] i.e. the liturgist (Ch. 43). The aptness of this description is best seen in the emphatic liturgical style, the terminology and imagery of the three main Johannine writings of the NT, John, Revelation and I John. John was written for liturgical purposes; its main sections had in all probability long been used in worship before the aged John committed the whole corpus in literary form to the care of his congregations.[69] This liturgical purpose is the best explanation for the dramatic construction of the book,[70] its liking for sacramental formulae, the solemn 'I' sayings,[71] the Johannine 'we', the veiled references to the beloved disciple, the enigmatic expression of 19.35 and finally, for everything that has been said about the 'unhistorical' character of the fourth Gospel and against its apostolic origin. The book of the Revelation is admittedly not an esoteric book of ritual from a Jewish-Christian sect in Asia Minor.[72] But it is not to no purpose that it contains more hymns than any other book in the NT, while its framework and its formal language[73] are unmistakably liturgical in character (Ch. 50). Much recent criticism has emphasized that I John is much more a public than a private letter.[74] That accords quite well with the liturgical structure of John and Revelation (cf. esp. I John 1.1 ff.). But these three main Johannine writings are not just related in style, they are related in theology, too, and they form with II and III John an individual group of writings which stand out very clearly from the other literature of the primitive Church. In view of all this we have sufficient ground to ascribe these five writings to a common author of remarkable individuality and great significance, and to identify him as the apostle John.[75] But we know from John 21 that the apostle had disciples who published his Gospel and enlarged it with an appendix. So we must be prepared to find that these disciples also took part in the transcription, the shaping and the publication of the writings themselves. It is impossible to separate the work of the Master from that of the disciples in detail, indeed we cannot recognize traces of any individual disciple in the work. So we have to sum up our position in the cautious thesis: the Johannine writings of the NT are to be ascribed to the apostle John or to his influence. In this sense we shall allow ourselves to speak of 'John' whenever a reference is made to the author of a Johannine text.

If the apostle John came from levitical circles and spoke the language of liturgy, we shall expect to find him specially familiar with the *priestly tradition*. The Johannine writings confirm this expectation.[76] We cannot easily deal with the relationship of John to the priestly tradition until we deal with individual problems (e.g. Ch. 13). But the points of contact are so numerous, in terminology, in formal language, and in style, that we shall have to confine ourselves to a particular group of writings, and even then select only the most characteristic comparisons. Appendix II sets these out in tabular form. Nowhere in rabbinic literature[77] or in pre-Christian hellenism is there a writing or a tradition which can exhibit anything like the same wealth of Johannine parallels. That fixes the place of John in the history of religion. He belongs to the priestly tradition. The Baptist's disciple John is an apocalyptist cast in a levitical-liturgical mould, just as Gamaliel's disciple Paul is an apocalyptist cast in a rabbinic-dialectical mould.

But to settle the question about his standing in the history of religion is but to decide a very peripheral matter. For the more fundamentally we come to know the Johannine theology the more clear it becomes that John is a 'thinker' *sui generis*. He stands unique and alone not only in the ancient world, but also in the primitive Church. That is why he is so hard to understand. And another difficulty arises. Paul was interpreted again by Luther, but John has never had a complete interpreter. In full awareness of all the doubts thus engendered we shall seek to find some clues to this puzzle of Johannine theology.

The starting-point of Johannine thought is a theological metaphysic. And like the rest of the thinkers of primitive Christianity, he has his theology of history. But he considers that the presuppositions of all history consist in certain primary data, divinely given, which take their effect in the course of history. Hence he starts the Prologue with a saying about Being[78] before he mentions Becoming at all.[79] In the same way the historical proposition in John 8.44 that 'the devil . . . stood not in the truth' is based upon the ontological assertion that 'there is no truth in him'.[80] All Becoming is an explication of Being. But 'from the beginning' (I John 1.1; 3.8; John 8.44) the world of Being, from which the historical order derives, is twofold (Ch. 13). The world of Light and Life, of Truth and divine Glory (John 1.14; 7.18) stands over against a world of darkness and death, of mendacity and self-glory (I John 2.21; 4.6). 'The light shineth in the darkness; and the darkness apprehended it not'—that is the basic theme of a history which embraces heaven and earth, from first days to last (John 1.5). So the twofold character of the beginning of history must needs affect the close of history: Light and darkness will finally separate (John 5.19–20). History is *krisis*, is separation of souls.

The decisive event of this history occurred when the primordial heavenly *Logos* became incarnate in the terrestrial mode of existence. (Ch. 26). Even in the story of the *Logos* on earth the nature of Christ is the real origin of all that he does, and the basis of all that happens round the figure of the Son. Hence the one great question that must be put to Jesus is: 'Who art thou?'; and hence, too, Jesus must always answer: 'I am . . .' He brings Life, because he is the Life. His Way is nothing other than the explicatory revelation of his nature. 'We beheld his glory' (John 1.14). In this sense the Evangelist records in John 1–12 the historical unfolding of his glory, while in 13–17 he tells of its mysterious veiling. But the historical road that Christ treads must also and especially spell crisis, separation of souls (John 3.19; 6.60 ff.; 12.31). Those who are of the truth hear the voice of the *Logos* (John 18.37), but the world does not know him (John 1.10). So stupidity, growing hostility and deadly enmity is the world's answer to the Son's revelation of his glory, and the incarnation ends in the passion (John 18–20; Rev. 12).

The coming of Christ is no isolated event for John, but an historical fact which reaches out beyond itself to an explication at the end of history. Those whom the Father has given to the Son are possessed of eternal life, and the Son will raise them up at the last day (John 6.39). 'The hour cometh, in which all that are in the tombs shall hear his voice, and shall come forth; they that have done good, unto the resurrection of life; and they that have done ill, unto the resurrection of judgement' (John 5.28 f.). That is the terse consistent, unambiguous eschatology of the Gospel. The Evangelist can afford to be brief, for instead of detailed pictures of the future he can announce the promise of the Spirit, who 'shall declare unto you (the disciples) the things that are to come' (John 16.13), and this promise is fulfilled in Rev. (Rev. 1.1, 10). Just as a rocket regularly discharges itself in ever new cascades of fire, so the basic vision of the Apocalypse unfolds itself step by step in ever-new series of visions (Rev. 4). The Johannine Christ unveils his glory in seven wonders. Revelation abounds in the number seven. Seven seals are opened (Rev. 5 f.). The seventh vision is unveiled in seven trumpet visions (Rev. 8.1 f.), and the seventh trumpet vision again is disclosed in the visions of the seven bowls (Rev. 10.7; 15.1, 7; 21.9). In this way does the coming of Christ undergo its eschatological explication in revelations, wars and catastrophes—until the final *krisis* comes, the final separation of souls (Rev. 20.7 ff.; 22.11 ff.; cf. Ch. 56 f.).

Chapter 7

IGNATIUS

J. v. Walther, 'Ignatius von Antiochen und die Entstehung des Frühkatholizismus', *Festschr. f. R. Seeberg*, II, 1929; V. Schultze, *Antiocheia,* 1930; C. H. Kraeling, 'The Jewish Community at Antioch', JBL, 1932; R. M. Grant, 'The Odes of Solomon and the Church of Antioch', JBL, 1944.

The most independent of all John's disciples was Ignatius of Antioch who died a martyr's death under the same emperor, Trajan, as the aged apostle.[81]

His *Logos* christology is Johannine. But while Ignatius is the first and most faithful interpreter of John 1, he developed the idea of the *Logos* with the aid of the parabiblical tradition to a cosmic doctrine of the creative Word of God. The creative Word once broke the silence of primordial time as now the saving Word has broken the silence of history (Eph. 19.1; IgnMg 8.2; Rom. 8.2). Any man who has received this Word understands its silence too! (Eph. 15.1 f.).

Ignatius' sacramental realism is also Johannine. Ever since Christ descended into the waters of his baptism, all water has been consecrated and purified (Eph. 18.2). The bread of the eucharist is the flesh of Christ and, therefore, the medicine of Life (Eph. 20.2). So the mystery of the sacraments is the beginning of a metaphysical penetration and renewal of the whole cosmos, a harbinger of the final eschatological transformation.

The liturgical standpoint of Ignatius is also Johannine. In the tradition of the primitive Church he is held to be the originator of the antiphon, and the creator of an eucharistic ritual,[82] certainly not without some basis in fact. In any event his epistolary style, his sacramental formulae, his Christmas hymns (Eph. 19), his ascriptions to Christ all betray the episcopal liturgist,[83] who developed Christian worship into an eucharist celebration of Christ's glory. Ignatius is thus an early witness, perhaps the originator of the impressive liturgical movement which goes on right through the old Syrian Church.[84] Indeed there is something of the spirit of the future eastern Church blowing through his prayers.

Ignatius is primarily a liturgist, only secondarily a theologian. He began to write at the time when he was deprived of his priestly offices in preaching and conducting services, i.e. on the long journey that led him to his fight with the beasts at Rome under the guard of his military band of ten men. On that journey he wrote his famous Letters to the Churches of Asia Minor,[85] a last bequest of a dying man to his Church, a last hymn to his 'God' Jesus Christ, for whom he was going to die. *Moriturus te salutat!*

Chapter 8

THE SPIRIT AND THE VISAGE OF THE 'THIRD RACE'

A. v. Harnack, *Mission und Ausbreitung des Christentums in den ersten drei Jahrhunderten.* I. 114, 1924; R. Delbrueck, *Spätantike Kaiserporträts,* 1933; H. P. L'Orange, *Studien zur Geschichte des spätantiken Porträts,* 1933.

'The way of the Greeks and the Jews is old. But you are . . . a third race.' Thus Peter in a late apocryphal writing to the Greeks.[86] The Christian gospel, in fact, painted new features into the visage of ancient man.

The portrait of Ezra (?, cf. Neh. 8.5 ff.) in the Synagogue of Dura-Europos on the Euphrates 245 A.D. (cf. C. Du Mesnil du Buisson, *Les Peintures de la Synagogue de Doura-Europos,* 1939, p. 92 ff.) strikes our eyes as that of a *vir desideriorum.* This picture is the only representative, perhaps the only really high quality artistic self-portrait of later Judaism so far known to us. Law and hope—these were the ·two great forces which dominated the Jewish people of those times. Loyalty and longing went to form those features.

How different is the head of Pericles on the marble bust in the Vatican—the classical self-portrait of classical Hellas.[87] Here man has found perfection within himself. Harmonious self-development of the personality, proportion in thought and will, in looks and suffering, heroic affirmation and impassionate mastery of fate, autarchy within the borders of humanity—that is the secret of the Periclean age, its 'noble simplicity and quiet greatness' (Winckelmann). Yet the infinite, the terrifying, the demonic was only banished, only bound time and again, but never really conquered in the Grecian world. The historians paint vivid pictures of the jealousy of the Gods deeply affecting world history; in the midst of the review of his enormous army and fleet Xerxes bursts into tears as the realization of the vanity of all earthly glory overcomes him like some enemy in the rear. Croesus paid for the wrongs of his ancestors in the fifth generation.[88] The problem of wrongdoing was paramount. The tragedians took up the theme. Aeschylus emphasized the ineluctable fate of the guilty as well as the remorselessness of the avenging spirits. Yet this broad-shouldered old Marathon warrior, this Atlas who wanted to save the world from collapse,[89] remained unbowed. But Euripides flinched under the problems.[90] Aristotle saw the import of tragedy in the quickening of fear, the trembling that comes in face of a fate that awaits us all, before a guilt from which none is guiltless.[91] So the hellenistic world dawns, the twilight of the Greek gods, the decay of classical man. Like some subterranean convulsion the approaching upheaval announces itself in the marble features of Medusa Ludovisi (cf. A. Springer-P. Wolters, *Die Kunst des Altertums*,[10] Verlag Alfred Kröner, Leipzig, 1915, fig. 814). Or possibly the figure may be that of a sleeping Erinus (cf. AeschEum 123 f.): ὕπνος πόνος τε κύριοι ξυνωμόται δεινῆς δρακαίνης ἐξεκήραναν μένος—Cp Helbig II p. 95 ff.; other interpretations in S. Ferri, *Bolletino d'Arte* 1931, p. 106 ff.). In a portrait of a poet from Naples (an hellenistic portrait of an unknown Greek of the third/second century in J. J. Bernoulli, *Griech. Ikonographie* II, 1901, p. 161 f.) the eruption has come, and the crisis occurred. This man knows that threefold evil of which Leibniz later wrote: the *malum morale*, the *malum physicum* and the *male metaphysicum*—and he can hardly bear the burden of his knowledge.

The Romans marched through the world with firm step. The idealized head of Caesar from the Naples National Museum is known everywhere—an unreflective, self-possessed, almost 'Prussian' soldier's face.[92] Such a man knows nothing of problems, but only recognizes tasks. His gaze is fixed on distant horizons unknown to Pericles. But who knows, by contrast, the ageing Caesar from his lifelike image on a coin? (cf. Bernoulli, p. 149 f.; 294.59; L. Curtius, RömMitt, 1932, p. 229, for a silver coin of the year of Caesar's death.) Here is the same face, though darkened with a world-despising melancholy. What happened to Greek man between Pericles and the late poet is here compressed into the inner experience of a single person. The aged Caesar has the same eye as the Roman at the height of his manhood, but now he looks cassandra-like into a future over which he has no more control. It is as if he sees with his inner eye the long succession of his heirs, and recognizes in their faces the downfall of his nation and empire. This is how the first emperor bade farewell to his work. 'The best men in this world go about in silent despair' (Kierkegaard).

The picture of Paul in the Domitilla catacomb is completely different. This is one of the oldest representations of Paul that we possess, probably the nearest to a real portrait, and in any event the most congenial [93] (a head of Paul, Cat.S. Domitilla, *c*. 375, cf. Wilpert, K.T., 179.2—E v.Dobschütz, *Der Apostel Paulus*, II, 1928, p. 13 f.). This shows us the visage of the Third Race. This Paul was perhaps once a man of the stamp of Ezra (of Dura), though something has happened to him. His spirit has been struck as by lightning (Gal. 1.15 f.; cf. Dante Par. 33.141), and now he flames like a torch that lights up the whole world till it is consumed in its own fire. This man shares the ancient's fear (II Cor. 7.5); he knows the ultimate extremes and devilries of existence as profoundly as any hellenistic artist or thinker, indeed perhaps more profoundly than them all. But he not only knows to the full the age-long tragedy of everything human; he has a message besides, and is himself a messenger of a divine revolution that has already taken place: 'The old things are passed away; behold, they are become new' (cf. II Cor. 5.17). This man sees the world's twilight, and how the ageing nations, empires and cultures sink into the shadows. He sees it more clearly, perhaps, than Caesar himself, for his eye is keener through his knowledge of scripture. But for him the glory of the Lord has risen high above the shadows of death, and he sees nations walking in that light and kings in the brightness of its uprising (cf. Isa. 60.1 ff.; Rev. 21.24; I Thess. 5.4).

Paul is like an apocalyptic trumpet blast. The Ambrose of the Milanese mosaic is like the quiet, soft singing of the liturgy [94] (St Ambrose Victor in *coelo aureo Oratorium in S Ambrogio*, Milan, 400–450, in Wilpert, M. T., 84.1.—Neuss p. 95; 142) *Te Deum laudamus. Gloria mundi* counts for him no longer; *gloria dei* is everything to him. 'And for the sick and dying we beseech thee, Lord have mercy upon us.' Care for his own personal life no longer counts for him, but the service of the world's suffering means everything. This is what those teachers look like 'who passing through the valley of weeping make it a place of springs, and are covered with many blessings' (cf. picture of Peter, catacomb of S Gennaro, Naples, fifth century, in H. Achelis, *Die Katakomben von Neapel*, Verl. K. W. Hiersemann, Leipzig, 1936, T 42).

When a new race is born, the women have to be changed. There are plenty of marble statues of Patrician women of Rome leaning on their chairs in gestures of inimitable grandeur. [95] The praying woman of Vigna Massimo is likewise a woman of the world, as her bearing and clothes indicate (cf. 'Head of Praying Woman,' catacomb of Vigna Massimo, Rome, 300–350, Wilpert, K. T., 176). But she has not been immortalized in marble. Her features, an unknown woman painted by an unknown hand, are simply recorded in a catacomb fresco. For she was outlawed from the palaces, and became a solitary in the catacombs, a stranger on the earth (I Pet. 2.11; Heb. 11.13; Herm.s 1.6). Her face is typical of the women who were hounded and tortured, interrogated and disrobed as a spectacle to amuse the rabble (I Cor. 12). She remained strong, though she suffered untold things. Both strength and suffering can be seen in her face. 'We were accounted as sheep for the slaughter. Nay, in all these things we are more than conquerors' (Rom. 8.36 f.). The woman at prayer in the Therme Museum has already become a conqueror (cf. 'Head of Woman at Prayer', sarcophagus n 455 in the Thermen Museum at Rome, fourth century, in O. Thulin, RömMitt., 1929, p. 246). Her eyes are withdrawn and look far beyond the sorrows of this world, and while the flames blaze up, her mouth is moved to speak by the Holy Spirit.[96] Her face is looking upwards: 'Lift up your heads, because your redemption draweth nigh' (cf. Luke 21.28).

We conclude our references to these representations with the huge statue of the emperor in Barletta. The unveiled vision of the last woman meets us again here, though this time the eye is turned from private life into world history. Pericles can see no farther than the frontiers of a city state; Caesar's vision was confined to the horizons of this world; but the glance of this Byzantine emperor stretches far into the beyond. The *ultima ratio* of ancient anthropology was the apotheosis of man, and the climax of leadership in the later ancient world was found in the cult of the emperor. But in this statue the process of divesting man—even the emperor—of divinity is complete. The divine He is all; the human I nothing. Yet authority in the *civitas terrena* begets an apocalyptic power and majesty in the service of the *civitas dei*. This man who is emperor by the grace of God holds in his left hand a globe; but in his right he clasps the labarum.[97]

What has happened to all these men? They are gripped by a revolutionary idea of history, filled with an apocalyptic theology of history, in which God and the devil, creation and sin, law and promise, Christ and emperor, primordial time and the end of the world, and last but not least themselves, the men and women of the third race, have their appointed place. They know where they are going. For they know the ways of God through the history of the universe. The NT has opened their eyes.

PART TWO

The Christocentric Theology of History in the New Testament

K. v. Hofmann, *Der Schriftbeweis,* I, II, 1857 ff.; B. Weiss, *Die Religion des NT*² 1908; K. Heim, *Die Weltanschauung der Bibel,*⁶ 1931; E. Stauffer, 'Prinzipienfragen der neutestamentlichen Theologie', ELKZ, 1950.

Section One

CREATION AND FALL

Chapter 9

THE PRIORITY OF THE DIVINE

K. Müller, *Die göttliche Zuvorersehung . . . nach . . . Paulus,* 1891;
J. Dalmer, 'Zur paulinischen Erwählungslehre', *Festschr.
F. H. Cremer,* 1895; W. Lütgert, *Das Problem der Willens-
freiheit in der . . . Synagoge,* 1906; H. E. Weber, *Das Problem
der Heilsgeschichte nach* R 9–11, 1911; H. Windisch, 'Die
Verstockungsidee in M 4', 12 ZNW, 1927; K. Galling, *Die
Erwählungstraditionen Israels,* 1928; E. v. Dobschütz, 'Prae-
destination', ThStKr, 1934; P. Adams, *The Call of Israel,*
1934.

THE fundamental datum of any theology of history, the primary
fact to which the old biblical tradition always goes back, is not sin,
nor even creation, but the absolute priority of God over the whole
world and its history: the priority of the divine. The God of the
great prophets proclaims 'I am the first' (Isa. 41.4; 44.6; 48.12).
And even hellenistic Judaism kept to the same idea in its own
understanding of its task: 'Let us begin with God.'[98] The old biblical
tradition articulates this priority of the divine by using four terms:
foreknowledge, predestination, preparation and pre-existence.

'All things were known unto him or ever they were created'.
Those are the words in which the divine priority is expressed in
Ecclus. 23.20. But such foreknowledge is more than the foresight
of a far-seeing man who can discern future developments, more
even than the knowledge a prophet has when he receives a revelation about future events from sources outside himself. The formulae
that are used about divine foreknowledge seem rather to pass as by
some necessity into an assertion about divine predestination. 'From
the beginning of the creation of the earth unto the end of the age . . .
all things he hath foreseen and foreordained.'[99] In its wider meaning
this predestination applies to everything that happens (Job 28.24

ff.). Nothing can happen without God willing it, willing it to happen so, and willing it beforehand.[100] But there is a narrower meaning which applies only to the volitional life of creation. No course of action that results from the exercise of will can be carried through in any part of the world unless God has willed it in its completeness beforehand [101] (TestG. 4.7). God called his prophet Jeremiah, as he called his servant in Second Isaiah while he was yet in his mother's womb (Jer. 1.5; Isa. 49.1; cf. ParalJer. 9.24 ff.). He even chose his servant Moses and marked him out from the very beginning of the world (AssMos. 1.14; 12.6 f.). And even when man says 'no' to God, God's will lies behind it; and the impenitence of the self-glorifying sinner is a divinely conditioned impenitence. That, at any rate, was what the prophets taught (Isa. 6.9 f.; Ex. 9.16; Ch. 45).

The idea of predestination in the old biblical tradition very soon became concentrated in the idea of a *preparatio* in virtue of which the future itself, and even the final gifts of salvation (Job 28.27; AssMos. 1.14) were got ready beforehand (PsPhil. 26.13). From here it is but a short step to the doctrine of the heavenly *pre-existence* of those decisive figures who were to appear in the course of salvation-history (IV Ezra 8.52). It is against this background that pre-Christian apocalyptic speaks about the pre-existence of Wisdom, of the Son of Man, and of the heavenly city (Job 28; Ecclus. 24; AEn 42; 48; 62.7; SBar 4). Similarly there was an old rabbinic saying that recognized 'ten things' as having been made on the evening of the day before God rested from his work of creation: the rainbow, Moses' staff, the tables of the law, the fountain in the desert, manna, hell-fire, etc.

The writers of the NT took up the inheritance of the old biblical tradition at all these points, and developed them further.

Jesus himself presupposed the traditional ideas about fore-knowledge and preparation, and probably also that of pre-existence as both known and valid (Matt. 13.35; 25.34; Luke 11.20 ff.; John 3.13; 8.58). It was clear to him that the road he must tread as Messiah is nothing other than the carrying through in actual historical events of the predestined purpose of God (Ch. 3). But what affected him in particular was the prophetic proclamation of the dark side of what was predestined. He took up the saying of Isa. 6.9 when he said 'Those men who do not belong to the *numerus praedestinatorum* shall see and not perceive, and shall hear and not understand, lest they should turn again, and it should be forgiven them' (Mark 4.11 f.).[102]

The *Petrine formulae* are based on the sayings about the Way of the Lord, and they see the divine predestination decisively illustrated in the passion: Jesus was betrayed and crucified 'by the determinate counsel and foreknowledge of God' (Acts 2.23; cf. 4.28).

When Paul talks about his own calling he uses the language of the OT prophets. God, who separated him from his mother's womb, was the one who had called him and led him step by step upon his way so far (Gal. 1.16 ff.; 2.2). But what the apostle says of himself is true, *mutatis mutandis* of everyone who is called according to the same purpose. For those whom God foreknew, he also foreordained and called, and them he has also promised to justify and to glorify (Rom. 8.28 ff.). From Jesus' saying about those who are hardened Paul develops the negative side of his concept of election, the teaching about hardening (Rom. 9.17 ff.). This brings us to the first enunciation of an all-inclusive understanding of history and its twofold way (Rom. 9.22 f.). 'Jacob I loved, but Esau I hated', says the Lord—even before they were born or were able to do good or evil (Rom. 9.11 ff.). So Paul's concluding sentence is: 'So then he hath mercy on whom he will, and whom he will he hardeneth' (Rom. 9.18). The Petrine traditions about divine providence are also developed in Paul in the particular form of the ideas of preparation and pre-existence. God has already, and long since, prepared his final blessings for the elect, and has shown them to the initiated in secret revelations (I Cor. 2.9 f.; cf. Gal. 3.19; 4.26). Finally, the bringer of salvation himself, the Messiah, has had a living and active existence in the heavenly world long before he began his earthly life (I Cor. 8.6; 10.4; Phil. 2.6; Col. 1.16). The Christian disciple and the apostle are alike in being predestined; but the Christ is pre-existent.

This christology of pre-existence is carried further by John,[103] who also develops Paul's idea of a double predestination along the lines of the priestly tradition and his own metaphysical ways of thinking (Ch. 6; 13). The result is something very much like a double preparation of the whole creation (cf. Rom. 9.22 f.). In the beginning God divided light from darkness—and the final purpose of history is to bring about an irrevocable separation of the powers' of darkness from those of light (John 1.4 f.; Rev. 22.14 f.).[104]

But when is the fundamental decision, the basic preparation made which has its expression all through history? 'Before the earth was, before ever the heavenward portals were standing . . . when the foundations of paradise were not yet laid . . . before the years of the present were reckoned'—this is the answer given in IV Ezra 6.1 ff. It is in this sense and against this background that the NT uses the formula 'from the foundation of the world'.[105] Before the foundations of the world were laid, God had appointed his Son to the work of salvation (John 17.24; I Pet. 1.20) and chosen his people that were to be saved (Eph. 1.4). Predestination is not just something that originates with the world, it is premundane. This is to give a supralapsarian answer to the question about the time of predestination. God did not first conceive his purpose for history after the fall. He must have decided on it long before man fell—for the divine plan of predestination is older than creation itself.

What makes the NT put so much emphasis on to this question of time? At first sight it would seem to be due to no more than merely systematic interest, or indeed a purely speculative one. Late Jewish apocalyptic shared with the NT in having no hesitation about engaging in such speculations. But it was their acknowledged interest in salvation-history that gave the writers of the NT their concern with the concept of predestination (cf. I Cor. 2.12). The knowledge referred to in Rom. 8.28 ff. is the basis of the 'persuasion', the certainty of salvation that finds expression in Rom. 8.38. So whenever the NT refers, as it frequently does, to foreknowledge, predestination, preparation or pre-existence, it is really building on the priority of the divine. Nothing less is at stake than the absolute temporal priority of God's purpose and rule over all the events of history—over the one great event to which we give the name of history. God is the first one; therefore he must, as he will, have the last word (Isa. 41.4; IV Ezra 6.6). God is the one who was, and the one who is to come; therefore he is the one who is, the Almighty.[106] So throughout the whole of history there runs like a golden thread a purpose that is single and irrevocable. God is the *alpha* and the *omega*, the beginning and the end (Rev. 1.8; 21.6).

If God's predestination was decided on long before the fall; if his will is operative in every act of every human will; if he even quickens and wills even man's self-glorifying rejection of himself, then it follows that God has also willed the fall. Accordingly, the NT teaches the supralapsarian *praedestinatio gemina*. This is a hard saying, a *logos skleros*. But Paul is quite clear about it (Rom. 11.22). But must God be thought unjust on these grounds (Rom. 3.5; 9.14, 19)? Paul refused to water down the harshness of such a predestination in the way that the *epigoni* have wanted to do ever since. He would have nothing to do with a speculative theodicy, nor would he allow an impertinent argument with God.[107] It is God himself who will 'justify' his horrible decree[108] by the inconceivable way in which he guides and controls the whole history of the universe (Rom. 11.25, 33).

So in the NT what follows from the basic conception of the priority of the divine is an exposition of a complete theology of history. God has been pleased to do his work in history in two ways, with his right hand and with his left.[109] But both these work 'together', as Paul puts it (Rom. 8.28; TestG. 4.7). The two hands work mutually together until the final work is accomplished in which the great 'master' will be truly praised (Rom. 11.36; Jude 25). Then what is the outcome of every new step which God takes in history? A new revelation of the glory of God! What is the outcome of the darkest deed of history which the inscrutable God decided on before all time and which he has brought to pass in this time— the hidden revelation of his glory in the cross? The *glorificatio dei!* So what must we conclude as the purpose of his premundane decree, the goal of all predestination and preparation? The final revelation of his glory both in his elect and through all creation, a revelation so compelling that every creature shall bow down before the glory that shall be revealed (Ch. 59).

Chapter 10

THE CREATIVE WORD

F. M. Lagrange, 'Vers le logos de St Jean', Rev. Bibl., 1923; A. B. D. Alexander, 'The Johannine Doctrine of the Logos', ExT, 1924–5; H. Leisegang, 'Logos', Pauly-W XIII, I, 1926; F. Aber, 'Memra und Schechina,' *Festschr. d. J. Th. Seminars Fraenckelscher Stiftung*, II, 1929; O. Grether, *Name und Wort Gottes im AT*, 1934; V. Hamp, *Der Begriff 'Wort' in den aramäischen Bibelübersetzungen*, 1938; L. Dürr, *Die Wertung des göttlichen Wortes im AT und antiken Orient*, 1938.

God spake, and the world began. That is what we read in both the OT and the NT. The formula makes certain historical presuppositions, and it has been left for Lorenz Dürr finally to clarify them with the necessary thoroughness. The theological presuppositions of the formula will become clear to us if we can make plain what are the triple relationships of Word, and Act and Will in biblical thinking.

God's Word is alway active in character.[110] Just as the rain comes down from heaven and does not return there until it has made things grow, so the Word which issues from God's mouth does not return empty, but accomplishes his commands and fulfils his will (Isa. 55.10 f.). The Deliverer-King of Isaiah 11.4 smites the earth with the word of his mouth, and in Wisd. 18.15 God's commandment is a sharp sword in the hands of the true *Logos* (cf. IV Ezra 13.9 f., 38). Similarly, according to Rev. 1.16, a sharp two-edged sword issues from the mouth of the Son of Man, and the Word of Rev. 19 smites God's enemies with the sword that 'proceedeth out of his mouth'. [111] Wherever God's Word penetrates nothing remains the same but things are turned upside down, sometimes by something new being started, sometimes by something old being ended, but for the most part by both of these happening together. For his Word is living and powerful and sharper than a two-edged sword.[112]

But God's action is always verbal in character. His acts are a testimony to his greatness, a proclamation of his will, both in the OT (Job 38 ff.; Wisd. 13 ff.) and in the NT (Rom. 1.18 ff.). God speaks in the very act of creation itself. And as he brings his works to pass he speaks to those who have eyes to see and ears to hear, and it is only the man who sees in those works the utterances of God that really knows and alone understands the Creator's work. In the same way God's action in history is a conversation with mankind (I Cor. 1.21; Ch. 18). Even the story of Christ has to be understood as a Word which God addresses to his creation. This is the reason why the Word made flesh says what he has to say to the world very much more through the actions he does, through the miracles he performs, and by the path he treads. He not only has the Word of eternal life; he is himself the Word of God (Ch. 29). That is why his entry into human history is the decisive intervention of God who, with his two-edged sword, precipitates the crisis of history (Matt. 10.34; Luke 22.36 ff.; John 3.19 ff.).

But why is it that the biblical writers lay so much stress on this idea of the Word? God's Word is concerned to effect his will, and he acts through his Word precisely because he has a will to effect and means to effect it. God wills his will, and by his Word and work calls into existence a creature with a will; and then by means of words and actions he is constantly calling on the volition of his creature. When God made the world he spoke and 'commanded' the dust to bring forth Adam.[113] He called the times into being, and they came; he once called the dead from the depths of the earth, and immediately they stood before him.[114] Every creative act of God is such a calling forth. That is the basic theological presupposition of what the Bible understands by the creative Word of God.

God created the world by his Word.[115] 'There was darkness and silence before the world was made. And the silence spoke, and the darkness shone—and the commandment sounded forth . . . .'[116] Primitive Christianity, understandably enough, retained this idea of the creative Word (II Cor. 4.6), but laid special stress on a consequence that rendered any metaphysical dualism impossible: creation out of nothing. 'God calls that which is not into being.'[117] God always creates by his Word. That principle applies logically not only to the act of creation itself, but also in a derived sense to the preservation of the world, and in the fullest sense to the continuation of the work of creation in history (Psa. 32.9; Jdth. 29.6; 16.14). Using the same formula about creation as Paul, SBar. 48.8 says: 'Thou callest into existence through thy Word that which is not.' And the silence of the primordial darkness, out of which God's creative Word once spoke, is repeated *mutatis mutandis* in the oppressive silence of the darkness in Egypt: 'A stilly silence enwrapped all things' until at midnight God's 'all-powerful Word' leaped from heaven 'bearing God's unfeigned commandment' like a stern warrior carrying a sharp sword.[118] God's Word, powerful in history, bears and determines the destiny of the world. II Pet. 3.5 ff. uses the same sort of language about cosmic history. God preserved the world until the catastrophe of the flood by the agency of his Word, and by his Word he preserves it still until the catastrophe of the end.

But alongside the idea of the creative Word of God there appears in the Pauline tradition another theme, at first almost unconsciously: God created the world by his Christ. Everything comes from God— but through Christ (I Cor. 8.6; Heb. 1.10).[119] God has also made the aeons through his Son (Heb. 1.2). The pre-existent one (Ch. 9) is the reflection of the divine glory, the first-born of every creature, the image that God stamps upon his creation (Col. 1.15 f.; Heb. 1.3). God always creates by his Christ. Through him he sustains the world, through him he continues its history. In this context Paul says not only that everything was created in Christ, but also that it had its 'origin' in him.[120] One of Paul's disciples goes even further in Heb. 1.3 and roundly declares that Christ 'upholds all things by the word of his power'. Christ is creation's life-giver! And in I Cor. 10.4 the pre-existent one is again identified with the rock which kept the Israelites from dying from thirst as they wandered through the wilderness.[121]

God creates through his Word. God creates through his Christ. In Paul both these statements appear alongside each other pretty well unconnected. It was John who brought them into an unity with his far-reaching identification of the creative Word with the creative Christ.

John begins his story of Christ with a story of creation *in nuce*. But he starts his creation story by quoting some words from the beginning of Gen. 1, the very words which gave the book its name in the Hebrew OT: 'In the beginning . . .' (John 1.1).[122] In view of the emphasis given to this reference we have to understand the idea of the *Logos* which John introduces into the self-same sentence, in terms of the story of Genesis and of its later development. This means interpreting the *Logos* as the creative Word of God that issued from the divine silence before the foundation of the world, that was the mediator of creation, and has ever since been the controller of history (John 1.3 ff.). But this *Logos* is Christ. I John speaks in exactly the same way of the *Logos*, which was from the beginning and is identical with the Son. Rev. 2 describes Christ as being the beginning of the creation of God.[123] Indeed, Revelation applies epithets to him which are frequently used of the creator God himself—'Beginning and end', 'first and last', '*alpha* and *omega*' (Rev. 1.17; 22.13). The Word (*Logos*) became flesh and tabernacled amongst men (John 1.14). But it was only a tabernacling. The world refuses to hear his voice (Ch. 29). So the *Logos* folds his tent up again and returns to his Father's mansions (John 10.18; 14.2 f.)[124] But the *verbum dei* will return to earth once more (Rev. 19.11 ff.; 21), armed like the all-powerful and destroying *Logos* in Wisd. 14.18 ff. Full many a time God has sent forth his Word. The *Logos* in Rev. 19 is God's Word for the end of history.

So in the Johannine understanding of the *Logos* the traditions of the earlier *Logos* theology and of the later christology meet—and the idea of the *Logos* becomes a sort of motto for the golden thread that runs through the whole of creation and right through the history of the world. It is understandable that from now on this great idea should dominate the Christian conception of creation, and even more, determine the Christian understanding of God's creative and reigning power[125].

Chapter 11

THE WORK OF CREATION

W. Caspari, 'Imago Divina Gn 1', *Festschr. f. R. Seeberg*, I, 1929;
H. Junker, 'Der Mensch im AT', *Festschr. f. F. Tillman*, 1934;
J. M. Nielen, 'Der Mensch in der Verkündigung des Evangeliums', ditto; R. Meyer, *Hellenistisches in der rabbinischen Anthropologie*, 1937; H. Engelland, *Die biblische Lehre von Schöpfung, Fall und Offenbarung*, 1938.

The Greek speaks of a cosmos, and for him the reality of the world is absolute. But the Bible speaks of a creation. With this one word the reality of the world is reduced to a relative order that goes back to, and points back to, an absolute subject who has established the world as an object over against himself, precisely as, and precisely as long as, he pleases. In this way a stop is put to both the alternatives between which the Greek had wavered despairingly. Man ceases being caught up in the stream of events (Wisd. 13.5; Rom. 1.25), but he also stops sinking into complete despair (Rom. 8.39; Col. 1.15 f.; 2.8 ff.). Everything that can be meant by the word 'world' is seen, in the light of the all-inclusive idea of creation, to be in the last resort conditional.

In essentials the early Church thought about the course of creation in the way that Genesis tells the story.[126] God gave his own judgement on the result of creation, and man has to confirm it: 'very good' (Gen. 1.31; cf. Isa. 40.26; Wisd. 1.14). God is the 'friend of all living' (Wisd. 11.24 ff.; cf. Job 38 f.). He feeds the ravens and protects the sparrows (Psa. 146.9; Luke 12.6). God loves little children (Psa. 8.3; Matt. 21.16; Mark 10.14 ff.); he delights in a man's strength (Job 40 f.; Judg. 14 f.); he is pleased with plenteousness (Psa. 64; 103). Nor is that all. God loves beauty[127]. He delights in the unfolding of the lily, beside which even Solomon is the veriest amateur (Matt. 6.28 ff.).[128] So the glory of God is revealed all through his creation (Psa. 138.14; Ecclus. 18.4; Rom. 1.20). It is in the light of such an understanding of nature that the biblical writers think of the purpose of God's work in creation. God has revealed his kindness and greatness there so that his creatures should praise his name in thankfulness and awe.[129] So the heavens declare his glory, along with the cherubim, the seraphim, the ophanim and all the hosts of heaven,[130] and, too, the inhabitants of the earth bend the knee before his glory. He has made the whole creation for his own name's sake. To him be glory for ever and ever (Did. 10.2 ff.).

On the last day of his creative work God made man, the crown of his labours. It is not only Genesis (1.26), but also apocalyptic thought that emphasizes the view that God's creative acts do not proceed from the higher to the lower, but in the opposite and upward direction. And Paul expressly argues against derogatory theories of man's origin in some alien nature.[131] Admittedly, man is made from the dust, and is earth born and earth bound (I Cor. 15.47; Gen. 2.7; Ecclus. 17.1; Lev. 17.11). But though he was made in this way man receives an inbreathing of the divine breath of life which quickens him into becoming a living soul.[132] It is in this context that the NT writers can speak of a 'divine race' of men; and Luke's genealogy of Jesus Christ is traced back to Adam 'the son of God'.[133] In a special and immediate way the first man comes from God and bears the marks of his origin (cf. Gen. 5.3) in himself. He is made in the image of God (Gen. 1.26 f.; Jas. 3.9).

But in what does the image of God in man consist? The biblical writers have given a good deal of thought to this matter, and their different answers have constituted something like a small anthropology of the primeval period. For example, it is suggested that the image of God in man consists in his being put into a place of dominion (Gen. 1.26, 28; 2.15, 19 ff.; I Cor. 11.3 ff.; Jas. 3.7). Man holds a divine office in this world, and is therefore invested with majesty and authority (Psa. 86 f.; I Cl. 61.2). Indeed, immortality was originally attributed to him; 'God created man for incorruption and made him an image of his own everlastingness.' That was the way in which the apocalyptic writers understood primordial history, and Paul entirely shared their point of view.[134] But biblical anthropology laid the greatest emphasis upon the mutual relationship between primordial man and his creator. God had 'set his eye upon men's hearts' (Ecclus. 17.8; Psa. 8.5; Acts 1.24). In making man, God had made a 'thou', and was himself the great 'thou' to whom man could pray. The thing that distinguishes man from every other creature that we know is that he can hear God's voice, and can pray for God's answers to his prayers. Biblical anthropology is well aware of the concept of *homo sapiens* (SEn. 6.5) and even of *homo faber* (Job 28; Ezra 4.2); but according to the Bible the most distinctive concept is that of *homo orans* (Ch. 24). But as *homo orans* man is a creature of an wholly distinct kind, and the very centre of creation. At this point the NT thinks no less anthropocentrically than does the OT.

That brings us to the last question, man's vocation. In the last resort man is like every other creature in being able to have no other task than that of glorifying God. If the angels in heaven sing the thrice-holy name of God, *homo orans* on earth should perform the same duty and 'add the voice of reverence to the choir of voiceless beings'.[135] But primordial man had not only to praise God in emulation of the heavenly beings, he had to hallow God's name in a quite distinctive way: in his theology—in the theology of creation! Angels have no theology. But God has given man a heart, and endowed him with eyes and ears and knowledge and speech, so that he can proclaim the greatness of God's works.[136] That, according to Ecclus. 17.1 ff., is the whole personal vocation of man, and the essential meaning of his theology (cf. Psa. 56.8; Job 32.5; Wisd. 13.5 ff.).[137] Paul took over these ideas and developed them: God spoke with the first man through his works so that man should tell of his maker and praise him for his creation (Rom. 1.20 f.). *Anima originaliter theologica.*

But all this applies only to primeval time. Man has long since proved himself untrue to his calling, and a theology of creation has long ago become problematical (Ch. 18). There is only one place in the world where the primordial destiny of mankind is fulfilled over and over again—in the lightheartedness of a child who praises the Creator in an unencumbered and thankful delight in the glory of the world (Psa. 8.3 LXX; cf. AEn. 106.11). Out of the mouth of babes and sucklings thou hast perfected praise (Matt. 21.16). This is no romantic reminiscence, but an accusing *Mene Tekel*!

Chapter 12

THE PRINCIPLE OF FREEDOM

W. Lueken, *Michael,* 1898; H. Diels, *Elementum,* 1899; M. Müller, 'Freiheit', ZNW, 1926; K. Galling, 'Die Geschichte als Wort Gottes bei den Propheten', ThBl, 1929; E. Schick, *Die Botschaft der Engel im NT,* 1940.

The order of God's creation is *a principio* an ordering of wills. That is why the later writings of Israel speak as 'anthropomorphically and 'personally' of world events as do the 'primitive spirits' of ancient Israel. God calls the light and tremulously it obeys. He calls the stars, and they answer: 'We are here' (BBar. 3.33; Jdth. 9.6). The same considerations explain why angelic figures play so surprising a role in later Judaism and in the NT. The angels are symbols of God's voluntarist world order! For angels are not only divine office-bearers and mediators (Ch. 51), but they are also independent, executant wills. God brings his will to pass all through the world by means of an hierarchy of mediatorial wills (Heb. 1.7, 14).

The course of divine history is *a principio* one determined by wills. God's will is carried out in and through the will of the creature. The creative act of God was continued in a history for which man's will was the responsible agent. It was man's duty to fill the earth and subdue it; he had to care for God's garden and give names to the animals; he had to subject land and sea to himself as farmer, and worker and king (Gen. 1.28; 2.5 ff.; Job 28; III Ezra 4.2; Acts 17.26). This makes very clear what the divine conditioning of history originally was. History is the continuation of the work of creation put into the hands of man who is possessed of a will.

But why is it that the NT writers lay so much emphasis on this voluntarist understanding of reality? It is because freedom is based on the principle of the will—*a principio*! God has established his world order in freedom. The angels are symbolic of that. God has also established the course of history in freedom. And man is symbolic of that. The right ordering of the cosmos depends on the free *subordinatio* of the heavenly beings; the course of history depends on the free subjection of the wills of mortal men.

God delights in freedom. The whole creation bears witness to that—'And how rich it is through freedom.'[138] God deals with his creatures through his Word because he wills that they have a will, and because he respects the freedom of their wills (Ch. 10). It is his will that the angels should bow before him and in their own free decision carry out his commands (ApMos. 7; 17). 'Everything is fulfilled in terms of a commandment'—the rotation of the stars as well as the flowing of the streams.[139] God takes pleasure in the indomitable will of the beasts of the desert. 'Who hath set the wild ass free? Or who hath loosed the bands of the wild ass? ... He scorneth the tumult of the city, neither heareth he the shoutings of the driver' (Job 39.5 ff.). Man's free will is what gives him royal dignity, and it constitutes the innermost secret of his having been made in the image of God.[140] It is God's will to have men who are free, instead of automata without wills, or even marionettes or pawns (PsSol. 9.4; Rom. 10.19). God despises tyranny because he desires loyalty. He does not compel, but rather wins over. He comes to us 'as one who will not overpower us to win us; for violence is not Godlike' (Dg. 7.3 ff.). He respects our freedom by leading men to their historical goal by means of discipline, education and the constant unfolding of his will (PsSol. 8.29; 18.4; I Cor. 11.32; Heb. 12.5 ff. Ch. 45). God has staked his honour in deciding to evoke the spontaneous love of his creation by his words and works. We can even say that he delights to hide himself behind the independent freedom of his world, behind the independent activities of his creatures, behind the self-unfolding and self-development of their powers. That is the *deus absconditus* of the NT. His glory lies in his hiddenness.

God so delights in freedom, so resolutely prizes the free fashioning of the will of his creatures that he refuses even to check the self-glorifying development of freedom in the sphere of the demonic (SBar. 56.11; HEn. 44.7; ApSh. 8; Schatzh. 4). He remains loyal to his own principle of freedom in not compelling men to keep back from their erroneous ways, but instead setting them a time for their voluntary homecoming (SBar. 24.2; Luke 13.1 ff.; Rom. 2.4; II Pet. 3.9). God lets evil have its course until it has reached its climax. He lets it vent itself in raging until it turns on itself.[141] The price that God has paid for this principle of freedom is that of a history filled with blood and horror (Ecclus. 33.14 f.; 42.24; TestA. 5; Job 39 ff.). But in his foreknowledge God foresaw these possibilities. And not only so, but he has provided for their being realized in his predestined plan of history; and no cry that it might stop that comes to him from his afflicted creation affects his will or his plan. And that is the measure of how dear to the Creator is the freedom of his creation.

But the God of the NT is no magician's apprentice who is dominated in the end by the powers he once controlled. By reason of his hidden *preparatio* he has long since contrived the means of deliverance which he will set in motion at the appointed time; and the pre-existent deliverer is already waiting for God's secret summons. The Word of God, which brought creation's freedom into being, retains its authority over the liberated powers (Isa. 40.8; Jas. 2.19; Mark 4.39; Jude 9; II Pet. 3.5 ff.; II Thess. 2.8; Heb. 1.3; Mark 13.31). The more self-willed the freedom of God's creation proves to be in its development, the more despotically the liberated creatures rave, so much the more certain is God's premundane plan put into operation and the more glorious will be his final victory. Such is the greatness of God. There is no limit to his love of freedom; and yet his omnipotence knows no bounds.

The principle of freedom is involved in that of the will. But with the principle of freedom there is also involved the possibility of rebellion on the part of the world-will that has been given its freedom. God has provided two foci for the will of his creatures. There is the will of the heavenly beings, which determines the destiny of the cosmic order; and there is the will of men which determines the course of history. Corresponding to this there is a twofold rebellion of the world-will that was created in freedom: we hear of a rebellion by Satan, and of a revolt by Adam.

Chapter 13

THE ADVERSARY

M. Dibelius, *Die Geisterwelt im Glauben des Paulus*, 1909; G. Kurz, *Der Engels- und Teufelsglaube des Apostels Paulus*, 1915; W. Bousset, 'Zur Dämonologie der späteren Antike', ARW, 1915; H. Gunkel, *Schöpfung und Chaos in Urzeit und Endzeit*,[2] 1921.

As far back as Isa. 14 there are traces of old traditions about the rebellion and fall of a heavenly being.[142] What is there said about Lucifer is taken over in VitAdEv. 12 ff. and applied to Satan and used in the construction of a theology of history. We are told that the devil belonged to the most glorious of the angels,[143] and was himself the leader of one of the angelic hosts. But in a decisive hour he refused to obey God. His words were: 'If he be wrath with me, I will set my seat above the stars of heaven and will be like the Most High.' But in his wrath God hurled him down into the depths.[144] The early Church, and Paul in particular, knew about these traditions of a pre-human catastrophe in the will of creation, and accepted them. It is quite plain that what is in Paul's mind in Phil. 2.6 ff. is this picture of Satan and his *superbia*, and it is that which he contrasts with such emphasis with the picture of Christ and his *humilitas*. More than once we read of Satan's rebellion in heaven.[145] But the most striking survival of that idea is seen when the name 'angel' is used of demonic powers (Matt. 25.41). When Paul talks of angelic beings that are demonic we have simply the survival of the idea that those demonic natures were once clothed with brightness and glory. that they have now lost it, and have nothing left but their name and a demonically perverted power (I Cor. 6.3; II Cor. 11.14; 12.7).

But apart from this main development we can trace a minor tradition. For alongside the ideas of freedom and a pre-human fall, which became the dominant teaching through Paul, there runs another tradition which tells of a primary antagonism in every creature.[146] There is frequent reference to this point of view, particularly in the priestly tradition. It is in the priestly code that we read about the separation of light from darkness, a separation which is taken as the basis of all further creative activity.[147] The basic presupposition of Ecclus. 42.24 links on to this: 'All things are double, one part set against another.'[148] The Testament of the Twelve Patriarchs has this passage in mind when it says 'There are two in all things, one against the other'.[149] But this way of thinking has nothing at all to do with a metaphysical or ontological dualism. Light and darkness are both created by God. Yet both are principles which run right through creation from the very beginning, and determine the future of all things. In our view John bases his teaching on this priestly doctrine when he asserts in John 1.5; 'The light shineth in the darkness; and the darkness apprehended it not.' The present tense of the first clause must be taken quite seriously.[150] The light is always shining—but the darkness has not yet apprehended it. This makes us see the basic antinomy of the Johannine metaphysic of history, that theological metaphysic of which we have already spoken (Ch. 6). God has created a world in which light and darkness stand in contrast to each other. The antithetic explanation of history is predetermined not only by the *gemina praedestinatio* (in the divine will) but it is also prepared in a *praeparatio gemina* (in the actual disposition of the creature's will)! (Ch. 9). How the events of history come to follow on these primary metaphysical data can be discovered from John 8.44: 'He (your father the devil) was a murderer from the beginning, and stood not in the truth, because there is no truth in him.' From the beginning the devil has been a villain and a murderer.[151] Yet at the beginning he was such only potentially. According to John, he actually becomes so because he did not stand firm in the truth when the pre-human fall took place.[152]

It is quite clear that the NT writers do not express themselves with complete unity about the origin of the demonic, nor deal with it as a particular theme. The reason is that these problems of origin are thrown into the background by most pressing and realistic questions about the wiles of the devil in actual life (Eph. 4.14; 6.11), and about the signs of his activity in the history of the world.[153] The primitive Church enunciated three fundamental principles for distinguishing demonic activity: the principle of self-glorification, of demonic opposition and of mendacity.

Satan means to become like God (Isa. 14.14; VitAdEv. 15; SEn. 29.4). The glory with which God has adorned his creation has become his temptation. Consequently, the freedom which God gave him works his ruin. The creature means to become something, something without God, something like God—and if need be, in spite of God. So the prime motive of demonic activity is self-glorification.[154] From now on the struggle between one glory and another, between the *gloria dei* and the *gloria mundi* is the dramatic theme of all history, even of the history of the Church.[155] The man possessed of a demonic spirit betrays himself in his determination to play the leading part, and in forming some special group to achieve his ends (I Cor. 1.11; II Pet. 2.1 ff.; Herm.m. 11.12 f.). So the NT opposes *superbia* in all its forms, among believers as well as among unbelievers (Luke 6.26; John 5.43; Gal. 5.26; I Tim. 3.6).

The devil is God's adversary, and consequently the enemy of God's creation. His very name betrays that.[156] He is envious of God (Wisd. 2.24; PsPhil. 60.3). All his thoughts and all his desires are set on theomachy.[157] He opposes himself to everything that God does, to prove that he is God and to put God's work in the shade, to disturb and destroy it (I Cor. 12.3; I John 4.3; Rev. 12.17). Moses and Aaron performed miracles in God's name. The devil immediately retaliated with miracle-workers of his own sort.[158] In Satan there is a survival of the primordial power of chaos and its hostility to creation (Gen. 15.11; John 8.44). The adversary is the spirit of constant negation—of negation most serious in its consequences for the cosmos and its history. Hence he answers every act of God with some counter-activity, every historical advance with a contrary motion (Gen. 3.15; Matt. 13.19, 25). But the more the adversary gets excited, the more it becomes plain that as he seeks his own glory by his opposition, he is exhausting himself in a negation that in the end can only reveal the profound vanity and unreality of his nature and the sole glory of God!

So the arrogant glory of the adversary can be nothing but illusory, and his theomachy nothing but a fight with illusory weapons (John 8.44; Luke 22.48). His antithesis stands in such servile dependence upon the thesis that it achieves nothing but a demonic aping and perversion of the divine. The adversary affects a piety that misuses the divine name, and works with Bible texts, orthodox ideas and theological pretexts (Matt. 4.6; II Cor. 10.5; I Tim. 4.7; 6.20). He dresses himself up as an angel of light, and his auxiliaries are the hypocrites who wear the garments of piety, the false brethren, false witnesses, false teachers, false apostles, false prophets and false Messiahs (II Cor. 11.13 ff.). He boasts of his great achievements (Gen. 11.4; Dan. 7.8; PsPhil. 6.1; Sib. 3.100; Mark 13.22). The satanic powers even undergo something akin to death and resurrection (Rev. 13.3). Yet with all this play acting at piety and miracle the adversary deceives the unwary as to his true nature and intentions (II Cor. 4.4). He bewitches his victims before he destroys them (Gal. 3.1; IgnE. 19.3).[159] The Father of Jesus Christ leads his people through Inferno to Paradise; but the father of lies dangles a heaven in front of his friends—till they fall down into Hell. Moreover, the two great powers of history, eros and mammon, serve him (PsPhokyl 194; I Cor. 7.5; Rev. 2.24; Luke 16.9 ff.). But it is in the ways of his associates that the entire inner deceptiveness of the satanic is revealed in the end (II Cor. 11.15; Acts 13.6 ff.; Did. 11.10; 12.5). 'But evil men and imposters shall wax worse and worse, deceiving and being deceived' (II Tim. 3.13). Satan, the misleader of the whole world, becomes at last the misled; he has deceived the whole world with his mendacity, but at last is deceived himself (Ch. 53).

In primitive Christianity there is no christology without demonology. But the first word and the last belongs to theology. Satan's fall from heaven is the sign that God retains the upper hand, however powerful and crafty his creatures may be. In the meantime God does not destroy the adversary, or thrust him out of creation into the void beyond, but assigns him to his place in the divine ordering of the world and appoints him to that office which he intended for him in his predestined plan for history. However much the idea of Satan has developed since the time of the Book of Job, the basic thought of Job 1.6 ff. remains true: Satan is an authorized minister of God.[160] God has even anticipated the demonic opposition of the adversary and the determined seductiveness of the tempter, and has systematically integrated it into his own world order (Rev. 2.10; 13.5 ff.). So really the devil is the power in God's world who always wills evil and yet always effects good. Satan does not escape from

God's *ordo*, but remains co-ordinated in it, *ordinatus* as Augustin says in his pregnant Latin. But the Creator is enthroned in awesome glory and lordly majesty over the creature who has become his enemy and who must remain his servant until he has done his work and departed.[161] Great and mysterious in his being God stands supreme even over that *dies ater* on which Satan tempted the first parent of mankind.

Chapter 14

SIN AND HISTORY

N. P. Williams, *The Ideas of the Fall and of Original Sin*, 1927; J.Freundorfer, *Erbsünde und Erbtod beim Apostel Paulus*, 1927; W. Staerk, 'Persönliche Schuld und Gesamtschuld', ZSTh, 1927; O. Kuss, *Die Adam-Christus-Parallele* . . . 1930; E. Hirsch, *Schöpfung und Sünde*, 1931; R. Otto, *Sünde und Urschuld*, 1932; J. Hempel, 'Sünde und Offenbarung', ZSTh, 1933.

The biblical doctrine of the fall is based upon a revelation—the revelation of an hereditary connection between man and man.

'I, the Lord thy God am a jealous God, visiting the iniquity of the fathers upon the children, upon the third and upon the fourth generation' (Ex. 20.5; cf. 34.7). This is the OT's fundamental proposition about heredity. To come into the historical order means to enter upon an historical inheritance, to take upon oneself the heritage of a guilty past. Present and future generations bear responsibility before God for the sins of the past. 'The fathers have eaten sour grapes, and the children's teeth have been set on edge' (Jer. 38.29 LXX; cf. Ezek. 18.2). Naturally enough, a statement like that aroused contradiction, and yet the idea of an historical heredity has established itself.[162] We talk in terms of an 'historical heredity'—and expressly distinguish it from any notion of biological heredity; for the bonds of historical heredity between men include their relationships in a biological heredity, though, of course, they can far exceed such biological ties. Our biological inheritance affects us only within the limits of consanguinity, but an historical inheritance has its effects in any sort of historical society, and is, indeed, the constitutive basis of both its existence and its destiny.[163] Anyone who wants to understand the story of Saul and his family and tribe must follow the history of one particular sin; and if anyone wants to read the story of that particular sin he must read the history of the whole house of Saul, and indeed, in the last resort, a whole chapter of the national history.[164] The story of this man's life, of his family, of his people, is the story of a particular sin.

The OT conceives the situation of all mankind in terms of this idea of an historical heredity. Man's history, with all its trouble and catastrophe, points back to some sin committed in primordial time, whose inheritance is like an avalanche rolling down the centuries with ever-increasing volume.[165] The world that we experience is no longer the world as God first made it; rather does it stand under a curse[166]. And yet all the retributive judgements that come upon us now are but trifles compared with the coming vengeance of God. For God will finally bring the primordial sin home to the generation that is alive at the end of time[167]. In short, the whole history of mankind is the history of a sin. That is what the story of the fall means in the old biblical tradition, and that, too, is the basis of what the NT teaches about original sin and the troubles of the world.

The NT makes only allusive references to the circumstances of the fall, and these are entirely within the framework of the old biblical tradition.[168] The decisive fact is that man has cast off the yoke of the divine supremacy because of his own self-glorification. From that very moment the adversary becomes the pitiless god of this world. [169] That is the situation caused by man's rebellion, a situation that is characterized by a threefold calamity: sin, sorrow and death—the three great afflictions that men have suffered since the days of the primordial fall.

The NT does not reach the concept of original sin, but it speaks with relentless realism of the tragedy of having to sin. The fall has given rise to a situation in which man no longer has a choice between the divine and the demonic,[170] but only between one sin and another. Man can fight this curse of having to sin by meeting it with a tragic 'no'. But he will come to perceive that even his refusal to act is itself a crime, and then he will fulfil the sinful necessity that is laid upon him with a tragic 'yes'. At every point of history he leaves behind him an accusing trail which the passing of the ages cannot obliterate. Whatever he does is always condemned to add something to the sin of the world (Rom. 3.10 ff.; cf. Ex. 34.7; Job 15.16). Ever since the beginning man's world has been 'under sin'—to use Paul's description of our plight.[171] Or we can put the point in the words of Ignatius and say that sin is the prison in which we were all born.[172]

We can, perhaps, move as we like in any direction within the prison;
we might even rattle the doors, but we cannot get outside. We remain
prisoners. But, according to the oft repeated conviction of the NT,
the tragedy of man's having to sin reaches its demonic fulfilment in
man's wanting to sin (cf. IV Ezra 3.26; 7.18 f.; SBar. 48.42 f.;
54.15, 19). 'Occasions of stumbling there must be,' said Jesus, 'but
woe to that man through whom the occasion cometh' (Matt. 18.7).
The NT writers see this demonic possibility realized[173] not just in
particular figures of history, but for them there is no heart in which
this 'radical evil' has failed to strike its roots. First and last and all
the time man means to be his own master, and the self-glorification
of his will finds no other way of effecting this than in a demonic 'no'
to God and a demonic 'yes' to the adversary, which only drags his
will deeper into that bondage which the first man brought upon his
kind. 'Ye are of your father the devil, and the lusts of your father
it is your will to do,' says the Johannine Christ.[174] 'The mind of the
flesh is death . . . is enmity against God,' says Paul. [175] But no man
goes to his destiny without being faced with the question. Every
member of Adam's race decides for himself to go the way of his first
parent. One by one we become subject to death through our own
sin.[176]

The second great affliction which mankind endures is the suffering
in human life.[177] It was sin which brought this suffering into our
existence, and it is sin which is continually heightening its effects
(cf. EpAr. 208). There is no suffering more bitter than the sorrow of
heart that one man causes another (Gen. 3.16c; Ecclus. 25.13). Jesus
has all this in mind when he speaks about the tribulations that have
gone on all over the world since creation began (Mark 13.19; cf. Rom.
8.18; Rev. 21.4). One particular chapter of the great book of the
world's suffering to which the biblical writers are specially sensitive
is that concerning the unrewarding hardship of man's labour. Ever
since Adam fell the ground has produced thorns and thistles,[178]
Lamech's hope when Noah was born was premature: 'this same
shall comfort us in our work and in the toil of our hands' (Gen.
5.29). Labour and sorrow are the pride of our life, says the Psalmist.[179] The curse of God lies on the fields where we work. But no
sorrow is deeper than man's struggle with the demonic strongholds
which sin has erected in this world (Eccl. 4.1 ff.). Jesus has set his
own seal on all these testimonies when he talked about the con-
suming care and the fresh anxiety of each new day (Matt. 6.34).
The same considerations were in his mind when he called the 'heavy

laden' to himself.[180] Paul frequently speaks of the sorrow written over all our work, even his own work, and he fights against the danger of becoming weary (Gal. 6.9; cf. III βασ. 19.4). But Lamech's hope does find a fulfilment in Rev. 14.13, and the promise of Rev. 21.4 is an answer to the Psalmists cry for help.

The third affliction which has overshadowed life and history ever since the fall is the inevitability of death. Death came into the world through sin, and now reigns over the whole race of mankind.[181] We have become slaves of mortality and are in bondage to the fear of death.[182] But just as every kind of sorrow and affliction that trouble men not only has its origin in sin but is constantly being intensified by it, so it is with the relationship of sin and death (I Cor. 15.56). The tragedy of having to sin reaches its climax in the tragedy of having to die. But the demonic character of the sinful will has its greatest triumph in offering a diabolic 'yes' to blood and violence.[183] Peoples and armies destroy each other in mutual murder. All through history there sounds a ceaseless rumbling of war and the noises of war, a moaning of the oppressed and the persecuted (Eccl. 4.1; Mark 13.7; Rev. 9.9 ff.; 21.4). Death is the rider on the pale horse who triumphantly gathers his harvest when the fourth part of the earth has become a vast mortuary (Rev. 6.8). Death is the 'last enemy' who still waits for his final harvest (I Cor. 15.26; cf. ApMos. 28; IgnE. 19.3). For all men are guilty of sin and without exception doomed to die (Ex. 34.7; Rom. 3.10 ff.). But God's visitation has its appointed time (Ex. 32.24). God is long-suffering. He has set limits to the time of the world's suffering.[184] He waits for the fruit of the tree for a long time; for a long time he lets the oppressed cry out in vain; for a long time he watches man's wickedness (Luke 13.1 ff.; Rom. 3.26; Rev. 22.11). But when the limit is reached, then he raises his hand (AssMos. 9 f.; IV Ezra 4.35; HEn. 44.7 ff.; Rev. 6.10 f.). 'And when he starts to scourge he will not stop short of death, and he laughs at the trials of the innocent' (Job 9.23 MT). That is why Paul warns the Gentiles: 'Do you desire, with your hardness and impenitence of heart, to treasure up for yourself wrath until the day of wrath?' (Rom. 2.3 ff.). There are respites in history, times of prosperous growth, of blossoming and ripening, when men regularly deceive themselves about the seriousness of their situation and say 'peace; peace' when there is no peace. There are also times of visitation when God lets all the forces of hell loose among men, and the very sun is darkened by the arrows of the Almighty. In the history of tribes and nations there is a law of ebb and flow, and it was in this context that Jesus said to his hard-hearted contemporaries: 'fill ye up then the measures of your fathers' (Matt. 23.32) 'that upon you may come all the righteous bloodshed on the earth and that has cried to heaven since the foundation of the world' (Luke 11.50 f.). God has not yet spoken his last word on that sin, whose history is our history (Luke 23.28 ff.; Mark 13.19; cf. VitAdEv. 49). All the calamities which meet and have met us are but the menacing heralds of a final, fearful visitation which God has appointed for the end of history (Rev. 1.7). When that time comes the avalanche of sin, sorrow and death, which ever since man's first sin has been sliding down history with unremitting, increasing and overpowering momentum, will finally come to rest in one mighty roll of thunder.

Chapter 15

HUMAN AND COSMIC HISTORY

F. F. Delitzsch, *Biblische Psychologie,*[2] 1861; F. Spitta, 'Die Tiere in der Versuchungsgeschichte', ZNW, 1904, 1907; W. Schubart, *Das Weltbild Jesu,* 1927; E. Lohmeyer, *Glaube und Geschichte in vorderorientalischen Religionen,* 1931; S. Herner, *Die Natur im AT,* 1941.

The history of man is the history of a sin, though the consequences of this sin stretch far beyond the bounds of human history. They enter the history of creation with their destructiveness. We have already spoken (Ch. 1) of the cosmic elements in apocalyptic thinking. Here, in the understanding of the fall, the presuppositions of this mode of thinking reveal their fundamental significance.

What does the old biblical apocalyptic have to say? Adam, the ruler of Paradise, was appointed as a free lord over the ministering animal kingdom, and he alone was responsible for its future (SEn. 56 f., 65). But the king of Paradise rebelled, and immediately the beasts were driven from Paradise, their nature was changed, they turned against their former ruler, distress and murder became their lot (Jub. 3.28; ApMos. 11.24; Eccl. 3.19 ff.; IV Ezra 9.20 ff.). Adam was the Atlas of the world. His rebellion spelt catastrophe for the whole life of creation.[185] 'For man's sake' the world was made (ArmEzra 7.11; SEn. 58). 'For man's sake' the earth was cursed with every sort of plant that it bore.[186] Not even the stars remained unaffected (GBar. 9). Every created thing came under the judgement (IV Ezra 7.11 f.; cf. SBar. 56.5 ff.). In every revolution of the cycle of life and death, wherever processes of construction and destruction go on, there from now on death and destruction have the last word. 'Mortality' or 'vanity' is the distinguishing mark of the new situation in the world (Eccl. 1.5 ff.; 3.19 ff.). But in the following era the sin which insinuates itself everywhere in the human situation retains its power to affect the cosmos itself. The sun's rays are polluted, the stars thrown from their courses, the rain is kept back, the vegetation withers and the earth trembles.[187] The earth is punished for man's sake and because of his wickedness, and it complains of the distress and violence that it suffers (GEn. 7.5; 10 f.; SEn. 57 f.). Creation's song of praise is drowned by the cry of distress that the earth raises because of the blood it has to drink.[188] But to whom does the earth cry? To God (cf. Gen. 4.10; Job 38.41; Psa. 146.9). Man does not hear this cry; but God does, as he heard the cry of Abel's blood and the cry of the young ravens. But this collective sharing of destiny by man and the cosmos reaches its limits when it brings about the break-up of the ages. The first man's sin brought much tribulation upon creation. The final judgement on man's sin, which has been accumulating ever since the flood, will be realized in catastrophes on a cosmic scale (VitAdEv. 49). But the new day that will dawn for man will also be a new day for creation itself; for then the earth will no longer bear thorns and thistles, but will yield fruit a thousandfold (Ch. 58).

In the NT likewise we keep on hearing about the cosmic consequences of, or accompaniments to, the history of man. Jesus does not only talk about God's care for the tiny birds (Luke 9.58; 12.24; Matt. 10.29 ff.; cf. SEn. 58.5). He can also see the growth of weeds, the enmity between man and beasts, the contrariness of the elements—and understand them all as secondary dislocations of the normal course of things, as the work of the 'enemy' who has attained power through the fall (Matt. 13.25 ff.; Mark 4.39). Hence his own invasion of Satan's empire is an event affecting the whole creation (Luke 10.18 f.). So the interconnections of human sin, man's salvation and cosmic destiny are not fully revealed until Jesus has spoken about the future when heaven and earth shall have passed away and given place to the *civitas christi* (Mark 13). The same presuppositions lie behind Mark's telling of Christ's first triumph and how the angels ministered to him, and how the wild beasts surrounded him who was Satan's conqueror, the king of Paradise incognito, the future restorer of that peace which had been lost to the whole creation. (Mark 1.13; cf. TestN. 8). John thinks of the whole creation as 'lying in the evil one', by whom he means the prince of the darkness who rules over this cosmic order (I John 5.18 f.; John 1.5; 12.31). Christ's final victory will have to be realized, and will be realized in cosmic upheavals (Rev. 9.1; 19 ff., etc.). In later writings this cosmic theology of history and eschatology is still further developed along the same lines (Heb. 2.14; 6.8; 8.13; II Pet. 3.5 ff., 10; IgnE. 19.2 f.; Barn. 6.18 f.).

But Paul more than anyone else gave full scope to these ideas. 'The creation was subjected to vanity, not of its own will, but by reason of him who subjected it in hope. For the creation itself also shall be delivered from the bondage of corruption into the liberty of the glory of the children of God. For we know that the whole creation groaneth and travaileth in pain together until now' (Rom. 8.19–22). 'We know,' says Paul; and in so doing clearly intends to appeal to a well-known and recognized tradition. No one acquainted with the presuppositions of apocalyptic thinking has any difficulty in recognizing what the apostle is talking about. The creation has been subjected to an inevitable doom not, like man, because of its own, but because of another's voluntary decision—because of man's decision, who is a free and responsible being. Hence, as in the earliest discussions of the problem, and as in the whole of Romans, the concept of creation embraces not only mankind (as Schlatter thinks) but also the whole created order.[189] The sin which was committed by man in his self-glorification is a destructive attack upon the whole life of God's creation! But what is the doom which mankind has brought upon creation? The curse of vanity and bondage to corruption—things which are not afflictions if the whole creation is itself to be annihilated in the end. But that is not so; annihilation does not have the last word. The curse is not spoken without a promise being made. The whole created order has a future before it. Creation has been subjected 'in hope'. But if we ask ourselves to what point this hope must attach itself, we have to answer that it relates to that point where the whole creation and its entire destiny is knit together for weal or woe. The rebellion of the first man brought destruction on the creation. But when the new man, the Son of God, is revealed at the end, then the whole creation will have its 'liberation day'. The despotic powers of this age that control its destiny are not eternal.[190] A new world of freedom and glory will appear. For the time being trouble and death are inseparable from creation, but such evils are no longer meaningless.[191] Admittedly, the glad praises of the stars and worlds that greeted the first days of creation are sung no more. Creation groans now in heavy chorus. But God hears its cry and will hear its prayer in due season. Its groans are those of a woman in travail (cf. Gen. 3.16). Affliction and mortality are but the birth pangs in which the new creation heralds its birth.

So under the sign of the fall and its universal consequences the glory of God reveals itself in all its mysterious majesty. God delights in beauty, and delights in it so much that he is prodigal with it in this passing world. The lilies of the field are never far from the curse or from destruction, yet God lavishes beauty on them and always produces new blooms and clothes them anew for their brief glory (Luke 12.27 f.). God delights in life, and his delight is strong enough to take the life of his creation through the pangs of death to a new beginning. The seed must die. But it will spring to life again and bear much fruit (I Cor. 15.36; John 12.24). This goes through the dying life of the fallen creation like a parabolic promise of things to come.

Chapter 16

TIME AND TIMES

E. v. Dobschütz, 'Zeit und Raum im Denken des Urchristentums', JBL, 1922; H. Schaedel, *Die nt Äonenlehre*, 1930; R. Löwe, *Kosmos und Aion*, 1935; K. Bornhauser, *Tage und Stunde im NT*, 1937; H. D. Wendland, *Geschichtsanschauung und Geschichtsbewusstsein im NT*, 1938; G. Delling, *Das Zeitverständnis des NT*, 1940; O. Cullmann, *Christ and Time*, (E.T.) 1951.

The dominant theology of the present day, more or less freely following Kant, thinks of time as a form of human sensibility. The NT conceives time to be the form of divine activity. Hence every NT saying about time is expressed by means of a time-coefficient, and without such time-coefficient it can be neither legitimately interpreted nor placed in its proper order. We moderns find it easy to talk in terms of time and eternity; the NT writers speak of time and times.

The NT has its own characteristic term for the totality of the world of experience: aeon or world-time. The word aeon can be used interchangeably with concepts such as universe, creation and cosmos. But when the NT writers refer to 'this aeon' they are not thinking of this world in any neutral fashion, but precisely on the mortal character of this world (Rom. 12.2; Eph. 2.2). They are thinking of the provisional character of this created order, and, in a manner quite in keeping with apocalyptic idiom, they are opposing the age to come to this present age (Matt. 12.32). They are thinking of cosmic history. This aeon has a beginning and an end (Jude 25; Matt. 13.39 f.). It points beyond itself to an aeon to come, and the whole series of aeons points backwards to the Creator of the ages (Heb. 1.2; 11.3), and upwards to their king (I Tim. 1.17). This means that the early Christian conception of the aeon has given chronological order primacy of place over every other principle of temporal order. Time is the fundamental order of any reality that can be experienced. That is the formal presupposition of the idea of universal history which has to be made at the very beginning of an apocalyptic theology of history. For it is the primacy of chronological order that makes it possible for anything to come and go in the course of universal history.

It is worth noticing that even the NT writings, which are obviously acquainted with Greek culture retain the apocalyptic idea of the aeon (Eph., Past.); indeed, that it is just such writings that develop the idea (Heb.). They knew very well that they had something distinctive and revolutionary to say to the Greeks with this concept. The Greeks knew 'how to interpret the face of the earth and the heaven', but they could not 'discern the signs of the times' (Luke 12.56; Matt. 16.3). It is possible to apply this saying of Jesus to the Greeks, for to the Greeks history[192] is only one phenomenon within the cosmos. But by contrast, for primitive Christianity, the cosmos is only one phenomenon within history. The Greeks heard the eternal harmony of the spheres. The NT writers heard the march of universal history.

But a number of particular times stand out from the whole course of this world history, smaller temporal units with clearly-defined boundaries, irremovable, whose contents are characteristic and unique. Such a temporal unit is called in the NT a *kairos* though it can equally well talk of an unrepeatable day, or hour, or year. Every possibility and task in history has its own time,[193] every historical phenomenon has its great time, every nation has its day (Dan. 7 f.; IV Ezra 12.44; Luke 19.42; 21.24), and every man has his hour (Luke

19.9). 'The noonday does not always burn. Nor do the rays of the sun constantly give light,' says SBar. (12.2 ff.) to the proud capital city of the world. 'Do not expect that thou wilt always be prosperous and rejoicing. For assuredly in its own season shall the wrath awake against thee!' But the biblical writers' favourite simile for this unique law of times is that of the changing seasons of the year with their tasks and rewards (Isa. 28.24 ff.; Psa. 125). Let us make use of the seedtime, says Gal. 6.9—'for in due season we shall reap without ceasing' (cf. Matt. 21.41).

There are years which are wholly dominated by what has already taken place ('Time shall succeed to time,' SBar. 42.6; John 4.36 f.), and others which pass completely in anticipation of something still to come; there are hours in which unpretentious decisions of inconceivable importance are made, and years of fulfilment which lavish benefits upon us (Mark 4.26 ff.). The adversary has his times, and his whole glory has its time (Rev. 12.12; 20.3). The time will come when the antichrist will cry out: 'Woe is me, that my time is past. I said, my time shall not pass by me' (ApEl. 40). It is the trick of time to speed so silently. Hence it pays to redeem the time (Col. 4.5; Eph. 5.16). God's government has its times, and the man who knows nothing of God cannot know how ultimately serious the *kairos* is. The NT talks about a year of the Lord (Luke 4.19), about times of forbearance, of visitation, of repentance, of testing (Luke 8.13), of restoration (Acts 3.20), about the eschatological day of the Lord (II Thess. 2.2; I Pet. 2.12) and about the day of judgement (Rev. 14.7; Rom. 2.5). Everything depends on our being ready in the hour of death, awake in the hour of the *parousia*, and on our not failing to grasp the irretrievable hour of God (Luke 19.42).

The universal understanding of time combines with this experience of hidden seriousness of times to make the idea of an universal and divine time-plan. 'He has weighed the age in the balance, and with measure has measured the times, and by number has numbered the seasons: neither will he move nor stir things, till the measure appointed be fulfilled' (IV Ezra 4.36 f.). The NT also talks about God's plan for the world which was before all ages, and endures for all the ages to come (I Cor. 2.7; Eph. 2.7; 3.21), and which is divided up into measured times and periods (I Thess. 5.1; cf. Acts 17.26). By his creative Word God calls the ages into existence when it pleases him, when he sees that their measure is full. 'Thou summonest the advent of the times, and they stand before thee; thou causest the power of the ages to pass away, and they do not resist thee'

(SBar. 48.2). Thus in Rev. 6.1 ff. God calls forth the apocalyptic riders one by one [194] with the word 'come'. The martyrs' cry for vengeance urges on towards the end (IV Ezra 4.35; Rev. 6.10). But the answer in Rev. is precisely the same as in IV Ezra: the prescribed measure is not yet full. [195] It is not for us to know times or seasons, which the Father has set within his own authority (Acts 1.7). Time is something reserved to God in his majesty (Mark 13.32). 'Do you think that it is time? I alone know when the time has come.'[196]

The apocalyptic idea of time is no mere formal category of transcendental philosophy. IV Ezra 13.58 speaks of 'times and the things that come to pass in them'. So, too, in the NT the ultimate question is about the historical content of times. Jesus Christ, the same yesterday, today and for ever. That, according to a creedal formula from the early Church, is the one and all-inclusive content of God's plan for time (Heb. 13.8). So, as the NT says, the coming of Christ stands in the middle of the predestined plan of history, the mystery, the wisdom, the dispensation of God. God established this plan before the ages were (Eph. 1.9; 3.9 ff.). He has only revealed it to his prophets piecemeal (Rom. 16.25; IgnE. 19.1; Tit. 1.2 f.). Yet the whole course of time since Adam's fall has facilitated the economy that has for its aim the new man (IgnE. 20.1). Mindful of the future coming of Christ, God withheld the cup of his righteous anger, so that the crucified Lord might drink it for the salvation of the lost world (Rom. 3.25 f.; otherwise Acts 17.30). In becoming man Christ set out upon the long-promised road through this world, to minister to its necessity. 'When the fulness of the time came, God sent forth his Son,' says Gal. 4.4 (cf. Mark 1.15; Luke 4.21). We know how intimately this time, so decisive for all history, is woven into even the smallest part of it (Ch. 3). 'My times are in thy hands' (*kairoi*, Psa. 30.16). This verse from the Psalms is like an invisible text over the path of Jesus from Nazareth to Golgotha (cf. ParalJer. 9.23). But what was done on Good Friday is not yet finished. The adversary is stricken but not yet destroyed (Matt. 8.29). Easter morning points to a distant future. The whole age of the Church that began on Whitsunday stands in the twilight of two aeons (II Cor. 5.7; 6.2; Ch. 34). 'Consider the time. For now is our salvation [197] nearer to us than when we first believed. The night is far spent, and the day is at hand' (Rom. 13.11 f.). The day and the hour no man knows. But we can be sure of two things: God 'hath appointed a day, in the which he will judge the world in righteousness' (Acts 17.31); and he prepared before the ages began the glory that is 'ready to be revealed in the last time' (I Pet. 1.5). It is to this future that the *ecclesia crucis* turns her eyes.

In this way the NT sees God's universal plan of salvation coming to its fulfilment. The pre-Christian era is one of promise. The time of Jesus is a time of prophetic fulfilment. The age to come will be the age of fulfilment. This completes the exposition of the idea of salvation-history, and prescribes the entire subsequent arrangement of our work.

Section Two

LAW AND PROMISE

Chapter 17

POWER IN HISTORY

E. Bickermann, 'Die römische Kaiserapotheose', ARW, 1929; A. Alföldi, 'Der neue Weltherrscher der Vierten Ekloge', Herm., 1930; F. J. Dölger, 'Zur antiken und frühchristl. Auffassung der Herrschergewalt von Gottes Gnaden', AC, 1932; R. Schütz, *Die Offenbarung des Johannes und Kaiser Domitian*, 1933; P. Touilleux, *L'Ap et les Cultes de Domitien et de Cybèle*, 1933; J. Vogt, *Ciceros Glaube an Rom*, 1935; W. Weber, *Princeps*, I, 1936; J. Straub, *Vom Herrscherideal in der Spätantike*, 1939; G. Kittel, 'Das Urteil des NT über den Staat', ZSTh, 1937; W. Böld, *Die antidämonischen Abwehrmächte in der Theologie des Spätjudentums*, 1938; E. Stauffer, *Christ and the Caesars,*[3] (E.T.), 1955.

THE fall has given rise to an historical situation so threatening as to call for emergency measures to prevent man's world from being swamped by the powers of destruction (cf. Ch. 13). The emergency measures have been taken in the establishment of the civil power; for according to the NT the civil power is the divinely ordained means for the due ordering of life in a world where chaos is constantly threatening.

To look for the beginnings of a theology of civil power is to be taken far back into the history and ideology of the great powers of the ancient world. The empire of the Pharaohs used to support its place and mission in the world with a metaphysic of empire: whenever the times are out of joint with strife and bloodshed the gods send a ruler to be a king and deliverer, to establish order and bring blessings.[198] But when the ruler fails chaos gets the upper hand.[199] The Assyrian and Babylonian kings had the same ideas about their mission in the world. Proof of this lies in the ritual surrounding the Assyrian throne and in the testimony of the Babylonian imperial inscriptions.[200] But we can see this most clearly in a Babylonian oracle that tells of some future inept conqueror and has this menacing announcement for its climax: 'Under his rule every man will be swallowed up by his neighbour.'[201] When the Persian kings entered Babylon they not only took over the political inheritance of the older empire, but also made the ideological inheritance of the ancient metaphysic of empire part of their own programme. So we find Cyrus saying in a cuneiform inscription: 'Marduk himself, the god of the Babylonian city and empire, has dethroned its former ruler because he has destroyed both the land and its people. Marduk himself has taken the Aryan ruler by the hand and raised him to the throne of Babylon, the capital of the world.'[202] Or again, Darius thought of his world mission in terms of the basic Iranian metaphysical idea that history is conflict. In his imperial palace at Persepolis he is depicted as being at war with some demonic colossus.[203] A contemporary bas-relief portrays his victory over a rebel who lies at his feet, while he, the great king, stands beneath the sign of his god, Ahura Mazda. The inscription on his tomb reads: 'When Ahura Mazda saw this world stricken by war he gave it to me and made me its king . . . in accordance with the will of Ahura Mazda I brought the earth back to its proper place . . . Ahura Mazda . . . increased the majesty of King Darius.'[204] There are many such pictures and texts to be found in the Iranian world, and they all say the same thing: the whole Persian empire with the great emperor at its head, with its peasants, priests and soldiers, its temples and fortresses are one single bulwark erected by the god of heaven as a protection against the powers of chaos.[205] *Imperium* is a necessity, otherwise man's world falls to pieces in a *bellum omnium contra omnes*.[206] That, so to speak, was the political testament of the oriental world empires right down to the time of Alexander, a testament that was executed in a new and unique way in the world empire of Rome. Wherever the *imperium romanum* went, there went also the *pax romana*. As long as the *imperium* lasted the world was protected against chaos. That was why the *imperium* had to stand as long as the world itself remained, and also why the Roman empire was to be an everlasting one.[207]

The people of the Bible had their place among the succession of empires in the ancient world. But they never became a master race. More than once they were themselves bowed beneath the bloody rule of a world conqueror. But in spite of that the biblical writers advocated the logic of imperialism with what practically amounts to a gruesome self-immolation. Thus as early as Genesis, and quite fully in the traditions that were built upon it, Joseph is portrayed as the loyal and powerful servant of the Egyptian empire. 'The land of Egypt was at peace . . . and Pharaoh's kingdom was well ordered, and there was no Satan and no evil person therein.'[208] Similarly, Yahweh's word comes through Jeremiah: 'I have made the earth, and I give it unto whom it seemeth right unto me . . . And now have I given all these lands into the hand of Nebuchadnezzar the king of Babylon, my servant . . . And all the nations shall serve him, and his son, and his son's son, until the time of his own land come: and then many nations and great kings shall serve themselves of him.' The kings and empires and peoples who oppose the imperial mission of the Babylonian king will be destroyed. But whoever bows down before the God-sent conqueror shall live and labour in peace (Jer. 27.5 ff. MT).[209] In like manner Second Isaiah greets Cyrus as the new ruler of the world by God's grace (Isa. 45, etc.). Similarly, just before the rebellion against Rome in 70 A.D., the Chief Priest Hananiah uttered this warning: 'Pray for the welfare of the government; for without a proper reverence for it the one would slay the other alive.'[210] But the government he speaks of is the Roman emperor: in spite of all their iniquity, heaven has given world dominion to the Romans (AZ 18a). Meanwhile the Maccabeans had tried to realize these imperial ideas on a small scale on a racial basis and within the framework of a Jewish national state. There is an ancient hymn which honours the government of Simon Maccabeus entirely in the style of such an imperial ideology: 'He made peace in the land . . . and every lawless and wicked person he banished.'[211] But the old biblical apocalyptic turned this imperial idea into eschatology (DaΘ. 9.26; Sib. 3.652 ff.; IV Ezra 5.3 f.). Each of the empires of this world has its appointed time (cf. Jer. 27.7; 25.12 MT). It is only the final kingdom that is everlasting, and that is no longer a kingdom of this world (Dan. 7 ff.). But until that kingdom comes the imperial powers of history remain an indispensable defence against the powers of chaos.[212] Indeed, at the end of the days, political power will be concentrated once again into the hands of a single person.[213] The last ruler of the world will rebuild the holy places, make rich gifts to God's temple, and proclaim: 'The name of God is one.'[214] Then men will say: 'The Lord has sent us a righteous king so that the land shall not be desolate.' But after this final triumph of political order the powers of chaos will break in—a sombre prelude to the setting up of the final and eternal kingdom.[215] In such ways the ancient idea of empire is itself built into a framework of a theology of history which both exceeds it and limits it; and out of the age-long metaphysic of power has grown up an apocalyptic theology of the kingdom.

The primitive Church took over this tradition and transformed it in the light of its christocentric theology of history into a porfound world-wide view of the mission and temptation of the state in history.

God himself is responsible for establishing the state. That is the first proposition of the *theologia imperii* held by the primitive Church. Right back in the days of creation God gave men 'dominion over every living thing that moveth upon the earth' (Gen. 1.28; TestZeb. 9.4; I Cl. 61.2). But it is only occasionally and comparatively late that the primitive Church goes back to these beginnings. The state that occupies the mind of primitive Christianity is not a divine 'order of creation' but an emergency measure taken in history by God. 'The powers that be are ordained of God' (Rom. 13.1). That applies unmistakably to the states that have appeared in history, the *de facto* possessors of political power, entirely independent of the question whether those in office at any time are themselves religious men or godless, heathens or Christians (cf. Jer. 27.5 f. MT) 'There is no power but of God' (Rom. 13.1). For God can establish kings and dethrone them according to his good pleasure (DaΘ. 2.21; I Pet. 2.13 f.). In his mercy he even calls or tolerates the unworthy (DaΘ. 8.11 ff.; John 19.10 f.). In this double sense every crown in history is a crown of God's grace. But God has given his officers a sword for their crown.[216] The state which the NT thinks about is based upon power (I Ezra 4.2 ff.; Rom. 13.4). This is what God wills, and also what is demanded by the historical situation. The days of Gen. 1.28 are past and an age of blood has begun.[217] The state can only fulfil its mission if it takes the sword into its hand.

But what is the historical task for which God has set up political power and equipped it with the sword? It is the fight against chaos. This is the meaning of II Thess. 2.6 f. in the unanimous opinion of the early Church, and of the reformers.[218] The *imperium romanum* with the *imperator* at its head is the defence which God has made to keep the powers of chaos at bay.[219] But the empire is not, as imperial religion itself would have it, an everlasting defence. The order of Rome will hold firm and keep the world stable until the demonic world sends its last and strongest champion, antichrist (cf. ApEl. 31). Then the empire will break up and chaos will reign until Christ himself takes over the government of the world. But until then it is the duty of the civil power to keep watch, sword in hand, against all arbitrary powers, unrighteousness and wickedness that threaten God's world and seek to upset the order that has been set up to meet the emergency of the fallen creation (Rom. 13.3 f.; I Pet. 2.14). So Tertullian concludes from Paul's *theologia imperii* that the Christian must hope that the empire and its emperor will remain unharmed as long as this world remains: for just so long will they themselves survive.[220]

The Bible recognizes the divine institution and historical necessity of the power-state—but it also recognizes the demonic character of power (Luke 22.25 ff., 53; I Cor. 2.8; 6.1), and where more than in political life does the historical necessity of having to sin come more clearly to light (I Ezra 4.37; Ecclus. 10.8)? When the NT speaks of an order of grace it does not exclude this demonic accompaniment of a divine task, but it includes it. Certainly God has sovereign power over all the kingdoms and rulers of the world. But, according to Luke 4.5, he has, as a temporary measure, handed over political power to Satan since the fall; and Satan gives it to whom he will. That is why Jesus refuses the way of power politics. For the price of gaining world dominion would have been to worship the demons of the world (Matt. 4.8 f.; Luke 4.6; John 18.36). The NT affirms the divine justification and the historical necessity of the sword— but it also recognizes that the sword is a suicidal weapon (Matt. 26.52; Rev. 13.10; cf. 22.11). The civil power cannot but fight with the bloodstained weapons of this world; hence it must in due course succumb to the same weapons. The NT recognizes the peculiar greatness but also the hidden tragedy of political life. The civil power is set up as a bulwark against the powers of chaos, but it can only keep these powers in check, never really subdue them. The fight against them will never come to an end, and in the end it must succumb to their final onslaught (II Thess. 2.7 f.).

So the emperor is a forerunner of Christ in a double sense: his empire is a promise of the coming kingdom of Christ in respect of its greatness and its task—but it is a cry for the coming of Christ's kingdom in regard to its limitations. This is what civil power means for the NT theology of history. Whenever the state thinks too highly of itself it betrays its own mission and in so doing gives concrete expression in the political sphere to the fall of man (Isa. 14).

The *civitas terrena* carries within itself a tendency to *parekbasis*,[221] to reach beyond itself, a tendency which leads to self-transcendence. For the glory with which God has equipped the civil power is always accompanied by the temptation to self-glorification. All too quickly the earthly monarch forgets that he holds his office from the heavenly King (SBar. 6 ff.; 83; ParalJer. 2.7). But at that point he goes beyond the historical task which God has set him (AEn. 89 ff.; PsSol. 2). He forgets that political weapons are impotent when it comes to the last and most specific dangers of men. But he appears as a deliverer and bringer of salvation, and calls himself a saviour (Acts 4.12). He forgets that he is a sinful fallen man in daily need of forgiveness for his political activity. He allows himself to be honoured like a God (Jdth. 6.2; Acts 12.19 ff.). He forgets that he is a mortal being whose political life is, therefore, inevitably temporary, and he enthuses about the imperishability of his work (Dan. 4.30; SBar. 82.2 ff.). He forgets the glory of God and strives with him for his honour (MEx. 15.11; PsSol. 2.29; II Mac. 9.8; Mark 13.14). Then the Church which gives glory to God alone is nothing but an offence to him, and he persecutes her with growing fury and makes himself into an enemy of God and an agent of the devil [222] (TestJud. 217 ff.; VitProph. 50; Rev. 11.7). But when, in its fight with the demons of chaos, the *civitas terrena* succumbs to its own demon then the historical role of civil power is changed into its opposite: from being a bulwark against antichrist it becomes the very fortress of antichrist himself (Dan. 8.9 ff.; 11.30 ff.; Rev. 13.14 ff.). The *civitas terrena* has become the *civitas diaboli*.

Chapter 18

THE FAILURE OF NATURAL THEOLOGY

E. Grafe, 'Das Verhältnis der Paulin. Schriften zur Sap'. *Festschr. f. C. v. Weizsacker*, 1892; H. E. Weber, *Die Beziehungen von Rom 1-3 zur Missionspraxis des Paulus*, 1905; H. Böhlig, 'Das Gewissen bei Seneca und Paulus', ThStKr, 1914; G. Kuhlmann, *Theologia naturalis bei Philon und bei Paulus*, 1930; G. Bornkamm, *Gesetz und Schöpfung im NT*, 1934.

Paul thinks much more negatively about what the world of nations has achieved in the spiritual realm than he does in any estimate of its political tasks. This faces us with the problem of natural theology which has been so hopelessly compromised in contemporary discussion by a general failure to take the effects of historical relativity into consideration. Paul and his disciples are not concerned to argue about the timeless possibility or impossibility of a *theologia naturalis*; they are much rather concerned to make plain how a theology of God's works and ways can be set in the context of an all-inclusive history of revelation so as to show how such a theology began, broke down and yet was finally reaffirmed.

Anima originaliter theologica. Man, like every other creature, was made to give glory to God. But it is his special duty in the created order to glorify God in his theological activity (see Ecclus. 17.8 ff.; Ch. 11). That is the reason why we find the old biblical apocalyptic with a fully developed terminology of seeking, discovering and apprehending God.[223] But since no one can of himself come to God, this can only happen by God's coming to us [224] (Sib. 3.15). This is the reservation which a true theology of revelation makes and which distinguishes it fundamentally from any programme of a purely natural theology (cf. Ch. 43). It was in very close association with these problems that the idea of a theology of history was developed. Its central idea was 'wisdom'. Thus in Ecclus. 14.20 ff. we read about the 'wisdom' of God that reveals her ways in the history of the world to the man who seeks her.[225] Wisdom knows both past and future—she understands the signs of the times, and knows beforehand what the issue of events will be (Wisd. 8.8; cf. Dan. 2.14; 13.7). But the same reservation has to be made here too, and such a theology of history is possible only by divine revelation (Wisd. 9.17; 10.1 ff.; 17.1 f.). In the wisdom of his ways God is speaking to man, and his speech is a summons, directed to man's will (Ch. 12). The man who obeys the summons comes to know God and to see the wisdom of his ways in the story of his own life and the history of his nation (I Mac. 2.61; PsPhil. 21.5 ff.; 32.12 f.). But the man who fails to obey the summons has to experience the reality of God in the anguish of his own body (II Mac. 7.17 ff., 37). The former offers adoration (Tob. 12 f.); but the latter is brought to destruction.

It was an independent development of such traditions that Paul asserted in Rom. 1.18 ff., the primary possibility of a theology of creation and outlined its task. God has made himself known to man (1.19). It is the history of such a revelation that makes any theology, including a theology of creation, possible. The revelation to which Paul here refers has been available to men ever since the creation of the world, for it takes place throughout the whole of the created order. Paul tells in traditional terms (GEn. 2 ff.) how the invisible God is visible in his works, and how he can be recognized by the intelligent spectator. But what is it that is revealed in creation?

It is God's divinity. It is the quality by reason of which he, and he alone, is called God: his glory. Consequently, the revelation of the divine glory in creation contains a demand within itself. It is intended to quicken men's hearts to glorify God in thanksgiving and praise. So the divine revelation in the created order does two things at one and the same time: it conditions the possibility of a theology of creation, and it sets the task of glorifying God. And the realization of the possibility is bound up with the fulfilment of the task. Theology is doxology or it is nothing at all. But Paul has something to say, too, about the possibility and the task of a theology of history.

He refers to it under the familiar title of 'wisdom' in a relative clause in I Cor. 1.21, a passage that has hitherto received far too little attention: 'For seeing that in the wisdom of God the world through its wisdom knew not God . . .' In the light of the tradition we have just referred to, it is at once apparent what a wealth of meaning these few words have as a technical phrase. Paul is thinking about the wisdom of the divine control of history [226] and says: when God gave the nations wisdom he presented them with the possibility and the task of discovering the wisdom of his dealings with them in human life and history, so that they might attain to a living and personal knowledge of God himself.[227] So in I Cor. 1.21 we have a counterpart to Rom. 1.18 ff. In the former passage (Rom. 1) Paul is writing about the possibility and task that was offered to man of attaining to a theology of creation; in the latter of the possibility and task of a theology of history.

Paul speaks about a possibility and a task that was offered, for these two possibilities and tasks are today irretrievably lost. But why so? Man declined to have as the guiding light of his own wisdom the wisdom of God which, in fact, illuminated him.[228] By so doing he was refusing to give recognition, adoration or praise to the divine majesty—not indeed by any open rejection, but in the covert form of falsification. Mankind is ungodly, not godless; a pseudo-theologian, not an atheist (Rom. 1.21, 23, 25). Why is that? Because man wanted his own wisdom to be his illumination (Rom. 1.22; I Cor. 1.19 ff.). So the fall of primeval man has its fulfilment in the fall of the nations (Wisd. 10.3, 5; SBar. 54.17 ff.). The need to vindicate human wisdom forms the starting-point of the pseudo-theology. And the consequence? God withdraws from the world of nations (cf. AEn. 42) and leaves the wisdom that seeks its own glory to its own light, and man thus loses the power of distinguishing between God and idols,[229] between the *gloria dei* and the *gloria mundi* between revelation and delusion.[230] His mind becomes confused, and the light of his own wisdom is extinguished (Wisd. 13 ff.; Rom. 1.21 ff.; cf. EpJer. 50 ff.). So beginning with a theology of creation we pass by way of natural theology to a theology of nature.

What comes out of it all at the end is a natural ethics, or rather a morality of nature, which arises because the faculty of distinguishing properly between the natural and the unnatural has been lost (Rom. 1.24 ff.). Such an ethics makes the concept of God serve the purposes of godlessness. Men justify what is against nature by the concept of the natural, and in the end there is no lack of philosophers to give the immoral a moral foundation.[231] Mankind has closed its eye to God's light, so as to be led by its own light[232], and has thus fallen victim to the delusions of a demonic will-o'-the-wisp (TestN. 3.3; cf. II Cor. 4.4; II Thess. 2.11). This is the situation of the world today. It does not know God (Psa. 78.6; I Thess. 4.5; Gal. 4.8; further Wisd. 13.1; Acts 17.23, 30). But that things have come to this pass is not God's fault, nor that of his creation, nor yet of his control of history; but man himself is to blame. He has absolutely no excuse (Wisd. 13.8; Rom. 1.20; cf. John 15.24 f.). Far from God being to blame, he has actually placed in men's hearts their own accuser—in the form of conscience.[233] Men can listen to the voice of conscience, or turn a deaf ear to it. But the time is coming when conscience will appear in court against man as a witness for the prosecution in the last judgement (Rom. 2.12 ff.).

Paul speaks three times in Rom. 1 about a divine *permissio*[234]. God 'gave them up' to those powers to which they had yielded themselves.[235] He gave the whole of humanity over to itself until it had reached the very point of destruction (Rom. 3.9 ff.; 11.32). For this reason natural theology and natural ethics are bound to be wrecked by the very effects they produce, and so produce that extremity for man which is God's opportunity (Acts 17.29 ff.). Men must use their powers to the utmost, they must make use of every device and try out their individual capacities to the last degree before their autonomy destroys itself by its own excess. Not till that happens will they be ready to listen to the message of the cross (Col. 3.9 ff.). For the Word of the cross is the *ultima ratio* which God has provided for the history of man.

But what is to come of the problem of natural theology? The Word of the cross marks the end of all the false attempts which are summed up in the concept of natural theology. But God takes nothing away from man without giving it back in a new and glorious form (Mark 10.29 f.; Luke 12.31). So the gospel of Christ is the starting-point of a new understanding of universal history in which the age-long ideals both of a theology of creation and of a theology of history find a surprising fulfilment (cf. Ch. 5; 45). 'In Christ,' says Paul, 'are all the treasures of wisdom and knowledge hidden.' And one of Paul's disciples writes in Heb. 11.3: 'By faith we understand that the worlds have been framed by the Word of God' (cf. Rom. 1.20; Luke 12.24; Matt. 6.26 ff.). And another of his disciples writes in Eph. 3.8: 'Unto me was this grace given, to preach unto the Gentiles the unsearchable of Christ; and to make all men see what is the dispensation of the mystery . . . that now . . . might be made known through the Church the manifold wisdom of God.'

Chapter 19

THE INADEQUACY OF LEGALISM

E. Grafe, *Die Paulin. Lehre vom Gesetz,*[2] 1893; J. M. P. Smith, *The Moral Life of the Hebrews,* 1923; W. G. Kümmel, *Rom.* 7 *und die Bekehrung des Paulus,* 1929; A. M. Brouwer, *Die Bergrede,* 1930; B. H. Branscomb, *Jesus and the Law of Moses,* 1930; S. M. Enstlin, *The Ethics of Paul,* 1930; R. Bultmann, 'Rom. 7 und die Anthropologie des Pls', *Festschr. f. G. Krüger,* 1932; W. Gutbrod, *Die Paulin. Anthropologie,* 1934; H. Windisch, *Der Sinn der Bergpredigt,*[2] 1937; P. Benoit, 'La Loi et la Croix', RevBibl, 1938.

In the NT teaching about the law we have a classical example of how Paul builds on Jesus. So we hope by a point-for-point comparison not only to make a contribution to the historical problem of Jesus and Paul, but also to find the proper way to a theological understanding of the apostle's teaching about the law, which, in spite of much labour, has not yet been adequately dealt with.

'Blessed is the man that . . . standeth not in the way of sinners . . . but his delight is in the law of the Lord' (Psa. 1.1 f.). These are the opening words of the first hymn in the Jewish hymn-book. Jesus refers to such sentiments more than once. The teacher of the law is convinced that he has the key of knowledge in his hands, and thinks of himself as the leader of the blind. The Pharisees encompass sea and land to make one new convert to the people of the law (Luke 11.52; Matt. 15.14; 23.15 f., 24). But all they do is to make a son of hell out of him (Matt. 23.15). For the instruction given by the Synagogue suffers from the fatal contradiction between teaching and life. 'All things whatsoever they bid you, these do and observe: but do ye not after their works,' Jesus tells the people (Matt. 23.3, 13). But he attacks the actual teaching too. For all its appearances of pious zeal the Halacha deals most impiously with the will of God (Mark 7.1 ff.; Matt. 23.23 ff.). But did Jesus know nothing of the example of moral earnestness and strenuous discipline which the really great teachers of the law gave to their disciples? He did recognize them for what they were, and called them the strong, the righteous or the healthy (Mark 2.17). He realized that they were different from the rest. But he knew, too, that many of them simply prided themselves on not being as other men were: 'God, I thank thee that I am not as the rest of men, extortioners, unjust, adulterers . . .' (Luke 18.11). A man like this no longer has his delight in God, but in his own piety, and in a thanksgiving of that kind a new 'fall' takes place, a new victory of self-glorification in its most dangerous form, viz. the form of pious self-gratification (Luke 18.9; cf. Matt. 23.6 f.). People of this sort have all they want. There is but one thing lacking—the approval of God (Luke 18.14). But Jesus does not just watch the Pharisees from a distance when they stand and pray (Luke 20.47). He knows what is inside a man (Mark 2.8; John 2.25)—and he calls the legally righteous 'whited sepulchres' (Matt. 23.27). A thin covering of righteousness hides what is really a grave full of death and decay. Behind a façade of security there hides a heart that has lost all its certainty.[236] The contradiction between teaching and life is a mere nothing compared with this conflict between the inner and the outer which is particularly widespread in those who take the law literally (Matt. 23.25 ff.; cf. Mark 7.6). Jesus calls them hypocrites and sons of hell (Matt. 23.15). What Jesus sees at work at this point is the deep mendacity of the adversary.

The righteousness which is of the law can win no entrance into the Kingdom of God (Luke 11.52). The Torah is divine law given by God to meet the emergency of man's historical situation; and it has therefore an historical task to perform. The function of the Torah was to bring man's satisfaction with this world to an end, and to quicken in him a thirst for righteousness (Matt. 5.6). But the Pharisees can go about with all the appearances of satisfaction, for they have turned the historical function of the law into its exact opposite. So the struggle between them and Jesus is necessarily a life-and-death struggle; and hence Jesus contrasts the illegitimate exegesis of the law—the Halacha—with its legitimate interpretation —the Sermon on the Mount (Matt. 5.27 ff.; cf. 7.29). But the mystery of the Sermon on the Mount is the paradoxical response it everywhere evokes. It makes man say 'no' to it, because it demands the impossible. But at the same time it calls forth an elemental 'yes', for what it requires is the only thing that is possible. This is the dire conflict into which Jesus thrusts men with his penetrating exegesis of the law—so that in their need men may learn the hunger and thirst which the Torah can only quicken, but never quench (cf. Matt. 5.20; 6.33). But who can quench it? There is none other than Jesus Christ himself (Luke 11.46; Matt. 11.28 ff.). So the Torah either takes us to Christ, or leads us astray.

The Scribes and Pharisees and their associates put up a very determined resistance to this encroachment on their preserves. Paul persecuted the Christians because he saw, as a rabbinic student and a Pharisee, that they shared Jesus' ideas about the Torah. Like Job of old, he protested his righteousness to the very last. But after Damascus he 'laid his hand upon his mouth' and kept silence, as Job did after he had seen God (Job 40.4; 42.1 ff.; cf. Isa. 6.5). After Damascus he gave up his glorying in the law so as to give all glory to God (Gal. 2.16; Phil. 3.7; Rom. 7), and became the first disciple of the Torah to pass from the law to Christ.[237]

When Paul writes about Pharisaic pride in the law he uses almost the same formulae that occur in the tradition about the teaching of Jesus.[238] He says that his one-time associates thought of themselves as 'leaders of the blind'. They boast of the law and of their learning in it (Rom. 2.17 ff.; cf. Ch. 43). But there is little to justify their pride (Rom. 2.5 ff.; 3.9 ff.), for their conduct is scandalous. Paul exposes the disastrous contradiction between their teaching and their life in almost the same words that Jesus had used (Rom. 2.21 ff.). But Paul also knows something of the fine and strenuous struggle which distinguishes the life of the true disciple of the Torah from that of the half-hearted majority. For he is one such disciple, the most zealous of them all (Gal. 1.14; Phil. 3.6 f., 9). For Paul it is an honour to belong to those who are called 'the people of the law' (Rom. 2.17, 28 f.). Many years after his conversion he can still say with Peter: 'We are Jews by nature, and not sinners of the Gentiles' (Gal. 2.15). But what is even more plain to Paul is the danger of that self-satisfaction which comes from pride in the law, the same danger that Jesus had himself pointed out. He knows why his fellow Jews, especially the 'zealous' among them, want nothing at all to do with *sola cruce*: 'They seek to establish their own righteousness' (Rom. 10.2 f.). The alternative that confronts man is that between the wisdom of the world and the wisdom of God (Ch. 18). But as the apostle knew well enough from his missionary experience, that particular issue is child's play compared to that which the Jews had to decide in their history—that between the righteousness that is of the law and the righteousness of God. Here for the first time in the history of the world the fight between the *gloria dei* and the *gloria mundi* reaches its utmost severity. Finally, Jesus exposed the tension between the inward and the outward for what it really was, whereas the Pharisees could only get more and more involved in it. Paul follows Jesus here too, and adds to his description of the outward condition of the Jew under the law in Gal. 2.15 a description of his inward state in Rom. 7.7 ff. Such a Jew is not content with the imperfections which Paul castigates in Rom. 2. Paul found no satisfaction in being able to pose as an unimpeachable Pharisee (cf. Phil. 3.6). He is a 'zealot' in the sense of Gal. 1.13 f. and Rom. 10.2 f. He means to take God's will revealed in the law utterly seriously. But that involves him in a conflict of which the contented and the compromisers have no inkling. The continuity of the old self has gone—and a tension has been set up between a self which says 'no' to the law and a self which says 'yes' to it. The divine law has to be translated into reality. But no sooner is that recognized than the adversary, who has such power in men's hearts, opposes it with his own 'no' (Rom. 7.8, 11). Certainly the inner man has his delight in the law of God (Rom. 7.22), but there is a law of perversity governing his will so that though he wants to do the good, he actually does evil (Rom. 7.15, 17, 21). Yet, in spite of this, man cannot fail to admit that God's commandment is right—and with such a judgement he passes a sentence of death upon himself (Rom. 7.16, 23, 25). This is the lost citadel where legalistic Judaism fights for its honour, the point of death to which the Torah brings mankind.[239]

After all this what can we say about the function of the law in the history of salvation? Paul calls the law a schoolmaster who with his rod drives the Jew under the law on to Christ.[240] The law has not been in existence from the very beginning, nor is it of final validity (Gal. 3.17; II Cor. 3.13 f.). It is an interim measure to expose sin and bring it to an end (Rom. 5.20; 4.15). Paul can go so far as to call it 'the strength of sin' (I Cor. 15.56). In the providence of God the law was meant to expose the latent crisis in which man has stood ever since the fall (Gal. 3.19 ff.; Rom. 7.7, 13 f., 23 f.), in that way performing a function exactly parallel to that of conscience among the Gentiles. By allowing sin to do its work it was meant to pave the way for the sole glory of the God of mercy. The way of the Torah is either a bypath or it leads to the cross. For 'Christ is the end of the law' (Rom. 10.4).

Chapter 20

CHRIST AND HIS KINGDOM IN THE OLD COVENANT

A. v. Undern-Sternberg, *Der . . . Schriftbeweis de Christo und de evangelio in der alten Kirche . . .* 1913; J. Jeremias, *Der Gottesberg,* 1919; O. Schmitz, 'Abraham im Spätjudentum und Urchristentum', *Festschr. f. A. Schlatter,* 1922; G. Wuttke, *Melchisedech,* 1927; F. Hvidberg, 'Die 390 Jahre der sogenannten Damaskusschrift', ZAW, 1933; W. Staerk, 'Eva-Maria', ZNW, 1934; H. Danthine, . . . *Les Arbres sacrés dans l'Iconographie de l'Asie . . .* 1937; R. Bauernreiss, *Arbor Vitae,* 1938; A. v. Blumenthal, '*Τύπος* und *Παράδειγμα*' Herm., 1928; L. Goppelt, *Typos,* 1939.

'Surely the Lord God will do nothing, but he revealeth his secret unto his servants the prophets' (Amos 3.5 MT). Apocalyptic made a maxim for its theology of history out of this prophetic saying: just as everything in the world has its origin in the Word and finds its realization in an act of revelation, so it is with the times of the Most High. They have their origin in words and premonitory signs, but their end is miracles and wonders.[241] Matt. 11. 13 is part of this same tradition: 'All the prophets and the law have prophesied until John.'[242] But what has God announced in words and prophetic signs, in the law and the prophets? The answer of the NT is: Christ and his kingdom.

IV Ezra gave first place to God's promise by word; and the same view is adopted by the writers of the NT. The OT was a prophetic book whose words had been fulfilled in the coming of Christ. The disposition to interpret the OT christologically has come most decisively from Jesus himself. And yet the very earliest statements that he made are not just conceived in terms of promise and fulfilment, but they tell how God would cause offence by fulfilling his promises in a way that would run counter to human expectations (Luke 7.22 f.; cf. 4.18, 29). But very soon after the death of Jesus this very necessary reservation on all proof by prophecy disappeared, and the primitive Church could the more happily set about constructing a new understanding of scripture centring in the coming of Christ (Luke 24.27). In Matt. the evangelist makes scriptural proof the theological clue of his presentation. The things he tells us of the life of Jesus are said to have taken place 'that it might be fulfilled as it was written . . .'[243] The fourth evangelist places little emphasis on particular applications of prophecy apart from his story of the passion, but even he shared with his predecessors the conviction that the scriptures were the book of life—though only when interpreted christologically (John 5.39). Paul gives further expression to this way of thinking when he uses his metaphor of the veil over the face of Moses (II Cor. 3.13 ff.). The scriptures of the OT had found their end and their fulfilment in Christ. The man who really understands scripture is the man who grasps the fact that now it has, to speak theologically, outmoded itself[244]. But the meaning of the OT remains hidden to the man who does not accept that fact, but instead tries to understand it as having its meaning and purpose within itself. For in the last resort the OT authors wrote 'for our sakes',[245] often to explain or exhort, sometimes also to warn. They wrote for our time in which the ages of history have found their fulfilment (I Cor. 10.11; cf. 9.9 f.; Rom. 4.23 f.). The old covenant was a time of promise, and therefore the book of the old covenant is inevitably a book of promises.[246]

But the events which constituted the story of our salvation in the OT were also promises, or *prodigia* [247] to use the word of IV Ezra. Thus Jesus can see Jonah as a prophetic symbol of the Son of Man (Luke 11.29 ff.; cf. John 3.14; 6.31 ff.). Paul describes man's first parent as 'the figure of him that was to come' (Rom. 5.14).[248] He was the first man, pointing beyond himself to his future counterpart, the second man. The exegesis of the early Church understood the curse in Gen. 3.15 (it shall bruise the serpent's head) as a *protevangelium*. Paul can even speak of the promise of the very event which evoked the curse. At one particular point the whole course of universal history was set on the road to destruction. At another particular point there can be, there must be, there will be an equally decisive turn to salvation. In the same way, though without the contrast of prophetic signs, the fate of the people of the old covenant is used in I Cor. 10.6 as a type to warn the Church of Christ. In the same way, though without using the word 'type', the apostle, in the richly suggestive midrash of Gal. 4.21 ff., uses the old covenant as a pointer to the new, the earthly Jerusalem as a sign of the heavenly, and the past struggles of the *civitas dei* as a sign of the future warfare of the *civitas christi*.[249] Paul has given a very thoroughgoing treatment to the story of Abraham in its character of a promise, first of all in Gal. 3, and then not long afterwards in Rom. 4. If Adam had been a kind of negative pointer to the future coming of Christ, Abraham is a positive sign,[250] for he points beyond himself and beyond the whole dispensation of the law to the future justification in the sign of the cross (Rom. 4.3). But even the law is not simply a schoolmaster to bring us to Christ, for the Torah contains prophecy in a hidden form. According to I Cor. 5.7 the annual celebration of the passover is a prophecy foretelling the true passover Lamb on the cross (Ch. 30). The great day of atonement which is celebrated year after year in accordance with the requirements of the law is, in the view of Rom. 3.25, a sign pointing to the cosmic day of atonement, Good Friday, when a new situation for the whole world was brought about (Ch. 35). Next, Paul's disciples developed their master's typological terminology. We get the idea of an 'antitype' (I Pet. 3.21; Heb. 9.24), and we read of the 'shadows' cast by the great events of the age of salvation (Heb. 10.1), and of the 'perfecting' of the story of salvation that was told in the OT (Heb. 7.11, 19). But they also developed Paul's thought as regards its content. According to Heb. 7 Abraham is put into the shade by his unknown contemporary Melchizedek, who was fatherless and a priest in perpetuity—and therefore the earliest figure of Christ as the great High Priest.[251] Heb. also deals with the great day of atonement, which Paul had treated with such pregnant brevity. In Heb. 9, the day of atonement is looked on as the anticipatory sign [252] of the atoning work which the heavenly High Priest has accomplished at the end of the ages (Heb. 9.11 ff., 26 ff.). It anticipates that work in two ways, as a promise of the one who is to come, and at the same time as a cry for help addressed to him (Heb. 10.1 ff.).

All pre-Christian history is the prehistory of Christ's coming, pointing by both word and deed teleologically to the cross. This is the great and basic idea which informs all these individual motifs, and which the early Church developed into a monumental synopsis of the OT story of salvation. With Adam begins the inheritance of human sin which reaches disastrously all through the history of the universe. But at the same time Adam is the original type of the Christ who was to come. For just as by one man the powers of death have gained their dominion, so by one man will the powers of life gain their victory throughout the world (IgnE. 18 ff.). The story of the old people of God began with Abraham, and it has been a story of election, of faith, and of conflict between the *civitas dei* and the *civitas diaboli*—and in it all there is given an unique promise of the coming *civitas christi* (Barn. 9.7 ff.). The law brings the crisis to its peak, the world's complete conviction of sin. But at the same time the old covenant is a sign of the new, and the propitiatory rites of the law are a prayer and a promise pointing beyond themselves to the atoning work of Christ. But prophecy tells us in its promises what path the Christ must tread according to God's premundane plan (IgnPhld. 9.2; JustinDial. *passim*).

This teleological interpretation awakened a remarkable response in the art of the early Church.[253] Hellenistic art and mythology was dominated by the principle of tautology. The departed one 'is' Osiris[254], the one rescued from hades 'is' Persephone[255], the deified ruler 'is' Zeus or Helios or Hercules or Aeneas.[256] But this exposes one of the basic presuppositions of ancient thought, that of the myth's indifference to time, or rather of the myth's timelessness. But the NT writers and the painters and sculptors of the early Church did their thinking essentially in terms of time, and thought of the history of salvation. So instead of a timeless tautology we now pass to a typology of salvation-history.[257] Joseph's sufferings are a sign of Christ's passion.[258] Isaac's road to the place of sacrifice is symbolic of the *via dolorosa* that Jesus trod: hence Isaac carries a cross instead of a traveller's pack.[259] Christ's saving work repaired the damage done by Adam's transgression; hence the skull of our first parent shows beneath the cross, and Adam is brought to Golgotha in accordance with God's secret plan, and will now be redeemed by the outpoured blood of Christ.[260] But these are individual motifs,[261] though they were very soon joined into typological cycles known as 'concordances of the OT and NT'.[262] We cite one example from the time of Constantine: Adam's expulsion from Paradise and the thief's reception there; the flood and the baptism of Christ; Isaac going to the sacrifice and Jesus carrying his cross; the selling of Joseph and the selling of Jesus; the passage of the Red Sea and Christ's descent into hell; Jonah's return to the light of day and the ascension of Christ.[263] So one after another the things that happened in the time of promise pointed beyond themselves to the time of fulfilment. But the painters and sculptors of the early Church were just as much at home in portraying the prophetic sayings of the OT. In the Priscilla catacomb at Rome there is the figure of the prophet Isaiah pointing with his raised hand to the Virgin Mary with her child and to his natal star.[264] On a later sarcophagus we find Moses with the law, though the law bears as a sign of its hidden theological meaning the Christ monogram.[265] The beginning thus is in the word—but the end is in work of revelation!

Chapter 21

THE PASSION OF CHRIST'S FORERUNNERS

W. Mundle, 'Die Stephanusrede, eine Märtyrerapologie', ZNW, 1921; F. J. F. Jackson, 'Stephen's Speech in Acts', JBL, 1930; W. Wichmann, *Die Leidenstheologie*, 1930; K. Galling, 'Jesaia-Adonis', OLZ, 1930; W. Nestle, 'Legenden vom Tod der Gottesverächter', ARW, 1936; E. Bickermann, *Der Gott der Makkabäer*, 1937.

The OT itself says of the children of Israel: 'They mocked the messengers of God, and despised his words, and scoffed at his prophets' (II Chron. 36.16). For later writers it was axiomatic that the people of God were basically opposed to whatever really emanates from God, and that therefore they had always persecuted God's true servants and ambassadors, and always would (App. 1).

Jesus inherited this kind of thinking. In Luke 11.49 ff. he quoted a now lost wisdom martyrology where the Wisdom of God recited the list of the persecuted servants and messengers of God from Abel down to Zechariah.[266] In Mark 9.13 he refers to a text of scripture which tells of the martyr's fate awaiting Elijah when he returned, a fate Jesus thought to have been fulfilled in the case of John the Baptist.[267] In the same style he gave in Mark 12.1 ff. a martyrological summary of the whole course of salvation-history.[268] But Jesus did not make use of these ideas or make these quotations just to revive a well-known tradition. The martyrs and confessors of the past were for him not only ambassadors of God; they were his own forerunners. The story of the war between God's people and the messengers God had sent, the tale of the martyrs from Abel to John the Baptist, had a goal to which, theologically speaking, the whole story had been pointing as its climax and to which it was now pressing with an eschatological speed: the killing of the Son. The Son is an ambassador, too, and that is why he will suffer the same fate as the prophets (Luke 6.23, 26; 13. 33 f.). Yet he is more than all the messengers of the past, and therefore the ancient hatred of the people of God will now reach its zenith and achieve its greatest triumph.[269] But with that the measure is at last full—and God will avenge the blood of his Son and all his forerunners on 'this generation' (Luke 11.50; 13.33; Mark 12.8 f.).

Jerusalem, the 'city of God', had become the *civitas diaboli*! This idea proved most efficacious, and after the crucifixion was a favourite theme with the Christian church in the sharp exchanges it had with Judaism (cf. Rev. 2.9 f.; 3.9; 11.8). The principal document of this struggle is Stephen's speech in Acts 7, which in form is a disputation, but in substance is a review of Israel's history in the manner of Mark 12.1 ff. The traditional arguments about persecution govern the exposition in 7.35, 39, 51, 52a, only to lead in the last sentence to a surprising turn of the argument: the prophets God's heralds, and not simply forerunners of Christ, they are his heralds who promised his coming, and they were persecuted precisely on that account.[270] So in the last resort the fight that the fathers fought was a fight against Christ![271]

In the epistle to the Hebrews the prophets are thought to be the messengers of the same Word that has now been proclaimed decisively to men in the coming of Christ (1.1 ff.). So wherever we find pre-Christian stories of martyrs we can recognize signs of the cross.[272] For the writer of Hebrews the evil entreating of Moses is the same thing as the reproach of Christ.[273] When Isaac was saved from death the writer saw in it a parable and promise of the raising of Christ from the dead.[274] Thus right through the story of the sufferings in Heb. 11 there runs like some blood-red thread the passion of Christ, to find its climax in Heb. 12.1.

The sufferings of the figures of the old covenant is the prologue to the story of Christ's passion. That is the basic thought of the passages we have reviewed, a thought which has its most powerful expression in the figure of the forerunner, as the NT calls him. According to Jesus this is Elijah, who is to prepare the way of the

Lord.[275] He is the man who in his own person sums up the pre-Christian era, because he brings it to an end.[276] He sums it up in himself so as to bring it to an end, and in order to make way for the new age—in which there is no room for himself. Just as Moses could only see the promised land from afar, so the Baptist could only behold the kingdom from afar off (Luke 7.28; John 3.27 ff).[277] This makes plain not simply the greatness and the tragedy of one human being, but the greatness and the tragedy of the whole OT dispensation. The last and greatest representative of the OT stands and greets the promises from afar off—and dies (cf. Heb. 11.13). For the new Elijah is Christ's forerunner in more than his appearance and his message. His martyrdom is the fulfilment of his office as the new Elijah: the blood-red sign of the cross at the end of the OT's story of our salvation, and at the beginning of the story of Christ. That is why the figure of the Baptist on the altar at Isenheim points with outstretched finger to the crucified: *Illum oportet crescere   me autem minui.*

Chapter 22

CHRIST'S WORK IN THE OLD COVENANT

H. St J. Thackery, *The Relations of St Paul to Contemporary Jewish Thought,* 1900; E. Becker, *Das Quellwunder des Moses in der altchristlichen Kunst,* 1909; L. Ginzberg, *Legends of the Jews,* III, 1911; VI, 1928. F. J. Dölger, 'Der Durchzug durch das Rote Meer als Sinnbild der christlichen Taufe', AC, 1930; 'Der Durchzug durch den Jordan als Sinnbild der christlichen Taufe', ibid.; J. Bonsirven, *Exégèse rabbinique et Exégèse paulinienne,* 1940.

The Christ was pre-existent, the agent of creation, the bearer and sustainer of creation's life (Col. 1.17; Heb. 1.3; cf. Ecclus. 43.26). This made it very easy to draw the further conclusion that the Christ was also the agent and the bearer of the OT story of salvation. Is this conclusion, in fact, drawn in the NT? Three passages can be quoted to support it.

In the very first verses of his Gospel John writes of the pre-existence of the *Logos* and of his agency in creation. In 1.6 ff. he goes on to talk about the Baptist and the incarnation of the heavenly *Logos.* In between he says that all things were made by him, and without him was not anything made that hath been made, that in him was life,[278] that this life was the light of men, and that this light shineth in the darkness.[279] Perhaps these words amount to an assertion of the control by the pre-existent Word in the history of salvation (cf. John 8.56 ff., but also 1.17). For we have here in brief the pre-history of Christ's saving work (i.e. before Christmas) as a counterbalance to Rev., which tells of the future saving work of Christ (after Good Friday and Easter Day).

Paul discusses Christ's activity in salvation-history in one passage only, but then with unmistakable clarity. In I Cor. 10.4 ff. the apostle is writing about one of the favourite themes of the old biblical tradition, the miraculous provision of water in the desert by Moses.[280] Like the writer of PsPhil. 10.7; 11.15 and other traditions, he presupposes that the rock which provided the miraculous source of water was not stationary, but moved about with the Israelites.[281] So he calls it a spiritual rock.[282] Then, applying traditional exegetical formulae, Paul identifies the rock with Christ.[283]

These ideas gained further currency among Paul's disciples. 'The prophets sought and searched diligently . . . what time or manner of time the Spirit of Christ which was in them did point unto, when it testified beforehand the sufferings of Christ, and the glories that should follow them' (I Pet. 1.10 f.).[284] OT prophecy is prophecy of Christ in a twofold sense, for Christ is both its subject and its object together. The prophets, filled by the spirit of Christ, foretold what should happen to him.[285]

Christ himself is active in the history of the old covenant, said Paul. It is Christ himself who speaks in the prophets of the OT, says I Peter. But John seems to unite them both in his assertion: in all the story of creation from the beginning until Christmas Day all true light and all true life come from Christ.

THE COMING OF CHRIST

Chapter 23

CHRISTOLOGY AND THE HISTORY OF RELIGION

H. Gressman, *Der Messias*,[2] 1929; A. J. Festugière, *L'Idéa religieux des Grecs et l'Évangile*,[2] 1932; S. Loesch, *Deitas Christi und antike Apotheose*, 1933; P. Volz, *Die Eschatologie der jüdischen Gemeinde*,[2] 1934; A. Christensen, *Le ... premier homme et le premier roi dans l'histoire légendaire des Iraniens*, I, 1917, II, 1934; K. Prümm, *Der Christliche Glaube und die altheidnische Welt*, I, II, 1935; L. Bieler, *'ΘΕΙΟΣ ΑΝΗΡ'* I, 1935, II, 1936; W. Staerk, *Soter*, I, 1933, II, 1938; H. S. Nyberg, *Die Religionen des alten Iran*, 1938; E. Stauffer, 'Zeitwende und Christuszeit', EMZ, 1942.

In Rev. 5 we are told about the book of the world's destiny, sealed with seven seals, and set by God's throne. An angelic herald makes a proclamation and cries out: 'Who is worthy to open the book, and to loose the seals thereof?' And there was no one in the heaven or on the earth or under the earth who was able to open it. And the seer of Patmos wept because of this. But then he heard another voice which said to him: 'Weep not: behold, the Lion that is of the tribe of Judah—the Lamb that hath been slain—hath overcome, to open the book and the seven seals thereof.' This is the contribution of the primitive Church to the question raised by the history of religion (cf. Mark 2.17; John 4.22 ff.; 10.16; 12.20 ff.). For the coming of Christ is God's answer to the questions raised by human history.

These questions can take many forms. For Babylonian religion it is the problem of death that is in the foreground. The hero Gilgamesh desperately tries to find the plant of immortality, and Ishtar, the goddess of life, descends in vain to the underworld to try to loose the dead from their captivity.[286] Buddhism sees all the problems of existence concentrated in its suffering. Buddha saw through this suffering and found a way to a solution, the way into the blessedness of Nothing or Nirvana.[287] But in the Buddhist communities of the Far East the great teacher of former times has become the heavenly rescuer (Amida Buddha), who will not himself pass into Nirvana until the last of his companions has found the way thither.[288] Sin is recognized as the basic problem in the Edda. The story of the gods is the story of a sin—and the end of the story is the twilight of the gods. Heroic Thor, gloomy Odin, and the whole world of the gods collapse under the heavy curse of their own sin.[289] In this way the truly profound spirits of the different peoples and times constitute a *communio peritorum*, an invisible community of the wise who have penetrated to the essentially calamitous character of everything in this world. They are realistic enough to know that there is no power in this world able to overcome the calamity. And this is, perhaps, the ultimate wisdom: no one is worthy! And it is, perhaps, out of this abysmal knowledge that the cry comes for a deliverer, the dream for a saviour: 'Who is worthy?'

Such a postulate of a deliverer or saviour was given a particularly concrete form in the picture of history that Iranian mythology painted for itself. We are told about the first man Gayomard, who as the masterpiece and the master of creation exercises authority in a paradisal world.[290] We are told about a first catastrophe, the origin of all the calamities in the world.[291] and about a sequence of deliverers (Saoshyants) who come with heavenly authority into the world of human destiny.[292] Zarathustra is one such deliverer, the 'saviour of life', as he called himself, who is honoured by his followers as a follower and successor of Gayomard.[293] But Zarathustra's work of salvation is unfinished, its completion being reserved to the end of the days. Then the final saviour will come, conceived of a pure virgin by the hidden seed of Zarathustra to bring the work of salvation to its completion.[294]

Among the mythologies of the world's high religions outside Christianity the Iranian was probably the only one to exercise any influence upon the formative stages of NT christology.[295] But it also exercised an influence on the bypath of the old biblical tradition. What do we learn there about heavenly and earthly deliverers in the past and in the future?

From the first to the last it is God the 'Lord' who is constantly proclaimed by the old biblical tradition to be the deliverer of deliverers. God himself is the 'saviour' that the prophets proclaim, the deliverer king whose coming they announce. But in later times there was a certain 'decentralization' of divine power, a transference of the divine work of deliverance to heavenly and earthly agents. As heavenly mediators of God's work in creation and salvation-history apocalyptic introduces angels (especially Michael, the angel of the people of God) and other mediatory beings such as *Logos* and *Sophia*. But, according to apocalyptic expectations, God has put his final work into the hands of the Son of Man, who is already standing at God's throne, and who will one day, like the last Iranian deliverer, bring man's original nature to realization in a renewed creation. But God has also brought earthly agents into the service of his plan of salvation, patriarchs (Enoch, Joseph), kings, prophets, intercessors, teachers, and last but by no means least, martyrs. Most of them were figures known already in the OT. But the post-canonical tradition adopted these men of God into its own use, and endowed the story of their work and destiny with manifold features beyond the limits of history.[296] There are journeys to heaven, journeys to hell, battles with demons and monsters, deaths bringing salvation, journeys back from the dead and suchlike things.[297] Even the future king of Davidic descent, the Messiah, was originally a terrestrial character.[298] He was the hope of national political circles. Admittedly, he is sometimes blended with the eschatological deliverer of apocalyptic, the heavenly Son of Man,[299] and sometimes the figure of the Messiah is deepened by traces of martyrology.[300] But his original political historical character always comes to the top.[301] Just about the time that Jesus came a secret messianic oracle had stirred men's minds very deeply.[302] Political leaders and revolutionaries came forward, until in 66 A.D. there was an organized resistance movement (cf. Acts 5.36 f., and also John 4.29; 7.26 ff.; Matt. 24.5; Mark 13.21). We then see the revolting spectacle of the cultured Jew Josephus making capital out of the secret hopes of his unhappy people, greeting the emperor as the fulfilment of all the messianic promises, and in return getting a handsome post as a prophet at the imperial court.[303] The rising itself was suppressed, but the political hope had not yet been extinguished. It flamed up once more with some power in the days of Bar-cochba and his aged apostle Akiba, who proclaimed him as the son of the star mentioned in Num. 24.[304] But even this last great messianic rebellion came to grief, Bar-cochba fell, and Akiba later suffered a martyr's death—a different man from

Joseph and a quite different end. Already in the ancient world there were two kinds of Jew. Yet hopes of a political messiah decreased.[305] A century after Akiba Johanan Bar-napaha drew the final conclusion from the historical experience of many generations: the children of Israel were in bondage in Egypt, and Moses rose up and delivered them. They were in bondage to the Babylonians, and Daniel rose up and delivered them. They were in bondage to the Greeks, and the Maccabees arose and delivered them. Now they were in bondage to the insolent Romans, and the Israelites said: 'We want no further deliverance by flesh and blood, but our deliverer is Yahweh Sabaoth, whose name is the Holy One of Israel.'[306] So the old biblical expectation of a deliverer comes back to the point from which it started. God himself is once more the one and only deliverer.

This was the sort of world in which the writers of the NT grew up, and to which, in due time, they brought their message of Jesus Christ. How did the new message of deliverance relate itself to the traditional hope of salvation? Three main ideas stand out at once in this debate in the field of the history of religion. First: Jesus is the fully authorized agent of God in salvation-history. God himself appears and acts in him. It is thus that NT christology adopts for its own purposes the whole range of old biblical predicates for God. Second: Jesus is the divine agent in whom the offices of previous agents, terrestrial as well as celestial, find their unity and their perfection, and in whom also there is a realization of the prophetic-apocalyptic expectations of a deliverer (Matt. 1.22; II Cor. 1.20). So, instead of the increasing decentralization of the various functions to be performed in salvation-history that was going on in pre-Christian apocalyptic, an opposite tendency now shows itself—a concentration of function. The NT saviour takes on himself all the very different motifs and characteristics of the old biblical tradition of a deliverer. Third: the mission given to Jesus in the history of salvation is an offence to the nationalist circles and parties. His kingdom is not of this world. And so the NT picture of the Christ has cast off all traces of a political and revolutionary Messiah.

But the situation in regard to the history of religion was very different in the hellenistic world to which Paul took the Christian gospel. Here, too, a number of ideas about a saviour were very much alive, but they were not so much related to the gods[307] as to divine men. Research over the past years has shown more and more clearly that the idea of divine men was an old and well-established tradition in the ancient world. We can hear of miraculous births, of lives full of miracles and heroism, and of the transfiguration and deification of the dying.[308] The heroes of prehistoric days were adored as god-men, but so, too, were the great poets and philosophers of history, and in particular the hellenistic kings and Roman emperors.[309] It is just at this point when the king or emperor is deified that the need of the hellenistic world for a saviour finds its most powerful and elemental expression. The ruler is the one who realizes every really attainable hope of a deliverer, he is the saviour of the world!

The NT writers radically rejected this apotheosis of human beings,[310] particularly the cult of the emperor. The rejection is expressed in three ways. First, they refuse the emperor any sort of divine honours or acclamation. None has the right to claim worship save God and his Christ. Second, the rejection is seen in the names and titles of honour that are bestowed on Christ. Titles taken over from the old biblical tradition and which had become a staple part of the christology of the primitive Church found a new use as providing an antithesis to hellenistic ideas. New hellenistic names and formulae were also added to the Church's vocabulary, names claimed for Christ alone, and making him a rival to the emperor. Third and last, the Church expressed its rejection of hellenism in the far-reaching form of interpreting the ancient world's adoration of its heroes, its apotheosis of the emperor and its expectation of a saviour in terms of its own theology of history as prophecies and anticipations of Jesus Christ and his saving work.[311] In this way Orpheus becomes a signpost to Christ, and finally the Christian emperor a type of the final saviour of the world.[312]

But when did the much discussed 'hellenization' of Christianity take place? Harnack looked for its beginnings in the second century, Bousset in pre-Pauline times at Antioch. Harnack has proved to be right. That at any rate has been the outcome of catholic research in recent decades: Catholicism developed as a synthesis of Christianity and hellenism. But primitive Christianity is both prehellenistic and antihellenistic.

Chapter 24

THE SON OF MAN

G. Dupont, *Le Fils de l'Homme*, 1924; C. H. Kraeling, *Anthropos and Son of Man*, 1927; H. Dieckmann, '"Der Sohn des Menschen' im J.', Scholastik, 1927; J. Jeremias, *Jesus als Weltvollender*, 1930; R. Otto, *Reich Gottes und Menschensohn*,[2] 1940; E. Sjöberg, *Der Menschensohn im aethiopischen Henochbuch*, 1946.

Of all the names and titles for Christ we have to give historical and theological primacy to the one which Jesus himself used to indicate his significance for the theology of history—that of the Son of Man. The one-time 'modern' quest for the historical Jesus interpreted the name 'Son of Man' in terms of Psa. 8.5, and was specially attracted to it as a guarantee of the complete unpretentiousness of the historical Jesus who was, and wanted to be, no more than a man among men. But the contribution of the history of religions has taught us better than that. 'Son of Man' is just about the most pretentious piece of self-description that any man in the ancient East could possibly have used!

At the end of his night visions of the four kingdoms the apocalyptist Daniel saw the throne-room in heaven, where God passed judgement on the kings of the peoples in order to transfer his own world dominion to the Son of Man.[313] There has been some discussion among recent exegetes whether this Son of Man must be thought of as an individual ruler, or whether as a symbol for the people of God, which, according to Dan. 7.27, is to assume worldwide dominion. What did the earliest interpreters, whose work Jesus would have known, have to say about this?[314] The answer is given in AEn. 46. Here, too, the subject of the text is a vision of the throne, which presupposes the vision in Daniel and in many respects reproduces it or embellishes it (Ch. 71). But here the Son of Man is quite unambiguously thought of as an individual. Indeed, it is precisely with the person of the Son of Man that the whole Enochian literature is concerned. In 46.1 the face of the heavenly man is compared to that of an angel.[315] In 48.2 ff. and 62.7 we read that the Son of Man has been pre-existent from the beginning and waits by the throne of God! Similarly, his relationship to the people of God, which has been such a puzzle to the modern interpreters of Daniel, is here transparently plain. The Son of Man is the *primogenitus* and the *princeps designatus* of the people of God (62.7). At the end of the days he will gather the quickened ones to himself and share with them the great banquet (62.13 ff.). And more than that, he will be the light of the Gentiles; the future of mankind rests on the Son of Man (48.4). In Dan. 7.10 the Ancient of Days is the judge of the world; but in AEn. 61.8 it is the Son of Man who acts as judge in the name of God. He will ascend the throne of his glory, and sweep off the earth all the agents of destruction that have afflicted the world since Adam, and will reign as king of a new Paradise in a world where affliction is no more (69.25 ff.).[316]

The sayings of Jesus in the synoptic Gospels about the Son of Man are not based on Psa. 8, but quite expressly (Mark 13.26 f.; 14.62) on Dan. 7, and the subsequent apocalyptic tradition.[317] Jesus claims for himself all the heavenly majesty of this Son of Man. Yet this celestial glory belongs to a man who, as the height of improbability, treads the way of suffering. The heavenly man in the form of a servant—that of the Son of Man of whom Jesus speaks. So on the lips of Jesus[318] the old apocalyptic idea is given a deep paradoxical meaning, which is developed in three groups of sayings: about the hidden majesty, the *via dolorosa* and the revealed glory of the Son of Man.

In the old biblical tradition the Son of Man is a ruler. But in Mark 10.45 the Son of Man is come 'not to be ministered unto, but to minister'. He is not concerned to gather the righteous together (as in AEn. 62.13) but he seeks the lost (Luke 19.10). He is not the king of Paradise (as in AEn. 19.29), but has less than the animal creation (Luke 9.58). For all that, this Son of Man is the *princeps* of man's world, and as such has authority over the Sabbath (Mark 2.28). For all that he is the representative of God and controls the issues of life and death, not only at some distant date and in heaven, but also here and now on earth (Mark 2.10). The miracles that are the accompaniments of the coming of the Son of Man (IV Ezra 13.50, etc.) serve to confirm the authority of Jesus (Mark 2.11 f.). Woe then to the man who is offended by the obscurity of the Son of Man. Whoever is offended in him, whoever betrays him, is lost (Luke 12.9; Mark 14.21). Blessed is the man who confesses the Son of Man and falls down before the hidden majesty of Jesus (Luke 12.8; cf. AEn. 48.2).

In AEn. the Son of Man is hidden before the throne of God. In the synoptic Gospels he is hidden while he is actually walking about among men. But this hiddenness reaches its climax on the cross. The Son of Man goeth, even as it is written of him (Mark 14.21). It is written of the Son of Man that he must endure much suffering and reproach (Mark 9.12; cf. 8.31 *'oportet'*). In Luke 18.31 ff. Jesus says: 'Behold, we go up to Jerusalem, and all the things that are written by the prophets shall be accomplished unto the Son of Man. For he shall be delivered up unto the Gentiles, and shall be mocked, and shamefully entreated, and spit upon; and they shall scourge and kill him: and the third day he shall rise again.'[319]

In later apocalyptic the Son of Man is said to rise from the depths of the sea.[320] In Matt. 12.40 the Son of Man rises out of the depths of the earth three days after his death.[321] But there is still a veil of secrecy over his heavenly majesty until the time that he comes on the clouds of heaven (Mark 13.26; 14.62; cf. Dan. 7.13) suddenly like a flash of lightning to be seen by all (Luke 17.24; cf. SBar. 53.8 ff.; 72.1 ?). That is the 'day of the Son of Man' (Luke 17.24; 21.34; cf. Ch.16). From now on it is the revelation of his glory that is taking place, now are realized the traditional expectations about the heavenly man (AEn. 69.29; Mark 13.31). The Son of Man will rid the world of all destruction and every agent of destruction (Matt. 13.41 f.; cf. AEn. 69.27 f.), will collect the new humanity together from the four ends of the earth (Mark 13.27; AEn. 57; IV Ezra 13.13), mount the throne of his glory to hold judgement and establish the Kingdom of God (Mark 8.38; Matt. 25.31; Mark 9.1; cf. AEn. 46.4 ff.). This is where the road ends that goes through the depths, and takes him in the form of the servant to the cross.

In the apocalyptic tradition the Son of Man is a pre-existent heavenly being. The sayings about the Son of Man in the synoptic Gospels seem to presuppose that, but make no express reference to it (Matt. 12.29). But the Johannine Christ speaks *expressis verbis* about the pre-existence of the Son of Man in heaven and of his descent to this world.[322] The invisibility of the heavenly Son of Man is continued in the obscurity of the earthly Jesus. But the descent of the Son of Man is but the beginning of the road that leads down into the depths of death, but thereafter takes the Son of Man once more up to his original glory in heaven (John 3.13 f.; 6.61 f.; Rev. 1.13, 17 f.; cf. Acts 7.56). From thence the Son of Man will come again to judge (John 5.27; Rev. 14.14; AEn. 69.27 ff.), to hold the eschatological banquet (John 6.27; AEn. 62.14) and to reveal his glory to all the world (John 8.28; cf. AEn. 62.3 ff.). Then all the angels will worship him as once they were meant to worship primordial man (John 1.51; cf. VitAdEv. 14).

The term Son of Man is reserved in the four Gospels to Jesus' description of himself,[323] and apart from that it is only the evangelists themselves who use the term, and even they do so but very occasionally (see above Acts; Rev.).[324] But the idea of the Son of Man lives on in the Pauline letters under a new christological word that gives linguistic expression to the same thing under the term 'Man' and its further development and correlatives.[325] This terminology gives a far more distinct expression to the antithesis between Christ and Adam than the name Son of Man could do.[326] What is the basis of the analogy? Adam is the head of the first humanity and the first creation;[327] Christ is the head of the second humanity and the second creation (cf. Col. 1.15 ff.). So Adam can be called the first man, and Christ consequently the second man.[328] And what is the basis of the antithesis between them? Between Adam and Christ there is an antithesis in regard to their origin (I Cor. 15.47), of nature (I Cor. 15.22, 45 f., 49) and of will (Rom. 5.18 f.; 8.20 f.). But both analogy and antithesis find in the end a dialectically rich expression in the idea that Christ is the express image of God. According to I Cor. 11.7 the first man is the image of God (Ch. 11). But this image is marred (Ch. 14 f.). Hence only Jesus Christ, the second man, is the image of God in a full and final sense.[329] In the fulness of time he appeared as the visible image of the invisible God (II Cor. 4.4 ff.), and as the beginning of a new humanity to restore God's marred image in us.[330] In this way Paul develops out of the idea of the Son of Man in the synoptics and John the basis of the doctrine of recapitulation (Ch. 57). He develops it, but has no need to introduce it. Jesus already had an idea of the Son of Man that comprised a whole theology of history in itself. In calling himself the Son of Man Jesus had already taken the decisive step in claiming cosmic history as his own.

Chapter 25

'CHRIST', 'LORD' AND OTHER TITLES

F. L. A. Hort, '*Μονογενὴς Θεός in Scripture and Tradition*', 1876; A. Seeberg, *Die Anbetung des 'Herrn' bei Paulus*, 1891; W. Wrede, 'Jesus als Davidsohn', *Vortr. und Stud.*, 1907; G. P. Wetter, *Der Sohn Gottes*, 1916; P. Th. Paffrath, 'Der Name "Sohn der Gottheit" ', in, *Festschr. f. F. Hommel*, I, 1917; W. Foerster, *Herr ist Jesus*, 1924; A. E. J. Rawlinson, *The NT doctrine of the Christ*, 1926; W. W. v. Baudissin, *Kyrios*, I–IV, 1929; E. Fascher, *Προφήτης*, 1927; E. Lohmeyer, *Kyrios Jesus*, 1928; E. v. Dobschütz, '*ΚΥΡΙΟΣ ΧΡΙΣΤΟΣ*', ZNW, 1930; W. Bousset, *Kyrios Christos*,[4] 1935.

The title 'Son of Man' is Jesus' own description of himself. It was never used to address, or to acclaim him, and as good as never to make confession of him. This meant that in the NT the title is supplemented, and in course of time replaced by a host of other titles, which for the most part originated as forms of address to the earthly Jesus or as acclamations of the exalted Christ. We can only take a short survey of them as we bring the prolific material into some sort of christological order and consider them as descriptions of a pedagogic, a prophetic, or a messianic sort, or as concerned with the theology of the passion or with the divine majesty.

The title first used to address Jesus was that of 'Rabbi' (Mark 13.1; John 1.38; Mark 10.51; 12.32). At the beginning of his ministry Jesus appeared to friend and foe alike as a master of scriptural exegesis, as a teacher of the law and of wisdom. Yet he was no professional theologian, and spoke with an authority of his own particular kind (Ch. 29). So even the title 'Rabbi' when applied to Jesus logically comes to have a meaning all its own.[331]

The same heightening of meaning applies to the title of 'prophet'. Is Jesus a prophet, either a new prophet[332] or some old prophet returned?[333] That was the question commonly asked by the nation. But the Church answered 'no' he is a prophet in an exclusive sense, the prophet that should come.[334] The prophet absolutely.[335]

Jesus himself never accepted either the pedagogic or the prophetic title. The first title he did accept as a valid and accurate description of his saving mission was that of 'Christ' (Mark 8.29). This gives a special authenticity to the title of Messiah as a predicate to describe Jesus Christ. The early Church laid claim to all the honours that this title involved. Particularly did she stress the Messiah's vocation to suffer (Acts 17.3). Yet she did not give up the Messiah's kingly office, titles like 'Son of David, Lion of the house of Judah',336 even though she rejected their traditional political interpretation (John 18.37; Acts 2.36). In the end, all on its own, the name 'Christ' took into itself the greater part of the content of the idea of the Son of Man.337 Admittedly, the hellenistic Churches would have known and understood little of all this, though that did not hinder the advancement of the name 'Christ'. The Hebrew name for Messiah was already in circulation without an article. The Church kept the name Christ by and large without an article too, and so it very soon passed from being an independent title to serve as a permanent member of a proper name. Thus it circulated in the Greek world in the form: Jesus Christ.

Most of Jesus' titles include in their meaning a reference to the passion motif.338 But the passion was so central for the primitive Church that it created a whole series of titles giving expression to her theology of the passion. Thus, following Wisd. 2 f., Jesus is called God's Righteous One, who was to be persecuted by his own people with all the apostates' hatred of God.339 Again, in the style of the Servant Songs (Isa. 42; 49; 52 f.; cf. also *pais* in Wisd. 2.13) Jesus is called the Servant of God (Matt. 12.18; Acts 3.13, 26; 4.27, 30; cf. 8.32) who was to bear the sin of those who deny him and persecute him.340 The picture of the Lamb without blemish that was slain belongs to this same circle of ideas (Ch. 30). Finally, Heb. speaks of the Mediator of the new covenant, of the High Priest who has saved the people of God with his own blood.341 Jesus suffered a martyr's fate, but he was no martyr among others. His was a higher office, since his person was more exalted (Heb. 7.26).

That leads us to the titles which refer to the person of Jesus Christ, and describe his divine majesty. The title 'Son of God' is one which describes his messianic office342, and serves first of all to emphasize his unique position though without intending to convey anything about his origin (Psa. 2.7; IV Ezra 7.28; Mark 14.61). This idea of the Son of God in its meaning of messianic office found its way into the christology of the NT, and not without the consent of Jesus himself (Matt. 16.16; Acts 13.33; Heb. 1.5). But it was not only used there in this sense.343 In the synoptic Gospels, as well as in John and Paul, the term 'Son of God' has a twofold meaning. It is a description of an office; but it is also an assertion about an origin. The Son of God is not only anointed by God. In some way he comes from heaven.[344] In the NT Jesus can be quite simply called 'God'.[345] In Psa. 44.7 f. the king anointed by God is twice addressed as 'God'.[346] Heb. 1.8 f. applies this psalm and therewith the divine titles in it to the Messiah. Paul goes a step further and in Rom. 9.5 transfers a doxological formula which originally applied to God the Father to God the Son[347]: 'Who is over all, God blessed for ever. Amen.'[348] The pastoral epistles abound in solemn formulae which are applied now to God and now to Christ.[349] In the Johannine writings we find such *theos*-predicates as regular christological titles.[350] John 1.1 lays down the divine nature of the premundane *Logos*.[351] In John 1.18 Jesus is called the 'only begotten God'.[352] Thomas makes his confession of the risen Lord in 20.28 with the words 'My Lord and my God.'[353] And in I John 5.20 Jesus is called the true God.[354] These christological *theos*-predicates had their origin in the liturgy, and it was here that in post-Johannine times they retained their special place (see Ch. 63).

But of all the christological titles the richest is that of 'Lord'. Its history is a compendium and at the same time a *repetitorium* of NT christology. For in a few years it passes through the main stages of the development of christological titles, and so takes us once more along the road from the pedagogic and monarchic to the divine honouring of Jesus Christ.

'Lord' is the favourite form of address for those disciples or suppliants who come to Jesus. It is a name of honour which in the first place refers to his authority as a teacher.[355] But it soon replaced the name of 'Rabbi' and acquired a meaning that went far beyond the bounds of a teacher's function.[356]

As far back as Psa. 110 the word *kyrios* is used to describe the majesty of the king who was the subject of divine favour. The psalm was very early given a christological interpretation (Mark 12.35 ff.; Acts 2.30 ff.; cf. SB. IV, 452 ff.) and in that way the word *kyrios* came to mean the kingly office of Christ. *Kyrios* meant ruler! Jesus was 'Lord' in this sense even in the days of his ministry, and he himself laid claim royal honours and rights when in Mark 11.3 he refers to the distraint of the beast on which the Messiah is to ride with the words: 'The Lord hath need of him.'[357] He is a king, though an uncrowned king. 'Lord, dost thou at this time restore the kingdom to Israel?' the disciples ask in Acts 1.6 (cf. Luke 2.11). His coronation takes place in quite another way: the risen Lord ascends to his heavenly throne and there takes his place at the right hand of God (Acts 2.36; cf. Rev. 19.16). In this way Psa. 110 is fulfilled!

The figure of a ruler is the normative one in Semitic religion used to describe the Godhead. God is a ruler, he 'lords it' over the world, and so is almost always called upon by the Semites as 'Lord' (Baudissin). This is also true of Israelite religion, and is the reason why the sacred name Yahweh is always replaced in the Hebrew OT by *Adonai* (..Lord), and translated in the LXX by *kyrios*. Where the Hebrew OT speaks about the day of Yahweh, the LXX talks about the day of the Lord. And in this way the title *kyrios* came to be identical in meaning with the name of God itself. The NT took over this linguistic tradition but at the same time it applied to Christ the title *kyrios* that in the OT had been used of God. The *parousia* of Christ thus becomes 'the day of the Lord' (Matt. 24.42; Acts 2.20b; n. 709). When the prophets require their hearers to call on 'the name of the Lord' they are understood to ask for a calling on the name of Christ (Acts 2.21; Ch. 63). The consequences of this *interpretatio christologica* are far reaching in the extreme. The name of God, and therewith the functions of God, are ascribed to Jesus (cf. Ch. 23). In the OT God is the Lord who in his mercy forgives sins.[358] In Acts 7.60 Stephen prays to his heavenly Master: 'Lord lay not this sin to their charge' (cf. Luke 23.42). The crucified Lord prays to the Father, in the words of the Psalmist: 'Into thy hands I commend my spirit' (Luke 23.46; Psa. 30.6a). Stephen prays: 'Lord Jesus, receive my spirit.'[359] Even the earliest Church in Jerusalem prayed to Jesus, and called on him as their Lord, their God: 'Maranatha—O Lord, come!'[360]

So by the time Paul began his work in the Church Christ was already seen to be possessed of all the necessary qualifications to bear the name of *kyrios*, even in the highest, divine sense. Paul found the name Lord as an element in the liturgical tradition that he stepped into, and he accepted it and developed its use (as against Bousset). So from the time when Paul wrote his letters onwards the title Lord was used much more frequently than any other, and at the same time attained a much deeper meaning, and this in four ways: first, Paul used the name *kyrios* in a wholly personal sense. After Damascus the apostle became the bondslave of Jesus Christ, but Jesus was the Lord who had the life and work of his bondslave entirely at his disposal, the one to whom Paul turned in everything that concerned his labours for his Lord (II Cor. 12.8). Second, though the name *kyrios* was particularly applicable to the exalted Lord, it also applied to the Christ who entered upon his passion at the Last Supper (I Cor. 11.23b), and Paul himself can call the crucified Lord the 'Lord of Glory' (I Cor. 2.8; cf. Acts 3.15). This means that Paul's use of *kyrios* takes on some colour from the theology of the passion. Third, the emphasis admittedly falls throughout on the unfolding of the risen Lord's power, and it is just in this connection that Paul made some significant developments in some points of the theology of the primitive Church. The exalted *kyrios* (Col. 2.15) has authority over all the powers that affect our destiny, he is 'Lord of Lords'.[361] The epistle to the Colossians shows us with what a sense of liberation this *kyrios* theology must have come to the hearts of hellenistic readers, enslaved as they were by a belief in fate. That leads us to the fourth and last point. In Paul's letters and in the Churches that he founded the use of *kyrios* had an unmistakably antithetic character (cf. Ch. 23). In the midst of a world that worshipped or feared Lords of every kind, Paul confessed his Lord, and the Church confessed him who was Lord of the world to come (I Cor. 8.5).

Chapter 26

'AND WAS MADE MAN'

H. Schumacher, *Christus in seiner Praeexistenz und Kenose*, I, 1914, II, 1921; R. Seeberg, '*O λόγος σάρξ ἐγένετο*' *Festg. f. A. v. Harnack*, 1921; F. Loofs, 'Das altkirchliche Zeugnis gegen die herrschende Auffassung der Kenosisstelle', ThStKr, 1927; W. Weber, *Der Prophet und sein Gott*, 1923; J. G. Machen, *The Virgin Birth of Christ*, 1930; W. Foerster, '*Οὐ ἁρπαγμὸν ἡγήσατο* bei den griech. Kirchenvätern', ZNW, 1930; M. Dibelius, *Jungfrauensohn und Krippenkind*, 1932; P. R. Botz, *Die Jungfrauschaft Mariens im NT . . .*, 1935; A. Kurfess, 'Vergils vierte Ekloge in Kaiser Konstantins Rede an die Versammlung der Heiligen', ZNW, 1936.

There are two demands that the pre-Christian story of the concept of destiny has to make upon the Church's soteriology. The whole world is so involved in Adam's sin that the situation can be redeemed, if at all, only by God himself. Then the fate of this world is so radically bound up with that of man that the actual work of deliverance can only be effected in terms of a human life. Both requirements are fulfilled in the coming of Christ.[362] To work that out was the first concern of NT christology.

Both these intentions are given their rightful place in Jesus' description of himself: he is at one and the same time a heavenly being and the new man, who begins the history of man over again at the old starting-point, but with a new start (Ch. 24). Paul pushes this double start through to its logical conclusion. He sees in Jesus the incorporation of a heavenly nature that mediated the creation of the world (I Cor. 8.6; Col. 1.16), and that since creation has sustained the world (Col. 1.17) and has already effectively intervened in the pre-Christian story of salvation (I Cor. 10.4). This heavenly man came to earth in the fulness of time so as to carry out the great work of deliverance towards which universal history had been directed ever since the beginning (I Cor. 15.47; cf. 8.6; Col. 1.15 ff.). But this descent was not accomplished in some brilliant and powerful epiphany; it meant rather a renunciation of the richness of heavenly conditions of existence in favour of the poverty of life on earth.[363] The heavenly Son of God came into history as the son of a woman, indeed as a member of a Jewish house (Gal. 4.4; cf. Rom. 1.3; 9.5). He took upon himself the form of sinful flesh, the burden of a life that has been afflicted hereditarily ever since the days of Adam (Rom. 8.3). In this way the Son of God comes to carry alien burdens, our burdens (cf. Gal. 6.2), and enters into the position of fallen man, who is under sin (Rom. 3.10) and the law and the curse (Gal. 4.4; 3.13), and he redeems that position. Up till now we have only lifted out the *disiecta membra* of Paul's Christmas gospel from his earlier epistles, and brought them together. Our reconstruction is confirmed and enlarged by the conspectus that Paul constructs for us himself in one of his later letters, in the hymn of the incarnation in Phil. 2.6 ff.: the logical starting-point is a participle which indicates the form in which the pre-existent one had his being.[364] The idea is developed by means of an ingressive aorist which tells us that he laid aside his former mode of existence.[365] The heavenly being accepts a metamorphosis for himself.[366] It takes him along the road of self-subjection to the bondage of corruption[367] and he was 'made in the likeness of men'.[368] But the pre-existent one did more than give up his previous position: he renounced all the possibilities of advancement that that position gave him.[369] In Phil. 2.6 the form of the pre-existent one is expressly distinguished from identity with God. The heavenly being thrust the temptation to *anabasis*, but rather laid his heavenly existence aside and entered on a *katabasis* which took him to his cross. To Satan's attempted self-exaltation God thus once replied with a plunge into the depths, into depths lower than Satan's were at first. To the Son's self-humiliation God replied with an exaltation to a height which went even above the original place that the Son held.[370] The Son now receives as a gift what he had scorned to snatch for himself before he started out on his cosmic *via dolorosa*,[371] viz. the place of honour as equal with God (Phil. 2.6), the name that is above every name (Phil. 2.9 ff.), the OT name for God—*kyrios*. In receiving this name Christ attains to the place of divine rule and honour which the Lord God claimed for himself in Isa. 45.23. But this honour of the Christ is not self-glorifying encroachment, not demonic seizure of God's honour, but on the other hand, a service to the *gloria dei* that God himself has willed.[372]

Matthew and Luke in the prefaces to their Gospels try another way of expressing the twofold concern of NT christology. Christmas Day is the day of the new creation, and the hour of Christ's birth is the long expected critical hour of cosmic history.[373] Why? The Spirit of God mentioned in Gen. 1.1 comes into action in a new Genesis (Matt. 1.18!) and a divine miracle (Luke 1.37) creates the new man who realizes the promise of Gen. 3.15 and fulfils the frustrated hope of Gen. 4.1. Like the first man, Adam (Luke 3.38), the new man comes directly from God. But he is not only, as Adam was, simply the recipient of the divine breath of life.[374] He was conceived by the Holy Ghost of the Virgin Mary (Luke 1.35; Matt. 1.18). So Jesus is at one and the same time both Adam's son and God's.[375]

This idea of parthenogenesis might very well have been suggested by similar ideas in the history of religions.[376] There is preparation and support for it in the stories of the miraculous births of Isaac, Joseph (Gen. 30.22), Samson, Samuel and John the Baptist.[377] Later on it was made much use of, developed and refashioned.[378] It was not universally accepted in the early Church. Possibly Paul had not learnt of it. But later still even John took no cognizance of it, to the very great astonishment of the early catholic readers and copyists (see John 1.13).[379]

John was much more disposed to push the synoptic understanding of the coming of Christ beyond its limits, by bringing the ideas of Paul and Jesus to their fulfilment in the idea of the incarnation: 'And the Word became flesh'. Matthew and Luke tell us that Jesus was conceived by the same Spirit that once was the agent of creation.

John 1 tells us that the divine *Logos* which was once the agent of creation now himself appears in the form of a creature.[380] Moreover, he appears in a form which for a long time has been alien and hostile to the Creator, the form of the historical. This incarnation does not turn out to be a marriage or fusion of heaven and earth, but much rather a shattering and a defeat of death that prevails in history.[381] There was no lack of prophets before the incarnation to proclaim God's word in the midst of an hostile world; but their proclamation could only aggravate the situation, never overcome it. But the Christ is more than one who proclaims God's Word. He is himself God's Word, the Word that God speaks, the revealing, saving, creative Word that does not return void (cf. I John 1.1 ff.; Rev. 19.13). So the *Logos* of creation has come in the flesh in its historical form and with its burdens so that, in the form of the historical, he might take the former creation to its appointed goal.[382] The incarnate *Logos* 'tabernacled amongst us', says John 1.14. Here in the event of the incarnation the principle of the incarnation becomes clear.[383] The God of the NT comes down out of heaven, and seeks man in his own world, meets him at the place where he stands, and finds him where he is at home.[384] The Son of God becomes man in order to find man.[385] He enters upon our earthly life with its mortality, descends to the depths where we are so as to raise us to the heights where he dwells (John 12.32; 14.2 f., 23; 17.24; Rev. 3.20 f.). In all this we hear nothing of the high ways by which those who seek after God ascend to the goal of their desires. And as the *Logos* pitched his tent amongst his disciples,[386] so Christ goes with his Church on its way through history (cf. Matt. 28.20 *vobiscum*), and so the Church tabernacles amongst the nations and goes with them through history as the tabernacle of God among men.[387] Phil. 2 tells of an exaltation: the path that Jesus follows through the depths leads at the last up to the place that the pre-existent one originally held. John tells us of the ascension, of Christ's return to the heavenly place from which he set out (3.13 f.; 6.62; cf. 10.17 f.). 'And now, O Father, glorify thou me with thine own self with the glory which I had with thee before the world was' (John 17.5). Paul's theology of history is dynamic, teleological, and the end is more impressive and glorious than the beginning. John's theology of history is static and aetiological. The end is but the realization of the basic metaphysical position, and we find that the situation is restored as it was at the start (Ch. 6; 56).

In Chapter 3 we made a distinction between the doxological, the antagonistic and the soteriological interpretation of Christ's life. Here, at the beginning of his life, all three modes of apprehension find expression in the understanding of his becoming man: the pre-existent one renounces his own glory, so as to bring about the glory of God (Phil. 2), and he reveals the eternal glory of God in the broken forms of our historical existence (John 1). His coming into the world is an invasion of enemy territory (Phil. 2.7 f.), and entry upon a state of war (John 1.11). He treads his earthly road so as to conquer the world's distress, and he does it for our sakes and for our salvation (Rom. 8.3; John 3.16). This threefold inter-pretation of Christ's life, which is stated basically in these propo-sitions, now finds its subsequent realization in what the NT tells us of the life of Christ and his passion.

Chapter 27

THE GLORY AND MAJESTY OF GOD

H. Schumacher, *Die Selbstoffenbarung Jesu bei Mt* 11. 27, 1912; G. P. Wetter, '"Die Verherrlichung" im J', Beitr. z. RelWiss., 1918; K. Zickendraht, '*ΕΓΩ ΕΙΜΙ*' ThStKr, 1922; G. Bertram, 'Die Vorstellung von Christus auf Grund biblischer Aussagen über sein Äusseres', ChrW, 1939.

The life of Jesus is a living doxology. The purpose of history is to establish the glory of God, and it is therefore the purpose of Jesus, of his activity and desire. That is the dominant idea of the synoptic tradition about Jesus. Deut. 6 is his favourite chapter from the OT. In the story of the temptation Christ fights for the integrity of the confession of monotheism, for the sole glory of the one God (Matt. 4.7, 10). According to Matt. 5.16 the final principle for the life of Christ's disciples must be to glorify God. In Luke the *glorificatio dei* runs like a golden thread through the whole presentation of the gospel. The praise of the Church is taken up and lost in the praise of men and angels who glory in the wonder of Christmas (Luke 1.46, 68; 2.14). At this point the story takes the decisive turn towards its proper goal! Even the story of the death of Jesus comes to an end in a doxological motif (Luke 23.47). The miracles which Jesus works during his ministry serve the glory of God. The people praise God (Luke 7.16; 18.43) and those who are healed give thanks

(Luke 13.13; 17.15; 18.43). Jesus himself awaits it and desires it to be so (Luke 17.17 f.; see Ch. 42). For only where God is glorified can man's salvation be effected. That is why in the Lord's Prayer the petition for the hallowing of God's name precedes the prayer for the coming of the Kingdom and all the other requests. For the same reason the divine doxology stands in the hymn of Christmas before the message of peace on earth. Likewise in Luke 17 the glory of God is the first thing (15 f.) and the healing of the leper the second (19). The faith which bows before the *gloria dei* is the faith that delivers men.

But this *gloria dei* is not only the chief thing for which Jesus lived and struggled; it is the reality which is revealed in him. *Ecce Deus*—that is the basic meaning of the gospel of Jesus Christ, right from OT times.[388] The Baptist is the forerunner of God in the sense of Mal. 3.1 just because and in so far as he is the forerunner of Jesus Christ (Luke 7.27). 'Immanuel' is the name given to the Christ: 'God with us' (Isa. 7.14; Matt. 1.23). We were without him; but now he is with us. The 'Johannine' saying in Matt. 11.27 drew all this together in the pregnant formula of the threefold relationship between Father, Son and world, which in turn is based upon the unique mutual relationship between God and Christ.[389] 'All things have been delivered unto me of my Father: and no one knoweth the Father save the Son, and he to whomsoever the Son willeth to reveal him.'[390]

John promptly developed this idea of God's honour and glory. It is zeal for God's house that 'eats up' Christ, John 2.17. He seeks the glory of him who sent him—even to the death of the cross, by which he must glorify God (7.18; 21.19). So Jesus answers the devil's company with the brief argument: 'I seek not mine own glory . . . I honour my Father' (8.49 f.; cf. Luke 4.8; otherwise in Luke 11.15 ff.). The spirits divide on the question that divides the worlds: 'self-glory or God's glory'; and it is on this basis that Jesus sees the fundamental opposition between the leaders of Judaism and the Christ of God (John 5.41 ff.).

In John, however, the idea of glorifying God is derived from the basic conception of the revelation of God's glory. That we should praise God's glory because of Jesus Christ presupposes that God discloses his glory to us in Jesus Christ. In this sense the Johannine Christ utters his perplexing formula: 'I am' (John 8.24 ff.; cf. Mark 13.6), which is derived from the name of Yahweh and which, according to OT tradition belongs to God as the absolute

Subject of all history (Ex. 3.14; Deut. 32.39; Job 33.31 LXX; cf. Ch. 6). Jesus does not displace God, he represents him, he can make himself equal, indeed identical, with God (John 5.18; 10.30). The incarnate Word is the completely valid bearer of divine revelation in the form of this world. Thus he says: 'He that hath seen me hath seen the Father' (John 12.45; 14.9 f.). In this way the Johannine Christ is properly given divine authority and name not only before the incarnation and after the ascension (John 1.1; I John 5.20), but also during his earthly life (John 1.18; cf. 10.33 ff.; 20.28). So it is that the revelation of God's glory in the manifestation of Christ is the basic theme of John: 'We beheld his glory, glory as of the only begotten from the Father' (1.14). The Johannine miracles are revelations, accomplished to make manifest his glory.[391] He does not perform the miracle of the wine at Cana or of the bread on the hillside just to cope with a difficult situation. The wine which he created was, indeed, too good (2.10) and much too rich [392] for the guests. And twelve baskets remained over from the bread which he created (6.13; cf. 21.11). He created so as to manifest his divine glory, and he revealed his glory here in superabundant profusion (cf. John 10.10). The God who reveals himself in the miracle of the wine and the miracle of the bread is the God who has fulness in himself, who delights in fulness and who pours out his fulness upon his perishable creation (Ch. 11). Even Christ's miracles of salvation are done for the sole purpose of serving the revelation of God's glory (John 9.3 ff.). Why does Jesus wait until Lazarus is dead before he intervenes with his miraculous powers (John 11.37)? Jesus tells the disciples: 'This sickness is not unto death, but for the glory of God, that the Son of God may be glorified thereby.' And to Martha he says: 'If thou believedst, thou shouldest see the glory of God' (11.4, 40). This is the profundity of God's way. His glory is most gloriously revealed where the situation is the most hopeless, where the possibility of being saved by worldly means is exhausted (Ch. 15). It is not revealed in a story that is nothing but light, but in a victory of life over death, of the mercy of God over the sins of the world (Ch. 51). The glory as of the only begotten from the Father is full of grace (John 1.14, 17).

Jesus preached the glory of God in a world that sought its own glory. He revealed God's glory in a world intoxicated with its own. So his life is one long battle—the decisive battle of the age-long war between the *gloria dei* and the *gloria mundi*, between the *civitas dei* and the *civitas diaboli*.

Chapter 28
THE KINGDOM OF GOD AND
THE DEMONIC POWERS

A. Jirku, *Die Dämonen und ihre Abwehr im AT,* 1912; B. Violet, 'Der Aufbau der Versuchungsgeschichte Jesu', Harnackeh-rung, 1921; S. Eitrem, *Die Versuchung Christi,* 1924; A. F. Macinnes, *The Kingdom of God in the Apostolic Writings,* 1924; A. v. Gall, βασιλεία τοῦ θεοῦ, 1926; O. Bauernfeind, 'Die Worte der Dämonen . . .', *Vortr. und Aufs.,* 1930; H. J. Korn, ΠΕΙΡΑΣΜΟΣ, 1937; E. Lohmeyer, 'Die Ver-suchung Jesu', ZSTh, 1937.

The Son of Man is connected with the Kingdom of God as early as Dan. 7.[393] Jesus claimed the title of Son of Man for himself (Ch. 24). He proclaimed the advent of the Kingdom of God (Matt. 4.17; 11.12). He joined both together and declared: the Kingdom of God comes in and with and as the coming of the Son of Man. 'For lo, the Kingdom of God is amongst you' (Luke 17.21). It is al-ready there, in his person and in his work.[394]

Hence the adversary, who never forgets his enmity against God and all that belongs to God (Gen. 3.15; Rev. 12.9). Hence the 'old dragon' is ready to use the same decisive counter-blow (Rev. 12.3 ff.). He sets every body and every thing in motion against God. The ruler persecutes the children of his territory (Matt. 2.16 ff.; Luke 13.31; 23.11), the pious, the theologians, the priests all accuse him, one of his own disciples betrays him, the populace throw stones at him (John 8.59; 10.31), the Roman judge condemns him (Matt. 27.19 ff.). The reasons for this hostility are different in every case, but the relentlessness of it is universal. People who are at enmity among themselves find themselves allied in the fight against Christ (Luke 23.12). A 'United Front' is formed, held together by nothing else than a defence against Christ. 'Not this man, but Barabbas' (John 18.40). But where does the unanimity of this mortal enmity come from? It is the spirit of the adversary, answers the NT, which is active in them all (Luke 22.3; John 1.5, 10 f.; 3.19 f.; 6.70; 17.12). Jesus tells his persecutors the same thing to their face in Luke 22.53: 'This is . . . the power of darkness.'

But the attack which the adversary launched against the life of Christ is nothing in comparison with the demonic assault on

Christ's will. This is the point upon which all the characteristic power, intelligence and the deceit of the old serpent who led the whole world astray (Rev. 12.9) is now concentrated. The synoptic story tells us that Satan tried on three different occasions to deceive and sap the will of the Son of God. Once at the beginning, a second time at the turning-point, and the third time at the very end of his life.[395] The end of it all was, in the words of John 14.30: Christ is the first and only one who has never fallen to the seductions of the old serpent, who has no need to fear when the accuser appears who accuses every son of man day and night (cf. John 8. 46). But the attacks of the adversary are shattered. The future course of history is decided—by Jesus' exercise of his will in his earthly life, and lastly by his prayer in Gethsemane.

Jesus was not content simply to be on the defensive against the assaults of the demons; he passed over to the attack. Hence the idea of the Kingdom in our Lord's teaching has an expressly polemical accent: 'But if I by the finger of God cast out devils, then is the Kingdom of God come upon you' (Luke 11.20). The Kingdom of God is present where the dominion of the adversary is overthrown.

Jesus enters the earthly sphere from heaven as the all-powerful contestant (Matt. 12.29 ff.; Luke 11.18 ff.; cf. I John 3.8; IgnE. 19.3). He knows the voluntary powers that have their fling in hatred of the elements, and he subdues them. The powers that are hostile to creation have found their master in him, and bow before him when he issues his commands.[396] He overcomes the demons who work mischief in the hearts of men. He restores to health all who have been overwhelmed by the devil (Acts. 10.38). The demons know right away who is in front of them and what lies before them, just as the prisoner instinctively knows the executioner (Mark 1.34): The fear of death gets hold upon them (Mark 1.24; cf. Jas. 2.19). Yet they make a legal protest—their time has not yet run out: 'Art thou come hither to torment us before the time?' (Matt. 8.29; cf. Mark 5.7, 10; Luke 11.24; Rev. 12.8). Jesus does not torment them (Mark 5.12 f.), neither does he carry out final sentence upon them yet. But wherever he meets them he drives them before him; for God is with him (Acts 10.38). His alliance with God is the secret of his victory (Mark 9.29). He drives the foe from his fortress with a divine invective that allows no gainsaying.[397]

Jesus beats the tempter back and attacks the demons. But even the fight with the demons has its temptation! It is the age-long temptation to drive out the devil with Beelzebub, to drive adversity from the world with adversity, sin with sin, demons with demons. But that only means that the form of adversity is changed, while the fundamental situation remains the same, indeed is only intensified and aggravated (cf. Luke 11.24 ff.). The Pharisees actually make this accusation against Jesus, and say that he fell to this temptation of casting out demons by the prince of demons (Mark 3.22). But Jesus had alone, at the very beginning of his ministry, put this temptation from him once and for all (Matt. 4.8 ff.). He trod a quite new road of historical activity, and for the first time in history took the line of radical renunciation of all demonic aids. God's work must be done and carried through by the use of divine powers, and nothing else whatever.[398] so that what results will prove to be for the first time really God's work, in no way dependent on or indebted to the Prince of this world. Hence Jesus alone proves to be stronger than the strong one whose demonic hand bears heavily on all the world and its history (Luke 11.22). But it is precisely for this reason that Jesus can now direct his attack against the strong one himself, the chief of the demons. He binds the strong man in his own house, so as himself to spoil his house—and there is no power on earth to stop him (Mark 3.27). For he does not fight with weapons borrowed from his demonic opponents. The weapons he uses are proof against every device of the devil.

To do this is to draw upon oneself the whole fury of the adversary (Rev. 12.4). Here God himself must be involved. Here is one who is a match for the adversary. 'Who then is this?' (Mark 4.41). No human being in the world or in history has proved a match for the adversary; only God is that. The irresistible power of the *civitas diaboli* is broken; the *civitas dei* must be at its dawn!

The kingdom has come, but it is not yet perfected (Mark 9.1; 13.26); The enemy is stricken,[399] but not yet destroyed! If the demonic spirit is expelled and the man celebrates his victory, it may well happen that the demon surprises him anew all unsuspecting right in the middle of his triumph, though now the demon is reinforced sevenfold—and the last state of that man becometh worse than the first (Luke 11.24 ff.). Matthew (12.45c) adds: 'Even so shall it be also unto this evil generation', and in doing so makes it plain that our proverb is a parable of the stress and danger of the fight against the demons in this age. To fight against demons in history is to engage with a hydra. A crop of new heads springs up every time one head is cut off. This reveals a situation that cannot be met by a merely human watchfulness, but can only be overcome by the intercession of Christ (cf. Luke 22.32). The blood of the crucified is the *remedium* which brings the fight against the hydra to an end. When Christ ascends the throne of God the 'old dragon' will be straightway cast down from heaven, down to the earth, and at the end of the days will be cast into the abyss (Rev. 12.8 ff.).

Chapter 29

'AND FOR OUR SALVATION'

E. Krebs, *Der Logos als Heiland im* 1 *Jh*, 1910; G. P. Wetter, *Phos*, 1915; J. B. Frey, 'Le Concept de "Vie" dans J', Biblica, 1920; K. L. Schmidt, 'Der joh. Charakter der Erzählung vom Hochzeitswunder in Kana', Harnackehrung, 1921; D. A. Froevig, *Das Sendungsbewusstsein Jesu und der Geist*, 1924; R. Bultmann, 'Untersuchungen zum J', ZNW, 1928; E. Stauffer, 'In Vollmacht', *Festschr. f. K. Heim*, 1934; H. Pribnow, *Die johann. Anschauung vom 'Leben'*, 1934; E. G. Gulin, *Die Freude im NT*, I, 1932, II, 1936; T. Arvedson, *Das Mysterium Christi*, 1937; G. Quell and E. Stauffer, *Love*, London, (E.T.), 1950.

The eternal Christ is the life of cosmic history (Ch. 10; 22). The incarnate Christ, if one can so summarize the soteriological interpretation of his life, is the life of salvation-history.

When Jesus says in Luke 7.34 f. 'Wisdom is justified of all her children' he is evidently quoting some wisdom book like the Wisdom of Ben Sira, or Ecclesiasticus.[400] He applies this saying to himself as the Son of Man, and to his relationship to the tax-gatherers and sinners. He is himself the Wisdom, which is now come down to men, and which is thrown away by the well-fed, but praised by the hungry. So he calls those that labour and are heavy laden to come to himself (Matt. 11.28), quite in the style of Ecclus. 24.19. But it is not the wise who gather round Jesus (cf. Matt. 11.25; Luke 5.31); it is rather the learners, who know about the final depths of human existence, about the hardships of man's toil and the burden of his guilt. To such as these Jesus reveals in himself a wisdom that is not of this world (cf. I Cor. 1.26 ff.; 2.6 ff.).

John carried these ideas further and, often in the language of the Testament of the Twelve Patriarchs, took them to their conclusion.[401] The creative Word takes on an historical form and is revealed in the context of salvation-history in the power of the word

that proceeds from the mouth of Jesus Christ. He speaks as one who
has 'authority', as one who is 'from heaven'.[402] His words are
'Spirit and Life' (John 6.63). Admittedly we read in John 6.60 that
many, even among his disciples, murmured at what he said—but
that is a token of the two-edged character of the true *Logos* (Ch. 10).
Jesus turned to the twelve on that occasion and said: 'Would ye
also go away?' But Peter answered: 'Lord, to whom shall we go?
thou hast the words of eternal life' (John 6.67 ff.). In the same way
the Church confesses in I John 1.1: 'we have heard the Word of life
with our ears and seen it with our eyes'.

The eternal Christ is the light that has lighted the creation from
the beginning. But since the incarnation he is the light that shines
in the darkness of man's world and the children of light gather
round it (John 1.7 ff.; 3.19 ff.; 8.12). And when he gives sight to the
man who was born blind we have only a parable of his being the
light shining in the history of our salvation. For it is not the fact
that the man born blind comes to see the sun that alone determines
his eternal destiny, but rather that he sees the Son and worships him
(John 9.35 ff.; cf. I John 1.1 ff.). So the incarnate *Logos* is called the
'true light' in John, the one true, real, the only light (John 1.9; cf.
6.32; 15.1; I John 2.8). Anything else that is called light is not really
light, and only deceives (cf. TestA. 4.3; TestIss. 4.6). Everything in
the world that is great, helpful or 'divine' is either just appearance
and delusion, or it is a parable,[403] pointing beyond itself to the real
and the true (I John 5.20). All reality in this world is but appearance,
all truth in this world is but a lie—or it has its basis and its end in
him, who is the historical realization of the truth (cf. TestL. 18.2).

'I am the Truth,' said the incarnate *Logos* in John 14.6. We
know or discover a number of truths; but here it is simply 'the'
truth that is mentioned. The 'harlot' reason will sell her truths to
anyone, and adapts herself to each man's fancy (John 18.38).But in
this saying 'the truth' speaks, and will permit no coquetry, and
demands decision (John 7.16 ff.). Many a person utters a truth and
his word returns to him void, because he will not give himself to it
with all his being (Matt. 12.36). But Christ speaks 'the truth' and
his word calls forth a revolution because he gives himself completely to the truth which he proclaims (cf. John 8.44). We are
chained and hindered because we have no desire for a knowledge
of 'the truth' (John 3.19 ff.; cf. Rom. 1.18). In contrast to us Christ
is a free man, and a liberator, since he desires to know 'the truth',
and 'the truth' is revealed in him; and 'the truth' makes us free (John

1.14, 17; 8.32, 36). If any man testifies to 'the truth' he accuses himself, since 'the truth' testifies against us (TestJud. 20.5; I John 1.8 ff.). But Christ testifies to 'the truth' and 'the truth' testifies to him.[404] We can only talk about 'the truth', and if we happen to express something of 'the truth', then we say more than we possess, more than we are. But the incarnate *Logos* is 'the truth'. He is more than he puts into words (John 16.12 ff., 25, 29 f.). In man's world truth and reality are everywhere two different things. But in him truth and reality are one (John 1.14, 17).

John draws together all he has to say about Christ as the bringer of life in the history of salvation in one proposition of christology: He is the life (John 11.25; 14.6). The life, which produced every creature, has appeared in a world subject to death, and it invades the sphere of history with its quickening power (John 1.4; 10.10; I John 1.1 f.). This *zoë* is more than *bios* which will only last as long as the elements that make up this mortal world, and will cease to be along with it (I John 3.17). The life that comes to light and activity in Jesus Christ is not of this world and will outlast it (John 6.27, 50 f.; 3.36). Jesus is the bread of life (John 6.26 ff., 35), and he bestows the water of life. Just as Wisdom makes her voice heard in the *ecclesia* of God, just as Jesus in the synoptics calls those who seek him to himself, so in John, Christ cries out in the temple: 'If any man thirst, let him come unto me, and drink.' The man who answers this summons, he and he alone finds the drink that quenches man's thirst for good and all (John 7.37; 4.14; 6.35). Nor is that all, for: 'Out of his belly shall flow rivers of living water' (John 7.38; cf. Ecclus. 24.30 ff.). For the life which the incarnate *Logos* inaugurates is a self-perpetuating, fruitful life. In this sense John calls Christ the vine, not only because it bears the grapes, gives them their nourishment and keeps them alive, but because he also gives life to the vine and makes it bear fruit. Without him we can do nothing. But the man who lives in and by the life of Christ will draw on his resources and will become a means of blessing to the brethren (John 1.16; 15.1 ff.; I John 1.3 f.).

In an old Wisdom myth we can read: 'Wisdom went forth to make her dwelling among the children of men, and found no dwelling-place: Wisdom returned to her place, and took her seat among the angels' (AEn. 42.2; cf. Job 28.12 ff.; IV Ezra 5.9 ff.). John also realized that the 'life' of the creation met with hatred and enmity in this mortal world (John 1.5, 10 f.; Rev. 3.20; 12.4 f.). Nevertheless, Christ goes his way in the hostile world. For 'love

this way the pattern of the martyr psalm (21) runs all through the passion narrative like some brilliant trail.[406] 'Behoved it not the Christ to suffer these things and to enter into his glory?' says Luke 24.26 as in confirmation. And so all through the synoptic Gospels the events of Good Friday are understood as the necessary fulfilment of the scandal which darkened the whole earthly life of Christ (Mark 14.27; Luke 13.32; 18.31), and as the lowest point of a road that, according to God's counsel and promise, would thereafter lead to the glorifying of Christ (Acts 2.23 f.; Phil. 2.8 f.; I Pet. 1.19 ff.). John conceived of Christ's passion as the last and decisive service to the glory of God (John 12.28; 13.31 f.; cf. 21.19). But the Father does not wait till Easter Day to reward this service, but does so on Good Friday itself in the glorifying of the Son (John 12.23; 17.1 ff.). So the doxological understanding of the cross has its final form in the Johannine story of the passion (John 18.37; 19.30). The ignominious raising on the cross is really a majestic elevation to glory (John 3.14; 8.28; 12.34). The sculptors of the early Church made these ideas their own, and like to represent the cross as a sign of triumph flying over the globe, òr as brilliantly illumined by a martyr crown.[407].

The antagonistic form of the *theologia crucis* thinks of the cross as the decisive turning-point in the history of the *civitas dei* and its fight with powers hostile to God. This mode of thought had its preparation in the basic apocalyptic ideas of universal history as warfare, and of the special place of martyrs in that war (Ch. 47). It has its basis in a saying of Jesus: Only when the night of death is past can the fire blaze forth that Christ must kindle on the earth— and will (Luke 12.49 f.). So the death of Christ brings about a new disposition of the battle, and a new situation in the world. This basic idea is presented in all sorts of ways in the christology of the primitive Church (e.g. Luke 2.34; Acts 2.23 f., 36; John 19.37; Rev. 1.7, 18; 2.26 ff.). But it was in particular Paul who took up the idea and developed it. The humiliation of the Son signified his subjection to the powers controlling this age (Ch. 26). His rising signified his elevation above those demonic opponents who seemed to be victors while he hung on the cross (II Cor. 13.4; Phil. 2.10 f.; Col. 2.15). The early Church put these thoughts into an eloquent formula when it intensified one of the favourite conceptions of the old biblical theology of martyrdom: Christ is the 'Victor' who has beaten down the ancient enemy in the battle of his passion.[408] That is the picture of Christ that later found its monumental expression in the Ravenna of Theodoric, and which was generally characteristic and normative for the young Germanic peoples.[409]

Meanwhile, the accent on a theology of history was also active from the beginning in the soteriological understanding of the cross. Here the events of Good Friday are understood as giving the answer to the question of sin, which ever since the fall had tragically encumbered history. These ideas have their antecedents too. In the pre-Christian martyr texts we can find ideas of representative and expiatory suffering associated with all sorts of suffering figures of the past or the future (cf. App. I. 44, 46). But Jesus was the first to associate these ideas with that of the expectation of the suffering Son of Man[410] (Ch. 24). It was in the light of this association of ideas that he himself understood the puzzle of what happened on Good Friday, and thereby himself laid the basis for the *theologia crucis* as part of a theology of history. 'The Son of Man came not to be ministered unto, but to minister, and to give his life a ransom for many.'[411] In this form the saying is found only in Mark and Matt. But Luke gives expression to the soteriological understanding of the passion when he reports Christ praying for his disciples during his passion, and for his enemies on the cross (Luke 22.32; 23.34; cf. App. I. 43, 45).[412] But all three synoptics agree in their account of the Last Supper—not indeed in every detail, but at any rate on the relevant decisive point: Jesus goes to his death 'for many'. Paul's account of the Last Supper comes as a confirmation on this same point. And John himself, who otherwise is content to go his own way, has chosen to retain from the sayings of the Last Supper the decisive *pro nobis*.[413] All these formulae refer back to Isa. 53, etc., but are here built into the idea of the passover: Jesus is the passover Lamb, whose blood will become the sign that the people of the new covenant will be 'passed over', a sign to preserve them against the wrath of God.

The *pro nobis* which Jesus uses in the words of institution of the eucharist straight away took the lead in formulating the soteriological thinking of the early Church.[414] The brief pre-Pauline creed in I Cor. 15.3 states that Christ died 'for our sins'. Paul presupposes this formula (I Cor. 1.13; Gal. 1.4; Rom. 14.15) and makes it the centre of his own Word of the cross (Gal. 3.13; II Cor. 5.21). Paul's disciples follow their master (Heb. 2.9; 10.12; Eph. 5.2; I Tim. 2.6; I Pet. 2.21). In Rom. 5.6 ff. and I Pet. 3.18 Christ dies for his enemies; in John he lays down his life for his friends (John 15.13), and the Good Shepherd gives his life for his sheep (John 10.11; cf. Rev. 1.5).

So the *pro nobis* of the creed runs like a blood-red thread right through the NT: the one represents the many (cf. John 11.50 f.). Christ, who brings life to many, on the cross becomes their burden-bearer.[415]

Hence the picture of the suffering and burden-bearing servant of God that was discernible in the background of the eucharistic sayings of Jesus comes more and more to the foreground. The creedal formula in I Cor. 15.3 is an indication of this when it refers to the witness of the scriptures in speaking of the sin-redeeming death of the one for the many, and in all probability intends us to think of Isa. 53. In Acts 8.32 ff. the interpretation of the same Servant Song in reference to Christ is systematically carried through. Often elsewhere Jesus is called God's servant (Acts 3.13; 4.27; cf. Matt. 12.18). There are motifs from the thought of Isa. 53 in Rom. 4.25; II Cor. 5.21; Mark 15.28vl and many other places. In I Pet. 2.21 ff. and right through Barnabas the picture of the crucified is drawn with features that are derived from the figure of the Suffering Servant. But the picture of the passover Lamb also kept its significance for the soteriological understanding of the cross. 'Our passover also hath been sacrificed, even Christ,' says Paul in I Cor. 5.7. Good Friday is the passover day of universal history; the passover blood that is shed on that day for us saves us from the destroyer not once only (Jub. 49.3; Heb. 11.28), nor yet for just a year (Jub. 49.15) but once and for all (cf. I Pet. 1.19). But John has fused the picture of the bleeding passover Lamb with that of the Suffering Servant (which even in Isa. 53.7 had been likened to a lamb led to slaughter) and conceived of the significance of the cross in the light of this synthesis. Christ is the Lamb of God that bears the sins of the world (John 1.29; cf. I John 3.5; Isa. 53.4, 12). He dies at the hour of passover, and the regulations of the old ritual for the passover have their fulfilment in him (John 19.36; cf. Ch. 40). He appeared to the seer on Patmos as the Lamb that had been slain (Rev. 5.6).[416] The lamb that had been slain and had purchased the new people of the covenant with his blood, now has his place on God's throne, and alone has authority to open the seal of the eschatological book of life (Rev. 5.9, 12; cf. AEn. 89.52). Once more we find united here all the motifs that run through the primitive Christian tradition from Mark 10.45 and 14.24; and like some distant echo of the words Jesus spoke just before his death there comes, in Rev. 5.13, the doxology: 'Unto the lamb be the blessing, and the honour, and the glory and the dominion, for ever and ever.'

In the art and poetry of early Christianity the soteriological under-standing of the cross finds most frequent expression in the picture of the tree of life. The tree of knowledge was once a catastrophe for man; but now the cross is planted as the tree of life that will bring healing to the whole world.[417] On the ampullae at Monza the cross is represented as a living tree.[418] Lastly, in early Germanic art the cross is intertwined with an ash tree which, like a pillar, supports the cosmos.[419]

Chapter 31

THE DESCENT INTO HELL

G. McN. Rushforth, 'The "Descent into Hell" in Byzantine Art', Papers of the British School at Rome, 1902; H. J. Holtzmann, 'Höllenfahrt im NT', ARW, 1908; W. Bousset, 'Zur Hadesfahrt Christi', ZNW, 1920; H. Diels, 'Himmels und Höllenfahrten von Homer bis Dante', NJbchKlAlt, 1922; A. Dieterich, *Mutter Erde*,[3] 1925; J. Kroll, *Gott und Hölle*, 1932.

The incarnation of Christ meant the coming down of a heavenly nature to this world. His death meant his going down into the underworld. So in the NT the descent into hell is the final realization of his coming down from heaven—his act of deepest renunciation. In this doxological sense primitive Christianity speaks far more often and much earlier than we commonly suppose of the descent of Jesus Christ into the realm of the dead. Jesus himself spoke about the 'heart of the earth';[420] the idea of Acts 2.24 is of hades as a womb that wants to grasp and keep hold of Jesus.[421] Paul mentions Christ's descent into the abyss.[422] and one of his disciples writes about his descent into the lower parts of the earth (Eph. 4.9). But this *descensus* from the very first was thought of very differently from that of the sons of Adam: the inscription on the door of hades that the lost soul read with dismay, had no validity for the Christian: *Lasciate ogni speranza voi ch'entrate.* The underworld had no power over Christ, because it had no right over him. God 'loosed its pangs' and freed Christ from the grasp of the world of death.[423] As God once brought Joseph up out of the grave into which his hostile brethren had cast him,[424] so now he brought Christ up from death's night, into which his own people had thrust him (App. IV).

Christ went down to hades undefeated, but he rose on high invincible (Rom. 10.7; cf. Psa. 70.20).

By itself the descent into hell is more than just the last act of self-humiliation done by the heavenly man before his rising to a place of divine honour; it is a work of liberation. In this way the doxological understanding of the descent into hell grows into an antagonistic interpretation. The all-powerful one, who even in his earthly life was able to chain Satan (Ch. 28), now enters the gloomy abode of the adversary. Hence the graves open and the dead rise up almost before the crucified has breathed his last (Matt. 27.52). He carries the keys of the underworld with him (Rev. 1.18; cf. 9.1), deprives the devil of the power of death (Heb. 2.14; cf. II Tim. 1.10) and leads captivity captive (Eph. 4.8 ff. quoting Psa. 67.19; cf. Phil. 2.10; Col. 2.15). Now the way to heavenly life is open. In this sense Ignatius calls Christ 'the door', through which the patriarchs and prophets go to the Father (IgnPhld. 9.1). 'He, for whom they rightly waited, when he came, raised them from the dead' (IgnMg. 9.2).[425]

The soteriological understanding of the descent into hell is concentrated in the motif of Christ's preaching in hades. Enoch had once preached in hades to the fallen angels of Gen. 6 the message of God's eternal wrath.[426] But now Christ has descended thither to bring good news to the dead, and so to open for them the way to eternal salvation.[427] Noah once called the corrupt generation of the flood to repentance.[428] But it was in vain. The flood swallowed up the unrepentant, and hades took their 'spirits' into its prison (Jub. 5.10; cf. GEn. 22.3 ff.). But now the crucified has gone after these spirits into their very prison, and has once more faced them with a decision in preaching to them the message of salvation.[429]

Later on, in the discussions that the Church had with the pagan religions of the ancient world, the idea of the descent into hell became a favourite theme of Christian poetry and art. That is understandable enough. For the most serious challenge of extra-Christian mytholology found its fulfilment at this point. The Son of God tcok no delight in the pleasant abodes of the blessed—he saw hell's might and history's distress, and heard creation's groanings. So he came down into the world of men and tabernacled amongst us, even in the Inferno. The incarnate Lord pursued man even to the abyss of the lost so as free them from their hellish prison. That is the basic idea of the paintings of the descent, the final consequence of the idea of an incarnation (II Cor. 8.9; Heb. 12.2).

Chapter 32

THE RESURRECTION

O. Schönewolf, *Die Darstellung der Auferstehung Christi*, 1909; E. Fascher, 'Die Auferstehung Jesu'. . . . ZNW, 1927; S. V. McCasland, 'The Scripture Basis of "On the Third Day"', JBL, 1929; H. Schrade, *Ikonographie der . . . Auferstehung Christi*, 1932; S. V. McCasland, *The Resurrection of Jesus*, 1932; M. Goguel, *La foi à la résurrection de Jésus dans le Christianisme primitif*, 1933; S. Lösch, *Diatagma Kaisaros*, 1936; G. Kittel, 'Die Auferstehung Jesu', Dtsch. Theol., 1937; E. Hirsch, *Die Auferstehungsgeschichten und der christliche Glaube*, 1940.

The NT speaks relatively little of the resurrection of Jesus, but mostly and with growing preference of his being raised from the dead (e.g. I Cor. 15.4). What happened at Easter was an act of God! In what did this act of God consist? The tomb, in which Jesus was laid on Good Friday, was empty on Easter morning.[430] So the evangelists report and so the creeds of the Church affirm.[431] Paul also presupposes that this is what took place.[432] Even Jewish polemic never dared to throw doubts on the fact of the empty tomb.[433] But Christ did not come from the grave, like Lazarus (John 11.44; cf. Matt. 27.52), in his previous body, but in a new one, to which the laws of gravity and mortality no longer applied. Ecclesiastical art was fond of expressing this by showing the risen one coming up through the unmoved and undamaged gravestone. This is thoroughly in keeping with the Easter message of the primitive Church[434] (in spite of Mark 16.4; John 20.1), for in John 20.19, 26 the risen Lord passed through doors that were locked. Any materialist conception of what took place on Easter morning is quite foreign to the NT—but so is any sort of spiritualization.[435] The risen Lord is no spirit,[436] but is rather to be thought of as having a spiritual body, which is as different from a purely physical body as it is from a purely pneumatic existence.[437]

Jesus was raised up. What does this divine act signify? Easter is the first decisive step that the Son took on the way to his final glory, after his descent to earth and to the darkness of hades. This is the doxological interpretation of the resurrection, as it is envisaged in the sayings of Jesus about the Son of Man, and as it is presented in the passion narratives of the evangelists. Christ's descent has passed its lowest limits, and his ascent has begun. In this sense Christ's appearances to his followers as recorded in the NT are the evidence, reverently received and then passed on, that God has fulfilled his OT promises in Jesus Christ, and brought his Messiah through the darkness of night to the light of day (Psa. 15.10; 17.6 ff.; 70.20; 114.3 ff.; Acts 2.24, 27; 13.35). After three days Jonah was brought back to the light (Matt. 12.40 f.). 'On the third day' God's people in the last days (after a period of catastrophes) will be quickened to life (Hos. 6.2; PirkREl. 51). So God's anointed was raised 'on the third day according to the scriptures'.[438]

The antagonistic *theologia resurrectionis* finds above all else in the resurrection of Christ his triumph over the powers hostile to the Christ, both human and super-human. Thus in the Petrine formulae Easter is God's confession of his true Servant, his betrayed, maltreated and unrecognized Messiah, and his answer to those who scorned and oppressed his Son (Acts 3.15; 4.10; 10.40). The OT is the starting-point for these ideas also. The traces of Isa. 53.4, 10 ff. are unmistakable, and the idea of the 'servant' is repeatedly used in this connection. God has raised and glorified his Servant Jesus, whom the people of God had rejected, delivered up for judgement and killed (Acts 3.13 ff., 26; cf. 4.27 ff.). This dramatic antithesis is transposed into a metaphysical key in OdSol. 22.3 ff.: it is God who scatters Christ's foes and gives him the power to break his chains (cf. Acts 2.24; II Cor. 13.4; Phil. 2.10 f.).

Christ was 'delivered up for our trespasses, and was raised up for our justification' (Rom. 4.25). This brings us to the decisive interpretation of Easter, the soteriological. For this double proposition from Romans is no pleonastic *parallelismus membrorum* but a creedal formula (cf. 4.24 and Ch. 63) whose two parts are precisely distinguished.[439] The first part is retrospective and deals with the cross and the expiation of past sin. The second is prospective and deals with the resurrection and the annulment of future sin. Rom. 8.34 continues the same movement of thought. We read of the cross, 'yea rather' of the resurrection, and finally of the intercession of the raised and exalted Christ (Ch. 33). 'Who is he that shall condemn? It is Christ Jesus, who maketh intercession for us!' It is for this reason that Paul's doctrine of justification is not complete without the resurrection. 'If Christ hath not been raised, your faith is vain; ye are yet in your sins' (I Cor. 15.17). So the confession of the risen Christ is of special importance. Faith, resurrection and justification belong together, according to Rom. 4.22–25 (cf. Rom. 10.9 f.). Without the resurrection the work of Christ is not finished, and salvation-history does not reach its goal. Without Easter there can be no *kyrie eleison*! For the Christ to whom the Church lifts up its need is the exalted Christ, the heavenly king and priest.

Chapter 33

THE ASCENSION

R. Holland, 'Zur Typik der Himmelfahrt', ARW, 1925; F. Büchsel, *Die Christologie des Hb.,* 1922; S. Mowinckel, *Das Thronbesteigungsfest Jahväs,* 1922; H. Schmidt, *Die Thronfahrt Jahves,* 1927; G. Bertram, 'Die Himmelfahrt Jesu vom Kreuz aus . . .' *Festschr. f. A. Deissmann,* 1927; H. Schrade, 'Zur Ikonographie der Himmelfahrt Christi', *Vortr. d. Bibl. Wbg.,* 1930; S. H. Gutberlet, *Die Himmelfahrt Christi in der bildenden Kunst,* 1934; E. Peterson, *Zeuge der Wahrheit,* 1937.

In its *kerygma* the primitive Church proclaimed the fact of Christ's ascension into heaven (Mark 16.19; cf. Ch. 63). Reports differ about precisely what took place, as they do about what sayings and events preceded it. But what is quite unmistakable in all the accounts is a reference by analogy or antithesis to the old biblical reports of ascents to heaven,[440] that is to say, to the Enoch tradition (App. VI). We read in Luke 24.50 ff. that the risen Lord blessed his disciples and then was taken from their sight. But they returned home and praised God. Acts 1 is more explicit[441] and describes vividly how Jesus spoke his last words and instructions and was then taken away by a cloud, while the disciples gazed after him until two angels came to them (Acts 1.9 ff.). Mark's longer ending relates as an artless story how the exalted Christ ascended his throne. We read in Matt. 28.9 how the disciples took hold of Christ's feet and worshipped him. In the fourth Gospel the 'farewell discourses' begin as early as Ch. 13 ff. and Christ talks here about his crucifixion and exaltation just as the patriarchs in the Testament of the Twelve Patriarchs talk about their departure.[442] After Easter he does not eat with them again (John 21.5, 12 f.). He keeps Mary Magdalene from touching him when she makes to do so (John 20.17). He gives the Spirit to the disciples and makes his final arrangements (John 20.22 f.; 21.15 ff.). The actual ascension is not described (on Rev. 12, *vide infra*). But the Christ talks about his coming ascent to the Father quite in the manner of the old biblical farewell discourses and testaments (John 20.17). So in the accounts of the ascension in primitive Christianity many different motifs from different traditions and different ways of presentation can be found alongside each other unmodified. It is easy enough to see that the essential thing is not how the ascension took place, but that it occurred! For the decisive, the theological question arises because of the 'that'. What significance has the ascension for the work that Christ did and the way that he trod?

The doxological interpretation answers: In the ascension Jesus attained to the highest point of his *anabasis*, the provisional end of his journey. He is 'exalted' into heaven (cf. John 3.13 f.; 13.1) and from thence will come again for the eschatological completion of his work (Acts 1.11; 3.21; John 14.3). Until then he has been received into the heavenly seclusion and will there remain,[443] just as, according to apocalyptic tradition, the eschatological city of God has been held ready from the very beginning, and just as Baruch, since his ascension, has been held ready for later times.[444]

The antagonistic understanding of the ascension links readily on to the formulae of the well-known enthronement psalm: 'Sit thou at my right hand until I make thine enemies thy footstool' (Psa. 109.1). This psalm was interpreted messianically in pre-Christian times (cf. Ch. 25), and now it is applied to Jesus Christ and his sitting on the throne.[445] The risen Lord's seizure of power is completed at his ascension! His victorious ascent is described with dramatic power as the giving of a name that is above every name, an elevation to the status of Lord (Phil. 2.9 ff.; Col. 2.15; Eph. 4.8 ff.). But who are the enemies whom God will put under his feet? They are the powers of hell. When will they be put under his feet? The answers vary somewhat but are not in any way contradictory. We read that the final subjection of God's enemies will only take place at the end of the days, though it is presupposed, in saying this, that the fundamental beginning has already been made (Mark 14.62p; Rev. 3.21; 14.14). We read again that the subjection has already taken place, though here the celebration of the triumph is held back until the time of the end (Eph. 1.20 ff.; Heb. 1.13; 10.12 f.; 12.2; cf. Ch. 54 f.). But wherever the emphasis falls, this much is clear: The Lord has from now on all authority in heaven and on earth, and he is 'with' his Church always, even unto the end of the world (Matt. 28.18 ff.). In this present age he does his work 'in and with and through' the labours of his Church. (cf. Acts 1.1 f.).

But what the primitive Church celebrated on Ascension Day was not just Christ's accession to power. The Church's intercessor had taken his place before God's throne! This is the soteriological significance of the ascension. From now on Christ is our Advocate at the right hand of God (Rom. 8.34; I John 2.1 f.; cf. Acts 5.30 f.), our High Priest who has passed into the heavenly places and intercedes for us before God's face.[446] But who is it that stands on the left of God's throne? It is Christ's counterpart, Satan, who accuses us before God (cf. Luke 22.31 f.; Rom. 8.33 f.). Christ and Satan— these two engage each other before God's throne for the future of the Church. But Christ has the last word—that much is certain to the whole NT (cf. John 12.31 f.).

In Paul's day there was a cultic hellenistic brotherhood that built an underground basilica in Rome. On its apse it carried a picture of the transfiguration of Sappho. The Christian Church was not long in building its catacombs and churches and decorating them with pictures of the transfigured Christ. In the throne-room of his palace the emperor received the homage of his people; but in his basilica Christ was enthroned in heavenly majesty and greeted those who believed on him. The imperial triumphal arches extolled the victories of the emperor over his enemies; but the 'triumphal arches' of the Christian basilicas celebrated the homage that the heavenly beings offered to the *kyrios pantokrator*.[447] This is none other than the Son of Man described in Rev. 1 with the features and insignia of the Ancient of Days, and who is honoured with the same formulae as God the Father. He says to the prostrate seer: 'I am the first and the last, and the living one; and I was dead, and behold, I am alive for evermore, and I have the keys of death and of hades.'[448] He has displaced Satan from before God's throne, the dragon from the heavenly realm.[449] The Church, persecuted by the ejected dragon and yet freed from a tremendous burden, sings its hymns to Christ: 'Now is come the salvation, and the power, and the kingdom of our God, and the authority of his Christ; for the accuser of our brethren is cast down, which accuseth them before our God day and night. And they overcame him because of the blood of the Lamb!' (Rev. 12.10 f.). This is the new situation for the world that dates from the ascension.

Chapter 34

THE COMING OF CHRIST AND
THE WORLD'S DISTRESS

H. Windisch, *Taufe und Sünde*, 1908; A. Juncker, *Jesus und das Leid*, 1925; A. v. Harnack, 'Κόπος', ZNW, 1928; J. Dey, *Παλιγγενεσία*, 1927; A. Kolping, *Neuschöpfung und Gnadenstand*, 1946.

We have spoken of a new situation for the world, created by the coming of Christ. The romantics see creation already transformed, and in particular think of themselves as already changed (cf. I Cor. 15.19; Rom. 8.24; I John 1.8). But the cynics maintain: 'From the day that the fathers fell asleep, all things continue as they were from the beginning of the creation' (II Pet. 3.4). But the writers of the NT are neither romantics nor cynics, but realists (Mark 10.5 ff.; Matt. 10.34; Luke 10.18 ff.). 'Awake up righteously and sin not,' Paul writes to the Corinthians (I Cor. 15.34; cf. 11.30; I Thess. 4.13; Rev. 12.12 ff.). In this way the apostle makes it clear from the very start that the three great afflictions of the world remain unresolved still, even after the coming of Christ: death, affliction and sin.

The creation still sighs under the curse of vanity and corruption (Rom. 8.19 ff.). Even the Church is no exception to the rule (Rom. 8.23; I Cor. 15.22; I Thess. 4.18). Neither Paul, nor John, nor Lazarus who was raised from the grave, nor those who were raised for a while according to Matt. 27.52 can escape death. Neither has the coming of Christ done any more to banish afflictions from the world (Rom. 8.22). Even the future will have its distress (Matt. 6.34). Poverty, distress and sickness will never cease so long as this world lasts (Mark 14.7; Luke 4.25 ff.). Indeed, Jesus talked of the ever-increasing tribulation of the future, worse than any since the world began (Mark 13.19). Is the Christian Church exempt from that? On the contrary: 'In the world ye have tribulation' (John 16.33; Rom. 8.17 f.). Neither is sin abolished (I John 1.8). It still dominates our mortal scene, unbroken in its power and reaching out to its fulfilment (Luke 17.27; Rev. 16.9; 22.11). Sin is still powerful in the Church of Christ (Rom. 16.20) even among the apostles themselves (Luke 22.34; Barn. 5.9). Indeed, the fight against sin has but entered upon its bitterest stage with the coming of Christ (Mark 14.38). We have seen already how acutely Paul has worked out the inner conflict in man before Christ (Ch. 19); the same conflict is not brought to an end, but rather intensified, according to Gal. 5.17 (Ch. 41).

This is the situation in the Church and in the world after Christ has come, died and risen again. Yet the apostle holds that the OT promises for the future have been fulfilled in the present: 'The old things are passed away; behold, they are become new.' For 'if any man is in Christ, he is a new creature' (II Cor. 5.17; cf. Isa. 43.18; 65.17; Gal. 6.15; Rev. 21.4 f.). What does Paul mean by calling the Christian a new creature? If we are to find the right answer to this question, we shall have to conduct a wide enquiry into the historical and morphological presuppositions that have gone to make Paul's ideas.

No one who reads the NT at all carefully can fail to be struck by the many concepts and phrases that are used to depict God's judgement on man's world, and of man's standing before God.[450] This distinctive terminology cannot be a pure accident. It is a language that belongs to a particular question, the biblical question: what does God think of a man's act or behaviour—what does he think of me? God is the measure of all things. So the question about God's judgement is *the* question above all other questions. So it also follows that any question about human nature as such, about man's own valuation of his conduct, is provisional and peripheral, since the one thing that is decisive is the question that our destiny turns on—what is our standing before God?

This problem of man's acceptance before God is the primary question raised by the old biblical theology. Sin is what God condemns; that is right which is so in the eyes of the law. He is clean who has pleased God by observing the ceremonial requirements of the law. The man who is 'cleansed' remains unchanged in his essential nature, but he is clean forensically.[451] Azariah prayed in the burning fiery furnace, prayed that God would regard the prayer of a contrite heart as if it were a burnt offering (Dan. 3.39). Moses 'is' as God to Aaron, because Yahweh has so designated him (Ex. 4.16; cf. 7.1). The king was called 'God's son', indeed, the 'begotten of God' from the day when God appointed him (Psa. 2.7). An historical event may be quite insignificant in the eyes of the world, and yet perhaps the more important in the eyes of God.[452] In the last result its future significance in history depends on that. Belshazzar's kingdom has its future decided in God's 'numbered, weighed, divided' (DaΘ. 5.25 ff.). A man may seem to be powerful and fortunate in the extreme, but everything turns on the invisible handwriting in which God has recorded his life (PsSol. 15.6). For his eternal destiny turns on that alone.

This forensic thinking is given a thoroughgoing scholastic expression in rabbinic terminology.[453] If an Azariah prays in the extremity of death that his prayer may be accepted as a sacrifice, SDt. 6.5 says this about martyrdom: God accounts it to the pious 'as if' they were killed every day (cf. Psa. 43.23). In such a context as this, rabbinic thinking loses all its reference to actuality. We 'are' what God judges us to be. Israel 'is' God's son, the man who keeps the law 'is' from heaven, and to be under the law 'is' the Kingdom of God in a world as alien from God as this.[454] In the legal customs of the Synagogue this same forensic thinking takes on a juristic character.[455] But the juristic way of thinking has its own repercussions on theological conceptions: God is himself the judge who, now or at the end of time, sits at the judgement seat and delivers his verdict. It is in this manner that on the great day of atonement God delivers his judgement, which determines the standing and destiny of man: 'On the day of atonement I declare you righteous and make you a new creature.' For man 'as such' it may be appointed as it will; 'before God's face' from now on he counts as a new creation.[456]

It is in the range of these questions and ideas that Paul, the disciple of Gamaliel, writes in II Cor. 5.17 about the 'new creature'.[457] So far as the actual state of affairs is concerned, everything can remain within the old order; that is the antecedent clause that saves us from romanticism. But everything has become new—forensically; and that is the consequent clause that delivers us from nihilism. Death, anguish and sin still rule in the world. But the question about the standing of sinful man before God, the question about guilt, that is solved, solved by God's mighty act on the cross. For the coming of Christ is God's answer to the problem of man's guilt, his 'yes' to man, who can do no other than confess his guilt before God (II Cor. 1.19; I John 1.9 ff.). God's time is now proclaimed, the time when we are acceptable *coram deo*—and so now is the day of salvation.[458] That is the new situation for the world, brought about by the coming of Christ—a new situation of man before God.[459]

The primitive Church articulated this condition of peace in very different concepts and images. It spoke of the merciful God's act of grace, of the divine remission of sins, of the work of atonement and the justification of the sinner. In all these formulae we find the same basic idea of the forensically new situation brought about by the coming of Christ.

As we know, the OT had itself spoken about the mercy, the love and the grace of God. The writers of the NT took over these concepts (Luke 6.36; 11.42; II Cor. 1.3; I Tim. 1.2), but only to use them in a quite new christocentric sense. Thus they speak of God's love in an inceptive aorist (John 3.16; cf. I John 4.9 f.; Matt. 18.33) of God's mercy with an explicit 'now' (I Pet. 2.10; cf. Rom. 11.30 f.), and of divine grace at the same time as of the coming of Christ: 'The law was given by Moses; grace and truth came by Jesus Christ' (John 1.17). Of course, this act of God in the history of salvation goes back to God's premundane decree (II Thess. 2.13 f.; Eph. 1.5 ff.; Ch. 9). But God's gracious will that predestinates us finds its first and its only realization in salvation-history in the mighty act of grace wrought out on the cross (John 1.14; Rom. 5.8; 8.28–39). For the God of the NT is no indulgent father winking at what his children do and incapable of anger—rather like the foolish taunt: *Pardonner c'est son métier.* 'We were by nature children of wrath' (Eph. 2.3; cf. Rom. 2.5; Heb. 10.31; John 3.36; Rev. 11.18). That is the minatory prelude to the primitive Christian gospel of peace which Paul condensed into a single sentence when he wrote: 'God appointed us not unto wrath, but unto the obtaining of salvation through our Lord Jesus Christ, who died for us' (I Thess. 5.9; aorist!). For, wrote Paul, using a well-trusted metaphor, God has 'blotted out the bond written in ordinances that was against us: and he hath taken it out of the way, nailing it to the cross', and so rid the world of it altogether.[463] According to Roman custom there was attached to Jesus' cross an accusation which gave details of his offence (Mark 15.26). But what offence, what sin is it that in accordance with God's counsel Christ has done away with on the cross? It is our sin, answers Paul, speaking for the Church. Our sins were written in invisible ink on the accusation over our Lord's head. Our guilt was done away and our sin forgiven on the cross.[464]

The message of God's grace and of the forgiveness of sins derives from Jesus himself and was the common ground of the primitive Church. But its most powerful representative was the apostle Paul, and its most forceful expression is found in his doctrine of atonement. This is contained *in compendio* in Rom. 3.25 f.: 'God set (him) forth to be a propitiation, through faith, by his blood, to shew his righteousness, because of the passing over of the sins done afore-time, in the forbearance of God.'[465] Good Friday is the atonement day for the history of the whole cosmos. For in the same way that the blood rituals of the Jewish day of atonement made expiations for the sins of the past year, or the blood of the martyrs for those of a whole epoch,[466] so the blood of the crucified makes expiation for every sin that has accumulated since the fall by the law of hereditary solidarity.[467] But now the state of war between God and the world has been brought to an end, once and for all. That is the meaning of Rom. 3.25, which is quite consistent with what Paul says in II Cor. 5 f. about the new forensic situation of the world (Ch. 34). By his universal work of atonement on Good Friday, God has made a new creation! So it is entirely in order that, just as the apostle has spoken about the 'new creature' in II Cor. 5.17, he should go on to talk about the atonement, and so make way for the message of the 'acceptable time' in II Cor. 6.2. In II Cor. 5.18 Paul affirms that everything that can be said about the new situation for the world has its origin and basis in the atoning work of God. Here, too, God is the absolute Subject. The apostle underlines this: 'Be ye reconciled to God' (5.19 f.). The motif of a state of peace, which at last becomes dominant at this point, returns in Rom. 5.10 and has its final expression in Col. 1.20 ff. In view of the death of his Son and of his blood that was shed, God reaches out to those who were once his enemies the hand of reconciliation, and on the cross concludes a universal peace (echoes in Eph. 2.16).

Following this idea of an universal day of atonement Paul talks of justification: 'Whom God set forth . . . for the shewing, I say, of his righteousness at this present season: that he might himself be just, and the justifier of him that hath faith in Jesus' (Rom. 3.26). Paul puts reconciliation in the first place.[468] For reconciliation is the universal, and justification the individual aspect of salvation. Reconciliation took place on Good Friday; justification takes place at baptism, or at the Last Judgement. The act of reconciliation on the cross is what makes the justification of the sinner possible. No one has seen this point more clearly than Anselm of Canterbury. God is just. He does not cancel the hereditary sin of the centuries, but lays them upon the crucified (cf. Ch. 16). And at this point we have a revelation of God's forensic righteousness.[469] Nevertheless, it is precisely in this way that God's will to reconciliation finds its realization. For in the name of the crucified the righteous God acquits guilty man of his sin and declares him righteous.[470] Here we have a revelation of the given righteousness of God.[471] This is the fruitful tension in the *iustitia dei* in Rom. 3.25 f.[472] At one and the same time it is *iustitia dei activa* and *iustitia dei passiva*—to make use of Luther's formal terminology.[473] God's *iustitia* is both forensic and given alike, forensic in the crucified one, given to us. 'Behold the severity and the goodness of God' (Rom. 11.22).[474]

At the very beginning of this whole way of thinking that leads from the common Christian conception of God's act of grace and forgiveness to Paul's doctrine of reconciliation and justification there stands Christ, proclaiming peace upon earth. At the end of this way of thinking there stands the idea of a *pax domini* (I Thess. 5.23; II Thess. 3.16; Rom. 1.7; 15.33). To Christ's peace we were called (Col. 3.15; cf. Isa. 9.5; 53.5)—that is the conclusion of Paul's doctrine of reconciliation and justification. 'The peace of God, which passeth all understanding, guard you hearts and your thoughts in Christ Jesus' (Phil. 4.7)—that is the conclusion of Paul's prayer. The post-apostolic age understood little of Paul's teaching about reconciliation. But it did understand his message of peace. What was said in Eph. 2.14 about Jesus Christ was that 'he is our peace'.

Chapter 36

DELIVERANCE FROM THE ENEMY

J. Wirtz, *Die Lehre von der Apolytrosis*, 1906; F. J. Dölger, *Sphragis*, 1911; F. J. Dölger, *Die Sonne der Gerechtigkeit und der Schwarze*, 1918; K. Latte, *Heiliges Recht*, 1920; E. Maass, 'Segnen, Weihen, Taufen', ARW, 1922; M. Sulzberger, 'Le Symbole de la croix et les Monogrammes de Jésus . . .' Byzantion, 1925; F. J. Dölger, *IXΘΥΣ*, 1 2–V 1922–40; J. Quasten, *Das Bild des guten Hirten . . . Pisiculi f. F. J. Dölger*, 1939; G. Stuhlfauth, 'Die Sinnzeichen der altchristlichen Kunst', ThBl, 1939; W. Elert, 'Redemptio ab hostibus', ThLZ, 1941.

The new situation for the world brought about by the coming of Christ is primarily characterized by the new relationship of God to man. But from such a new relationship there inevitably follows a new relationship between man and the adversary. For man in his indebtedness has fallen to the power of the adversary, and is no longer in a position to offer any sort of equivalent with which to resist the legal claims of the adversary (Psa. 48.8 f.; SDt. 329 on 32.39; Mark 8.36 f.). So it is only a matter of time before the devil tries to put his legal claims into operation. Jesus comes into this ambiguous situation on man's behalf and gives his life 'a ransom for many' (Ch. 30). In this saying there is the basis for the teaching of the primitive Church in regard to the saving work of Jesus Christ, which can be summed up under three inclusive heads.

Forgiveness of sins is redemption.[475] In Jesus Christ 'we have our redemption through his blood, the forgiveness of our trespasses', says Eph. 1.7 (cf. I Cor. 1.30; Rom. 3.24; Col. 1.14; Heb. 9.15; Luke 1.68, 77; Psa. 110.9). The idea of redemption can be understood in many different ways in the NT, and can mean the final deliverance from all the troubles of this world (Luke 21.28; Rom. 8.23). But here the issue concerns the decisive point where the universal work of redemption comes into operation—redemption is ransom (I Tim. 2.6; II Pet. 2.1). We were bought with a price (I Cor. 6.20; 7.23), but the price paid was the precious blood of Jesus Christ (I Pet. 1.18 f.). But from whose ownership are we ransomed? From the curse of the law, is the answer that Paul gives in Gal. 3.13 and further explains that this curse really means subjection to the demonic and elementary powers of this world (Gal. 4.3 f.; cf. Col. 2.20; Rev. 14.3). For whom are we ransomed? The answer is given in Rev. 5.9: for God! In this way the fundamentals of the early Church's theory of redemption are laid down. God takes his own world order so seriously that he sacrifices his son to save the world, without flouting its order. (cf. DaΘ 6.9; Esth. 1.19; 8.8).[476] Ransom is liberation from the power of darkness and translation into the Kingdom of Christ.[477] In Col. 2.13 ff. Paul writes about the blotting out of ordinances that were against us on the cross, so that he can go on to the idea of the disarming and subjection of the powers of hell (cf. II Tim. 1.10; IgnE. 19.3). So closely do forgiveness of sins, redemption and liberation go together in his thinking.[478] So deeply does the settling of the problem of sin concern the power relationships that obtain in universal history. Because the crucified has 'redeemed us from sin,' therefore are we delivered 'from every power of the devil'.

The coming of Christ has established a new relationship between God and man and the adversary. As a sign of this new relationship

God has sealed his saints with the sign of salvation, at the sight of which the destroyer himself has to give way.[479]

The name of Yahweh in the OT and the name of *kyrios* in the LXX are what keep the elect in safety and stave off destruction. But in the NT the name of Jesus takes their place. 'Neither is there any other name under heaven, that is given among men, wherein we must be saved' (Acts 4.12; cf. Rev. 3.12; II Tim. 2.19). Those who have been called are sealed with the name of Jesus at their baptism (Acts 2.38; Herm.s. 9.16). With this name the Lord marks out his own so that they can withstand every assault of the devil;[480] with it also the apostles bring the demons into subjection (Luke 10.17; Acts 16.18; cf. Jas. 2.19). The very watchmen of hell shrink back at the sound of this name.[481] In the last days the gates of the underworld will be undone and the demonic monsters will ascend to the earth and lay it waste, and strike terror into the hearts of men. But those who have been sealed will remain unharmed.[482]

The saints of Christ put themselves visibly under the saving sign of his name when they wore an amulet with the name of the monogram of Jesus Christ, or when they decorated their utensils and houses, their churches and tombs with the same sacred monogram. But this was neither magic nor mere symbolism. Such signs had a metaphysical meaning. They are prayers, by means of which the wearer besought the protection of his heavenly Lord against the demonic powers.

But the weapon that Christ used in his victory over hell was the cross. That is why signing with the sign of the cross was the most concrete form of sealing. The martyr and confessor were marked with the stigmata of Jesus (Gal. 6.17; IgnMg. 5.2; EusHE. 5.2.3; cf. TestJb. 5). When Jesus descended into hell those who were there and were saved had the sign of Christ made upon their forehead (EvNicod. 24). This *tropaion* is the only thing that can bring us safely through the crises and catastrophes of the last days. It is in this way that we can understand why we meet everywhere in the Church of the second century the *signaculum crucis*, crossing oneself before the baptized, the sick and the dying.[483] In every sort of danger and temptation to cross oneself is a 'shield against the devil'[484].

Early Christian art incorporated the same ideas when it painted and chiselled the sign of the cross or the divine monogram on the doors of houses, the walls of churches, gravestones and sarcophagi—all of them prayers in colours or stone. So, long before the figure of the crucified itself became an object of representation we can find the cross everywhere [485]—in the markets and streets, in the deserts and mountains, on ships and weapons.[486] Why? Because early Christian art is primarily prayer, and only secondarily an historical or theological representation—because it was primarily intended to speak to God, and only secondarily to men.[487]

The Gentile Church set up Christ's sign in a world where there was already a great number of ancient saving signs as well as names of new deliverers striving for the mastery.[488] What attitude did she take to these signs and names? Many of the traditional signs she took over without scruple into her own treasury and reinterpreted them christologically, e.g. the Indo-Germanic swastika, or the Egyptian symbol of life.[489] But the infant Church rejected the symbols of imperial self-glorification and political apotheosis as evil signs of a *civitas terrena* that had already become the *civitas diaboli*. So in the book of Revelation the name of Jesus is contrasted with the mark of the beast, antichrist, who, though he now oppresses God's Servant, will one day be destroyed.[490] Over against the children of darkness, who have power in this world and bear its mark, Ignatius sets the children of light, who bear the mark of God the Father through Jesus Christ; in due time everyone will come to his proper place.[491] The conscript Maximilian refused to put on the insignia bearing the name of the emperor, though it cost him his life. 'I already bear the *signum Christi*; I shall not put on the *signaculum* of this world.'[492] The courage and loyalty of such men were not in vain. A few decades after Maximilian had suffered martyrdom the monogram of Jesus Christ was taken as the badge of that same empire that for three hundred years had persecuted Christ and his saints.[493] Previously men, houses and churches had put themselves under the protection of Christ by using his sign; now the empire did the same, and sought to fulfil its mission in history *in hoc signo*, and to become a bulwark against the powers of chaos (Ch. 17).

Chapter 37

CHRIST THE PROTOTYPE

E. Lohmeyer, 'Σὺν Χριστῷ', *Festschr. f. A. Deissmann*, 1927; A. Marmorstein, 'Die Nachahmung Gottes in der Agada', *Festschr. f. J. Wohlgemuth*, 1928; J. Schneider, *Die Passionmystik des Paulus*, 1929; K. Mittring, *Heilswirklichkeit bei Paulus*, 1929; W. Schmauch, *In Christus*, 1935; A. Fridrichsen, 'Sich selbst verleugnen', Arbeiten a. d. nt Seminar zu Uppsala, 1936; W. T. Hahn, *Das Mitsterben und Mitauferstehen mit Christus bei Paulus*, 1937; E. Stauffer, *Das Gesetz der Stellvertretung*, Eckart, 1943.

The new world-situation, which in the first place effects a new relationship between God, the world and the adversary, brings with it new laws for our existence and changes the conditions of our life and our work. In Augustin's words, it creates a new *conditio*. 'For as in Adam all die, even so in Christ shall all be made alive'[494] (I Cor. 15.22). Adam's fall conditions our situation, and his way has become the law for us. So by a powerfully antithetic analogy the coming of Christ has become the fateful condition of our human situation. But Christ's way becomes a formative law for us (Rom. 5.12 ff.; I Cor. 15.48 f.). In this sense we can think of Christ's coming as a prototype.[495]

The primitive Church interpreted Christ's coming in a threefold way. In exact parallel to this it has given a threefold interpretation to the interpretation of it as a prototype.

'If any man would come after me, let him deny himself, and take up his cross,' said Jesus in Mark 8.34.[496] Here the *via crucis* is a prototype doxologically. The *katabasis* and the *anabasis* of Christ's way has to be carried out after the pattern of Christ's life. The prerequisite for the disciple to be taken at the last into Christ's glory is that he should drink the cup of suffering and undergo the baptism of death (Mark 10.37 ff.). Jesus calls his death a baptism, and Paul in turn calls our baptism a death, that has its fulfilment under the sign and the law of the crucifixion (Rom. 6.3 ff.; Col. 2.12). We are crucified and buried in the likeness of his death, so as to wake in the likeness of his new life (Phil. 3.10). In the first place this is to be understood ethically. Moral renewal is the form in which the renewal of life takes effect in this age (Gal. 2.19; Rom. 6.6; 7.4). But in the end the quickening to new life is an eschatological reality (Ch. 54 ff.). When Christ was raised from the dead on Easter Day he was a prototype pointing forward to the raising of Christians in general at the last day (Rom. 6.8; Col. 3.3 f.; I Thess. 4.14 f.; I Cor. 15.17 ff.; Col. 1.18; IgnTr. 9.2). The downward path through Inferno that God has trodden with his Christ on the way to Paradise is fundamentally the path that his Church must tread, and in the last resort is the road that universal history must take (Ch. 51).

The antagonistic conception of the new *conditio* is found concentrated in Paul on the idea of power (II Cor. 1.3 ff.; 4.7 ff.; 12.9 f.; 13.3 f.; cf. John 7.38; 15.1 ff.), and in John on that of victory. The disciple has to fight his life's battle on the same battleground between heaven and hell as the Master fought and won on (John 16.33; Rev. 17.14; 12.11 f.; cf. I Thess. 2.14 f.; Phil. 1.28; ActThom. 39). Again and again Christ's victory has to be repeated in our victory, and repeated in the same way and by the same means: in and through catastrophe. But like their prototype, Jesus Christ, the conquerors will be given the rod of victory and dominion, and will triumph over their foes (Rev. 2.26 ff.; 3.21; cf. Heb. 12.2 f.).

The soteriological understanding of our problem is based upon Jesus' saying about the service that finds its fulfilment in sacrifice. According to Mark 10.42 ff. the service of ministry of the Son of Man, which takes him to his death upon the cross, is the archetype of the disciple's service of his neighbour. The Johannine Christ gives a parabolic sign to his disciples of his death on the cross for them, and adds: 'I have given you an example, that ye also should do as I have done to you' (John 13.15). The inference is clearly drawn in I John 3.16: 'He laid down his life for us: and we ought to lay down our lives for the brethren.' Paul thinks of himself and of the Church as completely obliged to this duty. 'Be ye imitators of me, even as I also am of Christ' (I Cor. 11.1). What does he mean by this imitation of Christ? Precisely in the fact that he does not seek his own pleasure and profit, but that which tends to the salvation of the many (I Cor. 10.33; cf. 9.22 f.). Also in the Church's duty to fulfil Christ's law to the uttermost. But, according to Gal. 6.2, Christ's law can be put thus: 'Bear ye one another's burdens, and so fulfil the law of Christ.' The new world-situation finds its *principium*, its beginning and its norm in the vicarious carrying of its burden by Jesus Christ (cf. John 1.29). So it is vicarious bearing of burdens that is the office of those who are called by Christ's name. Sickness and sorrow and every sort of pain that God lays upon us become, in the law of Christ, our 'cross' that we must carry as our share of the agony of the world (II Cor. 1.5; Col. 1.24). Suffering is no longer our fate; it is our office, our burden-bearing office as we minister to the many (I Cor. 4.13). Gal. 6.2 speaks of a ministry to the brethren. But when we think of Christ's way as a prototype we can see another duty which has wider reference—the ministry of the Christian to his enemy, the ministry of the Church to the world. How does the Church perform this ministry? She does it by being the suffering and praying Church (Ch. 44; 46), by being at one and the same time *ecclesia pressa* and *ecclesia orans* (I Cor. 4.12 f.). She kneels before her crucified Lord and prays for the salvation of an hostile world. She stands at the altar and signs the lost world with the saving *signaculum crucis*.[497]

So much for the new situation brought about by the coming of Christ. It makes its appearance in the existence and history of the Church. It reaches its climax and conclusion in the end of history.

Section Four

THE CHURCH AND THE WORLD

Chapter 38

HOW THE EARLY CHURCH DESCRIBED HERSELF

H. F. Hamilton, *The People of God*, I, II, 1912; E. Gaugler, 'Die Bedeutung der Kirche in den joh. Schriften', IntKZ, 1924 f.; H. Gressmann, *The Tower of Babel*, 1928; W. Koester, *Die Idee der Kirche . . . bei Paulus*, 1928; E. v. Dobschütz, 'Die Kirche im Urchristentum', ZNW, 1929; Th. Dombart, *Der babylon. Turm*, 1930; E. Unger, *Babylon, die Heilige Stadt*, 1931; V. Burch, 'The "Stone" and the "Keys"', JBL, 1933; H. Schmidt, *Der heilige Fels*, 1933; F. J. Dölger, 'Domina mater ecclesia' . . . AC 1936; A. Wikenhauser, *Die Kirche als der myst. Leib Christi*, 1937; F. Wetzel und F. H. Weissbach, *Das Hauptheiligtum des Marduk in Babylon . . .*, 1938; E. Käsemann, *Das wandernde Gottesvolk*, 1939; Ph. Vielhauer, *Oikodome*, 1940.

PRIMITIVE Christianity has given an account of the historical situation of the Church in a wealth of concepts and images. We can get a brief review of them by arranging the profusion of material under seven heads represented in the seven words: '*ecclesia*', 'people of God', 'flock of Christ', 'God's planting', 'God's building', '*ecclesia femina*', '*corpus Christi*'.

The basic idea is that of the *ecclesia*, used, according to Matt. 16.18 (18.17) by Jesus himself of the Church that was to be. The Church that calls itself *ecclesia* means to be neither Synagogue nor anti-Synagogue nor yet para-Synagogue, but the covenant community of the Messiah, seeing its roots back beyond the age of the formation of the Synagogue in the very beginnings of Israel. She intends to revive the inheritance of the Mosaic covenant community and now at last bring its original purpose to its fulfilment: the hallowing of God's name.[498]

'I will be your God, and ye shall be my people'—so runs one of the fundamental original sayings of OT religion and history (Lev. 26.11; Ezek. 37.27; Zech. 8.8), which came vividly to life again in the apocalyptic period.[499] The primitive Church took these words as a promise that was only now being literally fulfilled for the first time (II Cor. 6.16b). The Church is the 'people' of God, the 'people of God's possession', to whom God will be Lord and Father in a quite unique sense, the 'priestly' people confessing and preaching God's name before all the world (II Cor. 6.18; I Pet. 2.9; Rev. 1.6; cf. Isa. 26.13; MEx. 15.2). In the midst of a dying world the Church is the coming generation that alone has a future before it when this world passes away: then God will dwell among them, and they shall be his people, and God himself shall be with them (Rev. 21.3; cf. Did. 10.5). In the same sense the Church of Christ is called the Church of the 'new covenant',[500] the 'true Israel',[501] 'the remnant',[502] 'the new tribe',[503] the 'elect generation',[504] the 'third race',[505] or the 'people of saints'.[506]

The picture of the 'flock' came to be used as a description of the people of God in the time when God was still calling kings and prophets from the pastoral life. We read of good and of worthless shepherds (Psa. 22; Isa. 40.11; Ezek. 34.23; Zech. 11.16 f.), and of the straying, forsaken flock (Isa. 13.14; 53.6; Jer. 13.17 ff.; AEn. 85 ff.). The NT writers (Paul!) no longer lived in this ancient Palestinian world of the shepherd and his pastoral experiences.[507] But for all that the traditional figures of the 'shepherd' and the 'flock' did not die out.[508] Indeed, in meeting the pastoral life of hellenism they gained new life and significance.[509] For this reason the picture of the Good Shepherd became a favourite theme of early Christian art.

From the remotest times the 'people of God' had been called a 'planting' of God in the old biblical tradition.[510] The writers of the NT applied this old and trusted metaphor to the Church of Christ. Jesus himself, linking up with Isa. 5, compared the story of the *civitas dei* with the destiny of a vineyard (Mark 12.1 ff.; cf. I Cor. 9.7). In John 15.1 ff. he illustrated his life-bearing function by the figure of the vine which bore fruit and gave the nourishment of life.[511] Revelation uses the picture of the paradise of God with the tree of life to depict the final *civitas dei*.[512]

The metaphor of a 'building' had a history which stretched far back into the usages of the ancient East.[513] We know of Iranian myths of the tower of the first king Yima;[514] and of Babylonian traditions of a 'world tower', a 'rock building' and the like.[515] The principal thing in the OT is Zion, the holy city with its temple on the holy mountain, a sign that there is the 'people of God' (cf. Matt. 4.5; 5.35). But Jesus commented on that. The ancient city of God had ceased to be such in the context of its significance for salvation-history (Ch. 21). James, the Lord's brother, prayed in vain for its deliverance (Ch. 4). The Church of Christ took its place[516] and in doing so pointed beyond itself to the heavenly Jerusalem, which would one day become the centre of the 'new creation'.[517] So the Church is to some degree the city of tents which the pilgrims inhabit who are looking for the city that is to come (Heb. 13.14; cf. 11.10; 12.22; Rev. 3.12; 22.19). Our 'capital city' is in heaven, says Paul.[518] Here we are but colonials waiting for our deliverer-king, the Lord Jesus Christ.

Many an ancient city had its tutelary goddess, who was looked on as the protectress or the symbol of her city. The old biblical tradition also frequently uses concepts like 'virgin', 'bride', 'wife', 'mother' in reference to the old or the new Jerusalem.[519] But in the thought of biblical monotheism these terms have only the force of images to describe the *civitas dei* poetically or parabolically. Such images play a considerable part in the parables of Jesus, in the closing chapters of Revelation, in the Vision of Hermas and also in early Christian mosaics (Mark 2.19 f.; Matt. 22.1 ff.; 25.10 ff.; Rev. 19.21 f.; Herm.v. 1., 2.4; 3.4.1). Ephesians interprets the saying from Genesis about the oneness of man and wife as a great mystery, and refers it to the relation between Christ and his Church.[520] In this sort of language the individual Christian is counted as a son of the *civitas dei* (Luke 13.34; cf. Matt. 2.18), and the Church appears as *mater ecclesia*.[521] We can recognize her, perhaps, in the Domitillan catacomb represented with her child in her arms. In Rev. 12.1 ff. Christ appears as the firstborn son of *ecclesia mater*.[522] For the woman with the crown of twelve stars is not some sort of meaningless theological echo of pre-Christian traditions (Gunkel), nor yet Sophia (Lohmeyer), and certainly not some young maiden who lays a trap for king Herod (cf. ThStKr., 1929, 457.1), but, as Luther knew, the *civitas dei*,[523] who first brings the Messiah into the world, and then his younger brethren (Rev. 12.17).

The figure of the body and its members as a picture of the corporate togetherness of a community is very ancient.[524] But the 'monarchic' understanding of the image, the formula of the body and the head, is also very early, and we meet it in the old biblical tradition.[525] This means that Paul was using a quite familiar image when he depicted the Church as a 'body' (Rom. 12.4 f.; I Cor. 12) and Christ as its 'Head' (Col. 1.18, 24). The *corpus christianum* is *corpus Christi* (I Cor. 10.16 f.; 12.13). He is the supreme head of his Church (Col. 1.18; cf. 2.10; I Cor. 11.3) and the conveyor of her life (Col. 2.19; cf. John 15.1 ff). This terminology is enlarged upon in Ephesians, though it is certainly done by mingling it with other concepts and ways of thought (1.22 f.; 2.16; 4.15 f.; 5.23, 30). In 5.28 the idea of the marriage of Christ to the Church is mixed with the idea of the 'body'. And in 4.12 the idea of *corpus Christi* is mingled with that of the building of the Church in the formula about the building up of the 'body' of Christ.[526] It was Ignatius who first made the traditional picture a completely Christian thing: the fate of the Head must be the fate of the members as well. So the cross of Christ is the norm for our existence, who are members of Christ (IgnTr. 11.2). Here for the first time the metaphor of *corpus Christi* is no longer used to describe a static relationship, but rather to express a theological understanding of history. 'The Church is the body of Christ. In the story of her suffering and her glorification the destiny of Jesus Christ in his passion, death and resurrection' comes to its conclusion.[527]

Almost every self-description used by the primitive Church contained an antithesis—in the sense of that antagonism between the *civitas dei* and the *civitas diaboli* which Augustin made the central theme of his chief work. The Church of Christ is at constant war with the Synagogue of Satan (Rev. 2.9; 3.9; cf. Ch. 47). The 'people' of God fence themselves off against the peoples of the world (II Cor. 6.14 ff.). The 'flock' of Christ is pursued by clawing beasts (AEn. 85 ff.; I Pet. 5.8; cf. Ch. 46). God's 'plant' is laid waste by God's enemies (Isa. 5.5; Matt. 13.39). God's 'building' has its demonic counterpart in the altar, the throne, the tower, the city of the adversary (Gen. 11; I Cor. 10.21; Rev. 2.13; 14.8; Herm.s. 1.6). But the counterpart of *ecclesia femina* is the '*ancilla sion*',[528] and above all others the 'whore' of Babylon.[529] In Revelation the city of God is the virgin adorned as the bride of the Messiah, while Babylon is the painted strumpet, intoxicated with wickedness and blasphemy, and drunk with the blood of the saints. The city of God is the mother of virgins (Rev. 12.5, 17; 14.4). Babylon is the mother of harlots (Rev. 17.5; cf. 2.20 ff.; 9.21; 22.15). The 'bride' of the Messiah waits in obscurity for the wedding day, arrayed in white linen (Rev. 19.8; 22.17). The strumpet Babylon gives herself airs in purple raiment on scarlet horses and commits fornication with the kings of the earth and confuses and destroys the inhabitants of the world with the wine of her fornication (Rev. 17.2; 18.3). So the carnival of the drunken whore staggers and totters to its death (Rev. 19.2). But the wedding procession of the Messiah's bride walks in white garments with 'Hallelujah!' sounding from their lips, surrounded by hymns and incense, and goes to meet the Bridegroom who rides forth from heaven on a white palfrey (Rev. 19.7).

Chapter 39

THE CHURCH'S MESSAGE

J. Schniewind, *Euangelion*, 1927 ff.; K. Holl, *Urchristentum und Religionsgeschichte, GesAufs* II, 1928; H. Preisker, *Die urchristliche Botschaft von der Liebe Gottes*, 1930; E. Molland, 'Das paulinische Euangelion', *Abd. d. Osloer. Akad*, II, 3, 1934; M. Dibelius, *Die Botschaft von Jesus Christus*, 1935; C. H. Dodd, *The Apostolic Preaching and its Developments*, 1936; F. J. Dölger, Θεοῦ Φωνή, AC, 1936; R. Asting, *Die Verkündigung des Wortes im Urchristentum*.

The first task of the Church is to preach the Word. What is the definitive content of the proclamation of the Word in the primitive Church: the message given by Jesus, or the message given about Jesus, an idea of God or the works of Christ? The characteristic terminology of the primitive Christian preaching must provide us with the answer.

The authoritative concept for what the Church had to say is called in the NT '*euangelion*'—good news. The expression is a *terminus technicus* in the cult of the emperor. The outstanding days in the life of the ruler were reckoned in the literature of ancient courts as festival days for the whole world, and in particular his birthday, his attainment of his majority and his coming to power.[530] Reports of such festivals were called '*euangelia*' in the inscriptions and papyri of imperial times.[531] The NT uses the term in this same sense, though with the distinctive difference that while there are many festivals to be celebrated (birth, start of the public ministry, the accession to the heavenly throne) there is no plurality of gospels. The primitive Church knows but one *euangelion*, and this one *euangelion* or gospel embraces all those festivals as constituting a unitary, unique event, the 'Christ-event', as we have called it.[532]

The concept of an evangel in the ancient world required for its content an historical event which brought in a new situation for the world. The NT idea of an evangel had as its content the Christ-event, which did bring in a new situation for the world. Terms like 'herald's message',[533] 'apostolic word', 'testimony',[534] demand and receive the same content. But we can find all those ideas together in I Cor. 15.1–15, all of them related to the pre-Pauline creedal formula of the death and resurrection of Christ, all joined in a passage where Paul talks of the tradition of the primitive Church, of the original tradition which in the last resort goes back to Jesus himself (cf. Ch. 30 ff.). We conclude: the message given by Jesus Christ was itself the message about Jesus Christ. The definitive content of the preaching of the primitive Church was not a gospel of the love of God and the love of one's neighbour (thus Harnack), and not simply a gospel of the holy God who condescended to sinners (thus Holl), but the gospel of the Christ-event. It was not just an event in man's spiritual history, nor just an event in revelation, but an event in salvation-history that stood at the beginning of the story of the Church. The event was the earthly path of the Son of God in the service of human need.

'Gospel' means good news. This concept has no place for preaching which is judgement and grace 'together'. What the NT writers have to say about the seriousness of our human situation is but the prelude to the gospel (Ch. 14 ff.), not its thesis, nor yet its dialectical antithesis (II Cor. 1.18 ff.).

The gospel of the NT is the witness of those who know to those who know (cf. Ch. 23). Only those who know the gravest realities can understand their testimony. Only the man who is *in extremis* hears God's voice and takes it seriously. That is why the witness of the primitive Church goes through history and among the nations as an unobtrusive and persistent *ceterum censeo* intelligible only in those short moments when the pomp of history and the self-conscious prattle of the peoples is painfully silenced. For the *Logos* of God is the *ultima ratio* of history.

The gospel of the primitive Church is an 'eternal gospel' (I Peter 1.25; Mark 13.31; Rev. 14.6). But its eternity takes on an historical form in its inexhaustibility, and is fulfilled in the fact that there is no time to which it fails to reveal its inconceivable scope, that to the questions of each new generation it brings its answer anew. So the gospel remains abidingly fresh, because and inasmuch as while the centuries pass it will always renew its freshness, glorious as on the first day. Barn. 10.11 recommends theologians to 'chew the cud' (of the Word of the Lord). In contrast to this John talks of an explication of the divine *Logos* in history, and unfolding of his treasures, which only dips deeper and wider into them (John 1.16 ff.; 14.24 ff.; 16.12 ff.; Rev. 1.1).

The NT writers never think of Christianity as absolute. They do not make the doubtful attempt to give absoluteness to some particular interpretation of life, or some special understanding of God. Indeed, men like Paul engage in bitter war against the temptation to give absolute status to some form of Christianity or some ecclesiastical system, and thereby to invalidate the sole efficacy and sufficiency of the *sola cruce* (Ch. 5). Rather did the primitive Church preach the gospel of salvation wrought out in the Christ-event, which had introduced a new situation between God, the world and the adversary, and had placed the destiny of mankind on a new footing. Every reality in the world and in history is in some way related to this central fact, relative to this absolute point of reference. In this sense we can speak of the absoluteness of Jesus Christ. But the NT connects this absoluteness with an historical fact that hides itself as such in the 'servant's form' of historical relativity. It is this Christ-event that the primitive Church proclaimed: an absolute in the form of the relative, the 'concrete absolute' (Heim). Christianity has played down now the absolute meaning, now the relative appearance of the Christ-event—but the NT will give up neither, but holds on to both with the same radical determination. That is the 'offence' of theology, the *scandalon* in which the hidden *sophia* of the gospel is wrapped up.

Chapter 40
THE SACRAMENTS

J. Leipoldt, *Dir urchristl. Taufe im Lichte der Religionsgesch.*, 1928; R. Plus, *Le Baptême dans l'Archeologie et l'Art chrétien*, 1932; J. Jeremias, *Hat die Urkirche die Kindertaufe geübt?*,[2] 1949; E. Stauffer, 'Zur Kindertaufe im Urchristentum', DPB, 1949; R. L. Cole, *Love Feasts*, 1916; H. Lietzmann, *Mass and Lords Supper*, 1926; K. Völker, *Mysterium und Agape*, 1927; A. Greiff, *Das älteste Pascharituale der Kirche . . . und das J*, 1929; W. v. Loewenich, *Das letzte Mahl Jesu*, 1939; O. Procksch, *Passa und Abendmahl*, in H. Sasse, *Vom Sakrament des Altars*, 1941; J. Jeremias, *Die Abendmahlsworte Jesu*,[2] 1949; G. Schmidt, 'Mnestheti', *Festschr. f. Meiser*, 1951; Stauffer, 'Zur sakramentalen Bedeutung des kirchlichen Segens', ditto, 1951.

Jesus himself accepted baptism of John, and gained his first disciples from the followers of the Baptist (Ch. 2). So it is in the highest degree credible that the baptism of repentance for the forgiveness of sins was also practised among Jesus' disciples, as is reported in John 4.2. But that report takes us back to the beginnings of the ministry, when Jesus was working alongside the Baptist. But from the time that the Baptist disappeared from the scene we hear no more of any sort of baptismal instruction or baptismal rites. It is, therefore, the more striking that the young Christian Church from its very beginning, in fact, kept to an established Christian baptismal usage (Acts 2.38, Rom. 6.3; I Cor. 1.13). How this Christian practice of baptism originated is a puzzle[535] that only begins to be solved if we come at last once more to conclude that the tradition of the risen Lord giving a missionary charge is to be taken seriously.[536] The commission to missionary activity is bound up in all the four Gospels with baptismal motifs (Luke 24.47; Mark 16.16; John 20.22; Matt. 28.19). And rightly so. For the commissioning of the apostles was directed to the gathering in of the people of the 'new covenant'. But the new 'people' of God needed a covenant sign, to take the place of the old covenant seal, the Jewish practice of circumcision (cf. Ch. 36). This covenant sign is Christian baptism—prepared for by late Jewish baptismal practices, stimulated by the baptism of John, and made necessary by the missionary command of the risen Lord.

Baptism in the primitive Church was the marking of men with the name of Jesus—precisely in the sense of that idea of a sign of salvation that we referred to above (Ch. 36) (Acts 2.38; 8.16; 10.48; 19.5; cf. I Cor. 1.13; 6.11; Did. 7.1). Paul had an even more concrete understanding of baptism: for him it was the marking of a man with the name of the crucified (Rom. 4.11; II Cor. 1.22) and in this way it was placing the baptized person under the sign of the cross. The death of Christ on the cross is the presupposition of baptism in the name of Christ (I Cor. 1.12 f.; cf. Barn. 11.1, 8). Again, the descent into the baptismal water, the element of death, is to be buried 'with Christ' (water=the element of death, see Ch. 46). But to rise up out of the baptismal water is a resurrection 'with Christ' (Rom. 6.4 ff.; I Cor. 10.2 ff.). The baptized is a risen person in the sense that he is accounted such. Henceforth he must prove himself as one quickened to a new life in an ethical sense (cf. Eph. 5.14). The day will come when he will be wakened to eternal life in the sense that he has been re-created so (Rom. 6.4 ff.; I Cor. 10.2 ff.). The early Church drew the consequences from this understanding of baptism. She made the sign of the cross over the person to be baptized (Ch. 36)[537] and called baptism a 'sealing' (Herm.s. 9.16.3). The baptized person is 'saved', is received into the congregation of the saints of the last days (Tit. 3.5; I Pet. 3.21; Eph. 1.13 f.; 4.30). But one reservation remains: the sovereign reservation of the Lord over against his Church and her sacrament: baptism does not save indubitably, and salvation is not absolutely bound up with baptism.[538] The Spirit blows where it listeth (John 3.8). There are baptisms without the Spirit, and the Spirit can come without baptism (Acts 8.16; 10.47). The Lord alone knows whose are his (II Tim. 2.19; John 13.18) and reserves to himself the right to seal the *predestinati* with the seal that is alone decisive.[539]

Did the first Christians already baptize their small children? Most probably so. For we find that already the oldest baptismal terminology uses the OT ritual formula 'the whole house', which demonstrably included the small children.[540] In any event we can recognize at least five points at the very beginning of Christianity where infant baptism could arise: (1) Baptism is a substitute for circumcision.[541] Anyone who remained uncircumcized was 'cut off' (Gen. 17.14). Who would be disposed to let his child go unbaptized *rebus sic stantibus*? (2) Christian baptism was prepared for by proselyte baptism. But proselyte baptism was performed on minors and infants.[542] (3) Baptism in the early Church was always performed by a baptizer[543] and in its whole ritual is neither an active perform-ance nor a sacramental activity of the person to be baptized, but rather a passive experience. For this reason it can much more readily pass into infant baptism than any sort of 'self-baptism' (e.g. JosVita. 2). (4) We know that Paul recognized and tolerated intercessory baptism for the dead.[544] The same non-voluntary conception of baptism made the emergence of infant baptism possible, and also permitted it, in the sense of an intercessory and sealing action. (5) We read of baptismal witnesses and intercessory prayers for the person to be baptized.[545] If a small child were to be baptized, the baptismal witnesses performed the duties of intercession, upon which the emphasis was now placed, and they became sponsors who would act on the child's behalf and be answerable for him. In view of all this it is quite probable and understandable that infant baptism very early was adopted as a custom, whether appeal was made to the Lord's saying (Mark 10.14) or not (cf. TertBapt. 18). Anyone who sees in this some declension from primitive Christianity has mis-understood baptism in voluntarist terms. The primitive act of bap-tism was a sealing with the sign of the cross. What was there to hinder the Church from permitting infants to be baptized in this sense? Nothing at all. What was there to urge them to it? Every-thing!

According to the evidence of the NT the Last Supper of Jesus with his disciples was a passover, celebrated on the eve of the passover feast,[546] and the synoptic reports of what was done at the Supper tell us how faithfully Jesus kept to the paschal customs of the fathers of Judaism.[547] The new significance of the passover meal was indicated by Jesus in the first place by the words of interpretation: 'This *is* my body; this *is* my covenant blood (the new covenant in my blood), which is shed for many (you) (for the forgiveness of sins)'. It is easy enough to determine what is *not* meant by this interpretative formula, by this determinative 'is': the 'is' in the eucharistic sayings is not to be understood as an analytic judgement, nor yet as some sort of teaching of a theory of transubstantiation.[548] It is much more difficult to answer the question: what positive meaning was intended by Jesus with his interpretative formula? The answer is to be found from the passover pericope in Ex. 13: Moses in God's name insti-tuted the rite of unleavened bread with these words: 'It shall be for a sign upon thine hand, and for frontlets between thine eyes for by strength of hand the Lord brought us forth out of Egypt.'[549] But this annual rite had a salvatory significance just as the historical sign of the 'passover' had in Ex. 12.13. If anyone missed it, he brought death upon himself (Num. 9.13 'cut off'; Jub. 49.3, 15, plague, death; cf. Wisd. 16.6 f.; 18.20 ff.). In the same way Jesus introduced the rite of the Last Supper as a sign and memorial of God's act of deliverance on the cross. The liturgical act is a sign and memorial of the event in salvation, and through its relation to that event begets the metaphysical efficacy of a saving sign. The breaking of the bread is a sign and memorial of the sacrifice of his body. The distribution of the cup is a sign and memorial of the sacrifice of his blood.[550] On the eve of God's act of deliverance in Egypt Moses celebrated the passover with the people of Israel, and in saving remembrance of that saving act the people of the old covenant from that time on celebrated the passover. On the eve of the divine act of salvation on Golgotha Jesus celebrated the Last Supper with his disciples, and in saving remembrance of that saving act the Christian covenant community from henceforth celebrated the eucharist.[551] 'This do'—that is not just permission, it is a command. The command to baptize is the eleventh, and the command to celebrate the Last Supper is the twelfth commandment.

Paul developed the tradition[552] of the Last Supper in seven points: (1) According to I Cor. 5.7 f. Good Friday is the passover day for universal history. (2) the passover is not the only type of the Lord's Supper, but the provision of manna in the wilderness serves as such too (I Cor. 10.2 ff.). (3) The one loaf created, according to I Cor. 10.16 f., the sacramental communion of the one 'body'. (4) The eucharist is always *manducatio indignorum et impiorum* but must never be *manducatio indigna et impia* (I Cor. 11.27). (5) In I Cor. 10.21; 11.20 Paul writes of the person of Christ as spiritual presence, which the Lord's Supper bestows upon us at the Lord's Table. (6) In I Cor. 10.3 f., 16; 12.13 and especially in 11.27, 29 Paul writes of the real and spiritual presence of Christ in the bread and wine. By *manducatio indigna* which makes no distinction between everyday food and sacramental, we sin against the body, which is found in the bread, and against the blood, which is found in the wine. (7) In I Cor. 11.24, 27, 29 ff. Paul speaks of a spiritual transference of life in the sacramental meal. The eucharist is instituted *in ruinam et resurrectionem* never as something indifferent, but always as something that either judges or saves us.[553]

John brings the eucharistic doctrine of the primitive Church to its completion. We can put his final interpretation again in seven points: (1) John has taken the coincidence of the crucified and the passover lamb chronologically. Even the prescription of Ex. 12.46 (Num. 9.12) is fulfilled in John 19.36; a bone of him shall not be broken.[554] (2) Because of the passover chronology, which perhaps goes with the levitical passover reckoning, the Last Supper in John 13 necessarily loses its specific character as a passover meal, and is seen in a new context reminiscent of TestL. 8.5. The 'feetwashing' now does the duty, performed in the synoptic Gospels by the Last Supper, of pointing to the imminence of the events of Good Friday.[555] (3) The liturgical accent shifts to the discourse on the 'bread of life' in John 6, which was the new Eucharistic-Haggada of the Johannine Churches (cf. Ch. 6). The miracle of the manna in the wilderness points typologically beyond itself to the incarnation of Jesus and the miracle of the five loaves.[556] Again, the miraculous bread of Jesus points beyond itself to the 'bread of life' in the eucharist.[557] Finally, the bread in the eucharist points beyond itself to the eschatological messianic feast. (4) The eucharistic bread which the believer eats is the body of Jesus, his flesh in a strict ontic sense ! (6.49 ff.). This illustrates the magnitude of the step that is taken in passing from an imputative to a creative understanding of the copula 'is'! (5) This (ontically understood) eucharistic bread cannot be distributed by Jesus during his earthly life.[558] For the disciples cannot eat the '*sarx*' of John 6.54 while Jesus is alive, but only the miraculous bread of John 6.11. The one who distributes the sacrament of the bread is rather the crucified and exalted Son of Man, who comes amongst us and shares the eucharist with us.[559] (6) The historical Christ said: 'I am the bread of life'—and interprets the incarnation in terms of the category of the bread from heaven. But the exalted Christ says: 'I am the eucharistic bread'—and interprets the eucharistic bread in terms of the category of incarnation. So in the eucharistic meal there takes place a sacramental reincarnation and indwelling of the *Logos* (John 6.35, 63, 68). The sacrament is the form in which the Christ himself comes to us in our world (I John 5.6). (7) The Christ of the eucharist is the bestower of life only in virtue of his unity with the Father (John 6.56 f.; cf. 1.16), and he bestows life only through the Spirit.[560] In this way John sees in the eucharist a realization of the real presence of the divine Trinity.

It is entirely in this Johannine spirit that Ignatius thinks of the sacrament as the new form of Christ's becoming flesh, and so as a sign of, indeed a participation in, the penetration of the whole creation with the life-giving powers of Christ (Rom. 7.3; cf. IgnEph. 18.2). There was a time when man enjoyed happy days in the shadow of the tree of life. But the wiles of the serpent led to his expulsion from Paradise and banishment to the world of death (Gen. 3; cf. Wisd. 1.14). But the time will come when man will once more enjoy the fruit of the tree of life and obtain eternal life, in the age to come. That at any rate is the promise of biblical apocalyptic (AEn. 25.4 f.; TestL. 18.11; Exr. 15 on 12.12; Rev. 2.7; 22.2). Ignatius applied these thoughts to the eucharist. The eucharistic bread is a foretaste of the future life, a 'medicine of immortality'.[561] The life-giving herb which man lost, and ever since has sought for tirelessly and in vain (Ch. 23), is now at last discovered!

Chapter 41

THE SPIRIT

M. Goguel, *La Notion Johannique de l'Esprit* . . ., 1902; W. Schauf, *Sarx*, 1924; F. Büchsel, *Der Geist Gottes im NT,* 1926; H. v. Baer, *Der hl Geist in den Lukasschriften,* 1926; R. B. Hoyle, *The Holy Spirit in St Paul,* 1927; H. Windisch, 'Die fünf johanneischen Parakletsprüche, *Festschr. f. A. Jülicher,* 1927; E. Fuchs, *Christus und der Geist bei Paulus,* 1932.

The most original saying of the NT about the Spirit takes up Joel 3.1 ff.: the time will come when 'I will pour out my spirit upon all flesh, and your sons and your daughters shall prophesy . . . and I will shew wonders . . . blood and fire and pillars of smoke . . . before the great and terrible day of the Lord come' (cf. Ezek. 37.5, 14). John the Baptist spoke of a baptism to come that would be with Spirit and with fire (Luke 3.16). Jesus himself promised those who confessed him before men that the Spirit would be with them (Mark 13.11; Luke 12.11 f.) and in the same way promised his disciples 'power from on high', the spiritual equipment for the discharge of their apostolic office (Luke 24.49; Acts 1.4 ff.). These promises are all thought of as fulfilled in Acts on the day of Pentecost (Acts 2.3 f., 13.16). The Spirit is the reality on which the Church is founded.[562] What the Spirit means for the story of salvation is made manifest in this generation, and is filled out in the history of the Church. This is the basic conception of the book of Acts.

Paul speaks of the start of the Spirit's work in the story of salvation in terms of an 'economic' understanding of the Trinity (Gal. 4.4 ff.; Ch. 65), though he talks of the operation of the Spirit in the Church and its history in terms of pre-Pauline traditions.[563] But his most distinctive contribution concerns the realization of the Spirit in the personal life of the believer. How does the Spirit make us sure that we are sons? Gal. 4.6 answers: in prayer! In affliction and joy alike there is something in me which cries 'Father'! What is it that does so? It is certainly not myself, but the Spirit in my heart. It is not the everyday self of the old man, but the spiritual self of the new man. It is not the self that is at home in the speech and the hearing of ordinary experience. It is a self that could come into existence only in a relation of intimacy with God. Its reality belongs exclusively to the dialogue that takes place between man the child and God the Father. Man's spiritual self is actualized in prayer (Rom. 8.15 f.; cf. I Cor. 14.14). 'The Spirit himself maketh intercession for us with groanings which cannot be uttered' (Rom. 8.26 f.). The man who lives out of this dialogue with God in prayer, lives a new life of which the world knows nothing (Rom. 8.2; 14.17; II Cor. 3.17; Gal. 5.22 ff.; I Cor. 2.13 ff.). But it is not as if the spiritual man were already taken out of the 'flesh', i.e. this world of death and its conditions. On the contrary. The Spirit brings man into a quite new place of conflict (Gal. 5.17; Ch. 34). The new situation, though it is no longer so desperate as that which confronted pre-Christian man, of which Paul speaks in Rom. 7.7 (cf. n.[239]), nevertheless needs to be taken with a new seriousness. The anthropology of Rom. 7 ends in a cry: 'Who shall deliver me out of the body of this death?' Gal. 5.16 is the transposition of this anthropology into the imperative: 'Walk by the Spirit, and ye shall not fulfil the lust of the flesh.' So the spiritual man is the subject of a new life, at war with the laws and powers of this mortal world. But in that new life there is already a foretaste of the powers of the age to come. That is why Paul calls the Spirit the firstfruits of the coming harvest. The Spirit is the herald of the new creation and promises us 'the redemption of our body' (Rom. 8.23; II Cor. 1.22; cf. I Cor. 3.15; 5.5). Thus all the tension of the intermediate situation in which the 'new man' finds himself receives precise expression in Paul's doctrine of the Spirit: The spirit-filled man is aflame with the fire of God. But he is not yet remoulded into the new form of his being.

In his own original fashion John has transformed the traditional view about the entrance of the Spirit upon his work in the history of salvation.[564] Pre-Johannine pneumatology made three distinctions in its conception of the Spirit—as it operated in the history of creation, in the history of salvation, and in the history of the Church. John brought all these three perspectives together in the proposition which constitutes the unexpressed premiss to John 20.22: the Spirit is a reality in and for universal history. It is this universal reality that is also, according to John, active in the present generation in the history of the Church[565]—but not only there: the Spirit bloweth where it listeth (John 3.8; cf. 4.23; 10.16). That is the reservation of universal history that the Johannine Christ makes over against the history of the Church.

A final sharpness of definition is given to the idea of the Holy Spirit in the NT by a complementary notion which is explicitly or implicitly related to it—the idea of the 'spirit of lies' (cf. Test Jud. 20.3). What is the *tertium comparationis* which makes it possible to correlate the Spirit of Christ and the spirit of lying? When the NT speaks of the communion of the Holy Ghost (II Cor. 13.13) it does not think of some company of persons who share some common idea or opinion and come together on that account. What comes first in the *communio sanctorum* is not individual personalities, but rather the one, supra-personal and all-inclusive Spirit, who lives in many and manifoldly different individual lives (Phil. 1.27; I Cor. 12.4 ff.). The same applies, *mutatis mutandis*, to the spirit of lying and the community which he creates (Rev. 17.13, 17; II Thess. 2.11 f.; Eph. 6.12). In this case also the reality is not individual persons, particular tenets, individual endowments, particular consequences, but rather the history, the experiences and the effects of a 'system' of a supra-personal spirit (cf. Ch. 53). Anyone who does battle with the men and the powers of the spirit of lying has to fight an army that betrays in its every movement and action the same unified strategy, the same superior strategist. Everywhere we can see a central will, an intelligent planning, one and the same personal spirit at work.[566] In a situation like this everything depends upon how we discern the 'spirits'—in the Church as well as outside (I Cor. 12.10; I John 4.1 f.). The primitive Church enumerated a whole series of distinguishing signs by which they could identify the adversary (Ch. 13). One of the most fundamental was his mendacity. But it was precisely his mendacity that was so masterly that no human being could possibly unmask it with the means of knowledge and the methods of proof that this world provides, and not even the distinguishing signs were adequate—so it was necessary that the Holy Spirit himself should open our eyes (I Cor. 12.10 f.).

Accordingly, this is the first mark by which we can recognize the Holy Spirit—that he makes us keen to observe the nature and the works of the spirit of lying. But it is also the comprehensive mark by which we can recognize the Spirit of God—that he brings the hidden things to light (TestJud. 20.5; Acts 5.3; 8.9 ff.; I Cor. 14.24). The Holy Spirit brings to the light of day this humbling truth about man and this destructive truth about the world (Eph. 5.13; John 16.7 f.). But this critical activity of the Spirit is, nevertheless, only the prelude to his positive work: the Holy Spirit testifies to the truth of God, his saving truth. And the truth of God which the Holy Spirit testifies to us and discloses is nothing other than Jesus Christ (I Cor. 12.3; I John 4.2; John 15.26; 16.14). The Holy Spirit brings the truth to light, and the Church can recognize him by that. And it is for this reason that John calls him the Spirit of truth (TestJud. 20.1; John 16.13; I John 4.6).

Chapter 42

FAITH

Ph. Bachmann, *Die persönliche Heilserfahrung . . . und ihre Bedeutung, f d Glauben n d Zeugnis d Apostel,* 1899; W. H. P. Hatch, *The Pauline Idea of Faith . . .,* 1917; E. Wissmann, *Das Verhältnis von Πίστις und Christusfrömmigkeit bei Paulus,* 1926; A. Schlatter, *Der Glaube im NT,*[4] 1927; G. Stählin, *Skandalon,* 1930; H. W. Heidland, *Die Anrechnung des Glaubens zur Gerechtigkeit,* 1936.

On the lips of Jesus faith is an audacious assertion of a possibility; in Paul and John it is an abasement before the glory of God; according to Heb. 11.1 it is evidence of the invisible, and in Revelation, finally, it is the fidelity of the martyr.

For the scribes of Mark 15.32 faith was thought of as a consequence of some miraculous experience (cf. Luke 4.9 ff.; John 20.29). Jesus himself, however, sees the relationship of faith and miracle in just the opposite way: faith is the presupposition of a miracle being done on me. But the miracle which the believer experiences, according to the synoptics, is different from that which the scribes acknowledge, in not being a demonstration, but a deliverance (Mark 5.36; Luke 8.50). Such faith is the assertion of a possibility against all probabilities, in spite of any contrary indication provided by our experience of life or the realities of the world, and in constant battle against temptation (Mark 9.23). What is it that differentiates this faith from mere illusion, which breaks down upon the hard rock of reality? It is not a faith that reaches vaguely into the void, but one that firmly trusts Jesus Christ. Such a faith has nothing else than Jesus Christ in the middle of a world which scoffs at all our hopes and fears. It fastens on to Jesus Christ with all its strength at its command, and if the demonic power of the storm becomes overpowering, then the last resources of man's nature give vent to the cry: 'Lord, I believe; help thou mine unbelief' (Mark 9.24; cf. 4.38 ff. p; Matt. 14.28).

But the assertion of a possibility which Jesus speaks about is not simply a faith that experiences a miracle of deliverance, it is also a faith that accomplishes miracle. This is confirmed to us by the saying of Jesus so frequent in the tradition and reported also by St Paul, about the faith that can remove mountains (Mark 11.23; Luke 17.6; Matt. 21.21; I Cor. 13.2). 'Nothing shall be impossible to you' (Matt. 17.20). What is it that distinguishes this faith from the self-intoxication that, in the words of Björnson, 'is beyond one's powers' and makes a man and his work end up in a fiasco? The 'faith' of Mark 11.23 f. is a faith that prays (cf. Mark 9.29; Luke 18.1; John 11.22 f., 41). Prayer is the source of its power, and the means of its strength—God's omnipotence is its sole assurance, and God's sovereignty its only restriction.

Faith seeks more than deliverance from sickness and danger. Its final fulfilment is the peace of God (Luke 7.48 ff.; 8.48; 17.19). God's sovereign omnipotence nowhere shows itself more purely or to better advantage than in the forgiveness of sins.[568] And nowhere does the unfathomable mercy of God reveal itself more brightly than in the hour of temptation. For then it is God himself who, for the sake of Jesus Christ, keeps our faith from destruction (Luke 22.32). In this sense the Christ-event is both the primary datum and the fulfilment of faith.

Luke 17.15 reports how one of the ten lepers who was healed turned back, glorifying God with a loud voice, and, when he saw Jesus, fell upon his face at his feet, and gave him thanks. Only this man, Jesus declared, had understood what had happened and given glory to God: 'Arise, and go thy way: thy faith hath saved thee' (cf. Ch. 27). This little story takes us on to the apostolic understanding of the idea of faith: faith is the adoring abasement of man before the revelation of the glory of God.

In Paul the accent falls upon the revelation of the Word. It is the Word of the gospel that calls out faith from men (Rom. 1.16; 10.8; cf. John 4.50). Hence faith is said to come from hearing, according to a formula that appears in a number of forms (Rom. 10.14 ff.; I Thess. 2.13; cf. John 4.41 f.; 12.38). But the hearing that is of faith expresses itself in the obedience of faith.[569] This obedience of faith has nothing at all to do with subjecting the human intellect to some dogmatic formula. What Paul has in mind is much more the subjection of man's self-glorification (cf. Rom. 10.3; Phil. 3.9) to the sole glory of God (II Cor. 7.15; 10.5 f.). This subjection of faith is the form by which we give his honour and his due to God who speaks to us.

John puts the emphasis upon revelation in act. In John it is not so much hearing and believing as seeing and believing that is the basic pair of related ideas (John 1.14; 20.8). The works which Jesus does are calculated to quicken faith (John 14.11, 29; cf. Acts 13.12). This forms the basis for a new idea of miracle. The synoptic Jesus works miracles of deliverance which presuppose faith. The Johannine Christ on the other hand works miracles of revelation which disclose his glory and in this way quicken faith. But although these two ideas of miracle are so different, they meet at the point where the evangelists work out in their miracle stories the way from faith to faith. Those who saw the miracle of healing on the mount of transfiguration were brought to a fuller faith, as were the leper, the nobleman and Martha, by the manifestation of Christ's power (Mark 9.24; Luke 9.43; 17.13 ff.; John 4.46 ff.; 11.3). But with John no less than with Paul the fulfilment of faith is an abasement before the glory of God, which was revealed in Jesus Christ (cf. Ch. 27). The blind man is born blind so that the works of God should be made manifest in him. He is made to see in order that he should look upon the glorious brightness of the Son of God (Ch. 29). He does, in fact, believe, and fall down at the Lord's feet (John 9.3, 35 ff.). Doubting Thomas saw and believed and adored (John 20.27 ff.).

The faith of which both John and Paul speak is the self-subjection of the *gloria mundi* to the *gloria dei*. But from this subjection God lifts man up to a new life (Rom. 3.27). There is a faith which is nothing more than optimism and self-confidence. But the apostles' faith is the faith of those who have fallen down and been raised up (Gal. 2.16; Phil. 3.9; Rom. 3.22 f.; 4.5, 9, 20; 10.4). This faith is the secret of the joyful heart for Paul, and for Luther and Paul Gerhardt (Phil. 1.25; Rom. 15.13). It is the source of a life that does not derive from this world, and so is stronger than anything worldly (I Cor. 16.13; Col. 2.7). 'The righteous shall live by faith,' says Paul in recasting a text from the OT (Gal. 3.11; Rom. 1.17; cf. Heb. 10.38). John directly joins faith and life together, without any interposition of the term righteousness. Those who believe have life in his name (John 20.31; cf. 3.15). But this life is the only kind of existence that can be said to have a future in this mortal world: it has eternity in itself. 'He that believeth hath eternal life' (John 6.47).

All this has nothing at all to do with the enthusiast's dreams of a better world or the romantic's sentimentality. The apostles know about the trials of temptation, but they also know of its necessity—for faith only remains faith, only really lives and grows as it is at grips with temptation.[570] In its fight with temptation faith frees itself from the calamitous presumption of doubt, and is free in the certainty that God can deal with every situation and any difficulty, that with him nothing is impossible, and that his unique majesty shines most brightly where man and his world are at an end of their resources and their understanding.[571] For this reason faith, when it has overcome temptation, is nothing more nor less than doxology.

Abraham 'in hope believed against hope' (Rom. 4.18). All faith is living in hope, living for an ultimate future in which temptation disappears as we come to see 'face to face' (Rom. 8.24; II Cor. 5.7; I Cor. 13.12; I John 3.2). To have faith is to bow the head before the hidden glory of God (II Thess. 1.4-8; II Cor. 3.18; 4.6; Col. 1.15; John 1.18; 5.37; 6.46). But to see is to lift one's eyes to the glory of God made manifest when the Lord appears in glory among his saints, and wondrous among those who believe on him (II Thess. 1.10; cf. Luke 21.27 f.).

The epistle to the Hebrews depends upon this eschatological understanding of faith. 'Now faith is the substance of things hoped for.'[572] So the fathers died without having received the promises; rather they saw them from far off and greeted them (11.15). Their sons now die in the same way, followers and witnesses to Christ who have spilt their blood for him, with their eyes set on the future that God provides: *Morituri te salutant!* (10.35 ff.). 'Faith is the proving of things not seen' (11.1). The devils also believe and shudder.[573] Their belief is the beginning of their destruction. But true faith is the beginning of a freedom, life and strength which lie at the further side of destruction; it is to be overcome by the invisible in such a way that this invisible reality has full authority over me, and is stronger than myself with all my individuality and self-will, more real but also more valuable than anything else in the world, than all the menaces and all the joys of this present age (Heb. 11.8, 27). The faith of those thus conquered is a power that overcomes all that is visible. It subdues lions and armies and kingdoms (11.33 f.).

It is only seldom that Rev. uses the word 'faith', and then always as a technical term for the faithfulness of those who are confessors and martyrs of Jesus Christ.[574] So at the end of the apostolic age the original meaning of the word (cf. *fides, fidelis*) once more passes into currency in the specific sense that it had in the pre-Christian martyr writings,[575] which it never quite lost in primitive Christianity, and which will of necessity always break out again in any time of persecution (cf. I Cl. 5.6). 'Here is the patience and the faith of the saints' (Rev. 13.10). The verb 'believe' is not used at all in Revelation. But in spite of that there is a christocentric belief in this book which we do not meet again in such depth and breadth until Augustin's *City of God*. Thus the language of Revelation is a necessary warning against the prodigality with which the idea of faith is used.

Chapter 43

THEOLOGY IN THE PRIMITIVE CHURCH

M. Wiener, 'Zur Geschichte des Offenbarungsbegriffs', '*Judaica*', *f. H. Cohen*, 1912; F. Kattenbusch, 'Die Entstehung einer christl. Theologie', ZThK, 1930; E. Fascher, 'Deus invisibilis', *Festgr. f. R. Otto*, 1931; O. Michel, 'Luther's "deus absconditus" und der Gottesgedanke des Paulus', ThStKr, 1931; R. Bultmann, *Glauben und Verstehen*, 1933; K. Mozley, *The Beginnings of Christian Theology*, 1936; O. Dilschneider, *Evangelischer Offenbarung*, 1939.

The spiritual history of Greece takes final form in natural theology.[577] The history of Jewish religion has its final form in a theology of a book.[578] The religion of the Bible is a religion of revelation.[579] The revelation which the NT proclaims is the self-revelation of God through *Logos*, through the Word of an historical revelation that God has spoken to us in the Christ-event (Heb. 1.1 f.; 2.3 f.; I John 1.1 ff.; Rev. 19.13). But man does not receive God's revelation as a welcome gift, not in the least (cf. Ex. 3 f.; Amos 7.14 f.; Jer. 1.4 ff.). He resists the moral demands which God's revelation makes of us, and passes over the seriousness of his situation in self-intoxication and self-deceit (John 3.19 f.; II Thess. 2.12; I Cor. 15.33 f.). He entrenches himself behind his natural theology (Ch. 18) or his religion of the law (Ch. 19). So the antagonism of everything human and worldly to God is made manifest in the very moment that God's word goes forth to his world. No amount of taking pains on man's part can overcome this antagonism. There is but one thing strong enough to overcome this resistance: the sovereign, revealing God himself.

God overcomes man's resistance in bringing to life in man his spiritual self, the spirit which confesses God whether with us, or without us, or even against us (Joel 3.1; Col. 1.9). Reason (*nous*) understands nothing about God. Blind and dumb it stands in history. But where the Spirit is, there 'Christian reason' comes to life. There man can comprehend history and understand it as an utterance of God. All through the process of history the divine Self is meeting the spiritual self of man and revealing to him the deep things of God. The spiritual man understands the wisdom of God's way, he recognizes the hidden plan of salvation which comes to its climax in the cross, and he lays hold of the *beneficia* of God (I Cor. 2.1–16; John 4.10). For where the Spirit is, there faith is quickened, there man keeps silence and listens, there man falls to his knees and looks (Rom. 11.22, 33; John 6.69; 9.35 ff.). Any man who has laid down his weapons before the all-subduing authority of the divine revelation is at the beginning of the road to theological knowledge (Gal. 4.8 f.; Col. 1.10; Eph. 3.9 f.; II Pet. 1.2). Every revelation of God contains a summons, an ethical demand.[580] That applies to the first step of the road, and to every subsequent step that is taken (Col. 1.9 f.; Eph. 1.19). If we become uncertain, God will then reveal to us what we are lacking—'only, whereunto we have already attained, by that same rule let us walk' (Phil. 3.15; cf. Rom. 1.17; I Thess. 3.10).

But wherever the divine revelation comes to be realized in faith and life, there it also finds expression in thought. 'Be not children in mind: howbeit in malice be ye babes, but in mind be men' (I Cor. 14.20; cf. 3.1). The faith of the primitive Church did not lull its thought to sleep, but woke it up, and set it in motion, so that we might apprehend with all the saints what is the breadth and length and height and depth of the mysteries of God (Eph. 3.16 ff.; 1.19).

The theology of the primitive Church was a process of ordering. What went on was not the making of metaphysical concepts, nor yet the construction of a system, but an ordering of thought, that sought to discover the actual relationships between the different elements of the world of human experience. The answer that was found as a result of the search was like this: God ordered all reality in history (Ch. 16). In this sense the theology of history is the primary and canonical form of Christian thinking and of all 'systematic' theology (Ch. 9–59). Any reality (such as man, the civil power, the Torah) is understood theologically when its place in this order of history, its place in the theology of history has been determined. But what is the actual place of the Christ-event in the theology of history? It is at the centre of history! The whole of history is ordered christocentrically. The Christ-event that has occurred in the world of our experience must be co-ordinated on this principle, and the world of our experience must be accommodated to our understanding of Christ. How did the writers of the NT reach this conclusion? Only by taking the fundamental fact of the NT revelation of God, the Christ-event, to its logical conclusion, and applying it with ruthless realism, in spite of all presuppositions of a metaphysical or pseudo-theological kind. He, Jesus Christ, was made unto us wisdom from God (I Cor. 1.30).

The Christ-event was a stumbling-block to the Jews (I Cor. 1.23). This was the point at which the conflict arose between revelation and the theology of a book, between faith and faith (cf. Mark 2.7; Luke 7.35; 10.21; John 10.33). Jewish realism sought after signs, palpable manifestations of Christ's power as a proof of his fitness before the tribunal of the OT and its official expositors (Matt. 12.38 ff.; I Cor. 1.22). But the essence of the revelation of Christ lies in its weakness (Matt. 4.1 ff.; Mark 15.32; Phil. 2.6 ff.).[581] Yet in the weakness of the revelation of Christ there is hidden an unique reality, of which Jewish reality knows nothing, for here a power comes into action which is stronger than anything else in the world (II Cor. 12.9; 13.4). It is in this sense that the primitive Church confessed: to us Christ is the mysterious revelation of the power of God (I Cor. 1.18, 24 ff.; 2.14 f.). This confession was made by means of an appeal to the OT! For the Church found all over the old biblical tradition secret witnesses of the mighty weakness of God, which pointed beyond themselves to the condescension of Jesus Christ. In doing this the primitive Church gave the established understanding and exegesis of the OT a thoroughgoing reorientation (II Cor. 3.13 ff.; 4.6): The cross is the secret of the OT (John 5.39; Heb. 1.1 f., 11 f.; I Pet. 1.10 f.; Barn. 2.6). In this way the OT was related to the Christ-event and became the Bible of primitive Christianity (Ch. 1).

The gospel of Christ was to the Greeks foolishness (I Cor. 1.22 ff.). At this point arose the conflict between 'revelation' and 'natural theology', between faith and knowledge (cf. II Cor. 10.5). Greek idealism sought after wisdom. But of what sort is the 'wisdom' that is referred to here? Classical philosophy dealt in concepts, abstractions and systems, and finds the ultimate 'metaphysical' reality in the timeless universal. *Universalissimum = realissimum*. The Greek talks about an impersonal absolute; the Christian of a personal God. With the Greek the cross is a parable, but for the Christian it is an event. Between these two there can be no sort of negotiated coexistence, for each of them makes quite totalitarian claims. Greek idealism neglects the gospel of the Christ-event as part of its intellectual presuppositions and, therefore, must reject the Christian gospel as an absurdity or else refashion it to suit its own premises. Paul dismisses the hellenistic presuppositions in considering the fact of Christ and must consequently reject its idealistic wisdom as foolishness (I Cor. 1.19 f., 27). To us Christ is the secret revelation of the wisdom of God (I Cor. 1.24, 30; 2.6 ff. Col. 2.2 f.). Following up this programme the apostle demanded a radical reconstruction of philosophical concepts and categories (Col. 2.8; cf. the two forms of wisdom in Athenag. 24.5): a break with a metaphysic of the 'supra-historical', the construction of an understanding of reality in terms of an universal history, which has its centre in the Christ-event, but in which also the facts and problems of the Greek understanding of the world have their place, though properly related to the centre (Ch. 5).

We have spoken about the essential correlation of faith and temptation (Ch. 42). A consequence of this is that thinking that treads the road from faith to faith has to fight a daily battle with temptation. Revelation is the light shining upon man's road through history, and man can set out upon the road in thankful confidence with this light in his hand. But again and again the way is beset with puzzles and darkness. The torch in his hand begins to flicker. God hides himself. It must be so. For in temptation theology passes into prayer, that asks God himself for the answer to the enigma of our historical experiences (cf. Psa. 72.2, 15 ff., 28). Only thought that prays can lead beyond the temptation and take us from one certainty to another.[582]

It is a precious thing to throw light on the works of God and confess them.[583] Theology is a return on man's part to his original destiny in creation, to the service of the glory of God (Ch. 11.18). It was in this sense that the apostles preached the mighty acts of God in redemption.[584] Josephus purged his doctrine of God from every idea which failed to agree with the idea of a transcendent God (cf. Ant. 1.15). But Paul fell down before the majestic wisdom of God's ways: 'To him be the glory for ever' (Rom. 11.33 ff.). God has made known to his saints, according to Col. 1.27, 'the riches of the glory of Christ' (cf. Ecclus. 43.33; I Cor. 2.10). So the Word of Christ has to resound through the Church in manifold forms, and God must be thanked in psalms and hymns and spiritual songs (Col. 3.16; Ch. 50). Ignatius, who himself wrote hymns in praise of God's grace, expressed this inward principle of the great early Christian thinkers in a superlatively good formula: 'The work is not of persuasiveness, but Christianity itself is a thing of might.' A proclamation of the Christ-event and an intellectual elaboration of its significance undertaken in this spirit was known in the early Church as 'theology'.[585]

Chapter 44

PRAYER

E. v. d. Göltz, *Das Gebet in der ältesten Christenheit,* 1901; K. Michel, *Gebet und Bild,* 1902; E. v. d. Goltz, 'Tischgebete und Abendmahlsgebete in der altchristl . . . Kirche', TU, 1905; W. Sattler, 'Das Gebet der Märtyrer', ZNW, 1921; H. Greeven, *Gebet und Eschatologie im NT,* 1931; J. Herrmann, 'Der at Urgrund des Vaterunsers', *Festschr. f. O. Procksch,* 1934; G. Harder, *Paulus und das Gebet,* 1936; E. Lohmeyer, *Das Vaterunser,* 1946.

'Father!' With this word the Lord's Prayer begins, and with this word Paul sums up the prayer that the Spirit offers.[586] There is a whole theology of prayer wrapped up in this one word. The God of the NT is a God to whom I can say 'thou'. That is the meaning of the dogmatic proposition about the 'personality' of God. Prayer in the NT is an appeal to the 'thou' who, in Ibsen's phrase is 'beyond me and above me', to whom I can flee—even from myself. Nor does this appeal echo out round a void, but it reaches God's ear (Job 27.9). But more, the one who prays receives an answer. Many a wish expressed in prayer remains unfulfilled, but every prayer to the Father is heard and none remains unanswered (Rom. 9.1 ff.; II Cor. 12.8; Heb. 5.7). But the answer comes to us from the very heart of God. The solitary man's cry of distress reaches God's heart! The God to whom we pray is no pitiless deity (PsSol. 5.5 ff.), but is the Father who can do all things, has control of every situation and is near me in every time of need. My prayer is a wrestling with his will (Gen. 32.25 ff.; Col. 1.29 f.), and the meaning of the wrestling and the fulfilment of the prayer is in God's being the victor in that wrestling (cf. Luke 22.44; Job 5.7 f.)! The Father, whom I address as 'thou', answers me with a 'thou' and when that happens my real self is brought to life for the first time. The living God deals with living men, and he finds them in this wrestling of prayer (Matt. 6.10; Mark 14.36 ff.; Job 1.21; Psa. 50.12). Only when I am entirely God's am I completely myself. Hence I am only fully myself when I pray. And, therefore, God wills my prayer.

The man who fulfils the original purpose of his life is *homo orans* (Ch. 11), and the original purpose of prayer is the hallowing of God's name (Acts 3.8 f.; 16.25). 'Thy name is holy, and thy saints shall praise thee daily' (XVIII 3; cf. Deut. 32.5; Psa. 71.17 ff.; Ecclus. 43.30; Tob. 13.7 ff.; Jdth. 16.13; PsSol. 8.24 ff.; 15.2; Rom. 15.9; Heb. 13.15). Formulae of praise begin many prayers and hymns in the OT and in later Judaism (Isa. 25.1; Tob. 3.11; 13.2; Jdth. 16.1; Dan. 3.26, 52; PsSol. 5.1; XVIII 1). 'Hallowed and glorified be thy great name' are the opening words of the Kaddish in the Jewish daily service.[587] A similar formula serves as the introit to the Lord's Prayer, 'Hallowed be thy name'.[588] The counterpart of these hymn-like introductory formulae are the doxological formulae with which many prayers close (cf. Man. 15; II Mac. 1.30; Dan. 3.88; PsSol. 5.19; 6.6; 8.34; 17.46; Deut. 32.43; I Cl. 61.3b). Even the Lord's Prayer was rounded off with such a formula in very early days (Matt. 6.13 vl; Did. 8.2; further Ezra 4.40). But the doxology is found in all sorts of places as an independent liturgical element in its own right, which provides the background of the whole service of worship (Isa. 6.3; I Chron. 29.10 ff.; Jub. 50.13 vi; AEn. 39.13; Luke 2.14; Rev. 4.8, 11; 5.12 f.; 7.12; 19.1 ff.; ApConst. 8.13.10 ff.). The most characteristic expression of the doxological significance of prayer is found in the monolatric formula: 'Thou alone'.[589] But even where there is no such formula, true prayer always includes in itself the confession 'Thou alone', for true prayer is always a fulfilment of the first commandment. 'Thou alone'—this is the theme on which a whole symphony of thanksgiving, confession, petition and intercession is constructed (cf. Phil. 4.6; I Tim. 2.1, etc.).

'In everything by prayer and supplication with thanksgiving let your requests be made known unto God'—so Phil. 4.6. Colossians is entirely in line with this theme (1.3, 12; 2.7; 3.15 ff.; 4.2). Indeed, this was the idea of prayer that the early Church had in all sorts of places, at table, at the eucharist, at the beginning of a letter to a Church, and also in the enthusiastic Church assemblies (Mark 8.6; Luke 24.30; Acts 27.35; I Cor. 10.30; Rom. 14.6; I Cor. 11.24; Did. 9; II Thess. 1.3; I Cor. 14.16 f.). What were the things for which the writers of the NT rendered thanks? Daily bread (I Tim. 4.3 f.), God's wonderful providences and saving acts (Luke 10.21; Acts 3.8 f.), his one, all decisive act of deliverance, the coming of Christ (Did. 9.2), the election and constancy of God (Phil. 1.3 ff.). Everything that God does for his Church is a summons to *glorificatio*, to *gratificatio* (I Thess. 5.18).

Confession, in the same way, is but another form of glorifying God. There are many places to which man can turn with thanks or petition; but when he has a heart burdened with guilt there is but one place he can go—to God (Psa. 31.3 ff.; 37.5; Prov. 28.13). 'Against thee, thee only, have I sinned' (Psa. 50.6; jXVIII 6; Luke 15.18 f.; cf. Lam. 3.42; Tob. 3.1 ff.; Barn. 2 f.; Acts 19.17 ff.; I Cl. 60.1 f.). Only God can forgive sins (Luke 5.21; cf. Psa. 50.7, 9; Dan. 9.18; Luke 18.13), and he does forgive them (I John 1.9). For it is not God's intention inevitably to punish, for the Father of Jesus Christ is a God who rejoices in repentance.[590] But what if our confession of sin is no more than words on the tongue? The NT gives us a sure criterion. If our confession is only half-hearted, then we are no longer willing to forgive our brother who has wronged us (Matt. 6.15; 18.21 ff.)! But if our confession is genuine then we pray: 'Forgive us our trespasses, as we forgive them that trespass against us' (Matt. 6.12; cf. 6.14; 5.23; Mark 11.25). The act of reconciliation with our brother, which needs to precede God's act of forgiveness,[591] is not a piece of magic of the *do ut des* kind, but rather the natural and indispensable expression of a thoroughgoing repentance which has once for all abandoned resentment and calculation of injury. We all have sins to confess, every one of us without exception; and that means we have every opportunity to become reconciled with one another in God's sight (Ch. 35). In this way becoming reconciled with our brother is nothing more or less than to offer prayer, a prayer of confession to the God of mercy.

Petition in the NT is no mere enumeration of covetous wishes, but a cry for help to the God who helps our necessities.[592] 'I put my life in my hand,' says Job.[593] The inner mortal tension of which Job speaks here can burst out in a single ejaculatory prayer, it can repeat itself, it can become a prayer that persists with me for hours, days, years, indeed a whole lifetime: 'Pray without ceasing' (I Thess. 5.17; Rom. 12.12; Col. 4.2). What did the early Church pray for? Day by day God gave the Israelites who wandered in the wilderness what bread they needed from heaven (Ex. 16.4; cf. III βας 17.6; Psa. 103.27): the original form of the petition in the Lord's Prayer runs: 'Give us day by day the bread we need.'[594] 'Deliver me from the hands of evil spirits . . . and let them not lead me astray from thee . . . from henceforth and for evermore' are the words of Abraham's prayer in Jub. 12.20 (cf. Jub. 1.20; 10.5 ff.; Ecclus. 23.1; PsSol. 5.5 ff.; IV Ezra 13.23). In the same way the Church prays in Matt. 6.13: 'Do not abandon us to the tempter, but deliver us out of his hand!'[595] Grant us the peace that is from above, and the salvation of our souls (cf. XVIII 18; Luke 11.4; II Thess. 1.11). Establish thy kingdom (jXVIII 10 ff.; PsSol. 17.45, Luke 11.2; Did. 10.6) and establish it soon (cf. Ch. 16)!

There are not many prayers for vengeance in the NT.[596] Another sort of prayer increasingly replaced them, viz. intercession.[597] Naturally enough, intercessory prayer in the first instance related to the smaller or wider circle for which the believer was responsible, his family (Ezek. 14.15 ff., IV Ezra 7.102 ff.; II Cl. 6.8), the Church (III Mac. 2.17 ff., 6.3, 15; MartPol. 5.1), his people, the state (Ch. 48 f.). But it comes in the end to be the people of God interceding for the whole of mankind (PhilSpecLeg. 1.97, 168, I Tim. 2.1 ff.; I Cl. 60.4). The people of the old covenant offered seventy bullocks for the seventy nations of the world (Succ. 55b). Jesus requires of his Church the offering of prayers of intercession for their enemies and their persecutors (Matt. 5.44 f.; cf. Luke 6.28). The Church of Christ took this demand in real earnest (I Cor. 4.12 f.; Rom. 12.14; Pol. 12.3).[598]

The primitive Church did not confine its prayers to a form of words only.[599] We have already referred to the early Christian tokens of salvation and the prayer-like character that they had (Ch. 36). But it was from the spirit of these salvation-tokens that the earliest Christian art developed,[600] viz. burial art (catacombs, sepulchral tablets, sarcophagi). They, too, shared in the character of prayer.[601] The most characteristic figures are those of men at prayer, who stand with hands uplifted in prayer, like some constantly recurring theme in solemn music. Sometimes it is the departed themselves who appear thus before God's face, sometimes it is biblical heroes like Noah, Daniel, or the three men in the burning fiery furnace, who by their attitude of prayer dominate the scene that is portrayed and give it its meaning.[602] But the first thing about them all is that they are not theological or historical representations contrived for the benefit of the onlooker, but carved and sculptured prayers offered to the all-seeing God.[603] That is why they are hidden away in the dark recesses of the tombs, like ejaculatory prayers in the silence of a room, and that is why, also, they are terse and stereotyped like a verbal formula, and like the salvation-tokens whose place they largely took.

'Mine house shall be called an house of prayer' (Isa. 56.7; Mark 11.17; cf. Acts 6.4; I Tim. 2.1). This promise, made about the temple, is now to be fulfilled in the Church of Christ. The *ecclesia orans* has to be the altar of God in the middle of a world that knows nothing about him, and wants to know nothing. The Church offers intercession for all men, and accordingly prays that they should all be saved, without exception. She brings the distresses of the oppressed to God in her priestly supplication, indeed she brings to the creator the unspoken cries and needs of the whole creation (Rom. 8.19 ff.; I Cl. 59.4 ff.). She bows vicariously in confession and thanksgiving before the God of all mercy. She stands in adoration at the altar of the world, voicing the praise of the glory of God for the whole created order.

Chapter 45

THE WILL OF GOD AND
THE WILL OF MAN

W. Wrede, 'Judas Ischarioth', *Vortr. und Stud.*, 1907; A. Schlatter, 'Herz und Gehirn im 1. Jahrhundert', *Festschr. f. Th. v. Haering*, 1918; H. Windisch, 'Das Problem des paulin. Imperativs', ZNW, 1924; E. v. Dobschütz, 'Die fünf Sinne im NT', JBL, 1929; D. Haugg, *Judas Iskarioth*, 1930; H. Preisker, *Geist und Leben*, 1933; J. Hempel, 'Berufung und Bekehrung', *Festschr. f. G. Beer*, 1935; H. Riesenfeld, 'Zum Gebrauch von Θέλω im NT', Arbeiten a. d. nt Seminar zu Uppsala, 1936.

The NT not only contains indicatives which proclaim God's work of salvation, but it has imperatives besides, which summon men to action. Orthodox dogmatics has for the most part so dealt with the indicatives of the gospel that the ethical imperative has suffered in consequence. Then the moralists have overstressed the imperatives of the NT because of their ethical concerns, and that has done considerable despite to soteriology. Recent theology has tried to embrace both theses of this antinomy in one dialectical paradox: Man must act, although God has already accomplished everything! What has the NT itself to say on this theme?

The NT propounds an exactly opposite thesis: Man must act, because God acts! Indicative and imperative belong together not in an antinomy, but for aetiological reasons. 'Work out your own salvation with fear and trembling, for it is God which worketh in you both to will and to work for his good pleasure.'[605] That is the surprising answer of the NT to our question about the relationship of divine to human action, of theology to ethics. The logic of this position is made more evident if we invert the two halves: 'God worketh in you both to will and to work . . . therefore work out your own salvation . . .! God works—thus the indicative. Therefore, you must work—thus the imperative adds.[606] It is abundantly clear that this proposition must be the starting-point, the key and the test of any treatment of man's will and God's will that purports to follow the NT: God's action is a summons.[607] God's active will summons man's will to action.[608]

The heart (*kardia*) is the human correlative to this idea of the divine summons to action. Wherever man is thought of as both subject and object of will at one and the same time, the OT and also the NT speaks of his heart. God knows and searches out our hearts in depths that remain closed to ourselves (Ecclus. 42.18; Luke 16.15; Rev. 2.23; Acts 15.9). His Word has power over our heart, more than we have ourselves, a power that does not exclude, but includes our freedom (Rom. 10.8; cf. Luke 1.17). His grace fortifies our heart, and endows it with a superhuman power of endurance (I Thess. 3.13; Heb. 13.9). His peace brings our heart into an abode of peace in the midst of this unpeaceful world (Phil. 4.7; cf. Eph. 3.17). His spirit takes possession of our heart and cries out to God from hidden depths in a language which we cannot speak; but God understands the spiritual prayer of the heart (Rom. 8.26 f.). Before his face the praying heart grows silent. 'Whereinsoever our heart condemn us, God is greater than our heart, and knoweth all things' (I John 3.19 f.). So in the last resort all the work of God is directed to the human heart. Why so? It is in the hearts of men that the decision has to be made as to the way man's world is to go, for it is in man's heart that choice is made between faith and unbelief. 'For with the heart man believeth' (Rom. 10.9 f.; cf. Mark 11.23). The gospel of Christ reaches its hearers through their hearts (Acts 2.37; cf. Psa. 108.16). The heart so conquered subjects itself to the mighty power of God (Rom. 6.17; Mark 12.30 ff.). Faith cleanses the heart (Acts 15.9; Matt. 5.8; Col. 3.22; Eph. 1.18; Heb. 10.22). But unbelief also finds a home in the heart (Mark 8.17; Luke 1.51; 9.47; 24.38; II Cor. 3.15; Eph. 4.18; Heb. 3.8). Even the hearts of the disciples on the road to Emmaus were too foolish and slow to find the way to faith, but as Jesus expounded the scriptures to them, their hearts burned within them! (Luke 24.25, 32). Yet the heart that does not want to be fortified through grace, fortifies itself against God, becomes hardened and stubborn, and refuses either to hear or see anything divine, but all the same in the last resort fumes against itself (Mark 3.5; 6.52; Rom. 2.5). For the heart of man is restless, till it finds its rest in God (Augustin). So in thinking of the problem of faith we come upon the whole problem of the human heart, which is made for God but insists on standing on its own, that is capable of self government, and yet of itself cannot attain to it. God alone has power over our hearts. And it is he who is really in control, both in the 'yes' and the 'no' that man's heart utters.

God is in control when our heart says 'no'. For it is God's pre-destinating will that has willed and brought into being man's contempt of God.[610] Just as a potter fashions vessels of dishonour, so God makes godless men (Rom. 9.21 f.; cf. Ch. 9). Here, incontrovertibly, is presupposed the *praedestinatio ad malam partem* (cf. I Pet. 2.8). God himself raised up Pharaoh—for what ends? To resist God! (Rom. 9.17). So in Rom. 9 Paul is stating the negative complement to Phil. 2.13.

But the divine predestination does not exclude the operation of man's will, but rather includes it.[611] For this reason the 'no' that man says in his heart is always a 'no' for which his will is responsible. 'How often would I,' we read in Luke 13.34, 'and ye would not.' Why not? Because they are in no need of God, because they want to achieve greatness without him (cf. Luke 7.30; 10.21; Acts 5.39; 7.51, John 1.5). Faith is subjecting our human self-glorification to the sole glory of God. What human heart wants that? So the demand of faith must be an immediate challenge to unbelief; and so the first response to God's appeal to man is 'normally' the blame-worthy 'no' of man's heart. No one has seen that more clearly than

Paul (I Thess. 4.7 f.; II Thess. 1.8; 3.2). And nowhere is it more powerfully stated and worked out than in Rom. (7.7 ff.; 8.7 f.) and especially in the chapters dealing with predestination: in Rom. 9.19 Paul deals with the men who by appealing to God's sole sovereignty try to escape responsibility for what they do. Paul rejects this favourite device most energetically, and in Rom. 10 bases his rejection, as Jesus himself had done, on the repeated affirmation that the reprobate had not exercised their will (10.2 f., 16, 21; cf. 11.30; I Pet. 2.7 f.). That is to say Rom. 10 is the negative complement to Phil. 2.12!

Human wilfulness finds its greatest triumph in the 'no' that man's heart addresses to God. By this man gets the freedom he wants, freedom without God, in opposition to God. But this self-glorifying freedom is really self-deception. The man who stubbornly asserts himself over against God is in truth no longer himself (Acts 5.3; 7.38 f., 42; Mark 8.33). To those who say 'no' to the divine call in the gospel God sends the power of seduction so that they come to believe in a false God, because they do not intend to believe the truth, but have their pleasure in unrighteousness.[612] The adversary's will operates in theirs (II Tim. 2.26; John 8.44; Rev. 17.17). For man is not so constituted as to have his will able to stand on its own; he is always possessed, whether by God or from the devil. But it is precisely there that man deceives himself in his stubbornness, and he means to deceive himself, because he means to have the freedom he has got.

The divine *praedestinatio ad malam* reaches its end when the demonic wilfulness of man's heart turns to hardness—when God hardens the heart. Here a flood of OT ideas come to mind (cf. Isa. 6.9 f. in Mark 4.12; Matt. 13.12 ff.; John 12.39 f.; Acts 28.26 f.). When he has told the story of Pharaoh Paul writes: 'Whom God will, he hardeneth.'[613] In Rom. 11.7 ff. he writes about the hardening of Israel, and then goes on to quote three passages, Isa. 29.10; Deut. 29.3; Psa. 68.24. The hardening referred to in each of these instances is a hardening of the will, which becomes an extreme form of wilfulness, and therefore blameworthy (cf. Mark 3.5; 8.17; Rom. 2.5). But God has both the first and the last word. His will operates even when our will says 'no' (Rom. 9.19 f.). But why does the NT lay such great stress upon this consideration? Because it provides the guarantee for the other proposition: God is operative beyond the 'no' of man's heart—his will operates when our will says 'yes'.

It is God who makes us both to will and to do (cf. EpAr. 195).

He triumphs over the 'no' of our heart, and evokes the 'yes' of our will (cf. II Thess. 3.5). He opens the heart that is closed, and in the darkened heart makes his light to shine (Acts 16.14; II Cor. 4.6; II Pet. 1.19). God's all-powerful will sets us free (Gal. 5.13; cf. 4.8 f.; Acts 26.18; Rom. 8.2). Where the Spirit of God is, there is freedom! (II Cor. 3.17). It is God's secret counsel that he does no violence to our wills, but wins them (Dg. 7.4; cf. I Pet. 5.2). God knows how to guide us so that we do not follow him of constraint, but freely.

The God of the OT willed our wills. The God of the NT wills *in* our wills. So here the Creator perfects, renews and surpasses his work in the actual re-creation of our wills (I John 3.9; 5.18; III John 11; John 3.6; Rom. 8.13 f.). 'The God of peace . . . make you perfect in every good thing to do his will, working in us that which is well-pleasing in his sight, through Jesus Christ' (Heb. 13.20 f.; cf. I Thess. 5.8 f.). The formula sounds like an echo of Phil. 2.12 f. and is as daring as it is precise: God has taken our wills up into his.

'We can do no thing against the truth, but for the truth' (II Cor. 13.8; cf. PsPhil. 15.5). For this reason everything depends on whether we say 'yes' to the will that is at work in us to make us will God's will (cf. Jas. 4.7 f.). Paul cannot escape his apostolic commission. Woe to him if he fail to carry it out willingly; blessed is he if he freely obeys (I Cor. 9.16 f.). Paul was apprehended by God. But his human will has not been put out of action thereby, but much rather brought into use, and raised to its highest power (Phil. 3.12 ff.). As the power of God's will grows the effort of man's will does not decrease, but grows.[614] That is the meaning of the imperative in Phil. 2.12.[615]

Chapter 46

THE MARTYR CHURCH

A. Schlatter, *Die Märtyrer in den Anfängen der Kirche*, 1915; F. J. Dölger, 'Gladiatorenblut und Martyrerblut', *Vortr. der Bibl. Warburg*, 1926; H. Delahaye, *Sanctus*, 1927; E. Lohmeyer, 'Die Idee des Martyriums im Judentum und Urchristentum', ZSTh, 1928; F. J. Dölger, 'Tert. über die Bluttaufe', AC, 1930; F. J. Dölger, 'Das Martyrium als Kampf mit dem Teufel', AC, 1932; H. Delahaye, *Les Origines du Culte des Martyrs*,[2] 1933; F. J. Dölger, 'Christophorus als Ehrentitel für Martyrer', AC, 1934; H. v. Campenhausen, *Die Idee des Martyriums in der alten Kirche*, 1936; G. Bornkamm, ''Ομολογία' Herm., 1936; H. W. Surkau, *Martyrien in jüdischer und frühchristlicher Zeit*, 1938; R. Schippers, *Getuigen van Jezus Christus in het NT*, 1928.

We have already remarked how the life of Christ constitutes a prototype for the life of the believer (Ch. 37). Nowhere is this prototype more concretely and seriously expressed than in the correlation between the passion of Christ and the sufferings of the martyr Church. Christ 'the faithful and true witness' is the prototype of the martyr.[616] But the confessors both suffer and die for the name of Jesus Christ.[617] Paul bears on his body the marks of Jesus (Gal. 6.17; cf. Ch. 36) which were apparently the marks of his sufferings as a confessor at Ephesus. The man who confesses Christ is taken up into the fellowship of Christ's sufferings; indeed his destiny is conformed to the death of Christ.[618] Hence the desire to emulate Christ must prove itself in a readiness for an *imitatio* of his passion.[619] But the passion of Christ was, as we have seen, envisaged under three heads: doxological, antagonistic and soteriological. The imitation of his passion naturally follows the same pattern.

The doxological form of the theology of martyrdom is based predominantly upon the old parallelism: *via crucis—via lucis* (cf. App. I. C). The way that leads through the depths of suffering to glory, 'which neither ear hath heard nor eye hath seen' (MartPol. 2.3), that is the way of Jesus Christ, and the way of his witnesses.[620] And a reflection of this heavenly glory lights up the death of those who witness unto blood.[621] Christ's messenger authenticates himself as such 'in demonstration of the Spirit and of power' (I Cor. 2.4):

Christ's martyr, however, authenticates himself as such in demonstration of an invincible suffering and death (MartPol. 10.10).
No threats or tortures of the adversary can shake him, and that is
a sign of salvation to the one who confesses Christ, an omen of
defeat for the one who persecutes Christ, a sign that is given by God
himself (App. I.13; II Thess. 1.4 f.; Phil. 1.28; cf. TertPat. 14;
also EvPt. 4.10?). For Stephen the heavens opened and he saw the
Son of Man (Acts 7.55 f.). Polycarp was lost in a prayer that lasted
for two whole hours, heard a voice from heaven which said: 'Be
strong, and play the man', and then the flames that sprang from the
stake made the appearance of a vault round him (Mart Pol.7.3; 9.1;
15.2). The martyrs mentioned in MartPol. 2.2 hold converse with
their Lord Christ, and no longer as men, but as angels behold the
glory of the other world. That is the end of those who resist unto
blood. The martyr confidently commits his soul into the faithful
hands of God (Ch. 25). Indeed, we often come upon the conviction
in our texts that the witness unto blood, in distinction from the
majority of believers, is carried up straight away from the place of
execution into heaven without passing through any intermediate
state (Phil. 1.23; 3.10 f.; Rev. 3.21; IgnR. 2.2; MartPol. 18.3). They
are taken from the world in their torments, but now they live in the
heavenly city, unharmed and joyful (I Cl. 5.4 ff.; Herm.s. 1.6; cf.
Matt. 7.14; Acts 14.22; Herm.v. 2.2.7; 3.2.1; MartPol. 19.2) They
held fast to God under torments, but now they have attained unto
God, says Ignatius.[622] For God's honour they endured shame and
dishonour,[623] and so there is certainly reserved for them in the world
to come a place of honour and a special prize (Matt. 5.10; 10.22;
II Cor. 4.17 f.; I Pet. 4.13; Rev. 2.10 f.; 21.7; MartPol. 17.1). They,
of whom the world was not worthy, will be deemed worthy of the
Kingdom of God, whenever God executes his justice and requites
the oppressor with oppression and sets the oppressed free.

Christ fought for the *gloria dei* against the demonic self-glory of
this world. That was why the prince of this world brought him to
the cross. The Church continues the fight that Christ began, and
that is why the adversary now directs his attacks to the Church of
Christ (cf. App.I.F.). Thus the doxological interpretation of
martyrdom finally comes to expression in an antagonistic conception: the 'tempter', the 'accuser', the 'opponent', the 'violent
enemy and slanderer and evil one, the opponent of the generation of
the righteous' puts everything in the world to action so as to effect
the downfall of the saints of God, or to destroy them (Matt. 24.9 ff.;

I Thess. 3.3, 5; Rev. 2.10, 13; Did. 16.4 f.; IgnR. 5.3; 7.1; MartPol. 3.1; 17.1; ApEl. 35 f.; EusHE. 5.1.5). Kings and dignitaries, the super-pious and the false prophets are all employed by the *civitas diaboli*.[625] Indeed, the adversary even incites the fellow tribesmen and fellow nationals of God's faithful people to act against them (Matt. 10.21; I Thess. 2.14). The Jews are his favourite instrument (Rev. 2.9; 3.9; MartPol. 12.2; 13.1; 17.2; 18.1), as casting suspicion on the innocent is his favourite weapon (App. I. 9). False accusations and false witnesses are the order of the day. Slander is one of the devil's original functions (I Pet. 4.14 ff.; Jas. 2.7). And so it came about that all the hatred of God in the world concentrated itself upon the Church of Christ; and the history of the Church in the first three hundred years, as Eusebius conceived and wrote of it, is a history of the Church under the cross (HE. 5. Prol.).

But the people of God withstood this general attack of God's enemies in the fearlessness of those who fear God (Phil. 1.14, 28): 'Be not afraid of them which kill the body,' said Jesus to his disciples. 'Fear him rather which hath power to cast into hell' (Luke 12.4 f.; cf. IV Mac. 13.14 f.; MartPol. 2.3; 11.2). The man who fears God must say 'no' to idolatry in every form; he may not bow before the 'abomination of desolation' in the temple, nor to the 'throne of Satan' in the pagan world.[626] In this way the antagonistic understanding of martyrdom concentrated more and more on the traditional picture of a battle of suffering (App. I.11, 37 ff.). The confessor or the witness unto blood is a combatant (I Thess. 2.2; Phil. 1.30; I Cl. 5.1 f.; 7.1; MartPol. 18.3; Heb. 12.4; TertMart. 3), and in particular one who fights with beasts.[627] His fight is a spectacle (Heb. 6.6; 10.32 f.; II Cor. 2.14; AugCivD. 14.9). Men and angels alike await the outcome with tension.[628] A great deal depends on it. Yet the fight goes on to its bitter end against the same superhuman opponent with whom Jesus had fought.[629] The man who confesses Christ will indeed triumph, but not through his own personal heroism (what use can that be against this enemy!) but because of the blood of the Lamb (Rev. 12.11; cf. 2.11; 3.21; Rom. 8.37 ff.). It is but a little thing for the Satanic powers of the world to get rid of God's witnesses. But the Christian who has confessed Christ in his death stands for a power in history that cannot be got rid of, a reality not of this world that the persecutor can never master.[630] The dead are stronger than the living, and the victims are victorious over those who murdered them!

The soteriological understanding of the suffering of the martyrs links on to the idea of the final massacre of the saints (App. I. 2.9). No one knows who will be the last martyr, or when his hour has come. But every martyr bears his contribution in reaching the limits of atrocities, in filling up the number of saints that are slain, and so the story reaches its end (II Thess. 1.6 ff.; Phil. 1.28; I Pet. 4.17 f.). Nor is that all. The witness who gives his life helps by his death to complete the toll of suffering that God has decreed for the world as punishment and expiation for its sin, so that the divine wrath should be turned and at long last the day of grace should dawn.[631] God needs men who will take upon themselves that burden of suffering in history that still remains to be borne.[632] It is Paul's hope and desire to be such a man, and to bear the afflictions of Christ in the service of his Church (Col. 1.24 f.; cf. Mark 10.43 ff.; Phil. 1.29; cf. App. I. 44). He suffered 'for them', and they gain consolation from his afflictions, and day by day receive new life from his dying daily (II Cor. 1.4 ff.; 4.12; cf. Eph. 3.1, 13). He even goes so far as to call himself an atonement for the cosmos and a ransom for the whole world.[633]. It is not just the Church of Christ that will benefit from the atoning power of the apostle's sufferings—the confessor suffers for mankind that despises him, the martyr dies for the cosmos that rejects him (cf. App. I. 45 ff.). The death of the martyrs is a plea for the ending of affliction, culminating as an intercession for the sins of many.[634]

Chapter 47

CHURCH AND SYNAGOGUE

J. Dalmer, *Die Erwählung Israels nach der Heilsverkündigung des Apostels Paulus,* 1894; W. Lütgert, 'Die Juden im NT', *Festschr. f. A. Schlatter,* 1922; F. W. Maier, *Israel in der Heilsgeschichte nach Rom.* 9–11, 1929; S. Loesch, *Epistula Claudiana,* 1930; H. Windisch, *Paulus und das Judentum,* 1935; J. Parkes, *Jesus, Paul and the Jews,* 1936; L. Rost, *Die Vorstufen von Kirche und Synagoge im NT,* 1938.

For the most part the different witnesses of the NT speak with a united voice. But in a few matters we can detect a clear and significant divergence of view, not only within the primitive Church and her story, but also within the sayings of one particular individual, even within one uniform literary work. A classical example of this is the attitude of the primitive Church to the Synagogue. Hence we shall do right to treat this theme genetically.

'Think not to say within yourselves, we have Abraham to our Father: for I say unto you, that God is able of these stones to raise up children unto Abraham' (Matt. 3.9; Luke 3.8). This saying of John the Baptist constitutes a revolution. It had for a long time been the widely-held conviction in Jewish circles that only a blood connection with the community of Israel brought one into the true people of God (Ch. 2). But the Baptist now threatened them with the possibility that God would not make up his 'people of promise', the true children of Abraham, out of the old 'people of God', but would gather them from the Gentiles.[635] Would the course of salvation-history pass by the doors of the Synagogue?

The answer that Jesus gave at the end of his life was 'yes'. Jerusalem has missed her hour! (Luke 13.25 ff.). She has said 'no' to God's call, constituted by the coming of Christ (Luke 14.24; 19.39 ff.; John 12.37). She has said 'yes', an autocratic, demonic 'yes', to the tradition of those who murdered the prophets (Mark 12.9 ff.; Luke 6.23). Zion became the mountain of the enemies of the Lord (Ch. 21). So Jerusalem must be destroyed, as all God's enemies must perish (cf. Psa. 68.24 ff.; Jer. 22.5 f.). But this is not the final judgement (cf. Isa. 6.10 ff.). From the very beginnings the polemic against the persecutor had threatened God's enemies and those who killed his saints: 'You shall look upon him whom you have pierced, and shall mourn for him' (App. I. 33). But Jesus tells his hostile fellow countrymen: 'Ye shall not see me, until ye shall say, blessed is he that cometh in the name of the Lord.'[636] Jesus' last word on the theme of Israel is thus a reservation; inexorable, but nevertheless full of promise.[637] All Jesus' thoughts about his people find expression here in Luke 13.33 ff. And we can say more than that: all the attitudes to the problems of persecution are contained in these sentences.

The attitude of the early Church in Jerusalem to the Synagogue was exemplified by two very different persons. Stephen the hellenist, based his position on the anti-Jewish sayings of Jesus (Ch. 21). James, a descendant of David, took his stand upon his brother's promises (Ch. 4). The most reliable historical information that we have about the two men tells us that the Jews killed the one as well as the other.

In the first letter that remains to us from Paul, the apostle appears as a sworn enemy to everything Jewish (I Thess. 2.14 ff.; cf. Rom. 2.4 f., 17 ff.). He takes Jesus' sayings about the persecutors and carries them further: they who persecuted the prophets have put the Lord himself to death, and persecuted his apostles (cf. II Cor. 11.24; Acts 17.5). And now they want to keep the gospel from the Gentiles and in that are 'filling up the measure of their fathers' (cf. Matt. 23.32). Indeed Paul, who had once lived in the ghetto and himself been a student of the law, does not hesitate to take over the formulae of the anti-Semitic propaganda of his time and use them for his own purposes.[638] In the ancient literatures Jews had been described as godless and as enemies of the human race (JosAp. 2.18). Paul put his judgement into the passive voice and made it a part of his theology of history in so doing[639]. When the Jew betrays his religious vocation there is nothing but a disagreeable fellow left! Scornfully reversing the Jews' estimate of themselves, Paul intensifies the ancient reproach to an accusation: they 'please not God, and are contrary to all men'! For that reason, says Paul in underlining the teaching of Stephen, 'the wrath of God is come upon them for ever'.[640]

Israel is finished (cf. Acts 28.25 ff.). But what will happen to the promises for the future which God made to the people of Israel? They retain their power. But they were not given to Israel after the flesh. This is what Paul shows in his letter to the Galatians—at a time when he was engaged in the hardest fight with the totalitarian claims in regard to salvation-history that were put forward by Jerusalem. God's promises to Abraham did not apply to all his offspring, but to one only; not to Israel, but to Christ (Gal. 3.16, 19). They do not relate to the present and earthly city of God, but to the future and heavenly (Gal. 4.22 ff.). This is by no means the first time that God has raised up children to Abraham from stones. From the very beginning his saving purpose has been directed to the Church of Christ, and to her alone. That is the common idea of Gal. 3.16 and 4.22 ff., and with this basic proposition Paul's antithesis to the Synagogue has received its sharpest possible expression. Yet only a little later, in Romans, there is an astonishing *volte face*.

The first eight chapters of Romans culminate in the triumph hymn of the elect (8.37 ff.). Then follows a silence, the great hiatus of the letter. Paul listens about him like some shipwrecked mariner who has escaped with his life on some small boat, while round about him the night is filled with the cries of the drowning. After a long silence and listening attentively the apostle continues, with the agonized confession of loyalty to Israel: 'I have great sorrow and unceasing pain in my heart . . .' (Rom. 9.2; cf. Ezek. 9.4; Matt. 5.4).

All polemic against his persecutors, every touch of anti-Semitism is now silenced. Paul prays for his people as Moses once prayed for Israel (Ch. 44). The mighty acts of God in Israel's history are not yet finished. Paul confesses himself in his prayer as one who, as a matter of course, rests on the ancient aspirations of his people. They are the people of Abraham, the people of adoption, of the covenants, of the promises, and such they remain in spite of everything (9.4 f.; cf. 3.2 ff.; 4.1).

By this means the polemical thesis as to the hopelessness of the outlook for Israel (I Thess. 2) is abandoned. Step by step the position of Gal. 3 is put aside. According to Gal. 3.16[641] the promises made in the time of Abraham applied to Christ alone. But according to Rom. 9.7 they do apply to the children of Abraham. Admittedly, in Rom. 9 it is only a remnant of Israel that is reckoned as the true children of Abraham, the people of promise (9.8 ff., 27 ff.; cf. 11.2 ff.). But in Rom. 11 Paul ascribes the promise to the whole racial community of Abraham (11.11 ff., 25 ff.). In Rom. 9 Paul talks about the casting away of the impenitent (9.32; cf. 10.21; 11.7 f.). But in Rom. 11 he sees in it but a merely temporary rejection.[642] But how will God win the impenitent people? The answer comes to Paul from one of the dominant themes of the OT.[643] God accepts the Gentiles into the people of Christ in order to make the people of God under the old covenant jealous (11.11 ff.). Thus they will come in due time out of their place of retirement to join themselves on to the people of the new covenant. Indeed, the apostle's mission to the Gentiles itself appears in this light as the only possible, if indirect service he can render to the future of his people. In divine emulation the apostle brings the Gentiles into the Church so as to make the people of the old covenant 'jealous' on their part, and so to prepare the way for their salvation and return (11.13 f.). So the Church had little cause to look down in self-satisfied triumph upon the tragic situation of the Synagogue. For all that it was believers from Israel who constituted the root of the divine tree. The 'remnant' out of Israel is the firstborn of the peoples in the church of the nations. So the holy city is not the dominant centre of the Church of Christ, but rather its starting-point in the story of our salvation (Rom. 11.16 ff.; cf. 15.27; II Cor. 8.14). The great mass of Jewry is rejected for the sake of the Gentiles. But the calling of the Gentiles is, from the divine point of view, the way to achieve the calling of Israel. The day will come when all Israel will hail Christ with the words of Luke 13.35: 'Blessed is he that cometh in the name of the Lord.'

So in Paul's attitude to the Jewish question the Spirit of Jesus triumphed over the spirit of anti-Semitism and the polemics of the oppressed (I Thess. 2), and the realism of his theology of history displaced his first attempts at allegory (Gal. 3.16) and spiritualization (Rom. 9.8). Israel is by race the children of Abraham and the people of the promise (Rom. 3.2 f.; 4.1; 9.4 f.). But these promises are irrevocable (Rom. 3.3 f.; 11.29). Israel after the flesh will one day taste the fulfilment of the promises, the whole of Israel, without exception or distinction (Rom. 11.26 ff.; 15.8). The dialectician becomes an apocalyptist: 'For I would not, brethren, have you ignorant of this mystery . . . that a hardening in part hath befallen Israel, until the fulness of the Gentiles be come in; and so all Israel shall be saved: even as it is written' (Rom. 11.25 f.). That is God's answer to the apostle of the Gentiles, himself of Jewish blood, as he wrestled in prayer. At the end of it all Paul winds up his account of the revelation he received with a doxology and an 'amen'.[644]

Chapter 48

CHURCH, NATION AND
INTERNATIONAL ORDER

H. E. Weber, *Die Beziehungen von R* 1–3 *zur Missionspraxis des Paulus*, 1905; E. Salin, *Civitas Dei*, 1926; M. Dibelius, *Evangelium und Welt*,[2] 1929; E. Peterson, *Die Kirche aus Juden und Heiden*, 1933; G. Bertram, 'Volk und Staat im NT' in *Volk, Staat, Kirche*, Lehrgang der Theol. Fak. Giessen, 1933; G. Stählin, 'Von der Dynamik der urchristl. Mission', *Festschr. f. K. Heim*, 1934; A. Schlatter, 'Der Kampf des Paulus gegen die Gleichmachung', Deutsche Theologie, 1934; J. Schneider, *Die Einheit der Kirche nach dem NT*, 1936; G. Bertram, *Volkstum und Menscheit im Lichte der Hl Schrift*, 1937; W. L. Knox, *St Paul and the Church of the Gentiles*, 1939; N. Johansson, *Parakletoi*, 1940.

'Ye, brethren, became imitators of the churches of God which are in Judaea in Christ Jesus; for ye also suffered the same things of your own countrymen, even as they did of the Jews' (I Thess. 2.14). With these words the apostle opens the eyes of the Gentile Christians to the fact that the relationship between the primitive Church and the Synagogue, between Paul and his people, is fundamentally paradigmatic, and (*mutatis mutandis*) can be repeated anywhere in the relation of the Christian to his people.

But this is to condemn the Church to a fate of painful isolation. The Church (*ecclesia*) is the society that is called out, it is the people of God, separated out from the ties of blood that bind the nations together. Its forms of life are different from the ways of the many (Rom. 12.2; I Pet. 1.14; II Cor. 6.14 ff.; I Cl. 29 f.). Its thought is in tension with the thought of the many (I Cor. 2.14). So the Church is always *ecclesia militans*. But its fight for God's honour brings it in opposition to the natural self-glorification of its own particular people (Rom. 3.9). Reaction is inevitable. So the Church is essentially *ecclesia pressa* (Ch. 46). 'For . . . hereunto we are appointed' (I Thess. 3.3). But we learn from Paul's own development that in such a situation the Church must never let herself become embittered (I Cor. 13.5), and from Rom. 9 ff. that the Church must never abandon her people before God. Then how did the apostle conquer a growing bitterness, how did he express loyalty to his people who, for their part, wanted to know nothing of him? He did it in intercession! (Rom. 9.3; 10.1). Hence the fundamental basis for the relation of a Church to its people must be intercession (I Cl. 53.5). It is only where the spirit of intercession dominates the relationship of the Christian to his people that he can preach the Christian message to his people aright. He has wrestled in prayer for the salvation of his people. In preaching he will try every practicable device to 'save' them (Rom. 11.14). Once more Paul is himself the example. His first and deepest concern, in which he shows himself a loyal disciple of Christ (Matt. 15.24; 10.6), is always concerned with his own people. Other peoples, whom he brings to the faith by his missionary journeys all over the world, are meant to shame his fellow countrymen and thereby stimulate them to believe (Ch. 47). For his own part he becomes a Jew to the Jew, a weakling to the weak, he makes himself their servant, subjects himself to the Torah, takes a supererogatory oath upon himself, circumcizes the half-Jew Timothy—and does it all with one purpose in mind: to win as many of his people as possible for Christ (Rom. 11.11 ff.; 3.31; 10.4; Acts 16.3; 19.8; 21.15 ff.; 28.23; I Cor. 9.19 ff.). 'Save' and 'win' are the main ideas that Paul uses in this context: it won't do for a Christian to tell his people the truth and then to wash his hands in innocency. It is of decisive importance that he leave nothing untried in his effort to win his people to the truth. Only when he has tried everything will he really have a share in the gospel himself

(I Cor. 9.23). What matters is not that the Christian should save himself, but that he should bring deliverance to his people. That is God's will (Rom. 11.11; cf. I Tim. 2.4), and the point of his being called in accordance with God's purpose[645], for which he makes us responsible (I Cor. 9.16; cf. Ezek. 33.8, 11).

It was in this way that the primitive Church thought of the relationships of the individual Christian to his people. It was by universalizing this principle that the NT obtained the pattern of the relationship of the Church to the international order.[646] Here, too, the first note is one of tension (I Cor. 16.9). Here, too, the tension is overcome by intercession (Col. 4.3 f.; I Tim. 2.1 ff.; I Cl. 60.4). Here, too, intercession is the fundamental basis of missionary activity (Col. 1.3 ff.; 4.12 ff.). Preaching and intercession belong together (cf. Acts 6.4). For it is only the praying Church that finds the right word to speak. And the preaching Church will always be thrown back, with ever-increasing intensity, upon prayer—and nowhere more than in those places where its word seems to take no root (see Ch. 5 on Col.). So it is no accident that the thanksgivings at the start of Paul's letters should regularly end up in intercession (e.g. Phil. 1.3 ff.). The labours of a missionary are an acted prayer. But they must also be a praying activity, and must employ every power and use up every opportunity to attain its end: the 'winning' and the 'saving' of the Gentiles (I Cor. 9.19 ff.). The apostle was given this objective by God himself (Gal. 1.16; 2.9). God himself shows the way and opens the doors (Acts 14.27; 16.9; II Cor. 2.12). Anyone who fails to recognize and make use of the openings into the hearts of the peoples which God makes for him is an unfaithful steward (I Cor. 9.17 ff.). So Paul became to them that were without law as one without law, that he might gain them who were without law. He refused to circumcize the Greek Titus. The fear of God drove him to 'persuade' his hellenistic hearers. If he could speak with the Jew about the law, he could equally talk with the Greek about his poets. He became all things to all men, that he might by all means save some (I Cor. 9.21 f.; Gal. 2.3; II Cor. 5.11; I Cor. 15.33; Col. 2.8 ff.; cf. Acts 17.28; 18.4).

Yet in spite of that Paul often says, and says with vehemence: My gospel will not 'persuade' men (I Cor. 2.4; Gal. 1.10; Col. 2.4; cf. IgnR. 3.3). He used the idioms of his hearers, as Luther did after him. But he never spoke just to please them. His missionary preaching was not decked out with ideas congenial to Jews and Greeks, but rather led through offence, scandal and crisis to a new understanding of the divine wisdom and reality (Ch. 43). God pursues mankind, the whole of mankind, with the gospel of Christ. But the peoples of the world take offence at the gospel, all the peoples without exception! And even more than this: each people takes offence in its own peculiar way, and has its own grounds for rejecting the word of the cross, its own reasons for holding back. So each people must find its own specific way through its peculiar hindrance. Every people says its own peculiar 'no' to Jesus Christ (Ch. 26), crucifies him afresh in its own way—and so comes, by its own road, to that point of extinction where all self-glory is at an end, and Jesus Christ is the *ultima ratio*. But it is along this road that the inexhaustibility of the gospel comes to light. For the universality of the gospel finds its historical expression in the fact that it has something specific to say to each particular people and to its particular questions. So we can say about the operation of the gospel among the various peoples of the world just what had to be said about its operation in the various epochs of history (Ch. 39). It serves the same final purpose: the unfolding of the mystery of Christ to the glory of God the Father (cf. Eph. 3.8 ff., 16.ff.).

It follows that the Church which grows from this missionary activity can be neither a national Church, nor yet a world Church. It must be a Church for the peoples of the world. The most powerful witness to this is the story of Pentecost, the story of the gathering of the dismembered unity of peoples into a new unity, the unity of the Church of the peoples. This unity is based upon the unity of the Spirit, and the unity of the Spirit is revealed in the unity of the *Logos* (the Word) which the spirit-filled witnesses proclaim (cf. Acts 4.12; Gal. 1.8 f.). But the apostles proclaim this one *Logos* (Word) to the peoples in the many tongues that have appeared in history since Gen. 11 (Acts 2.6, 8 ff., 11). So what the story of Pentecost has to say to us is this: if the same *Logos* (Word) be preached to the different peoples of the world in the same tongue, or if different *Logoi* (Words) be preached in different tongues, then the Spirit is not present. But if the same *Logos* (Word) is preached in many tongues, if the good news of the one Name under heaven reaches each people on the earth in its own tongue, then the Holy Spirit is at work (Acts 2.3 f.). This also brings to light the aggressive character of the Christian gospel, quite differently from those times when it is spoken in foreign tongues and passes over their heads. 'And they were all amazed, and were perplexed' (Acts 2.12, 37; cf. Heb. 4.12 f.). But the attack evoked a counter-attack. 'The others, mocking, said, they are filled with new wine' (Acts 2.13; cf. 17.32). In short: the Word of the cross gets its greatest power of penetration but also its acutest offence when the Church tells each people in its own idiom just what is at stake: *tua res agitur*!

The differences between one man and another are not done away in the Church (I Cor. 7.17 ff.; 11.2 ff.; 14.34 f.; Col. 3.18 ff.; Herm.s. 2.5 ff.). In the same way the division of mankind into peoples is not something that ceases to be in the Church. The many differences between one people and another are not blotted out—on the contrary they are rather made use of (Gal. 3.28; Eph. 2.15 f.). They lose their tragic quality in the inclusive unity of the Church of the peoples, where each has its particular place and significance, Jews and Greeks, Barbarians and Scythians, Cretes and Arabians (cf. Ch. 18). According to Gen. 11.4, self-glorification was the beginning of the confusion of tongues, and of the enmity between peoples in history (Ch. 38). But all the self-glorification of the peoples of the world is overcome when their tongues unite in the many-voiced choir which sings the glory of the mighty acts of God which he perfected in the cross (Acts 2.11, 22 f., 36). Is there a deeper community between peoples than exists in a common adoration of God?

Chapter 49

THE CHURCH AND THE ROMAN EMPIRE

A. Bigelmair, *Die Bedeutung der Christen am öffentlichen Leben . . .*, 1902; E. Klostermann und E. Seeberg, 'Die Apologie der Hl Katharina', *Schr. d. Königsb. Gel. Ges.*, I, 3, 1924; W. Bauer, *Jedermann sei untertan der Obrigkeit*, 1930; J. Behm, *Religion und Recht im NT*, 1931; H. Windisch, *Imperium und Evangelium im NT*, 1931; E. Peterson, *Der Monotheismus als politisches Problem*, 1935; E. Stauffer, *Gott und Kaiser im NT*, 1935; W. Elert, *Paulus und Nero, Zwischen Gnade und Ungnade*, 1948; H. v. Campenhausen, 'Zur Auslegung von Rom. 13', *Festschr. f. Bertholet*, 1950.

We have spoken elsewhere and in another connection of the primitive Christian theology of empire and the place of civil power in history (Ch. 17). But what has the NT to say about the place of the Christian in the state? In contrast to the little attention that has been paid as yet to the *theologia imperii*, the literature on this question of Church and State in the NT is vast. So we must confine ourselves here to a few necessary explanations.

'Give back to Caesar what belongs to him,' said Jesus, and in so doing laid the foundation for any practical discussion of the civil duties of Christians. 'Give back' were his words.[647] Our civil duty is a duty of giving back what is due. The Pharisees may have had many doubts about the emperor, but they used his money. We make use of the State (even when we entertain our doubts about it), and so cannot therefore avoid its claims on us (even when we have our doubts about them). We are debtors to the State, and so involved in her debts in turn. That is the least that can be said. But Paul goes a good deal further. He recognizes not only a duty to pay back to the State what is due, but also a Christian duty deriving from conscience. 'We must needs be in subjection . . . for conscience sake' (Rom. 13.5). For it is the King of kings, who has established the civil authority, who requires obedience from us.[648] Paul's disciples take the last step and resuscitate an idea that had had a wide currency in the theology of the State that belonged to the old biblical tradition.[649] We owe the State not just our obedience, but our prayers as well.[650] The Church must praise God that he has blessed the work of Caesar. She must thank God for the *pax Augusti*. She must be the intercessor for the authorities of the State. For that is the most distinctive, and sometimes the only, thing that the Church can do in politics, viz. to intercede for the civil powers before God. She intercedes, says the martyr Justin, even when the State despises her prayer. Indeed, then the Church prays aright for the first time, since it is then that the authorities have most need of the intercessions of the Church.

The intercession of the primitive Church for the magistrates was shaped by three considerations which all derive from the NT *theologia imperii*. The civil power is the divinely-ordained ordinance to protect human life from the powers of chaos. Therefore, the Church prays that the civil power be maintained (TertScap. 2). Political life is specially open to the tragedy of having to sin. For how can political power and significant action in world history be achieved save through injustice and violence (Ecclus. 10.8)? So the Church prays in representative confession for the *gratia dei* to come to the ruler by God's grace and through his action in history (I Tim. 2.1 ff.). The *civitas terrena* has a tendency in it to self-aggrandizement, which can only lead to self-immolation. So the Church prays that, for the sake of the mission it has to do, the State will be kept safe from the temptation to self-glorification (I Cl. 61).

A Church that educated its members in this sort of spirit deserved praise as the training ground of a new conception of the State. Instead, the primitive Church had to suffer the constant accusation of being the enemy of the State (Luke 23.2; John 19.12 ff.; Acts 17.7; 24.5). What was the reason for that? The accusation itself was old, one of the many slanders that the anti-Semitists used (Dan. 6.22 f.), but now turned by the Jews themselves upon Jesus and the Christian community (John 19.19). It was a convenient catchword on the lips of those who could not judge for themselves, and a welcome weapon in the hand of the disaffected and the enemies of Christ. But among all the senseless political accusations there was one charge which the first Christians took upon themselves, and which they had to take, because it accorded with the facts: the first Christians rejected any attempt to deify the State. 'Give back to God what belongs to him.' Jesus himself had put this restriction on his injunction to perform the duties of citizenship. We have a debt to pay back to God. What is it? The first petition of the Lord's Prayer gives the answer: it is a debt of thanksgiving! It consists in the hallowing of his Name. That is what we owe to God (Ch. 44). Honour belongs to him, and to him alone. Obedience properly belongs to the State so long as it does not interfere with giving sole honour to God alone. That is the reservation Jesus made against the deification of the civil power.[651]

'There is no power but of God' (Rom. 13.1). True! Again and again God has let authorities be called into existence and become established, that have fallen to the temptations of demonic self-glorification, encroached upon the sole glory of God and hindered his being glorified, scorned the prayers made for them, and demanded adoration for themselves (MartPol. 8.2). In such circumstances God does not ask of his Church a 'yes' but a 'no' to the civil authority. In what form did the primitive Church make this 'no' a reality? Not by actions of protest, but in the simple but strong confession: 'We must obey God rather than men' (Acts 4.19; 5.29; cf. I Mac. 2.19 ff.; II Mac. 7.30; San. 49a). The Maccabeans answered the fury of God's enemies and the slayers of the saints with a holy war, a war begun in God's name and by his commission, a war which was blessed by him (I Mac. 5.55 ff.; Heb. 11.33 f.). For his own person Jesus repudiated the holy war (Matt. 26.52 ff.). The early Church answered Caesar's attack upon the sole glory and worship of God with the fearlessness of those who fear God—entirely in the spirit of I Peter 2.17: 'Esteem the emperor as the emperor. But fear God.'⁶⁵² Will the emperor declare war upon his own citizens? Indeed yes, and he will himself take care that the restriction which the Church's theology of history put upon the State should not be forgotten (Ch. 17), and so God's martyrs leave this *civitas terrena* with this confession on their lips: 'Our citizenship is in heaven' (Ch. 38). Will the emperor destroy God's altar? Then the blood of the servant of God who has been slain will ascend like incense to the presence of the thrice-holy One! 'Fear God, and give him glory' (Rev. 14.7; 15.4).

Chapter 50

THE CHURCH IN HISTORY

Th. Schermann, *Die allgemeine Kirchenordnung, frühchristl. Liturgien und Kirchl. Überlieferung*, I, 1914; II, 1915; III, 1916; H. Gunkel, 'Die Lieder in der Kindheitsgeschichte Jesu', *Harnackfestg.*, 1921; F. J. Dölger, *Sol Salutis*,² 1925; W. O. E. Oesterley, *The Jewish Background of the Christian Liturgy*, 1925; J. Kroll, 'Die Hymnendichtung des frühen Christentums', Antike, 1926; W. Andrae, *Das Gotteshaus und die Urformen des Bauens im alten Orient*, 1930; A. Duhm, *Der Gottesdienst im ältesten Christentum*, 1930; I. Elbogen, *Der jüdische Gottesdienst*,³ 1931; A. Z. Idelsohn, *Jewish Liturgy*, 1932; F. Jeremias, 'Das orientalische Heiligtum', Angelos, 1932; J. D. Stefanescu, 'L'Illustration des Liturgies . . .', Annuaire de l'Institut de Philologie et de l'Hist. or. 1932, 1935; E. L. Sukenik, *Ancient Synagogues in Palestine and Greece*, 1934; J. Leipoldt, *Der Gottesdienst der älteste Kirche*, 1937; J. M. Nielen, *Gebet und Gottesdienst im NT*, 1937; J. Michl, *Die 24 Ältesten in Ap*, 1938.

The NT writers do not enlarge upon the nature of the Church and the legal claims that arise therefrom. It is much more urgent, in their view, to talk about the Church's task. But what is the all-inclusive office of the Church, according to the mind of the primitive Church? After all that has been said there can be no doubt about the answer. The mission of the Church in history is to give glory to God.

From all the peoples God has called his Church from those who can join in the angel's doxology as they see the coming of Christ (Ch. 35). The Church's faith is an obeisance before God's glory (Ch. 42). The Church's theology is thinking and speaking to God's glory (Ch. 43). The Church's prayer is a fulfilment of the first commandment (Ch. 44). The Church's life is meant to be an honouring of God's name (Matt. 5.16). The Church's suffering is endured for the sake of giving glory to God's name alone (Ch. 46). The Church's struggle with the world is a fearless defence of God's honour against the self-sufficiency of the Synagogue, the self-glorification of the peoples and the self-deification of the civil powers (Ch. 47 ff.). 'Too long, too long, has the glory of heaven been hid' (Hölderlin). That is the *ceterum censeo* of the Church in history. But it is in worship that the Church finds the final fulfilment of its mission.

'Speak to one another in psalms and hymns and spiritual songs . . . giving thanks always for all things in the name of our Lord Jesus Christ to God, even the Father' (Eph. 5.19 f.; after Col. 3.16 f.). The primitive Church faithfully obeyed this injunction (I Cor. 14.15 f., 26). And alongside the psalms and spiritual songs there very soon appeared choruses and responses with prescribed forms of words.[654] We hear of daily office hymns and antiphonies for use before sunrise on Sundays.[655] The infant Church gratefully borrowed from the rich treasures of the Psalter.[656] The five songs found in the first chapters of Luke were given a fixed place in the liturgy, five different variations on the theme of God's glory.[657] As the decades passed new treasures of hymnody were acquired, particularly in the Syrian Church.[658]

In all these songs of praise there was a natural tendency to heighten the sublimity of the christological phrasing.[659] Even the creedal formulae of the primitive Church were liturgical elements in hymnodic form[660] fashioned for assisting in the glorification of God (Ch. 60). Contrition for man's wickedness (I Cor. 14.25; Did. 4.14) goes along with belief in the holiness of God[661] (Phil. 2.11) in the same way that surrender of man's self-glorification and the recognition of the *gloria dei* accompany each other (Heb. 13.15).

A wealth of liturgical formulae gives emphasis to the hymnodic character of the whole act of worship.[662] Many different accents came together in the worship of the early Church: the Trisagion of the Seraphim, the 'Hallelujah' (Praise ye the Lord) of the people of the old covenant, the *'Gloria in Excelsis'* sung by the angels at Bethlehem, the 'Hosanna' of the Easter pilgrims at Jerusalem, and the '*kyrie eleison*' from the hearts of the burdened and oppressed. (TertOr. 3.27, 29; ApConst. 8.6). All these combine to form an imposing symphony of praise in the high 'priestly' prayer of the Antiochene liturgy (ApConst. 8.12, 6 ff.; cf. 13.13).[663]

When the Synagogue celebrated the passover, it was as a memorial feast in praise and thanks to God. It was thus that the seven Hallel psalms were sung,[664] as they were sung at the end of the Last Supper by Jesus and his disciples (Mark 14.26; cf. Acts 2.46 f.). The Didache calls the eucharist a 'thankoffering', and a crown of thanksgiving surrounds the sacred meal (Ch. 40; cf. JustApol. 1.65.3; 66.1). Did. 14 speaks of a sacrifice at the Lord's Supper—but without any implication of a repetition of the sacrifice on Calvary such as featured in later eucharistic doctrine, but rather as a thanksgiving of the participants which, in God's sight, was the true sacrifice of thanksgiving (cf. Hos. 14.3; Psa. 49.23; Dan. 3.40; Heb. 13.15). So the primitive Christian eucharistic prayer, as the sacrifice of praise, came to replace the theurgy of ancient cults as well as the sacrifices of the temple (Mal. 1.11 ff.; Did. 14.3).

The worship of the primitive Church at every point took it back to the coming of Christ, the Christ-event. So it is the good news of the gospel that constitutes the real centre of her services of worship.[665] The Word of Jesus Christ must have its course, said Luther, in the German Mass (WA. 19.80). It must dwell amongst us richly, declared Paul (Col. 3.16; cf. 1.27). So it came about that the prophecies and histories of the OT were read and expounded;[666] the sermon set forth the mighty acts of God in the fulness of time (Acts 13.15 ff.; Ch. 39); the correspondence of the apostles, new and old alike, the epistles, which are very much like sermons when read to the congregations, these were read and so, with their message, their thanksgivings and doxologies, helped to bring out the full meaning of Christian worship.

But Christian worship was 'also', most certainly, a service to the world (Ch. 48). Yet the primitive Church did not serve mankind in solemn rites and cultic practices, in pious instructions and edifying spirituality. Christian worship rooted men out of their self-centred individualism into an *extra nos*—away from all that is subjective—up to that which is simply objective. This was its service to humanity. It summoned the nations to worship the crucified. This was its service to God's glory. 'Lift up your hearts,' said the 'High Priest' in ApConst. 8.12.5; The congregation answered: 'We lift them up unto the Lord.'

The historical function of the early Church finds its fulfilment in worship. But the significance of her worship finds its mature expression in apocalyptic.[667] John, the liturgiologist among the apostles (Ch. 6), indicates the place that the worship of the Church has in universal history. The Church on the mainland of Asia assembles for worship on the Lord's Day, while John is alone on the island of Patmos (1.10). But then it is that all earthly limitations are removed and the heavenly temple itself is opened to the inward eye, as once it was opened to Isaiah (Isa. 6.1; cf. Acts 22.17 f.). John saw the 'tent of witness', the 'ark of the covenant', the 'altar',[668] the 'seven lamps',[669] the 'censer of sacrifice' whose smoke filled the whole temple (Rev. 1.12; 6.9; 7.15; 8.3 f.; 11.19; 15.5 ff.; cf. Dan. 3.53). Men and beasts alike prostrate themselves before God and the Lamb and adore. Angels and martyrs play on their eternal harps (Rev. 5.8; 7.9 ff.; 14.2 f.). The lonely figure on Patmos is both witness of and sharer in the worship of heaven itself.[670] The heavenly trumpets sound.[671] The 'trisagion' is sung (Rev. 4.8). The praises sung by the creatures, the stars and the worlds surge round the Creator like some fugue of Bach's that knows no end (4.11; 5.13). The heavenly choir sings the *agnus dei* (Rev. 5.9 ff.). The drama of salvation rolls onward like Palestrina's *Marcellus Mass* (Rev. 12.1 ff.). The 144,000 voices sing a new song in words no human ear can learn (14.3). The angel proclaims an eternal gospel in unearthly glory like the final chorus of Handel's *Messiah* (19.1 ff; cf. TestL. 18.5). The final Church comes together for the 'great eucharist',[672] a Church of priests who are to serve God throughout eternity (20.6; 22.3 f.). That is the liturgy of universal history that the seer of Patmos knew, and shared in. But the brotherhood is also gathered round him, invisible, here and now a Church of priests (1.6; 5.10; cf. Dan. 3.82 ff.). It receives the heavenly epistle (1.11) and shares in the heavenly worship with its solemn 'yea' and 'amen' and 'maranatha': 'even so, come quickly Lord Jesus'.[673] So the apocalyptic liturgist understands the doxology of the persecuted Church (*ecclesia pressa*) in the framework of a liturgy that embraces all worlds and times.

Early Christian sepulchral art grew out of the spirit of apocalyptic salvation tokens (Ch. 36; 44). The ecclesiastical art of early Christianity grew out of the spirit of apocalyptic liturgy.[674] The building erected for worship embodies a vision of the city of God, with its walls and stones rising up like the city in Rev. 21.16, or the tower of the Church in Herm.s. 9.[675] The place of divine worship is a piece of heaven on earth, the place where God's glory dwells in the midst of a self-glorifying world. Both basic forms of ecclesiastical design develop out of the apocalyptic dialectic of the earliest liturgy: in the east the primary movement in the liturgy of architecture is a climbing upwards, while in the west it is a going forwards. Here Christ's poor honour their God, who loves beauty and plenitude and liberality (Ch. 11), with all the art and pageantry they can command (cf. Mark 14.3 ff.). They decorate their churches in his honour with mosaics and frescoes, which in their fundamental significance are nothing else than prayers, though not prayers for protection as the salvation-tokens were, nor supplications as were the pictures in the catacombs,[676] but hymns of glory, elements of an unspoken but dynamic and ceaseless liturgy which formed the other-worldly context of the earthly congregation.[677] While the believers passed down the nave of the Church towards the altar the glorified virgins and martyrs passed down the side walls of the church in double procession to the same altar.[678] While the believers knelt at the altar before the Sacrament, the four and twenty elders knelt on the triumphal arch above them and cast their crowns at the feet of the Lamb.[679] While the believers sang their hallelujahs, the angels sounded their trumpets before the triumphant Christ on the walls of the apse.[680] But the most monumental expression of this correlation between earthly and heavenly worship is to be found in the 'Glorification of the Crucified', which was found some decades ago in Sta Maria Antiqua. It is only in parts, yet possesses in spite of that a singular beauty and greatness. It anticipates the altar at Ghent. At the foot of the cross, which stretches like some world tree from earth to heaven, mankind swarms in a surging mass, the multitude which no man can number, out of every tribe and people and tongue, the small and the great—'mankind brought home'.[682] Over this seething mass of mankind the multitude of the heavenly host moves in solemn procession to the cross. But the seraphim circle round the head of the crucified and sing the 'thrice holy' that, like the *cantus firmus* of Bach's *Matthew's Passion* drowns the antiphonies of the heavenly and earthly choirs.

We have spoken of the historical mission of the State and of its temptation (Ch. 17). We have now spoken of the historical mission of the Church. But what is the temptation to which the Church is exposed in history? It is the temptation to pious self-glorification, the same temptation to which the Synagogue succumbed (cf. Rom. 2.17, with 11.18). It would be a sad thing were the Church to fall a victim to it too! This temptation meets the Church in a thousand different forms, a thousand different dangers threaten her mission, dangers by comparison with which all the threats to her stability are entirely secondary. The Church looks down upon the Synagogue, boasts of herself, instead of grieving over the Synagogue, and with her in true godly fear (Ch. 47). The Church no longer has her desire set upon her Lord, but upon her own piety. She says: 'I am rich, and have gotten riches, and have need of nothing'—but does not know that she is pitiable and destitute, and poor and blind and empty (Rev. 3.17; cf. Matt. 23.15, 30). The Church becomes too important in her own estimation. She safeguards her historical existence instead of justifying it. She believes on herself and talks of ecclesiology instead of christology. She holds her form to be more important than her mission, and takes her dogmatics more seriously than her God (cf. Luke 11.52; Rom. 2.20). Questions of form and education become questions of faith (1 Cor. 1.11 f.). She 'excuses' herself if God's call is addressed to her (cf. Luke 14.15 ff.). She entrenches herself behind theological axioms against the divine revelation (Luke 10.21; II Cor. 10.5). The place where God's honour dwells becomes a breeding place of pious titles (Mark 12.38 f.; Matt. 23.8 ff.). The 'we' overshadows the 'he'. Self-edification supplants the glorifying of God. Where the flame burns itself out upon the altar those who seek edification gather so as to intoxicate themselves for an hour by its light.[683] So in the end even the artistic development of church buildings ceases to serve the worship of God and instead ministers to pious self-intoxication. It becomes a development in self-glorifying splendour (cf. Mark 13.1 ff.), a mere aesthetic end-in-itself—and so betrays its doxological mission.

That is the temptation of the Church in history. The Church of Christ has not always seen through this temptation and overcome it. Often enough it has fallen to it, even in the days of the primitive Church—a divine sign that the Church in this age cannot be the end of God's dealings with us. But how can the Church meet this temptation in this age? There is but one possibility. There must go through all the life of the Church, like one single prayer, the words of the fifth Hallel psalm: 'Not unto us, O Lord, not unto us, but unto thy name give glory'! (Psa. 113.9).

Section Five

THE PRESENT AND
THE FUTURE

Chapter 51
THE WAYS OF PROVIDENCE

K. Gronau, *Das Theodizeeproblem in der altchristlichen Auffas-sung*, 1922; E. Seeberg, *Über Bewegungsgesetze der Welt und Kirchengeschichte*, 1924; L. Baeck, 'Natur und Weg', *Festr. f. M. Schaefer*, 1927; E. Seeberg, *Ideen zur Theologie der Ge-schichte des Christentums*, 1929; E. Stauffer, 'Das Problem des teleologischen Denkens bei Paulus', ThStKr, 1930; E. Schlink, 'Zum Begriff des Teleologischen', ZSTh, 1933; W. Eich-rodt, 'Vorsehungsglaube und Theodizee im AT', *Festr. f. O. Procksch*, 1934; F. Billicsich, *Das Problem der Theodizee*, I, 1936.

THERE are two ways of formulating a theology of history. It is possible to follow the actual passage of universal history, and much as we have done hitherto, trace out the carefully-planned course of salvation-history from the creation through the fall and the 'acts of salvation' right up to the founding of the Church. Or it is possible to examine the world process for its ever valid laws, those principles that are continually being thrown into clear relief, in accordance with which the divine providence controls the course of history. In that case we come upon a series of higher laws which control everything that happens, whether it happens by causality, by will or by accident, and directs the outcome to an end. For this reason we would call them 'guiding principles'. Augustin referred to them as 'laws of providence' (*leges providentiae*). They are called the 'ways of God' in the Bible.[684] What, then, are the 'guiding principles' which the NT writers discovered as they looked back upon the course of history? We have naturally learnt a good deal about them in the course of the previous discussion, and so all that we need to do here is to bring them together before our mind's eye, and give them some conceptual formulation, so that we can see their significance for our understanding of divine providence and its rule of law.

God allows his creation to go its self-chosen way. That is the point of the first *lex providentiae*, the 'principle of freedom' (Ch. 12). But out of the many he chooses for himself a few, who are put under his special guidance. So all through history there goes a law of 'selection' (IV Ezra 5.23 ff., 7.49 ff., 9.21 f., ApSedr. 8). The *praedestinatio gemina* means at one and the same time both election and rejection (PsSol. 15.6, 9; Rom. 9.21 ff.). God's activity in history means both deliverance and destruction, destruction of the many, and deliverance of the few (Wisd. 17 f.; PsSol. 3.5 ff., 9 ff.; Rom. 9.33; II Cor. 2.16; Barn. 8.6, 14.5). That applies to the story of the old people of God (PsSol. 2.33 f.; Heb. 11.8 ff.; Rom. 9.6 ff., 11.2 ff.), and to the historical effects of the advent of Christ (Luke 2.34). In the synoptics Jesus himself speaks of the division which his coming everywhere occasioned (Luke 10.21, 14.16 ff.; Matt. 7.13 f.), while John's Gospel is completely dominated by such thoughts (Ch. 6). All previous selection in history had been anticipation; all future judgement is but the revelation of the crisis which is now accomplished, a crisis ultimate for all its unpretentiousness (John 5.23 ff., 12.48; cf. DaΘ. 5.25, 30). 'Many are called, but few are chosen' (Ch. 56).

But the elect are not called for their own sakes, but for the service of the few for the many (John 1.6 f.; Acts 9.15; Gal. 1.15 ff., 2.8 f.). God's intercourse with mankind is determined by the 'law of mediation' (cf. Ch. 12, 23). The Bible knows nothing of a *deus ex machina*. It speaks rather of a host of mediators through whom God effects his will in creation.[685] There is a whole hierarchy of them. At their head stands Christ, in whom all the different functions of a mediator are united and intensified. In his coming the principle of mediation begets its decisive meaning. Before him the angels, kings and prophets of the OT are subordinated to him, as after him is the Church with its apostles and all who join in its prayer (Ch. 4). For God deals directly neither with mankind in the mass, nor with the individual privately. God's activity in history requires more than a double, it always creates a triple relationship: God, man and the contemporary situation. God seeks a vessel for his blessing. When he calls he reaches with his hand for an instrument that has been destined to the task from eternity, and prepared for it from the mother's womb. That is why predestination to the service of God's world and work and glory is the only and the irremissible condition of authentic historical action (I Mac. 5.6 f.; AssMos. 1.14, 12.7; cf. ParalJer. 9.29). And that is why for the apostles the certainty they had of their calling was the secret of their effectiveness in history (Gal. 1.15; I Cor. 15.8 ff.; II Cor. 3.5 f.). But when the task that God has set in history is done, then comes the time of which Savonarola later spoke: 'God throws away the hammer which he has used' (Matt. 11.2; John 3.30; but cf. Matt. 25.21; John 4.36 f.).

Evil too, has its place from God. Even the secret paths of the adversary are taken up into the all-inclusive historical purpose of God; even the principle of demonic reaction is enlisted in the service of divine salvation (Ch. 13). The more the adversary undertakes, the more gloriously does God reveal his unlimited superiority whose secret lies in the 'law of reversal'.[686] The Bible illustrates what the divine 'reversal' of opposing forces means in two conspicuous examples: the story of Joseph and the passion of Jesus (see App. 4). 'And as for you,' says Joseph in Gen. 50.20, 'ye meant evil against me; but God meant it for good.' 'They let me down into the grave; but the Most High raised me up,' we read in TestJos. 1.4. The Petrine formulae take this antithesis from Joseph, the suffering man of God, and apply it to Jesus Christ, the dying Servant of God: 'Whom ye crucified, whom God raised from the dead' (Acts 4.10). The resurrection is God's *opus proprium*, but even the crucifixion itself is God's work, his *opus alienum* which he carries through in the process of overcoming his enemies. Thus the divine providence is in complete control over every step of the path that Christ trod (Acts 2.23 f.; cf. I Pet. 2.4). But the real opponents of Christ are neither Romans nor Jews, but the demonic powers of this age. It was they who brought Jesus to his cross. Yet even they have their place from God, and are *ministri dei* on his left hand, for without knowing it, and without willing it, they have, by their very misdeed, brought God's providential plan of salvation to its fulfilment.[687]

'For he was crucified through weakness, yet he liveth through the power of God' (II Cor. 13.4; cf. I Pet. 3.18). The guiding principle revealed here we have called (Ch. 26) the principle of depth. It is announced in the trials of the pre-Christian martyrs and confessors (Wisd. 3.1 ff.; TestJb. 4). It comes to full expression in the life of Christ (Luke 12.49 f., 24.26; Phil. 2.5 ff.; Heb. 2.9, 5.4 ff., 12.2). It affects the life and the work, the suffering and the dying of Christ's disciples (II Cor. 1.9, 4.10 ff., 8.2, 12.9 f.; Col. 2.12). God makes himself known in an antagonistic form, *sub contrario* (Luther). So he lets men try all sorts of powers and experience all sorts of catastrophes, right to the very point of death (PsSol. 12.4); but then he displays the wealth of his goodness and power (Psa. 22.4, 49.15,

129.1 ff.; Hos. 6.1 f.). So God plunges men into blindness, only to make them see; and into death, only to make them live (John 9.1 ff., 11.4; Rom. 4.17, 8.18; Heb. 11.19). With a modern dramatist we can put it all into biblical language by saying that the 'way of life' goes through the 'hell of death', and that 'in the valley of the shadow' we reach 'the unveiling of the eternal light'.[688]

The ways of God always have an end which controls their direction from the beginning. There is a 'teleological' principle in all God's providential sway. In predestination this teleological character is carried as far back as the plan and the coming to be of the cosmos. Nor does the early biblical tradition pass by the purposefulness of the natural order or the possibility of a teleological proof for the existence of God (Ecclus. 39.16 ff.; Gnr. 12 on 2.4). Still more in the course of history the experience of everyday life led to teleological thinking and the formation of stereotyped questions and modes of speech.[689] It is not 'whence' but 'whither', not 'from what' but 'for what' that leads us to a decisive understanding of God's ways (John 9.2 f.). In the NT it is particularly the coming of Christ that cannot be understood save in reference to teleological questions (Rom. 14.9; II Cor. 5.21). This explains the striking number of final clauses, many of which point beyond all historical teleology to the eschatological end of God's ways, which lies beyond history (SBar. 4.1 ff.; Rom. 11.32 ff.; I Cor. 15.28). The *terminus technicus* among early Christians for this eschatological goal was the word *telos* (e.g. Mark 13.7). But just as teleological clauses are thus often intensified into eschatology, the reverse can also happen and the eschatological concept of *telos* be reduced to teleology (John 13.1; Luke 22.37; I Cor. 10.11; Rom. 10.4; II Cor. 3.13). Teleology and eschatology are two different things, but they nevertheless belong together. Eschatology is the limiting instance of teleology. But both ways of looking at history, the teleological and the eschatological, have this conviction in common: the ways of providence can be understood only in terms of their goal. What, then, are the goals which God pursues down his historical ways?

'In the way of thy judgements, O Lord, have we waited for thee' (Isa. 26.8). A law of retaliation operates in God's providential rule. (DaΘ. 4.37, Psa. 18.10; 144.17; Wisd. 17.1; PsSol. 8.7, 10.5; Rev. 19.2). Man is punished 'through the sins with which he has sinned' (PsPhil. 44.10, cf. Beil. 1.27). That applies to the past and the present, and must also apply to the future (Jub. 4.31 f.; PsPhil. 9.8; Rev. 13.10; cf. Rom. 1.24; Acts 23.3). But the history of the world is not always judgement. There are long periods when God holds back and lets unrighteousness have its way, and at such time the problem of theodicy is paramount (Psa. 72). But then the day of visitation draws near, and the agonizing problem of theodicy is solved at a stroke.[690] God's judgement has its appointed times! (Chs. 14, 16). Admittedly, not every offence meets its deserts in this age. But there is a recompense (SBar. 48.27; I Cor. 3.17; Gal. 6.7 f.; Rom. 12.19; Heb. 11.6). God has put off the final reckoning until a 'last time' (IV Ezra 7.38, 44; II Thess. 1.5 ff.; Rom. 2.2 ff.). All the times of judgement that occur in history point beyond themselves to this eschatological time, which is the limit of the divine will for requital, but not the final goal of the divine providence.

'All the paths of the Lord are loving kindness and truth' (Psa. 24.10). Even under the old covenant in the guidance that God gave men experienced and confessed the rule of a fatherly mercy (Tob. 3.2). It was precisely in the tokens of mercy that they recognized the marks of God's activity in history (Psa. 66.2; PsSol. 8.32; IV Ezra 5.40, 7.132 ff.): 'All God's ways are love.' The primitive Church understood the sayings of the OT about the mercy of God as a promise that had been fulfilled in the coming of Christ. The 'ways of blessing', which the OT confessed, had come to their goal in the cross (I Cl. 31 f.). Here the mercy of God finds its full realization (John 3.16 f.). Here the principle of justice is taken up and in this (Hegelian) sense taken into the 'principle of mercy' (Rom. 4.16; Gal. 2.16). That is why, paradoxically enough, Paul can speak of justification, of the *iustitia dei* where he is really meaning God's act of acquittal (Ch. 34 f.). But the victory of the *gratia dei* on the cross is the determining ground and pledge of the final victory of God's mercy in history (John 6.38 ff.; Rom. 8.23, 11.11–36). In the hierarchy of ends which God is concerned to establish mercy stands higher than the principle of retribution. But the chief end of God's ways in history is the revelation of his glory.

God's counsel is marvellous, and he promotes it gloriously.[691] If 'freedom' is the basic principle in all the rule of providence, then we may say that the regulative principle is the revelation of God's glory. The coming of Christ serves to reveal his glory (John 1.14; Luke 23.47; Phil. 2.10 f., 4.19; Col. 1.26; I Tim. 3.16). The judgements of God serve it (Isa. 63.1 ff.; PsSol. 2.17, 29 ff.; Matt. 24.30; Rev. 14.7, 15.7). His mighty acts of mercy serve it (III Kings LXX 19.12 f.; Matt. 20.15; John 5.20 ff.; Rom. 3.19 ff., 5.17, 9.23; Eph. 2.6 ff.). Where severity and kindness go together in the course of history, there God is certainly at work, and there the depths of his glory are revealed (Ex. 15.11, 34.10; Psa. 77.13 ff.; Wisd. 10.7; Rom. 11.22, 25 ff.). But where the justice of God is transposed into his mercy, there his glory triumphs most majestically, and there we catch a glimpse of the future (I Thess. 5.9 f.; II Cor. 4.15; Rom. 3.3 ff., 11.36, 15.6 ff.). All the *leges providentiae* serve the revelation of God's glory; they are all but means to an end, but roads to a goal. The revelation of glory is an end in itself, and the final end (Num. 14.21). But by these objectives history will in the end be taken beyond itself. For in this age there is not room for the glory of God. That is why the traces of God's ways which illuminate this world altogether amount to no more than a promise of the perfected glory of God in the age to come. For the present, God's light shines in the darkness; but then there will be no more night, and the nations will walk in the brightness of his glory (Ch. 59).

The NT teaching about providence comprises the sum total of the history of the past and the present—yet at the same time a statement of future history. For God is 'faithful in all his ways' (PsPhil. 13.10; cf. Deut. 32.4; JustinDial. 92.5). The writers of the NT already knew the God who was and who is. Now they came to know the God who holds the future in his hand.

Chapter 52

LIFE AFTER DEATH

J. Frey, *Tod, Seelenglaube und Seelenkult im alten Israel*, 1898; L. Ruland, *Die Geschichte der kirchlichen Leichenfeier*, 1901; W. Bousset, 'Die Himmelsreise der Seele', ARW, 1901; L. Ruhl, 'De mortuorum iudicio', RVV, 1903; H. Gressmann, 'Vom reichen Mann und armen Lazarus', AAB, 1918; P. Feine, *Das Leben nach dem Tode*,[2] 1919; E. Rohde, *Psyche* [10] I, II, 1925; W. Mundle, 'Das Problem des Zwischenzustandes' . . ., *Festschr. f. A. Jülicher*, 1927; H. Kees, 'Die Himmelsreise im ägypt. Totenglauben', *Vortr. d. Bibl. Wbg.*, 1930; P. Le Seur, 'Zur biblischen Verkündigung vom Tode', Pastoralblätter 85, 1942–43.

In the parable of the rich man and Lazarus Jesus presupposes that immediately after death men will be taken to the place of fire or to the fields of the blessed (Luke 16.22 ff., 23.43). In other parables we are told that only after sentence at the last judgement will men reach the 'furnace of fire' or the world of light (Luke 13.28; Matt. 13.39 ff., 50; 22.13; 24.51; 25.30). How can this contradiction be understood? It disappears as soon as we set Jesus' sayings in the light of apocalyptic imagery and its associated concepts. The older Enoch tradition particularly helps us to clarity here[692]: After death men go to Sheol, each 'to his own place' (Luke 16.28; cf. Acts 1.25), borne thither by angels, or carried off by emissaries of the devil (Luke 16.22; cf. ApMos. 37; VitAdEv. 47; Jdth. 9; otherwise TestAbr. B.9; ApShed. 16). In heaven, according to both Enoch and Luke, there is a fountain of water that springs up, while hell, for both writers, is the place of torment by fire (GEn. 21.3 ff.; 22.2, 9; AEn. 108.4 ff.; Luke 16.23 f.). Occasionally we are told that the amount of torment corresponds to the amount of sin (GEn. 21.6; Matt. 5.26). But in any event, the condition which begins at death is not everlasting, but lasts only till the great judgement day (GEn. 10.11 ff.; 22.4). Not till then does the separation of spirits come into force, about which Jesus speaks in Matt. 13.25 and elsewhere (Isa. 66.24; GEn. 27.2 ff.; AEn. 56.8, 99.6, 11, 108. 12 ff., Mark 9.43 ff.). Then some pass to the glory of the world to come, while others go to Gehenna (Ch. 56).

Paul presupposes the same tradition, though it did not occupy much of his attention, as he expected a speedy advent of the Lord (I Thess. 4.17, 5.10). Moreover, in I Cor. 15.51 ff. he reckons himself among those who will experience the *parousia* before they die, and announces to those who will still be alive the mystery of their 'change': Already in the present they are filled with the Spirit that will endure into eternity. Meanwhile, however, they carry this Spirit in the mortal vessels of a natural body. But on the day of the *parousia* this perishable covering will be covered, absorbed and replaced by an imperishable covering of a spiritual body. So, like others who remain alive to the last day, the apostle is spared the state intermediate between earthly and heavenly corporality, the state of bodilessness. (cf. TestAbr. 7 twds. end). In I Cor. 15.52b that is a confident certainty that is referred to as entirely self-evident. In II Cor. 5, however, it is so far only a wish expressed in prayer. Anxious questions open up in front of the apostle and trouble him.[693] But however this question may be answered, in any case death means our departure to the Lord who is in heaven. That is already the essential meaning of II Cor. 5.6 ff.[694] In the captivity epistles that is the wholly dominant certainty: Thus 'to depart' and 'to be with Christ' in Phil. 1.23 are unmistakably identical in meaning. And according to Col. 3.3 f. (Ch. 33) the entry of those who die into the full communion of Christ means their entry into the hidden life of God's own world (cf. I John 3.2, 14; John 5.24 f.; 8.51; 11.26).

Later writings display a considerable development of the problem together with copious additions of traditional material. But the basic formula is the same in all the changes of concepts and thought forms and is: the dead 'sleep' (Dan. 12.2, 13; TestZeb. 10.4 ff.; IV Ezra 7.95; SBar. 21.24; I Thess. 4.13 ff.; II Pet. 3.4). They sleep under God's eyes and in his protection. Jesus commends his spirit into God's hands, with the words of the early biblical evening prayer (Psa. 31.5; Luke 23.46; cf. I Pet. 4.19; I Cl. 27.1); and Stephen, with the same words, commends his spirit into Jesus' hands (Ch. 25). Anyone who falls asleep in Jesus sleeps in peace (Isa. 57.2; Wisd. 3.3; AEn. 100.5; SBar. 11.4; VisEsr. 64. Mercati; Rev. 14.13; Heb. 4.9 ff.). He sleeps till the final reveille sounds.[695]

In pre-Christian apocalyptic we meet occasionally with the idea of purgatory.[696] Does the NT know, and does it adopt this notion? In Luke 12.58 f. Jesus reckons with the possibility that the sinner can expiate his sin in Sheol and so escape Gehenna.[697] In I Cor. 3.15 Paul says about the man whose work is unable to survive the fire that 'he himself shall be saved; yet so as by fire'—as a brand from the burning.[698] According to I Cor. 5.5 the incestuous person is to be delivered to Satan for the destruction of the flesh, so that the spirit may be saved in the day of the Lord.[699] These formulae and customs remained alive in the Pauline churches (I Tim. 1.20). One of Paul's disciples has given expression to their theological presupposition: the dead are to receive the judgement in the flesh, but [700] in the spirit they are to receive life (I Pet. 4.6).

NT theology is *theologia in conspectu mortis*. So one of its cardinal questions from the beginning was 'What will happen to our dead?' The NT Church answered the question with thoughts new and old. But she never made the claim to be able to give inside information about the beyond. Yet the NT Church could prepare the dying for the passage through the dark portal. She signed him with the sign of the cross (Ch. 36). That was enough.

Later Judaism produced all sorts of apocalypses purporting to come from above, in which life after death in its different forms is graphically described (cf. IV Ezra 7.75 ff.; GBar. 2 f.; 10 ff.;

TestAbr. B.9). By contrast the writers of the early Church speak of such things with the greatest reserve. Why? Because they are agreed upon one basic conviction: death is not a final solution. The post-mortem state is only temporary, pointing beyond itself to a future and final state. So the interest of the earliest Christian thinkers concentrated upon that.

Chapter 53

THE FINAL REVELATION OF ANTICHRIST

W. Bousset, *Der Antichrist*, 1895; A. Dell 'Mt.16.17 ff.', ZNW, 1914 and 1916; V. Hartl, ''O κατέχων ἄρτι', ZKTh, 1921; B. Rigaux, *L'Antéchrist*, 1932; D. Haugg, *Die zwei Zeugen*, 1936; H. Schlier, 'Vom Antichrist', *Festr. f. K. Barth*, 1936; O. Cullmann, 'Le Caractère eschatologique du Devoir-missionaire . . . de St Paul, Étude sur le Κατέχον de II Thess. 2', RHPhR, 1936; E. Stauffer, *Christ and the Caesars*, (E.T.), 1955.

Iranian eschatology in confident optimism reckons on a gradual recession of demonic power, until finally at the end of the day the last remnants of wickedness will be done away (Bundehesch, I, 4 f.). But the biblical writers think more realistically, more pessimistically. The movement of hostility to God, which infects the whole of universal history since the fall, does not abate, but grows. Even the coming of Christ has not conquered it, but only aggravated it (Ch. 21; 28; 46). The mystery of lawlessness is already at work in the present (II Thess. 2.7; I John 2.18 ff.; Barn. 4.3). But this demonic counter-movement will reach its peak in the time of the end (Dan. 8.23; Matt. 24.12; Did. 16.4). As always, the founder of this movement is the adversary himself (II Thess. 2.9; Rev. 16.13). But in the time of the end this movement will be focused in the 'antichrist'.[702] How does antichrist conduct his campaign against God's affairs and God's people? He fights with two weapons, and they are power and lies.

Antichrist is the strongest world power in history. In him all political power is concentrated (DaΘ. 7.23; 8.5 ff., 23; Did. 16.4; Barn. 4.5). In him the demonic is raised to a higher power, though its demonic character is betrayed by its hostility to the created order. Under the assault of antichrist the last defences that the

Creator has erected against the powers of chaos break down completely.[703] Even political order collapses (Ch. 28). The *civitas antichristi* spreads devastation and terror all around (Dan. 7.7 ff.; 12.1; Mark 13.15 ff.; II Thess. 2.7; Did. 16.4). But just as Herod and Pilate, Pharisees and Sadducees became friends in the lifetime of Jesus of Nazareth because they opposed Christ (Ch. 28), so in the time of antichrist everything that comprises the world unites against the Church (Dan. 7.21, 25; 11.33; Matt. 16.18; cf. OdSol. 24.5 ff.). Denunciation, defection, betrayal will gain ground in the Church itself in the last testing time (Dan. 11.30 ff.; Mark 13.9 ff.; Matt. 24.12; II Thess. 2.3; Did. 16.5). Will the Church itself fall too? 'The gates of hades shall not prevail against it' (Matt. 16.18). But the spirit of lying is more dangerous than brute force, and the adversary menaces the faithful with it (Ch. 13; 41). The antichrist is the 'world deceiver' who deceives the unsuspecting by the deceptive brightness of his appearance (Did. 16.4). He misleads them with words and wonders (Mark 13.22; II Thess. 2.9 f., ApEl. 32 f.). His forerunners are false messiahs, and his followers comprise false prophets and false theologians.[704]

These two weapons of antichrist, great power and much cunning, appear combined into a system in Rev. 13 ff.: The antichrist is the eschatological world power that takes the lying spirit into his service! Just as in the traditional persecution literature the enemy of God is compared with ravenous beasts (App. I. 37, 46), so here antichrist appears in the guise of a seven-headed monster. His origin is in the deeps of chaos. Satan himself, depicted as the dragon of hell, gives authority over to him (13.1–10). Antichrist announces the mobilization of the *civitas diaboli* (16.14), directs the movements of the assembled hosts (16.16), and forms the political united front. The dwellers on the earth will be all of one mind because they will be of one mind with antichrist. They will perform his will, and give their power and their kingdom to the beast (17.12 f., 17). The angel of the Lord seals the elect with the sign of Christ (Ch. 36). But the false prophet insists that the whole world shall be signed with the mark of antichrist (13.16; 14.9). Anyone who does not bear this mark is not able to buy or to sell in the kingdom of antichrist. But the military, political and economic alliance is consummated in a religious united front—the devil's counterpart to the universal mission of the *civitas dei* (cf. Mark 13.10). This religious united front is the work of the false prophet, who looks like a lamb, but talks like a dragon (Rev. 13.11–8; cf. 16.13; 19.20; 20.10). He is the religious and political herald of antichrist, for whom he recruits adherents by misleading miracles. His favourite theme is a perverted Good Friday, of antichrist's mortal wounds and their miraculous healing (Rev. 13.12). Apostasy works havoc in the Church like some devastating plague (Rev. 17.8 ff.). But God does not permit him to take those who have been sealed with the invisible sign of salvation (Rev. 14.1; EphrGr. III. 143. A.Assem.).

Why does antichrist persecute the people of God? Because he wants to banish God's glory from the world![705] Why does he fight against the worship of God? Because he wants a cult of his own person![706] From time immemorial individual possessors of power or workers of miracle have allowed themselves to be honoured as divine beings (Isa. 47.7; Dan. 4.30; 6.8; Jdth. 6.2; Acts 8.9 f.; 12.21 f.; cf. 14.11; 28.6). But antichrist outstrips them all. In his self-proclamation the history of human self-apotheosis reaches its demonic peak (cf. Mark 13.6, 14, 22). He proclaims himself as God (II Thess. 2.4). He says 'I am the anointed one' (ApEl. 31.40) and 'I am God, and before me there has been no God' (AscIs. 4.6). Christ came in the name of the Father, and the world has not received him. But when antichrist comes in his own name, men will receive him (John 5.43; cf. IrenAdvHaer. 5.25.4). Men will look on him and pray to him (Rev. 13.12 ff.). 'Who is like unto the beast?' (Rev. 13.4). 'He is God, and beside him there is none other.'[707]

In antichrist there is the final revelation of creaturely sovereignty. But the self-revelation of the demonic passes with historical necessity through self-advertisement to self-judgement. The powers hostile to creation that were set in action by the adversary come in the end to vent their fury against themselves: murder, hunger, earthquakes and world catastrophes are but different forms of this eschatological self-destruction of the *civitas diaboli*. (AEn. 80.2 ff.; Mark 13.7; Rev. 16.18). The end of lying is in self-refutation, and of the devil's deception the disillusionment of those who were led astray. When the birds fall dead from the sky and the seas dry up, then sinners will lament: 'What have you done to us, you son of lawlessness? . . . Woe to us that we ever hearkened to thee. Behold, now are we full of misery and distress!' But antichrist himself answers: 'Woe is me . . . for now I perish with you' (ApEl. 40).

This is utter and complete crisis. Antichrist, the grave-digger of this age, has appeared and completed his work. Universal history has come to its dead end. But now the hour of the Son of Man has come.[708]

Chapter 54

THE FINAL REVELATION OF CHRIST

A. Wünsche, *Der Auferstehungsglaube und sein Beweiserbringung,*
1904; F. Tillmann, *Die Wiederkunft Christi nach den paulin.*
Briefen, 1909; H. Windisch, *Der messian. Krieg und das*
Urchristentum, 1909; E. Peterson, 'Die Einholung des Kyrios',
ZSTh, 1930.

Christ once came to the earth as the *rex absconditus* but at the end of
history he will come in state as the *rex triumphans* the *deus salvator
revelatus.*[709] How did the primitive Church conceive the details?
In the very early days the Church made up a sort of mosaic picture
out of a number of motifs from different sources. We will summarize
them without troubling ourselves about their differences and incon-
sistencies. A divine injunction gives the signal to begin, and the
archangel repeats the injunction in a voice that resounds through
the universe like thunder (I Thess. 4.16; cf. Rev. 6.1; 7.2). The
stars leave their courses (Mark 13.24 f.; cf. Rev. 16.18), the heavens
are opened,[710] and the sign of the Son of Man appears.[711] The
trumpet sounds (PsSol. 11.1; IV Ezra 6.23; ApAbr. 31a A; Acht-
zehngeb. 10; Matt. 24.31; I Thess. 4.16; I Cor. 15.52; Did. 16.6) and
the saints come up out of their graves and join the host of Christians
who are still alive (Dan. 12.1 f.; Mark 13.27; I Thess. 4.16 f.; I Cor.
15.23; John 5.25; Did. 16.6 f.). Then follows the revelation of the
Son of Man in all his splendour (Col. 3.4; Heb. 12.14; I Pet. 4.13;
5.1). He appears in the brightness of his glory on the clouds of
heaven, surrounded by his angels (Dan. 7.13; IV Ezra 13.2 ff.;
Mark 13.26; 14.62; Matt. 24.26 f.; II Thess. 1.7; Did. 16.7). But
those who have confessed Christ, whether they have risen from the
dead or remained alive, are taken up together on clouds into the
air to be ceremoniously received by their Lord.[712] The populace of
ancient cities used to take great pains to welcome their governors
with an impressive escort. The population of Jerusalem once greeted
the Son of David and the Saviour at his first advent with acclamation.[713] Faithful Christians have waited all their lives long for
the advent of their Saviour-King from the heavenly city (Phil. 3.20
f.; cf. Matt. 25.1, 6). Now they go out through the gates of the *civitas
terrena* to escort the Ruler of the *civitas dei* in triumph to the earthly city.

The resurrection of the saints which is a part of the picture of the *parousia* has nothing whatever to do with the Greek belief in the essential immortality of the soul (Ch. 32). It happens because Easter happened, and it is exclusively confined to those who confess Christ (I Cor. 15.23). But it must not be conceived as a resurrection of the flesh, as though the conditions of our life before death were to be reconstituted (Ch. 58), but is to be associated with a change from which even those who remain alive are not exempt.[714] When the heavenly Lord makes his triumphal entry then 'he shall fashion anew the body of our humiliation, that it may be conformed to the body of his glory' (Phil. 3.21; cf. Rom. 8.17; Col. 3.4). When that happens the glorified sons of God will see the glory of the Son of God face to face (cf. I Cor. 13.12; II Cor. 5.7), for only transfigured eyes will be able to look upon the whole glory of the Transfigured One. Paul presupposes this as an axiom, while John makes it quite explicit: 'It is not yet made manifest what we shall be. We know that, if he (Christ, cf. I John 2.28) shall be manifested, we shall be like him; for we shall see him even as he is.'[715]

Christ will make his triumphal entry into a world where antichrist reigns. So the last act of the drama of the *parousia* is necessarily the overthrow of the powers hostile to God. According to Dan. 7.11 ff. it is God himself who undertakes the liquidation of these world powers, though later apocalyptic ascribed it to the Son of Man (AEn. 46.4 ff.; 51.2 f.; cf. 90.37; IV Ezra 13.3 ff.). This latter opinion influenced the primitive Church. When the prince of Luke 19.27 has withdrawn into his kingdom then the Son of Man calls out: 'Howbeit these mine enemies, which would not that I should reign over them, bring hither, and slay them before me.' That was the common practice of victorious rulers in the Near East (cf. Ch. 17), and that will the Son of Man also do (cf. II Thess. 1.7 ff.; 2.8; Phil. 2.10 f.; 3.21; Eph. 1.21). The most imposing treatment of the campaign of the coming Christ occurs in Rev. The sounding of the seventh and last trumpet in Rev. (10.7) 11.15 ff. announces Christ's public assumption of power. Rev. 17.14 tell us of the victory of the King of kings and Lord of lords and his elect over the united forces of the *civitas diaboli*. In 19.11 the doors of heaven open and the King of kings rides out armed for battle with antichrist and his hosts (cf. III Mac. 3.25). His name is 'the Word of God', and out of his mouth proceeds a sharp sword (cf. Ch. 10). The multitude of the heavenly host ride behind him. Antichrist summons the kings of the earth and assembles their armies for the last fight (cf. Psa. 2.2; IV Ezra

13.5 ff.). He loses the battle and finally, along with the false prophets, he is plunged into the burning pit (cf. Dan. 7.11; AEn. 90.25). But his commander-in-chief, Satan, is only chained and shut up in the abyss for the present (Rev. 20.2 f.). With this the age of demonic rule is over (cf. Luke 4.6), and all the kingdoms of the world are in the hand of the Lord. How long?

Chapter 55

THE KINGDOM OF CHRIST AND THE FINAL CONFLICT

J. Sickenberger, 'Das tausendjährige Reich in der Ap', *Festschr. f. S. Merkle*, 1922; A. Wikenhauser, 'Das Problem des tausendjährigen Reiches in der Ap', Röm. Quartalschr., 1932; J. W. Bailey, 'The Temporary Messianic reign in the Literature of Early Judaism', JBL, 1934; A. Wikenhauser, 'Die Herkunft der Idee des tausendjährigen Reiches in der Ap', Röm. Quartalschr., 1937.

According to the book of Daniel the kingdom of the Son of Man is to be everlasting (Dan. 2.44; 7.14, 18, 27; cf. Luke 1.33), but in the later apocalyptic tradition the messianic kingdom will precede the final everlasting kingdom (of God or of the Son of Man).[716] So the messianic kingdom will be an interim affair, 'the end of what passes away and the beginning of that which is incorruptible' (SBar. 74.2). The rabbis talk about 'the days of the Messiah' and think of them as the close of this age.[717] Jesus speaks of 'the days of the Son of Man' and thinks of them as already in the age to come.[718] Nevertheless, he might well have been thinking of them as an initiatory period which would come to an end, and there is some support for this view in the fact that both Paul and John have no hesitation in envisaging an end of his kingdom.

Paul has it that the glory of Christ, though not his kingdom, will last for ever (I Cor. 15.23 ff.). As a matter of fact it is no more possible to obtain an exact chronological scheme for the duration of Christ's kingdom from Paul than it is from, say, SBar. 30.1. What Paul does tell us is that he must reign till he hath put all his enemies under his feet (I Cor. 15.25 cf. Psa. 109.1). Such a phrase means that the summit and end of Christ's kingdom is the final abolition of the hostile demonic powers, the powers that have been in conflict with Christ ever since his temptation, that won a suicidal victory over the Holy One at the crucifixion (I Cor. 15.24 ff.) and that were bound, but only bound, before the reign of Christ began (Ch. 54). When Christ's royal work has attained this goal, then will come the *telos*, which Paul distinguishes sharply from the *parousia*.[720] Then Christ will lay his crown at the foot of God's throne, and the *civitas christi* will become the *civitas dei* that knows no end (I Cor. 15.24).

The book of Revelation pushes these thoughts to their limits, and puts the duration of the future kingdom of Christ at a thousand years (cf. SEn. 33.1). Satan will be chained for a thousand years (20.2 f.). Christ will reign with his elect for a thousand years (20.4 ff.). The city of God on Zion's hill will be his residence (20.9). The token of his fellowship with the saints is the messianic meal (19.9). Admittedly, this happy time is but the final calm before the final storm. When the thousand years are over Satan will once more be let loose for a short while (20.3, 7; cf. Dam. 4.13 ff.; 20.13 ff.). So the final conflict begins, no longer initiated by antichrist, but by the adversary himself. But this demonic assault is but the final flicker of an already exhausted torch. Satan deceives the whole world of men and leads them together to attack the *civitas dei*.[721] But a fire from heaven will destroy the power of the adversary at the walls of the Holy City (20.9; cf. Ezek. 38.22; 36.6; Dan. 2.45; IV Ezra 13.11; Matt. 16.18). And now the adversary suffers the same fate as antichrist a thousand years before him. He is cast into the same lake of fire and brimstone to eternal torment (20.10; cf. John 12.31; 16.11). Death and hades soon follow (Isa. 25.8; Rev. 20.14; 21.4). And now the head of the old serpent is crushed finally and for all time (cf. Gen. 3.15; Ecclus. 36.5 ff.; PsSol. 2.25; TestA. 7.3; Luke 10.18 f.; Rom. 16.20; Rev. 12.7 ff.; 20.2 f.). Christ has performed his cosmic service. He does not disappear (Rev. 20.6; 21.23; 22.3), but he yields up his office (cf. SBar. 30.12). God himself takes over control, and he will reign over his saints, and with them and through them, from everlasting to everlasting (Rev. 5.10; 22.5).[722]

Chapter 56

THE PARTITION OF SOULS

G. P. Wetter, *Der Vergeltungsgedanke bei Paulus*, 1912; W. Sattler, 'Die Bücher der Werke und das Buch des Lebens', ZNW, 1922; H. Braun, *Gerichtsgedanke und Rechtfertigungslehre Bei Paulus*, 1930; F. V. Filson, *St Paul's Conception of Recompense*, 1931; E. B. Allo, 'St Paul et la "Double Résurrection" corporelle', RevBibl., 1932.

Universal history is a process of selection (Ch. 51). The historical selection can take the form of deliverance and destruction as in the days of Noah (Heb. 11.7; I Pet. 3.20 f.; II Pet. 2.5 f.), but it can also be realized in reception and rejection as in the time of John the Baptist (Luke 7.35; Matt. 3.7 ff.). The activity of God always leads to a *krisis*, a partition of souls. Even the Christ is 'set for the falling and rising up of many' (Luke 2.34). But the partition which is begun in the time of Jesus is continued in the whole of human history between the crucifixion and the end. Thus the Church is called out from the mass of mankind (Luke 3.17; John 6.66 ff.) and the history of the Church itself is, once again, a continuing process of selection, until from the multitude of those who are called only the small number of those who are chosen remains.[723] The nearer the Church comes to the end of its history, the more destructive will persecutions and the final 'offences' prove to be (Matt. 24.10; Did. 16.5; Barn. 4.3; II Thess. 2.3, 10 ff.). Here the sifting of history reaches its climax, and there comes the revelation of the divine rejection, which is carried through in destruction. Thus at the end of the seven visions of antichrist the Son of Man casts a sickle upon the earth, and the earth is reaped. Sin is over-ripe. The clusters of the vine of the earth are cut and cast into the winepress of the wrath of God, until the blood from it floods the earth (Rev. 14.14–20). These pictures of the coming revelation of God's wrath are ancient ones which John uses and concentrates upon the figure of the Son of Man (Joel 4.13; Isa. 63.3 ff.; Mark 4.29; Matt. 13.30). But this judgement of wrath in Rev. 14 is still not the last judgement. The condemned have still not seen the dread judge himself, and the great crisis has still to be enacted in universal catastrophes. At this point world history is world judgement, and the great catastrophes of the end are thought of as the last questions God addresses to the peoples. But these questions will spell destruction for the nations for they but serve to reveal and complete the hardheartedness of the self-sufficient (Rev. 16.9 ff.; cf. TestL. 4.1). They die with a curse on their lips. So at the time of the end God cleans up the world of men with his judgements of wrath, until at last the trumpet sounds for the last judgement (Rev. 20.11).

Every crisis which occurs in the course of history is a foreshadowing of the final crisis or judgement (II. Thess. 1.5 ff.; Phil. 1.28; Matt. 13.30, 38 f., 47 ff.; 22.14; cf. SBar. 85.12 ff.). When that comes, all mankind will be summoned once more, small and great alike, and all their deeds will once more be tried.[724] The fallen angels of premundane times, as well as the evildoers of Sodom and Gomorrha, will then for the first time receive their final sentence (Matt. 11.24; Jude 6; II Pet. 2.4, 9). The God who is both judge and divider[725] has not yet spoken his last word. Therefore everything in life and history comes to this great terminus (I Cor. 4.5; Heb. 9.27). 'That which I find you doing, on that will I pass judgement,' says Jesus in an *agraphon* (ClAl. Quis. div. salv. 40.2). And in Did. 16.2 we read: 'For the whole time of your faith will not profit you, if ye be not made perfect in the last time.'

The NT is quite prepared to use the pre-Christian formula to state the criterion by which the heavenly judge acts: the Lord rewards 'every man according to his work' (Jer. 17.10; Psa. 61.5; Rom. 2.6; Matt. 16.27; II Tim. 4.14; Rev. 2.23; 20.12; 22.12; cf. II Cor. 5.10; I Pet. 1.17). But it is not that this formula is simply pre-Christian; it would be unChristian were it understood in terms of the primitive biblical tradition as a judgement on good works in the one case and on evil deeds in the other. The early Church thought otherwise, and interpreted the formula in terms of justification. It was faith's 'yea' that led to an acquittal (John 5.24, 29), while the 'no' of the self-sufficient man led on to condemnation (John 5.23; 12.48). The saints bear the sign of the cross on their foreheads (Ch. 36), and in their hands they carry the white stone on which already their new name is inscribed.[726] The Son has lived with them, and ruled for a thousand years. No one will ever judge them again (I Thess. 4.17). The rest have rejected the work of Christ and relied upon their own achievements, and on their achievements they will be judged (II Thess. 1.6 ff.; II Cor. 11.15; Jude 15; Mark 4.24; 3.28 f.; Matt. 12.31 f.). But such a judgement will lead inevitably to condemnation, for even the noblest deeds and characteristics are tainted with the poison of self-sufficiency, and are therefore *splendida vitia*.[727]

So a difference in destiny follows hard upon the partition of souls (DaΘ. 12.2; John 5.29; Matt. 25.46). According to the basically distinctive principle of all divine revelation the sight of the heavenly judge must spell bliss for the elect and torment for the damned.[728] Now the elect pass into the new world to enter into the joy of their Lord (Matt. 25.21 ff.; 5.8; I John 3.2), while the damned are cast into that place where there is weeping and gnashing of teeth (Heb. 10.27; Luke 13.28; Matt. 13.39 ff., 50; 22.13, etc.; Rom. 9.3; Matt. 7.23; 25.41; Mark 9.48), which is the second death (Rev. 14.10 f.; 20.6; 21.8; 22.15). And now the 'last enemy', death itself, can be done away. Death, too, is cast into the lake of fire where antichrist has been since the millenium began, and Satan since it ended (I Cor. 15.26; Rev. 20.14; 21.4; cf. Matt. 25.41). The story of the adversary is over; the demonic world is destroyed.

Chapter 57

UNIVERSAL HOMECOMING

A. Pott, *Das Hoffen im NT in seiner Beziehung zum Glauben*, 1915; E. L. Dietrich, *Die endzeitliche Wiederherstellung bei den Propheten*, 1925; Th. Hoppe, *Die Idee der Heilsgeschichte bei Paulus*, 1926; L. Brun, 'Übriggebliebene und Märtyrer in der Ap', ThStKr, 1930; E. K. Dietrich, *Die Umkehr im AT und im Judentum*, 1936; H. Pohlmann, *Die Metanoia als Zentralbegriff der christl. Frömmigkeit*, 1938.

The idea of eternal damnation finds frequent and quite clear expression in the NT (Mark 9.48; II Thess. 1.9; Heb. 6.2), and in particular John has developed it with ruthless consistency (John 3.36; Rev. 22.15).[729] Nevertheless, the primitive Church never gave up the hope that in his will to save the all merciful and all powerful God would overcome even the final 'no' of the self-sufficient world.[730]

Jesus requires his followers to pray for those that persecute them (Ch. 44). In God's presence the elect ought not, and dare not, assume that any man is lost. But intercession for the lost has no meaning without the certainty that God does not give up even the most lost as lost (Luke 15.1 ff.). The Prodigal Son says: 'I will arise and go to my Father . . .' Without such a return home [731] salvation is impossible, for God desires that men should want to come home. But when a man does return, when he gives up his proud autonomy and humbles himself before the sole glory of God, then nothing is impossible; for the God of the Bible delights in such a home-coming. [732] The thief on Golgotha repented, confessed his lost condition, and turned to the saviour on the cross—and he died comforted (Luke 23.40 ff.). But does death finally exclude such possibilities? No. For in Luke 12.58 f. Jesus speaks of a purgatorial and expiatory suffering (Ch. 52). And not only so, but the authority and intercession of the Church, according to Jesus' words, reach beyond this life and beyond this world (Matt. 16.19; 18.18 f.; John 20.23). But do they reach beyond the last judgement? Are there possibilities of intercession, repentance and salvation after the eschatological judgement day? No. At any rate, the sayings of Jesus that have come down to us never refer to them, and often speak against them (Mark 9.47 f.; Matt. 25.41). In this matter Jesus seems to take his stand unreservedly upon the basis of pre-Christian apocalyptic (AEn. 50.2 ff.; SBar. 85.12 ff.; cf. Ezek. 14.13 ff.; IV Ezra 7.102 ff., but also AEn. 108.15).

Paul is quite confident that there will be possibilities of salvation for men after death. That much is evident all through the first epistle to the Corinthians. [733] It is possible that even in I Cor. 13.13a he means that, even in the world to come, hope for the future will not cease. [734] However that may be, in I Cor. 15.29 Paul presupposes that the potency of intercessory baptism of the dead reaches even to Sheol and there benefits men who in this mortal life have not been sealed with the name of Christ. [735] In the same chapter Paul speaks of the destruction of the hostile demonic powers, which by their fall disturbed the original course of universal history (I Cor. 15.24, 26). But after this great clearance all other creatures find their way back to themselves and to their Creator in their subjection to the Son, who finally subjects himself to the Father 'that God may be all in all'. [736]

The ideas about the future that are being worked out in I Cor. come to full expression in the epistle to the Romans. Man's fall into sin is absolutely universal (Rom. 3.4, 19 f., 27; cf. Eph. 2.8 f.). But will the divine deliverance include all? Paul answers 'yes'. [737] God's irresistible grace and will is destined to overcome the most obdurate opposition (11.25 f.; cf. 3.3 ff.; 11.29; 15.8). None is to remain outside. In the first place double predestination appears to be God's final purpose (9.13, 18, 22 f.). But in the end it reveals itself as God's plan for history, a plan whose aim and outcome is the total victory of the divine purpose of salvation (10.19; 11.11 ff.). Once Paul had written: 'the scripture hath shut up all things under sin, that the promise by faith in Jesus Christ might be given *to them that believe.*' (Gal. 3.22). But now the last reservation has disappeared: 'God hath shut up all unto disobedience, that he might have mercy upon all' (Rom. 11.32). The universalism of the divine creativity requires and guarantees the divine salvation. 'Of him and through him and unto him are all things.' The principle of the *gloria dei* requires and guarantees the final victory of the divine and universal mercy (Ch. 51). 'To him be the glory for ever' (11.36).

The new serenity which Paul gained in Romans comes to its full maturity in his last two letters written to a Church, that have come down to us. In Isa. 45.23 f. God calls out to the nations: 'Unto me every knee shall bow, every tongue shall swear.' That is an invitation, though it leads on to a threat: 'All they that were incensed against him shall be ashamed.' In Rom. 14.11 Paul has turned the invitation into a summons, the grave summons to the last judgement! But in Phil. 2.10 f. this same formula is applied to the exalted Christ: 'In the name of Jesus every knee shall bow, of things in heaven and things on earth, and things under the earth, and every tongue confess that Jesus Christ is Lord.' There is here no limiting clause to the affirmation of universality, no threatening tone. None hold aloof; all bend the knee, angels in heaven, men on earth and shades of the underworld (cf. Phil. 3.21). Even they join without exception in the chorus of those who confess Christ. We hear of no destruction of demonic powers, as in I Cor. 15.24 ff. (Rom. 16.20). Here subjection means as much as overcoming—an overcoming of demonic antagonism in the will—'to the glory of God the Father'. The God who cut Rahab in pieces is glorious; but the concluding triumph of the divine glory is the overcoming of satanic will-power. In Phil. 2.11 the doxological ideas of Rom. 11.36b have the last word. By contrast the motif of a theology of creation from Rom. 11.36a controls the movement of thought in Col. 1.15 ff., now significantly turned in the same way into christological form. Christ is the first-born of all creation, and in him were all things created; therefore all things have been created unto him. Christ is the ground of all being (cf. Ecclus. 43.26)—whether thrones, or dominions, or principalities or powers. Therefore he is the reconciler of all. He disarms the powers of hell, but he does not destroy them (Col. 2.15). He is the universal peacemaker, and everything is included in his peace (Col. 1.16, 20).[738]

Chapter 58
THE NEW CREATED ORDER

A. Wünsche, *Die Sagen vom Lebensbaum und Lebenswasser,* 1905; R. H. Charles, *Eschatology,*[2] 1913; R. Knopf, 'Die Himmels-stadt', *Festschr. f. G. Heinrici,* 1914; F. Dijkema, 'Het hemelsch Jerusalem', Nieuw Th. Tijdschr., 1926; G. Sevenster, *Ethiek en Eschatologie in de syn. Evangelien,* 1929; H. E. Weber, *'Eschatologie' und 'Mystik' im NT,* 1930; A. Schweitzer, *The Mysticism of Paul the Apostle,* 1930; F. Guntermann, *Die Eschatologie des hl. Paulus,* 1932; G. v. Rad, 'Es ist noch eine Ruhe vorhanden . . .', ZdZ, 1933; B. Aebert, *Die Eschatologie des J.,* 1937.

This world cannot receive the promises of God (IV Ezra 4.27; cf. Rom. 8.24). So the way to the final realization of God's purpose for the future necessarily goes through the destruction of the world in its present form (SEn. k. Rd. 65.10vl). There is already truth in the saying 'the fashion of this world passeth away' (I Cor. 7.31; cf. Rom. 12.2; Did. 10.6), though before the new age can begin it must be fully and finally demolished (I Cor. 6.13; 13.8 ff.). With great dramatic power the Persian, Jewish and Christian apocalyptic describes the course of this dissolution. 'The heavens shall pass away with a great noise, and the elements shall be dissolved with fervent heat, and the earth and all that is in it shall be found as chaos.'[739] Rev. 21.4 states the outcome of this process of disintegration with considerable theological emphasis when it says: 'The first things are passed away' (cf. 20.11; 21.1b). With this the last negative conditions for the creation of a new heaven and a new earth are fulfilled (Rev. 21.1a). But how will God's new creation be fashioned? The primitive Church answered this question with critical reserve, with negative definition and with some positive promises.

Critical reserve against unbridled speculation about the future was nothing very remarkable even in pre-Christian apocalyptic, but in the NT it is quite normal. Only very few secrets of the other world are disclosed.[740] How are these few secrets differentiated from the mass of revelations given by the apocalyptic fanatics? By the reserve with which the NT speaks of them; and that reserve is due to the insight that the Last Things are of necessity ineffable (II Cor. 12.1 ff.; I John 3.2; ArmEzra 5.40). But with this critical note of reserve there is always mingled an undertone of joyful expectation (I Cl. 34.8; II Cl. 11.7). But why must the Last Things remain secret? The answer is that the Last Things are too great, too glorious for our thought and our speech (II Cl. 14.5).

Hence the primitive Church often speaks of the future in negatives. Yet it is precisely these negatives that belong to the most important things we can know about the world to come. Sin will have no place in the new creation (I Cor. 6.9 f.; Rev. 21.27; 22.15; II Pet. 3.13), and with its passing there goes the real centre of all the troubles of the universe, and all the innumerable troubles of the world will disappear. The weeping of children, the heartaches of mothers, the toil of man, the needs of the hungry and the sick, the alarms of war, the groaning of creation, all the sufferings of this present world order will come to an end (Isa. 11.6 ff.; 65.23; SEn. k. Rd. 65.9; Mark 13.7; Rom. 8.19 ff.; Rev. 7.17; 21.4). But the most important thing of all is that the curse of corruption, the world's mortality, is taken away (Rom. 8.20 ff.; II Cor. 4.18; cf. Job 6.8; 8.13; Rev. 21.4; IV Ezra 7.31; SBar. 21.22 f.; otherwise Isa. 65.20; SBar. 73.3). Henceforth 'there shall be time no longer'. Days and hours and years cease and the one unending age begins.[741] The meaning that runs through all these negations is that the Creator says an eschatological 'no' to this world in all its sin and suffering and death. 'If in this life only we have hoped in Christ, we are of all men most pitiable.'[742] This 'no' has nothing whatever to do with world negation, escapism or other-worldly romanticism. The NT writers sorrow over the creation, because they love it with a love that is deeper than enthusiasm, because it is a discerning love (Ch. 23). They have been given to see the power of the demonic in men, the tragedies of the world and of history, and the problematical character of all earthly greatness—and that is why they sorrow (Ezek. 9.4; Matt. 5.4).

But for this reason the eschatological negations of the NT are but the prolegomena to positive affirmations about the shape of the world to come. The future creation will be so new and so great that all the troubles of the past will be forgotten (Isa. 43.18 f.; 65.16 f.). Wherever men have made history with fire and sword, wherever bloody revolutions have promised to lead on to a paradisaical future, there the accusation has always been made: the price of Paradise is too high, the price of misery and dread. But here another power is at work, and another future on the way (Rom. 8.18; II Cor. 4.17; cf. Jer. 38.15 f.; I Pet. 1.3 ff.). God 'makes all things new' (Rev. 21.5; cf. Jub. 1.29). God does not restore the *status quo ante*, but neither does he change everything. God destroys his creation, but only to re-establish it in its perfected form. This is the reason why the NT writers are constantly finding new images and formulae to depict the seed-like character of universal history.[743] 'That which thou thyself sowest is not quickened, except it die' (I Cor. 15.36). So it is that this whole world in its transitoriness, frailty and shame is destined to die. But because it is a seed planted by God, it will rise from this death to incorruption, power and glory (I Cor. 15.42 ff.).

The new creation is God's 'no' to the troubles of this world, but it is also his 'yes' to his original purpose in creation (Barn. 6.12 f.). The sign of this is God's adherence to the principle of materiality (cf. Ch. 32). A materialist eschatology promises a perpetuation of our corporality (cf. Rom. 13.14; I Cor. 6.13). A spiritualist eschatology seeks release from corporality (cf. I Cor. 6.13; 15.12, 50; Rom. 7.24; 8.3; John 3.6). But the realistic eschatology of the NT promises us the redemption of the body itself (Rom. 8.23). God's final purpose is the reconstruction of the material world,[744] and it is in this sense that the early Church confessed the resurrection of the flesh. The same desire is expressed[745] in the proclamation of a new heaven and a new earth, and it is thought of as coming to its final realization now. 'I create new heavens and a new earth: and the former things shall not be remembered, nor come into mind,' Yahweh promises in Isa. 65.17 (cf. 66.22). When the elements are dissolved in fervent heat, then this promise will be fulfilled, and God will establish a new creation 'where righteousness dwells' (Mark 13.31; II Pet. 3.12 f.; cf. Rev. 21.1). In this age, however, righteousness neither does nor can dwell (AEn. 42.3), and that is why the moral purpose of universal history cannot be attained until the cosmic goal is reached.

There is no room for God in this age. Therefore, the form of this world will be forcibly shattered at the final revelation of God. But in the world to come that whole creation will be 'room for God'. The temple, which in this world is the sign of God's need of room, will disappear (cf. HEn. 5.13; Num. 7.1). In the new age there will be no more temple (Rev. 21.22), for God's presence will fill the whole world (Rev. 21.3). The city of God will come down out of heaven (Rev. 21.2), and end the opposition that has dominated the whole of this age, the opposition between heaven and earth, between God's world and man's world (II Cor. 4.18). Creation's original need is supplied, the need of God. God himself shall be with us (Rev. 21.3). He has, of course, been with us since the coming of Christ (Ch. 26.28). But in this present age such a fellowship with God is always under the sign of what is hidden and contested, of what is fought and opposed (cf. Rom. 8.24, 31 ff.; I Cor. 15.19), and so it is but the promise of the manifest and perfect fellowship which will first become possible in the world to come (Rev. 21.7).

Chapter 59

THE FINAL GLORY OF GOD

A. v. Gall, *Die Herrlichkeit Gottes,* 1900; W. W. v. Baudissin, ' "Gott schauen" in der at Religion', ARW, 1915; F. Nötscher, *'Das Angesicht Gottes schauen' nach biblischer und babyl. Auffassung,* 1924; J. Abrahams, *The Glory of God,* 1925; J. Horst, *Proskynein,* 1932; J. Schneider, *Doxa,* 1932; H. Kittel, *Die Herrlichkeit Gottes,* 1934; E. Lohmeyer, 'Und Jesus ging vorüber', Nieuw Th. Tijdschr., 1934.

What is the meaning of creation and history? The revelation of God's glory, or *doxophany.* The *gloria dei* is revealed in the structure and life of creation, but also in the majestic serenity with which, day after day, God makes his sun to rise upon the just and the unjust (Ch. 11 ff.). It is revealed in his dealings with Israel, and in the secret and devious ways that he has used with the world of nations. It is God who glorifies himself, but he seeks this self-glorification in the glory, in the freedom and fulness and greatness and beauty of his world, in the blessing which he pours upon his creatures. He is glorious as creator; but more glorious as saviour. He is glorious in his wrath; but more glorious in his all-conquering faithfulness and grace. So the coming of Christ is the fulfilment of doxophany in this world. The life, death and resurrection of Jesus Christ is the paradoxical self-revelation and self-glorification of God (Ch. 51). As John put it, 'We beheld his glory'.

What is it to be a creature? To glorify God, to share in doxology. Every creative act calls something into existence for the glorifying of God, and every act of divine self-revelation is meant to recall the creature to this glorification. God placed man in the creation that he might glorify God on its behalf (Ch. 11). But in demonic self-glorification man rebelled against his creator and became unfaithful in his devotion to God's glory (Ch. 14, 18), and ever since history has been a conflict between the *gloria dei* and the *gloria mundi*. The conflict reached its climax and its turning-point when the revelation of God's glory was made in its completeness (Ch. 27). The divine doxophany in the advent of Christ calls the Church into being, which prostrates itself before the glory of God's mercy in the cross (Ch. 42). So the original destiny of mankind comes to realization in the historical function of the Church, i.e. in the service rendered by the *ecclesia christi* to the *gloria dei* (Ch. 50). 'Where then is the *gloria mundi*? It is excluded' (Rom. 3.27). That is the message of the apostle Paul.

But the revelation of God's glory in the advent of Christ is doxophany in a world that has no room for the full revelation of divine glory. In the same way the glorifying of God in the Church of Christ is doxology in a world that seeks its own glory. So both Christ's advent and the Church point beyond themselves to another world. When the doxophany comes at last into unlimited display—then the doxology will also come into unlimited activity. When God unveils his face and pours out the fulness of his glory over heaven, earth and hell, then at last will every creature prostrate itself before his glory and exalt his name.

The final revelation of the *gloria dei* begins with the personal activity of God in the ordering of history. Revelation shows (as also Mark 13; I, II Thess.; I Cor. 15) how God calls up his different ministers one after another in a rising order of importance, and appoints them to perform their service to his final mighty act. At the same time and in parallel order the demonic powers are conquered, until at the last Christ himself appears and overcomes the most deadly foe. But every one of God's ministers who has made his contribution to the end of history retires into the background, until at last the greatest of them all, the Christ himself, resigns his office. That is God's hour. In all that has happened since the beginning God has been the absolute subject, though he has hidden himself behind the arbitrariness of his creation. He has accomplished his historical purposes by the conversion of the opposing powers. He has achieved his salvation through the principle of the mediator. But now, when all his ministers have finished their service of preparation, he forsakes his hiddenness for the light, and takes affairs personally in hand. God is all in all. This is the self-revelation of God for which creation waits, and towards which universal history has marched since creation first began (Jer. 16.21; SDt. 6.4; Luke 13.21; I Cor. 15.28; Rom. 11.36; John 5.20).

The eschatological self-revelation of God attains its second phase in the unveiling of his face. 'Let me see thy face' is the favour that Moses asked of God, the only favour, but the greatest possible. But he asked too much (Ex. 33.17 ff.; I Tim. 6.16). But his prayer is no longer silenced. Job would sacrifice everything if only he could see God with his eyes (Job 19.26; cf. 22.26; 42.5). And the Psalmist sings that he will waken before God's likeness, and be satisfied with his glory (Psa. 17.15; cf. MidrPs. 4.7). 'Show us the Father, and it sufficeth us,' says Philip (John 14.8). The day is coming when God will answer this prayer of the centuries (Matt. 5.8), and then we shall see him face to face (I Cor. 13.12; Rev. 22.4). Then we shall be satisfied (Jude 24).

The third phase of the divine self-revelation is the radiation of his brightness through all the world. Heaven and earth will be flooded with the brightness of his countenance,[746] and so there will be no more night in the world to come, neither will men need a sun any more (Rev. 21.25; 22.5; cf. SEn. 65.9). For the Lord God will cause his unveiled face visibly to shine upon us, and his glory will illumine the new creation (Isa. 60.19; Rev. 21.23; cf. Num. 6.25). The new Jerusalem shines resplendent in the glory of God, and nations walk in her light (Isa. 60.1 ff.; Rev. 21.10 f., 24). For God will implement his oath in Num. 14.21: 'All the earth shall be filled with the glory of the Lord.'

The self-revelation and self-glorification of God has its fulfilment in the resplendent perfection of the creation. God, who delights in plenty and greatness and beauty, builds himself a world to the glory of his name. The new mankind will gather together in festival raiment, and the new world is likened to a bride adorned for her husband (Rev. 3.5; 21.2). But the Creator himself reveals the riches of his glory in pouring them out on his creation. The work of his left hand is done. All that God does henceforth are works of his right hand. Now for the first time God is wholly himself.

How does the creation respond to the final revelation of God and his glory? It prostrates itself in adoration. We know that faith, too, is an adoration, but so is prostration before the doxophany of the invisible God (Ch. 42). That is why faith is always at war with temptation and unbelief. But when God himself uncovers his face, then faith will be turned to sight, and temptation will be taken away from us (I Cor. 13.10 ff.; II Cor. 5.7). Then we shall be in the presence of his glory in exceeding joy (Jude 24), for wherever God looks down from above, there is peace and exultation (ClAlPaed. I 8.20.1). In that day unbelief will be put to shame. Then the self-will of those hardened hearts, that no warnings or threatenings could move, will melt like ice in the sun. Then the progressive unveiling of the divine glory will constantly inspire new believers, and every new step of the final revelation will release a new confession (Luke 13.35; Rom. 3.4). We can imagine how the universal home-coming will be accomplished! As the last veil falls, then the last creature bends the knee before the revealed glory of God.

Paul speaks of the liberty of the glory of the children of God, in which every creature will share in the world to come (Rom. 8.21). According to Rom. 9 ff. that is the final end of divine predestination, and the ultimate triumph of the divine will, that God coerces no one, and yet surrenders no one, but wins them all. No one will be forced; yet even the most stubborn heart will at length be overcome by the supreme revelation of the glory of God. Then God, who delights in liberty, and wills it, will have overcome the last 'no'; the creation will have found its liberty in a spontaneous 'yes' to God. Then God will be the one and all of a liberated world.

Self-glorification comes to an end when every creature praises God's glory with united voice (cf. Psa. 68.34 f.; Jer. 9.22 f.; II Cor. 10.17; Rom. 3.27). Then the whole cosmos is a temple of God and the new age one continual Sabbath (Rev. 21.3; Heb. 4.9). The people of God will be a people of priests, and clouds of incense will ascend continually to heaven (Ex. 19.6; Isa. 61.6; I Pet. 2.5, 9; Rev. 19.3; 20.6; 22.3). The peoples will fall down and offer sacrifice before his face (Psa. 86.9; Rom. 15.16; Rev. 15.4; 21.24). *The antiphony of universal history leads into a symphonic doxology*. At last God has attained the *telos* of his ways: the revelation of the *gloria dei* achieves its end in the hallowing of his name.

PART THREE

The Creeds of The Primitive Church

F. Kattenbusch, *Das ap. Symbol* I, 1894, II, 1900; W. M. Peitz, *Das Glaubensbekenntnis der Apostel, Stimmen der Zeit,* 1918; A. v. Harnack, 'Zur . . . Auslegung des . . . ap. Glaubensbekenntnisses', SAB, 1919; H. Lietzmann, 'Die Urform des ap. Glaubensbekenntnisses', SAB, 1919; H. Lietzmann, 'Die Anfänge des Glaubensbekenntnisses', *Festg. f. A. v. Harnack,* 1921; R. Seeberg, 'Zur Geschichte der Entstehung des ap. Symbols', ZKG, 1922; H. Lietzmann, 'Symbolstudien', ZNW, 1922 ff.; P. Feine, *Die Gestalt des ap. Glaubensbekenntnisses in der Zeit des NT,* 1925; C. Fabricius, 'Urbekenntnisse der Christenheit', *Festschr. f. R. Seeberg* I, 1929; E. v. Dobschütz, *Das Apostolicum in biblisch-theologischer Beleuchtung,* 1932; O. Cullmann, *The Earliest Christian Confessions,* 1949.

Chapter 60

THE USE OF DOGMATIC FORMULAE

W. Brandt, "Ὄνομα en de Doopsformule in het NT", ThT, 1891; A. Seeberg, *Der Katechismus der Urchristenheit*, 1903; H. Jordan, *Rhythmische Prosa in der altchristl. lat. Literatur*, 1905; F. Wieland, *Mensa und Confessio*, 1906; G. Klein, *Der älteste christliche Katechismus . . .*, 1909; A. Seeberg, *Die Taufe im NT*,[2] 1913; R. Schültz, *Der parallele Bau der Satzglieder im NT*, 1920; E. Norden, *Agnostos Theos*,[2] 1929; F. J. Dölger, 'Die Eingliederung des Taufsymbols in den Taufvollzug . . . .', AC, 1934.

THE Apostles' Creed first attained its present form in the fourth or fifth century A.D., but its theological content is in the last resort derived from the NT (see Kattenbusch, Feine, v. Dobschütz). Did the apostolic age merely prepare the theological material, or did it in addition create dogmatic formulae, which in structure and importance could be regarded as antecedents to the Apostles' Creed? A. Seeberg was the first to broach this question with clarity and emphasis, and R. Seeberg has pursued his brother's enquiries further. Meanwhile, the problem has been placed in a new light by methods of Form Criticism,[747] by liturgical science,[748] and not for the last time by a rigorous analysis of the Apostles' Creed and its antecedents (see Jordan, Holl, Harnack, Lietzmann). It is thus possible for us today to take up A. Seeberg's work with new tools in our hands. In this connection there are two preliminary questions to answer, about the use and then about the form of dogmatic formulae in the primitive Church. What have our sources to tell us about the situation that produced creedal formulae, about how they first appeared in the practice of the primitive Church, about the where, when and how of their adoption? That is the question about use. And what are the morphological criteria by which we may recognize dogmatic formulae embedded in the primitive Christian writings? That is the question about form.

We will treat first of all the problem of use.

The liveliest and most original species of theological speech in early Christianity was missionary preaching. But even this mode of proclamation, for all the freedom of its development, was tied to a dogmatic centre, to the *kerygma* which stated the decisive acts of our salvation in stabilized concepts and sentences. (Acts 4.10; 8.12; 9.20). Paul is at pains to state expressly that his own missionary preaching was based upon the *kerygma* of the whole Church, and that he reproduced the 'official' version of the *kerygmatic* formulae word for word (I Cor. 15.1 ff., 11, 14). But even the most distinctively Pauline element in his missionary preaching, the cross, had already been given its specific expression in a stabilized formula, which Paul referred to as 'the word of the cross', and used in a number of different modifications in his letters (Ch. 63).

In the very first Christian communities the impression made by the missionary preaching was given a fixed form, and later deepened by systematic theological *'instruction'* (Acts 2.41 f.; Matt. 23.10; Gal. 6.6; I Cor. 12.28; Dg. 1). In this instruction the presentation of the christocentric interpretation of the OT was a major concern, but even more place was given to the story of Jesus and his earthly life.[749] For this purpose the use of catechismal formulae as introductory material and as an aid to memory was indispensable. We hear of elementary catechical instruction which contained among other things the fundamental propositions of Christian ethics, sacramental teaching and eschatology.[750] We hear, too, of instruction for the advanced and of different types of teaching, which became more and more important in this upper grade of theological education.[751] The discussions between the different Christian schools, but more particularly their common struggle with heretical schools of thought, led inevitably to the formation of formal academic doctrines. But in the course of the Church's doctrinal disputes these academic doctrines have attained a dogmatic and authoritative importance of many kinds.

One of the many places where dogmatic formulae originated, though perhaps the most important of all, was in the *baptismal practice* of the primitive Church. John's baptism had included a confession of sin (Mark 1.5). The primitive Church kept strictly to this custom,[752] but enlarged the baptismal ritual with a confession of faith, a confession by those about to be baptized of Jesus as Lord (Rom. 10.9; cf. Eph. 4.5; I Pet. 3.21 f.; Acts 8.37 vl.). This confessional formula followed and corresponded to the immersion of the catechumen while calling on the name of the Lord—the baptism into the name of the Lord Jesus (Acts 8.16; 19.5; I Cor. 1.13). But we very soon find this formula of the Lord's name being displaced by the triadic baptismal formula, in the name of the Father, Son and Spirit (Matt. 28.19; Did. 7.1, 3; JustinApol. I 61.3; TertPrax. 26; ApConst. 7.41). And in correlation to this triadic baptismal formula a triadic confession of faith was formed (cf. TertSpect. 4; ApConst. 7.41).

A great demand for the further development of confessional formulae was made by the needs and customs of the *Church's worship*. From the very beginning the Assyrian *terminus technicus* for the act of confession [753] was nothing else than 'to invoke God in the cult'. So the act of confession is basically an act of acclamation, a contribution to the filling of worship with doxological meaning.[754] For this reason the Creed had its fixed place in Christian worship from the beginning (I Cor. 12.3; cf. II Cor. 1.20). But first and foremost it was in the framework of the eucharistic liturgy that confessional formulae very quickly became important.[755] The Creed has doxological significance and a liturgical form. The liturgy in turn has dogmatic content and is studded with various confessional forms (I Cor. 16.22; Rev. 22.20). Many confessions were hymn-like, and many hymns were creed-like (Col. 3.16; Eph. 5.19; PlinEp. 10.96 Merrill; EusHE. 5.28.4 cf. Ch. 43). Parochial preaching also fastened on to these stable confessional formulae and used them as the normal basis of homiletical exegesis.[756]

So much for the sources of dogmatic formulae in the primitive Church.[757] The water, which springs from these sources, for a long time goes its own way, each brook in its own bed, until at last all the different currents flow together into one stream, the stream of the *dogmatic tradition*. Astonishingly early in the history of primitive Christianity there appeared an authoritative teaching tradition in which dogmatic formulae of the most varied stamp and importance had their fixed place. For a long time 'tradition' has been thought of as a malevolent invention of Catholicism, but we know today that the principle of 'tradition' is older than Christianity itself. Thus we read in Jub. 7.38 of a pre-Mosaic legal tradition stretching back past Enoch and Methuselah and Lamech right down to Noah and his sons and grandsons. In Ab. 1.1 this principle of tradition is applied to the law given on Sinai: 'Moses received the Torah on Sinai and delivered it to Joshua, and Joshua to the elders, the elders to the prophets, and the prophets to the men of the Great Synagogue . . .'[758] Later apocalyptic joined these two lines of tradition: In HEn. 48.10 the chain of tradition runs from God *via* Metatron, Moses, Joshua, the Elders, the Prophets, the men of the Great Synagogue, Ezra,

Hillel, Abbahu, Zera down to 'the men of faith'.[760] In SEn. we hear of a secret tradition—Adam, Seth, Enosh, Kenan, Mahalalel, Jared, Enoch—and then onwards from generation to generation.[761] In the same sense, indeed with the selfsame formulae and words, Paul introduces the account of the Last Supper in I Cor. 11.23. Even before Paul the individual points of doctrine had been arranged within the tradition according to their meaning and significance. According to I Cor. 15.3 the christological formulae concerning the death and resurrection of Christ belonged to the most important part (cf. I Cor. 3.11). The tradition is the stream which carries dogmatic propositions down the centuries. But it is at the same time the guarantee which authenticates their normative importance (I Tim. 3.15 f.; II Tim. 2.2). That is why the Roman Church of the year 90 A.D. attached the greatest importance to tracing the line of tradition from God and Jesus through the apostles and bishops down to the Church of its own day.[762] *Church and dogma belong together*.

Let us now ask on what principles these confessional formulae were formed.

By what means can we recognize dogmatic formulae within the theological tradition of primitive Christianity? The confessions are embedded in the mass of theological expositions like crystals in a mass of amorphous stone. The stone can consist of the same chemical material as the crystal, or it can be composed of other elements. The crystal itself can be formed and constructed in different ways; it can be so mutilated that we can only recognize one characteristic facet, one specific angle. That makes it the more necessary to sharpen our eyes to detect the crystal and the laws of its formation. The signs of the crystal in the stone of primitive Christian literature, characteristic marks of a formal confessional passage, are very different in different instances. We can give twelve morphological criteria (App. III). Naturally enough the whole twelve never appear in any one instance, but there is seldom one only. Mostly there are a number together. For example, in the much-quoted formula of I Cor. 15.1 ff. the following criteria named in App. III appear: 1, 5, 6, 7, 8, 9, 12. Where the indications are so strikingly numerous, we may be reasonably sure of our conclusion. And at the same time we acquire a means for the discovery of other confessional formulae whose structural laws do not come so clearly and instructively to light.

But what are the main themes, we may now ask, of those confessional formulae which we find stamped upon the usage of the primitive Church?

Chapter 61

THEOLOGICAL SUMMARIES
OF HISTORY

E. Le Blant, *Étude sur les Sarcophages Chrétiens Antiques de la Ville d'Arles,* 1878; D. Kauffmann, 'Sens et Origine des Symboles tumulaires de l'AT dans l'Art Chrétien primitif', REJ, 1887, p. 33 ff.; 217 ff.; K. Michel, *Gebet und Bild . . .,* 1902; R. Pfender, *De la Prière juive à la Prière Chrétienne,* 1903; P. Drews, *Stud. ӡ Gesch. d Gottesd.* II, III, 1906; A. Baumstark, 'Das eucharist. Hochgebet und die Literatur des nachexil. Judentums', Theol. und Glaube, 1910; W. Bousset, 'Eine jüd. Gebetssammlung im 7 Buch der Const Ap', NGG, 1915; A. Baumstark, 'Eine Parallele zur Commendatio animae in griechischer Kirchenpoesie', OrChr., 1915; A. Kiefer, *Aretalog. Studien,* 1929; A. Baumstark, 'Paradigmengebete ostsyrischer Kirchendichtung', OrChr., 1932; H. Gunkel, J. Begrich, *Einleitung in die Psalmen,* 1933.

From the very earliest times the gods of the ancient East were honoured in a liturgical series of ascriptions of glory. These are sometimes found in the first person of divine revelation, sometimes in the second person singular of hymns, and sometimes in the third person of doxology and homiletics. The characteristic tense is the present, due to the timeless attributes and the recurrent activities of the deity.[763] In the hellenistic world these ascriptions of glory and similar liturgical elements were more or less transformed. Likewise in the world of the primitive biblical tradition we meet with kindred series of ascriptions, though they are now directed to the one true God.[764] But these attributive lists have also become a compendium of a theology of history, for the characteristic tense is not the present,[765] but the perfect, due to the unique character of events in the history of creation and salvation.[766] Nor is the recital confined to the mighty acts of God, but the deeds of the great men of God in the past are recounted in the same form. We shall call such a cursory recital of the events or figures of sacred history a 'summary' (cf. App. VII).[767]

The primary source for the summaries of the primitive biblical tradition is probably the liturgy, where the mighty acts of Yahweh from the creation or the exodus down to the present time were celebrated in summary divine speeches in the first person, in prayers and hymns in the second person singular, and in sermons and instructions in the third person.[768] But the summaries about men of God, especially confessors and martyrs, have their origin here too.[769] Next prophecy seized on these theological paradigms of history and transformed them into an instrument of controversy.[770] So in their speeches the prophets recited now the gracious acts of Yahweh alongside Israel's offences, and now the men of God on whose intercession the godless nation vainly relied. Later still we find summary-like material of all sorts in the life of the community, as parts of oaths, ejaculatory prayers and addresses of all kinds. The summaries in such cases were not always recited in full from beginning to end, but were often quoted in a shortened form: the first and second, or the first and last line of a well-known summary.[771]

In Luke 11.49 ff. Jesus refers to the abbreviated form of a martyr summary (itself now long since lost) that stretched from Abel to Zechariah.[772] Hebrews gives a complete summary of the men of God, which in form and content alike is rooted in pre-Christian tradition (Heb. 11). The theme is announced at the start by the much-quoted definition of faith (Ch. 42). Now, to interpret and fortify the definition, a history of faith is recounted.[773] First of all we hear of the first object of faith, the creation, and only then (cf. Psa. 135.7 f.; II Ezra 19.6 f.) is the main theme taken up: the story of the men of faith, the loyal and the heroic, the confessors and martyrs from Abel down to Syrian times. The material is derived from the OT and the primitive biblical martyr texts (App. I. 1 ff.). In form, the arrangement is anaphoric.[774] Finally an *applicatio* in the manner of I Mac. 2.61; IV Mac. 16.22 forms a transition to the *paranesis* (12.1). But the end, to which the whole story of the witnesses to faith leads, is the cross of Christ (11.25 f., 35, 40; 12.2 ff.). So the summary in Heb. 11 is a compendium of a theology of history with the necessary Christian adjustments (cf. John 1.1 ff.). Heb. 11 is the heir of a very old tradition, but also the beginning of a new one: the first epistle of Clement expressly starts from Hebrews using the same pattern of events and the same forms of speech (9.3 f.; 10.7; 12.1; 17.1; 18.1; 36.2 ff., etc.). But it has its own summaries too, and we can find no fewer than seven summary-like sections embedded in the letter (I Cl. 4.1–6, 4; 7.5–7; 9.1–12, 7; 17 f.; 31.1–32, 4; 45.2–8; 55.3–6): materials towards compiling a theological compendium of the ways of God in history.[775] The *disjecta membra* of I Clement, which owe their insertion to the spirit of Heb. 11, are finally in the same spirit united again in the summaries of Clement of Alexandria.[776]

Heb. 11 is the only summary that has come down to us intact from the primitive Church,[777] but certainly not the only one in use. For very early in its history the Church had an immense store of summaries at its disposal, which centuries after still betrayed their origin in the primitive biblical tradition.[778] We shall mention only liturgical hymns and prayers, [779] paranetic and exorcist formulae, and especially the much discussed summary-like prayers for the sick and the dead, and graveside prayers.[780] Formal language and a wealth of paradigm are native to these summaries.[781] Often they have taken over a primitive biblical set of *paradigmata* unaltered and unenlarged.[782] Elsewhere the pre-Christian arrangement is typologically related to the coming of Christ by being set in a Christian context. Thus the Church's graveside prayers are addressed to the God who has revealed his power in the pre-Christian story of salvation, and in the sign of the cross has won a victory over death that will hold for the future. Finally, an additional section was sometimes added to the lists of attributes that were taken over, and these, in traditional summary style, emphasized the chief events of the life of Christ,[783] or the acts of God or the men of God that began the age of the new covenant. Not till then was the christianization of the primitive biblical summaries complete.[784]

The liturgical wealth of *paradigmata* passed almost entirely into Christian art. And here, too, we find the same sequences, and for the most part the same preference for primitive biblical examples.[785] 'As thou didst save Noah from the flood, Jonah from the belly of the monster, Susanna from false judgement, Daniel from the lion's den, the three men from the burning fiery furnace, so now deliver our brethren from the power of death'. So ran the normal primitive Christian graveside prayer. Primitive Christian sepulchral art uses the same *paradigmata* in the same formal style and in the same sense on the walls of the catacombs and sarcophagi—sculptured prayers for the eternal salvation of the dead. The great prayer of the eucharist in the ApConst. celebrates the God who created the world, and made man, who showed his glory to Abel and Noah, to Abraham and Melchizedek, to Isaac and Joseph, to Moses, Aaron and Joshua at the exodus and in the wilderness—and it also celebrates Jesus Christ, the Virgin's son and miracle worker, crucified and buried, risen and exalted. Christian ecclesiastical art celebrates these same figures and events on the walls of churches, offering pictorial prayers to the glory of the Father and the Son. So the praises of the people of the old and the new covenants (Rev. 7) join together to make one single celebration in picture and in word.

Chapter 62

MONOTHEISTIC FORMULAE

E. Peterson, *Εἷς Θεός*, 1926; O. Procksch, *Das Bekenntnis im AT*, 1936; K. Tallqvist, *Akkadische Götterepitheta*, 1938.

The monotheism of the OT is not a thesis being proved to us, but a 'confession' demanded of us (Ex. 20.2 ff.). Accordingly, its appropriate expression is not in theoretical propositions, but in confessional formulae: 'The Lord our God is one Lord' (Deut. 6.4). This confession involves giving God the glory in a world and in an age which denies God his glory (Dan. 3.45; cf. DaΘ. 4.30; Isa. 14.14; Ezek. 28.2), renouncing all self-glorification (Josh. 7.19; Psa. 38.18; 92.1 f.), a denial of all that constitutes the world and makes divine pretensions (Ex. 20.3 ff.; 23.13; Deut. 5.9; Psa. 20.7), and an unconditional acceptance of God and his ways in the very hour of tribulation (Deut. 6.5, 13 f.; Isa. 26.13). The time will come when God's sole majesty will be known and acknowledged through all the world. 'In that day shall the Lord be one, and his name one' (Zech. 14.9). But until that day the uniqueness of God will be acknowledged only in the confessions of his Church. So to fulfil the first commandment by the doxological confession of the one true God is 'the rightful honour and service of God' (cf. Luther, WA. 30.134).

Monotheistic formulae were of considerable importance in later Judaism, for there is nothing in which Judaism is so united as in loyalty to the confession 'God is one'.[786] In such confessions the first commandment is often quoted or paraphrased (EpAr. 132; PsPhokyl. 8; PhilDecal. 65). More frequently it is (Deut. 6.4) the 'shema' that is cited, the original monotheistic formula of Jewish orthodoxy.[787] For the rest the forms taken by monotheistic confessions of faith are manifold. Sometimes it is simply 'God is one' (JosAnt. 4.201; Peterson pp. 277, 281, 285). Sometimes it is in the abbreviated form 'the only one' (ApAbr. 17; cf. Bonwetsch p. 28). Again, we come on creedal phrases such as 'the only God' or 'the true and only God' (PhilLegAll. 2.1 f.; JosAnt. 8.335, 337). And we find such formulae in syncretistic texts as well as in Jewish writings— a proof that the monotheism of the Bible was not without effect upon its polytheistic environment.[788] But it was scarcely more than just another ingredient in the great mixture of religions.[789] The faith of monotheism really attained its victory by the message which was rejected by the Synagogue as a decline into polytheism— the gospel of the primitive Church.

Jesus answered the question about the first and greatest commandment in the same words as the scribe.[790] Paul often makes use of monotheistic formulae, which apparently very soon came *via* the Synagogue into usage by the Church (I Cor. 8.4; Gal. 3.20; Rom. 3.30; 16.27; I Thess. 1.9). The early Church used the traditional formulae of the one, the true and only God now in a doxological and now in an apotropaic sense.[791] Such monotheistic formulae are not in any way compromised by the Church's christology. This is perfectly plain in those doxologies which may well be the most characteristic creations of the primitive Church—the hymn-like praises of the one God 'through Jesus Christ' (Jude 25; cf. Phil. 2.11). For it was through the coming of Christ that the glory and the sole majesty of the one God came to its full revelation and effect (cf. Acts 14.15; 17.23 ff.; 22.14; 24.14).

Besides the formulae about the uniqueness of God, the NT contains a great variety of formula-like affirmations about God, which for the most part seem to have come from the liturgy of the Synagogue. There are the bipartite 'I' formulae—'I am the first and the last', 'I am alpha and omega',[792]—the tripartite formulae concerning God—'who was, and is, and is to come',[793]—and the tersanctus (Isa. 6.3; Rev. 4.8). There are also the formulae 'the Father of mercies and God of all comfort' (II Cor. 1.3; cf. Ex. 34.6; Psa. 145.9 f.; EJsv. 'Ab Ha-Rachamim'), titles such as almighty, vindicator and saviour, or epithets like 'the Living One' (II Cor. 6.18; Heb. 11.6; Rev. 1.8; I Tim. 1.1; 4.10), and the devotional name 'Father' (*abba*).[794] The NT lays special stress on formulae concerning God's creativity (Acts 14.15; 17.24). Paul is only following the custom of his fathers when he writes in Rom. 4.17 of the 'God who quickeneth the dead, and calleth the things that are not, as though they were'.[795] But in I Pet. 4.19 God is called tersely and all inclusively 'the Creator'.

We have by now indicated all the essential elements of the first article of the Creed, not only in the thought, but also in the dogmatic formulae of the early Church. Where the assertion of God's creativity accompanies a confession of God's uniqueness, we can detect the origin of the 'first article' of the Creed in its primary and yet remarkably full form. 'Above all else believe that God is one, that he has created the universe and established it, and brought it into existence out of nothing, and that he comprehends everything, though himself incomprehensible.' So runs the first commandment in the Shepherd of Hermas.[796] The name of 'Father' is missing. Again, in the Apostles' Creed the confession of the uniqueness of God is lacking. By contrast both elements are found in the creeds of Irenaeus of Lyons and Cyril of Jerusalem.[797]

Chapter 63

CHRISTOLOGICAL FORMULAE

A. Seeberg, *Christi Person und Werk nach der Lehre seiner Jünger*, 1910; K. Holl, 'Zur Auslegung des 2 Artikels', *GesAufs.*, II, 1928; E. Stauffer, 'Vom λόγος τοῦ σταυροῦ und seiner Logik', ThStKr, 1931.

Christological formulae are so profuse in the NT that they far out-number all other creedal formulae put together. But this serves to strengthen our thesis that it is not the idea of God, certainly not ecclesiology, but the coming of Christ that constitutes the central theme of primitive Christian thought (Ch. 39). The theological stress in these christological formulae is laid in turn upon the doxo-logical, the antagonistic and the soteriological conceptions of the mystery of Christ,[798] though often enough they are fused together.

The most elementary forms of the confession of Christ are the christological titles, and their beginnings go back to the earthly life of Jesus. Admittedly, the term 'Son of Man', which Jesus brought into use himself to describe his person, was never used to address him,[799] and never attained the full function or significance of a confession of Christ.[800] By contrast, however, the titles like 'Christ', 'Son of God' and 'Lord',[801] by which the disciples and suppliants addressed him, were very quickly used after Easter as a form of acclamation, and soon gained currency as a confession.[802] New titles kept on being added, in particular the predication of *theos*.[803] Sometimes a single title appears as an independent monument of confessing Christ, sometimes it would be joined with other titles. But most commonly one or more titles were joined with the christo-logical creedal formula which took shape very soon after Easter.

The story of the formation of christological formulae begins with the Petrine formulae of Acts.[804] Their antecedents go back to the Joseph tradition of the primitive biblical literature (cf. App. IV). This already was telling of the destiny of a man of God to be tested by suffering, by means of a somewhat formal double schema. The first part (written originally in the second-person plural) spoke of man's will to destruction, and the second of God's work of deliverance. The central theological idea of this double schema is that of divine providence. We hear a good deal of detail about the way from shame to glory, about the antagonism between the elect and their foes, and about the final salvation which God will attain through catastrophe and opposition.[805] The same double schema dominates the eight Petrine formulae which run like some thread of gold through the opening chapters of Acts.[806] In these formulae it is no longer the suffering of Joseph but the passion of Christ that finds expression. But it is the same notion of divine providence that is the light shining through the darkness of God's ways. Here, too, we have the varying emphasis on the doxological, the antagonistic and the soteriological aspects. The Petrine formula is found in its simplest and most transparent form in Acts 4.10. In 2.36 the formula widens to have two predications of Christ (*kyrios* and *christos*). The passion formulae are expanded in 2.22 ff.; 3.13 ff.; 4.27 f.; 13.23 ff. by the insertion of short 'summaries' which recall in swift sequence particular 'stations' of Christ's road, thus: John, the miracles, Herod, Pilate, cross, burial, descent into hell. The missionary address to the heathen in Acts 10.37 ff. sees our formulae changed from its primary polemical form into its secondary historical form, in which it includes a summary about Christ that stretches from John the Baptist to the last judgement.

According to Acts 13.23 ff. Paul himself used the Petrine formulae at the beginning of his Christian work.[807] There may be a gleam of a pre-Pauline passion formula in Rom. 8.34, reciting the death and resurrection, the exaltation and the heavenly intercession. In any event the passion formula in I Cor. 15.3 f. has come from the primitive Church, according to the explicit statement of the context. This is certainly not so old or original as the Petrine formulae (for it lacks the polemical and missionary second-person plural which the Petrine formulae have from their use in controversy with Judaism). But still the double appeal to scripture in I Cor. 15.3 is original enough.[808] This formula is also a quadripartite summary, beginning with a descending movement in the death and burial, and continuing with an upward movement in the resurrection and the appearances of the risen Lord. So the structure is clearly worked out in the manner of a doxological passion theology. Yet the soteriological motif receives emphatic expression in the first part with its 'for us' (cf. Isa. 53.4 f.). Otherwise this creedal formula in I Cor. 15.3 is on a par with the Petrine formulae. In Peter's speeches in Acts it is normative for the whole system of thought.

The pre-Pauline creedal formulae are passion formulae, at the most expanded with some particular references to the public ministry of Jesus. At first Paul simply took over these passion formulae (I Cor. 15.3 f.) or somewhat developed them (Rom. 4.24 f.), but increasingly substituted for them a new type of christological formulae—incarnation formulae. Other changes accompanied this one. Pre-Pauline formulae dealt with the divine providence which exercised its sway over the passion of Christ, while the Pauline formulae speak of a heavenly pre-existence from which Christ comes at the moment of his incarnation to tread his earthly way.[809]

The Pauline incarnation formulae fall into three groups. First there are the antinomies of the incarnation, formulae which describe the mystery of Christ's person in pairs of contradictory terms: he is David's son and God's Son, man and God at one and the same time.

The paradoxes of the incarnation are formulae which speak of the hidden connection between the 'way' and the 'work' of Christ, in II Cor. 8.9; Gal. 4.4 f.; 3.13; II Cor. 5.21; Rom. 8.3 f. They are without exception constructed on the same double schema (App. V). The antecedent clause relates the paradoxical way of salvation, the burden of the unencumbered. In reciprocal correlation the last and consequent clause speaks of the paradoxical work of salvation, the unburdening of the encumbered.[810] In their context in Paul's letters these formulae provide the clues to the development of thought, no less than the Petrine formulae in their context in Acts provide similar clues there. What we have here in Paul is without doubt the parallel to the Petrine formulae, the formal expression of the Pauline 'form of teaching' (cf. Rom. 6.17), the 'word of the cross' (cf. I Cor. 1.18).

The third main group of the Pauline christological formulae is made up of summaries of the incarnation. Such a formulae is evidently worked into Rom. 10.6 ff. We can recognize it by the terminology of the framework,[811] and can reconstruct it in its main features. It first tells of Christ's descent from the heavenly world (10.6), then of his descent into the realm of hades (10.7), and finally of the testimony to the risen and ascended Lord (10.9, 12 f.). So this formula also finishes up by using a traditional title (cf. Acts 2.36; 5.31; 13.23). The Christ summary, which can only be assumed from Rom. 10.6, can be found quoted *expressis verbis* in Phil. 2.6 ff.! Heavenly existence, becoming man, the earthly road, the cross, the exaltation, the universal dominion—these are the chief landmarks of the cosmic way of the Christ, which is again represented in our two-versed formula as the double journey of descent and ascent. To become man is itself seen as a path of suffering, the 'passion before the passion', the 'acceptance of the cross before the crucifixion' (E. Seeberg). But God's answer to the self-humiliation of the Son is to exalt the crucified to the same place of honour at which the heavenly Christ had once declined to grasp. And this formula ends in the traditional style with a title, with the eschatological confession of Jesus as the Lord (2.10 f.). In Phil. 2.6 ff. doxological and antagonistic elements are mixed up together. The soteriological motif, which dominates the paradoxes of the incarnation, and can also be detected in the framework of Rom. 10.9 ff., is completely absent here. This motif has its first thematic treatment in Col. 1.13 ff., the last and the most forcible of the incarnational summaries. This formula is also given in two strophes, the first telling of the significance of Christ for cosmic history, and the second of his meaning in the history of salvation. Paul includes the beginning of all things: 'Who is the image of the invisible God, the firstborn of all creation.' That is how the first verse begins—with a relative clause in the present tense, whose titles refer to the person of Christ. Then the verse proceeds with a causal clause, which refers in the past tense to the works of Christ in creation. The second strophe takes the theological summary of history further. It, too, begins with a relative clause in the present tense, and contains some titles which apply to the person of Christ. Then it also continues with a causal clause in the past tense which tells of the work of Christ in salvation, which he effected by his incarnation, death and resurrection (cf. Col. 2.9 ff.). The hymnodic formula concludes with a reference to the end of all things (1.20).

Amongst Paul's disciples the incarnational formulae completely dominated the field. The incarnational paradoxes can be found in Tit. 2.13 f.; I Pet. 2.24; 3.18; Heb. 2.14 f. and later in Barn. 5.11; 7.2; 14.4 f. (see App. V).[812] The incarnational summary became an even more favourite formula, and it was always combined with one or more titles.[813] We can see here, in numerous items and part formulae, how the construction was begun of a 'Christ summary' which, all in all, embraced more or less the following landmarks of the way of the Christ: pre-existence, the work of creation, becoming man, life, opposition, passion, Pilate, crucifixion, work of redemption, burial, descent to hades, conquest of death, resurrection, post-resurrection, appearances, ascension, enthronement, benefits of salvation, foundation of the Church, return, judgement of the world, subjection of all things.

In John the formation of series of summaries recedes in favour of individual title-formulae, which glorify particular moments of the cosmic way of Christ: the work of creation (Rev. 3.14; cf. John 1.1 ff.), incarnation (John 1.14; I John 4.3; II John 7), the work of the passion (Rev. 5.9 f., 12 f.), conquest of the powers of death (Rev. 1.17 f.; 2.8; cf. 3.7, 21a), enthronement (Rev. 11.15; 12.10 ff. cf. 3.21b), ascription of divine dignity (Rev. 2.1, 12, 18; 3.1). The Johannine Christ takes the name and title of God (*theos* Ch. 25), but he also lays claim to the most universal divine titles (Rev. 1.8; 21.6). He is the first and the last, the *alpha* and the *omega* (Rev. 1.17; 2.8; 22.13). So the significance of Christ for cosmic history which the disciples of Paul for the most part express only in long chain-formulae (only once is there a brief triple formula, Heb. 13.8) John condenses into one pregnant double attribution.

In the early Church Ignatius is the most significant heir to and creator of christological creedal formulae. From the sayings of the Lord he adopted the idea of the Son of Man; from the Gospels he took the statement about the *parthenogenesis*; from the Pauline epistles he took the formation of antinomies; from the Deutero-Pauline epistles the christological summaries, and from the Johannine tradition the predicate '*theos*'—and from all these elements he formed an abundance of liturgical incarnational formulae with a soteriological accent (Eph. 7.2; 18 f.; IgnMg. 11; IgnTr. 9; IgnSm. 1; IgnPol. 3.2). The combination of titles and verbal creedal formulae grew into a fixed style. Among the titles the most frequent to be found are God, Son of God, *kyrios* (Lord), Christ, Son of David, *anthropos* (man), less frequently Son of Man, Physician, etc. In the summary-like formulae the following in particular stand out: pre-existence, *parthenogenesis*, becoming man, baptism, earthly way, passion, Pilate, Herod, crucifixion, work of salvation, Easter foundation of the Church, quickening of the dead, universal renewal.[814] One can see how the early forms of a 'second article' of the Creed gradually crystallize out of the abundant wealth of formulae which the early Church possessed.

Chapter 64

RUDIMENTS OF THE THIRD ARTICLE

Th. Schermann, *Die Gottheit des heiligen Geistes*, 1901; H. B. Swete, *The Holy Spirit in the Ancient Church*, 1912; A. v. Harnack, 'Das Alter des Gliedes "Heilige Kirche" im Symbol', *Festschr. f. A. Schlatter*, 1922.

We shall search the NT in vain for anything that can be called a 'third article' of the Creed. Yet we can find individual elements of the third article in something like formulae in the literature of the early Church—in part as the final part of a christological formula, in part also as independent items in 'amorphous' texts.

Without any doubt the formula concerning the raising of the dead has the longest history of all the individual elements of the third article. Since the days of the Maccabees it was one of the chief creedal propositions of loyal Judaism, often testified to, and defended with much passion.[815] The primitive Church took the confession of the resurrection of the dead into its catechism as a dogma of traditional orthodoxy (Mark 12.18 ff.; Acts 23.6; 24.21; Heb. 6.2; cf. Acts 24.15). But this ancient creedal item gained a new foundation in the message of Easter (I Cor. 15.1 ff.; Acts 4.2; otherwise 26.23), and this new christological foundation comes into currency in the history of the creeds by a sentence about the resurrection of the dead being added to the article about Christ: 'who moreover was truly raised from the dead ... His[816] Father, I say, will raise us— in Christ Jesus, apart from whom we have not true life' (IgnTr. 9.2). One can see here how already the hope of the resurrection of the dead has been enriched by the promise of eternal life. The belief in the resurrection of the flesh cannot be found in the NT, and, in its literal meaning, is directly opposed to Paul's eschatology (Ch. 58). Yet in the creeds of the primitive Church it gained an astonishingly early circulation in the traditions of Rome, Gaul and Jerusalem.

Formulae concerning the forgiveness of sins had their place in the oldest baptismal rites. John the Baptist preached a baptism for the remission of sins, and Peter did precisely the same in the name of Christ, and evidently, too, in the framework of his Petrine *kerygma*.[817] We hear of a confession of sins at baptism (Mark 1.5) and can venture the guess that it was answered by a formula promising grace. It is no longer possible to say with any certainty just when the affirmation of belief in the forgiveness of sins found its way into the Creed. But we can find the forgiveness of sins as early as the middle of the second century in the framework of the Roman baptismal creed, and of the creedal formula of the EpAp.[818]

The Spirit was one of the matters of controversy in the creedal discussions in later Judaism (Acts 23.8). According to Mark 3.29 the attitude that anyone took to the 'Holy Spirit' was, even in the lifetime of Jesus, reckoned to provide a criterion of faith. The man who blasphemed against the Holy Spirit was doomed to damnation. Out of that negative warning it is possible to draw by analogy the positive conclusion stated in I Cor. 12.3, that confession of the Holy Spirit was already a part of the Creed in the earliest Churches, i.e. it was a part of the requirements for entry into the Church and for reception of eternal life (cf. Mark 16.16). In the same way we can note that the Holy Spirit is expressly mentioned in the baptismal formula of Matt. 28.19. Paul has much to say about the unity and uniformity of the Spirit in the Church (I Cor. 12.4, 11 f.; Phil. 1.27; cf. Acts 4.32). Eph. 4.4 ff. puts the Spirit in the framework of a sevenfold formula. John in one place joins the Spirit with the two chief sacraments and speaks of the agreement in witness of the Spirit, the water and the blood (I John 5.7 f.; cf. I Cor. 12.13). In these instances there are clear tendencies to an expanded formula. But the baptismal formula of Matt. 28 has not been affected by such development (see Did. 7.1; Justin, Tert., etc.). In Matthew there is simply the name Holy Spirit, and this short form became normative for the oldest catholic creeds. Only in the creed of Cyril do we find, after the confession of the Holy Spirit, an expansion in the line of these examples, in the phrase 'one baptism of repentance for the forgiveness of sins'.

When do we find the first mention of the Church in the Creed? We have already seen in Ch. 60 that the Church is accepted as the foundation and guarantee of the Creed in I Tim. 3.15 and elsewhere. But before that the Church was already one of the elements confessed in the Creed! Acts 24.14 f. is admittedly only a confession of loyalty to the persecuted flock of Christ, where the concept of the *ecclesia* is not mentioned as such. Yet this homologue acquires a certain dogmatic nuance through the confession of faith in the resurrection of the dead which comes at the close. In Paul's letters there is a good deal of reference to the unity of the Body of Christ— more frequent and formal than the references to the unity of the

Spirit (Gal. 3.28; Rom. 12.5; Col. 3.15; I Cor. 10.17; 12.12 f., cf. Eph. 2.15 f.; 4.4). In John 11.52 we read about the worldwide character of this unitary Church (cf. Did. 9.4). But in all this, again, there is no explicit mention of the idea of the *ecclesia*. In contradistinction we do find it in Col. 1.18—and there it is found in the framework of a christological formula that itself has the character of a creed (cf. Eph. 1.20 ff.). This is the point on which Ignatius fastens when he concludes his summary christological formula in IgnSm. 1.2 with the words: 'in the one body of his Church.' The baptismal creed as early as the first decade of the second century (Harnack op. cit.) drew on this development for its final summary, when it confessed: 'I believe . . . one holy Church.'

Chapter 65
THE BEGINNINGS OF A TRINITARIAN CREED

K. Künstle, *Das Comma Johanneum*, 1905; M. Dibelius, 'Die Christianisierung einer hellenist. Formel', NJbchKlAlt, 1915; A. Seeberg, 'Zur Entstehung der triadischen Gottesvorstellung', in R. Seeberg, *D. Alfred Seeburg*, 1916; J. Haussleiter, *Trinitarischer Glaube und Christusbekenntnis in der alten Kirche*, 1920; D. Nielsen, *Der dreieinige Gott in religionshistorischer Beleuchtung*, I, 1922; J. Lebreton, *Histoire du Dogme de la Trinité* I,[8] 1927, II,[2] 1928; A. Rawlinson, *Essays on the Trinity and Incarnation*, 1928; O. Moë, 'Hat Paulus . . . ein trinitarisches Taufbekenntnis gekannt?', *Festschr. f. R. Seeberg*, I, 1929; E. v. Dobschütz, 'Zwei- und dreigliedrige Formeln', JBL, 1931; G. Ongaro, 'L'autenticità e integrità del comma trinitario in Matt. 28.19', Biblica, 1938.

The formulae of the old biblical tradition, in which confession was made of the one God, could quite easily be developed into twofold or threefold forms, or even into a form with more than three members. On the analogy of the correlation formula one God–one name (Ch. 62) other double formulae came into use: one God–one temple,[819] or one God–one people of God.[820] Triadic formulae appeared as combinations of such double formulae: one God–one name–one Israel, or one God–one Israel–one temple.[821] Even four- and five-membered formulae were devised: one God–one law–one world–one end (SBar. 85.14), or one God–one people of God–one city of God–one temple-one altar (JosAnt. 4.200 f.). Practically all these formulae begin with a confession of the oneness of God,[822] and that oneness was not compromised in any way by the designations in the following members of the formulae, but on the other hand confirmed by them.[823]

The primitive Church used these formulae as the means of giving expression to the relation of God to his Christ: one God–one Teacher, or Lord, or Mediator (Matt. 23.8 ff.; I Cor. 8.4 ff.; I Tim. 2.5). There is no trace of ditheism in that;[824] on the contrary, the oneness of God is confirmed by the oneness of his Christ (cf. Ch. 62).

Furthermore, the primitive Church displayed a special tendency to form threefold formulae.[825] Jesus himself spoke of the trinity of Father–Son–angels.[826] But this particular triad never attained to any significant importance alongside the formula that dominated all others: Father–Son–Spirit.[827] This formula was never used by Jesus in his earthly life. But, according to Matt. 28.19, it very quickly secured a firm place in the primitive Christian baptismal rite, and on that basis came to determine the whole creedal development of the early Church (Ch. 60). Paul and others repeatedly use this same formula, though in somewhat different terms.[828] But the chief examples, however, are in the liturgical texts of the early Church, which abound in threefold doxologies to the praise of Father, Son and Spirit.[829] Normally these formulae, particularly the baptismal formulae, are called trinitarian formulae. But the description is, at the very least, unthoughtful. They are triadic formulae, for they speak of three; but there is nothing here of a threefoldness or a triunity.[830] This can be seen from the previous history of the formula. Neither in the Jewish triple formula, God–temple–Israel, nor in the Christian triad, God–Son of Man–angel, is there any real thought of a triunity.[831]

The baptismal formula gives us the framework, as A. Seeberg recognized, in which later on the titles and epithets ascribed to God (Ch. 62), the attributes and summary material of the confession of Christ (Ch. 63), and the formulae used for the Church, the forgiveness of sins and the resurrection (Ch. 64), were inserted. It was in this manner that the earliest baptismal creed,[832] the old Roman Creed, and the Apostles' Creed itself have developed. But even here there is never an assertion of a triunity. It is simply that this triple basis forms for most of the baptismal creeds that principle that determines the construction, and that holds for the creeds of ancient Egypt and south Gaul, as for the old Roman and the Apostles'

Creeds. But even this trichotomy was never universal.[833] Instead we can trace the same ingenuous alternation between formulae with three and more sections, which struck us in the history of the triple formula and its development (JustinApol. 1.6, etc.). And we are bound to draw the same conclusion: As with the triadic baptismal formula, so with the triadic baptismal creed—it does not amount to a proper trinitarian creed.[834]

Yet later on, especially in the century of the trinitarian councils, the lack of a trinitarian creedal formula in the NT was felt to be a serious impediment. An attempt to remove this impediment is the so-called '*Comma Johanneum*'—an addition to I John 5.7 f. which originated in Spain in the fourth century.[835] The original text of I John 5.7 f. dealt with the unanimity of the witness of the Spirit, the water and the blood (Ch. 64). This original form of the text is to be found in the Egyptian and Syrian manuscripts, in the earliest Fathers and the whole of the East. The Spanish version of the text expanded that particular triad into a trinitarian confession of faith [836] by the use of a brilliant stylized insertion. We append here the expanded text in English translation, and arrange it schematically, italicizing the words which belong to the original text of I John.

> '*There are three which bear witness* in heaven
>   The Father, the Word and the Spirit,
>   And these three are one.
> And there are three which bear witness on earth,
>   *The Spirit, the water and the blood*
>   *And these three agree together.*'

It is easy to see that this is the same tendency in the tradition of the text as can be detected in John 1.13. At that point it was the absence of a witness to parthenogenesis that was regretted, and such a witness was provided by a small textual alteration (Ch. 26).

In this instance the Spanish readers of the Bible in the fourth century have created a trinitarian formula by means of a thoroughgoing expansion of the text—and by doing so have given involuntary proof that what is true for us was also true for them: among all the wealth of formulae in the NT they found no trinitarian creedal formula.

Chapter 66

TOWARDS A HISTORY OF DOGMA

R. Seeberg, *Lehrbuch der Dogmengeschichte*, I,[3] 1922; A. v. Harnack, *Die Entstehung der christlichen Theologie und des kirch⁊ lichen Dogmas*, 1927; W. Bauer, *Rechtgläubigkeit und Ketzerei im ältesten Christentum*, 1934; E. Seeberg, *Menschwerdung und Geschichte*, 1938.

There was a time when theologians sought to represent the history of primitive Christianity as an epigenetical process, a sort of progressive theological development. The matrix in which the process took place was Judaism, which had 'a law' but 'no theology'.[837] At the beginning of Christianity stood Jesus of Nazareth, who preached the love of God and the love of one's neighbour, and at all events the imminent end of the world. He went about doing good, and called himself the Son of Man, and 'thereby' indicated that he meant to claim no more than that he was simply a man among men—Jesus, the first Christ. On Good Friday the light from this unique figure shone for the last time, thereafter to be for ever extinguished. But then the dejected disciples were suddenly seized by a wave of ecstatic experiences and, uplifted by them, they saw their deceased Master in a glorified form; the Easter and Whitsun legends went into circulation, and there arose the enthusiastic primitive Church with its pneumatic preaching, its congregational singing, praying and speaking with tongues. Then Paul intervened, that unhappy man with his morbid sense of sin, his Greek ideals of salvation, his rabbinic dialectic—the theologian of the Christ with a great conversion experience in his heart. He it was who made a theology out of the religion of Jesus of Nazareth, a theology of Jesus the crucified. Next John appeared on the scene, that great anonymous figure and mystic of Asia Minor, who completed the apotheosis of the Christ and so brightly gilded over the historical figure of Jesus of Nazareth that it became completely unrecognizable. Finally, Catholicism arrived with its Church doctrine and creedal formulae. So the history of the Christian religion had a most promising beginning as a new piety. But then it took a fatal turn and became the story of a theology, and finally it came to an unhappy end as the history of dogma. This is the epigenetic theory of the history of primitive Christianity.

But we have reached another conclusion. So far as their definitive contents are concerned we can see the christological affirmations and formulae of the early Church in a state of preformation in the interpretation of himself offered by Jesus Christ. In this sense we thus oppose the epigenetic theory of primitive Christianity and its history with what may be called the 'preformatory' understanding of them.

Jesus called himself the Son of Man. Certainly. But the idea of the Son of Man was a central theological concept in pre-Christian apocalyptic. There it stood for that heavenly man who existed from the beginning and would appear at the end of the days in all his glory to accomplish God's judging, saving, creative work. Jesus adopted that idea from apocalyptic theology, without any curtailment, but also not without an explicit accentuation, a paradoxical profundity. This heavenly man must pass through the depths of earthly suffering for the sake of the world's distress. His way lay through rejection and death to the accomplishment of his work and the full revelation of his glory. Thus the concept of the Son of Man is the fundamental christological term in the NT. Its problems are the ones to receive explanation in the theological discussions of the following decades. The so-called history of religion in primitive Christianity is a history of theology from its beginning, from the self-interpretation of Jesus.[838]

The primitive Church sang and prayed. Certainly. But she sang of the mighty acts of God, and her prayer was worship and invocation of Christ; it was confession of the Lord. Enthusiasm and hymn, Spirit and confession belong together. So in the first beginnings of the Church there grew up a wealth of dogmatic formulae. In this the idea of the Son of Man was presupposed theologically, though not repeated in creedal fashion. Instead it was the subject of further explication in formulae. Peter unfolded the paradox of Christ's way in the antagonistic formulae of the suffering and the subsequent glory of Christ. The primitive Church unfolded the secret of Christ's work in the summary-like formulae of Christ's death (burial, resurrection, revelation, exaltation) and intercession for us. She held to her inherited preference for triadic formulae. She revived the ancient creedal formulae of belief in one God and in the resurrection of the dead. The apostles preached a baptism 'for the forgiveness of sins', and baptized into Jesus Christ, and very quickly in the name of the triad Father-Son-Spirit. So the story of the Church's dogma runs like a golden thread through the history of Christian theology from the very beginning. The dogma is as old as the Church herself. But both the dogma-making Church and the Church-making dogma are pre-Pauline in origin.

Paul presupposes the theology of the Son of Man, and builds upon the dogmatic tradition of the primitive Church. But he took the passion formulae of the first apostles, which were conceived in terms of the concept of the Son of Man, and expanded them into formulae about the incarnation. Becoming man is itself part of the passion, itself an event in salvation history. The Son of God becomes a son of man burdened with the curse, so that the children of men, set free from the curse, might become the sons of God. This is the meaning of the Word of the cross, the paradoxical incarnation formula to be found in the greater letters of St Paul. The later letters probe even deeper. The doxological incarnation formula in Philippians puts the adversary's self-glorification in antithesis to the self-renunciation of the Son, and follows the course of Christ's way from the divine pre-existence through his human suffering and death upon the cross to the divine power of the exalted Lord. Finally, the incarnation formula of Colossians, expressed in terms of universal history, recounts the history of Christ's work from the creation through salvation to the re-creation of all things. That constitutes Paul's final contribution to the history of dogma in the primitive Church. For the rest the apostle left behind him a school of disciples who continued the dogmatic tradition of their Master and developed his dogmatic formulae in manifold ways.

In John the story of the primitive Church's dogmatic development reaches its immanent goal. Three marks characterize the Gospel of John, all three alike essential to the 'preformatory' understanding of the dogma of the Christ and its history: First, there is 'more' to tell about Jesus than any one Gospel can contain. Next, Jesus had 'more' to say than any one disciple could comprehend. Third and lastly, for this very reason Jesus promised the Church his Spirit, who should lead her into the fulness of the truth about Christ: 'He shall bring to your remembrance all that I said unto you.' 'He shall not speak from himself; but whatsoever he shall hear, these shall he speak ... He shall glorify me: for he shall take of mine, and shall declare it unto you.' As if in confirmation of this last promise John goes back behind Paul and the primitive Church to the idea of the Son of Man, to develop it in two directions. Jesus Christ is truly God; with the Father from the beginning; the only begotten; eternally enjoying mutual relationships with the Father;

the 'first', the 'last' and the 'living' one; the bringer of life to the world. His Church makes confession of him in the words of Thomas' avowal: 'My Lord and my God.' Jesus Christ is truly man, revealed among men in the form of a man, seen by men, heard by us and touched by our hands, entering into our own destiny of death, burdened with our sin, the burden-bearer of the world. Whoever 'confesses that Jesus Christ is come in the flesh' has the 'Spirit of truth'. This is the twofold confession that John makes and in turn demands, a confession of the true divinity and the true humanity of Jesus Christ. Whoever fails to keep this double confession intact in both its clauses has the spirit of untruth in him. For he would be attacking the paradoxical glory of the Son of Man, and shaking the very foundations of our eternal salvation.

NOTES

1. Cf. the work of A. Deissmann and his disciples (Bertram, Euler, Hasenzahl, Korn).

2. See T. Rostovtzeff T. XLVII f. and J. Hempel, ZAW, 1933, p. 289.

3. Here, more than anywhere else, ways of thought come into play which derive from a Zarathustrian understanding of reality. Apocalyptic does not think dualistically. But in wrestling with the problem of theodicy it has reached a point where it cannot but adopt a demonology; and in this way the OT monotheistic theology of history has been built, by the introduction of ancient Persian ideas, into a dynamic monotheism, an understanding of the world and its history that can be called 'antagonistic'. In this sense pre-Christian apocalyptic is a symbol of the first meeting in history of biblical and Iranian ideas, of the Semitic and the Indo-Germanic spirit (cf. Ch. 23 f.; 53).

4. G. Wodtke, ZNW, 1935, p. 61 f. Others refer the scene to 26.12, which seems to be confirmed by the recent cleaning of the picture, see ThLZ, 1940, p. 116.

5. According to Exr. 26, on 17.8 'all the tents of Israel' were watered by the miraculous spring.

6. Cf. KW, s.v. εἰκών ; on the effect of haggadic tradition on the representation of the Exodus see C. du Mesnil du Buisson ‚*Les Peintures de la Synagogue de Doura-Europos*, 1939, p. 30 ff.

7. JosAnt. 18.117.

8. Summarized in W. Bienert, *Der älteste nichtchristliche Jesusbericht*, 1936, p. 111 ff.

9. E.g. O. Wulff, *Altchristl. und byz. Kunst*, I, 1914, Ill. 289. For like traces in the literary picture of the Baptist in Slavonic Jos. see Bienert, op.cit. p. 113 ff.

10. LidzGinza p. 51; 190 ff.; 240; Jos. p. 70 ff.

11. JosVita 11; Bell 2.129; JustinDial. 80; Hegesipp in EusHE. 4.22.7; EpiphHaer. 17, etc.

12. Cf. PirkREl. in W. Meyer ad. loc. J. Lévi (REJ, 1889, p. 86 ff.) thinks both passages are Christian interpolations, intended to contrast Adam's vain repentance baptism with Christ's baptism in the Jordan. Yet it is a repeatable baptismal rite that appears in both VitAdEv. and PirkREl., and not a unique act of baptism in the sense of Mark 1.

13. Sib. 4.168 f.: θεὸς δώσει μετάνοιαν οὐδ' ὀλέσει. παύσει δὲ χόλον πάλιν . . . JosAnt. 18.117 certainly engages in polemic against the idea of the παραίτησις ἁμαρτάδων, but such polemic proves only how ancient and strong was the connection between the ideas of baptism and forgiveness in the tradition of the Baptist.

14. Isa. 1.16; Dam. 10.11 ff.; Sib. 3.592 f.; PsPhokyl 228 (cf. Bergk ad. loc). On proselyte baptism see KW, s.v. βαπτιστής. In the OT it is God himself who confirms the purificatory rite to his impure people (Isa. 4.4; Ezek. 36.25). The Baptist fastens precisely on this.

15. Otherwise the imagery of the shoes (Matt. 3.11) would be impossible.

16. Ezekiel is of priestly descent, see Ezek. 1.3. For the place of Ecclus. in the history of religion see Ecclus. 7.29 f.; 38.12; 45.7; 50.1 ff.

17. Cf. with reserve, V. Aptowitzer, *Parteipolitik der Hasmonäerzeit*, 1927, p. 95 ff.; 104.

18. Related material in StrB. I p. 12 f.

19. In Dam. 10.11 ff. special regulations for plunge baths.

20. On Thielscher, Winkel and Thiel see ThLZ, 1931, col. 437 f., 1937, col. 275 ff.; 1939, col. 115 ff.

21. Passion sayings like Mark 8.31 show that even among the sayings about the Son of Man there are many secondary or transformed *logia*, which need to be dropped or restored. Cf. n. 405.

22. Cf. ἀρξάμενος in Acts 1.22; 10.37 ff. with ἀρχή in Mark 1.1 (and ἀπ' ἀρχῆς in Luke 1.2). The likeness between Acts 10.37 ff. and the mosaic picture which results from Mark has been noticed also by W. Gutbrod.

23. Acts 1.1 ἤρξατο! Christ's works before Easter are, accordingly, only the prelude to the works which he will accomplish after Easter.

24. John 1.1: ἐν ἀρχῇ.

25. On the historicity of the number 12 see J. Jeremias, *Jesus der Weltvollender*, 1930, p. 71, 4.

26. Cf. e.g. R. Bultmann, *History of the Synoptic Tradition*,[2] on Mark 14.66 ff.

27. Cf. Bar. 3.26 ff.; AssMos. 12.7 f.; I Cor. 1.26 and esp. Bar. 5.9: ὅτε ... τούς ... ἀποστόλους ... ἐξελέξατο ὄντας ὑπὲρ πᾶσαν ἁμαρτίαν ἀνομωτέρους ... τότε ἐφανέρωσεν ἑαυτὸν εἶναι υἱὸν θεοῦ.

28. Kattenbusch, ThStKr, 1922, does not mention Luke 22 at all. Haller (op. cit. p. 4) has done with the saying once he has established that it contains nothing about infallibility in the sense of the Roman dogma.

29. Cf. the accusation of Satan and his defence, also the pardoning and commissioning (διακρινεῖς τὸν οἶκόν μου) of the High Priest in Zech. 3.1 ff., and the office of Moses in AssMos. 11.16 f.; 12.6 f.: *me constituit pro eis ut pro peccatis eorum (orarem)*. In Luke 22.32b I adopt the reading with sa, e, d, D, and Blass (evangelium secundum Lucam, 1897): σὺ δὲ ἐπίστρεψον καὶ στήρισον ; on the grounds for this see ZKG, 1944, p. 20.

30. No more than the office of the High Priest in Zech. 3.4 f., or of Moses in AssMos. 12.6 f. Hence Kattenbusch considers the attempt to justify Peter quite erroneous.

31. Like Michael for the threatened people of the covenant, TestL. 5.6.

32. Cf. Zech. 3.2: ὡς δαλὸς ἐξεσπασμένος ἐκ πυρός.

33. Cf. the pastoral and illuminatory office of God's chosen one, SBar. 77.13.

34. On the office of the 'keys' see StrB. I p. 736 ff.; PsClemRec., Frankenberg, 1.34, 2.30. Harnack, SAB, 1927, p. 423 ff., is unsatisfactory, being without knowledge of pre-Christian tendencies.

35. Cf. Acts 5.1 ff., and also the accord between Paul and the Church in I Cor. 5.2 ff.; between Qenez and the Qahal in PaPhil. 26.

36. I Cor. 15 and John 21 may be the confirmation and fortification of Luke 22 (cf. the 'repetition' of the calling of the disciples before and after Easter in Matt. 10.1 ff.; I Cor. 15.5; IgnTr. 28.18 ff.; Acts 2.1 ff., etc.). Possibly Luke 22 and Matt. 16 are secondary antedatings of the calling in I Cor. 15. That would account for the silence of Mark 1.1–16.8, and point to the conjecture that the

original ending of Mark (now lost) contained an account of a 'calling' in the manner of I. Cor. 15.5 (John 21); cf. Mark 16.7; Luke 24.34; EvPt. 14.60; E. Hirsch, *Die Auferstehungsgeschichte und der christliche Glaube*, 1940, p. 18; Stauffer, ZKG, 1944, p. 13 ff.

37. God = Shepherd in Psa. 79.2; AEn. 89.28, etc.; Moses = Shepherd in Isa. 63.11; Moses' successor = Shepherd in IV Ezra 5.18; SBar. 77.13 ff. Shepherd and rock in Gen. 49.24?

38. Num. 27.18 ff.; AssMos. 1.7; 10.15; AbRN. 1.1 ff. Likewise the pardoned High Priest of Zech. 3 has a successor in office—self-evidently. Cf. further App. VI.

39. Ex. 4.16; 7.1 (Moses = God!); Deut. 34.10; AssMos. 1.14; 11.4 ff.

40. Num. 27.18: ἐπιθήσεις τὰς χεῖρας σου . . . καὶ δώσεις τῆς δόξης σου ἐπ' αὐτόν. AssMos. 12.2: *et Moyses prendit manum ipsius (Josuas) et erexit illum in cathedra ante se*; *Sifr Pisk* in Charles ad. loc.; San. 13b–14a. Cf. also Akiba, etc.: 'Thou art not standing before Rabbi Akiba, but before him who spake, and the world came to be'; KW, II, p. 345, 49.

41. Matt. 23.2; I. Elbogen, *Der Jüd. Gottesdienst*,[2] 1924, p. 473, 483; S. Risom in *Mélanges Holleaux*, 1913, p. 257 ff.; E. L. Sukenik, *Ancient Synagogues in Palestine and Greece*, 1934, p. 57 ff.; apparently at Dura over the chair of the Ruler of the Synagogue there was a representation of the original, the *Cathedra Mosis*; see, Rostovtzeff op. cit. p. 322 f., 369.

42. See Jub. 7.38 f. and also below Ch. 60; n. 758 ff.; App. VII.

43. On the picture of the rock and its rich history see Exr. on 10.1 f. (Patriarchs = the rocks of the world); TertPud. 21; 'Ephraem' in S. Euringer, *Festschr. f. A. Ehrhard*, 1922, p. 146, 148 ff.; further G. Dalman, *Neue Petrusforschungen und der Heilige Felsen von Jerusalem*, 1912, p. 134 ff.; J. Jeremias, *Der Gottesberg* 1919, p. 155 f.; K. Heim, *Das Wesen des Ev. Christentums*, 1925, p. 31; Joach. Jeremias, *Golgotha*, 1926, p. 68 ff.; H. Schmidt, *Der Hl. Fels*, 1933, p. 62 f.; 96 ff., 100 ff.

44. Cf. John 21.22 (otherwise Mark 10.39); also 19, 35 and II John 1 (ὁ πρεσβύτερος); Acts 2.1 ff. (ἄγγελοι; cf. Deut. 32.8; AssMos. 11.17 *Nuntius*). Here we may possibly have (before Ignatius and otherwise than in Antioch) the beginnings of a monarchical episcopate, and (before I Cl. and otherwise than in Rome) the beginnings of a primacy—conceived in the spirit of the priestly tradition. See Ch. 2; 6. More detailed treatment by Stauffer, ZKG, 1944, p. 14, 17 f.

45. Thereupon Moses becomes the type of Peter (*traditio legis*, the miracle of the spring of water), the *Cathedra Mosis* the *Cathedra Petri* (PsClemHom., Lagarde, p. 3, 8; 6.27; 7.4; 12.21; PsClemRec., Frankenberg, Ch. 3.16, 30, 75; Recogn Gersdorf 10.68, 71. Cf. Herm. v. III, 1.8 ff.; TertMonog. 8), and the seat of the Ruler of the Synagogue the prefiguring of the chair of the Christian bishop (cf. W. Neuss, *Die Kunst der alten Christen*, 1926, p. 63 f.).

46. EusHE. 5.8.3; cf. 3.39.15 and the antimarcionite prologue to Mark in Huck's *Synopsis*,[9] p. VII f. M. Dibelius brushes these reports aside with the remark that Papias presupposes that Peter travelled with a secretary (*Gesch. der Urchr. Lit.* I, 1926, p. 44). But ἑρμηνευτής does not mean 'secretary' here, but *meturgeman* (cf. Elbogen, *Gottesdienst*, p. 187 f.) and, as W. Stein has observed, Papias lays stress on the point that Mark kept strictly to the rules which the Synagogue prescribes for the duties of a *meturgeman*; see T. Meg. 4.41 (SB. IV.

187): The *meturgeman* is not entitled to omit anything . . . or alter anything. EusHE. 3.39.15: ἑνὸς γὰρ ἐποιήσατο πρόνοιαν, τοῦ μηδὲν ὧν ἤκουσεν παραλιπεῖν ψεύσασθαί τι ἐν αὐτοῖς.

47. Such ideas were a long way from the mind of his brother Jesus, Luke 13.22 ff.; cf. John 4.21.

48. Cf. Holl, Haller, Lohmeyer, and to the contrary Kittel. For extra-canonical material on the Jerusalem primacy of James see Hennecke, *Apokr.*, p. 103 ff., and further PsClemRec. 1.68 (*c.* 135 A.D.), 1.43.73; EusHE. 2.1.3 f.; 7.19; EpiphHaer. 29.4; 78.14 and n. 68 below.

49. Even his external appearance was a contradiction of Greek ideals and must have been a thoroughgoing abomination to the numerous anti-Semites of his time. cf. II Cor. 10.10; E. v. Dobschütz, *Paulus*, II, p. 1, 45.

50. The genuine hellenistic elements in his thoughts and ideas reached him through the medium of late Judaism. See G. Kittel, *Die Religionsgeschichte und das Urchristentum*, 1932, p. 42 ff., and Nock, op. cit. This applies in particular to his metaphors of the stadium, which have been accepted as evidence for Paul's hellenism since Wendland; see KW, s.v. ἀγών, ἄθλησις, βραβεῖον.

51. There is an abundance of material for comparison in W. Bacher, *Die exegetische Terminologie der jüdischen Traditionsliteratur* I, 1899. Even Paul's form of dialogue, which Bultmann has again tried, though vainly, to trace to the diatribe, and which Wernle wants to explain psychologically, derives from the debates on the law which Saul as a youth had experienced and taken part in.

52. W. Bacher, *Die Agada der Tannaiten*, I,[2] 1903, p. 22 ff., 263 ff. A. Schlatter, *Jochanan ben Zakkai*, 1899; EJ., s.v. Akiba. Rabbi Akiba belongs to that eventful time when the Synagogue began, when the rabbis were in fruitful interrelation with apocalyptic (cf. IV Ezra; HbEn; Dura). Formally his thought and speech show him as essentially a scripture dialectician, but in regard to his material he is, like Paul, an apocalyptic.

53. The vast majority of Pauline scholars talk incessantly of Paul's 'experience on the Damascus road', of some burdensome adolescent sin, of a crisis, a 'conversion' with all its parapsychological accompaniments, of the solitude of the Arabian desert and the years of remote meditation when the Pauline picture of Christ grew out of the vision of Christ on the Damascus road—and this in spite of the fact that in his letters Paul never derives a single christological proposition from his experience on the road to Damascus. Why this uncritical violence to our most authentic sources, and notably among the critical scholars? Because 'the transcendental light' that surrounds the story of the Damascus road must be 'removed'. 'The historical critic . . . under the guidance of the law of the immanent development of the human spirit by causes existing in this world must (*sic*) endeavour to understand the vision as an immanent, psychological act of his own spirit.' Thus (against F. C. Baur!) the founder of Damascus psychology, C. Holsten in *Die Christusvision des Paulus*, 1868, p. 65. But it follows from II Cor. 11.32 that Paul did not meditate in Arabia, but worked there. But it is possible that some new discoveries enable us to answer the question how the conflict with the Nabatean king arose. For the excavations in Petra, Abdeh, etc., show that the cult of the glorified ruler or lord flourished vigorously under Aretas and the other Nabatean princes. The inscriptions tell of the royal Σωτήρ and Κύριος, of 'God our Lord . . .' (G. Dalman, *Neue Petraforsch.* 1912, p. 100, 103, 105). They go so far as to call the not-long-dead founder of

the ruling dynasty 'our God Obodat', and we know that statues, altars, sacrifices and a temple of the dead were erected to him (H. Vincent, etc., in RevBen., 1905, p. 52, 214; *Neue Petraforsch.* p. 57, 92 f.; C. Watzinger, etc., *Petra*, 1908, p. 91; C. Watzinger and K. Wulzinger, *Damaskus*, 1921). It is thus possible for Paul to have been in conflict with the ancient ruler-cult as soon as this (cf. I Cor. 8.5).

54. We have no literary deposit of the long Arabian and Syrian missionary activity of Paul. The surviving letters all seem to fall in the decade between 50 and 60. So it can only be with the greatest reserve that we can trace a 'development' out of these documents in so short a span of time.

55. The so-called apostolic decree of which Acts says so much and Galatians nothing, is, in my view, the draft of an agreement which James brought to the Council of Five, but could not get accepted (KW, s.v. εἶς). James somehow managed to keep the news of the defeat which he had suffered behind closed doors from his supporters outside. This gives a natural explanation why James' party could later engage in propaganda (*optima fide*) in Antioch, and awaken echoes with it—and above all why Acts itself could think of the abandoned draft as a decree signed by both sides (15.2 ff.; 16.4; 21.25).

56. It is renewed in Luther's *sola fide*, which in our day has been so subjectively misused that we are driven to formulate a more unambiguous formula for interpreting Paul. Hence *sola cruce*.

57. Cf. now W. L. Knox, *St Paul and the Church of the Gentiles*, 1939, p. 149 ff.

58. To the Pauline School belong I, II Tim., Tit., Heb. and Eph. (see the synoptic tables on Col/Eph. in E. I. Goodspeed, *The Meaning of Ephesians*, 1933, p. 82 ff.). I Peter is a document representing the fusing of Petrine and Pauline traditions, first circulated in Antioch and then more widely in Rome (cf. Ch. 4; 64). James fought against the extreme Paulinists who saw no road from the theology of *sola cruce* to ethics (cf. Rom. 3.8).

59. cf. E. Hirsch, op. cit. p. 142; otherwise below in n. 703.

60. Funk-Bihlmeyer, *Die ApVäter* I, 1924, p. 138 f.

61. Chronicle of Georgios Hamartolos in Funk-Bihlmeyer op. cit. p. 139.

62. Cf. G. Hamartolos op. cit. and the argument on John in RevBen. 1928, p. 198; 206 ff.

63. Ibid: Παπίας γὰρ . . . αὐτόπτης τούτου γενόμενος . . . φάσκει ὅτι ὑπὸ Ἰουδαίων ἀνηρέθη.

64. Ὑπὸ Ἰουδαίων not only in G. Hamartolos op. cit., but exactly the same in the parallel quotation from Papias in Philippus Sidetes; see Funk-Bihlmeyer, p. 138. Jülicher, Knopf, Hirsch, etc., give the quite careless rendering 'by the Jews'.

65. MartPol. 13.1 shows how easily and readily the Jews of Asia Minor could instigate a rising against the Christians.

66. EusHE. 3.29.2 ff., admittedly recognizes two Johns in Ephesus, who could have been mistaken for one another. But the quotation from Papias which he makes use of is obscure, his own interpretation is tendentious (Alexandrian antipathy to Rev.), and his assertion that there were two graves of a John has been contradicted by excavations on the spot (see Schultze op. cit. II, 104 ff., 450; on the earliest entombments, see the interim reports by J. Keil in JahreshÖstArchInst., 1929, 1932, 1933 (a Johannine mausoleum and a Johannine church!)). In spite of this the Alexandrian theory of mistaken identity

keeps cropping up. E. Schwartz ('Über den Tod der Söhne Zebedaei', AGG, 1904, p. 5 f.) holds that Gal. 2.9 refers to John Mark, not to John the Apostle. B. W. Bacon (*The Fourth Gospel in Research and Debate*, 1909; see E. Hirsch, *Studien zum vierten Evangelium*, 1936, p. 142) applies Mark 3.17 not to John the Apostle and his brother James, but to John the Apostle and James the brother of the Lord, and E. Hirsch (op. cit. p. 141) refers Mark 10.39 and Papias' report of the martyrdom to the same two persons. According to J. Behm (Feine-Behm, *Einleitung in das NT*,[8] 1936, p. 101 f.), Papias' note refers to John the Baptist, and not to John the Apostle. Jülicher-Fascher (*Einleitung in das NT*,[3] 1930, p. 127) says the original apostle John of Palestine is wrongly identified with an Ephesian presbyter of the same name. Against this Hirsch (op. cit. p. 153 f.) states the original apostle John has been confused with another John who was first a presbyter in Jerusalem and later was a figure of some importance in Ephesus. Who would like to turn this kaleidoscope further?

67. John 3.24, 26 ff.; 18.15; correspondingly John follows the Sadducean chronology of the passover (cf. SB. II, p. 852 f.).

68. On the 'phylactery' see Polykrates of Ephesus in EusHE. 3.31.3: ἱερεὺς τὸ πέταλον πεφορεκώς =Rufinus: *sacerdos dei pontificale petalum gestans* (on this Cod. P. petalum =*vestis in quo scriptum nomen dei vel tetragrammaton*); EusHE. 5.24.3 Rufinus: *fuit summus sacerdos et pontificale petalum gessit*. Similar reports are made of James the Just, see Th. Zahn, *Forsch*. VI 212 f.; C. Schmidt TU, IV, 1, 1950, p. 324 (Signs of the status of Primate: cf. above n. 44, 48). A picture of a Petalon of the year 1697 is in the catalogue of the *Lipperheideschen Kostümbibliothek*, II, 1902, p. 55. On the title *Theologos* see PhilSidetes op. cit. and n. 585.

69. Cf. John 21.24; RevBen. op. cit., p. 198. Hence the so-called 'disorder' in John.

70. Cf. H. Windisch, *Eucharisterion für H. Gunkel*, 1923, p. 191 ff.; R. H. Strachan, *The Fourth Evangelist, Dramatist or Historian*, 1925; C. R. Bowen, 'The Fourth Gospel as Dramatic Material', JBL, 1930; H. D. A. Major, T. W. Manson, C. J. Wright, *The Mission and Message of Jesus*, 1938. Further, A. Greiff, *Das älteste Pascharituale der Kirche . . . und das J*, 1929; Bauer, *John*[3], as above.

71. Cf. KW, s.v. ἐγώ—R. Bultmann's, *Johannesevangelium*, 1939, p. 167 f., is diligently made use of, though not actually quoted. On the formula-like language of John, see e.g. G. P. Wetter, *Der Sohn Gottes*, 1916, p. 2 f. Perhaps John 14.31 (᾽Εγείρεσθε, ἄγωμεν ἐντεύθεν) is connected with the liturgical origin of John. How uncertain in any event any literary operation is in John (Bultmann has attempted one again) can be seen from the fate of Hirsch's theory of its formation and his source analysis. According to Hirsch, John was expanded by editorial insertions about 140 A.D. in Asia Minor, and then introduced into use by the local Church. An example of such an editorial insertion may be seen, he thinks, in John 18.32 (*Studien zum 4 Ev.*, 1936, p. 36, 140, 185). But there has recently been published a papyrus originating in Egypt about 130 A.D. and it contains John 18.31 ff., and even the disputed verse 32! (C. H. Roberts: An unpublished fragment of the Fourth Gospel, in the John Rylands Library); H. Lietzmann, ZNW, 1935, p. 285; 1936, p. 118. On this evidence John was at that time (130 A.D. or earlier) in circulation as far as Egypt, and already contained verses 18.31–33 in their present form.

72. The opinion of the ethnologist A. van Gennep op. cit. with reference to primitive parallels.

73. The theologian H. Lietzmann has put the inflexible language of Rev. on a level with idiom of the least literary papyri, see his *Einl. i.d. Altertumswiss.* I, 5, (1923) p. 248. The philologist E. Norden detects here a consciously concise style, see *Agnostos Theos*, p. 382 f., 387. On the framework of Rev. see Ch. 50. On the liturgical imagery see I. Peschek, *Geh. offenbarung und Tempeldienst*, 1929, *passim*.

74. Cautious analyses by E. v. Dobschütz, ZNW, 1907; R. Bultmann, *Festschr. f. A. Jülicher*, 1927; E. Lohmeyer, ZNW, 1928.

75. The relation of the Apocalyptist to Ephesus and the Churches attached to it in Asia Minor (Rev. 1.4; 2.1, 5) corresponds to the position of the Evangelist to his disciples and Churches (John 21.22, 24; RevBen. op. cit. p. 198), as does the fact that (in striking contrast to the pre-Christian apocalyptists, such as the authors of AEn., IV Ezra, SBar.) he makes no use of a name of some author of antiquity or of the familiar *vaticinia ex eventu*, but rather speaks on his own authority to his followers. The character of I John accords with this, for it reads very much like an archiepiscopal pastoral letter, and finally there is also his description of himself as ὁ πρεσβύτερος in II John 1 and III John 1. On ἄγγελος in Rev. 2.1 see SB ad. loc., and also *nuntius* in AssMos. 11.17. ApConst. 7.46 mentions a disciple of John who succeeded him in office. He, too, was named 'John'. Did this name become the traditional name in the early days taken over by the successor as he took over office? Does this provide the real basis for the phantasies of Eusebius?

76. As far back as 1902 A. Schlatter showed that John was a Palestinian Jew, by comparison with the language of MEx. (*Sprache und Heimat des 4 Evangelisten*, p. 8 ff.). But John does not belong to rabbinic tradition, for he is fond of the I-formulae, which not only are not to be found in rabbinic material (even SB, and SchlJ. offer no material for comparison), but were expressly forbidden. Yet neither can the Johannine I-formulae be traced from hellenistic influences; for hellenism knows nothing of the critical I-sayings without a predicate (also G. P. Wetter, ThStKr., 1915, p. 233 f.; E. Schweizer op. cit. p. 128; E. Percy op. cit. and R. Bultmann, *Das Evangelium des Johannes*, p. 167 f., 265, offer no parallels). Rather does John's liking for I-formulae point back to the OT and to apocalyptic (see KW, s.v. ἐγώ), and the only proper place to recognize as the stream in which John stands is that of the old biblical apocalyptic.

77. The OdSol. and certainly the Mandaean literature do not belong here. They are essentially later than John, perhaps not even possible without his influence already operative (cf. ActJ.!) and comprise apocalyptic concepts in the false dress of Gnosticism. But John was the first great anti-gnostic of the Church, and not, as Bultmann supposes (KW. I, p. 245, 249), a peculiarly individual modification of Gnosticism. The anti-gnostic character of John receives better treatment in Schweizer op. cit., though he treats questions of date somewhat superficially. The most thoroughgoing treatment is the patient research of Percy, who checks Bultmann's 'parallels' item by item, until practically nothing remains, see op. cit. p. 299 f. In general the question of the influence of John and of intermediaries down to Manda must be postponed until the publication of the Johannine apocrypha discovered by Giovanni Galbiati. References to the Testaments of the Twelve Patriarchs are, in my opinion, exceedingly sporadic in what Johannine literature we possess (e.g. Percy, p. 67 f., 123 f.), but Bultmann indicates a possibility in his bold words on

John 1.21: 'There is no evidence of a hope in "the prophets" in Judaism' (cf. TestB. 9.2 and Ch. 25).

78. John 1.1 ἐν ἀρχῇ ἦν, differing from JosAnt. 1.27 (ἔκτισεν) and the common copy in Gen. 1.1 (ἐποίησεν).

79. John 1.3: ἐγένετο.

80. There is a parallel to the main clause in GEn. 5.4 οὐκ ἐνεμείνατε . . . ἀλλ᾽ ἀπέστητε—but not to the metaphysical causal clause!

81. For the relations of Ignatius to John see E. v. d. Goltz, TU, 1894, p. 118 ff.; F. Haase, *Altchr. Kirchengeschichte nach oriental. Quellen*, 1925, p. 103. On Ignatius' place in the history of religion see, with reserve, H. Schlier, *Untersuchungen zu den Ignatiusbriefen*, 1929, and H. W. Bartsch, *Gnost. Gut und Gemeindetradition bei Ignatius . . .*, 1940; for theological understanding F. Loofs, *Dogmengeschichte,*⁴ 1906, p. 98 ff. For other early Christian literature see R. Knopf, *Das nachapost. Zeitalter*, 1905.

82. According to SocHE. 6.8, Ignatius composed the first Christian antiphons after the type of the angelic chorus in heaven (cf. Trall. 5). The anaphora of the Jac. Church in Antioch was traced back to him, see F. E. Brightman, Eastern Liturgies, 1896, p. LVIII. In addition Th. Zahn. *Ignatius von Antiochen*, 1873, p. 69; A. Baumstark, *Die Messe im Morgenland*, p. 28 ff. Can there be a reference to Ignatius in EusHE. 5.28.5 as well?

83. For Ignatius, as already for John, the central place in the worship and the life of the Church belong together. So it is no accident that it should be John's disciple, the liturgist Ignatius, who appears as the founder of the monarchical episcopate (cf. Eph. 20.2; IgnSm. 7 f.).

84. Cf. Zahn, op. cit. p. 338 ff.; Brightman, op. cit. p. XXXV ff.; 3 ff.; 470 ff.

85. Among them the 'Johannine' Churches of Ephesus, Smyrna, Philadelphia, and to the Johannine disciple, Polycarp (cf. Rev. 2.1, 8; 3.7; EusHE. 3.39.1).

86. E. v. Dobschütz, 'The Gospel of Peter', TU, 11.1, 1893, p. 21; 49 f.; A. v. Harnack op. cit. I, p. 259 ff.

87. R. Delbrueck, *Antike Porträts*, 1912, Plate 13.

88. Herodotus 1.32.91; 7.45 f., 59 ff.

89. Cf. A. Hekler, *Die Bildniskunst der Griechen und Römer*, 1912, Plate 14; and his *Bildnisse berühmter Griechen*, 1940, Plate 3.17.

90. E. Löwy, 'Zum Bildnis des Euripides', Jahresh. d. Österr. Arch. Onst., 1930, p. 129 ff. Cf. AeschEum. 916 ff. with EurTro .1249 ff.

91. AristPoet. 6 ff.; Rhet. 2.5, 8.

92. L. Curtius, *Ikon. Beitr. II (Caesar) Röm. Mitt.*, 1932 p. 235 ff. R. West, *Röm. Porträtplastik*, 1933, p. 78 f. (The ideal picture of Divus Julius, executed in the time of Trajan 'but nevertheless probably after an authentic likeness'). As a supplement to what is said about the ageing Caesar, cf. the coinage portraits in H. A. Grueber, 'Coins of the Roman Empire', in the BM III, 1910, Plate 54.15; West op. cit., Plate 67, 28 (death mask?).

93. This fresco to a certain extent draws the inner character in the outward appearance which tradition has recorded. See above, n. 49.

94. On the value of the picture as a portrait see Neuss, p. 95; 142.

95. E.g. Agrippina the Elder in the Capitol Museum in Rome.

96. Cf. MartIs. 5.14; MartPol. 14 ff. For the typical feminine character cf. the praying woman in Neuss op. cit. Plate 1.

97. For typical examples see EusHE. 9.9.9 ff.; the gigantic bust of Constantine in the Capitol; A. Alföldi, 25 *Jahre Röm-Germ Komm*, 1929, p. 42 ff., RömMitt., 1933, p. 82 ff.; R. Delbrueck, *Die Münzbildnisse von Maximinus bis Carinus*, 1940, p. 237, 20 e. Rs; Plate 3.12.

98. Aristobulus on EusPraepEv. 13.12.6.

99. AssMos. 12.4: *praevidit et pronovit* (so Hilgenfeld, etc.; Charles reads *promovit*); also IV Ezra 6.1 ff.; Ecclus. 23.20.

100. That is not fatalism. The fatalist sees everything that happens in the world and its history subjected to the oppressive coercion of an impersonal fate, while the biblical writers know of the guiding will of a personal God who hears and answers our prayers (Ch. 44).

101. That is not determinism. The determinist conceives of human decision as being effected by sub-personal causal factors that are alien to the will. This reduces the will to an appearance (as among the Essenes, according to JosAnt. 13.172). By contrast the scriptures conceive of our will as conditioned by a will of a supra-personal kind, by the will of God, who wills man's will, and by his willing first quickens man to his specific reality.

102. These words impressed themselves upon the consciousness of the early Church as few others contrived to do. Matt. 13.14 f. amplifies them with an explicit quotation from Isa. ('obduracy!'). Luke advances the same idea in another place or another form (Luke 17.1; Acts 28.25 ff.). Paul treats the central conception of 'hardening' in Rom. 9.13 ff, The saying appears in literal form again in John 12.37 ff.—almost the only extensive OT quotation in John.

103. Isa. 1.1; 3.13. On predestination cf. Rev. 17.8, on preparation Rev. 12.6 (counterpart in Acts 1.25), on pre-existence Rev. 21.2.

104. All these ideas can be found together once more in the early Church: foreknowledge (Heb. 11.40); predestination (Eph. 1.9 f.; 3.9 f.); preparation (II Cl. 14.5; of works Eph. 2.10) and pre-existence (Heb. 11.10, 16; of the Church II Cl. 14.2 f.).

105. πρὸ καταβολῆς κόσμου; cf. I Cor. 2.7: προώρισεν ὁ θεὸς πρὸ τῶν αἰώνων . . In the compounds πρόθεσις, πρόγνωσις, etc., πρό bears the same sense, but so, too, has ἀπό where the formulae ἀπὸ καταβολῆς κόσμου or ἀπ' ἀρχῆς is used in the same context of ideas, as Rev. 13.8; 17.8; II Thess. 2.13.

106. Isa. 44.6; Aristobulus on EusPraepEv. 13.12.5; Sib. 3.16; IV Ezra 6.6; Rev. 1.4, 8; below n. 793.

107. Rom. 9.20; cf. Isa. 29.16; Jer. 18.6, but also Job 13.7 ff.; 27.8 ff.; 42.5.

108. Calvin, *Inst.* 3.23.7; *Decretum quidem horribile, fateor*.

109. *Opera propria und opera aliena*.

110. Cf. the Hymn of the Word of Marduk, in Dürr op. cit. p. 8 ff.

111. II Thess. 2.8; Rev. 19.15, 21. Thus the Word in John 1 is something totally different from the 'word' which Faust can value so impossibly high, in order to play it off against the 'deed'. For God's Word contains the deed within itself (Deut. 8.3; Wisd. 16.12, 26; Heb. 6.5).

112. Psa 18.8 f.; 90.9b; IV Ezra 6.43; 8.22; Mark 4.14 ff.; Matt. 12.36 f.; Col. 1.25; Rev. 19.11; Heb. 4.12 (ἐνεργής); OdSol. 12.3 ff. So the Word of God is sharply distinguished by John from mere λαλία, and by Ignatius from the human φωνή (John 4.42; 8.43; 6.68; I John 1.1 ff.; IgnR. 2.1; cf. 3.2 f.

113. Thus IV Ezra in a pregnant recasting of Gen. 2.7.

114. SBar. 48.2; ParalJer. 2.8; IV Ezra 4.37 ff.; I Thess. 4.16.

115. Psa. 32.6; Gen. 1.1 (ברא); Wisd. 2.1; IV Ezra 3.4; 7.30; Akiba in jSan 18a: 'who thus spake, and the world came to be'.

116. Σκότος καὶ σιγὴ ἦσαν πρὸ τοῦ γενέσθαι τὸν αἰῶνα. καὶ ἐλάλησεν ἡ σιγὴ καὶ ἐφάνη . . . σκότος . . . καὶ προστεταγμένον ἦν PsPhil. 60 according to TSt. II. 3, 1893, p. 185. Cf. IV Ezra 6.38 f.: *Locutus es . . . et tuum verbum opus perfecit* (Arab Gild: thy word becomes an act) *et . . . tenebrae circumferebantur et silentium.*

117. Rom. 4.17; cf. II Mac. 7.28; SBar. 48.8; Heb. 11.3; Herm.m. 1.1.

118. Wisd. 18.14 ff. (cf. Dan. 4.13 ff.); the personal character of this Word or *Logos* is as important for the history of our problem as is his relationship to God, whose work he accomplished here (cf. Ex. 12.12, 29).

119. In I Cor. 8.6 the middle member of the formula for the divine nature found in Rom. 11.36 is applied to Christ, as in Heb. 1.10 is the whole characterization of God given in Psa. 102.27. Cf. Wisd. 18.14 ff. with Ex. 12.12 f.

120. Συνέστηκεν Col. 1.16 f. Cf. σύγκειται of the Word of God that maintains the world in Ecclus. 43.26.

121. The figure of the pre-existent, world-creating and all-powerful Wisdom was no less significant for the development of NT christology than the old biblical theology of the *Logos*; cf. e.g. Prov. 8; Job 28; Ecclus. 24; AEn. 42; BBar. 3 (Ch. 23 ff.). Further, in the pre-Christian era an important reciprocity of motif had developed between *Logos* and *Sophia*, e.g. Ecclus. 24.3 ff., where *Sophia* (!) says: ἀπὸ στόματος ὑψίστου ἐξῆλθον (cf. OdSol. 12.7 f.). From the literature on the subject see H. Windisch, *NT Studien f. G. Heinrici*, 1914; R. Bultmann, *Eucharisterion für H. Gunkel*, 1923.

122. Josephus begins his *Antiquities* (1.1) with the same formula and the same chapter as also the Synagogue began its lectionary for the ecclesiastical year.

123. Rev. 3.14; cf. *Sophia* in Prov. 8.22. On John 1.2 πρὸς τὸν θεόν cf. Prov. 8.27, 30: παρ᾽ αὐτῷ.

124. Wisdom thus tabernacled in Israel, according to Ecclus. 24.8; and according to AEn. 42.2 she thus returned to her heavenly throne.

125. IgnMg. 8.2; Rom. 8.2; Eph. 19.1 (also Paul in Rom. 16.25). Another spirit is concealed in similar formulae in OdSol. 16.8, 20 f. The apologists and Alexandrians reinterpreted the biblical λόγος προφορικός in the sense of the hellenistic λόγος ἐνδιαθετός ('in the beginning was Meaning'). Gnosis transformed the primordial silence and God's Word of the creation story into an ultimate dualism of σιγή and λόγος. The Church energetically resisted these metaphysical speculations. The variant reading to IgnMg. 8.2 is one instance of this resistance. In Ign. we read of the λόγος ἀπὸ σιγῆς προελθών. That was intended to be wholly in accord with the old biblical tradition, though to a later age it could well have a Gnostic sound. So some orthodox protagonist who wanted to defend Ignatius against false suspicion added a negative to the sentence: ὁ λόγος οὐκ ἀπὸ σιγῆς προελθών!

126. E.g. Heb. 1.4. Elsewhere (Job 1.10; 3.4; John 17.24; I Cl. 60.1) other traditions exercise their influence (Job 38.4 ff.; II Mac. 2.29).

127. πάντα καλὰ λίαν Gen. 1.31 (for טוֹב מְאֹד Mas!); cf. Wisd. 13.3 ff.; I Tim. 4.4; KW, s.v. καλός.

128. Quite differently IgnR. 3.3: οὐδὲν φαινόμενον καλόν.

129. Psa. 18.1 ff.; 88.13; 95.11 ff.; 145.10; Isa. 40.12; Ecclus. 18.6; 43.31; Dan. 3.59; HEn. *passim*; Rom. 1.23; Rev. 4.11; 5.13; rabbinic material in EJ VII, 568.

130. Tob. 8.5; ApMos. 7; TestAd. 1 f.

131. See Lietzmann on I Cor. 15.46.

132. Gen. 2.7 (πνοὴ ζωῆς); Wisd. 15.11 (πνεῦμα ζωτικόν); IV Ezra 3.4; VitAdEv. 13; I Cor. 15.45.

133. Acts 17.29 (not 17.28); Luke 3.23, 38.

134. Gen. 3.19; Wisd. 2.23; ApMos. 14; Rom. 5.12 ff.; 6.23; 8.20; Ecclus. 17.2 f., 6 speak summarily and therewith indifferently of the time before and after the fall. Cf. A. Struker, *Gottebenbildlichkeit des Menschen in den . . . ersten 2 Jh*, 1913.

135. Psa. 104.1; JosAp. 2.171; Luke 11.2; Jas. 3.9a; Did. 10.3. Cf. Milton, *Paradise Lost*, 9.197 f.

136. ἵνα διηγῶνται τὰ μεγαλεῖα τῶν ἔργων αὐτοῦ.

137. The motif of seeking God (Wisd. 13.6, etc.), which is reflected in Acts 17.25 ff., is of another sort.

138. Marquis Posa in *Don Carlos*, III, 10: 'Look around upon His glorious natural order. It is grounded in freedom, and how rich it is through freedom . . .'

139. Κατὰ ἐπιταγὴν τὰ πάντα γίνεται. ἴδετε, πῶς ἡ θάλασσα καὶ οἱ ποταμοὶ ὡς ὁμοίως ἀποτελοῦσιν . . . τὰ ἔργα ἀπὸ τῶν λόγων αὐτοῦ. ὑμεῖς δὲ οὐκ ἐνεμείνατε . . . ἀλλὰ ἀπέστητε καὶ κατελαλήσατε . . . κατὰ τῆς μεγαλοσύνης αὐτοῦ (GEn. 5.2 ff.).

140. ArmEzra at 6.54 f. and 8.1 f. God's foreknowledge does not encroach upon human freedom. *Nam quamquam praescientia eius magna ist, tamen liberam suam* (!) *voluntatem largitus est hominibus. . . . ut scirent, quod faciunt* (at 8.1 f.; cf. Akiba, in Ab. 3.19). Man was created good, but the good which he received as for his benefit he has misused for his destruction. *Cur non datum est nobis eiusmodi cor, ut sciamus tantum bonum et id tantum faciamus . . . Sed quando accepimus mali scientiam, ad illud propensi sumus, quod tu odisti . . . Dedi ei potestatem facere quidquid velit . . . At ille talem potestatem a me accepit, quem bonum creaveram, non bene usus est et peccavit. Non malum quidquam creavi, sed omnia, quae feci, valde bona feci . . . Bonum bene factum in malum mutarunt. Non igitur qui bene formet, causa est, sed qui non bene fruitus est, contumelia affecit creatorem eorundem* (at 8.59 ff.). The 'Augustinian' ideas are noticeable! For this reason research on ArmEzra would prove profitable.

141. Isa. 5.19; SBar. 21.19 f. ; Luke 22.53 ; Psa. 80.13; Acts 14.16; Rom. 1.24, 28; Rev. 6.11.

142. Isa. 14.13 ff: Εἰς τὸν οὐρανὸν ἀναβήσομαι, ἐπάνω τῶν ἄστρων . . . θήσω τὸν θρόνον μου . . . ἔσομαι ὅμοιος τῷ ὑψίστῳ. Cf. Ezek. 28.16 f.; Job 38.7; AEn. 18.15; 21.6; hellenised in Sib. 3.118.

143. Cf. S.B. I, p. 137 ff.; II, p. 167.

144. Later paraphrases in SEn. 29.3; cf. 31.3 ff.

145. A fall from heaven appears in Luke 10.18; Rev. 9.1; 12.9; John 12.31 vl. The idea of a (later) catastrophe to the Sons of God, the stars, or the elemental spirits are in Gen. 6.2; Jub. 5; AEn. 6; 81.6; I Cor. 11.10; II Pet. 2.4; Jude 6.13; Mark 4.39; Col. 2.8; IgnE. 19.3, etc.

146. Job 9.13; 26.12; 38.8 ff.; Jub. 2.2; AEn. 42 (cf. Dg. 7.2). In PsPhil. the demonic world is called a κτίσμα δευτερεῦον, formed ἀπὸ τῆς ἐν τῷ

χάει ἀνακρούσεως (TSt. op. cit.). The anthropology of IV Ezra 3.20 ff.; 4.30 (*granum seminis mali ab initio*!) and of ApAbr. seems to have been influenced by similar ideas.

147. Gen. 1.1–7, especially 1.4: διεχώρισεν ὁ θεὸς ἀνὰ μέσον τοῦ φωτὸς καὶ ἀνὰ μέσον τοῦ σκότους.

148. Ecclus. 42.24: πάντα δισσά, ἕν κατέναντι τοῦ ἑνός; 33.9 ff: ἀπέναντι τοῦ κακοῦ τὸ ἀγαθόν, καὶ ἀπέναντι τοῦ θανάτου ἡ ζωή, οὕτως ἀπέναντι εὐσεβοῦς ἁμαρτωλός. καὶ οὕτως ἔμβλεψον εἰς πάντα τὰ ἔργα τοῦ ὑψίστου, δύο δύο, ἕν κατέναντι τοῦ ἑνός (cf. PhilRerDiv. 163; 207 ff.; AugCivD. 11.18). In Ecclus. 43.23 it is said of the conquest of the primordial chaos: λογισμῷ αὐτοῦ ἐκόπασεν ἄβυσσον (cf. 43.26).

149. TAss. 5.1: δύο εἰσὶν ἐν πᾶσιν, ἕν κατέναντι τοῦ ἑνός. Also TestN. 2.7: κεχώρισται ἀνάμεσον φωτὸς καὶ σκότους. The antagonism between God and Beliar, truth and untruth runs through the whole corpus (cf. App. II). Possibly this, as Josephus says of the 'determinism' of the Essenes, is no more than the anthropological consequence of the metaphysical presuppositions.

150. φαίνει: cf. for this so early a work as A. Hilgenfeld, *Ev. u Briefe Johannis*, 1849.

151. ἀπ᾿ ἀρχῆς I John 3.8; John 8.44—in antithetic correlation to the christological ἀπ᾿ ἀρχῆς in I John 1.1; 2.13; yet limited by John 1.3.

152. Cf. the demonic ἄγγελοι in Rev. 9.11; 12.7 ff!

153. Cf. I Cor. 12.10 (διάκρισις πνευμάτων).

154. Self-glorification=κενοδοξία (Phil. 2.3)=καύχησις (Rom. 3.27); cf. ὕβρις in the Greek world.

155. BBar. 3.26 f.; Matt. 4.9; Rev. 13.12; II Thess. 2.4. Who has issued from the mingling of the sons of God and the daughters of men, according to Gen. 6.4? The ἄνθρωποι ὀνομαστοί!

156. Cf. W. Bauer, WB, s.v. διάβολος, σατανᾶς, κατήγωρ, ἀντικείμενος ἀντίδικος, (ἀντίχριστος).

157. GBar. 2 (πύργος τῆς θεομαχίας); Acts 5.39. There is important comparable material in S. Loesch, *Deitas Christi und antike Apotheose*, 1933.

158. Ex. 2.8 ff.; Jub. 48.2, 10; Dam. 5.18 ff.; TestSol. 25.3 ff. (PlinNatHi. 30.1.11). II Tim. 3.8 rests on these interpretations of Ex. 2.

159. He keeps the truth from them, and deceives them about the seriousness of their situation (Jer. 8.10 f.; Gal. 6.7; I Cor. 6.9 f.; 15.32 ff.; I John 1.8). He loves half-truths and superficial talk (Herm.m. 11.2 f., 13).

160. Cf. II βας. 24.1 with I Chron. 21.1. God holds Satan by the reins (ApAbr. 10), and holds the demonic will in impenetrable limits. Abundant material in W. Böld (Cf. head of Ch. 17).

161. I Cor. 2.6 ff.: ἀρχόντων . . . καταργουμένων.

162. The contradiction is in Jer. 38.30; Ezek. 18.20; Deut. 24.16; 4.14.6; rabbinic references in KW, s.v. εἷς. Rejection of the contradiction appears in Jer. 39.18; Isa. 65.6 f.; cf. Psa. 16.14; 108.13 ff.; John 9.2; Akiba in Ab. 3.20, etc.

163. Prov. 28.2; Dan. 6.25; Esth. 9.13 f.; Ex. 32.34; Job 9.22 f. Particular examples are: Sodom (Gen. 18.20), Nineveh (Jonah 4.11), Abimelech (Gen. 20.9; 26.10), Levi (Gen. 34.39; TestL. 6), Pharaoh (Ex. 12.29 ff.), Korah (Num. 16.22, 27 ff.), Achan (Josh. 7.24), David (II βας 24.17).

164. I βας. 15.26 ff.; 16.31; II βας. 9.21.

165. Gen. 3 tells the story of this event. On the role of the adversary see Wisd. 2.24; ApMos. 16; VitAdEv. 16; GBar. 4 p. 86–7. On man's freedom see Ecclus. 15.14; IV Ezra 3.7; SEn. 65.2; ApSedr. 8; On the principle of self-glorification see Ecclus. 10.13.

166. Gen. 3.14 ff.; Wisd. 1.13 f. (cf. Gen. 2.17; 3.3, 19, 22, 24); 2.23 f.; Ecclus. 25.24; Jub. 3.23 ff.; ApMos. 13 f.; 24; 28; IV Ezra 3.7, 21 ff.; 4.30; 7.12, 118 f.; SBar. 48.42 f. (54.15); 56.6; TestAbr. 8.

167. VitAdEv. 49: *Propter praevaricationes vestras generi vestro superinducet . . . iram iudicii sui, primum per aquam, secundum per ignem.*

168. The most rewarding is Rom. 5.12–21. As a supplement cf. Rom. 7.9; 8.20; II Cor. 11.3; I Tim. 2.14; Rev. 12.9; John 8.44; Mark 1.13.

169. Eph. 2.2; Heb. 2.14; Luke 4.6; I Cor. 2.6; I Cor. 4.4; John 13.31; Rom. 8.20 f.; Col. 1.16; IgnE. 19.3; Freer logion on Mark 16.14.

170. Adam's descendants' sin, according to Rom. 5.14 μὴ . . . ἐπὶ . . . τῷ ὁμοιώματι τῆς παραβάσεως Ἀδάμ.

171. ὑφ' ἁμαρτίαν Rom. 3.9; 7.14; Gal. 3.22; cf. the simile of the brutal tyrant and warlord in Rom. 5.21; 6.23.

172. IgnE. 19.3; cf. ApConst. 8.12.33: δεσμὰ τοῦ διαβόλου.

173. Pharaoh (Rom. 9); Judas (Luke 22.47 f.; John 13.30; on νύξ cf. Wisd. 17.13).

174. John 8.44 (on ἐπιθυμίας cf. PsSol. 2.24).

175. Rom. 8.6 f.; cf. 6.12; Eph. 2.2 f.; also Gen. 6.5, 13 f.; 8.21; Mark 7.21.

176. This is the meaning of ἥμαρτον Rom. 5.12; ἐπί with its relative pronoun refers back to the preceding θάνατος (ἐφ' ᾧ = ἐπὶ θανάτῳ) and does not mean, as translations mostly suppose, 'on the basis of' but 'in the direction of' (cf. Phil. 4.10; II Tim. 2.14). This is the meaning which ἐπί had in the old biblical text which Paul had in mind in Rom. 5.12, and which he in part makes verbal use of (ἐπ' ἀφθαρσίᾳ, Wisd. 2.23 f.); it is also required by the *chiasmus* of the phrases in Rom. 5.12:

$$\begin{array}{l} \text{διὰ ἁμαρτίας} \longrightarrow \text{θάνατος} \\ \text{ἐπὶ θανάτῳ} \longleftarrow \text{ἥμαρτον} \end{array}$$

Here ἐπί is the reciprocal preposition to the διά of the first phrase. So we must accordingly paraphrase: 'death, to which they fell man by man through their sin'.

177. Gen. 3.16; Eccl. 4.1; SEn. 65.9; Job 2.13 (πληγὴ δεινή); III Mac. 4.4 (κοινὸν ἔλεον).

178. Gen. 3.18; cf. ApMos. 24: ἔσῃ δὲ καμάτοις πολυτρόποις· καμῇ καὶ μὴ ἀναπαύου, θλιβεὶς ἀπὸ πικρίας . . . κοπιάσεις πολλὰ καὶ . . . εἰς τέλος μὴ ὑπάρξεις.

179. Psa. 89.10: κόπος καὶ πόνος (cf. Eccl. 1.13 ff.). Luther misunderstood the passage.

180. Matt. 11.28 (κοπιῶντες . . . ἀναπαύσω ὑμᾶς). But cf. also POxy 1.1 and thereon J. Leipoldt, *Der Gottesdienst der ältesten Kirche*, 1937, p. 19 f.

181. Wisd. 2.24: φθόνῳ δὲ διαβόλου θάνατος εἰσῆλθεν εἰς τὸν κόσμον; Rom. 5.12: διὰ τῆς ἁμαρτίας ὁ θάνατος (εἰς τὸν κόσμον εἰσῆλθεν). ApMos. 14: κατακυριεύειν; Rom. 5.14, 17: βασιλεύειν.

182. Rom. 7.24; 8.21 ff.; I Cor. 15.21 f., 49; Gal. 4.9; Phil. 2.7; Heb. 2.15.

183. PsSol. 2.23 ff. (ἐν ἐπιθυμίᾳ ψυχῆς); cf. Matt. 26.52; Rev. 13.10.

184. Gen. 8 f.; Jub. 6; PsPhil. 3, 9 f.; Mark 5.45; Rom. 3.26 (ἀνοχή); POxy 403.9 f. (ὀργὴ κατέχεται).

185. Here we could do no more than sketch in the dominant themes. In Ecclus., SBar., etc., there can be seen traces of another outlook, which deserves serious notice: self-glorification, affliction and death had their origin before the fall of man. Man was destined to overcome this situation, but he missed his destiny and thereby further intensified the universal affliction. On the correlation of Adam and Messiah see B. Murmelstein, WZKM, 1928, p. 242 ff.; Pesikt. 23.

186. Gen. 3.17; 5.29; Isa. 11.6 ff.; Jub. 3.25; Sib. 3.787 ff.; Schatzh. p. 7 (the 'whole earth'); otherwise ApMos. 24 (according to the LXX).

187. GBar. 8; AEn. 80; 101.2; M. Sachs, *Tefillah Vetachanunim*, 1939 (=Sachs, Tef) p. 354: אָדָם וּבְהֵמָה תּוֹשִׁיעַ יְיָ. Similarly, the flood and the threatened punishment on Nineveh drew the non-human creation in to share its suffering, Gen. 6 ff.; Jonah 3.7 f.; 4.11.

188. See KW, s.v. βοάω.

189. The earliest exegesis of Rom. 8.19 ff. is quite in the spirit of the apocalyptic tradition in thinking of a creation-wide catastrophe (Iren. C. Haer. 5.32.1, 36.1, 3). It was the same later on in the East with Theodore of Mopsuesta, etc. (K. Staab, *Pauluskommentare aus der griechischen Kirche*, 1933, p. 137 f.; Catena, p. 246.22, 29, Cramer), in the West with Thomas Aquinas (Marcion expunges the verses, Pelagius wavers between interpreting 'creature' (22) as 'the whole creation' and 'mankind', see TSt. 9.2 (1926) p. 65 f.). Luther also translated the text in terms of universal history, and so interpreted it: *per ipsum* (Adam) *omnis creatura* (=*totus mundus*) *licet invita fit vanitas* (see Glosses und Scholia ad. loc.). Lutheran exegesis has followed the same lines (Bengel, Delitzsch, Althaus, and further, Lietzmann, Billerbeck and even Jülicher, who did not recognize the antecedents of the problem, and so could only explain Rom. 8.19 ff. as a poetic 'mixture of phantasy and feeling'). Similarly, the reformed tradition from Calvin to Barth. To the same effect is the research into the history of ideas (κτίσις=בְּרִיאָה cf. בָּרָא in Gen. 1.1: KW, s.v.). On the contrary, A. Schlatter repudiates this interpretation in terms of universal history (following him are W. Gutbrod and others), and most pointedly in his last literary observation on the matter: *Gottes Gerechtigkeit*, 1935, on Rom. 8.22: 'To ascribe a common sighing and groaning together to the whole world of being demands a highly-excited phantasy.'

190. I Cor. 2.6; Gal. 1.4; Col. 1.15 ff.; 2.15; cf. δουλεία, etc., in Rom. 8.21; Gal. 4.9; Phil. 2.7.

191. So IV Ezra 9.22: *sine causa*.

192. So it comes about that a quite new conception of history permeates the western world with the spread of Christianity; W. Windelband, *Präludien*, II[7.8.], 1921, p. 156; J. Behm, *Das Geschichtsbild der Ap*, ZSTh. 1925; cf. N. N. Glatzer . . . *Geschichtslehre der Tannaiten* 1933.

193. ἴδιος καιρός cf. Gal. 6.9 f.; Tit. 1.3; II Thess. 2.6.

194. The Bamberg Apocalypse rightly makes each one ride alone over the earth (ed. H. Wölfflin, 1918). Each rider has his ἴδιος καιρός. Dürer thinks differently!

195. Yet God never appears as the slave of his own programme. He can shorten the times (Gen. 6.3 LXX; AEn. 80.2; SBar. 20.1; PsSol. 17.21; Mark 13.20; Rev. 22.20; Barn. 4.3; Ch. 45), and also prolong them (Gen. 6.3 according to I Pet. 3.20; II Thess. 2.6 f.; Herm.s. 8.11.1; Ch. 14, 61).

196. F. Hebbel, Jdth. 3.2.

197. So E. v. Dobschütz op. cit. p. 219.

198. See the prophecy of Nefer-Rehu (pap. Golenischeff) in A. Erman, *Die Literatur der Ägypter*, 1923, p. 151 ff.: 'The whole land is ruined . . . the sun is covered up . . . Asiatics have come down to Egypt . . . no cry for help is heard . . . one man takes the life of another . . . a king will come from the south . . . the victor's wall will be built and the Asiatics will not be permitted to come down (again) to Egypt . . . Justice will once more come into her own, and injustice will be driven out . . .' Cf. the 'Potter's Oracle', AOT, p. 50.

199. See the prophet's words to a weak king (pap. Leiden in Erman op. cit. p. 130 ff.): 'Behold, the time will come, that the king's land shall be pillaged . . . the Palace is razed to the ground in a single hour . . . they are as scared sheep without a shepherd . . . every man is against his neighbour . . . all these years are rebellion . . . the younger generation, which we have decimated, has become inverted, and will destroy the very place where they have grown up . . .'

200. S. Langdon, 'Die neubab. Königinschriften', OLZ, 1924; K. F. Müller, *Das ass. Ritual*, I, 1937.

201. AOT, p. 231; cf. 228.

202. F. H. Weissbach, *Die Keilinschriften der Achämeniden*, 1911, p. 3 ff. On the self-consciousness and the sense of mission belonging to the Aryans, see p. 71 and W. Brandenstein, 'Die neue Achämenideninschriften', WZKM, 1932, p.27. On the reflex effect on other peoples cf. Isa. 45.1, and Jean, *Milieu Biblique*, II, p. 395.

203. The conflict of gods, heroes, rulers or knights with demonic monstrosities is a favourite theme of ancient art. E.g. Gods: AOB, fig. 326; 380; .397; 400. Heroes: JeremiasATAO,[3] 1916, fig. 4; 45. Non-Christian rulers: A. U. Pope, *A Survey of Persian Art, IV*, (1938) Plate 123 G.L; W. Wruck, *Die syr. Provinzialprägung von Augustus bis Trajan*, 1931, p. 162; M. Wegner, *Die Herrscherbildnisse in antoninischer Zeit*, 1939, Plate 53; R. Delbrueck, *Die Münzbildnisse von Maximinus bis Carinus*, 1940, Plate 18, 81. Cohen, *Christian Princes*, VI, p. 514; J. Kurth, *Die Mosaiken von Ravenna*,[2] 1912, p. 133; F. J. Dölger, AC, I, p. IV f.; P. Perdrizet, *Rev Ét Grecques* 1903, p. 46 ff.; E. Peterson, Εἷς θεός, 1926, p. 94 ff.; 109; 124; A. Graber, *L'Empereur dans l'Art Byz.* 1936, p. 237 ff.; H. Schlunk, 'Kunst d Spätantike im Mittelmeerraum = Kat. d. Ausstell z. VI Arch. Kongress Berlin', 1939, fig. 54 (Berliner Frühchr. Byz. Sammlg. Inv. 9300). Christus Triumphans Garrucci, Storia IV, 243; VI, 457; 473; A. Orlik, *Nord. Geistesleben*,[2] 1925, fig. 25 f.; J. Reil, *Christus am Kreuz* 1930, Plate IV ff.; ThStKr. 1937, fig. 5; E. Weigand, ByzZ., 1932, p. 75 ff.; 81.

204. Weissbach, op. cit. 89; also 'Die Keilinschriften am Grabe des Darius', SächsAk., 1911. Similar motives in the newly-discovered Darius inscription in Brandenstein op. cit. 27; 31 ff.; 53; 73. Byzant. Gegenstücke zu Abb. 52 die Arkadiusmünzen in J. Sabatier, *Monn Byz.*, I, 1862, pl. IV 2.11.

205. Cf. Brandenstein op. cit. p. 78 (Canal construction); Chr. Bartholomae, *Die Gathas des Avesta*, 1905, p. 6 ff.; 20 f. (Stockfarming against nomadic economy); F. Wolff, *Avesta*, 1910, Vendid. 3.31 f. (Agriculture against demonic power).

206. Hobbes, *Leviathan*, 13 (Molesworth p. 99 f.); cf. also LutherWA., 18.66.10, etc.

207. On the ultimate effects of Alexander, cf. F. Kampers, *Al. d. Gr. und die*

Idee des Weltimperiums in Prophetie und Sage, 1901; ibid., *Vom Werdegang der abendl. Kaisermystik,* 1924; E. Bikerman, *Institutions des Seleucides,* 1938. On the Roman conception of Caesar and Empire, see A. Alföldi, *Röm.Mitt.,* 1934, p. 1 ff.; 1935, p. 1 ff.; 1937, p. 48 ff. For the Roman idea of an *Imperium Aeternum,* cf. Delbrueck op. cit. Plate 15.49; Dölger op. cit. p. 119; JosAnt. 10.209 f.; AugCivD. 20.19.3. On the christianization of the ancient idea of Empire, see A. Alföldi, *Pisciculi f. F. J. Dölger,* 1939, p. 1 ff.; A. Dempf, *Sacrum Imperium,* 1929.

208. Jub. 40.9; 46.2; cf. Deut. 33.17; TestN. 5.6 f. (also n. 203). Later on Joseph the 'Politician' is a favourite figure of Jewish tracts, e.g. Philo, De Josepho; L. Ginzberg, *Legends of the Jews,* II, 1910, p. 73 ff.; G. Friedländer, *Pirke de Rabbi Eliezer,* 1916, p. 303 ff.; E. Stein, *Philo und der Midrasch,* 1931.

209. Cf. H. Gunkel, *Die Propheten,* 1917, p. 31 ff.; O. Procksch, *Der Staatsgedanke in der Prophetie,* 1933. Philo speaks of Augustus in the same spirit: ὡς μικροῦ σύμπαν τὸ ἀνθρώπων γένος ἀναλωθὲν ταῖς ἀλληλοκτονίαις (!) εἰς τὸ παντελὲς ἀφανισθῆναι, εἰ μὴ δι᾽ ἕνα ἄνδρα . . . ὃν ἄξιον καλεῖν ἀλεξίκακον (!) . . . ὁ ἰασάμενος . . . παραλύσας . . . ἀνελών . . . εἰρηνοφύλαξ (Legat. 144 ff.). Also now H. Leisegang, JBL, 1938, p. 390 ff.

210. Ab. 2.3a. With Strack read בַּלְעוֹ, not as Marti-Beer בַּלְעֻנוֹ. For the point here concerns not some ironic Jewish self-characterization in regard to some passing political squabble, but an ancient fundamental proposition about the theology of the State (cf. n. 198 ff.; 208 f. and Az, 4a; Ber. 58a). On Ananias see Bacher, *Agada* I,² p. 51 f. It is noteworthy that it was precisely a priest who gave validity to such a proposition. Nevertheless, it was a custom down to the Jewish rebellion to make a daily sacrifice in the temple at Jerusalem for the emperor, JosBell 2.409 f. (Cf. the prayer for the imperial sovereign in Elbogen, *Gottesdienst,* p. 203; 274; Sachs, Tef. p. 300, and also n. 649).

211. I Mac. 14.4 ff.; cf. TestL. 8.11 (Hasmoneans as forerunners of the final kingdom).

212. Cf. Psa. 100.8; II Mac. 4.6; Sib. 3.175 ff.

213. Significantly in the hand of a Persian king! For the role of the Persians in Jewish (and Christian) eschatology cf. Micah 5.4; SBar. 70.7; San. 98b; MidrHL. 14.1; Yoma. 10a; also H. Lessmann, *Die Kyrossage in Europa,* 1906, H. Windisch, 'Die Orakel des Hystaspes', Verh.d.kon.Akad.te Amsterdam, 1929, p. 45 ff.

214. Cf. Isa. 45; Ezra 1; n. 787.

215. ApEl. 30 f. = a Jewish product (cf. temple, temple treasure, rebuilding, oblation, heathen = lawless monotheistic confession = n. 787), and worked into a Christian framework. The Christian Prince of Peace of the West is portrayed after the pattern of the Persian King of Peace in 25 f. The whole work will have to be properly analysed. A provisional analysis can be found in Weinel, *Eucharisterion für H. Gunkel,* 1923.

216. Rom. 13.4 διάκονος; 13.6 λειτουργός; cf. Wisd. 6.4 ὑπηρέτης.

217. Cf. Gen. 9.1 ff; further LutherWA., 42, p. 361: *Ad hunc modum constituit hic locus* (Gen. 9.6) *Politiam in mundo, quae ante Diluvium non fuit.*

218. For the history of the exegesis see W. Bornemann, *Thess.,* p. 400 ff. and 538 ff. On the effects of II Thess. 2 on the German ideology of the State, see the *Ludus de Antichristo* (ed. F. Wilhelm, 1912), which often has verbal likenesses to II Thess. 2. Modern exegesis begins with H. Gunkel, who sees in κατέχων a

mythological-apocalyptic figure (*Schöpfung und Chaos*, 1895, p. 223 ff.). E. v. Dobschütz picks up the interpretation in terms of the theology of the State again, but holds that 'the idea of κατέχων is completely lacking in the rich apocalyptic literature of Judaism', and so sees in II Thess. 2.6 f. 'an idea of Paul developed ad hoc' (*Thess.*, 1909, p. 280; 283). M. Dibelius on the other hand has produced a rich collection from the history of religions illustrating the idea of a shackled demon, unhappily though it cannot be used to decide this exegetical question (*Thess.*,[2] 1925, p. 40 ff.). A. Hans moves backward rather than forward (KW, s.v. ἔχω). W. Böld was the first to turn the work in the history of religion on to the antecedents of the NT, and by his collection of relevant material to lead us to a line of tradition that stretches from the ancient East through Paul down to the exegesis of the early Church, and establishes the equation κατέχον = *imperium*.

219. *Imperium* = κατέχον. *Imperator* = κατέχων. The same correlation of the two figures is found in TertScap. 2.

220. TertScap. 2 (*quousque saeculum stabit: tamdiu enim stabit*); Apoll. 32: *clausulam saeculi . . . Romani imperii commeatu scimus retardari* (cf. II Thess. 2.6).

221. AristPol. 3.7.7; 6.1.1 ff.

222. TestJud. 21.7 ff.; Th. Schermann, *Proph.Vit.*, 1907, p. 50; Rev. 11.7.

223. Wisd. 13.11: ζητεῖν, εὑρεῖν, διερευνᾶν, νοεῖν, θεωρεῖν, εἰδέναι (cf. II Chron. 15.15; Acts 14.17; 17.27). GEn. 2 ff.: ἴδετε, νοήσατε, διανοήθητε, κατανοήσατε, καταμάθετε, γνῶτε.

224. The favourite example is Abraham, see Jub. 11.16 f.; 12.4 f.; ApAbr. 7 f.; MaaseAbr. in StrB. III 34 f. Job is led the same way in TestJb. 2 ff. He draws the logical conclusion, makes an end of the demonic cult, and restores the worship of the one true God.

225. Leading ideas: διανοούμενος ἐννοηθήσεται, ἰχνευτής.

226. See the context (2.6 ff!) and σοφία in Rom. 11.33; Col. 2.2 f.

227. Thus the apparent overlapping of prepositions and the concept of Wisdom disappears in a transparent co-ordination (ἐν τῇ σοφίᾳ τοῦ θεοῦ . . . διὰ τῆς σοφίας τὸν θεόν).

228. Rom. 1.18, 25, 28; I Cor. 1.21; cf. III Ezra 4.33 ff.; SlTestAss. 5.2 (Charles p. 287); II Cor. 10.5; I John 1.6.

229. ἐδοκίμασαν . . . ἀδόκιμον νοῦν Rom. 1.28; cf. 2.18; Phil. 1.10.

230. The principles of divine creation and lordship of history are, objectively considered, unchanged since Gen. 8 f. (TestN. 3). That is why Paul uses the present tense in Rom. 1.20 (as GEn. 2.ff). But, considered subjectively, man lost the power to see these things—eyes he has but sees not. Cf. Luther quoted in E. Seeberg, *Menschwerdung und Geschichte*, p. 222: 'There (in Christ) thou findest God most certainly; else shalt thou go hither and thither through the whole creation, groping here and there, and yet never find him; even if he be really and truly there; for he is not there for you.'

231. Rom. 1.32 συνευδοκοῦσιν; cf. TestA. 6.1 vl; TacitGerm. 19.

232. Cf. BB. 10b: All the works of charity done by the Gentiles are sins; for they do them only to attain greatness.

233. When was conscience brought into being? In anything that can be called 'law' Paul does not see (as is usual today) something that can be called a primordial datum of creation, but rather something by which God enters as revealer into history, and institutes as a provisional measure. That applies to the

Torah (Gal. 3.19; 5.20; Ch. 19), but also (according to the position adopted in Rom. 1.32 and 2.14 f. in the whole theology of history in Romans) to the law of Gentile peoples (φύσει = 'originally', see Wisd. 13.1; Gal. 2.15; Rom. 11.21). According to Rom. 3.19; 7.13 the Jewish law had the historical and eschatological function of bringing sin to light (cf. PsPhil. 11.2: 'I put my word in thy mouth . . ., the eternal law, and by it I will judge the world. That is to say this will serve as a witness: If men say "We did not know thee", I will nevertheless afflict them . . .'). According to Rom. 2.15 f. the law of the Gentiles has the same function (cf. TestJud. 20.5; AEn. 96.4: 'Woe to you, ye sinners! Your heart convicts you; and these (your) speeches will then become witnesses against you to recall (your) evil deeds'). The same motif, transposed into the realm of the timeless, is found in PhilPostCain. 59: ὁ νοῦς ἑκάστῳ μάρτυς ἐστιν . . . καὶ τὸ σύνειδος ἔλεγχος . . . ἀψευδέστατος.

234. παρέδωκεν, Rom. 1.24, 26, 28.

235. The NT does not know the great conception of Amos 9.7 (cf. Acts 7.42; 14.16).

236. Cf. Johanan ben Zakkai Ber. 28b.

237. Rom. 11.i, 16; cf. 16.5: Ἀπαρχή = The first fruits, which are the promise of the coming harvest.

238. It is the Pharisaic terminology itself which is adopted here in polemical form; cf. also Luke 18.11 with SachsTef. p. 170.

239. The autobiographical interpretation of Rom. 7 (Holsten, op. cit. p. 106 ff.; Deissmann, *Paulus*,² 1925, p. 73) comes to grief on Phil. 3.6. The rhetorical-universal interpretation (Kümmel op. cit.; Bultmann, ThR, 1934, p. 233) founders on Gal. 2.15. It also ignores the fact that the characteristics of *homo sub lege* in Rom. 7 must logically include the pre-Christian Paul (cf. Augustin ad loc: *Quo loco videturmihi Apostolus transfigurasse in se hominem sub lege positum, cuius verbis ex persona sua loquitur*; MPL, 40 Sp. 103). But its chief fault is to neglect the distance in time which separates the theological anthropology of the NT from the metaphysical anthropology of existentialism, and will not permit it to be reduced as a mythological residue, or at best turned into something 'contemporaneous'. Rom. 7 can only be understood in terms of the history of salvation: it is a chapter about the Jewish man who fights under the banner of the Torah, and therefore fights to the bitter end, because he is fighting in a lost position (by way of comparison it may be noted how SBar possibly disavows the capitulation of legal righteousness that is threatened in IV Ezra). Thus Augustin MPL, 40 Sp. 66 (*In prima ergo actione, quae est ante Legem, nulla pugna est cum voluptatibus . . . in secunda, quae sub Lege est, pugnamus, sed vincimur; in tertia pugnamus et vincimus: in quarta non pugnamus, sed perfecta et aeterna pace requiescimus*). LutherWA., II, p. 492 (*Opera peccati, quae dominante concupiscentia fiunt . . . Opera legis, quae foris coercita concupiscentia fiunt . . . Opera gratiae, quae repugnante concupiscentia, victore tamen spiritu gratiae fiunt. Opera pacis et perfectae sanitatis, quae, extincta concupiscentia, plenissima facilitate et suavitate fiunt, quod in futura vita erit, hic incipitur*). Stauffer, KW, s.v. ἐγώ ('In him (Paul) there has been decisively fulfilled the divine intervention in salvation-history through the people of the Torah, which lasted from the age of the law to the age of the Spirit'). Benoit, op. cit. p. 497 ('Paul speaks to us in terms of salvation-history and describes to us the stages of the world's history').

240. Gal. 3.24; cf. ῥάβδος in I Cor. 15.21; ῥάβδος παιδείας in PsSol. 18.7;

μάστιξ παιδείας in PsSol. 7.9. Luther ('taskmaster') is much nearer the Pauline idea than the humanist Lessing with his 'step-at-a-time' progress in the 'education of mankind'.

241. IV Ezra 9.5 with Gunkel according to Äth; otherwise Violet.

242. Cf. JustinAp. I 12.10: θεοῦ ἔργον ἐστί, πρὶν ἢ γενέσθαι εἰπεῖν (cf. John 13.19) αἱ οὕτως δειχθῆναι γινόμενον ὡς προείρηται.

243. Cf. PsPhil. 12.3: *ut completur (sic!) verbum*; W. Bacher, *Terminologie* I, p. 170 f.: לקים מה־שנאמר

244. τέλος τοῦ καταργουμένου; ἐν Χριστῷ καταργεῖται.

245. Cf. Rom. 15.4: εἰς τὴν ἡμετέραν διδασκαλίαν: further Gnr. 1.1; San. 37a ללמדך ; In the technical formulae of the Haggadic schools Paul interprets the OT words for 'sting', for 'Lord' in I Cor. 15.55 and II Cor. 3.16 f. respectively. (Cf. the same formulae in *Dam* passim.) Further see n. 249.

246. According to John 8.56 many OT personalities have seen Christ in visionary experience. Possibly Matt. 13.17; I Pet. 1.10 ff.; Heb. 11.13—in any case ParalJer. 9.13 ff. (cf. VitProph. p. 44); ActVerc. 24 (in Hennecke, p. 244) make the same point.

247. See IV Ezra 9.5. The source of this idea is the schematic correlation of primordial time and end time, which Gunkel has worked out in *Schöpfung und Chaos*.

248. In hellenism *typos* is the (timeless) model, while for Paul it is the (historical) premonitory sign.

249. Cf. PsCypOr., *De montibus Sina et Sion* (Hartel, III, 3, p. 104 ff.). In Gal. 4.26 Paul uses the same exegetical language of the schools as he does in I Cor. 15.56; II Cor. 3.17 (see n. 245; 283). Cf. TestD. 5.12; Schatzhöhle, p. 5.

250. Paul himself abandons in Rom. 9.7 the hazardous exegesis of Gen. 12.7 which he used in Gal. 3.16.

251. Cf. Schatzh. p. 34, and the SlMelch. legend, 3.1 ff., 34; 4.7 (Bonwetsch).

252. Heb. 9.9 παραβολή: 9.23 ὑπόδειγμα.

253. Cf. TestL. 14.4; Dam. 6.4.

254. Cf. J. Leipoldt, *Die Religionen in der Umwelt des Urchristentums* (Bilderatlas), Fig. 1; 12, O. Weinreich, NJBWissJgdb., 1926, p. 641 f.; 644.

255. Ibid., cf. F. Gerke, ZKG, 1940, p. 22; 27; 29.

256. A. Heckler, *Bildniskunst* 1912, T 180 (Claudius as Jupiter); quite the best is Gallienus, who in quick succession lets himself be honoured as Hercules. Alexander, Augustus, Mercury, the Sun, the *'genius populi Romani'*, Demeter (!), Athene (!), Zeus Panhellenius; see R. Delbrueck, *Die Münzbildnisse von Maximinus bis Carinus*, 1940, p. 48 f.; 119 ff.

257. The relation between Moses and Peter becomes tautologous (Neuss, Kunst, p. 53; E. Becker, Quellwinder, ö 131 ff.; cf. n. 45), as does that between Noah and Orantes (K. Michel, *Gebet und Bild*, 1902, p. 61; Neuss op. cit. p. 37; Gerke op. cit. p. 42; 99 f.).

258. Aphraates, *De pers.* 9; Maximian's episcopal chair in Ravenna.

259. See E. Le Blant, *Les Sarcophages Chrétiens de la Gaule*, 1886, p. 101; 4.

260. The literary evidence for this idea goes back a long way, cf. K. Holl, *GesAufs*, III, 1928, p. 34 ff.; the earliest and long since established iconographical proofs appear first in the ninth century: cf. W. Neuss, *Die katal. Bibel illustration*, 1922, p. 125; J. Reil, *Christus am Kreuz*, 1930, p. 29.

261. Further τύποι of Christ, not always unquestioned, in WilpertK. passim.

262. J. Reil, *Die altchr. Bildzyklen des Lebens Jesu,* 1910, p. 63.

263. Cf. WilpertM., *Textbd.* p. 202 ff.

264. The texts presupposed are Isa. 7.14. LXX; Num. 24.17; Matt. 1.18; 2.2; perhaps also ParalJer. 9.20; AscIs. 11. Cf. Schermann, VitProph. p. 10; 45; 62; 72; TU, 31.3, 1907, p. 87.

265. Le Blant, p. 6; yet the interpretation in terms of Moses is contested, see Wilpert, *Sarcofagi,* T, 153.

266. The quotation is set in the framework of a controversial speech which is full of persecution polemic (cf. App. I. 25). Wisdom is also the subject of the prophetic mission in Luke 7.35. Abel is a favourite figure in pre-Christian theology of martyrdom (App. I. 5; VII, at the end). Zechariah is the priest of II Chron. 24.21 (for discussion on the point see Sh. H. Blank, 'The Death of Zechariah in Rabbinic Literature', HebUnColAn., 1937–8, p. 327 ff.). On the other hand commentators quite early identified him with the father of John the Baptist (Luke 1.5), and thus destroyed the ancient value of the quotation (see Orig; ProtevJa.; other refs. in E. Klosterman ad loc.).

267. Mark 9.13 is an unidentifiable reference (cf. Ch. 1). The OT alone tells of the sufferings of the historical Elijah (I Kings 19.2 ff.) and of his reappearance at the end (Mal. 3.231 cf. Ecclus. 48.10; ApP. 2). Yet there are Christian texts which permit us to argue back to these pre-Christian traditions of the martyrdom of the returning Elijah (Rev. 11; ApEl. 35; D. Haugg, *Die zwei Zeugen,* 1936). This process has manifest confirmation in the allusions in Dam. 20.13 f. In fine, Jesus is here understanding his OT in the manner of post-canonical tradition of interpretation (cf. also J. Jeremias, *Deutsche Theologie,* 1929, p. 115). Matt. 17.12 takes offence at this, and, according to a well-known custom, omits the words which mention the scripture reference (even the οὐκ ἐπέγνωσαν indicates retreat from it).

268. Cf. App. I.29.

269. Cf. Matt. 22.6; I Thess. 2.14 ff.; 3.3; II Thess. 1.6 ff.; Barn. 5.11.

270. Cf. IgnMg. 8.2 (also Jas. 5.10?). Further n. 246.

271. Cf. Barn. 5.11 f. (also Heb. 9.26?). Rev. 13.8 is not to be classed here, but has to be interpreted in terms of 17.8.

272. The suggestions of post-canonical martyr-literature are particularly numerous, see 11.4 (cf. 12.24; I John 3.17): 11.37 ff. We frequently find the decisive formulae in the traditional style (cf. App. I.19), so in 11.24 ff., 35, 39 f., further 12.2; 13.13 f. For the Summaries see Ch. 61; App. VII.

273. Heb. 11.26 (christological interpretation of χριστός by Psa. 88.52 f.!).

274. Heb. 11.19; cf. IV Mac. 7.12. On the Isaac-Christ typology see n. 258.

275. Mark 9.13; Matt. 11.10, 13 f.; 17.13 (christological interpretation of κύριος by Mal. 3).

276. R. M. Rilke, *Stundenbuch* (of Michelangelo).

277. In MEx. 19.17, etc., Moses is the bride's best man, who leads the young covenant community to his God at Sinai. In John 3.29 the Baptist is the bride's best man, and Christ celebrates the marriage feast with the messianic community (cf. Mark 2.19; Matt. 25.1 ff.); the bride's man, however, has done his duty, and must retire!

278. Not with the Curetonian Syriac: ἐστιν !!

279. Without temporal boundary, cf. Ch. 13.

280. For the literary tradition see Ginzberg op. cit. III, p. 50 ff.; VI, p. 21

(n. 129); KW, s.v. εἰκών, p. 384; Rostovtzeff, *Excavations*, 1936, p. 353 f. (MEx. 15.27; Tos on Succ. 3.11–16). Exr. on 17.8 has been overlooked hitherto (see n. 5).

281. See Bachmann-Stauffer ad. loc. W. L. Knox, *St Paul and the Church of the Gentiles*, 1939, p. 122 ff.

282. Ab. 5.8 reckons him as one of the ten pre-existent means of salvation.

283. ἡ δὲ πέτρα ἦν ὁ Χριστός; the analogy of I Cor. 15.56; II Cor. 3.14 suggests this reading (cf. n. 245; 249). The naturalness with which Paul carries through this figure is the more comprehensible when we remember the role which Wisdom played in the old biblical tradition, not only at creation, but also in Israel's history, and especially in the miracle of the water (cf. Wisd. 11.4; Phil., etc., in Bachmann-Stauffer op. cit.). In Paul the pre-existent Christ takes the place of Sophia, in I Cor. 8.6 in the work of creation, and here 10.4 in the OT story of salvation.

284. רוּחַ יְהֹוָה = πνεῦμα κυρίου = πνεῦμα χριστοῦ!

285. Cf. Heb. 1.1 ff. (Rev. 19.10c?); IgnMg. 8.2 and often in the early Church. In the OT stories of creation and salvation Christ is the real foundation. Correspondingly, in primitive Christian art the OT God appears in the form of Jesus Christ, see e.g. B. WilpertM., Plate 8; 14; 19.1.

286. S. Gressmann, AOT, p. 150 ff.; 206 ff. Further, F. Schmidtke, 'Gilgameschs Strebung nach Erlösung von dem Tode', in F. Taeschner, *Or. Stimmen zum Erlösungsged*, 1936.

287. Legendary elaboration of Buddha's life, see *Buddhatscharita*, 70–249 (C. Capeller, Buddhas Wandel, 1922, p. 9 ff.). In the relevant pictorial world the mother of the exalted one with the wonder-child on her lap played an important role. See H. Haas, *Die Buddhalegende auf den Flachreliefs von Boro-Budur* (Java), 1923.

288. Texts in H. Haas, *Amida Buddha unsere Zuflucht*, 1910, p. 43 ff. In China the goddess of mercy grew out of the figure of Amida Buddha; she was called Kwan Yin, and was a favourite theme of painters; see H. Hackmann, *Laienbuddhismus in China*, 1924, p. 10; 44; 67.

289. See the Voluspa in F. Genzmer, *Edda* II,[3] 1938, p. 34 ff.

290. See Yasna 26.5; 67.2; Bundehesch 24.57; K. F. Geldner, *Die zoroastrische Religion*, 1926, p. 47 f.; Schaeder in R. Reitzenstein and H. H. Schaeder, *Aus Iran und Griechenland*, 1926, p. 213. Distantly related to Gayomart is the primordial king Yima, see Yasna 9.4; 32.8; Videvdat 2.1 ff.; Geldner op. cit. 25 f.; Christensen op. cit. II.23.

291. Cf. Bundehesch 4.12, etc. Otherwise Yäst 19.30 ff.

292. Yasna, 26.10.

293. For Zarathustra's self-interpretation see Gatha 6.1 f.; 10.11 ('Healer of life' is a standing self-description). For Zarathustran mythology see Geldner, op. cit. 33, etc. Formerly the place of primitive Christianity in the history of religions had been thus portrayed: The religion of the ancient world is essentially mythological, the stories of the gods; the revolutionary fact about Christianity was its application of the ancient mythology (selected and adapted) to a certain historical figure of flesh and blood, thus historicizing the myth. In this way the victory of Christianity over the ancient religions became intelligible, but not its conflict. But nowadays we are coming to see more and more clearly that in the pre-Christian history of religion there was a quite elementary

correlation between myth and the world of concrete experience, so that we can talk about historical concretions of the myth, and about mythological trans-figurations of historical figures already in the ancient world: Zarathustra, divine humanity, apotheosis of the king are but some of the clues to this reality. But that means that the conflict of primitive Christianity with the faiths of the ancient world becomes intelligible—and the question as to the basic reason for her victory is raised anew. The only solution now possible is to be found in the realm of destiny, and no longer simply in terms of a history of ideas.

294. Yäst 13.142 (Mother of the final saviour—'all-conquering lady'); Bund. 33.79; Geldner, op. cit., 45 f.; E. Lehmann, *Textbuch zur Religionsgeschichte*, 1912, p. 285–288.

295. It is known that Aryan-racial elements also played some part in the populating of Palestine; for all that they had hardly affected the exclusive families to which Jesus, Paul and John belonged (cf. Ch. 5 f.; 25; n. 33, 6; J. Jeremias, *Jerusalem zur Zeit Jesu*, II, B, 1929, p. 80 ff.). Elements of Aryan culture are also to be found in pre-Israelite Palestine (cf. Jean, *Milieu Biblique*, III, p. 100; A. Jirku, 'Der Name der Stadt Jerusalem', WZKM, 1939, p. 208), in the Philistine border, and fully in hellenistic and Roman times. So far Indian influences have not been established, see H. W. Schomerus, *Ist die Bibel von Indien abhängig?*, 1932, p. 138 ff. But the meeting of the Iranian and the biblical worlds can be historically fixed, and the consequences of the meeting are evident in apocalyptic ideas; cf. most recently R. Otto, *Reich Gottes und Menschensohn*,[2] 1940.

296. But in the old biblical tradition we never find an actual apotheosis of these figures in the hellenistic sense of worshipping and praying to them as gods.

297. On the OT men of God in hellenistic literature see Bieler, II. A.

298. מָשִׁיחַ =χριστός =unctus (ArmEzra 7.28!) is the king's title, cf. PsSol. 17.32; Acts 4.26; Luke 23.2.

299. Thus in AEn. and the Test. 12. In IV Ezra the Messiah is the precursory deliverer, and the Son of Man the final one. Thus each can be introduced in his own place in the same picture of the end.

300. Acts 3.18; Luke 24.26, 46; cf. SB. II p. 284 ff.; Acts 26.23; Psa. 88.52; Heb. 11.26; 13.13.

301. Thus especially in rabbinic orthodoxy, see JustinDial. *passim*; San. 98; J. Klausner, *Die messian. Vorstellungen des jüd. Volkes im Zeitalter der Tannaiten*, 1904.

302. E. Norden, N. Jbch. KlAlt., 1913.

303. See JosBell. 3.399 ff.; 4.622 ff.; 5.2 ff.; 6.312 ff.; 7.71. Further R. Laqueur, *Der jüd. Historiker Flavius Josephus*, 1920; W. Weber, *Josephus und Vespasian*, 1921; EJ, s.v. Josephus.

304. J. Taan, 68d. The Haggada calls him, in this sense, Barkochba's armour-bearer, see HamRealEnzJdt., s.v. Akiba.

305. Several rabbis explain offhand: Israel has had her Messiah already—in the days of Hezekiah! (San. 94a; 99a).

306. MidrPs. 36.10; cf. App. VII.

307. See J. Leipoldt, *Sterbende und auferstehende Heilandsgötter* 1923.

308. Cf. Loesch and Bieler, op. cit.; O. Weinreich, 'Antikes Gottmen-schentum',NJBWissJgdb., 1926; E. Fascher, Προφήτης, 1926; H. Windisch, *Paulus und Christus*, 1934 p. 59 ff., 70 ff.; KW, s.v. θεῖος.

309. Cf. the 'ascension' of the king Etana (Jean, *Milieu Biblique*, III, 40.135), the worship of King Sulgis (Ibid. 134), the apotheosis of Hercules (Roscher, I,[2] 2293), of Germanicus, etc. (J. J. Bernoulli, *Röm. Ikonographie* II, 1886, Plate 30), of Titus (JeremiasATAO, fig. 185), of Antoninus and Faustina (P. Wendland, *Hellenist. Röm. Kultur,*[2,3] 1912, Plate V2), of Sappho (J. Carcopino, *La Basilique Pythagoricienne de la Porte Majeure*, 1926, Plate 24). The ascension of Constantine in Cohen VI, p. 172; 568 shows Christian influences.

310. Cf. MartPol. 17.3; Acts 14.8 ff. and also S. Eitrem, 'De Paulo et Barnaba deorum numero habitis', Arb a. d. nt. Sem zu Uppsala, 1939.

311. Cf. n. 203; EusVitConst. 18 ff. on Virgil's *Fourth Eclogue*; h.e 9.9.9 (Constantine as λυτρωτής, σωτήρ, εὐεργέτης) ; Rom. Delbrück, *Späatantike Kaiserporträts*, 1933, Plate 2.18 ff. (Dominus noster Const.); DeissmannLO, p. 319 f. (Correlation between Christ's *parousia* and that of Caesar!)

312. On the Orpheus question see ClAlStrom. 1.1 ff.; EusDeLaudeConst. 14.5; WilpertK., T. 37; 229; F. Gerke, ZKG, 1940, p. 44; O. Kern, *Orpheus*, with a lecture by J. Strzygowski, 1920; R. Eisler, *Orpheus the Fisher*, 1921; Ibid, 'Orphisch-Dion. Mysterienged. i.d. chr. Antike', Vortr. B Wbg., 1925 (with reserve). Other extra-biblical *typoi* I Cl. 25 ff.; Phoenix, Pfau, etc.

313. DaΘ. 7.13: Ἰδοὺ μετὰ τῶν νεφελῶν τοῦ οὐρανοῦ ὡς υἱὸς ἀνθρώπου ἐρχόμενος ἦν . . .

314. Among the rabbis the idea is met only in quotations (exegetically in Brierre-Narbonne, 1933, p. 76 ff.; polemically in j Taan, 2.1) and always in the sense of 'heavenly man'. I Cor. 15.46 indulges in polemic against the idea of primordial men (see n. 131).

315. Contrariwise in Asenath, p. 59.5, Michael is described as *vir de coelo*, cf. Ezek. 1.26.

316. It follows from IV Ezra 13 that all these traditions remained alive well into NT times. In HEn. 70 f., etc., another figure (cf. n. 314!) takes on the place and the features of the Son of Man: Enoch Metatron (see H. Odeberg, III Enoch, 1928, p. 47; 146). The expression Son of Man sinks once more here to its everyday meaning of Psa. 8 (see HEn. 6.4 f.; 48.8D; but also AEn. 60.10). In ArmEzra there are traditions at work in which the figures of primordial man and the primordial king have been fused together; see ArmEzra 6.54: *Finxisti hominem et urbi similem* (!) *plantasti paradisum* (counterpart AEn. 87.3, etc.) *et collocasti eum intra . . . et principem et regem super omnia . . . constituisti*; 7.11: *et regnat regnum bonum.*

317. It is the more likely that Jesus here drew upon the Enoch tradition, because he shows acquaintance at other points with the traditions at the source of AEn; cf. e.g. Otto, op. cit., p. 310 ff. ('The same school').

318. On Mark 10.45 see Ch. 30.

319. Jesus here uses the same formula as in Mark 9.13 to refer to the apocalyptic writings (προφῆται), and these speak in the well-known formulae of martyrdom on the destiny of the Son of Man—an indication that even in pre-Christian times the expectation of the Son of Man had already absorbed some of the motifs of the ideas of martyrdom. Cf. P. Billerbeck, *Nathanael XXI*, 1905, p. 107 ff. and below.

320. IV Ezra 13.3, 25, 52 (*de corde maris*).

321. Matt. 12.40. In the Gospel to the Hebrews the risen Lord says (to James the Just!): *resurrexit filius hominis a dormientibus*; see JerVirIn. 2.

322. John 3.13 f.; 6.62; also 8.56 ff. is according to AEn; ApAbr. 31 a saying about the Son of Man. Do we find as early as Mark 12.36 f. the idea of the pre-existent Son of Man asserted over against the popular idea of Messiah?

323. Also EvHebr., see n. 321. For isolated use of the idea in early Christian creeds see Ch. 63 (n. 800). On the history of the idea of the Son of Man in Judaic Christianity see n. 838.

324. This is clear evidence that the idea must go back to Jesus' own speech, and not just to the secondary record of the Church.

325. Ἄνθρωπος, δεύτερος Ἄνθρωπος, Ἄνθρωπος ἐξ οὐρανοῦ, ἔσχατος Ἀδάμ, κεφαλή, εἰκών.

326. Namely for hellenistic ears, cf. IgnEph. 20.2!

327. Nur. on 6.2; cf. Levy Wört, s.v. ראשׁון; Murmelstein, WZKM, 1928, p. 242 ff.

328. I Cor. 15.47 f. Men between these two do not count as such, for they are not men in the special sense in which the title *anthropos* is applied here; cf. *homo* in IV Ezra 13 (and Ἄνθρωπος in I Tim. 2.5?). In PsClemHom. 3.22 (Lagarde) Adam also bears the title υἱὸς ἀνθρώπου; cf. πρῶτος Ἀδάμ in I Cor. 15.45 and also IV Ezra 3.21; GBar. 9; JosAnt. 1.82.

329. According to Col. 1.15 he is the *primogenitus* of creation; cf. Heb. 1.2 f. In Heb. 1.6 the pre-existent one appears in his divine likeness in the place of Adam; cf. VitAdEv. 13 ff.

330. Col. 3.10; II Cor. 3.18; cf. I Cor. 15.49; Rom. 8.29 and IgnE. 20.1.

331. Matt. 23.8 ff.; IgnE. 15.1; cf. the title יורה היחיד in Dam. 20.1, 14, 32 and Staerk ad loc.

332. Matt. 21.46; John 9.17; Luke 24.19; 7.6. Martyrdom motif in Luke 13.33; 24.19 f.

333. Mark 8.28; Matt. 16.14; Mark 6.14 f.; cf. 9.4, 11.

334. John 6.14; cf. Luke 7.19 f. ὁ ἐρχόμενος; Heb. 3.1.

335. ὁ Προφήτης John 7.40; cf. 1.21, 25. Once more we find the 'priestly' tradition here, and its hope for a 'levitic' deliverer of prophetic coinage; cf. Deut. 18.15 f.; Ecclus. 50.1 ff.; TestL. 8.151, 18.3 ff.; TestB. 9.2; TestJud. 24 (original text); AssMos. 11.16. The title had not been fulfilled (cf. Acts 3.22 f.; 7.37), though it was thought otherwise in Jewish Christianity (and Islam), see e.g. PsClemHom. 20.19; Rev. 1.37, 50 for the saving *parousia* of the one and the true prophet.

336. On 'Son of David' see Matt. 21.9; also PsSol. 17.21; Prayer 18: 14; John 7.42. In spite of Mark 12.37 Jesus did not himself repudiate these forms of address. 'The root of David' and 'The Lion of Judah', see Rev. 5.5; also Acts 2.30; 13.23; Rom. 1.3 and Luke 11.22; Rom. 9.5. Such titles of majesty are in the first place traditional names for indicating the succession of the Messiah. But in the NT they have beyond that a thoroughly genetic significance. Our oldest witness, Paul, speaks in Rom. 1.3 of genealogical descent of Jesus from the house of David (here κατὰ σάρκα, unlike IgnSm. 1.1, is tied up with the idea of 'seed' and so is strongly genealogical, like Rom. 9.3, 5). The same tradition is at work in Matt. 1.16, where, in the same genealogical way, Jesus is called the son of Abraham and the son of David. Both Matthew and Luke tell us who, according to the oldest tradition, was the final connecting-link between the ancestor David and his offspring Jesus: Joseph (cf. the Ebionites in Justin-Dial. 48, etc.). But Joseph is not only of Davidic descent according to Matt.

1.16; Luke 3.21, but also according to Luke 1.27, while Mary, according to Luke 1.36, possibly comes from the tribe of Levi, quite independent of the fact that in terms of Jewish principles she had no influence in determining the tribal status of her children (BB 110b; otherwise ProtEvJa. 10.1; Luke 2.4 f. in Syr^sin and Tatian). Jesus was reckoned as an offspring of David. Is this tradition historically credible? Entirely so. For from the very beginning great emphasis was laid upon keeping the blood pure and upon proper proofs of tribal standing. This was the more so because within salvation-history a considerable number of special privileges were bound up with considerations of blood. In NT times the old family trees had been lost or destroyed, though oral tradition had kept them alive, and they were readily quoted (Phil. 3.5; JosVita 1). In particular the heirs of the house of David naturally preserved their family traditions with pride and great expectation (cf. HamRealEnzJdt., s.v. Hillel). Even among the sons and descendants of Joseph the Galilean carpenter there was an oral tradition about their Davidic origin quite independent of the synoptic genealogies and their disagreements, and which was not disowned even in face of great danger (Hegesippus in EusHE. 2.23.13 ff.; cf. 3.12; EpiphHaer. 29.4; Julius Afric in Eus. 1.7.13 f.). The house from which Jesus sprang must have been one of the most exclusive of families, and in any case have repudiated any sort of mixing with non-Jewish blood (cf. n. 295). So the Davidic descent of Jesus means that, in spite of the different Semitic (Talmudic material in Hennecke, *Handb.*, p. 51 ff.; adopted from Celsus in Orig., I, 28.32) and anti-Semitic combinations, he was of pure Jewish blood (otherwise E. Hirsch, *Das Wesen des Christentums*, 1939, p. 158 ff.; W. Grundmann, *Jesus der Galiläaer und das Judentum*, 1940, p. 166 ff.).

337. The passive meaning: the one anointed by God, always remains basic.

338. Cf. also concepts like ἅγιος θεοῦ, μάρτυς πιστός, which at least in the NT become the vehicles of the idea of the passion.

339. Acts 3.14; 7.52; cf. Matt. 27.19; Luke 23.47; JustinDial. 16; allusions to Wisd. 2 in Matt. 27.40, 43, 54. Further, H. Dechent, ThStKr., 1927–8, p. 439 ff.

340. Cf. Driver, Dalman, Euler at the top of Ch. 30. H. W. Wolff, *Isaiah 53 in primitive Christianity*, 1942.

341. Heb. 12.24; 13.11 f.; cf. μεσίτης in Gal. 3.19; I Tim. 2.5; Heb. 8.5 ff.; 9.15.

342. Application to the persecuted saints in Wisd. 2.18; cf. Matt. 27.43.

343. It is quite misleading to equate 'Son of God' with 'Child of God'. Jesus spoke to the disciples about 'his' Father and 'their' Father, never about 'our' Father in heaven (survey in Jackson-Lake, *Beginnings*, I, 402.1). He prays alone, he prays for them in their fellowship, but he never prays a common prayer together with them. He is not 'a' son, but 'the' Son (cf. Luke 10.22; John 20.17).

344. Cf. Ch. 26 and titles like Son of Man, Word and Wisdom.

345. It is quite a familiar thing for the NT to apply theological names and formulae from the OT to christological usage. Cf. e.g. the theological σωτήρ in Luke 1.47; Tit. 3.4 with the christological σωτήρ in Tit. 2.13; 3.6. On names and formulae with *kyrios* see below.

346. John 10.35 ff. points to Psa. 81 (82), where the concept of deity is the fixed description of those in authority. In Ex. 4.16 (cf. Exr. ad. loc.) the con-

cept of deity is a relational one, which passes from Moses to Aaron, cf. Ex. 7.1; ApAbr. 4; Asenath 22.

347. Cf. Rom. 1.25; II Cor. 11.31; Eph. 4.6.

348. Rom. 9.5a and 9.5b belong morphologically and christologically together, like Rom. 1.3 and 1.4.

349. In Acts 20.28 an almost *patripassian* formulation has unintentionally occurred. Cf. the modalist phrasing of Abgar in EusHE. 1.13.7: ὁ θεὸς . . . καταβὰς ἀπὸ τοῦ οὐρανοῦ.

350. This is involved in its liturgical character, cf. Ch. 6.

351. θεός predicatively, anarthrous. Bultmann translates differently.

352. Thus according to the most reliable text and many remarkable patristic citations.

353. The christological use of *theos* cannot be easily explained as one form of ancient apotheosis of men. The early Church rather fought with the same intensity as the OT against any idolization or worship of men (cf. n. 296). If in spite of that she preached the divine majesty of Christ and prayed to him, we can only seek sufficient ground for that in the self-testimony of Jesus Christ in his word, his way and his work.

354. In view of the preceding Χριστός and the following ζωή only Jesus can be meant here.

355. Luke 11.1; 12.41; Matt. 18.21; cf. John 13.13. In such contexts κύριε means no more than διδάσκαλε.

356. Cf. Mark 4.38, διδάσκαλε with Luke 8.24 ἐπίστατα and Matt. 8.25 κύριε, σῶσον, ἀπολλύμεθα.

357. Cf. Matt. 21.3 ff., and on the requisitioning E. v. Dobschütz, ZNW, 1931 (not 1930!), p. 112.

358. Cf. Luke 23.34 and James in EusHE. 2.23.

359. Acts 7.59; cf. κύριε ὁ θεός in Psa. 30.6b.

360. I Cor. 16.22; Did. 10.6 (cf. Ap. 22.20; Acts 7.59 f.). The call to prayer comes from the liturgical formulary of the Synagogue (Schubert-Christaller, p. 36), and its aramaic grammatic form (in the margin of the Greek text!) shows that it had already found its way into the primitive Jerusalem liturgy (cf. Bousset's unhappy attempts to avoid this conclusion, e.g. *Kyrios Christos*, 1913, p. 103; 1931, p. 84; to the contrary F. Büchsel, *Theol. des NT*, 1935, p. 177.3; K. G. Kuhn in KW, s.v. μαραναθά). Agreeing with this is the fact that the name *kyrios* has its established place in the pre-Pauline text of the eucharist and in the pre-Pauline creed (I Cor. 11.20, 23; Ch. 63).

361. Col. 1.16 κυριότητες.

362. That is why the NT teaching about Christ's saving work rests upon the doctrine of his divinity, and the teaching about his divinity depends upon the doctrine of his divine origin.

363. I Cor. 4.8; II Cor. 8.9, 13 (περίσσευμα); 13.4 and Orig. on Matt 13.2 (Klosterm. p. 183), where Jesus says: διὰ τοὺς ἀσθενοῦντας ἠσθένουν.

364. ἐν μορφῇ θεοῦ ὑπάρχον like II Cor. 8.9 πλούσιος ὤν.

365. ἐκένωσεν like II Cor. 8.9 ἐπτώχευσεν.

366. μορφὴν δούλου λαβών.

367. Cf. Rom. 8.24; Gal. 4.9; I Cor. 2.8.

368. ἐν ὁμοιώματι ἀνθρώπου like Rom. 8.3 ἐν ὁμοιώματι σαρκὸς ἁμαρτίας.

369. Οὐχ ἁρπαγμὸν ἡγήσατο τὸ εἶναι ἴσα θεῷ, ἀλλὰ ἑαυτὸν ἐκένωσεν.

The word ἁρπαγμός is unusual (hence the conjecture of ἅρπαγμος, ThStKr, 1932, p. 373 ff.) and ambiguous. It can mean a *res rapta* (something held on to exultantly, such as some prize booty) but it can also mean a *res rapienda* (something that can be snatched for oneself, like some small object of plunder). The meaning of ἁρπαγμός in Phil. 2.6 f. can be determined only in light of the context. In the context the pre-existent one is contrasted by the οὐκ—ἀλλά of the sentence with another figure who in similar circumstances considers equality with God to be something to plunder. Perhaps it is Adam (cf. Gen. 3.5; Rom. 5.12 ff.; Ch. 20)? But Adam is a terrestrial being, whereas the pre-existent Son of God is a heavenly figure. In Gen. 3.5 equality with God consists in knowledge, while in Phil. 2.6 it lies in having a place of divine honour (cf. κενοδοξία 2.3). The concept that Paul has before his mind's eye must, therefore, be that of a heavenly being who wants a place of honour equal to God's. That suits Satan, who was not satisfied with his heavenly nature, but strove after equality of status with God, and now atones for his κενοδοξία by his descent to the deeps (Ch. 13). His opposite is Christ, who in the same tempting situation demonstrated his ταπεινοφροσύνη and has no wish to grasp God's status for himself. So the old contention about ἁρπαγμός is over: equality with God is not a *res rapta*, not (as Barth lays down ad. loc., and which Stählin has regrettably repeated) a position which the pre-existent Christ had and gave up, but it is a *res rapienda*, a possibility of advancement which he declined. With this exegesis agrees not only the whole context of the hymn, but also the oldest interpretation and adaptation of Phil. 2 viz. Heb. 12.2 and the martyr's letter from Lyons in EusHE. 5.1 ff.

370. Διὸ καὶ ὁ θεὸς αὐτὸν ὑπερύψωσεν.

371. Antithesis: ἐχαρίσατο—ἁρπαγμός.

372. Antithesis: εἰς δόξαν θεοῦ—κενεδοξία. The passage Phil. 2.6–11 is neither pre-Pauline (Lohmeyer), since it is one of the characteristically Pauline incarnation formulae, while passion formulae are characteristic of the pre-Pauline period, nor post-Pauline (Barnikol), for it is found worked into Rom. 10.6 ff. (see below, p. 224), but creedal hymn, which Paul composed at an earlier date and quotes here.

373. Matt. 2.29 f.; IgnE. 18.2; 19.2 f.; also Rev. 2.1, 28; 12.16; Dg. 7.2. On the origins of the star motif cf. Yäst 8 (Lommel, p. 46 ff.); VirEcl. 4.6; A. Jirku, *Die Wanderungen der Hebräer*, 1924, p. 15; Gen. 37.9 (cf. Neuss, Kunst, p. 101, Text); Num. 24.17; TestL. 18.3, Dam. 7.18.

374. πνοὴ ζωῆς Gen. 2.7; cf. 15.11.

375. Yet in spite of excluding the blood relationship of Joseph, Matthew and Luke still hold on to his Davidic sonship, not only in the successive or genetic sense, but also in a new legitimizing sense: Joseph of David's house had, according to Matt. 1.20, 24 f. recognized Mary as his wife, thus legitimizing her son according to BB 8.6, and so 'planting' him in the house of David (see SB and Schlatter ad loc.).

376. Cf. n. 264; JustinDial. 69 f.; E. Norden, *Die Geburt des Kindes*, 1924, p. 67 ff.

377. Cf. Moses in PsPhil. 9.2 ff.; Melchizedek in Melch 3 (Bonwetsch): Brierre-Narbonne, 1933, p. 31.

378. See Matt. 1.16, vl.; IgnE. 18.2; JustinDial. 43, etc.; ProtEvJa. 19 f.

379. Why this reserve? Very likely because the Virgin's Son is God on his

Father's side, man on his mother's side, yet not quite either in the full sense. So the idea of *parthenogenesis*, which we find in the early narratives of the synoptics, does justice to neither the complete divinity and divine sonship (cf. John 2.4) nor yet the full humanity and Davidic sonship (Rom. 1.3).

380. The gospel of the incarnation thus spells rejection for the metaphysical doctrine of the schoolmen: *Finitum non capax infiniti*; cf. John 1.5, 10 f., etc.; 20.27; I John 1.1; 4.3; II John 7.

381. See n. 380, cf. John 1.14.

382. κένωσις is the motto of Phil. 2. Another motto, with an equally long history, is required for John 1: κρύψις. The Johannine Christ is not God on his Father's side and man on his mother's, but fully God and fully man (as in Paul), and not simply by turns (so Phil. 2; but see n. 390), but contemporaneously: 'very God and very man together' (cf. John 1.14, 18).

383. See E. Seeberg, op. cit., p. 15 ff.

384. Cf. E. Lohmeyer, 'Und Jesus ging vorüber'. Nieuw ThTijdsskrift, 1934, p. 224.

385. Cf. Dg. 7.4; God sends his divine Son ὡς ἄνθρωπον πρὸς ἀνθρώπους.

386. John 1.14, 18. In the same way the God of the OT tabernacled in the midst of the pilgrim people, and Wisdom in Ecclus. 24.8 tabernacled in the Holy City.

387. Thus at the end God will pitch his tent in his world (Rev. 21.3). The God of scripture is not remote from the world, but neither is he deep down in in our hearts; he is the Lord of heaven who tabernacles amongst us.

388. See Isa. 40.9: εὐαγγελιζόμενος . . . Ἰδοὺ ὁ θεὸς ὑμῶν.

389. Cf. Akhenaton's 'Hymn to the Sun', in A. Erman, *Die Lit. d Ägypter*, 1923, p. 358.

390. Paul would also accept the christological '*Ecce Deus*'; see II Cor. 5.19; Rom. 5.8; Col. 1.19 f.; 2.9. The rulers and children of this age know nothing of it (I Cor. 2.8 f.; II Cor. 4.4). But those who have the Spirit confess the δόξα θεοῦ ἐν προσώπῳ Χριστοῦ. (II Cor. 4.6; cf. 3.18; 5.16; I Cor. 2.10 ff.).

391. The synoptics are fond of salvation miracles; John favours revelation miracles (2.11; cf. 20.30 f.). Cf. Mark 4.38 f. with John 6.19 f.

392. According to John 2.6 something over 100 gallons.

393. For the correlation of the Kingdom of God and the Son of Man (Christ) in the NT see Mark 9.1; 13.26; Rev. 3.20; 11.15; 12.10; Matt. 16.28; Luke 22.29 f.; John 18.36 f.; Luke 11.14 ff.; Matt. 20.21; Luke 23.42; Rev. 1.9; Col. 1.13. Even the Gnostics could describe the Christian message as 'the gospel of the Kingdom of the Son of Man', see Hennecke, p. 70.

394. Cf. Sachs, *Tef.*, p. 152 (אֱלֹהֵינוּ חַיֵּי עוֹלָם נָטַע בְּחוֹכֵנוּ); p. 486 (בְּקִרְבְּךָ). Admittedly POxy 654.16 had already interpreted ἐντὸς ὑμῶν in Luke 17.21 to mean man's inward nature; and Luther (against the Vulgate which rendered *intra vos*) even translated it 'within you'. But against this gnostic interpretation represented in the Oxyrhyncus papyrus stands the most ancient interpretation of this saying of Jesus: Luke places the saying in the framework of a brief story and shows that it was a polemical utterance directed against the Pharisees. But to suggest that in such circumstances Jesus would tell the Pharisees that they had the Kingdom of God in their hearts is an absurdity that we cannot ascribe to the evangelist. Accordingly, Luke could only have meant 'among you' by the phrase ἐντὸς ὑμῶν. (So also M. Dibelius, *Jesus*, 1939, p. 63.) Against Luther's

translation there is also the Semitic translator of the passage. Syrˢⁱⁿ renders ἐντὸς ὑμῶν as *bainath-khum*, Delitzsch as בְּקִרְבְּכֶם, that is to say, both support 'among you'! Christ is the Αὐτοβασιλεία (Orig).

395. In Mark 1.12 it is Satan 'in his own person' who answers the baptismal proclamation with a demonic counter-attack. In Matt. 16.23 he speaks through the mouth of the trusted disciple. In Luke 22.31, 44, 46 the demonic attack on the Son's will takes its most dangerous form, that of a fight between two wills, self-will and God's will (cf. Heb. 2.17 f.; 4.15; 5.7 f.).

396. Mark 4.39; cf. Dg. 7.2 of Christ: ᾧ τὴν θάλασσαν ἰδίοις ὅροις ἐνέκλεισεν . . . ᾧ πειθαρχεῖ . . . θάλασσα.

397. As the Father had given the Son authority over the adversary, so the Son gives it to his disciples, see Luke 10.17 ff.; Mark 16.17; Rom. 16.20.

398. Cf. Luke 24.21; John 6.15; 18.36 f.; Acts 1.6.

399. Luke 10.18; John 12.31 (syr. and o.l.codd. think even here of the rebellion in heaven and read βληθήσεται κάτω).

400. In Ecclus. 24 we are told of the pre-cosmic *Sophia* who came forth out of the mouth of God and called the creation into being (3.9 cf. Prov. 8.22 ff.; Job 28.27). She had her throne in the heavenly places (4 cf. AEn. 42.1 f.). But then, according to the will of the Most High, she took up her abode upon earth, in the people of Israel (8 cf. BBar. 3.37 f.; HEn. 48 D), and was manifested in the form of the Torah (23 cf. BBar. 4.1). Then she lifted up her voice in the midst of 'her people' and called to her 'children' προσέλθετε πρός με (1 f., 18vl, 19 Prov. 8.4 ff.; 9.4 ff.). She promised them food, abundance, splendour and inexhaustible wealth of knowledge (17 ff., 21, 25 ff.; cf. Psa. 64.10; BBar. 4.3 ff.). For *Sophia* is 'light', 'fountain' and 'vine' all at once, the origin and giver of all true life, and in this sense the bearer of the life of salvation (17.25 ff.; cf. Prov. 18.4; 9.11; Psa. 35.10; Ezek. 47.1; Zech. 13.1; SBar. 77.13 ff.; BBar. 4.1 f.).

401. In the Testaments of the Twelve Patriarchs the cardinal concept of *Sophia* is, be it noted, almost entirely absent (it appears only in TestL. 13.7 f.; TestZeb. 6.1). But the idea of a bearer of life is still powerful, and is applied to the Torah (TestL. 14.4b), to historical figures (TestL. 4.3; 18.2; cf. Ecclus. 50.6 ff.; Dan. 2.14; AssMos. 1.14; 11.16 f.), and sometimes it is transferred to the priestly assistants at the time of the end (TestL. 18.2 ff.). The images of 'light' and 'fountain' and 'vine' also survive (TestZeb. 9.8; TestJud. 24.4; TestL. 2.12). At the same time new ideas make their appearance, such as 'word', 'love'. To replace 'wisdom' comes the term Ἀλήθεια (TestA. 5.1 ff.; TestR. 3.8 f.; cf. III Ezra 4.33 ff.); the formula in Dam. 2.12 f. is almost Johannine: רות קרשו והוא אמת

402. John 3.13; 4.41 f.; 7.14 ff., 46; cf. Prov. 18.4; AssMos. 11.16; Mark 1.27; 10.2 ff.; Matt. 5.17 ff.; 7.29.

403. Paul and his disciples talk of history as having a quality of christological promise, John of creation as being a sort of christological parable. Φῶς, ζωή, ἀλήθεια are what they are anywhere in the world only because they are related to that which is 'the light', 'the life' and 'the truth'. Without this christocentric reference they would remain ψεῦδος.

404. John 18.37; 8.13 f.; 5.31 f.; further, R. Schippers, *Getuigen van Jezus Christus*, 1938, p. 165.

405. Luke 18.31 ff.; cf. Mark 9.12. It is obvious that announcements of the passion such as that in Mark 8.31b have been recast *ex eventu*.

406. The 'last word' of the crucified is a problem in itself (cf. App. VI). Jesus cried out. He was thought to say 'Eli' (see Mark 15.34 it. Hebrew: 'My God'!). Some interpreted it ironically of Elijah. Peter and Mark (see Mark 15.34b) understood his cry rightly as the beginning of a prayer from the Hebrew OT, and they complete it with reference to the situation with Psa. 22.2. (John 16.32 defends it from early misinterpretation in the spirit of Wisd. 10.13 f.; TestJos. 1.6: μόνος ἤμην καὶ ὁ θεὸς παρεκάλεσέ με). EvPt. 5.19 goes back to Psa. 21.2 A Σ (So finally Hasenzahl, op. cit., p. 77 ff.). On the effect of other martyr motifs in the passion story cf. H. W. Surkau, *Martyrien in jüdischer und frühchristlicher Zeit*, 1938, p. 82 ff.

407. Cf. Neuss, Kunst, fig. 52; 154; p. 129; Wulff, Kunst, I, p. 199; WilpertM., T, 29; Campenhausen, *Passionssarkophage*, fig. 9. On the whole field see G. Schönermark, *Der Kruzifixus in der bildenden Kunst*, 1908.

408. ActThom. 39: ὁ εἰς πολλοὺς ἀγῶνας ὑπὲρ ἡμῶν (!) ἀγωνιζόμενος. ὁ ἀληθὴς ἀθλητὴς ἡμῶν καὶ ἀήττητος· ὁ στρατηλάτης ἡμῶν ὁ . . . νικήφορος . . . ὁ ἀγαθὸς ποιμὴν ὁ . . . τὸν λύκον νικήσας. Psa. 90.13; cf. Heb. 12.2 f. and KW, s.v. ἀγών.

409. cf. n. 203.

410. It is entirely in accordance with this view that the decisive saying on this subject, Mark 10.45 makes no claim, as is usual (even with sayings about the Son of Man), to any reliance upon a more ancient tradition.

411. Mark 10.45. Previously attempts have been made to discredit the ransom saying as a secondary addition to Mark. But the idea of suffering goes right through the context from 10.32 on, and reaches its climax in the ransom saying. Most play has been made with the absence of any parallel saying in Luke. But Matthew has the saying in the same context and in the same form. Luke has been following another traditional source from the outset here (Luke 18.31 ff. does not derive from Mark 10.32 ff.), lacks some considerable elements entirely (the sayings about the cup of suffering and the baptism of his death) and only later on does he introduce the saying about service (or ransom) in another context. But the idea of service was to be found in Isa. 40 ff. worked out to its conclusion in the concept of vicarious suffering (Isa. 53.11; εὖ δουλεύοντα πολλοῖς; cf. John 13.1 ff.). It is quite consistent with all this that the new context in which Luke places the saying about service is the narrative of the passion!

412. Here, too, Isa. 53, etc., is in the background.

413. Mark 14.24: ὑπὲρ πολλῶν; Matt. 26.28: περὶ πολλῶν εἰς ἄφεσιν ἁμαρτιῶν; Luke 22.19 f.: ὑπὲρ ὑμῶν; I Cor. 11.24: ὑπὲρ ὑμῶν; John 6.51: ἡ σάρξ μού ἐστιν ὑπὲρ τῆς τοῦ κόσμου ζωῆς.

414. Equivalent forms: διά (I Cor. 8.11); περί (I Pet. 3.18), etc.

415. Isa. 53.4 f.: οὗτος τὰς ἁμαρτίας ἡμῶν (MT: חֳלָיֵנוּ; Matt. 8.17: τὰς ἀσθενείας ἡμῶν; John 1.29: τὴν ἁμαρτίαν τοῦ κόσμου) φέρει καὶ . . . παιδεία εἰρήνης ἡμῶν ἐπ' αὐτόν. Cf. Isa. 53.12; Ezek. 4.4 ff.; Gal. 6.2; Mark 10.42 ff.; John 13.15 f.; 15.13.

416. Cf. persecuted but victorious lamb in TestJos. 19.8A.

417. Legends in VitAdEv. (Meyer, p. 52 ff.; Stockbauer, op. cit., p. 141; J. Reil, op. cit., p. 42 f.

418. See Neuss, *Die Kunst der alten Christen*, fig. 183; also Reil, op. cit., p. 51. Further development with the wooden cross (e.g. Springer, II, 1924, p. 429), another form, an independent 'tree of life' at the side of the cross itself (e.g.

Wulff, p. 535). For the idea of the 'tree of life' see Danthine und Bauernreiss at the top of Ch. 20; F. Kampers, Mittelalt. *Sagen v. Paradies u. v. Holze des Lebens,* 1897; Z. Mayani, *L'Arbre Sacré . . . chez les Anciens Sémites,* 1936.

419. On poetry cf. e.g. C. W. M. Grein, *Dichtungen der Angelsachsen,*[2] 1863, I, p. 178 ff.; 188; II, p. 140 ff. On the pictorial arts see e.g. K. Lentzner, *Das Kreuz bei den Angelsachsen,* 1890; W. Viëtor, *Die northumbrischen Runensteine,* 1894. Traditions about the hanging of Odin or Baldur on the tree of the world are in W. Schultz, *Altgerm. Kultur,*[4] 1937, p. 79; 99 f. with fig. 201.

420. Matt. 12.40 f. καρδία (γῆς)=picture of the underworld in Jonah 2.4 (cf. IV Ezra 13.25, 51); similarly κοιλία (ᾅδου) in Jonah 2.3. hades=stomach cavity of the dragon Satan in GBar. 5.

421. Read with Pol. 1.2 ὠδῖνας τοῦ ᾅδου; cf. *Terra Mater* and 'the lap of mother earth' in Psa. 17.6; IV Ezra 4.41 f. (Ecclus. 51.5; Jonah 2.3 MT?).

422. Rom. 10.7; cf. Job 28.22; Jub. 24.31; IV Ezra 4.8. Does the pre-Pauline creed in I Cor. 15.4 reflect the descent into hell (with the word ἐτάφη)?

423. Acts 2.24; on λύειν cf. ApAbr. 10.

424. TestJos. 1.6: ὁ ὕψιστος ἀνήγαγέν με.

425. From the period of the early Church cf. AscIs. 9.16, etc.; MelSard. 8.4 (Goodspeed); EusHE. 1.13.20; EvNicod. 2.5 (Tischendorf, p. 306 ff.); Act-Thom. 10.115; cf. 256, 265; Schatzhöhle, p. 70 f. In addition the syncretistic motif of saviour who needs saving (cf. Ischtar AOT, p. 206 ff.) is to be found in gnostic poetry (ActThom. 108 ff.); traces in the mandaean writings.

426. AEn. 6 f.; 10; 12 ff.; GEn. 12.5 (οὐκ ἔσται ὑμῖν εἰρήνη οὔτε ἄφεσις); 16.4.

427. I Pet. 4.6. According to Ecclus. 25.5 the descent of *Sophia* (AEn. 42.2) goes right into the abyss. It would, therefore, seem to be presupposed that she carries with her into the darkness the light of the law or of God's Word; cf. Job 38.16; BBar. 3.30; IV Ezra 4.8; HEn. 48D; Rom. 10.7 and early addition in Ecclus. 24.32 which removes the motif from the past into the future (C. Schmidt, TU, 43, p. 473.2; cf. 86 f.).

428. JosAnt. 1.74; II Pet. 2.5; I Cl. 7.6; cf. Noah's intercession in Ezek. 14.14; II Cl. 6.8.

429. I Pet. 3.19 f. (in contrast to AEn. 65.11: From these things there is no conversion for ever). From the early Church cf. EvPt. 41 f.; JustinDial. 72.4; EpAp. 27 (Duensing, p. 23); Sib. 8.310 ff.; 1.377 ff.; IrenCHaer. 4.27.2; Schatzhöhle, p. 70 f.

430. Cf. the grave in AOB, fig. 242.

431. By the antithesis of ἐτάφη and ἐγήγερται in I Cor. 15.4.

432. In comparing Christ's burial with immersion in the waters of baptism (Rom. 6.4; Col. 2.12) he uses the baptismal immersion as an analogy of Christ's emergence from the tomb. He thus leaves the tomb behind empty. For the Christ who was raised up on Easter Day is for Paul the prototype of the Christians who will be raised up on the last day (Ch. 37). But on the last day the graves will be empty (cf. John 5.28 f.; Matt. 27.52; Ch. 58 ff.).

433. By their desperate recourse to a story of theft the Jews tried to trifle with the fact, but the only result was that they had themselves to recognize the fact of the empty tomb as something incontestable (Matt. 28.15). Perhaps it is possible to associate the inscription fron Nazareth published in 1930 with these rumours of the theft of Christ's body, as Cumont and Loesch suggest. The problem of the inscription is the question as to how and where it was actually

found in Nazareth (cf. F. Cumont, RevHist., 1930, p. 241 f.). But among other things its genuineness is supported by the fact that such cautionary warnings were by no means uncommon in ancient Judaism, cf. S. Krauss, *Synagog. Altertümer*, 1922, p. 230; 233 f.; 235.

434. Dürer in Preuss, op. cit., fig. 68. Cf. Fra Bartolommeo in K. Künstle, *Ikonographie*, I, 1928, fig. 280 and the closed door of the tomb on the ivory table of the Bayr. Nationalmuseums in Schönewolf, op. cit., p. 75.

435. Cf. I Cor. 15.5 ff.; Luke 24.34; Gal. 1.15 (antimaterialistic), but also Acts 1.3; 10.41; Luke 24.36 ff.; John 20.27 (antispiritualistic).

436. Luke 24.37: $\pi\nu\epsilon\hat{\upsilon}\mu\alpha$ (vl. $\phi\acute{\alpha}\nu\tau\alpha\sigma\mu\alpha$); IgnSm. 3.2: $\delta\alpha\iota\mu\acute{o}\nu\iota\upsilon\nu$ $\dot{\alpha}\sigma\acute{\omega}\mu\alpha\tau\upsilon\nu$.

437. For, according to I Cor. 15.35 ff., 49, he is the prototype of our future $\sigma\hat{\omega}\mu\alpha$ $\pi\nu\epsilon\upsilon\mu\alpha\tau\iota\kappa\acute{o}\nu$. I Cor. 15.12 ff. tells us that in Christ God has wrought something that he has never accomplished before. This disposes at one and the same time of two misinterpretations of the Easter occurrences: the metaphysical (which thinks of Easter as simply a pattern of the essential immortality of the soul) and the occult (which views Easter as a materialization of a departed spirit).

438. I Cor. 15.4; cf. Luke 9.22; 18.33; 24.7, 46; John 2.19; Mark 8.31; 9.31: instead of a scripture proof text.

439. And are then expanded like the prepositional modifications in Rom. 3.25 f.

440. There are numerous instances of ascension to heaven in ancient art and literature (cf. n. 309), and not a few in the old biblical tradition: temporary ascensions, often thought of as bodily journeyings (GEn. 12.1; ApAbr. 15; TestAbr. 8). Final ascensions, originally conceived as bodily journeys (see App. VI). The rabbis disowned these traditions in contending against the Christian gospel of the ascension: 'if a man says . . I will ascend into heaven, he will not accomplish it' (j Taan 2.1).

441. Acts 1.2: $\dot{\alpha}\nu\epsilon\lambda\acute{\eta}\mu\phi\theta\eta$ instead of $\delta\iota\acute{\epsilon}\sigma\tau\eta$.

442. On farewell scenes and speeches in the ancient world see Stauffer in RAC, s.v. 'Abschiedsreden'.

443. Col. 3.3 f.; $\dot{\epsilon}\nu$ $\tau\hat{\omega}$ $\theta\epsilon\hat{\omega}$ = בָּאלֹהִים = with God = in heaven—as in Paral-Jer. 9.6: $\kappa\acute{\upsilon}\rho\iota\epsilon$ . . . $\hat{\omega}$ $\pi\hat{\alpha}\sigma\alpha$ $\kappa\tau\acute{\iota}\sigma\iota\varsigma$ (not, as Harris, $\kappa\rho\acute{\iota}\sigma\iota\varsigma$) $\kappa\acute{\epsilon}\kappa\rho\upsilon\pi\tau\alpha\iota$ $\dot{\epsilon}\nu$ $\alpha\dot{\upsilon}\tau\hat{\omega}$ = אֲשֶׁר בּוֹ = with whom (aeth!). Cf. also Wisd. 3.1; ParalJer. 5.32; AEn. 39.7; 40.5; 48.6; 62.7; John 1.1, 18; Eph. 3.9; IgnE. 19.

444. SBar. 13.3 etc.; cf. AEn. 42.2; 70.3; SEn. 67, etc. (late revised form, in Melch. 4, Bonwetsch).

445. Christ's royal session at the right hand of God's throne is mentioned by Mark 12.36; 16.19; Acts 2.29 f.; Rev. 2.28; 3.21.

446. Christ standing to intercede at the right hand before God's throne is mentioned by Heb. 7.25; 9.24 (otherwise 8.1); Rev. 12.5; Acts 7.55 f.; cf. Enoch (AEn. 64.5; 67.2; 89.52); Michael (TestL. 3.5; 5.6), etc.

447. Cf. E. Strong and N. Joliffe in Journal Hellenistic Studies, 1924, I, p. 65 ff.; J. Carcopino, *La Basilique Pythagoricienne de la Porte Majeure*, 1926; Alföldi, RömMitt., 1935, p. 132 f.

448. Traces of the Ancient of Days and of the insignia of Yahweh, e.g. in Rev. 1.12, 13b, 14 ff. A. v. Gennep (see head of Ch. 6) thinks that in Revelation we have a picture of the worship of a Johannine community, but is certainly wrong. But quite likely our chapter with its blending of the picture of God and of

Christ has had an effect on the later representations of Jesus' outward appearance, and especially on the representations of early Church and Byzantine art. (see ZNW, 1910, p. 241); cf. G. Millet, *Monuments de l'Athos*, I, 1927, pl. 110; *L'Anciendes Jours*; Wµlff, op. cit., p. 565. So the *ecce deus* of NT christology finds its fullest expression in art.

449. Rev. 12.1 ff.; cf. the persecution of the lamb in TestJos. 19.8A and the withdrawal of the lamb to God's throne in AEn. 89.52 (Rev. 5.5 ff.).

450. E.g. λογίζεσθαι; ἀρέσκειν; εὐδοκία; δεκτός; παρὰ θεῷ; ἐνώπιον, ἐναντίον, ἔμπροσθεν τοῦ θεοῦ.

451. Lev. 11 f.; Num. 19 (cf. SNu. 1.23 on 19.2); Psa. 51.9; Ezek. 36.25. The old biblical conception of the sacraments is strongly theonomic, and avoids any kind of magic or moralistic false interpretation.

452. I Kings 16.10 ff.; Wisd. 2.15 ff.; Esth. 3.13d–g; Micah 5.6; Zech. 9.9; AssMos. 12.7 f.; cf. I Cor. 1.27; Rom. 2.29.

453. SB. III, 121; II, 40.

454. Akiba in Ab. 3; SB. I, II; II, 360; 605; III, 15 ff.; 673 ff.

455. Akiba in San. 19a; Juda in Ab. 1; SB. on Matt. 1.25; also I, 590; II, 542; 556 ff.; Bacher, *Agada der Tannaiten*, p. 283; 323; 350.

456. Rabbi Isaac (*c.* 300 A.D.), etc., in SB on John 3.3; cf. II, 162; III, 15 ff.; 673 ff.; Sachs, Tef. p. 220; 636 (*liphnê*!); A. Büchler, *Atonement in the Rabbinic Literature*, 1928.

457. Elsewhere, too, formulas of assurance control thought, see Rom. 4.6 ff.; Luke 15.21 (cf. JosBell. 1.635); 3.22; 12.32; 6.21 (cf. PsSol. 8.33). Nevertheless, the NT has not just taken over the OT principle of validity, but radicalized it, cf. n. 474; 482.

458. This is the meaning of II Cor. 6.2—the authentic exposition of II Cor. 5.17!

459. The gospel of the new relationship between God and man is not the only thing that the NT writers have to say about the new world situation, but it is the greatest. To romantics and millenarians, to moralists and activists such a gospel seems confined. But Anselm's saying applies to them: *Nondum consideras ti, quanti ponderis sit peccatum* (cf. Gen. 39.9; Psa. 50.6; Dan. 9.7; also JosAnt. 7.320). But this gospel meant a great deal to the Reformers. For to them the question of man's standing before God became again one that was bound up with existence itself, and so became the fundamental question of all theology. So, with the NT in their hand, they fought for an understanding of the new situation of the world in terms of its 'standing' or 'validity' as over against one based on its pure essentiality: *Extra nos* the decisive change in things has taken place, *coram deo*.

460. So Luke 10.4 ff.; in Matt. 10.11 this is made to depend on a moral judgement in Matt. 10.11.

461. This is why Isa. 52.7 is expanded in Acts 10.36 by the addition of διὰ Ἰησοῦ Χριστοῦ to εἰρήνη.

462. The doxology in Luke 2.14 is in the form of a two-part antiphony, whose second line runs:

ἐπὶ γῆς εἰρήνη ἐν ἀνθρώποις εὐδοκίας
בָּאָרֶץ שָׁלוֹם בְּאַנְשֵׁי רְצוֹנוֹ

The subject here, then, is neither *bona voluntas* understood moralistically, nor yet international peace in a pacifistic sense, but the *benevolentia* of God (cf. Delitzsch, and KW, s.v. εὐδοκία).

463. Col. 2.14. In ApAn. 12 (TU, 2.3a, 1899, p. 55) the apocalyptist prays: 'Oh, that thou wouldest blot out the roll of my writing.' In the prayer of preparation for the day of atonement are the words: 'Our Father, Our King, destroy thou our condemnation (רֹעַ גְּזַר דִּינֵנוּ) . . . cancel (מְחוֹק) all the documents (שְׁטָרֵי) of our offences (Sachs, *Tef.*, p. 590). In HEn. 26.12 the seraphim, on the day that God assumes power, burn the charges against Israel. When the Roman emperors took the throne they made a point of announcing a remission of taxes, and as a sign of it they had the tax tables burnt (cf. O. Jaeger, *Geschichte des Altertums*,[6] 1903, fig. 511). In Exr. on 12.12 we have the parallel drawn in parabolic form, and the divine remission of debt compared with the imperial (I. Ziegler, *Die Königsgleichnisse des Midrasch*, 1903, overlooks this).

464. Cf. Matt. 26.28; John 1.29. The χάρις, which finds its pinnacle in the acquittal of men, is, as Augustin understands it, an antecedent (I John 4.10; Rom. 9.11 ff.), and irresistible (Rom. 11), indeed an invincible (cf. Rom. 3.8; 6.1) and inexhaustible (Eph. 2.4 ff.; I Pet. 4.10) grace. But it is in no sense *gratia infusa*. It is an event that happens exclusively *extra nos*. Precisely on this account it is removed from the ups and downs of our subjective states, and the conflicts of our experience (cf. I Cor. 15.10; II Cor. 12.8; Heb. 13.9; Acts 20.24, 32). The Father, who loved us, and sent us in his grace his eternal comfort, accompanies us throughout our lives, and keeps faith with us; he comforts our hearts and strengthems us in every good word and work (II Cor. 1.3; II Thess. 2.16 f.; cf. I Cor. 10.13; Rom. 1.7). On the actualization of grace see n. 607.

465. Ἱλαστήριον in hellenistic literature stands for the expiation that man provides for the appeasement of the gods. But this usage does not fit here, since it is God himself who erects the altar of expiation. So the roots of our idea are not in hellenism. We must look for them in the LXX.

466. In the LXX the word ἱλαστήριον belongs to the technical terms associated with the great day of atonement, and indicates the cover of the ark which Moses once made at God's command (Ex. 25.17 ff.). On the great day of atonement (*Yom Kippur*) this cover (כַּפֹּרֶת) was sprinkled with the blood of the sacrifice to secure atonement with God and the purification of the people (Lev. 16.11 ff.; ἱλαστήριον has the same meaning in PhilCher. 25; VitMos. 2.95 ff. and Heb. 9.5). The *Yom Kippur* is to some extent raised to a higher power in the ἐνιαυτὸς ἀφέσεως, which was proclaimed every 7×7 years, and was taken to restore the *status quo ante* (Lev. 25.9 f.). IV Mac. uses the noun ἱλαστήριον in the context of a theology of martyrdom (cf. Ch. 30). God (*he* is the subject here) has not only allowed, but actually willed the death of the seven martyrs. For he has saved Israel διὰ τοῦ αἵματος τῶν εὐσεβῶν ἐκείνων καὶ τοῦ ἱλαστηρίου τοῦ (!) θανάτου αὐτῶν. (Reading with א, Fritzsche, Rahlfs—against A. Swete, Deissmann, Büchsel, KW: τοῦ ἱλαστηρίου θανάτου. *Homoioteleuton!*). Through these martyrs God begins a new epoch in the history of Israel (IV Mac. 17.20, 22; 18.4 f.; cf. the similar II Mac. 7.37 f; 8.2 ff.; also the traditions of the martyrdom of Akiba, etc., on the great day of atonement, MidrPr. on 9.2; MidrHL. on 7.9). The *Yom Kippur* of Lev. 16 is valid for a year (retrospectively). The great day of atonement of Lev. 25 is valid for half a century. The death of the seven martyrs is valid for a whole epoch—an epochal day of atonement.

467. The historically inclusive day of atonement works retrospectively. But what comes of the debt with which man is burdened after the atonement has been effected? Paul had already put this to himself and pointed the way to an answer in Rom. 8.34 (cf. I John 2.1 f. and Ch. 33). Hebrews has taken this to its conclusion (7.25 ff.; 9.12 ff., 24 ff.).

468. Ritschl (op. cit.) starts with 'justification'.

469. Rom. 3.25: εἰς τὸ εἶναι αὐτὸν δίκαιον.

470. Justification is a forensic idea. The basic idea is of a God who judges and passes judgement on man. In this sense we find the term already in our rabbinic saying about the great day of atonement (Ch. 34). Paul uses the word in the same sense (*iustificare* accordingly means 'to declare righteous'). But this sentence is not based upon man's works, but upon the work of Jesus Christ. So justification is not (to use the language of Ritschl) an analytic judgement announcing the righteousness of the innocent, but a synthetic judgement, which ascribes righteousness to the guilty. Justification is not based on man's nature as such. But neither does it change this conception in any way! So justification is never to make righteous, and so altering the essential condition of man, but always a declaring righteous, that determines man's standing before God. So Luther's translation rightly speaks of a 'righteousness that counts with God' (Rom. 3.21). So the justified person is righteous and sinful together, righteous before God, but in himself a sinner. And this he is, first and last and all the time. For God certainly acquits man of his debt. But he does not set him free from his inherited necessity of having to sin. The man who is justified, just because he is justified constantly returns to God with the cry: God be merciful to me, a sinner (Luke 18.13). The disciple must always pray: Forgive us our trespasses (Matt. 6.12). And the Church's prayer must always be: *Kyrie eleison!* (Rom. 8.34; Heb. 7.25 ff.; 9.12 ff.). 'When our Lord and Master Jesus Christ spoke the words: "Repent", he meant that the whole life of believers should consist of repentance' (Luther, Thesis 1).

471. Rom. 3.25: εἰς τὸ εἶναι αὐτὸν . . . δικαιοῦντα θεοῦ; cf. Rom. 3.24 δικαιούμενοι δωρεάν; Rom. 1.17; 3.21 f.: δικαιοσύνη θεοῦ.

472. εἰς οτ πρὸς ἔνδειξιν τῆς δικαιοσύνης αὐτοῦ.

473. Cf. F. Loofs, ThStKr., 1917.

474. The whole work of atonement and justification is in the last resort meant to serve the glory of God (Luke 2.14). The Pharisee in Luke 18.11 derives his great delight from himself. There are deeper thinkers in the Synagogue than this self-righteous Pharisee (see n. 232; 236). But even the most profound book of late Judaism, IV Ezra, thinks in terms of a surviving remnant of the righteous, who are to take their places in heaven with all the pride of a victor (7.92 ff., 139). But in Rom. 3.27 Paul exclaims: ποῦ οὖν ἡ καύχησις? ἐξεκλείσθη! On this view of things the whole of mankind is under sin, and none is great save God himself. Rom. 3.21 ff., indeed the whole epistle to the Romans is one unparalleled doxology to God, who is himself righteous, and yet proclaims the sinner righteous. God's honour requires that the weight of guilt should not be taken lightly. But the same God also engages his honour in saving men from their hopelessly heavy indebtedness. The solution which his omnipotence finds is the work of atonement. So the cross is the token of God's honour (Anselm). The cross is the end of self-glorification (cf. Luke 7.35). For we have to admit that God is in the right, and in face of the cross acknowledge his severity and

his goodness, and confess in our prayers of confession and thanksgiving that without God we were lost, hopelessly at the very point of death (Luther). The work of atonement and justification is the decisive victory of the divine glory (Calvin).

475. λύτρωσις, ἀπολύτρωσις.

476. Cf. DaΘ. 6.9; Esth. 1.19; 8.8; SBar. 48.27: 'My statutes require their right, and my judgement its own in its turn.'

477. Luke 1.71, 79; Acts 26.18; Gal. 1.4; Rom. 6.18; 8.2; Col. 1.13 f.; I Pet. 2.9; Rev. 1.5; ApEl. 20 f. Comparative hellenistic material to be found in K. Latte, op. cit., p. 108 ff. and DeissmannLAE, p. 275 ff.

478. On Col. 2.12 ff. see F. J. Dölger, *Die Sonne der Gerechtigkeit*, 1918, p. 129 ff. Here are the presuppositions behind the passionate fight against the hellenistic and judaic (AEn. 60.11 f.; TestSol. p. 31 f.; 51 f.) astrology; see Gal. 4.9; Dg. 7.2; Athenag. 16; TheophAutol. 1.35; Tatian. Graec. 9, p. 107; KgP. in ClAlStrom. 6.5.39 ff.

479. For a history of the forerunners of Christian signs of salvation cf. circumcision (Gen. 17.13 f.; Ex. 4.24 f.; Rom. 4.11; Barn. 9.8; Schubert-Christaller, p. 54; TertMarc. 3.22), passover blood on the door-posts (Ex. 12.13) tetragram or the sign of the law on the door-post, clothing, phylactery, hand, etc. (Ex. 28.36; Wisd. 18.24; Pes. 7.7; JosAnt. 4.213; Meg. 24b; EpAr. 158; cf. JosAnt. 8.47 f.; TestSol. 1.6 ff.; TestJb. 47). This can be transposed into eschatology (Isa. 44.5; Ezek. 9.1 ff. (תָו =σημεῖον), in Dam. 19.11 f. (=תיו) messianically interpreted, according to the exegesis of the early Church =*crux Christi*). There is a confrontation of saving and damning signs in PsSol. 15.6 ff.

480. Tim. 2.19; cf. OdSol. 4.7 f.; 8.15. Similar material in C. Schmidt, *Kopt. Gnost. Schriften* I, 1905, p. 295 f. On the attack of the powers of hell upon the elect see Luke 11.4; 22.31 ff.; John 16.33; Rev. 12.7 ff.; Rom. 8.23; II Cor. 12.7; I Pet. 5.8.

481. OdSol. 42.20; cf. the Naassener hymn in HippRef. 5.10.2.

482. Rev. 7.3; 9.1 ff.; 14.1 ff.; 22.4; ApEl. 20 (cf. Matt. 16.18; Luke 22.31 f.). In PsSol. it is the righteous that are sealed, but in Rev. 14 it is the justified. This is the way in which the NT gives its radical treatment to the principle of validity!

483. See EgCO. 45 f. = TU 6.4, 1891, p. 93; 99 (catechumen; cf. Barn. 9.7 f.; 11.1); ActThom. 49 (the possessed); ActJ. 115 (self-crucifixion of the dying); ApConst. 8.12.4 (τρόπαιον τοῦ σταυροῦ); A. Deissmann, *Ein Originaldokument aus der diokl. Christenverfolgung*, 1902; H. Koch, *Die altchr. Bilderfrage nach den lit. Quellen*, 1917, p. 47 ff.

484. HipCan. 29.2.247 ff. = TU., op. cit., p. 134 f.; TertCor. 3, etc.

485. Ph.Schaff., *Gesch.d.alten Kirche*, III,² 1869, p. 878; Dict. AC, s.v. *croix*. On fish, star, sunbeam and other marks of salvation see Dölger and Stuhlfauth, op. cit.

486. The mock-crucifix in J. Leipoldt, *Umwelt* (Bilderatlas) fig. 80, is one of the oldest proofs for the existence of crucifixes. Further see Reil, op. cit.

487. At first we find the literary testimony to using the sign of the cross as a prayer, and after that come the first crosses on Christian monuments, and finally the representation of the crucified and the crucifixion. This order is significant for the origins and development of Christian art generally; cf. n. 603.

488. Indirect evidence in Lev. 19.28; Deut. 14.1 f.; II Mac. 12.40 ff.; Barn. 9.8.

489. Cf. the swastika from Teleilat Ghassul in East Jordan, 4000–3000 B.C. (discovered 1929–32, cf. A. Jirku, *Forschungen und Fortschritte*, 1938, p. 220), which Stuhlfauth was unaware of when he wrote (op. cit., p. 219 f.): 'the swastika was unknown to the culture of Mesopotamia . . . just as it was to that of Palestine.' On the analogy of the cross and the sign of life, cf. SocrHE. 5.17 and Irene with the sign of life in El. Bagauat in Wulff, op. cit., p. 99.

490. Rev. 13.16 f.; 14.9; cf. Bousset, *Antichrist*, p. 132 ff.; also the imperial temple in DeissmannLAE., p. 289, and the antithetic correlation of Rev. 7 and Rev. 13 in iconography, see Neuss, 'Die Apokalypse in der altspan. Buchillustration', Tafelband Nr 236 and 261.

491. Mg. 5.1; cf. Wisd. 3.9; OrigCel. 6.27. Prudentius opposes the very painful branding in the heathen cults with the suffering of the martyrs (Peristephanon 10.1080, 1091 ff. Bergmann, p. 409 f.).

492. F. J. Dölger, AC, 1930, p. 268 f.

493. On Julian's antipathy to the cross see Stockbauer, op. cit., p. 85; 93 f.

494. I Cor. 15.22. Deissmann has given a mystical interpretation to the formula ἐν Χριστῷ. E. Lohmeyer, *Grundlagen paul.Theol*, 1929, p. 139 ff., and Schmauch, op. cit., argue against this position and speak with more accuracy of a 'Christ-metaphysic'. We go a step further and see in this phrase an expression of a christocentric theology of history. For Paul uses the formula ἐν Χριστῷ in antithetic analogy with ἐν Ἀδάμ (cf. also ἐν νόμῳ Rom. 2.12; 3.19). But it is impossible to talk of a mystic communion with Adam. Adam is much rather a fateful and determinative symbol raised over a whole world.

495. The old biblical tradition planted the idea of μίμησις θεοῦ (EpAr. 188; 190; 192; 207; Sota. 14a; cf. Luke 6.36; Matt. 5.44 f., 48; Eph. 5.6; IgnTr. 1.2). The NT speaks about following and imitating Christ (John 8.12; Rev. 14.14; IgnPhld. 7.2). Christ is the 'type' (cf. Adam in Rom. 5.14). Christians are his μιμηταί (I Cor. 11.1; I Thess. 6; Literature in PrBau., s.v.). He is the original picture, we are mere copies (I Cor. 15.49; II Cor. 3.18; Phil. 3.21; Rom. 6.5; cf. ὑπόδειγμα in John 13.15; ὑπογραμμός in I Pet. 2.21; I Cl. 16.17): 'The thing that happened in Christ, that God himself came in the flesh, that he died and rose again, is constantly repeated in the life of the Christian' (E. Seeberg, *Wer ist Christus*, 1937, p. 43). But it does not happen to us precisely in the same way as it took place in Christ, but because it happened in his coming. Christ's coming is not a pattern, but a principle in the strongest assertion of both meanings of that word: beginning and norm. The way of Christ is the *nomos* which henceforth stands above the guiding principles of our own way of living. We are Χριστονόμοι (Gal. 6.2; IgnR. Inscr.). Christ is the firstborn, we are his younger brethren, who must be made like him (Rev. 1.5; Col. 1.18; Rom. 8.29; Phil. 3.10). He is the firstfruits, which promise a harvest to come. But there are other formulae in which the way of Christ is seen as a prototype, and particularly in the phrase σὺν Χριστῷ (see Lohmeyer, *Festschr. f. A. Deissmann*). We die with him, we live with him—'conformed' to him, as Paul himself puts it (σύμμορφοι in Rom. 8.29; Phil. 3.21; σύμφυτοι τῷ ὁμοιώματι τοῦ θανάτου αὐτοῦ in Rom. 6.5; further ὁμοίωμα in IgnTr. 9.2) not contemporaneous with him, as is taught in Bultmann's school. To disregard time reference at this point is to destroy the whole conception (cf. Ch. 16). For the formula σὺν

Χριστῷ expressly points back to the historical priority of the coming of Christ (Rom. 5 f.) and excludes any sort of metaphysical contemporaneity.

496. Cf. Luke 14.27p from Q. The saying is thus given a fivefold place in the tradition.

497. Even the 'descent into hell', which the apostles make in their μίμησις Χριστοῦ, serves their mission in the history of salvation, see Herm. 9.16.5 ff.

498. Ἐκκλησία in the LXX is the *terminus technicus* for *Qahal* which is the covenant community united in the worship of the Lord, and assembled together to worship him. Less frequently the LXX uses the word ἐκκλησία (as an alternative for the word συναγωγή) as a translation for the idea of 'gathering' (עֵדָה, כְּנִשְׁתָּה, cf. AEn. 46.8). Which meaning fits ἐκκλησία in Matt. 16.18? K. L. Schmidt goes for 'gathering' (כְּנִישְׁתָּא), admittedly not without reservation and reinterpretation. Delitzsch on the other hand stands for the covenant community (קְהִלָּה). This is correct, for the context demands this expression as a correlative to the ideas of the Messiah and the Son of Man (Ch. 4; 28). The use of ἐκκλησία in the OT formulae in Acts 7.38 and Heb. 2.12 agrees with this, as does a parallel enquiry into the idea of the assembly (συναγωγή, כנישתה, עדה). In the NT συναγωγή is almost always used for the Jewish synagogue, often in a polemical tone (Matt. 19.17p; 23.6p; Acts 22.19; 26.11; only once does συναγωγή stand for a Christian place of assembly, in the Ebionite passage Jas. 2.2). How fundamental this aversion from the word 'synagogue' is in the NT is indicated by the translation of Psa. 74.2 in Acts 20.28. The MT says 'assembly' (עדה), the LXX συναγωγή; Acts 20 quotes the relevant words and applies them to the Christian Church, but translates with the word ἐκκλησία, not with συναγωγή.

499. Jub. 1.17, etc. Cf. Sachs, *Tef.*, p. 316.

500. Acts 3.25; Gal. 4.24; Heb. 8.6. Cf. Jer. 31.31 ff. (quoted in Mark 14.24; Heb. 8.8 ff.; 10.16) and the Damascus community's description of itself in Dam. 6.19; 19.34; 20.12.

501. Not in tribal history, but salvation-history, see Gal. 6.16; Rom. 9.6; cf. 2.28 f.; Rev. 2.9; Herm.s. 9.17.1; Luke 3.8; Rom. 4.16 f.; Gal. 3.7; Heb. 2.16.

502. Isa. 10.22 quoted in Rom. 9.27; cf. Rom. 11.4 f.

503. JosAnt. 18.64: τὸ φῦλον τῶν Χριστιανῶν.

504. I Pet. 2.9 (MartPol. 14.1 γένος δικαίων); cf. Th. Spoerri, *Der Gemeindegedanke im* 1P, 1925.

505. See n. 86.

506. People of the saints (Dan. 7.27; Ex. 28.36; Rev. 13.7; Eph. 1.18) = those sanctified by God (Did. 10.5), the predestined (Rom. 1.7; Col. 3.12) = the sealed (Rev. 7.4; I Cl. 59.2). The angels are likewise called ἅγιοι θεοῦ (Psa. 67.36; II Thess. 1.10): the *numerus praedestinatorum* is the replacements for the ejected angels, and the elect saints will in the time to come be the associates of the heavenly host.

507. The figures of fish, fishing and fishnets had their origin in the circles about Jesus and the original apostles. They then quickly became ecclesiological images, and were mingled with ancient traditions in Christian art; cf. G. Dalman, *Arbeit und Sitte in Pal VI*, 1939, p. 356 ff., and Dölger, *Ichthys*, at the top of Ch. 36.

508. John 10.12 ff.; I Pet. 2.25; Heb. 13.20; Matt. 9.36; 26.31; John 21.15 ff. (cf. Psa. 76.21; SBar. 77.13); Acts 20.28; I Pet. 5.2 f.; Eph. 4.11.

509. Herm.v. 5; s. 6 f.

510. Isa. 5.1 ff.; 27.2 ff.; Psa. 79.9 ff.; PsPhil. 12.8 f. The *massa perditionis* is a dying forest (Wisd. 4.3 ff.; Ecclus. 10.15 ff.; PhilExsecr. 171 f.). The people of God is a Garden of Paradise (PsSol. 14.3 f.; cf. OdSol. 38.20 f.).

511. To the same circle of imagery belong the cornfield (Mark 4.3 ff.; I Cor. 3.6 ff.; II Tim. 2.6), the fig tree (Luke 13.6 ff.), the mustard seed (Matt. 13.32), the olive tree (Rom. 11.16 ff.; cf. Ezek. 17, etc.), the harvest (Rev. 14.14 ff.; cf. Joel 4.13), the elm and the vine (Herm.s. 2 ff.; 8). Cf. Sprenger, *PalästJbch*, 1913, p. 79 ff.; H. Beer, Ἀπαρχή, 1914.

512. Rev. 2.7; 22.2; The idea of God's planting is confused with that of God's building in Isa. 5.2; ArmEzra 6.54; Mark 12.1; I Cor. 3; Rev. 21 f.; Herm.s. 1 f.

513. See the picture of the tower of Nineveh, eighth–seventh century B.C., in Th. Dombart, Der bab.Turm. Further Gressmann, op. cit.

514. Vendid. 2.1 ff. (Yima saves the remnant of mankind in his cubic stronghold); Bwd. 29.4 (stronghold beneath the hill Yimyan); cf. Geldner, p. 28 ff.; Christensen, II, p. 23 ff.

515. See Gressmann, Jeremias, Wetzel and Weissbach, op. cit; Th. Dombart . . . 'Zum Babelturmproblem', Festschr. f. F. Hommel, I, 1917; A. J. Wensinck, . . . 'The Navel of the Earth' . . . Ak.te, Amsterdam, 1934. A rich source for oriental motifs in biblical and Christian transformations is *Schatzhöble* (ed. C. Bezold).

516. Matt. 5.35; Rev. 11.2; 20.9. WilpertM., Pl. 73 f. Particular building materials, particular buildings, pieces of construction and individual builders were drawn into this circle of imagery; cf. PrBau. or KW, s.v. ἀκρογωνιαῖος, ἑδραίωμα, θεμέλιος, κεφαλὴ γωνίας, λίθος, ναός, οἰκοδομή, οἶκος θεοῦ, πέτρα, στῦλος, τέχνιτης. The tower of Babel in Gen. 11 led to the scattering of the peoples. The old biblical apocalyptic used the picture of the tower as a figure of the temple and of the paradisal city (AEn. 87.3; 89.50 ff.; cf. Barn. 16.5; Lueken, Michael, p. 125). In Acts 2 the Church creates a new community of peoples, in which the confusion of tongues is overcome. In direct consequence of this the Church appears later on under the figure of a tower (Herm.v. 3; s. 9; cf. Eph. 2.20 ff. and Ephraem in ZNW, 1914, p. 8 f.). In Gen. 11.4 the tower of Babel is meant to reach up to heaven—a sure sign of man's self-glorification. In an apocalypse of the early Church (Sib. 5.252) the future city of God reaches up to the clouds—a true token of God's glory.

517. Gal. 4.26; Heb. 12.22; Rev. 3.12; 21.2 ff.; cf. Isa. 54.11 ff.; Tob. 13.16; IV Ezra 7.6; 8.50 ff.; 10.27; 13.36; SBar. 4.1 ff. The ancient east thought of the world as a foursquare building, just as Iranian mythology conceived of Yima's castle. The future Jerusalem is pictured as foursquare in Ezek. 48.16; Herm.v. 3.2.5, cubic in Rev. 21.17, as is the Holy Rock in Herm.s. 9.2.1 f.

518. Phil. 3.20: πολίτευμα does not mean 'behaviour' nor yet 'colony' (Dibelius), but on the contrary the capital or native city, which keeps the citizens on its registers (Tert. Erasm. Stephen; LutherWA., 26.425). Philo understood in this way the whole group of ideas associated with πολίτευμα (e.g. Jos. 69; ConfLing. 78). This meaning is really required by the construction in Phil. 3.20 (ἐξ οὗ = ἐκ τοῦ πολιτ. not = ἐκ τῶν οὐραν.), by the context (locality, political situation), the terms of advent theology (ἐν, ὑπάρχειν, κύριος, σωτήρ), and the situation in which the letter was written. Philippi was a Roman military colony granted the municipal rights of the *ius italicum* i.e. free from the general super-

intendence of the Governor and immediately related to the capital Rome (see PaulyW, s.vv. *Coloniae ius italicum municipium*). The legionaries at Philippi were proud of their Roman citizenship (Acts 16.12, 21). Paul based his remarks on that: As *milites Caesaris* you are citizens far from your imperial city of Rome. As *milites Christi* you are citizens of the distant capital and native city, where your Lord has his residence. Cf. DionChrysOr. 30.26 ff.; III Mac. 3.23; I Pet. 2.21; Herm.v. 3.2.1 f.; Dg. 5.9 f.; TertMarc. 3.25, etc. Cf. J. A. Bengel and E. Peterson on Phil. 3.20 and particularly W. Ruppel, Philol., 1927 (πολ. in Phil. 3.20 = fatherland).

519. Hos. 2.21 f.; Isa. 54.4 ff.; 62.4 f.; Ezek. 16.7 ff.; Isa. 37.22; Akiba in MEx. on 15.2; Cantr. 8.6 f.; cf. Exr. on 12.2; Lvr. on 9.1; Asenath, p. 15 f.; 17; 19; 21.

520. Gen. 2.24; Eph. 5.31 f.; cf. II Cor. 11.2 f.; this is individualized in mystical terms in ActThom. 6 f.; 14, etc. *Ecclesia Femina* in art see WilpertM., Pl. 47.1; DictAC. IV, Sp. 2228 f.; WilpertM., T. 46 (?); 47.2; F. Gerke, *Christus in der spätantiken Plastik*, 1940, Pl. 97. Cf. the silver medallion of Priscus Attalus (409–416 A.D.). Rome, enthroned, holds a globe with the words INVICTA ROMA AETERNA (416 A.D.: Alaric sacked Rome!), Regling, p. 123; Bernhart, p. 66.

521. Hos. 2.2; BBar. 4.4; IV Ezra 9.38 ff.; Herm.v. 3.9.1 ff.; IV Ezra 2.2, 15; Gal. 4.27; II John 1. Also I Cor. 15.8 belongs to the same circle of ideas, cf. ApP. 11.26; EusHE. 5.1.45 f.; further A. Fridrichsen, "Ἔκτρωμα Eusb., op. cit., is able to speak of the virgin mother Church τῇ παρθένῳ μητρί cf. Test Jos. 19.8A). Cf. DictAC, s.v. *église*, p. 22, 30 ff.; Eisler, *VortrBWbg*, 1925, p. 387.

522. Cf. Rom. 8.29 and the lamb in AEn. 89.52; TestJos. 19.8A.

523. Cf. Rev. 12.1c with Gen. 37.9 and Rev. 7.4 ff. On the iconography see n. 574 and L. Burger, 'Die Himmelskönigin der Ap i.d.Kunst d'. M.A., 1937.

524. See Lietzmann and Schlatter on I Cor. 12.12.

525. TestSeb. 9.4: πᾶν ὃ ἐποίησεν ὁ Κύριος κεφαλὴν μίαν κέκτηται, καὶ ... σύμπαντα μέλη μιᾷ κεφαλῇ ὑπακούει.

526. The ancients buried their tribal members in their closed cemeteries, the early Church laid the οἰκεῖοι τῆς πίστεως to rest there. In this way the solidarity of the *corpus christianum* found expression even in burial customs (E. Kohlmeyer).

527. Cf. E. Benz, *Ecclesia spiritualis*, 1934, p. 26 f.; 302 ff. on the Franciscan theology of history.

528. Gal. 4.25; cf. the divorce of God's unfaithful bride in Jer. 3.8; Schatzh., p. 67.

529. Isa. 23.12; 47.1 ff.; Sib. 3.75 ff., 385; 445; 459 and most particularly 356:
'Ὦ χλιδανὴ ζάχρυσε Λατινίδος ἔκγονε 'Ρώμη,
Παρθένε, πολλάκι σοῖσι πολυμνήστοισι γάμοισιν
Οἰνωθεῖσα, λάτρις νυμφεύσεαι οὐκ ἐνὶ κόσμῳ,
Πολλάκι δ'ἁβρὴν σεῖο κόμην δέσποινά τε κείρει ...

530. In Vendid. 19.43 ff. before the birth of Zarathustra it says: 'He is born, the victor over Daevas (Demons), the enemy of Drug.' Similarly, VirEcl. 4 announces the birth of the child ruler, when the golden age will begin (9). When he is born into the waiting cosmos, snakes and poisonous plants will disappear, and the oxen will no longer fear the lion (22 ff.). All traces of ancient ills and illusions will be obliterated on earth (13.31). When the young ruler

reaches manhood, earth will become a Paradise (37 ff.). And finally his en-thronement will be a festival day for every creature: *Aspice, venturo lactentur ut omnia saeclo* (48 ff.; we take *adgredere . . . honores* to refer to the seizure of power, as already Constantine in Eus.: ἀλλ' ἄγε τιμῆεν σκῆπτρον βασιληίδος ἀρχῆς δεξιτερῆς ἀπὸ πατρὸς ἐριβρεμέταο δέδεξο (oration on the salvation of the saints (20); cf. 18 f. and AugCivD. 18.23). On the spread of this expectation see Alföldi, Herm., 1930.

531. The inscription from Priene says of the birthday: ἦρξεν δὲ τῶι κόσμωι τῶν δι' αὐτὸν εὐαγγελί[ων ἡ γενέθλιος] τοῦ θεοῦ ‹ =of the Emperor› (DittOr. 458.40 ff.). The inscription from Sardes says of the day when his majority is proclaimed: τὴν ἡμέραν τὴν ἐκ παιδὸς ἄνδρα τελησοῦσαν αὐτὸν ἱερὰν . . . ἐν ᾗ τε εὐαγγελίσθη ἡ πόλις (AJA, 1914, p. 314). Of the day that he is proclaimed Emperor a certain papyrus says: γνώστης ἐγενόμην τοῦ εὐαγγελίου περὶ τοῦ ἀνηγορεῦσθαι Καίσαρα (Deissmann LAE, p. 371).

532. Cf. Acts 10.36 and n. 461.

533. God must be the absolute subject of the proclamation and this is the presupposition of apostolic legitimacy. But where God is the absolute subject of preaching, there its theme, its object is Jesus Christ. While the hellenistic world delighted to engage in philosophical dialogues *de deo* (cf. περὶ θεοῦ in JosAp. 2.168 f., 179) the writers of the NT pronounced the Word of God. That is why we never have the expression περὶ θεοῦ (only περὶ πατρός in John 16.25). Of course, the preposition is frequently found in combination with Christ's name (e.g. Acts 22.18; John 1.15): When God speaks to us he speaks to us about his Son (Rom. 1.2 ff.; I John 5.9), whether it be with the men of the OT (ἐπαγγελία) or with the NT characters (εὐαγγέλιον). But where a word fails to have the coming of Christ as its theme, it is not *verbum dei*, but the private opinion of a false prophet or apostle.

534. On ἀπόστολος and μάρτυς see KW, s.v. and Schippers at Ch. 46.

535. It remains a puzzle even when we take into account comparative baptismal practices in the ancient world, and even more puzzling when we look back to John's baptism, which so suddenly disappears, without leaving any further traces, from the Gospels.

536. Luke 24.27; Mark 16.15; John 20.21; Matt. 28.19a; I Cor. 15.1 ff.; Gal. 2.9. Only Matt. 28.19 mentions an express injunction to baptize, while I Cor. 1.17 knows nothing of such a command. On baptismal formulae see Ch. 60.

537. Cf. the formulae of absolution and rites of exorcism in Mark 16.16 f.; JustinApol. I, 61.2; ApConst. 7.41.1 f.

538. Mark 16.16; Luke 3.7 ff.; I Cor. 10.1 ff.; Jude 5; II Cl. 6.9. Differently PsClemHom. 13.21.3: No baptism no salvation!

539. II Tim. 2.19; John 13.18; Rev. 7.2 f. After this proviso what is the meaning of baptism, which remains whatever the circumstances? It is the visible act of reception into the visible Church (John 4.1; Matt. 28.18 f.; Eph. 4.5; Acts 2.41; Did. 9.5; cf. circumcision in Ex. 12.43 f., 48) and as such it is prayer to be received into the company of the redeemed (Luke 3.21; Acts 22.16; I Pet. 3.21 f.; JustinApol. I, 65.1; cf. the prayer value of the symbols of salvation, Ch. 36).

540. I Cor. 1.16; Acts 16.15, 33 f. Cf. Gen. 17.12 f.; 23, 27; Ex. 12.27, 30; I Kings 1.21 ff., etc. Even the ἅγια τέκνα of I Cor. 7.14 have to be baptized

just as surely as the 'children of the saints' had to be circumcized in the OT. In IgnPol. 8.2 children were only expressly so called because they were fellow residents in the same οἶκος.

541. Rom. 4.11; Col. 2.11; Did. 9.5; Barn. 9.6 ff.; further, the correlation of circumcision and proselyte baptism in Jebamot 46a.

542. See Ketubbot 11a and Jebamot 78a in Jeremias, Kindertaufe, p. 12 f. Unfortunately the quotations are not very ancient.

543. In the early days astonishingly little depended on the person who was performing the act of baptism, see John 3.22 f.; 4.2; Acts 8.13 ff.; 10.48; I Cor. 1.17. Differently IgnSm. 8.2.

544. Prayers for the dead were a widespread feature of late Judaism (ApEzra., Tischendorf, p. 25; ApSedr. 5; 8; San. 37a; jSan. 10.4; Gnr. 98.3). The intercessory formula μνησθῇ is found everywhere on tombstones (cf. e.g. B. C. du Mesnil du Buisson, *Biblica*, 1937, p. 170 ff.). We hear of the sacramental significance of the Kaddisch as *oratio pro defunctis* (Elbogen, *Gottesdienst*, p. 95 f.). But there is evidence also for *oblationes pro defunctis* (II Mac. 12.40 ff.; Tob. BA 4.17; Succ. 20a; Tanch. Hanina. 1; Sachs. Tef. p. 741; further material in A. Marmorstein, ZNW, 1931, p. 277 ff.). Paul writes about the Corinthian baptism of the dead quite in the spirit, indeed in the same form as the argument of II Mac. 12. Accordingly, he conceives the Corinthian *baptismum pro defunctis* as an analogy to the Jewish *oblatio pro defunctis*: i.e. as an act of intercession (cf. Bachmann-Stauffer on I Cor. 15.29).

545. SB. I 102 ff.; cf. I Tim. 6.12 (?); Did. 7.4; JustinApol. I, 65.1.

546. Mark 4.12; Luke 22.8; Matt. 26.17; EvEb. (EpiphHaer. 30.22.4) say it *expressis verbis*; I Cor. 11.23 ff. corresponds to the course of the passover meal; John has a different chronology, though he preserves in 6.4 the temporal and material relation between the eucharist and the passover (is John 13.26 also an instance of a passover motif?).

547. We briefly recount the traditional elements: The evening hour, the passover lamb, bread, thanksgiving and blessing, passover hymn (Ex. 12 f.; Wisd. 18.9; Psa. 112–117). On the use of more than one cup which has caused so much trouble to ancient copyists and modern critics of Luke 22.17 ff., see Pes. 10.1 ff. On the motif of remembrance (Luke 22.19, etc.), which many regard as secondary and some as an hellenistic intrusion, see Ex. 13.3; Deut. 16.3; Jub. 49.15. The use of explanatory words is also a long established custom at the passover (Ex. 12.27; 13.14; cf. 13.8 f., 15 f.). Even the formal structure of Jesus' interpretative formulae is traditional (cf. n. 549; Ex. 24.8 ἰδοὺ τὸ αἷμα τῆς διαθήκης ; . . . הָא לַחְמָא עַנְיָה in G. Dalman, *Jesus-Jeschua*, 1922, p. 127 f.; also Deut. 16.3 ἄρτος κακώσεως). And the reference to the atoning blood of the covenant has its history too: in Midr. Ex. 12.6 the blood of the passover lamb is considered as atoning covenant blood; cf. the sin and guilt offering at the passover, Num. 28.22; Ezek. 45.22 ff., and the blood of the covenant in Ex. 24.8; Zech. 9.11. Further, see Stauffer, review of Jeremias, *Die Abendmahlsworte Jesu*, in DLZ, 1952.

548. There are seven grounds for refusing to press the ἐστιν in the eucharistic sayings: (1) As he speaks the words, Jesus is sitting alive, still a man of flesh and blood in the midst of his disciples. So he cannot say at that moment the bread 'is' his body. (2) The blood of Jesus is not yet poured out at that hour. So he cannot say at that moment the wine 'is' his outpoured blood. (3) The copula is

simply an aid to the translator, and had no place in Jesus' own words. Cf. Dalman, op. cit., p. 129, 145; Jeremias, op. cit., p. 80 ff. (4) In the dominical sayings the copula is often not used in a literal sense. Thus, in Luke 8.21p, when Jesus points to the bystanders and says: ἴδε ἡ μήτηρ μου (cf. John 19.26 f.) and adds: those which hear the word of God, and do it, οὗτοι εἰσιν μήτηρ μου καὶ ἀδελφοί μου. (5) The copula formulae had already achieved before Jesus a non-literal meaning in the passover tradition, see n. 547. (6) Both copulas in Jesus' sayings at the Last Supper have manifestly a non-literal sense. This is shown in Luke 22.20: 'This cup is . . . the covenant'. Jesus could not have meant that a cup 'is' a covenant. Again, the cup-formula is expressly made in analogy to that over the bread. This is done by the use of 'In like manner' (ὡσαύτως cf. I Cor. 11; JustinApol. I 66.3). Consequently, it appears that neither can the bread 'be' the body of Christ. (7) It is not the *substantia* of the bread and the wine that are the saving signs, but the act of breaking the bread and pouring out the wine, and it is these actions which stand in correlation to the offering of the body and blood of Christ. In each case it is not the 'substance' but the event which is the *tertium comparationis*. This means that every interpretation of ἐστίν in terms of substance is positively excluded.

549. Ex. 13.9, 16: καὶ ἔσται σοι σημεῖον ἐπὶ τῆς χειρός σου καὶ μνημόσυνον (ἀσάλευτον) πρὸ ὀφθαλμῶν σου . . . Cf. Deut. 6.8 f.; 11.18; EpAr. 157 ff. Also Sachs. Tef. p. 278 (אוֹת) and 610 (זִכָּרוֹן לְיוֹם רִאשׁוֹן . . . . זֶה הַיּוֹם).

550. Cf. n. 548, 7.

551. Thus the foundation of the new passover celebration on Maundy Thursday points beyond itself to the foundation of the new covenant on Good Friday—most expressly in Luke, who enlarges the idea of covenant blood by the conception of the καινὴ διαθήκη in the sense of Jer. 31.31: 'Behold, the days come . . .'. These days are henceforward just at hand. But the fulfilment of the covenant, founded on Good Friday, comes with the fulfilment of the kingdom. So the Last Supper points away from Good Friday to the messianic covenant feast in the new age (Mark 14.25). The eucharist is εἰκὼν τοῦ μέλλοντος (cf. Wisd. 7.20—again this is most clearly expressed in Luke): the passover, which Jesus eats 'before his passion', demands its 'fulfilment' in that passover which Jesus will eat in the future in his glory (Luke 22.15 f.). On the festal meals of the early Church see Acts 2.42, 46 f.; 20.7, 11; 27.35; Cole, Lietzmann, Völker, op. cit.

552. Paul himself in I Cor. 11.23 emphasizes his reliance upon a tradition which reaches back in unbroken succession to the words of institution which Jesus used on Maundy Thursday evening (cf. Ch. 60). Hence his eucharistic text has most affinity to that of the Lucan tradition: ὡσαύτος, memorial motif, cup after supper, καινὴ διαθήκη, etc.). On I Cor. 10.16 see Psa. 115.4; on ἀναξίως (*indigne*, not *indignus*!) see Num. 9.6 ff.; Did. 10.6. Moreover, according to 11.25, Paul does not understand the ἐστίν in a 'substantial' sense (cf. I Cor. 10.16: ποτήριον, ἄρτος = κοινωνία ἐστίν). For Paul, too, the celebration of the eucharist is a sign and memorial of what happened on Golgotha (on καταγγέλετε in 11.26 cf. the passover Haggadah Ex. 12.27; 13.4). The Lord's Supper is a feast to commemorate Good Friday, not Maundy Thursday (so, too, JustinDial. 41: εἰς ἀνάμνησιν τοῦ πάθους; JustinApol., I, 66.3: εἰς ἀνάμνησιν μου). With all this the so-called analogy to the memorial meals that took place in the ancient world, and upon which from time to time much

importance has been placed, is seen to be a very weak one. But in real affinity with the synoptic tradition the Pauline eucharist is not only a memorial celebration, but at the same time an anticipation, a premonitory sign of the coming of Christ in the messianic meal at the end of the world. 'Ye shall eat it in haste'— that was how God's wandering people ate their passover (Ex. 12.11). 'Till he come'—that is how Christ's 'strangers and pilgrims' celebrate the Lord's Supper.

553. On Heb. 6.2 ff. cf. SBar. 29.8; Wisd. 16.26; Barn. 1.7. In the Did. pre-Pauline and Pauline motifs both persist: Memorial motif (9.2 f.), futurist motif (10.5 f.), fellowship motif (9.4; 10.5; cf. IgnPhld. 4.1), Spirit motif (10.2 f.; non-substantial here also: the table-companions do not offer thanks for the elements received, but for what God has given them through Christ, cf. Wisd. 16.7). The doxological motif is dominant (9 f.; 'Εὐχαριστία'! cf. Pes. 117a).

554. There is a typological interpretation of the same rubric in Jub. 49.13.

555. TestL. 8.5: ἔλουσέ με ὕδατι καθαρῷ, καὶ ἐψώμισέ με ἄρτον καὶ οἶνον. On feetwashing see finally Lohmeyer, ZNW, 1939, p. 74 ff.

556. On John 6.14 cf. TestL. 18.11; SBar. 29.8; Sib. 7.149; I Cor. 10.3, 11.

557. Cf. Wisd. 16.6 f. (σύμβολον σωτηρίας); 6.20.

558. For this reason John is only being consistent when he abandons a report of the Last Supper like that of Mark 14.22.

559. John 6.27 ff.; Rev. 3.20; ἐσφράγισεν in John 6.27 follows TestJb. 5 in referring to the sealing for death; cf. EusHE. 5.2.3.

560. John 6.32; 49; cf. Deut. 8.3; Wisd. 16.6 f., 12, 20, 26; PhilFug. 137; Heb. 6.5. Where there is no lively faith man remains lost, even as Judas remains lost (John 6.63; cf. 13.18 ff. τρώγων!). This avoids any possibility of sacramental magic.

561. Eph. 20.2 φάρμακον ἀθανασίας, ἀντίδοτος τοῦ μὴ ἀποθανεῖν; cf. Heb. 6.5.

562. Witness (6.10); comfort (9.31; cf. παράκλητος in John 15.25 f.); word (10.44); guide (13.4; 16.6 f.); decision (15.28; 20.28); prophecy (21.11).

563. New covenant (Jer. 31.31 ff.; II Cor. 3.6); revelation (I Cor. 14.2, 26); word (I Cor. 2.4; 12.8; Gal. 3.2); confession (I Cor. 12.3; cf. I Peter 4.14); miracle (I Cor. 2.4; Gal. 3.5); official authority (I Cor. 5.3 ff.; 7.40; II Cor. 6.6); doxology (I Cor. 14.15, 26; Col. 3.16).

564. See KW, s.v. ἐμφυσάω.

565. Apocalyptic (Rev. 1.10; 2.7; 14.13); liturgy (Rev. 1.7; 22.17); lifebearer (John 7.38; cf. Ecclus. 24.23 ff.; Ch. 29); paraclete (John 14.16 f., 26; 15.26; 16.7; cf. Luke 12.11 f.; Acts 9.31; Rom. 8.26; further Acts 9.31; John 14.26; similarly Ab. 4.11; I John 2.1; POxy. 850.10). On the Spirit in the realm of the trinity as historically revealed see Ch. 65.

566. Cf. LutherWA., 18.139.

567. Cf. IV Ezra 7.127–139 and in addition the fine Armenian version: *Scio et ista ratione credo, quod in miserando misericors est Altissimus.*

568. Mark 10.26 asks: τίς δύναται σωθῆναι? ApSh. (Christian!) explains δικαιοῦμεν οὐδαμῶς ἁμαρτωλόν. Jesus proclaims: πάντα δυνατὰ παρὰ θεῷ.

569. Ἀκοὴ πίστεως (Cl. 3.2); ὑπακοὴ πίστεως (Rom. 1.5; 16.26).

570. Psa. 83.8 (ἐκ δυνάμεως εἰς δύναμιν); Mark 9.24 (πιστεύω, βοήθει μου τῇ ἀπιστίᾳ); Rom. 1.17 (ἐκ πίστεως εἰς πίστιν) 4.18 ff. (παρ' ἐλπίδα ἐπ' ἐλπίδι); II Cor. 3.18 (ἀπὸ δόξης εἰς δόξαν); John 1.16 (χάριν ἀντὶ χάριτος). Cf. Rom. 8.24 f., 38; John 20.29.

571. For this reason πιστεύειν θεῷ (Gal. 3.6; Rom. 4.3; I John 5.10). Human

fides is based upon the *fides* of God (cf. I Cor. 10.13; Rom. 3.3; 9.33; 10.11; I John 1.9—to the contrary II Thess. 2.11 f.; I John 4.1). Inevitably this faith may be blind. But God's way leads men from blind faith through the experience of salvation-history to conscious and confessing faith (Rom. 4.5, 17, 25; Col. 2.12; John 11.25 ff.; 20.27 ff.).

572. Heb. 11.1; on ὑπόστασις cf. JosAnt. 18.24.

573. Jas. 2.19; cf. the conviction of those who despised God, who 'had to believe on him', Wisd. 11.13; 12.27; II Mac. 9.8, etc.

574. πίστις four times in Rev. (2.13, 19; 13.10; 14.12), otherwise only once in the Johannine corpus (I John 5.4). πιστός (=loyal) eight times in Rev.

575. Cf. πιστός in Wisd. 2.9; πίστις in IV Mac. 15.24; 16.22; 17.2.

576. Cf. II Thess. 1.4; II Tim. 4.7; I Pet. 1.9; Heb. 6.12; 11.35 ff.; 12.2.

577. Philosophy of religion climbs through the world of the relative up to the Absolute, like climbing the steps of a pyramid: *ad initia . . . rerum redit aeternamque rationem . . .* (SenEp. 90.29). Philo calls this inductive *regressus* the way κάτωθεν ἄνω and sees its culmination in mystical ecstasy (PhilPraemPoen. 41 ff.). Similarly in Norden, *Theos*, p. 14 ff.

578. The Torah is the embodiment of the knowledge of God (Ecclus. 24.23; BBar. 4.1; Rom. 2.20). ידע comes to have the meaning of 'determine by exegetical proof' (cf. Bacher, *Terminologie*, II, s.v.). 'Thou desirest to know him who spake, and the world was? Study the Haggadah!' (SDt. 11.22). On this basis the scribes maintained their unique theological competence, even over against God in heaven. In the scriptural discussions of the schools no consideration was given 'even of a voice from heaven', and God had to resign himself to this: 'My children have gained a victory over me' (BM. 59b). Indeed, the rabbis could only think of God as himself a teacher of the Torah: the Holy One is seated in heaven and studies the scripture and the Mishnah. He holds daily disputation there with the scribes, and daily proclaims a new Halacha. (e.g. Gnr. on 18.17).

579. Ἀποκάλυψις is self-revelation, self-disclosure. In natural religion man is the subject of the act of knowledge, as he is in scriptural religion. In the act of revelation God himself is the subject. His authoritative revelatory form is the Word, which makes the language of creation and the call of history alike intelligible (Amos 3.7; Deut. 4.32 ff.; Isa. 40.26). After the prophetic era the living Word of revelation was silent (cf. I Mac. 4.46; 14.41). It was apocalyptic that thereafter kept alive, and with complete clarity, the concept of revelation: αὐτὸς ἀνέδειξεν αἰώνιος αὐτὸς ἑαυτόν (Sib. 3.15; cf. ApAbr., etc., in Ch. 18).

580. John 3.21; 7.17; III John 11; cf. SlTestA. in Charles, p. 287.

581. The Synagogue drew the consequence and repudiated the Christ for the sake of its Bible. The counter movement did not fail to come, and soon Marcion repudiated the OT for the sake of his Christ.

582. It was in this fashion that Job prayed to God in the extremity of his unavoidable doubt, and God justified the doubter in answering him (Job 27.1 ff.; 42.8). Similarly, Paul prayed in the hour of temptation and wrestled with God as to the puzzle of contemporary history—until God himself revealed the hidden plan (μυστήριον) of history, in which all problems have their solution (Rom. 9.3; 10.1; 11.25 ff.; cf. II Cor. 12.8 f.; Jas. 1.5). Paul the thinker stands awed before the depths of God's wisdom, which opens before him here (Rom. 11.33 ff.). Who can penetrate to the bottom of this deep?

583. Tob. 12.6 f.: τὰ ἔργα τοῦ θεοῦ ἀνακαλύπτειν καὶ ἐξομολογεῖσθαι ἐντίμως.

584. Μεγαλεῖα in Acts 2.11 (cf. Ecclus. 42.21); μεγαλύνειν in Acts 10.46; μεγαλειότης in II Pet. 1.16.

585. Οὐ πεισμονῆς τὸ ἔργον, ἀλλὰ μεγέθους ἐστιν ὁ Χριστιανισμός . . . (IgnR. 3.3). The issue here is not the greatness of man (as most translators think), but the greatness of God, as in IgnE. Inscr. Pls. E. 1.19; Wisd. 13.5; cf. KW, s.v. (Prov. 18.10 vl; Eccl. 2.9 vl); PrBau, s.v. (μέγεθος τοῦ θεοῦ in the Phrygian Inscr.). θεολόγοι were called in Asia Minor God's heralds, sebastologians, hymnodists, mystarchs, who expounded and glorified their God's θειότης; θεολογία then becomes the language of a revelation by means of which they proclaim the greatness of their God, in his name. It is in this sense that the words θεολόγος, θεολογία, θεολογεῖν are used, e.g. by Papias (TU. 5.2, 1888, p. 170); JustinDial. 56); ClAl. (Strom. 1.13.57.6; 28.176.1 f.); EusHE. 1.2.3 ff.; 5.28.4 f.; 10.3.3; 10.4.70; and Chrys. (Deissmann LAE, p. 353.1). Theology of this sort, if it is to be true to itself, must be in the last resort a work of the Spirit (cf. Acts 2; Col. 3.16). To be a theologian accordingly means to proclaim the glory of Christ in the name of God, and to develop the proclamation in the realm of thought.

586. Luke 11.2; Mark 14.36; Gal. 4.6; Rom. 8.15. Harnack, along with others, has put his faith in the fatherhood of God as the revolutionary factor in the gospel. But the name of 'father' had already won and kept a firm place in the language of prayer in the old biblical tradition. Cf. Jer. 3.4; Isa. 63.16; Ecclus. 23.1; Tob. 13.4; jXVIII, 4.6.

587. SB. 1.411; cf. Tob. 8.5; GEn. 1.2 (Angel = ἀγιολόγοι) ; 9.4 (with *Synkellos!*); AEn. 39.9 ff.; 61.12; Sachs, Tef. p. 24; 108; 148; 244; 256; 258; 276; 292; 314.

588. Luke 11.2 is a doxological formula (cf. n. 587) with a concern to show that every creature joins in the *trisagion* (cf. Ch. 59). The position adopted in KW, s.v. ἀγιάζω: 'The logical subject of the hallowing is God, and God alone, not man' is untenable in terms either of the problem itself or of the formula.

589. II Mac. 1.24 f.; Add. Esth. 13.14; Isa. 26.13; Dan. 3.45; Rom. 16.17; I Tim. 1.17; 6.15 f.; Jude 25; Rev. 15.4; I Cl. 59.3 f.; 61.3; II Cl. 20.5; cf. jBer. 13a (He shall call on *me*); Bundehesch 4.12 (Justin); Poim. 13.20 (Parthey).

590. See n. 732.

591. According to the most ancient text of Matt. 6.12: ἀφήκαμεν (B ℵ).

592. θεὸς βοηθόος = the God who hastens to my aid at my βοῇ.

593. Job 13.14: נַפְשִׁי אָשִׂים בְּכַפִּי. On this formula, which is found elsewhere, the rabbis based an axiom: 'A man's prayer is only heard if he puts his soul in his hand' (Taan 8a; on the formula cf. Psa. 119.109; Lam. 3.41; on the content see II Mac. 3.14 ff.; Esth. 4.17l, 4.17k; Luke 22.44; Mark 14.35; Heb. 5.7 f.).

594. Luke 11.3: ἐπιούσιος from ἐπ-ιέναι (Delitzsch: חָקֵנוּ from חֹק); cf. Prov. 30.8; PsSol. 5.16 f. Cf. KW, s.v., where all possible meanings are discussed.

595. On μὴ εἰσενέγκῃς see Matt. 26.41; I Peter 5.8 ff.; Orig. Comm. Psa. 17.29; Sachs. Tef., p. 20. On πονηρός see Matt. 13.19, 38; Eph. 6.16; I John 5.18 f.; Sachs. Tef., p. 152; otherwise מִכָּל־רָע, ibid., p. 150, = ἀπὸ παντὸς κακοῦ (Psa. 120.7).

596. The recompense for which the biblical characters pray is often nothing more than the unavoidable correlation of the divine act of deliverance (TestJos. 19.3 f.; GEn. 8.4; IV Mac. 9.24; cf. the plaint of the advocate in AEn. 89.57, 69; HEn. 44.10), often also simply a postulate of a theodicy (IV Mac. 11.23; 12.18 f.; a prayer of revenge from Rheneia is in Deissmann LAE, p. 424: ἵνα ἐγδικήσῃ(ς) τὸ αἷμα τὸ ἀναίτιον καὶ τὴν ταχίστη(ν); EJ, s.v. Ab. Harachamin; Sachs, Tef., p. 592), often quite basically a form of divine revelation (Deut. 32.43; I Mac. 7.38; II Mac. 2.2 ff.; AssMos. 9.7 ff.). Τὸ τάχος ἐπιφάνηθι! (III Mac. 6.9; cf. 15.4 f.; 2.19). Similar motives are found in the NT: Rom. 12.19 (cf. Gen. 4.10; AEn. 22.5); Heb. 11.4 (cf. Ex. 22.20 ff.; Deut. 24.15; Mal. 3.5; Job 31.38); Jas. 5.3 ff. (Cf. XVIII 12; I Cl. 59.3 f.). The elect in Luke 18.7 cry to God day and night to avenge them (cf. Luke 18.3, 5; KW, s.v. βοάω). But Rev. 6.10 is moulded in the spirit of Luke 9.54 and of the ancient prayer of revenge (cf. Rev. 8.3 ff.; IV Ezra 4.33 ff.; 15.8; GEn. 9.1 ff.; HEn. 44.7; for liturgical echoes see A. Baumstark in *Festg. f. A. Ehrhard*, 1926, p. 59 f.). Nevertheless, these motives in the NT remain as isolated examples (see Luke 9.55 and the curtailment of Psa. 2 in Acts 4.25 ff.).

597. In the old biblical tradition Moses is the great original of the advocate who is ready to sacrifice himself (Ex. 32.32; Jub. 1.19 ff.; AssMos. 11.9 ff., 17; PsPhil. 12.8 ff.; 15.7). 'Undaunted the servant speaks to his Lord, and pleads forgiveness for the many, or else be destroyed with them' (I Cl. 53.5). Alongside Moses stand Aaron, Jeremiah and Ezekiel as conspicuous examples of the same thing (Num. 17.9 ff.; Jer. 18.20; 29.7; VitProph., p. 44; II Mac. 15.12 ff.; Ezek. 3.17 ff.; 4.4 ff.; Wisd. 18.21 ff.). These are all come of priestly descent. Priesthood and intercession go together. The Servant of Isa. 53.12 prays for his persecutors (Ch. 30). Job prays for the friends who have plied him with questions so harshly (Job 42.8; otherwise Ezek. 14.14). Abraham prayed for the godless Sodomites (Gen. 18.22). In a later apocalypse we read of a daily intercession by the patriarch for the damned in the place of torment (ApAn. 16 f. = TU, 1899, p. 154 f.; cf. ApEzra, ibid; ApSh. 8).

598. In the NT Jesus is the prototype of the intercessor, who prays for his persecutors: 'Father, forgive them . . .' (Luke 23.34 according to א, lat, etc.). Similarly, the martyr Stephen died emulating his Master with a like intercession (Acts 7.60; cf. 3.17). But the spirit of Moses comes to life again in Paul's intercession for his own people (Rom. 9.3; cf. 10.1; 9.15 proves that Paul had Moses' prayer in mind). The two chief motives, from the Christ-Stephen and the Moses-Paul traditions respectively, appear in a unity in Hegesippus' picture of James the brother of the Lord (EusHE. 2.23). He prays for his Jewish compatriots and is for that reason called Oblias (for the etymology see Stigloher, ad. loc., and Hennecke, p. 104), *monumentum populi* (cf. στήριγμα λαοῦ Wisd. 49.15). He prayed, till they killed him: 'Father, forgive them . . .' The 'bulwark of the people' has fallen. And very soon destruction comes upon Jerusalem (cf. n. 703).

599. On thought as prayer see Ch. 43. On work as prayer and creative prayer see Psa. 89.17; 117.25; 127.1 f.; Wisd. 37.15; 38.9 ff., 34; I Mac. 3.60; PsSol. 5.9 ff.; Luke 11.3; 14.28 ff.; Heb. 11.33 f.; Jas. 1.17; 5.13 ff.; I Cl. 59.4.

600. Loculus plates with Noah: see Roller, *Catacombes*, I, pl. XI. 15 ff., with praying figures see, ibid., XI.3, catacomb pictures with salvation symbols see Wulff, I, p. 88, sarcophagi with salvation symbols see Neuss, Kunst, fig. 71 ff.

601. In this way we reach by another route and with a much more sure result to the same interpretation as Le Blant and Kauffmann have reached about sarcophagi (see Literature for Ch. 61) and K. Michel and Wilpert about the catacombs.

602. Cf. Roller, *Catacombes*, I, pl. XI.3; 83 f.; further W. Neuss, 'Die Oranten in der Altchristl. Kunst'. *Festg. für P. Clemen*, 1926, p. 9, etc.

603. At this point we come upon the metaphysical significance of primitive Christian art, which has been recognized both by the realists (P. Styger, *Die altchr. Grabeskunst*, 1927) and the symbolists (cf. here O. Casel, JbfLtgw, 1932). We cannot here go into the whole story of how this metaphysical, prayer-like art came later on to make use of realistic-historic and also symbolic-theological motifs, and only thus reached its final development.

604. The formal style of the pictures in the catacombs of Rome may be compared with the descriptive prolixity with which the same scenes were depicted at the same time at Dura.

605. Phil. 2.12 f. The γάρ in 2.13 is not a straightforward continuation. That would demand δέ, as parallels in Josephus show (Ant. 5.349: ἐγὼ μὲν . . . σιγὴν . . . ἦγον, θεὸς δ' ἐστὶν ὁ καλῶν; cf. 20.48). It is only if we take the γάρ seriously as used aetiologically that the relationship of the human will to the divine is understood in the way that the NT conceives it (cf. γάρ in Matt. 4.17 and Rom. 6.14b; ὅτι in I John 4.7). God is at work, and our salvation is at stake (cf. I Thess. 5.9). Hence the need for fear and trembling (Barth at this point merely toys with the text). God's work is a Word to our wills. Hence the imperative. God's ἐνεργεῖν calls our wills so that he may become effective in our ἐνεργεῖν. Hence the appeal to κατεργάζεσθαι. On ἔργον see n. 607; on θέλειν see n. 608.

606. Cf. οὖν, ὥστε, διό in Rom. 6.12 ff.; 12.1 f.; II Pet. 3.17 f.; εἰς, ἵνα, ὅπως in Rom. 7.4; 8.3 f.; Gal. 2.19; II Cor. 5.15; Eph. 5.26 f.

607. Thus God's action becomes effective in man's. God himself is at work in our work (Phil. 2.13; IV Ezra 8.52; Phil. 1.6; Col. 1.29; I Cor. 12.6; Eph. 2.10; 3.20; John 3.21; further KW, s.v. ἔργον). The grace of God is potential energy which seeks actualization (I Cor. 15.9 f.; II Cor. 12.8 f.; Rom. 15.15 f.; II Tim. 1.6). The Spirit is at one and the same time a gift and a task (Gal. 5.25). Divine election means being called to serve (Ch. 52). It is only through the deepest passivity that man can reach his highest activity. Paul has given this classic expression in his own correlation-formula, which finds particularly powerful statement in Phil.: Phil. 3.12 ff.; cf. I Cor. 8.3; 13.12; Gal. 4.8 f.; echoes in I Tim. 6.12. On λόγος, etc., see Ch. 12.

608. Basically the NT has two concepts for God's will, βουλή and θέλημα (see KW, s.vv., and Riesenfeld, op. cit.). They are related to each other something like foreknowledge and predestination (Ch. 9). βουλή in Psa. 32.11; Acts 2.23; 4.28; 20.27; Heb. 6.17 is the premundane decree of salvation and plan for history (cf. βούλημα in Rom. 9.19; βούλεσθαι in II Pet. 3.9). In distinction from that θέλημα is the technical term for the evocative will of God by means of which that salvatory decree attains fulfilment (a challenging appeal to the will in Col. 4.12; I Thess. 4.3; 5.18; obedient realization by the will in jXVIII 13; Luke 12.47; Matt. 7.21; 12.50; 21.31; John 7.17; 9.31; I John 2.17; Heb. 10.36). This concept of will is to be found wherever the struggle between God's will and man's is being discussed. Thus used of God's will in Matt. 6.10; 26.42;

20—N.T.T.

John 4.34; 5.30; 6.38 f.; I John 5.14. Of man's will in Mark 14.36; Matt. 26.39; Luke 12.49; 13.34; 22.42; Rom. 7.15 ff.; Gal. 5.17; I Pet. 3.17; Rev. 2.21; 22.17. That is the idea of will in Phil. 2.12 f. (ὑπακούειν, θέλειν).

609. God keeps his eye set upon our heart (Ecclus. 17.8), and man's heart should find its delight in God (Deut. 6.5; Psa. 32.21; 56.8; Prov. 23.26). Those who seek God beget living hearts (Psa. 21.27; 68.33). But our heart is a defiant and dispirited thing. Who can fathom it? (Jer. 17.9; cf. Psa. 94.8; Prov. 16.5). Only God knows it through and through, and God has power over our heart, where we have no power or possibility left us, save in prayer (Psa. 50.12; III βασ 3.9; Job 36.5: δυνατὸς ἰσχύι καρδίας). Man's heart in God's hand is like clay in the hand of the potter (Psa. 32.15; I βασ 10.9; Prov. 16.2). It is the steel which glows in God's fire and will one day be recast in his fire (Ch. 41).

610. ἀνάγκη γὰρ ἐλθεῖν τὰ σκάνδαλα (Matt. 18.7).

611. Πλὴν οὐαὶ τῷ ἀνθρώπῳ δι' οὗ τὸ σκάνδαλον ἔρχεται (Matt. 18.7).

612. II Thess. 2.9 ff.; II Cor. 4.4; Rom. 1.21 ff. On the antithetical pair of concepts ἀλήθεια-ἀδικία cf. the Freerlogion Mark 16.14 (5.Jh.s. Klostermann, ad. loc.).

613. Notice καρδία in Ex. 9.12; θέλειν in Rom. 9.18.

614. So in biblical imagery (as also in Augustin's and Luther's) God appears as the rider who with his paramount will overcomes the at first contrary will of his beast, masters it, guides it, continually spurs it until the will of the rider is completely implanted in that of the animal; see Psa. 31.8 f.; Prov. 26.3; Eccl. 12.11 ff.; SB., II, 769 f.; PsSol. 16.41; PhilSom. 2.294; ApSh. 7; Acts 26.14; I Cor. 15.56; II Tim. 2.26 cf. KW, s.v. κέντρον (further AeschEum. 400, etc.) and F. Smend, *Angelos*, 1925, p. 36 f.

615. A number of long paragraphs have had to be sacrificed at this point for the sake of brevity, because, in my view, they could not themselves be shortened. Cf. my preparatory work in RGG,² s.v., Sittlichkeit, KW, s.v.v. ἀγαπᾶν, ἀγωνίζεσθαι, γάμος, ἵνα and the literature referred to there.

616. On the problem of the concept of martyrdom and its development see first F. Kattenbusch in ZNW, 1903, p. 111 ff., and finally v. Campenhausen, Schippers, etc., and KW, s.v., μάρτυς. On the history of the concept see App. I.34, *Acta Pauli*, 1936, p. 4.28.

617. Mark 4.17; 3.13; Matt. 10.22; Luke 6.22; Acts 9.16; 21.11; I Pet. 4.13 f., 16; Jas. 2.7; Rev. 9; cf. n. 623.

618. Phil. 3.10; Rev. 1.9; cf. Mark 8.34; Matt. 5.10 ff.; 10.24 f., 38; John 21.19; MartPol. 19.1. II Tim. 3.10 f.; I Pet. 2.21 (ὑπογραμμόν).

619. I Thess. 2.14 f.; IgnE. 10.3; Rom. 6.3; MartPol. 1.2. The idea of μίμησις often comes to the fore in all sorts of related expressions. The πρωτομάρτυς Stephen accentuated the conflict with the Jews in an aggressive speech as Jesus himself had done (Ch. 21). He died with almost the same words on his lips in prayer as are recorded of Jesus in Luke (Acts 7.2 ff., 59 f.; cf. Ch. 25). After that the similarity of the passion of the martyrs with that of Christ is a favourite theme of Christian martyrology (EusHE. 2.23.20 ff.; 5.1 ff.; LutherWA., XVIII, 215 ff.). In a lonely place outside the city the Bishop Polycarp awaited his hour, united in prayer with a few loyal friends (MartPol. 5.1). His own housemates betrayed him; his persecutor was called Herod; they went out armed in the late evening as though to pursue a robber. 'May God's will be done', said Polycarp, as they approached him (6.2; 7.1). So the fate of the

bishop-martyr took its course, step by step repeating typologically the passion of Christ, even to the thrust in the side after his execution (16.1). And yet in all this the dividing line between the crucified and his witnesses unto blood is most emphatically preserved (17.3).

620. So Ignatius says, as if it were a parting formula (cf. App. I 19): καλόν μοι ἀποθανεῖν εἰς Χριστόν . . . ἢ βασιλεύειν τῶν περάτων τῆς γῆς (Rom. 6.1; cf. EusHE. 5.1 ff.; parting formula applied directly to the life of Christ in IgnPol. 4.3).

621. Even in the hour of extreme affliction the confessor knew a consolation, a certainty of victory, that no one else knew: I Thess. 2.2 f.; II Cor. 1.3 ff.; 4.7 ff.; 6.4 ff.; 7.4 ff.; Rom. 12.12; Heb. 11.34; cf. Rom. 8.36 f. (ἐλογίσθημεν ὡς πρόβατα σφαγῆς—ἀλλ' ἐν τούτοις πᾶσιν ὑπερνικῶμεν) with Sachs. *Tef.* p. 144 (כְּצֹאן לַטֶּבַח—וּבְכָל זֹאת שִׁמְךָ לֹא שָׁכַחְנוּ). The Spirit, alive in the gospel of Christ, speaks through the mouth of those who confess Christ and rests on those who remain loyal to Christ's name under abuse and persecution (Luke 12.11 f.; I Pet. 4.14). The service of the Word finds its fulfilment in the ministry of suffering, and the witness unto blood is a word of God (Col. 1.24 f.; IgnR. 2.1).

622. Rom. 1.2; 4.1 (ἐσχηκότες—ἐπιτυχεῖν); cf.Heb. 11.27, 33 (ἐκαρτέρησεν—ἐπέτυχον).

623. Cf. n. 617 and Rom. 8.36; Phil. 1.20, 29; 2.3; I Cor. 13.3 (Heyschtext); John 21.19; IgnR. 2.2; 4.1 f.; MartPol. 14.1 f.; AthenagSuppl. 37; ActApoll. 37; EusHE. 5.2.2 ff.

624. II Thess. 1.5 ff. Here the motifs of the old biblical persecution polemic come to life again (cf. App. I 25). The persecutors will share in the sight of the martyrs being exalted, and will be horror struck, and in the end will miserably come to nought (Rev. 3.9). Indeed many tyrants taste a dreadful end within this present age (Acts 12.1, 21 ff.; Rev. 13.10; 16.5 f.; EusHE. 7, passim; LactDeMortPersec, passim; cf. n. 625).

625. John 16.2; MartPol. 2.4; τύραννος in EusHE. 9.2; 10.4.60; 11.1 ff.

626. Mark 13.14; Rev. 2.13; MartPol. 9.2 ff.; Herm.s. 1.6; cf. App. I.16. Ancient Christian art has happily expressed the relationship between the old biblical and early Christian martyrs in representing the three young men of Dan. 3 as turning their backs on the bust of an emperor (!). See e.g. WilpertK. 123.1; Sarcofagi, T. 82.

627. IgnR. 5.1 f.; Probably I Cor. 15.32 is intended to be equally metaphorical, as the reservation κατὰ ἄνθρωπον λέγω leads us to understand.

628. I Cor. 4.9 ff.; cf. ApEl. 35; IgnTr. 9.1 of Christ: ἀπέθανεν, βλεπόντων τῶν ἐπουρανίων καὶ ἐπιγείων καὶ ὑποχθονίων.

629. Rev. 11 f.; I Pet. 5.8 f.; MartPol. 19.21; Herm.s. 8.3.6 vl; ApEl 37 f.; ActThom. 39; Test40Mart. 1.1, 5; EusHE. 5, prol. 4; Aug. De. Agone. Chr., MPL. 40.289 ff.

630. MartPol. 19.2; EusHE. 5, prol. 4; 5.1.23, 42.

631. Rev. 6.10 ff.; MartPol. 1.1 f. Cf. the idea of purification in I Pet. 4.17; Heb. 12.5 ff.; I Cl. 6.1;

632. Col. 1.24: ἀνταναπληρόω; cf. Phil. 2.30 and Gal. 6.2: ἀναθληρόω.

633. I Cor. 4.13 περικάθαρμα and περίψημα. Both expressions are found in the same sense in the LXX (περικάθαρμα in Prov. 21.18; cf. 11.8; περίψημα in Tob. 5.19). The first had its place also in the atonement rites of the Grecian Thargelian festival (cf. L. Deubner, *Attische Feste*, 1932, p. 179 ff.). The latter

is adopted by Ign. in E.8.1. The death that Ignatius dies as a martyr will serve as redemption price for the Church in Ephesus (cf. 18.1; Barn. 6.5). But Paul's thought in I Cor. 4.13 is more universal.

634. Acts 7.60; EusHE. 2.23. The redeeming work of Christ is the only thing that serves for the salvation of the world. But the passion of the martyrs effects in the first place their own salvation; it is a contribution to the cancellation of their own debt. 'For he that hath suffered in the flesh hath ceased from sin' (I Pet. 4.1; cf. Herm.s. 8.3.6; 9.28.3 ff.). This basic principle found its most colourful expression in the early Church in the metaphor of blood-baptism. Jesus called his own death a baptism, and in doing so was thinking of the descent into the waters of death in the underworld (Luke 12.50; cf. Gen. 7.11; Psa. 41.8; 68.2 f., 15; SBar. 53 ff.; I Pet. 3.20; II Pet. 3.6; Herm.v. 3.2.2; 3.5.5; s. 9.16.5 ff.). In the same sense he asked the two sons of Zebedee 'Are ye able to be baptized with the baptism that I am baptized with?' (Mark 10.38). This gave the notion of death as a baptism its sure place in the Christian theology of martyrdom (MartIs. 5.13; Mark 14.36; 10.38 f.; MartPol. 14.2; speak of the 'cup of death'). For the same reason the bloody end of Perpetua and Felicitas was regularly pictured as a baptism of blood (PassPerpFel. 21; further Windisch, *Taufe und Sünde*, 415.1). Similarly, Tertullian with Luke 12.50 in mind calls the death of martyrs a 'second baptism, namely the baptism of blood' (TertBapt. 16). Eusebius speaks of a 'baptism by fire' (EusHE. 6.4.3; MartPol. 11.1). But in all these metaphors the thing that is significant and gives the early Church its conviction is that martyrdom, like baptism itself, serves for the expiation of sin (MelSard, Fragment 12; cf. PassPerpFel. 18; ActPl-Thecl. 34). That is why the efficacy of baptism by water can be either renewed or even substituted for by blood baptism (Tert., op. cit.). For all that, however, blood baptism, no more than water baptism, is an independent means of self-expiation, but always a baptism in the name of the Lord Jesus Christ. The martyrs, like everyone else, have washed their robes in the blood of the lamb, and not in their own blood (Rev. 7.14).

635. On this basis the Baptist had already taken the step which Jean (*Milieu Biblique*, III, 1936, p. 593 f.; 614 f.) has described as the first and decisive step in forming the Church: the establishment of a 'people of God' on a basis other than blood relationship.

636. Luke 13.35; on $\ddot{\epsilon}\omega\varsigma$ cf. the positive $\ddot{\epsilon}\omega\varsigma$ in Deut. 29.3; otherwise, the negative $\mu\acute{\epsilon}\chi\rho\iota\ \tau\acute{\epsilon}\lambda o\upsilon\varsigma$ in Wisd. 16.5; 19.1.

637. Cf. Luke 22.29 f., where $\kappa\rho\acute{\iota}\nu\epsilon\iota\nu$ means not 'judge' but 'rule', see Ch. 55.

638. Ancient complaints about the 'Jewish pestilence' are in Lösch, op. cit., 9.24 ff.

639. The great figures of Jewish history found the same favour 'before God and men' (I $\beta\alpha\sigma$. 2.26; Prov. 3.4; DaG. 6.22 f.; JosAnt. 6.205; SB. 2.152 f.; cf. Luke 2.52; Rom. 14.18). Today the Jew is disliked all over the world, but is therefore so much the surer of divine favour (Esth. 3.13d–g; Wisd. 2.15 ff.; cf. Ch. 34).

640. $\epsilon\grave{\iota}\varsigma\ \tau\acute{\epsilon}\lambda o\varsigma$ I Thess. 2.16 as in TestL. 6.11; Barn. 4.7; Herm.s. 8.6.4; cf. ApAbr. 28 and $\mu\acute{\epsilon}\chi\rho\iota\ \tau\acute{\epsilon}\lambda o\upsilon\varsigma$ in n. 636.

641. $\sigma\pi\acute{\epsilon}\rho\mu\alpha$ = singular!

642. Rom. 11.1, 11 f.; notice $\ddot{\epsilon}\omega\varsigma$, $\ddot{\alpha}\chi\rho\iota$ in 11.8, 25 and further n. 636.

643. Rom. 10.19 παραζηλοῦν; cf. Deut. 32.21; GBar. 16.

644. Rom. 11.33 ff.; cf. מִשְׁפָּטֶיךָ תְּהוֹם רַבָּה in Sachs, Tef. 354. In the early Church anti-Jewish forces very quickly got the upper hand. The theological polemic and political hunting of Jewish circles against Christianity did not diminish with the fall of Jerusalem (cf. the acrimonious stories about Jesus in the Talmud and the equally hostile role of Judaism in the trial of Polycarp, Ch. 47). The Jews attacked Jesus as one who was devil-possessed (John 8.48 f.). John, himself later destroyed by the Jews, described Judaism as the Synagogue of Satan, and Jerusalem as the new Sodom (Rev. 2.9; 3.9; 11.8; cf. above 1.7). JustinDial. renewed the anti-Jewish persecution-polemic of Luke 13 and I Thess. 2 with formulae from Wisd. 2.12. Marcion dragged the whole OT story into the mire. Barnabas allegorized and spiritualized it far worse than Gal. 3 f. Rom. 11 became incomprehensible. Very soon the international Church looked down on the old people of God in the same way that the Strassburg Ekklesia looked down on the Synagogue of the broken staff.

645. ἵνα and other final modifications fourteen times in I Cor. 9.13 f.

646. Popular Jewish theology was dominated by the idea: The world exists for the sake of the people of God (AssMos. 1.12; I Ezra 6.55). But a 'Copernican revolution' had already taken place in Second Isaiah. The people of God exists for the sake of the world (Isa. 49.6; 60.3; Rom. 2.19; the idea was later on narrowed down again, see KW, s.v. λαός). Apocalyptic carried on these traditions in producing the formula: the people of God is a φυτὸν δικαιοσύνης, bearing its fruit as a blessing for the whole world (GEn. 10.16 ff.; Jub. 1.16; 36.6; cf. Isa. 60.61; 61.3; AEn. 84.6; Gen. 22.18; Acts 3.25. The NT writers took over these same traditions: the Church exists for the sake of the world!

647. Mark 12.17 ἀπόδοτε! On the idea of returning what is due see Luke 20.25; Matt. 22.21; Rom. 13.7; Vulg., Iren., Orig., Aug. There is a catena on Matt. 22.16 f. in Cramer, p. 181 (ἀπόδοτε . . . οὐ γάρ ἐστι τοῦτο δοῦναι); Hilarius: *Caesari quae eius essent redhibenda decernit . . . Deo autem quae eius sunt propria reddere nos oportere . . . . . .* For Dibelius that does not mean Rome and the Christians, p. 3 n. 2, which in any case refutes itself.

648. Cf. Prov. 24.21; JosBell. 2.140; I Pet. 2.13 ff.; Tit. 3.1; MartPol. 10.2.

649. E.g. Jer. 29.7; 36.7 LXX; II Ezra 6.10; BBar. 1.10 ff.; Ab. 3.2; Philo and Josephus passim; Elbogen, Gottesdienst, 203; 274; 549.

650. I Tim. 2.1 ff.; cf. I Cl. 60 f.; Pol. 12.3; TheophAutol. 1.11; TertApol. 30. Further above n. 210.

651. Paul is silent about this reservation in Rom. 13. So it seems in Rom. 13.2 as though obedience to God in every case demands unconditional obedience to civil authority, allowing of no denial. This silence is doubly noteworthy because Paul did not at that time, as some have maintained, in any way underestimate the possibility of conflict between the empire and the Church, but rather it is the case that in the immediate context he is writing about slanders and persecution in Rome (Rom. 12.14 ff., like I Pet. 2.13 ff., belongs to Rom. 13.1 ff.). Meanwhile the early Church took good care that the reservation against the apotheosis of the State was not forgotten. The earliest commentator on Rom. 12 f. wrote briefly and pregnantly: Τὸν θεὸν φοβεῖσθε, τὸν βασιλέα τιμᾶτε (I Pet. 2.17; cf. φοβήθητε in Luke 12.5; τιμή in Rom. 13.7). And the earliest expositor of the saying about God and Caesar makes Jesus' reservation plain with a remarkable clarity and courage: θεὸν μόνον προσκυνοῦμεν, ὑμῖν δὲ πρὸς

τὰ ἄλλα χαίροντες ὑπηρετοῦμεν, βασιλεῖς καὶ ἄρχοντας ἀνθρώπων ὁμολο-
γοῦντες (JustinApol. I 1.17.2 ff.).

652. Donata in PassSanctScilit; cf. MartPol. 10.2; ActApoll. 37; Athenag
Suppl. 37.

653. It must never be forgotten that it was already the custom in the Synagogue for the one who led in prayer to be very often himself an hymnographer,
cf. Elbogen, *Gottesdienst*, p. 484.

654. Antiphonies were already much in use in the liturgy of the Synagogue,
but there were no congregational hymns, see Elbogen, op. cit., 249; 494 ff.

655. I Cor. 14.16; PlinEp. 10; dance motif in Herm.s. 9.11.5 and ActJ. 94.

656. Jas. 5.13; ConstAp. 8.13.16; cf. the OT Psalms in Sachs, *Tef.*, passim;
further, PsSol., passim; AEn. 39.9 ff.; HEn., passim.

657. Cf. H. Gunkel, op. cit.

658. Certain Bible manuscripts contain a selection of odes (Rahlfs, II, 164 ff.).
In heretical circles the production of hymns after the manner of OdSol., ActJ.
and ActThom. got so much out of control that the Church issued a warning
against it, and commended the Psalms of David.

659. The first time that Christ is called God is in a liturgical formula (Rom.
9.5; cf. Pliny, op. cit.; EusHE. 28). In the same way the name of θεοτόκος (for
Mary) was taken from the liturgy and used in the formulation of dogma.

660. On the place and formation of the Shema in the liturgy, see Elbogen,
op. cit., 14 ff.; 24 f.; 235 f.; 247; 496.

661. As early as the rite of baptism, see Mark 1.5; TertBapt. 20; TertSpect. 4;
ApConst. 7.41.4.

662. On the antecedents see Oesterley, op. cit.; Elbogen, op. cit., 67; 93;
241; 489; 578; E. Schubert-Christaller, *Der Gottesdienst der Synagoge*, 1927, 17 f.

663. F. E. Brightman, *Liturgies Eastern and Western*, I, 1896, 3 ff. P. Drews
has investigated the early origins of this ideal formula (*Studien zur Geschichte des
Gottesdienstes*, II, III, 1906), and A. Baumstark its association with Antioch
(*Messe im Morgenland*, 1921, p. 29 ff.; *Geschichtl. Werden der Liturgie*, 1923, p. 17).

664. Psa. 110–116; further Elbogen, op. cit., 249.

665. See Brightman, op. cit., glossary of technical terms, s.v. κηρύσσειν.

666. See Elbogen, op. cit., 156 ff., 257; Luke 4.17; Acts 13.15; JustinApol.,
I, 67.3 f.; A. Baumstark, *Werden der Liturgie*, 15 ff.

667. On liturgy and apocalyptic in Daniel see Elbogen, op. cit., 243. On
Revelation see Gennep at head of Ch. 6 and I. Peschek, *Geheime Offenbarung und
Tempeldienst*, 1929; E. Peterson, *Das Buch von den Engeln*, 1935.

668. On the correlation between heavenly and terrestrial sanctuaries see
Ex. 25.9, 40; 26.30; Acts 7.44; Heb. 8.5. In the Synagogue the κιβωτός was the
shrine for the Torah and the point of orientation for the sanctuary, cf. Elbogen,
op. cit., 469 ff.; Rostovtzeff, Dura, 1936; 320 ff.; 343.

669. On the correlation between celestial and terrestrial lamps see Ex. 25.37
ff. On the whole subject cf. E. Lohmeyer, *Kultus und Evangelium*, 1942.

670. On the correlation between terrestrial and heavenly worship see n. 668;
669; 671, further Isa. 6.1 ff.; Elbogen, op. cit., 47 f.; 58 ff.; K. Schneider,
Kyrios, 1938, p. 311. The worshipping community thought of the heavenly
worship of God as a magnified form of the earthly, and correspondingly conceived of its own worship as an attenuated copy of the heavenly, and as one
element in the worship of the cosmos.

671. On the correlation of terrestrial and celestial trumpets see Ex. 19.16 and Num. 10.10. On the festival trumpeting in the worship of the Synagogue see Elbogen, op. cit., 140. Further cf. Hamburger, 257, 11; CGC, 27 (Palestine), 289 f.

672. Rev. 3.20; 19.9; cf. 7.16; 22.17. On the formal diction and its antecedents see Isa. 55.1 and the passover Haggada in SB. 4.41 ff.

673. Rev. 1.7; 22.17 ff.; cf. PsSol. 17.44 ff.; XVIII, 9 f.; Schubert-Christaller, op. cit., 36; Sachs, *Tef.*, 738!

674. On the effects of Revelation on iconography see the works of W. Neuss also, Sorsch, *Fortschr.*, 1930, p. 34), further R. le Nail, *L'Ap d'après d'Iconogr.*, I, 1916; M. R. James, *The Apocalypse in Art*, 1931; Stefanescu, op. cit., OT XXI, XXXVII, etc.

675. E.g. the cruciform domed church at Firsandyre, Springer, II, 1924, Ill, 15.

676. This doxological display was prepared for in sepulchral art, cf. the liturg. sarcophagus in Wulff, I, T. VI. 2 and the gesture of adoration made by the praying figure, ibid., Plate IV; further O. Casel, JbfLtgev., 1932, p. 69.

677. The whole doxological purpose is also facilitated by the series of historical portraits out of the OT (e.g. Maria Maggiore in WilpertM., Plate 8 ff.) and by the theological representation of the Good Friday mystery (e.g. Aquileia in Ch. Cahier and A. Martin, *Mélanges d'Archéologie* IV, 1856, fig. 57).

678. It is tempting to look in the neolithic stone alleys for the origins of that procession which wound its way through the rows of pillars and the sacred places of the Basilica.

679. Cf. S. Prassede in R. Kömstedt, *Vormitte alt. Malerei*, 1929, fig. 126. Particularly beautiful is the miniature in W. Neuss, *Die Ap in der Bibelillustration*, I, II, 1931, fig. 239.

680. In S. Michele, in Wulff, II, 427; cf. Cefalu in H. Preuss, *Bild Christi*, 1932, n. 20.

681. See above n. 670.

682. Cf. Rev. 7.9; 19.5; WilpertM., T. 672: 'Every station of life is represented: workers in short smocks, well-to-do in doublet and hose, philosophers in their pallium—and at the head a (princely) personage . . .', R. Guardini, *Der Engel in Dantes Göttlicher Komödie*, 1937, p. 85 (on *Paradiso*, p.23): 'The "procession" is a primordial form of life's pyramid. In it greatness, victory, dominion are experienced. So this procession is a heavenly triumph. But it is also much more: it is the harvest of history, mankind restored.'

683. John 5.35. For the cultic-enthusiastic origin of ἀγαλλιάομαι see KW, s.v.

684. Here are a few issues in the history of the concept and its problems: nature: Job 26.4; Prov. 8.22 = JustinDial. 61.3; 129.3. History: II Βασ 22.31; Jdth. 9.5; EpAr. 141. Proverbial wisdom: Job 5.27; 8.8 ff.; Ecclus. 14.21 f.; 16.20 ff.; Prov. 20.18. Rabbi's office: Ber. 7a; SB. 1.152; 435 ff.; 2.71; 3.245, 294. Prophecy and apocalyptic: Isa. 55.9 = JustinDial. 14.5; IV Ezra 4.2, 11; 5.34; SBar. 14.8 f.; 75.1 ff. Primitive Church: Rom. 11.33 (cf. Ecclus. 42.21); Eph. 3.8 ff.; Rev. 15.3 f.; I Cl. 31.1.

685. Psa. 76.20; PsSol. 8.15, 19; 17.21, 42; SBar. 5.3; 6.4 ff.; Gal. 3.19 f.; Matt. 5.13 ff.; Herm.s. 2.5 ff. Notice the words governed by διά c Gen. (=on the way over); διὰ χειρός (by the mediation of); ὑπέρ (=in the service of). On μεσίτης see Ch. 24.

686. Cf. Rom. 8.28 and also Phil. 1.12 ff.; TestB. 3.4 f.; TestG. 4.7 (συνεργεῖν),

together with לטב in Nahum (Taan, 21a) and Akiba (Ber. 60b); in the same connection the stoic ἐπ' ἀγαθῷ, e.g. DionChrysOr 30.8.

687. I Cor. 2.6 ff.; cf. J. A. Quenstedt, *Theologia Didactico-Polemica*, 1685, 534, on God's *directio* (in reference to Gen. 50.20; Acts 4.28; Rom. 8.28).

688. G. B. Shaw, *Major Barbara*, the end.

689. See KW, 3.326, 18 ff.; 329.26 ff.

690. Tob. 3.5; PsSol. 2.8; SBar. 5.2; 44.4 ff.; Rev. 18.5, 20; 16.5 ff. (the same 'yea' as in 1.7).

691. Isa. 28.29.

692. In GEn. 22.3 ff. the *angelus interpres* shows the apocalyptist a number of rock dwellings and explains; Οὗτοι οἱ τόποι οἱ κοῖλοι, ἵνα ἐπισυνάγωνται εἰς αὐτοὺς τὰ πνεύματα τῶν ψυχῶν τῶν νεκρῶν, εἰς αὐτὸ τοῦτο ἐκρίθησαν ὧδε ἐπισυνάγεσθαι πάσας τὰς ψυχὰς τῶν ἀνθρώπων. καὶ οὗτοι οἱ τόποι εἰς ἐπισύσχεσιν αὐτῶν ἐποιήθησαν μέχρι τῆς ἡμέρας τῆς κρίσεως αὐτῶν καὶ μέχρι τοῦ διορισμοῦ καὶ διαρισμένου χρόνου, ἐν ᾧ ἡ κρίσις ἡ μεγάλη ἔσται. The souls of the dead then gather together at some intermediate point and there, in an intermediate incorporeal state, await the final judgement (AEn. 51.1; 102.5; IV Ezra 4.35; 7.32; SBar. 21.23; 23.4; 30.2). Indeed, there are several such gathering points, different 'waiting rooms' for differing groups of men, each clearly divided off from the other. That is the picture of Gen. 22.8 f., and the presupposition of Luke 16.26 (though otherwise John 14.2 f.).

693. II Cor. 5.2 ff. (on καταποθῇ see I Cor. 15.55). Two images are intimately mixed up here. The earthly body is but a perishable covering (cf. II Cor. 4.7). That is the first picture (AEn. 62.15 f.; SEn. 22.8 ff.; ApAbr. 13; Rev. 3.4 f., 18; 6.11; 7.14). Within this temporary covering the imperishable spirit dwells, which God has given to the Christian as a pledge of eternal life (5.5; cf. Rom. 8.23). That much is certain. But will Paul's generation see the end of all things, and undergo the transmutation of the earthly body in their own lifetime? Or must the spiritual ego experience the decay of the corruptible body, and then await the end of all things and the imperishable body? That is the disquieting question. The earthly body is but a temporary lodging—that is the other picture (BBar. 2.17; II Pet. 1.14; on οἰκητήριον cf. GEn. 27.2). In virtue of God's preparation for us in heaven we are already provided with our final home. That much is sure. But what remains an unanswered question is when shall we enter our heavenly home (cf. Luke 16.9; John 14.2 f.).

694. Cf. Rom. 8.38; 14.8 f. and further Wisd. 3.1; IV Mac. 17.18 f.; Luke 23.43; I Cor. 3.22.

695. SBar. 30.1; John 5.28 f.; anticipatory resurrections in Matt. 27.52; John 11.43. But the 'rest' is not thought to be spent in an unconscious state. The fathers, patriarchs and prophets who 'fell asleep' live and act in the time between their death and their resurrection (IV Mac. 7.19; 16.25; Matt. 22.32; Luke 9.30). They have put off their fleshly garment and already wear the garments of light that belong to angelic beings (Rev. 4.4; 6.11; AscIs. 9.9). The souls of the martyrs 'rest' beneath the altar and cry out from thence to heaven (AEn. 22.5 f.; IV Ezra 4.35; Rev. 6.9 ff.). But evildoers 'rest in torment' till the judgement day, which will bring them new and greater and eternal torments (SBar. 36.11; Jude 6; II Pet. 2.4).

696. Thus in VitAdEv. 47 God gives fallen Adam into the care of the archangel Michael, with the words: *Sit in custodia tua usque in diem dispensationis*,

in suppliciis ad annos novissimos quando convertam luctum eius in guadium. (Temporal chastisement for sin *before* death in AEn. 22.10; cf. I Cor. 11.32.)

697. φυλακή = Sheol, cf. AEn. 22.4 ff.; 51; I Pet. 3.19; not Gehenna as in AEn. 27; Sib. 4.185; Matt. 10.28; 23.33.

698. Cf. Amos 4.11; Zech. 3.2; ὡς δαλὸς ἐξεσπασμένος ἐκ πυρός and the same formula in Sachs, Tef., 712.

699. Cf. Dam. 20.3 ff. and the burning of the unfaithful in PsPhil. 26.1 with the declared purpose: *ut pauset ira mea ab eis.*

700. When they hear the preaching of the gospel in hades.

701. This is the information given in ApP. in its more ancient version (Ethiopian) with one special sentence about hell sending forth all its inhabitants on the day of judgement to the forum of God (Ch. 4). But it goes on to spend many pages describing the punishments of the damned and the bliss of the saints after the last judgement (5 ff.). The later version, however (Greek text of Akhmim), changes the whole account from the future tense into the present, from the eschatological into the *katabasic* (6.21 ff.; cf. TestAbr. B. 10 f. = TSt. 2.2, 1892, p. 114 ff.). The interest in the age to come has receded. The picture of what is to happen at the end has become a picture of 'the other side', very much in the style of Greek descriptions of descents into hades and their accounts of the dead. Here we go beyond the limits of primitive Christianity.

702. The *name* cannot be definitely established before the Johannine epistles, though its appearance there presupposes a considerable history (I John 2.18, 22; 4.3; II John 7; cf. the marginal gloss in Dan. LXX 8.23 Swete; on 'Beliar' see Bousset, Antichrist, 86 f.). The *idea* is ancient. The figure of antichrist is described in its main features as early as Dan. 8.23 ff.; PsSol. 2 and other places, where historical and mythological elements are fused into a single picture of the enemy of God. It seems that this enemy of God was very early used as the antitype of the forerunner of the divinely sent deliverer-king (cf. Dan. 7.7 ff.; PsSol. 17.11, 21). This expectation established itself in the early Church, and the idea was filled out with all sorts of features, new and old (cf. Mark 13.21 f.; Matt. 24.11; Rev. 14; Did. 16; II Thess. 2). Indeed, later texts describe how he looks, with most circumstantial detail (ApEl. 33 f.; ApJ. 7 Tischendorf 74 f.; ApEzra, ibid., 29; further Weinel in *Eucharist. f. Gunkel*, p. 144 ff.). He is, as his name indicates, the opponent of the Christ who is to come, and his appearance is correspondingly given down to the last detail as a perverted copy of Christ (ApEl. 32 ff.). In this way the figure of the demonic opponent of God is more and more turned into the central figure of eschatological theomachy.

703. Rev. 11.3 ff. E. Hirsch, *Studien zum vierten Evangelium*, 1936, p. 142, 164, thinks that what we have got at this place is an allegorical account of the double martyrdom of the sons of Zebedee. We think this double martyrdom very uncertain and are more inclined to agree with Haug. op. cit., that in Rev. 11 it is an eschatological vision, with motifs from the stories of Moses and Elijah (plagues and rain) and other traditions as well. Yet the main theological motif which underlies the plan of the whole chapter is the old biblical idea of the unknown man of God, for whose sake cities and peoples and empires, indeed the world itself, continue in existence (cf. Gen. 18.32; Ecclus. 48.10; SBar. 2.2; 34 and the thoroughgoing scheme in AEn. 47; AssMos. 8 f.; II Mac. 15; Dam. 20.13 ff.; JosAnt. 18.119; 20.203; Orig. on Matt. 3.35; EusHE. 2.23; ApEl. 26 ff.). Haug overlooks this, hence his erroneous comment, p. 85, 87.

704. Mark 13.22; Matt. 24.11; II Thess. 2.3 ff.; I John 2.18 ff.; 4.3; II John 7; II Pet. 2.1; 3.3; Did. 16.3; cf. II Cor. 11.14; II Tim. 3, 4; Rev. 2.19. The last and most powerful of the rulers of the earth will not be brought to destruction by force of arms. The powers of chaos unite in vain to storm the defences of his kingdom. Only when the antichrist has performed his wonders will the unconquered ruler bend his knee in supplication. It is in this way that II Thess. is interpreted in *Ludus de Antichristo* (ed. F. Wilhelm, 1912, p. 14 ff.).

705. Antichrist says 'Church' but means 'God'. So it is only a question of time before the war of antichrist against the Church issues into a war against God himself. The older apocalyptic like to show this in the typical example of Antiochus Epiphanes. He erected the abomination of desolation in God's temple (Dan. 8.11 ff.; 9.27; 11.31; 12.11; I Mac. 1.57; 6.7; II Mac. 5.16 f.). He prided himself against the God of gods (Dan. 11.36; II Mac. 5.16 f.). He made sensational speeches, using fine words, which are an abomination before God (Dan. 7.8, 11 f.; cf. GEn. 5.4). The old biblical writings tell of similar attacks on God's honour by Heliodorus (II Mac. 3.13 ff.), Ptolemy (III Mac. 1.12 ff.) and Pompey (JosAnt. 14.66, 72; Bell 1.152; PsSol. 2.2 ff.; 17.11 ff.). The primitive Church held all these stories as merely chapters in the preface to the story of antichrist. When he appears he unites in himself every motif of blasphemy against God: Mark 13.14 (the masculine ἑστηκότα in connection with the neuter βδέλυγμα betrays the fact that the passage is about a person, and not an object); II Thess. 2.3 f. (cf. Iren. c. Haer. 5.30, 4); Rev. 13.5 f.

706. According to Maase Abr. (in SB. 3.35) once declared to Nimrod: 'I am he who created the heaven and the earth and all the host of them.' With the same sort of divine self-proclamation appeared Pharaoh and the King of Tyre, Sennacherib and Nebuchadrezzar (MEx. 49a on 15.11; further Ex. 29.9; 28.2, 9; IV βασ 18.35; Isa. 14.14). 'I am God, and I sit upon God's seat in the midst of the sea' (Hiram in Schatzh., p. 43). Antiochus and Pompey, and also Theudas and Simon Magus, have a liking for such I-formulae (Acts 5.36; 8.9 f.). According to Celsus the sorcerers used to cry: 'I am God, or the Servant of God or a Spirit of God' (OrigCels. 7.8 f.).

707. Rev. 13.4; AscIs. 4.8; primitive acclamation formulae which were used in Egypt of the triad Amon, Ra and Ptah (Jean, *Milieu Biblique*, II, p. 354), in Babylon of Marduk (A. Ungnad, *Rel. d. Bab. u. Ass.*, 1921, p. 40; 172; 197), in Jdth. 6.2 of Nebuchadrezzar are employed for Yahweh in Ex. 15.11.

708. On the question as to what point (in terms of the calendar) the early Church expected the end of the world there is not room for discussion. I refer to P. Feine, *Theol. d. NT*, p. 442 f.

709. The revelation of Christ's glory is depicted in the NT chiefly through four old biblical ideas: The day of the Lord=day of Yahweh in Amos 5.18; Isa. 2.12; Zeph. 1.7=the day of Christ in I Thess. 5.2; II Thess. 2.2 (cf. Ch. 25; 28). The day of the Son of Man (cf. Luke 17.24 with AEn. 61.5). *Parousia* and Epiphany (TestL. 8.15; TestJud. 22.2; AssMos. 10.1, 12; SBar. 30.1). Even the last two ideas have their old biblical antecedents, though they conform to the idiom of the Gentile Church as it was assimilated to the court language of Greece and Rome (Ch. 23). In the Diadochian and imperial times *parousia* meant the ceremonial entrance of the ruler into his city or province (Adventus, see the recently discovered dedicatory inscription of the triumphal tower in Gerasa for the 'Advent' of Hadrian, 130 A.D., Watzinger, D,

II, 920. There he was hailed as θεός and σωτήρ (cf. Vespasian's entry into Rome, JosBell. 7.68 ff.). The day of entry could be reckoned as a 'holy day' and was often used as the starting-point of a new time reckoning (DeissmannLAE, p. 314 ff.). In connection with the idea of *parousia*, indeed in alternation with it, we find the term Epiphany in use. The sovereign was held to be Θεὸς Ἐπιφανής, God manifest (DittSyll.³ 760.6). 'In the first year of the Epiphany of Gaius Caesar', was the way the inhabitants of Cos calculated their time after the visit of a prince of the house of Augustus (Paton and Hicks, *Inscriptions of Cos*, p. 391). The primitive Church spoke of the *parousia* of her heavenly Lord (παρουσία in Matt. 24.27 = ἡμέρα in Luke 17.24) and in so doing referred to his eschatological advent (Matt. 24.3; I Thess. 3.13; I Cor. 15.23; transferred to antichrist in II Thess. 2.9). It was not until the time of the Christian emperors that a typological co-ordination was achieved out of this antithesis. Thus the oppressed peasants of Egypt affirm in a papyrus of the sixth century that they await the *parousia* of the Dux with unceasing prayer, 'just as the inhabitants of hades sigh for the *parousia* of Christ' (DeissmannLAE, p. 319). The NT uses the word 'epiphany' in the same sense and in the same connection as the word *parousia*, see II Thess. 2.8 (further with Deissmann: DittSyll.³ 1169.34; παρουσίαν παρεφάνιζε); Tit. 2.13; cf. I Tim. 6.14; II Tim. 4.8 (further II Thess. 1.17: ἀποκάλυψις). But the heavenly Christ has already appeared once on earth on Christmas Day, admittedly in the form of a servant. Hence the Pastorals can describe the incarnation in a derived sense as an epiphany (II Tim. 1.10; cf. Tit. 2.11; 3.4). And even the term *parousia* was, at any rate up to the time of Ignatius, carried back to the incarnation itself (II Pet. 1.16?; IgnPhld. 9.2). After that we hear of a first and a second *parousia* (JustinDial. 1.14; ApSh. Inscr; ChrysHom. 75.2; cf. SEn. 32.1; 42.5). On the idea of *parousia* see now A. Baumstark in RAC, s.v. 'Advent'.

710. Did. 16.6: σημεῖον ἐκπετάσεως ἐν οὐρανῷ?

711. Matt. 24.30; according to Chrys. and others the cross; otherwise Sib. 4.172 f.

712. I Thess. 4.17 ἀπάντησις; cf. D* G and Matt. 25.1 ὑπάντησις.

713. See Peterson, op. cit., and KW, s.v. ἀπάντησις.

714. The Iranian tradition already had not only a regular succession of resurrection events (cf. I Cor. 15.23 f.) but also a metamorphosis of those resuscitated: 'First of all the skeleton of Gayomart will rise, then those of the first pair of human beings, then the rest of mankind . . . the body will walk perpetually in purity . . . and the heavenly creator will prepare clothing for it' (Bundehesch. ⟨Justi⟩ 31.72, 76; cf. 30, p. 47). From the time of Daniel onwards the old biblical apocalyptic spoke of the imperishable brilliance which would irradiate the saints on the resurrection day (Wisd. 3.7; AEn. 108.11 ff.; IV Ezra 7.88; AEn. 39.7; 62.15 f.). They would be like the angels (AEn. 104.6; 51.4), and shine like the stars (Dan. 12.3; IV Ezra 7.97; AEn. 104.2; IV Ezra 7.125). In TestB. 10.8a we read about the day of resurrection: Τότε πάντες ἀλλαγησόμεθα, οἱ μὲν εἰς δόξαν, οἱ δὲ εἰς ἀτιμίαν. The Seer of SBar. asks: 'In what form are they likely to live, who remain alive in thy day? Dost thou change them who have been in the world, as thou dost change the world itself?' He receives the answer that the dead will first of all come out of their graves in their previous condition, so that after God's judgement they might be changed. 'The wicked will be disfigured, but the pious will be glorified'

(cf. Ch. 56; 58). 'Then their brightness will be step by step transfigured and their countenances will change to a luminous beauty, so that they can accept and receive the immortal world . . . And time will not alter them, for they will live in the high places of that world and resemble the angels and be as the stars. And they will be changed into any form they choose: from beauty to splendour and from light to the brilliance of glory . . . And then the glory of the righteous will be greater than that of the angels' (51.3 ff.). Primitive Christianity adopted these traditions in speaking of the brightness of the stars, the glory of the angels and the radiant garments of the resurrected saints (Matt. 13.43; Luke 20.36; Rev. 3.4; 7.9). The problem of metamorphosis was particularly studied by Paul (II Cor. 4.17 f.; 5.1 ff.; proleptic glorification in Rom. 8.30; II Cor. 3.18; by degrees in SBar. 51.3, 10; mystical transformation in OdSol. 15.8). Πάντες . . . ἀλλαγησόμεθα, says Paul in the words of TestB. 10. 'With what manner of body do they come?' he asks, in the manner of SBar. 49.2, so as to continue in the words of SBar. 51.3 ff. (I Cor. 15.35; 40 ff.). The negative premiss of his argument runs quite in the style of SBar. 51.3b: 'Flesh and blood cannot inherit the Kingdom of God' (I Cor. 15.50). The positive basis (similar to Bundehesch 31) is the resurrection of Christ, which has its fulfilment in his *parousia* (I Cor. 15.23, 44 ff.). Paul knows nothing of a restitution of the earthly body for the time between the resurrection and the last judgement (I Cor. 15.52 cf. SBar. 50.2 ff.). The bodily form in which the dead appear is fashioned after the pattern of Christ's spiritual body of glory (I Cor. 15.49; read φορέσομεν with B; φορέσωμεν is an unsuccessful attempt to moralize).

715. I John 3.2; cf. PsClemHom. 17.16 and POxy 655b in Windisch ad. loc.

716. In Dan. 7 it is the Son of Man who follows after the fourth and last world empire. In IV Ezra it is the Messiah of the tribe of David who puts an end to the fourth world empire, and saves the remnant—and rules them 'until the end, the day of judgement comes' (12.31 ff.; AEn. 91.12 ff. speaks of a 'week' of righteousness before the 'week' of the last judgement without mentioning either the Son of Man or Messiah; cf. the seven years in IV Ezra 7.26 ff. and Sib. 5.351: ἔσσεται ἧμαρ ἐκεῖνο χρόνον πολύν). Then for the first time, after a final crisis, the Son of Man will appear on the clouds of heaven and establish his eternal dominion (IV Ezra 13.3 ff. after Dan. 2.45; 7.13, etc.). In IV Ezra 7.26 ff. the traditions of an earthly Messiah and a supernatural Son of Man appear united, and the messianic reign is fixed at 400 years (see Gen. 15.13; Psa. 89.15). Then Messiah dies and all mankind with him. God himself holds the judgement of the world (as in Dan. 7.10). Then at last the 'age to come' arrives in power. SBar. has enhanced the supernatural qualities of Messiah, though even he speaks of an end of his government. We read of a paradisaical age when the earth will be abundantly fruitful and of the messianic feast (cf. Isa. 25.6). 'And it shall come to pass after these things, when the time of the advent of the Messiah is fulfilled, that he shall return (to heaven) in glory.' Then follows, as in IV Ezra, the resurrection of the dead and the segregation of the spirits (29 f.; cf. 49 ff.; 74.1; otherwise 73.1).

717. San. 98b; SB. 4 799 ff.

718. Luke 17.22 (ἡμέραι τοῦ υἱοῦ τοῦ ἀνθρώπου betrays a blending of the motifs of the Son of Man and Messiah, as in IV Ezra 7; SBar. 29 f.); Matt. 19.28 (παλιγγενεσία implies a renewal of the creation after some catastrophic destruction, cf. PhilVitMos. 2.65; IV Ezra 7.31 f., 75; I Cl. 9.4; Papias in EusHE.

3.39.1: *creatura renovata*). Otherwise the period of government which begins with the *parousia* is called the Kingdom of God or the Kingdom of the Son of Man (cf. Ch. 28). The Father has given authority over to the Son, and the Son has passed it on to the twelve. When he enters upon the throne of his glory they will sit on twelve thrones ruling over the twelve tribes of Israel (Dan. 7.9, 18; Wisd. 3.8; Luke 22.29 f.; Matt. 19.28; κρίνειν means here, as in Wisd. 3.8 'rule', not 'judge'. The same is true of I Cor. 6.2 f.; Rev. 20.4; see Klosterm and Bchm. against Ltzm. and Lohm. ad. loc.). For the rest, Jesus had a liking for the picture of the messianic meal, which we meet first in SBar. 29 (Luke 14.15, 24; Mark 14.25; Matt. 22.2 ff.; 25.10 ff.). The disciples are to eat and drink with him at his table in his kingdom (Luke 22.30).

719. I Thess. 4.17; 5.10; cf. SBar. 30; Matt. 28.28 (in the NT there is no evidence of the death of the eschatological Christ, as in IV Ezra 7.21). On the participation of Christians in the dominion of Christ see II Thess. 1.5 ff.; I Cor. 6.2 f.; 15.50; Rom. 5.17; cf. AEn. 13 ff.; II Tim. 2.10 ff.

720. Εἶτα τὸ τέλος in I Cor. 15.24 does not concern the last group of those who are raised from the dead, but simply the end of history; see ArmEzra 6.28: *atque sic veniet finis*; SyrEzra 7.33: *et veniet consummatio*; if (both?) these formulae were to be thought secondary, they could well gain significance as early inter pretations of I Cor. 15.24.

721. Rev. 20.8 f.; cf. EEn. 56.6. Satan's generals are called Gog and Magog, see Ezek. 38.2 LXX; Sib. 3.319, 512. The rabbis allotted seven years to Gog and Magog, see Exr. 15 on 12.2; Lvr. 11 on 9.1 and jScheb. 35c25 in SB. 1.517.

722. The idea of a (millenial) *civitas christi* between the old age and the new gained a very lively currency in the early Church (IV Ezra 2.28; TestIs. 8.11; II Pet. 3.8; Barn. 15.4; Iren. AdvHaer. 5.28.3). Millenianism plays an important part in the writings of Papias (TU. 5.2, 1888, 170). Χιλιάδα τινά φησιν ἐτῶν ἔσεσθαι μετὰ τὴν ἐκ νεκρῶν ἀνάστασιν, σωματικῶς τῆς Χριστοῦ βασιλείας ἐπί ταυτησὶ τῆς γῆς ὑποστησομένης (Papias, according to EusHE. 3.39.12). Papias describes the paradisal fertility of these days in language that is highly reminiscent of SBar. 29.5 ff. There the description of the messianic kingdom includes: 'On a single vine there will be a thousand branches, on every branch a thousand clusters, and to every cluster a thousand grapes.' In Papias this information is multiplied and reads thus—Jesus is brought back! *Vineae nascentur, singulae decem millia palmitum habentes . . . et in uno vero palmite dena millia flagellorum et in unoquoque flagello dena millia botruum, et in unoquoque botruo dena millia acinorum . . .* (EusHE. 3.39.1). One can see how pre-Christian traditions were taken up and developed by the early Church.

723. Ezek. 9.6; Matt. 13.13, 20, 24 ff.; 47 ff.; 22.14; Matt. 10.22; II Thess. 1.5; I Cor. 11.19, 32; Phil. 1.28; Rev. 2 f.; I Pet. 4.17; Windisch, ad. loc. compares with MartPionii. 4.14 ff.

724. The earth gives up her dead, and now not only those who confess Christ, but all without exception (John 5.28 f.; cf. TestB. 10.8a). This is the second resurrection (cf. ἀνάστασις πρώτη in Rev. 20.5 f.). The books are opened (Dan. 7.10; Rev. 20.12). What is written in them? In the Book of Life are the names of the elect (Ex. 32.32; Dan. 12.1; Psa. 68.29; Sachs, *Tef.* 590; Luke 10.20; Phil. 4.3; Rev. 3.5; 13.8; 17.8; 20.15; 21.27; Herm.v. 1.3.2). But in the Book of Judgement are written the evil deeds of the godless (EEn. 69.27; 89.62; 90.20; SBar. 24.1; Rev. 20.12; AscIs. 9.22; TestAb. 10 f. refers to the

Book of Good Deeds and the Book of Evil Deeds). On that day the persecutors will recognize with moanings him whom they pierced (App. I and Rev. 1.7; cf. John 19.37). The accused will lament over themselves: 'All the sins which I committed in this world I have forgotten; ἐνταῦθα δὲ οὐκ ἐληθαργήθησαν!' (Rev. 1.7; TestAb. 10; cf. I John 2.28).

725. The last judgement is the boundary line between the *civitas christi* and the *civitas dei*. Who will be the judge? Neither Christ (who ends his reign at that point) nor yet God himself (who begins his reign then)? Both these answers have their roots in pre-Christian apocalyptic, and both are attested in the NT. In Dan. 7.9 the Ancient of Days himself sits upon the seat of judgement (cf. EEn. 47.3), and this tradition finds an echo in Rom. 14.10; Jas. 4.12; Luke 12.5; Heb. 10.31; Rev. 20.11. But it is the Son of Man who holds judgement in EEn. 69.7, and it is this view which is carried on into Christian eschatology, symbolics, poetry and art. But it takes up into itself the idea of the judgement of God (John 5.22, 27; Matt. 25.31 ff.; II Cor. 5.10; Rev. 22.12; II Tim. 4.1).

726. Rev. 2.17. ψῆφος is the voting tablet (cf. Acts 26.10), 'white' indicates acquittal (cf. IV Mac. 15.26), the 'new name' is the sacred name which the elect receive in υἱοθεσία (cf. Gen. 32.29; Isa. 62.2; Matt. 16.18 and the later monastic names). Lohmeyer contends differently ad. loc.: 'With the manna . . . fell . . . from heaven "precious stones and pearls" at the same time; this rabbinic tradition could well have given rise to the saying about the white stone . . . The name is naturally that of Christ; it is "new" provided that it is . . . written on the stone in a form of signs and numbers previously unknown.' Beatus long ago put it briefly and rightly: *nomen christianum = adoptio in filios dei* (H. A. Sanders, *Beati in Apocalypsin libri duodecim*, 1930).

727. The rabbis had already given expression to this, though polemically, and not as a confession.

728. Rev. 6.17; 7.15; ArmEzra 7.42; cf. Bundehesch 30.269, 20; Wisd. 11.5 ff.

729. The duality for a theology of history that is found in John 1.5; 8.44 prevents the universalist motif of John 1.29; I John 2.2; Rev. 15.4; 21.24; 22.2 from having full effect.

730. There are motifs in the old biblical literature that point in this direction. God's creation must come to grief on the stubborn fact of sin, were not God's justice to give place to his mercy (IV Ezra 7.138; Pesikt. 16 f.; cf. Ezek. 18.23; Wisd. 11.23 ff.; PsSol. 17.34 f. ?). But God does not allow his creation to perish. He made the world in the dimension of justice, and judges it in the dimension of mercy (IV Ezra 7.132; 8.47; Ab. 3.19 f.). God's mercy is first of all applied to the chosen people. But the elect are meant to come before God in intercession for those that are depraved (VitAdEv. 46 f.?; IV Ezra 7.132; San. 37a; ApAn. 16 f. = TU., 1899, 154 f.; ApSh. 5; 8; 14: here the interceding apocalyptist turns for support to Michael, not to Christ—a proof of the pre-Christian origin of this motif; otherwise TestIss. 8.12). The mercy of God and the intercession of the elect—these are the hope of the world.

731. תְּשׁוּבָה ('μετάνοια' is a bad translation and 'repentance' even worse).

732. XVIII, 5 (הָרוֹצֶה בִּתְשׁוּבָה); TestAbr. 12; Lam. 3.33; Manasseh 6 ff.; Jonah 3.10; Jer. 18.7 f.; Ezek. 33.11; Luke 13.6 ff., 35 (cf. Luke 12.58 f. μέχρι!); 19.42; Matt. 12.39 ff.; n. 781.

733. We have already discussed, in Ch. 52, the two suggestions of purgatory

in this epistle. But in neither instance is the context that of effecting an universal salvation, but rather that of contrasting divine grace which is immutable with an individual who has been completely swept off his feet.

734. But in its full meaning μένειν can only apply to ἀγάπη; see I Cor. 13.13b; II Cor. 5.7; Rom. 8.24 and KW, s.v. ἀγαπάω.

735. See n. 544.

736. I Cor. 15.28; ἐν πᾶσιν neutral like πάντα in I Cor. 15.27 f.; 8.6; Rom. 11.36; Col. 1.16, 20; the formula in Col. 3.11 has a different wording and meaning.

737. See πάντες Rom. 3.23 f.; 5.18.

738. The idea of an universal salvation did not die out even among Paul's disciples. The author of I Tim. 2.1 ff. directly connects the motif of intercession in Rom. 9.3 with the universal salvation in Rom. 11.36, and so provides us with an authoritative testimony as to the earliest exegesis of Rom. 9–11: he exhorts to intercession 'for all men' (cf. ApEzra, Tischendorf, 24 f.). The pathos of such intercession is, however, rooted in the conviction: Christ has given his life a ransom not only ἀντὶ πολλῶν (Mark 10.45), but ὑπὲρ πάντων (so Heb. 2.9; I Tim. 2.6). (Θεὸς) πάντας ἀνθρώπους θέλει σωθῆναι (cf. OdSol. 9.13). Our text says 'God wills' not merely 'God would like'. The word is θέλει, and it means the irresistible will of God, which is stronger than anything we can .mean by 'world', and which has power over every creaturely will, and so carries its own guarantee of fulfilment within itself (the counterpart to this is βούλεσθαι in II Pet. 3.9; cf. Ch. 45). In this sense (contrary to B. Weiss, ad. loc.) God is called in I Tim. 4.10 'the Saviour of all men, specially of them that (now) believe', but not only of believers (cf. I Tim. 6. 13). In this sense the *numerus praedestinatorum* in Heb. 12.23 are thought of as the Church of the firstborn (in Jas. 1.18 as the firstfruits of his creatures). In fine: the Church of God is not the end, but the beginning, the beginning of a renewal and redemption of all mankind (cf. PhilSpecLeg. 4.180; Rom. 11.1, 7, 16, 18). Another disciple of Paul uses the descent into hades to support the basic conception of God's will that all should be saved (cf. Rom. 10.7; Eph. 4.8 f.). The God-fearers of the old covenant are not alone in hearing the message of salvation and receiving the sign of the cross (so Herm.s. 9.16.7). Even the wicked and disobedient generation of the Flood are among those who hear the gospel preached in hades, and a future prospect is opened up for them (I Pet. 3.19, in contrast to EEn. 65.11: no return throughout eternity). None is finally condemned (cf. EvPt. 41 f.; also ApAn. 16 f.; TestAbr. 12). The message of the cross reaches everyone, ἵνα κριθῶσι μὲν κατὰ ἀνθρώπους σαρκί, ζῶσι δὲ κατὰ θεὸν πνεύματι (I Pet. 4.6 following I Cor. 5.5 cf. I Tim. 1.20; TestIss. 7.13). The final and most daring thought of Paul is the future outlook of Col. which has affected Eph. and in that epistle is given conceptual formulation in the apt word 'recapitulation' (later supplanted by the unsuitable idea of *apokatastasis*). It is the mystery of God's will 'to sum up (recapitulate) all things in Christ, the things in the heavens, and the things upon the earth' (Eph. 1.9 f., cf. ἀνακεφαλαιοῦσθαι, i.e. recapitulare in ProtevJa. 13.1; Justin IrenAdvHaer. 4.6.2). Christ takes up universal history, which since Adam has been set on the way to death, so as to give it henceforth an all-inclusive end in salvation (cf. Eph. 1.20 ff.; 2.14 ff.; 3.10; also IgnE. 19.3; Barn. 6.13; JustinDial. 100). Μακροθυμεῖ εἰς ὑμᾶς, μὴ βουλόμενός τινας ἀπολέσθαι ἀλλὰ πάντας εἰς μετάνοιαν χωρῆσαι

(II Pet. 3.9). That is how the last letter of the NT changes the formula of I Tim. 2.4 (cf. Ezek. 18.23; I Cl. 7.4; TestAbr. 12). God's programme, issuing in his decree, is that none should be lost, but that every moment should provide an opportunity to return home.

739. II Pet. 3.10 (read ἀγρά; cf. IV Ezra 7.30; II Cl. 16.3; πᾶσα ἡ γῆ ὡς μόλιβος ἐπὶ πυρὶ τηκόμενος); related passages in Windisch, ad. loc.

740. Cf. I Cor. 2.10 and the history of the formula in Bachmann-Stauffer, ad. loc.

741. EEn. 72.1; SEn. 65.6 ff.; Rev. 10.6; cf. Beda in Lohmeyer, ad. loc.: *mutabilis saecularium temporum varietas cessabit.*

742. I Cor. 15.19; cf. SBar. 21.13: 'For if there were this life only, which belongs to all men, nothing could be more bitter than this.'

743. Mark 4.26 ff.; Matt. 13.24 ff.; John 12.24; I Cor. 15.20, 23; cf. also Sprenger, PJB, 1913.

744. See Luther on Rom. 8.21 Gloss: *Terra et coelum transibunt non secundum substantiam sed secundum corruptibilitatem.*

745. Cf. the heavenly city (Isa. 65.18 f.; SBar. 4.1 ff.; Gal. 4.26; Heb. 11.10; Rev. 21.2, 16 ff.) and the paradise of the last times (Rom. 8.21; Isa. 11.6 ff.; 65.25; Mark 1.13; Barn. 6.17 ff.; Isa. 4.2 MT; Ezek. 47.12; Exr. on 12.12; Rev. 2.7; 21.2; 22.1 f., 14, 19).

746. Rev. 10.1; 18.1; cf. Ex. 34.29 ff.; II Cor. 3.7 ff.; 4.6; also PhilDecal 105.

747. For the literary species of the OT and NT H. Gunkel has asked the question as to their *sitz im leben* (location in life); E. Norden, *Theos*, p. 380 ff. has searched the NT for formally expressed confessions of faith.

748. Drews, Schermann, Baumstark, etc.

749. II Tim. 3.14 ff.; Acts 18.25 f.; Luke 1.4 (further Jackson, *Beginnings*, 2, p. 489–510).

750. Matt. 18.20; I Cor. 11.2, 16; Heb. 5.12; 6.1 f.; the same trichotomy appears in the Did.: 1 ff. = ethical catechism; 7 ff. = liturgy; 16 = apocalypse.

751. Heb. 6.1; Rom. 6.17 τύπος διδαχῆς. There arose a Pauline (Tit. 1.9), a Johannine (II John 9 f.) and a Roman (Rom. 6.17) school, and soon in addition an Alexandrine, which admitted hellenistic as well as Jewish influences upon itself; cf. W. Bousset, *Jüd.christl. Schulbetrieb in Alexandria und Rom*, 1915. Heretics (the Gnostics!) also founded schools (Heb. 13.9; Rev. 2.14, 24).

752. TertBapt. 20; Absolute renunciation in ApConst. 7.41.2.

753. Sakaru = זכר in the OT = ὁμολογεῖν in LXX and NT. Cf. also W. Maurer, *Bekenntnis und Sakrament*, 1939, 7 ff.

754. Also in the Synagogue, see Elbogen, *Gottesdienst*, 24 f.; 235 f.; 247, etc.

755. I Cor. 11.26 (?); JustinApol. 1.67.2; further the detailed eucharistic confession in the Papyrus on Der-Balyzeh in Th. Schermann, *Ägypt. Abendmahlsliturgien des 1 Jahrtausends*, 1912, p. 10.

756. Tit. 1.9; cf. the analogous structure of I Thess. 4.14 ff.; I Cor. 15.1 ff.; Heb. 1.1 ff.; I John 1.1 ff.; Rev. 1.4 ff. and above all II Cl. 1.1.

757. Naturally confessions of faith had their place, not only in the life of the community, but also in that of the individual. We may refer to exorcism (cf. Jas. 2.19; DeissmannLAE, 217), the rite of ordination (cf. I Tim. 4.14; II Tim. 1.6; II Tim. 2.2 mentions a catechism by which the ordinand was bound, I Tim. 6.12 an ordination confession), martyrdom (cf. Ber 61b; MartPol. 8 ff.; further the doxological triad of the dying man in 14.3). The confession of

Christ and the baptism of blood belong together just as baptismal confession and water baptism (Rev. 3.8; Heb. 10.25). TertSpect. 25 explains: The mouth that has responded to the trisagion in the liturgy with 'Amen' cannot confess any other than God and his anointed in the moment of martyrdom or in eternity. 'Confessor', 'professor' became technical terms for those who had made their confession *in conspectu mortis*. Indeed, in the Syrian Church the notion of 'confessor' actually got the meaning of 'witness by blood' (equivalent to μάρτυς!); see P. Peeters, AnBoll. 39, 1921, p. 53 ff.

758. Further material in W. Bacher, *Tradition und Tradenten in den Schulen Palästinas und Babyloniens*, 1914, 25 ff., and, E. Kohlmeyer, ThStKr., 1931, 237 f.

759. Cf. SEn. 33.10 (Michael = 'mediator' of the secret revelation).

760. Further material in H. Odeberg, ad. loc. (bHag. 14b; jHag. 77b, etc.).

761. Cf. the list of priests in Melch III (Bonwetsch)—Seth-Enosh-Russij-Amilan - Prassidan - Maleleel - Seroch - Arnsan - Aleem - Enoch - Methusaleh - Nir-Melchidezek, etc.

762. I Cl. 42.2, 4; cf. Schatzh. 53: 'Because every one of the divine teachers of the Church had given her true doctrine as her foundation . . .'

763. Hymns to Enlil, Horus, Osiris, Nile, Sun, Amon Ra, etc., in Jean, *Milieu Biblique*, II, p. 40; 42; 105; 119; 151 ff.; 350 ff.; SophAnt. 781 ff. (hymn to Eros); ApulMet 11.5 (Isis liturgy). On self-revelations of an ethical kind see KW, s.v. ἐγώ. There are not so many formulae telling in the past tense of a chain of divine acts in a mythical prehistory, see A. Erman, *AegRel*,[2] 61; A. Ungnad, *Rel.der Bab.*, 172 ff.; H. Gressmann, *AOT*,[2] 1926, 1 ff.; 129 ff.

764. On the term ἀρεταλογία in Ecclus. 36.13 cf. Isa. 43.21; I Pet. 2.9 and Kiefer, op. cit.

765. So e.g. in Psa. 75; 134.6 ff. (Present-beginning; past-continuation, as in Akhenaton's 'Hymn to the Sun'), Sachs, *Tef.* 18 ff.; 54 ff.; 158 ff.

766. Cf. Gunkel, op. cit., 51 f.; 76 ff.; 78: The 'appearance of the sacred legend in hymns . . . is a distinctively Israelite feature, for which there is no parallel in Babylon or Egypt.' The first germ of these summaries of the history of salvation is in all probability the formula of Yahweh's deliverance from Egypt, see Ex. 20.2 ; Deut. 5.6; 6.4 ff., 20 ff.; Psa. 106.1 (ἐξομολογεῖσθε); 106.31 f.; 76.12.

767. The problem of the summaries is a typical example of how research suffers when the individual scholar or exegete fails to look beyond his specialism or his confessional boundaries. Archeologists (Le Blant, Kauffmann, K. Michel. Wilpert, Wulff, Neuss), liturgiologists (Drews, Elbogen, Baumstark), students of religion (Kiefer), literary critics (Gunkel) have dealt with the subject one after another, mostly without knowledge of work already done. NT literature up to the present (even Bousset, op. cit., and Dibelius, ThR., 1931, 228 f.) has so far shown practically no signs of any knowledge of all this material and research and offers either no observations at all (Windisch,[1] Rohr, SB, O. Michel) on Heb. 11, or else comments quite insignificantly (Windisch,[2] cf. N. Peters, 1913, on Ecclus. 44 ff.).

768. Cf. Wisd. 18.9 (τοὺς ἁγίους πατέρων ἤδη προαναμέλποντες αἴνους), II Ezra 19.3 ; III Mac. 2.20 (αἰνέσεις) ; PhilSpecLeg. 1.97; 210 f. ; further Kauffmann, op. cit., 245 ff.; Michel, op. cit., 123; Elbogen, *Gottesdienst*, 112 f.; 276 ff.; 223; 550 f.; 217; Sachs, *Tef.* 38; 56; 80 ff.; 216; 666 ff.; Baumstark, *Theol und Gl.*, op. cit.; Fiebig, *Judentum*, 26; 28; 64.

769. Ecclus. 44 Inscr. πατέρων ὕμνος. Ecclus. 44–50, the greatest of all surviving summaries, offers but scant appreciation of the men of God from Enoch until the day of the prophets, and finally gives as its crowning conclusion a glorification of Simon the High Priest. The Abodah of the day of atonement was later constructed on the same schema, and it runs through the men of God from the beginning until Moses in order to finish with a glorification of Aaron and his cultic functions on the day of atonement (see Elbogen, *Studien z.Gesch. des jüd. Gottesdienstes*, 1907, 58 ff.; 66 f.). Does Ecclus. 44 ff. constitute the first 'Abodah'? On patriarchs or patriarchal women in stereotyped formulae see Sachs, Tef. 236; 741 f. On martyr-summaries and martyrologies see Elbogen, *Gottesdienst*, 203; 228.

770. Cf. H. Gunkel, *Die Propheten*, 1917, 138 f.: 'In the end a religious philosophy of history has grown up out of prophecy . . .' It is noteworthy that the two prophets who opened up the new paths, Jer. and Ezek. both came from priestly families and therefore were specially trusted from the very beginning with the liturgical traditions of their people. Philo had a liking for the series of paradigms, and used a name for them which otherwise he reserved for the harmony of the spheres, τάξεις ἐναρμόνιοι, and he used them from time to time as introductions for his tractates (PhilPraemPoen. 7; cf. PhilVirt. 198 ff.)

771. Cf. App. VII; SEn in the longer version has a series of seven, though the shorter text has only 1 and 2; Peah 2 quotes from the stereotyped succession list of Ab. 1.1. only the first and the last.

772. On Zechariah see above n. 266; on μεταξὺ τοῦ θυσιαστηρίου καὶ τοῦ οἴκου cf. Yoma 103; Luke 13.1; Acts 5.37 and the scholium from MatthAcApost in Preuschen, ad. loc.

773. Heb. 11.2; cf. the introductory words in I Mac. 2.51 and the transition from the main introductory thesis to historical proof in IV Mac. 1.7 f., 12; 2.16 ff.; 3.6 ff., 19 ff.

774. Seven times a summary starts with πίστει, leading up to the end of the first section with κατὰ πίστιν (11.13–16). Then follows an elevenfold πίστει and at the end (11.32 ff.) a general survey in style of I Mac. 2.61. On 11.37 f. cf. PsSol. 17.16 f.

775. I Cl. 31.1: ἴδωμεν, τίνες αἱ ὁδοὶ τῆς εὐλογίας. ἀνατυλίξωμεν τὰ ἀπ' ἀρχῆς γενόμενα; cf. Psa. 77.2 ff., etc.

776. See App. VII; further AugCivD. 10.

777. There are only summary-like elements or items in the speech of Acts 7, as also in the short list of those who despised God in Jude 5 ff. (on the theme see MEx. 49 on 15.11; on the introductory formula see Psa. 76.12; Deut. 6.21; 32.7; IV Mac. 18.14; for the unchronological series see Ecclus. 49.16 ff.; Judth. 9.2 ff.). II Pet. 2.4 ff. has not developed the items into a summary-like series, but rather prevented it.

778. Barn. 11 is not a summary, but a list of places; cf. SB. 3.198 f.

779. Cf. K. Michel, op. cit., 31; 61; 64; A. Baumstark, *Werden der Lit*, 1923, 14; 17; *Messe im Morgenland*, 25 f.; 126 ff.; Edessen, 'Martyrologium', ActBoll. Nov 2, 1 p. LXIII.

780. Exorcist paradigm-series in K. Michel, 19 ff.; E. Peterson, 1926, 83; homiletic series in Michel, 44.

781. Cf. n. 773 ff.; further the traditional introductory and application formulae in I Cl. 9.2; 13.1; the transition from general to special in I Cl. 45.2 ff.

(like Ecclus. 44.15 f.); the phrase *qui es amator paenitentiae*, in PsCypr. 2.2 =
TU. 4.36, 1899, 26 (cf. n. 732); the predication of φιλάνθρωπε ActCypr. 5 in
Th. Zahn, *Cyprian von Antiochen*, 1882, 145 (cf. Wisd. 11.26). Bousset's ob-
servations and theses in literary criticism point in the same direction.

782. Thus the prayers of martyrs in Le Blant, op. cit., XXIX f.; K. Michel,
25; cf. 30; three patriarchs in the liturgy for the dead, three wives of patriarchs
in the marriage liturgy, see James, TsT, 2.2.128 f. and Brightman, *Eastern
Liturgies*, p. 57 (cf. n. 769). Exclusive NT series of paradigms are infrequent,
cf. Michel, 25; Äg Kirchenordnung in Achelis, 51 f.

783. Cf. the praises of the ruler's virtues, AOT,[2] 23; 25; PhilLeg. 144 (cf.
above n. 210).

784. The form of the summary survives in early German texts (see e.g.
C. W. M. Grein, *Dichtungen der Angelsachsen*, II,[2] 1863, 54 ff.; W. Schultz,
Altgerm.Kultur,[3] 1935, 88; 90), baptismal hymns (see Stauffer, ZKG, 1933,
560 ff.) and most noticeably in the present-day liturgies of the Synagogue and
of the Roman Church.

785. An early Christian glass bowl has in the centre (!) the sacrifice of Isaac,
and on the rim Daniel, the three young men, Susanna, Jonah, Lazarus, etc.,
and in addition notes which read like the formulae of the *commendatio animae*:
Daniel *de lacu leonis*, etc.; see the reproduction in Le Blant, op. cit.; photograph
in P. Styger, *Altchr. Grabeskunst*, fig. 30. There are similar bowls in London
and Cologne. K. Michel (p. 64) discusses the correlation between prayer
inscriptions in the form of a summary and picture-paradigms. There are illus-
trations in Stefanescu, *Annuaire de l'Institut . . .Or*, 1935, CXXIII; on the summary in the anaphora of the Liturgy of St Basil, see ibid., 487. On the consequences see Neuss, Kunst, 30 ff.; Styger, 141.

786. JosAnt. 5.112; θεὸν ἕνα γινώσκειν τὸν Ἑβραίοις ἅπασιν κοινόν.

787. See Elbogen, *Gottesdienst*, 14 ff.; 496; SB. 2.28 ff.; SDt 6.4 f. Akiba died
with the אחד of the Shema on his lips (Ber. 61b). Related formulae in Sachs,
Tef. 10; 12; 36; 96; 148; 262. The apologetic, polemic and propaganda of the
Jews preached the monotheistic confession of faith as the most exalted expression of the most exalted religion (PhilOpMund. 171; PhilLegGai. 115;
JosAnt. 3.91; Sib, Aristobulus, etc., in KW, s.v. θεός p. 98, 197). In their
everyday piety the Jews used monotheistic formulae to fight against the demonic
powers (cf. Peterson, op. cit., 280 ff.). Jewish eschatology revived the idea of the
future found in Zech. 14.9; see ApEl. 31 (christianized in ApEl. 26); TgJ I on Ex.
17.15 f. (Bacher, Tannaiten, 142); Sachs, Tef. 172; 202; 316; 464; 466; 608; 710.

788. Norden, *Theos*, 145.

789. See Leipoldt, Umwelt (Picture Atlas), fig. 76 f.; 79; 81.

790. Mark 12.28 ff.; cf. 10.18; Luke 10.27; Naassenerev in Huck[9] 143;
εἷς ἐστιν ἀγαθός, ὁ πατήρ μου ἐν τοῖς οὐρανοῖς.

791. I Tim. 1.17; John 17.3; Rev. 15.4; Jas. 2.19; Peterson, op. cit., 1 ff.;
M. J. Rostovtzeff, *Dura*, 1934, 240: εἷς θεὸς ἐν οὐρανῷ; O. Casel, JbfLygw,
XII, 1932, 68.

792. Rev. 1.8; cf. Gatha (Bartholomae) 4.8; 9.3 ff.; Isa. 44.6; Fiebig, *Judentum*,
26; Schubert-Christaller, op. cit., 13; KW, s.v.

793. Rev. 1.8; cf. Gatha 2.4; 6.10; 10.7 (Bartholomae); Yasna 39.2 (Wolff);
Yasht 13.154 (Lommel); Sachs, *Tef.* 12; 66; Schubert-Christaller, op. cit., 8;
10; n. 106 above; Greek parallels in KW, s.v. εἰμί.

794. Luke 11.2; Matt. 23.9; Gal. 4.6; Rom. 8.15; cf. Ecclus. 23.1; XVIII 4.6; Elbogen, op. cit., 30; KW, s.v. ἀββά; on II Cor. 1.3 cf. also Sachs, *Tef.* 94; 118; 152; 304.

795. Cf. II Mac. 7.28 f.; XVIII 2. In Rom. 11.36 (cf. I Cor. 8.6) Paul uses the language of hellenism, see Lietzmann ad. loc. and M. Dibelius, NJbchKlAlt, 1915.

796. Cf. Dg. 3.22 ff.; GP in ClAl 6.5.39; also 6.6.48.

797. A. Hahn, *Bibl. der Symbole*,² 1877, 1; 45 ff.; 62.

798. To these correspond the doxological (John 16.14), the exorcist (Mark 16.17) and the confessional (Acts 4.12) usage of the Christ-formulae.

799. Cf. the striking avoidance of the title of 'Son of Man' in John 9.35 ff. An apocryphal exception which proves the rule is to be found in HippRef. 5.26.30.

800. They are only tendencies in that direction; cf. Acts 7.56; EusHE. 2.23; I Tim. 2.5 (?); IgnE. 20.2; PsClemRec. 3.48.

801. 'Prophet' is a word we do not find at all in the creedal history of the primitive Church, and 'teacher' occurs but spasmodically and with indirect testimony (Matt. 23.8).

802. Confession of Christ is to be found as early as the original form of Peter's confession (Mark 8.29; Luke 9.20) and in the early confessional conflicts as John 9.22, but it can also be found in the later christological discussion with Docetism (I John 2.22). But the title Christ very quickly hardened into a regular part of the proper name (Ch. 25). In this form it took root in the development of the creeds and gained a place as a dogmatic concept and criterion (cf. Acts 4.12; 8.12; I Cor. 1.2, etc.). The predicate 'Son of God' (MartPol. 17.3; cf. John 9.35 vl., and the liturgical interpolation of Acts 8.37) is often very closely connected with the confession of the Christ (Mark 16.16; I John 2.22 ff.; cf. IV Ezra 7.28; Mark 14.61). But even the double predicate Son of God-Son of David is not infrequent (Rom. 1.4; cf. 9.4 f.; IgnE. 7.2; 18.2). And here the inner antinomy of the concept of the Son of Man (divine exaltation and human dishonour) is turned into the paradoxical unity of a conceptual antithesis—for the first time, and in exemplary fashion, in the history of the creeds! The confession of Jesus as Lord is already contained in the ancient prayer 'Maranatha' (see above n. 360). In Rom. 10.9; I Cor. 12.3 there is a clear testimony to the confession of Jesus as Lord, and this is put in eschatological terms in Phil. 2.11 (cf. Isa. 45.23; Zech. 14.9). All three titles are united in the Apostles' Creed, and in ApConst. 8.12.30 are joined to θεός.

803. It was first of all applied to Christ in connection with liturgical formulae. In Rom. 9.5 a doxology to God is used as a doxology to Christ. In Tit. 2.13 f. a doxology to God is changed into a doxology to Christ. After John 20.28 in the story of the creeds of the primitive Church there was no stopping the attribution of the word God to Christ (I John 5.20; Did. 10.6; PlinEp. 10; IgnE. proem; cf. 15.3; 19.3; IgnTr. 7.1; IgnSm. 1.1; 10.1; ActThom. 26; SyrInscr. in Peterson, op. cit., 13; JustinApol. 1.6). Later on the predication of 'God' held the central place in the Nicene Creed, and in the creed of Cyril of Jerusalem (*c.* 340).

804. In the previous literature, even in the writings of Jackson-Lake, Bauernfeind and Dibelius, the Petrine formulae have remained to all intents and purposes unnoticed.

805. The influence of the story of Joseph (cf. Yoma 35b) on the history of

the passion and its developments has already been worked out, at any rate in respect of particular incidents (Silberlinge, Rock; cf. E. Nestle in, ZNW, 1902, 169; 1910, 241; Murmelstein, in *Angelos*, 1932). So far as I know, no one has yet remarked on the significance of the Joseph-tradition for the formation of christological formulae.

806. It is to be noted that our formulae appear exclusively in the first and oldest part of Acts (on Acts 1–15 see Feine-Behm, *Einl. i.d. NT*,[8] 1936, 86 f.). That in itself speaks for its early date.

807. Luke may have himself been responsible for this report, in order to make the pictures of Peter and Paul as alike as possible. In any event he has put it to good use in this particular direction.

808. Cf. App. IV, Acts 12.23 ff. Here proof by the text of scripture has replaced the idea of foreknowledge which is found in Acts 2.22 ff.; 4.27 f. (cf. Ch. 3). In other respects also the formulation of Acts 13.23 ff. looks like a combination of the Petrine formulae with the schematism of I Cor. 15.3 f. ($\mu\nu\eta\mu\epsilon\hat{\iota}o\nu$, $\mathring{\omega}\phi\theta\eta$!). Perhaps Paul makes some allusion to the creedal formula of I Cor. 15.3 f. as early as I Thess. 4.14 (cf. n. 756).

809. In the primitive Church no one thought that the question of pre-existence was a real point of division: the sayings about the Son of Man presupposed pre-existence. The Petrine formulae, on the other hand, are quite silent about it. But, again, Paul certainly bases his teaching on it. In contrast once more, the 'deutero-Pauline' I Peter pays no attention to the idea. Like the Petrine formulae, he prefers the idea of foreknowledge—which is nevertheless a favourite idea of Peter himself.

810. Cf. Isa. 53.5: $\pi\alpha\iota\delta\epsilon\acute{\iota}\alpha$ $\epsilon\mathring{\iota}\rho\acute{\eta}\nu\eta\varsigma$ $\mathring{\eta}\mu\hat{\omega}\nu$ $\mathring{\epsilon}\pi$' $\alpha\mathring{\upsilon}\tau\acute{o}\nu$, $\tau\hat{\omega}$ $\mu\acute{\omega}\lambda\omega\pi\iota$ $\alpha\mathring{\upsilon}\tauο\hat{\upsilon}$ $\mathring{\eta}\mu\epsilon\hat{\iota}\varsigma$ $\mathring{\iota}\acute{\alpha}\theta\eta\mu\epsilon\nu$; 53.12: $\mathring{\alpha}\mu\alpha\rho\tau\acute{\iota}\alpha\varsigma$ $\pi ο\lambda\lambda\hat{\omega}\nu$ $\mathring{\alpha}\nu\acute{\eta}\nu\epsilon\gamma\kappa\epsilon\nu$ $\kappa\alpha\grave{\iota}$ $\delta\iota\grave{\alpha}$ $\tau\grave{\alpha}\varsigma$ $\mathring{\alpha}\mu\alpha\rho\tau\acute{\iota}\alpha\varsigma$ $\alpha\mathring{\upsilon}\tau\hat{\omega}\nu$ $\pi\alpha\rho\epsilon\delta\acute{o}\theta\eta$.

811. $\mathring{o}\mu o\lambda o\gamma\acute{\eta}\sigma\eta\varsigma$, $\pi\iota\sigma\tau\epsilon\acute{\upsilon}\sigma\eta\varsigma$, $\sigma\omega\theta\acute{\eta}\sigma\eta$.

812. There are traces of Isa. 53 in Barn. 5.2, 5; 12.5.7; late traces of the paradoxical incarnation formula, e.g. ActThom. 48; ApConst. 8.12.31 ff. (cf App. V).

813. I Tim. 3.16; 6.12 ff.; II Tim. 1.10; 2.8; 4.1; Eph. 1.20 ff.; Heb. 1.3 f.; 2.9; 6.2; Dg. 11.3; ActThom. 48. In addition the forms in I Pet. 1.20 f.; 2.22 ff.; 3.18 ff. are 'deutero-Pauline' and are to be classed with the foregoing for the presupposed idea of pre-existence (see Windisch on 1.20). But their emphasis is laid on the idea of providence (cf. n. 809), their interest is concentrated on the passion, and they are written in the second person plural. In all this they are reminiscent of the Petrine formulae, and represent the Petrine tradition within the Pauline school of thought.

814. Cf. also Th. Zahn, *Ignatius von Antiochen*, 1873, 590 ff. There are further developments of the Ignatian formulae, joined with other traditions, in the christological summaries of the Antiochene ideal liturgy in ApConst. 8.12.30–34.

815. II Mac. 7.28 f.; 12.45; Acts 23.8 ($\mathring{o}\mu o\lambda o\gamma ο\hat{\upsilon}\sigma\iota\nu$).

816. Read $ο\mathring{\upsilon}$ instead of $\mathring{o}\varsigma$.

817. Mark 1.4; Acts 2.38; 5.31; cf. Cyril's creed in Hahn, op. cit., 64.

818. Hahn, op. cit., 12 ff.; EpAp. 5 (Duensing 7).

819. PhilSpecLeg. I, 67; JosAp. 2.193.

820. IV Ezra 8.7. Schubert-Christaller, op. cit., 30. The hellenists expanded the formula in a cosmic and cosmopolitan fashion: One God—one humanity

(PsOrph in JustinCoh. 15; cf. PhilSpecLeg., I, 208; Acts 17.26); One God—one world (PhilOpMund. 61.172; PhilConfLing. 33.170).

821. See ERE 6.295; Sachs, *Tef.* 348. The formula which Pseudo-Peter quotes in his 'Letter to James'—one God—one law—one hope—is also originally Jewish, see PsClemHom., Lagarde, 3.17; cf. SBar. 84.15.

822. SBar. 30.2 is unique: one people of God, one community of mind—one hope.

823. Cf. the uniqueness of Metatron in HEn. 48.1 (C) and 48.9 (D).

824. For such correlative uniqueness applies *mutatis mutandis* also to the mutual relationships between shepherd and flock, and the bread and the body of Christ (John 10.16; I Cor. 10.17).

825. These do not have their origins in the ancient world's fondness for divine triads, but in the elementary and in particular quite formal preference for the number three as such, in the same preference from which the Jewish threefold formulae (and perhaps the polytheistic triads) also derive. This follows from the consideration that we can find in the NT many examples of impersonal threefold formulae which have been constituted by magnitudes or determinants that have nothing to do with the divine nature, as, for example, the trinity of faith—hope—love (I Thess. 1.3; 5.8; I Cor. 13.13; Col. 1.4 f.), or the formula 'of . . . through . . . unto' (Rom. 11.36; cf. Eph. 3.12).

826. Mark 13.32; Luke 9.26; cf. I Tim. 5.21; Rev. 1.4 f.; 3.12.

827. In late Judaism the Spirit is only one divine hypostasis among others. But whereas the functions of the other hypostases, such as *sophia, logos*, are transferred to Christ in the NT, Spirit retains a relative independence alongside Christ, relative in the strictest sense: a relation which is calculated always to preserve the reference back to the *relatum*. Just as the Christ is the Son of the Father and fulfils the Father's works at their proper time, so is the Spirit the Spirit of the Son and carries on the work of the Son, in this age when the time of the Spirit has come.

828. God—Lord—Spirit in II Cor. 13.13; I Cor. 12.4 ff. (II Thess. 2.13 is uncertain; I Cor. 8.6 is only enlarged to a triadic form in later manuscripts); Jud. 20 f.; I Cl. 58.2. God—Christ—Spirit in II Cor. 1.21 f. God the Father—Christ—Spirit in I Pet. 1.2.

829. JustinApol. 1.65.3; ClAlPaed. 12.101; ApConst. 8.6.13, etc. Triadic formulae were also very much in circulation in heretical circles on the fringe of the primitive Church. Thus we hear in ActThom. 27.49 of a sealing in the name of the Father, and of the Son, and of the Spirit. Doxologies with the same triad can be found in OdSol. 23.22; PsClemHom. 3.72. In the eucharistic liturgy of the Acts of John glory is given to 'the Father, the Logos and the Spirit'. We know independently from Augustin (Ep. 237) that the Priscillians took this same eucharistic hymn into their liturgy, just as Priscillian himself, the Spanish heretic of the fourth century, was notorious for his addiction to the Apocrypha. But it was not only triadic formulae that found expression in the Apocrypha and in the heretical writings, but even the theological problems of the Trinity as well. The idea that the interrelationships of the holy three are like those that obtain within a family rests upon Semitic presuppositions of thought ($\pi\nu\epsilon\tilde{\nu}\mu\alpha$ = רִיּה = *femininum*; cf. Gen. 1.2). God is the Father. The Spirit is the mother. Christ is the son (EvH., in Klostermann, *Apocrypha*, 2.3.6 f., n. 4 f.; formerly in the doxology in ActThom. 39 and in the Valentinian baptismal

liturgy in EpiphHaer. 34.20.2). Actually the Christian idea of the Trinity is here falsified through the syncretistic idea of the divine triad, in particular the family triad. The formal statement of the Egyptian Gospel points in another direction, speaking of the identity of the Father, Son and Spirit (τὸν αὐτὸν εἶναι πατέρα. τὸν αὐτὸν εἶναι υἱόν, τὸν αὐτὸν εἶναι ἅγιον πνεῦμα; EpiphHaer. in Klostermann, op. cit., 15). If Epiphanius (ibid.) be right, the Sabellians used this Gospel and other apocrypha as the source for their modalistic errors.

830. It is not possible to read this from the singular εἰς τὸ ὄνομα (Matt. 28.19); cf. the Syriac in Rev. 17.8 (Nestle!) and לְשֵׁם? in Levy, *Wörterbuch*.

831. Moreover, the NT does not, any more than late Judaism, remain in any way bound to triple formulae. As early as Eph. 4.4 ff. a sevenfold formula is elaborated : One God (thrice qualified with ἐπί, διά, ἐν)—one Lord—one Spirit—one body—one baptism—one faith—one hope (there are other series in the letter conditioned by the context). Each member of this sevenfold series is accentuated by the prefixing of the well-known motif of uniqueness. That indicates the source of our formula. Here the essential elements of the older Jewish and Christian formulae of uniqueness are joined in a trinity and a quaternity, and then both of them into a septenary (Dibelius, op. cit., refers on the contrary to the Stoic formulae of the unity of the cosmos). I Cl. 46.6 enlarges the holy triad by adding another member—μία κλῆσις. Justin combines the triads of Mark 13 and Matt. 28 into one four-membered formulae: Father, Son, Angels, Spirit (Apol. 1.6; also 61? cf. Angel and Spirit in the creedal reference in Acts 23.8). Does this amount to an assertion of 'fourfoldness'? Most certainly not. It amounts but to a quaternity. If Justin had really conceived the triad of the baptismal formula as Trinity, he would not have widened and weakened it without any reservations by introducing into it a fourth member quite foreign to the Trinity (the angels).

832. On the creedal form of the Egyptian liturgy see Lietzmann in *Harnack-ehrung*, 1921.

833. There is a five-sectioned creed as early as the second century, see EpAp. 5 (Duensing 7); Th. Schermann, TU 36.6.1b, 1910, 30. In the fourth century Cyril used a creed of seven sections, which echoed Eph. 4.4 ff. not only in the number 7, but also in the baptismal theme.

834. The complicated doctrinal propositions about the metaphysics of the Trinity which were used by ecclesiastics and hellenists would have been understood only with difficulty by the writers of the NT. Yet the NT is all too rich with theological expressions which give expression not only to the threeness and the homogeneousness of God, Christ and the Spirit, but also to the quite unique relationships that obtain between them. These ideas are, indeed, anticipated in the OT (Isa. 48.16; 61.1). The testimony that Jesus bore to himself built further on that foundation (Luke 4.18 f.; Mark 3.28 ff.; cf. Matt. 11.27). The primitive Church knew that God was active in Christ to reveal himself and accomplish his ends (Acts 2.33; II Cor. 1.21; John 16.13 ff.; 20.21 f.; cf. Matt. 3.16; further KW, s.v. θεός 103 ff.; 107 ff.). All three natures are thought of in personal terms (even the Spirit, as the combination of πνεῦμα with the construction εἰς τὸ ὄνομα proves; cf. Matt. 28.19; I Cor. 1.13 ; TertPrax. 26: *ter ad singula nomina in personas singulas tinguimur*). In Gal. 4.4 ff. Paul gives us a complete picture of the way in which the threefold relationship of God—Christ—Spirit has been unfolded in the history of salvation. John speaks

of such a relation in the history of revelation: the Father will be 'declared' by the Son, and the Son by the Spirit (John 1.18; 16.13 f.). Here we are at the beginnings of a trinitarian theology (cf. John 10.30; 17.11, etc.). But even here we do not yet have a normative trinitarian formula. Theologically there is preparation for the doctrine of the Trinity in the NT, but regarded in the light of the history of the Creed, there is in it only a triadic, and not yet a trinitarian confession of faith.

835. On its origin in Spain see Lebreton, op. cit., 1.645 ff.

836. The addition is first testified in the heretic and lover of the Apocrypha, Priscillian. It speaks of the three divine persons in the nomenclature which is known to us in the Priscillian eucharistic doxology, which was derived from the Acts of John (cf. n. 829).

837. A. v. Harnack, op. cit., 3 f.

838. While the substance of the idea of the Son of Man formed the original material for the Church's christology, the term itself very soon lost its meaning. The Synagogue passed its own verdict upon it in pursuit of its anti-Christian polemic (jTaan 2,1: If a man says: 'I am the Son of Man', he lies) or else debased it (in HEn. Son of Man = a child of a man). But the great Church also ceased to use it: Acts and Revelation still used it in its full apocalyptic meaning, in accounts of visions! Paul used the idea of man (*anthropos*). Ignatius (Eph. 20.2) used it in its everyday meaning of a man's son. It is found in isolated and insignificant instances in Gentile Christian gnosis; see Hennecke Apokr. 70 (kopt. Marienev): 102 (HippRef. 5.26); 190 (ActJ. 109); 435 (Celsus in Orig. 8.15). It was only in Judaistic Christianity that the apocalyptic idea of the Son of Man had a short-lived survival: In the Gospel to the Hebrews the risen Lord says to James the Just: 'My brother . . . the Son of Man is risen from them that sleep' (HierVir. I 11.2). In Hegesippus the same James cries out before his martyrdom: 'What do you ask me about Jesus, the Son of Man?' (Eus. 2.23). In the EvPet (*c.* 135 A.D.) Adam and Christ appear (thus uniting Iranian and biblical apocalyptic) as different incorporations of a pre-existent heavenly nature, which bore the name of 'the Son of Man' (PsClemHom. 3.22, Lagarde; PsClemRec. 1.60.3, Frankenberg).

[The quotation on the title leaf of this book comes from IgnR. 3.3 and is translated on p. 176, and discussed in n. 585.]

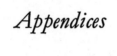

Appendices

APPENDIX I

The Principal Elements of the Old Biblical
Theology of Martyrdom
(*Chief passages and proof texts*)

A. *The shape of martyrdom*

1. The people of God is the martyr nation among the Gentiles (Psa. 73.3 ff.; 78.1 ff.; 79.9 ff.; 82.3 ff.; Jdth. 9.8; Isa. 42.1 LXX; AEn. 85 ff.; 89.59 ff.; IV Ezra 3.27 ff.; MEx. on 20.23; SB, II, 284).

2. Those people of God who are loyal to the Torah are persecuted by the Gentiles and their accomplices (DaG, 3; 9; 11 f.; I Mac. 2.27 ff.; II Mac. 5.27; 7.2, 30; IV Mac. 5.16 f.; PsSol. 17.19; AssMos. 8.6; MartIs. 2.8 ff.; PsPhil. 6.9, 16; San. 49a; Cantr. 8.6 f.).

3. Those people of God who are loyal to the Torah are persecuted by their apostate fellows (Psa. 21; 40.9 f.; 68; II Chron. 24.1; Wisd. 2 f.; 5; PsSol. 4; 12; Dam. 1.20; IV Ezra 7).

4. The people of God persecute the messengers of God (III βασ 19.2 ff.; Ex. 17.4; 32.9; Num. 14.10; 17.14; Jer. 6.10; 9.25; 11.19; Isa. 40 ff.; II Chron. 36.16; Jub. 1.12; MartIs. 3; 5; ParalJer. 9.20 ff.).

5. The blood of Abel cries to heaven till the end of time (AEn. 22.7; TestAbr. 11).

6. Even the picture of Messiah has traces of the martyr in it (SB, II, 273 ff.; IV Ezra 7.29; 10.1, 16, etc., in Jeremias, *Deutsche Theologie*, II, 1929, 106 ff.).

7. Even the picture of the Son of Man has traces of the martyr in it (Joachim, Jeremias, briefly: Motifs from the Servant Songs in the texts about the Son of Man in AEn. 37 ff.; Traditions about the past earthly life, the present heavenly existence and the future return of the Son of Man in AEn. 39.4 ff.; 71.14 ff.; 90.31, etc.).

B. *The fate of martyrdom*

8. The confessors live in the desert, far from the wickedness and pursuits of the world (I Mac. 1.56; PsSol. 17.16 f.; AssMos. 9; MartIs. 5.11 ff.; PsPhil. 6.7 ff.; Dam. 6.5).

9. The persecutors use suspicions and slanders, false accusations and false witnesses against those who are faithful to God (Jer. 15.15; Psa. 26.12; 34.11; DaΘ. 6.5 f.; Wisd. 2.22; III Mac. 7.11; Ps. Sol. 12.1ff.; MartIs. 3.8 f.).

10. The martyrs are treated undeservedly like thieves and killed and

in this sense suffer innocently (Psa. 34.7, 19; 58.4 f.; Wisd. 2.19, 22; 3.5; PsSol. 12.4; II Mac. 7.40; IV Mac. 12.14).

11. The martyrs frequently suffer and die in the arena, which was a recognized institution also in Palestine in hellenistic times (III Mac. 4.11 [IV Mac. 5.1; 15.20]; cf. Jer. 12.5; Eccl. 9.11; I Mac. 1.14; II Mac. 4.12 ff.; IV Mac. 4.20; JosAnt. 12.241; 15.268 ff., 341; remains in Jerusalem, Samaria, Rabbath-Ammon, Gerasa, etc.).

12. Martyrs are often scourged and crucified, and 'cross' therefore appears occasionally as the inclusive term for a martyr's fate (AssMos. 8.1; JosAnt. 12.256; Gnr. on 22.6; further A. Schlatter, *Die Märtyrer in den Anfängen der Kirche*, 1915, 70 and n. 259 above).

13. The martyr's death is a sign of his coming victory (Dan. 3; Wisd. 2.17; MartIs. 5.7; Ber. 61b; AZ. 18a).

14. Lists of martyrs kept memory fresh about the typical murder of the saints in history (IV Mac. 16.20 f.; 18.11 ff. L. Zunz, *Die gottesdienstl. Vorträge der Juden*, 1832, 142; Elbogen, 203; 228 ff.; Kaufmann, REJ, 1887, 250; SB, I, 582).

15. History has also seen some miraculous deliverances which God has wrought for his faithful ones (Dan. 3.49 f.; III Mac. 6.18 ff.; 7.16; PsPhil. 6.9, 17 f.; Gnr. on 15.7; 22.19).

C. *God's Glory and the shame and glory of martyrdom*

16. The martyrs suffer for the name of the one true God, and glorify him in their death (DaΘ. 3.17 f.; Dan. 6.11, 14, 17; 11.31 ff.; I Mac. 1.54; 6.7; II Mac. 6.1 ff.; III Mac. 7.16; IV Mac. 8.24; Wisd. 2.18; 3.6; PsSol. 2.2; AEn. 108.10; MartIs. 2.7 ff.; TestJb. 3 f.; PsPhil. 6.4; IV Ezra 7.89; Ber. 61b; Ekar. on 1.16).

17. The martyrs willingly drink the cup that God has prepared for them (MartIs. 5.13).

18. The martyr's strength derives from the fearlessness of those that fear God (Dan. 3.12, 17 f., 95; II Mac. 6.26; 7.30; IV Mac. 13.14 f.; MartIs. 5.10; PsPhil. 6.4; AbRN 4=SB, I, 581).

19. The martyrs prefer eternal to temporal glory (the oath of renunciation: (I Mac. 1.66; 3.59; IV Mac. 15.2 f., 8, 16, 26 f.; AEn. 108.10; AssMos. 9.6; TestJb. 18; MartIs. 5.8 f.; VitProph. 51).

20. The martyr's road leads through short tribulation to eternal glory (Wisd. 3.2 ff.; IV Ezra 7.88 ff., etc.).

21. The saints that have been slain are at peace (Deut. 33.3; Wisd. 3.1 ff.; IV Mac. 17.19).

22. The martyrs pass at death directly to heaven (Wisd. 5.15; IV Mac. 5.37; 13.7; 17.18; 18.23).

23. The martyrs' road leads from the circumscribed to the spacious (IV Ezra 7.6 ff., 96; 13.19 f.; TestAbr. 7; TestIss. 12a).

24. The martyrs will receive a place of honour and an honourable

reward in the world to come (Dan. 12.1 ff.; II Mac. 7.9; 28 f.; Wisd. 2.16; 3 f.; 5.15 f.; PsSol. 14.1 ff.; AEn. 108 ff.; JosAp. 2.218; Kohr. on 9.10).

D. *The slaughter of the saints and the revenge of God*

25. The martyrs throw contentions, curses and prayers for revenge at those who slaughter the saints ('Persecution polemics': Jer. 18.20 ff.; Psa. 68.29; II Mac. 7.31; IV Mac. 11.23; TestL. 16.2; IV Ezra 4.35; Inscr. at Rheneia, Deissmann, LAE, 423 ff.; HEn. 44.7; Taan, 18b).

26. The blood of the martyrs will be the destruction of their persecutors (Deut. 32.43; IV Mac. 11.23; RH, 23a; KW, s.v.).

27. Those who slaughter the saints are punished for their offences, and come to a miserable end (Psa. 34.8; I Mac. 2.62 f.; 6.11 ff.; II Mac. 3.28 f.; 4.38; 5.9 f.; 9.4 ff.; 13.8; Wisd. 3.10 ff.; PsSol. 2.25 ff.; 14.7, 9; MartIs. 2.14; PsPhil. 9.8; 44.10).

28. The way of the slayer of the saints passes through a brief triumph to eternal torment (II Mac. 6.12 ff.; SBar. 13; JosAp. 2.218; Taan, 18b).

29. The turning-point of history can only come when the measure of atrocities is full, and when the last slaughter of a saint has been accomplished (Dan. 9.25 ff.; Wisd. 5.17 ff.; II Mac. 6.12 ff.; 7.37 f.; 8.2 ff.; III Mac. 3.8; 6.18 ff.; IV Mac. 12.17 f.; AEn. 89.75; AssMos 9 f.; Dam. 20.1, 14 f.; IV Ezra 4.36; SBar. 13; JosAnt. 18.116; SB, II, 274 ff.).

E. *Witness against the accused and the contest at law*

30. God's messenger is involved in the controversy between God and man as the witness (עד, μάρτυς) for the prosecution against the ungodly and is therefore persecuted (IV βασ 17.13 ff.; Psa. 118.22 ff.; I Mac. 2.56 [cf. Num. 14.9 f.]; IV Mac. 12.16, vl.; 16.16 ff.; Jub. 1.12; SDt. on 32.1).

31. The eye-witnesses' accounts of the slaughter of the saints count as evidence for the prosecution at the last judgement (II Mac. 7.6 [cf. Deut. 31.21; 32.36, 43; also IV Mac. 18.18; AZ, 17b/18c]; AEn. 89.63, 76; GEn. 104.11; SBar. 13.3 ff.).

32. The names of the saints that have been slain are recorded and at the last judgement serve as evidence against the persecutors (MidrPs. on 9.13).

33. At the last judgement the persecutors will look with dread upon the transfigured martyrs (Zech. 5.1 ff.; Wisd. 5.1 ff.; AEn. 108.15; IV Ezra 7.37 ff., 83; ApEl. 41; Succ. 52a).

34. The persecuted and murdered saints will reappear in the controversy between God and the world of men as witnesses for the prosecution against their persecutors (Wisd. 5.1 ff; AEn. 22.7; GEn. 99.3 [in C. Bonner p. 43] AEn. 108.15; IV Ezra 7.37 f.; TestAbr. 11; ApAbr. 25; ApEl. 41).

F. *Warfare and Victory*

35. Martyrdom is one of the forms taken by the war between the

civitas dei and the *civitas diaboli* (Wisd. 2.10 ff.; PsSol. 17.16 ff.; IV Mac. 11.7 f. vl; MartIs. 2.5; VitProph. 41; 44, etc.).

36. The princes who slaughter the saints are, and are called, tyrants (II Mac. 7.27; IV Mac. 1.11; 15.2; VitProph. 50; MidrPr. on 9.2).

37. The persecutors are ravenous beasts (Jer. 51.34; Psa. 7.3; 9.30; 21.13 ff.; 34.17; 90.13; AEn. 87 ff.; 89.13 ff., 55 f.; PsSol. 2.25; TestJud. 21.7 ff.; VitProph. 50).

38. The martyr is a combatant (gladiator, boxer, wrestler: IV Mac. 6.10 f.; 9.8, 23; 11.20 ff.; 17.8 ff.; TestJb. 4.27; PhilMigrAbr. 74 f.).

39. Martyrdom is a fight with beasts (IV Mac. 9.26 ff.).

40. The suffering of martyrdom is a wrestling with Satan (TestJb. 27).

41. The whole cosmos watches the bloodstained spectacle of the martyrs' suffering and war (III Mac. 4.11; 5.24; 7.14; IV Mac. 15.20; 17.14; cf. AEn. 9.1 ff.; HEn. 44.10; Ekar. on 1.16 ff.).

G. *Expiatory suffering*

42. The martyr makes atonement in the first instance for his own sins (II Mac. 7.18, 32; Wisd. 3.5 f.; PsSol. 10.2 f.; PsPhil. 6.11; SNu. on 15.31; Haggad Beresch 56 = SB, I, 225).

43. The martyr prays for his people (II Mac. 7.37 f.; IV Mac. 6.28).

44. The blood of the martyr atones for the sin of his people (Deut. 32.43; II Mac. 7.37 f.; IV Mac. 1.11; 6.28 f.; 12.7 f.; 17.21 f.; SB, II, 274 ff.; 281 f.; MidrHL. on 7.9; MidrPr. on 9.2).

45. The martyr prays for his persecutors (Isa. 53.12 MT; II Mac. 15.11 ff.; TestB. 3.5 ff.).

46. The blood of the martyr atones for the sin of the persecutor (Isa. 53.4 f., 12 LXX; TestB. 3.8A; Sota. 14a).

47. The blood of the martyrs serves to sustain the world (San. 93a; Gnr. on 8.21).

APPENDIX II

Comparative tables of the formal styles of the Testament of the Twelve Patriarchs and the Johannine writings

TestN 2. 7: ὡς κεχώρισται ἀνάμεσον τοῦ φωτὸς καὶ . . . σκότους, οὕτως κεχώρισται ἀνάμεσον ἀνδρὸς καὶ ἀνδρός

John 1. 5: τὸ φῶς ἐν τῇ σκοτίᾳ φαίνει, καὶ ἡ σκοτία αὐτὸ οὐ κατέλαβεν

TestL 14. 4 β: τὸ φῶς τοῦ νόμου . . . τὸ δοθὲν . . . εἰς φωτισμὸν παντὸς ἀνθρώπου

John 1. 9: τὸ φῶς τὸ ἀληθινόν, ὁ φωτίζει πάντα ἄνθρωπον

TestB 9. 2: σωτήριον . . . ἐν ἐπισκοπῇ μονογενοῦς προφήτου

John 1. 14: ὡς μονογενοῦς παρὰ πατρός

TestL 8. 15: παρουσία αὐτοῦ ἀγαπητὴ . . . ὡς προφήτης ὑψίστου

TestL 8. 11: σημεῖον δόξης

TestG 4. 6 f.: ἀγάπη καὶ τοὺς νεκροὺς θέλει ζωοποιῆσαι καὶ τοὺς ἐν ἀποφάσει θανάτου θέλει ἀνακαλέσασθαι . . . τὸ . . . πνεῦμα τῆς ἀγάπης ἐν μακροθυμίᾳ συνεργεῖ τῷ νόμῳ τοῦ θεοῦ εἰς σωτηρίαν τῶν ἀνθρώπων

TestB 10. 3: ποιήσατε ἀλήθειαν

TestA 5. 3: ἀλήθεια . . . φῶς

TestA 4. 3: δοκοῦν opp. ἀληθινόν

TestL 2. 3e: κρίσιν ἀληθινήν

TestJos 1. 3: ἔμεινα ἐν τῇ ἀληθείᾳ κυρίου

TestA 3. 2: οὐκ εἰσὶ τοῦ θεοῦ, ἀλλὰ ταῖς ἐπιθυμίαις αὐτῶν δουλεύουσιν, ἵνα τῷ Βελίαρ ἀρέσωσιν

TestJud 19. 4: ἐτύφλωσε . . . με ὁ ἄρχων τῆς πλάνης καὶ ἠγνόησα . . . ὡς σάρξ ἐν ἁμαρτίαις φθαρείς

TestD 3. 6: ἀεὶ μετὰ τοῦ ψεύδους ἐκ δεξιῶν τοῦ Σατανᾶ πορεύεται

TestJud 24. 1: πᾶσα ἁμαρτία οὐχ εὑρεθήσεται ἐν αὐτῷ

TestIss 1. 10: μηδὲ δόξαζε σεαυτήν

TestL 18, 5. 14: ἐν ταῖς ἡμέραις αὐτοῦ . . . ἀγαλλιάσεται Ἀβραάμ

TestJ 25. 3: ἔσονται . . . μία γλῶσσα

TestR 3. 1: ὕπνος = εἰκὼν τοῦ θανάτου

TestB 3. 8: ὁ ἀναμάρτητος ὑπὲρ ἀσεβῶν ἀποθανεῖται

TestJos 10. 3: ὑψοῖ καὶ δοξάζει αὐτόν

TestS 2. 7: ὁ ἄρχων τῆς πλάνης . . . ἐτύφλωσέ μου τὸν νοῦν, μὴ . . . φείσασθαι

TestL 2. 3e: ὅλος ἐλουσάμην ἐν ὕδατι ζῶντι

TestD 2. 1; 3, 6: πνεῦμα τοῦ ψεύδους . . . ἐκ . . . Σατανᾶ πορεύεται

John 1. 21: ὁ προφήτης εἰ σύ;

John 2. 11. σημείων . . . δόξαν

John 3. 16: οὕτως γὰρ ἠγάπησεν ὁ θεὸς τὸν κόσμον, ὥστε τὸν υἱὸν τὸν μονογενῆ ἔδωκεν, ἵνα πᾶς ὁ πιστεύων εἰς αὐτὸν . . . ἔχῃ ζωὴν αἰώνιον

John 3. 21: ποιῶν . . . ἀλήθειαν

John 3. 21: ἀλήθεια . . . φῶς

John 6. 32: ἀληθινόν

John 8. 16: κρίσις . . . ἀληθινή

John 8. 31 ff.: ἐὰν . . . μείνητε ἐν . . . λόγῳ . . . ἐμῷ . . . ἀλήθειαν

John 8. 42 ff.: εἰ ὁ θεὸς πατὴρ ὑμῶν ἦν . . . οὐ γινώσκετε . . . ὑμεῖς ἐκ . . . τοῦ διαβόλου ἐστὲ καὶ τὰς ἐπιθυμίας τοῦ πατρὸς ὑμῶν θέλετε ποιεῖν. ἐκεῖνος ἀνθρωποκτόνος ἦν ἀπ' ἀρχῆς . . . ψεύστης ἐστὶν καὶ ὁ πατὴρ αὐτοῦ . . . ἐκ τοῦ θεοῦ οὐκ ἐστέ

John 8. 46: τίς . . . ἐλέγχει με περὶ ἁμαρτίας;

John 8. 54: ἐὰν . . . δοξάσω ἐμαυτόν

John 8. 56: Ἀβρ. . . . ἠγαλλιάσετο ἵνα ἴδῃ τὴν ἡμέραν . . . ἐμήν

John 10. 16: γενήσεται μία ποίμνη

John 11. 13: (κοίμησις) θανάτου—κοίμησις ὕπνου

John 11. 51: ἔμελλεν Ἰησοῦς ἀποθνήσκειν ὑπὲρ . . . ἔθνους

John 12. 23, 34: δοξασθῇ . . . ὑψωθῆναι

John 13. 2: διαβόλου . . . βεβληκότος εἰς . . . καρδίαν, ἵνα παραδοῖ αὐτόν

John 13. 10: ὁ λελουμένος . . . καθαρὸς ὅλος

John 15. 26: πνεῦμα τῆς ἀληθείας . . . παρὰ . . . πατρὸς ἐκπορεύεται

TestJud 20. 5 : πνεῦμα τῆς ἀληθείας (μαρτυρεῖ πάντα καὶ) κατηγορεῖ πάντων

John 15. 26; 16. 8: πνεῦμα τῆς ἀληθείας . . . μαρτυρήσει περὶ ἐμοῦ . . . καὶ ἐλέγξει τὸν κόσμον . . .

TestL 10. 1: ὅσα . . . ἤκουσα . . . ἀνήγγειλα ὑμῖν

John 16. 13: ὅσα ἀκούει . . . ἀναγγελεῖ ὑμῖν

TestJud 25. 4: οἱ ἐν λύπῃ τελευτήσαντες ἀναστήσονται ἐν χαρᾷ

John 16. 20: ἡ λύπη ὑμῶν εἰς χαρὰν γενήσεται

TestJos 1. 6: μόνος ἤμην, καὶ ὁ Θεὸς παρεκάλεσέ με

John 16. 32: οὐκ εἰμὶ μόνος, ὅτι ὁ πατὴρ μετ᾽ ἐμοῦ ἐστιν

TestL 18. 8: δώσει τὴν μεγαλωσύνην κυρίου τοῖς υἱοῖς

John 17. 22: δόξαν ἣν δέδωκάς μοι δέδωκα αὐτοῖς

TestJud 24. 2: ἐκχεεῖ πνεῦμα χάριτος ἐφ᾽ ὑμάς

John 20 22: ἐνεφύσησεν καὶ λέγει . . . λάβετε πνεῦμα ἅγιον

TestN 2. 10: οὐδὲ ἐν σκότει ὄντες δύνασθε ποιεῖν ἔργα φωτός

I John 1. 6: ἐὰν . . . ἐν τῷ σκότει περιπατῶμεν . . . οὐ ποιοῦμεν τὴν ἀλήθειαν

TestJos 20. 2: Κύριος ἐν φωτὶ ἔσται μεθ᾽ ὑμῶν

I John 1. 7: ἐὰν . . . ἐν . . . φωτὶ περιπατῶμεν ὡς αὐτός ἐστιν ἐν τῷ φωτί

TestD 6. 2: ἐγγίσατε τῷ . . . ἀγγέλῳ τῷ παραιτουμένῳ ὑμᾶς ὅτι οὗτός ἐστι μεσίτης θεοῦ καὶ ἀνθρώπων. L 3. 5β ἄγγελοι . . . ἐξιλασκόμενοι

I John 2. 1: παράκλητον ἔχομεν πρὸς τὸν πατέρα . . . καὶ αὐτὸς ἱλασμός ἐστιν περὶ τῶν ἁμαρτιῶν . . . τοῦ κόσμου

TestS 4. 7: ἀγαπήσατε . . . τὸν ἀδελφόν

I John 2. 10: ἀγαπῶν τὸν ἀδελφόν

TestS 2. 7: πνεῦμα τοῦ ζήλου ἐτύφλωσέ μου τὸν νοῦν, μὴ προσέχειν αὐτῷ ὡς ἀδελφῷ

I John 2. 11: μισῶν τὸν ἀδελφὸν . . . ὅτι ἡ σκοτία ἐτύφλωσεν τοὺς ὀφθαλμοὺς αὐτοῦ

TestB 7. 5: οἱ ὁμοιούμενοι τῷ Καῖν ἐπὶ φθόνῳ καὶ μισαδελφίᾳ . . . κολασθήσονται

I John 3. 11 ff.: καθὼς Κάϊν . . . ἔσφαξεν τὸν ἀδελφόν . . . ὁ μισῶν τὸν ἀδελφὸν οὐκ ἔχει ζωὴν αἰώνιον

TestJud 21. 1: ἀγαπᾶτε ἵνα διαμείνητε

I John 3. 15: ὁ μὴ ἀγαπῶν μένει ἐν τῷ θανάτῳ

TestG 4. 6: τὸ μῖσος τοὺς ζῶντας θέλει ἀποκτεῖναι

I John 3. 15: ὁ μισῶν . . . ἀνθρωποκτόνος ἐστίν

TestG 6. 1: Τέκνα . . . ἀγαπήσατε ἀλλήλους ἐν ἔργῳ καὶ λόγῳ

I John 3. 18: Τεκνία, μὴ ἀγαπῶμεν λόγῳ . . . ἀλλὰ ἐν ἔργῳ καὶ ἀληθείᾳ

TestJud 20. 1: δύο πνεύματα . . . τὸ τῆς ἀλεθείας καὶ τὸ τῆς πλάνης

I John 4. 6: τὸ πνεῦμα τῆς ἀληθείας καὶ τὸ πνεῦμα τῆς πλάνης

TestS 3. 1: Τέκνα . . . φυλάξασθε
ἀπὸ τοῦ πνεύματος τῆς πλάνης
TestZeb 8. 5 : ἀγαπᾶτε ἀλλήλους

I John 5. 21: Τεκνία, φυλάξατε
ἑαυτὰ ἀπὸ τῶν εἰδώλων
II John 5: ἀγαπῶμεν ἀλλήλους

TestR 2. 1: τῶν ἑπτὰ πνευμάτων
TestR 6. 8 : Λευί . . . ἀρχιερεὺς
χριστός, ὃν εἶπεν ὁ Κύριος
TestB 4. 1: ἴδετε . . τὸ τέλος . ., ἵνα
στεφάνους δόξης φορέσητε

Rev. 1. 4: τῶν ἑπτὰ πνευμάτων
Rev. 1. 6: ἐποίησεν ἡμᾶς βασιλείαν,
ἱερεῖς τῷ θεῷ
Rev. 2. 10: γίνου πιστὸς ἄχρι θανάτου, καὶ δώσω σοι τὸν στέφανον
τῆς ζωῆς

TestL 3. 5 f.: ἄγγελοι . . . προσφέ-
ρουσι . . . Κυρίῳ ὀσμὴν εὐωδίας
TestL 3. 8: ἐν (οὐρανῷ) εἰσι θρόνοι
. . . ἐν ᾧ ἀεὶ ὕμνοι τῷ θεῷ προσ-
φέρονται
TestJ 23. 3 : ἐπάξει . . . λιμὸν καὶ
λοιμόν, θάνατον καὶ ῥομφαίαν
TestL 8. 5: περιέθηκέ μοι στολὴν
ἁγίαν καὶ ἔνδοξον
TestL 3. 9: Ὅταν . . . ἐπιβλέψῃ
Κύριος ἐφ'ἡμᾶς πάντες . . .
σαλευόμεθα καὶ οἱ οὐρανοὶ καὶ ἡ
γῆ καὶ αἱ ἄβυσσοι ἀπὸ προσώπου
. . . αὐτοῦ σαλεύονται

Rev. 5. 8: ζῷα . . . ἔχοντες . . . φιάλας
. . . γεμούσας θυμιαμάτων
Rev. (4. 4) 5. 8: (ἐπὶ τοὺς θρόνους
. . .) πρεσβύτεροι . . . ᾄδουσιν
ᾠδὴν καινήν
Rev. 6. 8: ἀποκτεῖναι ἐν ῥομφαίᾳ καὶ
ἐν λιμῷ καὶ ἐν θανάτῳ
Rev. 6. 11: ἐδόθη αὐτοῖς ἑκάστῳ
στολὴ λευκή
Rev. 6. 12 ff: σεισμὸς μέγας ἐγένετο . . . καὶ ὁ οὐρανὸς ἀπε-
χωρίσθη . . . καὶ πᾶν ὄρος καὶ
νῆσος . . . ἐκινήθησαν καὶ οἱ
βασιλεῖς . . . λέγουσιν . . .
κρύψατε ἡμᾶς ἀπὸ προσώπου τοῦ
καθημένου

TestJos 19. 8 : εἶδον . . . παρθένος
. . . (καὶ ἐξ αὐτῆς) ἐγεννήθη ἀμνός
. . . καὶ ἦν ἐξ ἀριστερῶν αὐτοῦ ὡς
λέων
TestL 4. 1: τοῦ πυρὸς καταπτήσ-
σοντος . . . οἱ ἄνθρωποι ἀπειθοῦντες
ἐπιμενοῦσι ταῖς ἀδικίαις. διὰ τοῦτο
ἐν τῇ κολάσει κριθήσονται
TestJos 19. 8: ὥρμων πάντα τὰ
θηρία . . . καὶ ἐνίκησεν αὐτὰ ὁ
ἀμνός, καὶ ἀπώλεσεν αὐτά

Rev. 12. 1 ff: ὤφθη . . . γυνὴ . . . καὶ
. . . δράκων ἕστηκεν ἐνώπιον τῆς
γυναικὸς τῆς μελλούσης τεκεῖν

Rev. 16. 8 f: ἐν πυρὶ . . . ἐκαυμα-
τίσθησαν οἱ ἄνθρωποι καὶ . . . οὐ
μετενόησαν δοῦναι αὐτῷ δόξαν

Rev. 17. 11. 14: τὸ θηρίον εἰς . . . ἀπώ-
λειαν ὑπάγει . . . μετὰ τοῦ ἀρνίου
πολεμήσουσιν καὶ τὸ ἀρνίον νική-
σει αὐτούς

TestL 18. 12: ὁ Βελίαρ δεθήσεται
ὑπ' αὐτοῦ

Rev. 20. 2. 10: ἔδησεν αὐτὸν . . .
καὶ . . . διάβολος . . . ἐβλήθη εἰς
. . . λίμνην

TestL 18. 6: οἱ οὐρανοὶ ἀνοιγήσο-
νται, καὶ ἐκ τοῦ ναοῦ τῆς δόξης

Rev. 21. 2 ff: τὴν πόλιν τὴν ἁγίαν
. . . εἶδον καταβαίνουσαν ἐκ τοῦ

22—N.T.T.

ἥξει ἐπ᾽ αὐτὸν ἁγίασμα μετὰ φωνῆς πατρικῆς

οὐρανοῦ . . . καὶ ἤκουσα φωνῆς . . . ἰδοὺ ἡ σκηνὴ τοῦ θεοῦ . . . ὁ νικῶν . . . ἔσται μοι υἱός

TestJ 25. 3: ἔσεσθε εἰς λαὸν Κυρίου . . . καὶ πνεῦμα πλάνης . . . ἐμπλη-θήσεται ἐν πυρὶ εἰς τὸν αἰῶνα

Rev. 21. 3, 8: λαοὶ αὐτοῦ ἔσονται . . . καὶ πᾶσιν τοῖς ψευδέσιν τὸ μέρος . . . ἐν . . . πυρί, ὅ ἐστιν ὁ θάνατος ὁ δεύτερος

TestJ 24. 3: ἔσεσθε αὐτῷ εἰς υἱούς

Rev. 21. 7: αὐτὸς ἔσται μοι υἱός

TestL 2. 5: ἐπέπεσέ με ὕπνος, καὶ ἐθεασάμην ὅρος ὑψηλόν, καὶ ἤμην ἐν αὐτῷ

Rev. 21. 10: ἀπήνεγκέν με ἐν πνεύματι ἐπὶ ὅρος . . . ὑψηλόν

TestD 5. 12: τῆς νέας Ἰερουσαλὴμ . . . ἥτις ἐστι δόξα θεοῦ

Rev. 21. 10 f.: τὴν ἁγίαν Ἰερουσαλὴμ . . . ἔχουσαν τὴν δόξαν . . . θεοῦ

TestL 18. 4: ἀναλάμψει (ὁ ἱερεὺς καινός) ὡς ὁ ἥλιος . . . καὶ ἐξαρεῖ πᾶν σκότος

Rev. 21. 23 f.: οὐ χρείαν ἔχει τοῦ ἡλίου . . . ὁ λύχνος αὐτῆς τὸ ἀρνίον . . . νύξ . . . οὐκ ἔσται ἐκεῖ

TestJ 15. 3: διάδημα, τουτέστιν τὴν δόξαν τῆς βασιλείας

Rev. 21. 24: οἱ βασιλεῖς . . . φέρουσιν τὴν δόξαν αὐτῶν

TestL 18. 10: ἀνοίξει τὰς θύρας τοῦ παραδείσου

Rev. 21. 25: οἱ πυλῶνες . . . οὐ μὴ κλεισθῶσιν

TestL 18. 11: δώσει τοῖς ἁγίοις φαγεῖν ἐκ τοῦ ξύλου τῆς ζωῆς

Rev. 22. 2: ξύλον ζωῆς ποιοῦν καρ-πούς . . . εἰς θεραπείαν

TestD 5. 13: Κύριος ἔσται ἐν μέσῳ αὐτῆς, καὶ ὁ Ἅγιος Ἰσραὴλ βασι-λεύων ἐπ᾽ αὐτῆς

Rev. 22. 3, 5: ὁ θρόνος τοῦ θεοῦ . . . ἐν αὐτῇ ἔσται . . . καὶ βασιλεύ-σουσιν εἰς τοὺς αἰῶνας

TestJ 24. 1: ἀνατελεῖ ὑμῖν ἄστρον ἐξ Ἰακώβ

Rev. 22. 16: ἐγώ εἰμι ἡ ῥίζα . . . Δαυίδ, ὁ ἀστήρ

Longer passages for comparison

See TestN. 6.4 ff. and John 6.18—TestL. 8.5 and John 13.1 ff.—TestL. 2.3 (vl) and John 17.1 ff.—TestL. 2.3 ff. and Rev. 1.10 ff.—TestJud. 21.7 ff. and Rev. 13.1 ff.—TestD. 5.10 f. and Rev. 19.11 ff.

APPENDIX III

Twelve Criteria of Creedal Formulae
in the New Testament

1. Often the most reliable guide is the language of the immediate context: the creedal formulae or their constitutive elements are inserted and introduced by such words as 'deliver', 'believe' or 'confess', e.g. Rom. 10.9.

2. The presence of a creedal formula can often be detected by contextual dislocations. Frequently when such a formula is inserted the context or the formula or both suffer changes, e.g. I Tim. 3.16 (!).

3. Frequently the creedal formula fails to fit into the context syntactically, e.g. Rev. 1.4.

4. The creedal formula often exhibits a different linguistic usage, terminology or style from its context, e.g. I Cor. 16.22.

5. We can often see how quite different passages repeat the same creedal formula with very little difference in each case, e.g. II Cor. 5.21; 8.9.

6. Creedal formulae often strike us by their simple and clear syntax. They avoid particles, conjunctions and complicated constructions, and prefer parataxis to hypotaxis. Their thought proceeds by thesis rather than by argument, e.g. Acts 4.10.

7. Creedal formulae often stand out by reason of their monumental stylistic construction. They favour an antithetic or anaphoral style, e.g. I Tim. 3.16.

8. Creedal formulae are often rhythmical in form. But, unlike Greek poetry, its rhythm is not determined by quantity, but by the number of stresses or even of words, e.g. I Cor. 15.3.

9. The creedal formulae are often arranged in lines and strophes, e.g. Col. 1.15 ff.

10. Creedal formulae are often marked by their preference for appositions and noun predicates, e.g. IgnE. 7.2.

11. Creedal formulae often favour participles and relative clauses, e.g. Rom. 1.3.

12. For the most part creedal formulae refer to the elementary truths and events of salvation-history as norms, e.g. IgnTr. 9. 1 f.

APPENDIX IV

The Petrine Formulae and the Joseph Tradition

(Passages are for the most part abbreviated. Ideas and constructions in the Joseph tradition which recur in the Petrine formulae are underlined)

Man's act and God's decree	God's work and goal
Gen. 50. 20: ὑμεῖς ἐβουλεύσασθε κατ᾽ ἐμοῦ εἰς πονηρά	ὁ δὲ θεὸς ἐβουλεύσατο περὶ ἐμοῦ εἰς ἀγαθά, ἵνα διατραφῇ λαὸς πολύς
Gen. 49. 23 ff.: εἰς ὃν διαβουλευόμενοι ἐλοιδόρουν	καὶ ἐβοήθησέν σοι ὁ θεός

Gen. 45. 4f.: ἐγὼ Ἰωσήφ, ὃν ἀπέδοσθε εἰς Αἴγυπτον

Gen. 45. 8: οὐχ ὑμεῖς με ἀπεστάλκατε ὧδε ἀλλ' ἢ ὁ θεός

εἰς δοῦλον ἐπράθη Ἰωσήφ

Wisd. 10. 13 f.: (σοφία) πραθέντα δίκαιον οὐκ ἐγκατέλιπεν

I Mac 2. 53: ἐν καιρῷ στενοχωρίας ἐφύλαξεν ἐντολήν

Jub. 39. 11 f.: The Egyptians cast Joseph into prison

Jub. 39. 18: The chief butler forgot Joseph in prison

ΛEn. 89.13 f.: The twelve sheep gave up one to the wolves, and that sheep grew up among the wolves

TestS 2. 7 f.: ἐστήριξα τὰ ἥπατά μου ὥστε ἀνελεῖν αὐτόν

TestJos 1. 4 ff.: Οἱ ἀδελφοὶ ἐμίσησάν με αὐτοὶ ἤθελόν με ἀνελεῖν εἰς λάκκον με ἐχάλασαν μόνος ἤμην ἐν ἀσθενείᾳ ἤμην ἐν φυλακῇ ἤμην δοῦλος

εἰς ζωὴν ἀπέστειλέν με ὁ θεὸς ἔμπροσθεν ὑμῶν

Psa. 104. 17 ff.: ἀπέστειλεν ἔμπροσθεν αὐτῶν ἄνθρωπον κατέστησεν (βασιλεὺς) αὐτὸν κύριον καὶ ἄρχοντα

ἀλλὰ ἐξ ἁμαρτίας ἐρρύσατο αὐτόν καὶ ἔδωκεν αὐτῷ δόξαν αἰώνιον

Ecclus. 49. 15: (Ἰωσήφ) ἡγούμενος ἀδελφῶν, στήριγμα λαοῦ

καὶ ἐγένετο κύριος Αἰγύπτου

and God favoured Joseph, God was with him

Jub. 40. 3: And God favoured Joseph

Jub. 43. 18: God (has) sent (me) on beforehand, so that many people may be kept alive

And the Lord brought the eleven sheep, to pasture with it among the wolves

ἀλλ' ὁ θεὸς τῶν πατέρων ἐρρύσατο αὐτόν

ὁ δὲ Κύριος ἠγάπησέ με
ὁ δὲ Θεὸς τῶν πατέρων ἐφύλαξέν με
καὶ ὁ ὕψιστος ἀνήγαγέν με

καὶ ὁ Θεὸς παρεκάλεσέ με
καὶ ὁ Κύριος ἐπεσκέψατό με
καὶ ὁ σωτὴρ ἐχαρίτωσέ με cf. supra Jub 39 f.)
καὶ ὕψωσέ με

TestB 3. 6 ff.: Ἰωσήφ ἐδεήθη, ἵνα μὴ λογίσηται Κύριος αὐτοῖς ἁμαρτίαν, ὅτι ἐποίησαν πονηρὸν εἰς αὐτόν. Ὁ ἄμωμος ὑπὲρ ἀνόμων μιανθήσεται, καὶ ὁ ἀναμάρτητος ὑπὲρ ἀσεβῶν ἀποθανεῖται

Asenath 6: Ἰωσὴφ ὁ υἱὸς τοῦ
ποιμένος ἐκ τῆς Χαναάν

PhilJos 99: ὁ ἀρχιοινοχόος ἐκλαν-
θάνεται τοῦ ἐπικουφίσαντος κατὰ
πρόνοιαν θεοῦ βουληθέντος

νῦν ὡς ἥλιος ἐκ τοῦ οὐρανοῦ ἥκει,
ὅτι υἱὸς θεοῦ ἐστί

τὰς εὐπραγίας μὴ δι᾽ ἀνθρώπου
γενέσθαι μᾶλλον ἢ δι᾽ ἑαυτοῦ

ibid. 122 f.: τοιαῦτα τῶν εὐσεβῶν τὰ
τέλη

ἀντὶ μὲν δούλου
ἀντι τῶν εἰς ἀτιμίαν ἐσχάτων

ibid. 236: οὐκ ἐπιβουλαῖς ἀδελφῶν
πεπονθὼς ἢ κατὰ πρόνοιαν θεοῦ

ibid. 241: νομίζω τῶν συμβεβηκό-
των οὐχ ὑμᾶς ἀλλὰ θεὸν αἴτιον
γεγενῆσθαι βουληθέντα

δεσπότην ἔσεσθαι

τὰ πρῶτα τῶν ἐπὶ τιμαῖς φερόμενον

τὰ μακρὰν ἐμβλέποντος

με τῶν αὐτοῦ χαρίτων ὑπηρέτην
γενέσθαι

ibid. 244: ὁ τὰς ἐσχάτας συμφοράς
τε καὶ δυσπραγίας μεθαρμοσάμε-
νος εἰς τὰς ἀνωτάτω καὶ πρώτας
εὐτυχίας θεὸς ἦν, ᾧ πάντα δυνατά

ibid. 246: ἐπὶ θεὸν ἀναφέροντος τὰ
τέλη τῶν κατορθουμένων

ibid. 266: τοῦ θεοῦ τοῦ τὰ πονηρὰ
βουλεύματα ὑμῶν

JosAnt 2. 20: ὡς ἐπ᾽ ἐχθροῦ καὶ
ταῖς χερσὶν αὐτῶν κατὰ θείαν
βούλησιν παραδοθέντος

ibid. 2. 26: Ἰώσηπον οὐδὲ πονηρὸν
γεγεννημένον διαφθεροῦσιν

ibid. 2. 74: Ἰώσηπον μηδὲν ὑπὸ οἰνο-
χόου ὠφελούμενον

εἰς ἀγαθῶν περιουσίαν μεθαρμο-
σαμένου

ὁ θεὸς ἀπέλυσε

ibid. 2. 94: γεγενημένος σωτὴρ ὁμο-
λογουμένως τοῦ πλήθους

ibid. 2. 161 ff.: πονηροὺς γεγονέναι
θεοῦ βουλήσει, συναιτίους τῶν τῷ
θεῷ βεβουλευμένων, τῆς τότε
ἀβουλίας μετάνοια μὴ προχωρῆσαι
τὰ βεβουλευμένα

εἰς τοιοῦτον ἐπελθούσης τέλος

χαίροντες οὖν ἐπὶ τοῖς ἐκ θεοῦ
γεγενημένοις

Gnr. on 40. 23: The chief butler
has forgotten thee

I alone have not forgotten thee.

Acts 4. 10: σέσωσται ἐν ὀνόματι
Ἰησοῦ

      ὃν ὑμεῖς ἐσταυρώσατε

ὃν ὁ θεὸς ἤγειρεν ἐκ νεκρῶν

Acts 2. 36: Ἰησοῦν ὃν ὑμεῖς
ἐσταυρώσατε

καὶ κύριον αὐτὸν καὶ χριστὸν ἐποίησεν ὁ θεὸς

Acts 3. 13 ff.: ὁ θεὸς τῶν πατέρων
ἐδόξασεν

τὸν παῖδα αὐτοῦ Ἰησοῦν, ὃν ὑμεῖς
μὲν παρεδώκατε, ὑμεῖς τὸν ἅγιον
καὶ δίκαιον ἠρνήσασθε
τὸν ἀρχηγὸν τῆς ζωῆς ἀπεκτείνατε

ὃν ὁ θεὸς ἤγειρεν ἐκ νεκρῶν

Acts 2. 22 ff.: Ἰησοῦν ἄνδρα ἀπο-
δεδειγμένον ἀπὸ τοῦ θεοῦ . . .

τοῦτον τῇ ὡρισμένῃ βουλῇ καὶ
προγνώσει θεοῦ ἔκδοτον διὰ χειρὸς
ἀνόμων προσπήξαντες ἀνείλατε

ὃν θεὸς ἀνέστησεν λύσας τὰς ὠδῖνας
τοῦ ᾅδου

Acts 4. 27 f.: συνήχθησαν ἐπὶ τὸν
παῖδά σου Ἰησοῦν
ποιῆσαι ὅσα ἡ χείρ σου καὶ ἡ
βουλὴ προώρισεν γενέσθαι

ὃν ἔχρισας

Acts 5. 30 f.: ὁ θεὸς τῶν πατέρων
ἤγειρεν Ἰησοῦν, . . .

ὃν ὑμεῖς διεχειρίσασθε κρεμάσαντες ἐπὶ ξύλου

τοῦτον θεὸς ἀρχηγὸν καὶ σωτῆρα
ὕψωσεν, τοῦ δοῦναι μετάνοιαν τῷ
Ἰσραηλ καὶ ἄφεσιν ἁμαρτιῶν.

Acts 10. 37 ff.: ἔχρισεν ὁ θεὸς (Ἰησοῦν) ὃς διῆλθεν εὐεργετῶν . . .
ὅτι ὁ θεὸς ἦν μετ᾽ αὐτοῦ . . .

ὃν καὶ ἀνεῖλαν κρεμάσαντες ἐπὶ
ξύλου

τοῦτον ὁ θεὸς ἤγειρεν ἐν τῇ τρίτῃ
ἡμέρᾳ

Acts 13. 23 ff.: ὁ θεὸς ἤγαγεν
σωτῆρα Ἰησοῦν

οἱ ἄρχοντες τοῦτον ἀγνοήσαντες
ᾐτήσαντο Πιλᾶτον ἀναιρεθῆναι αὐτόν, ἐτέλεσαν τὰ γεγραμμένα,

ὁ δὲ θεὸς ἤγειρεν αὐτὸν ἐκ νεκρῶν.

APPENDIX V

Paradoxical Incarnation Formulae
in Paul and his Successors

II Cor 8. 9: πλούσιος ὤν / ἐπτώχευσεν / δι᾽ . . . ὑμᾶς

Gal 4. 5: θεὸς ἐξαπέστειλεν υἱόν
/ γενόμενον ἐκ γυναικός / —
/ γενόμενον ὑπὸ νόμον / —

Gal 3. 13: Χριστός / γενόμενος
κατάρα / ὑπὲρ ἡμῶν

ἵνα ὑμεῖς / τῇ ἐκείνου πτωχείᾳ /
πλουτήσητε

ἵνα / — / τὴν υἱοθεσίαν ἀπολάβωμεν
ἵνα / — / τοὺς ὑπὸ νόμον ἐξαγοράσῃ
ἡμᾶς / — / ἐξηγόρασεν ἐκ κατάρας
τοῦ νόμου
ἵνα εἰς τὰ ἔθνη / ἐν Χριστῷ / γένηται
εὐλογία
ἵνα / διὰ πίστεως / ἐπαγγελίαν πνεύματος λάβωμεν

II Cor. 5. 21: τὸν μὴ γνόντα ἁμαρτίαν / ἁμαρτίαν ἐποίησεν / ὑπὲρ
ἡμῶν

Rom. 8. 3 f.: θεὸς πέμψας υἱόν /
ἐν ὁμοιώματι σαρκὸς ἁμαρτίας /
— / καὶ κατέκρινεν ἁμαρτίαν / ἐν
σαρκί / περὶ ἁμαρτίας

T 2. 13 f.: μεγάλου θεοῦ κ. σωτῆ-
ρος / ὃς ἔδωκεν ἑαυτὸν / ὑπὲρ
ἡμῶν

Heb. 2. 14: (ὁ υἱὸς) αἵματος καὶ
σαρκὸς μέτεσχεν /

Barn 5. 11: υἱὸς θεοῦ / ἦλθεν ἐν
σαρκί / εἰς τοῦτο

Barn 7. 2: υἱὸς θεοῦ / ἔπαθεν / —

Barn 14. 4 f.: ὁ κύριος / ἐφανερώθη /
(δι᾽ ὑμᾶς ὑπομείνας)

(κύριος) / ἡτοιμάσθη / εἰς τοῦτο

ApConst. VIII 12. 31ff.: ὁ θεὸς
λόγος
/ γενόμενος ἐκ παρθένου / —
/ γενόμενος ἐν σαρκί / —
/ παρεγένετο / (δι᾽ ἡμᾶς) /
ὁ ἀπαθής / σταυρῷ προσηλώθη / —
ὁ ἀθάνατος / ἀπέθανεν / —

ἵνα ἡμεῖς / ἐν αὐτῷ / γενώμεθα
δικαιοσύνη / θεοῦ

ἵνα ἐν ἡμῖν / τοῖς περιπατ. κατὰ
πνεῦμα / πληρωθῇ δικαίωμα νόμου

ἵνα ἡμᾶς / — / λυτρώσηται ἀπὸ
ἀνομίας

ἵνα / διὰ θανάτου / καταργ. τὸν τ.
κρ. ἔχοντα τοῦ θανάτου

ἵνα / τὸ τέλειον τῶν ἁμαρτιῶν / ἀνα-
κεφαλαιώσῃ

ἵνα ἡμᾶς / ἡ πληγὴ αὐτοῦ / ζωο-
ποιήσῃ

ἵνα κἀκεῖνοι / τοῖς ἁμαρτήμασιν /
τελειωθῶσιν // καὶ ἡμεῖς / διὰ
κληρον. / διαθήκην λάβωμεν

ἵνα τ. δεδαπ. καρδ. θαν. / λυτρ. ἐκ
σκότους / διαθ. διαθήκην

ἵνα (ἡμᾶς) / — / πάθους λύσῃ
(ἵνα ἡμᾶς) / — / θανάτου ἐξέληται

APPENDIX VI

Valedictions and Farewell Speeches

Old Biblical Tradition	*New Testament*

Heaven reveals the approach of death.

Deut. 32.48; Jub. 35.6; AEn. 91.1; TestL. 1.2; VitAdEv. 30.45; IV Ezra 14.14; SBar. 76.2 f.; SEn. 64.1; Melch. 2.3; TestAbrA. 1; TestIss. 11b.	John 12.23, 28; 13.1, 3; 17.1, 27 (Acts 20.22 ff.; 21.11).

The one prepared for death calls together those who are left behind

Gen. 49.2; Deut. 31.28; Josh. 23.2; Tob. 14.5; Jub. 20.1 ff.; AEn. 91.1; TestL. 1.2; VitAdEv. 30; PsPhil. 23.1 f.; 33.1; IV Ezra 14.27; SBar. 77.1; SEn. 57.1; PhilVitMos. 288 ff.; JosAnt. 4.309 ff.	Acts 1.4; Matt. 28.10, 16 ff.; John 13.1 ff. (Acts 20.1, 17).

He announces his forthcoming ascension.

III *Baσ* 2.2; Jub. 36.1; AEn. 91.1; TestR. 1.3; TestZeb. 10.4; Ass-Mos. 1.15; PsPhil. 33.2; TestIss. 13a.	Mark 14.37, 41; John 12.32 ff.; 16.28; 20.17.

He will then be beyond their ken, and it is better so.

Deut. 34.6; ApMos. 40; 42; PsPhil. 33.6; IV Ezra 14.23, 36; SEn. 1.9.	John 13.33; cf. 7, 34 ff.; 8.21; 20.15; Luke 24.31.

He performs a final footwashing.

TestAbrB. 3; TestAbrA. 3.	John 13.5.

He takes a last meal with his friends.

Gen. 27, 25, 33; Jub. 35.27; 36.17; TestN. 1.2 ff.; 9.2; cf. SEn. 56.1.	Luke 22.15 f.; John 13.2 ff.; Luke 24.43; Acts 10.41; (20.11).

He says farewell to friends or foes as, e.g.:
A theological review of history.

Deut. 32; Josh. 23.14; 24; Jub. 20.5; VitAdEv. 32 ff.; PsPhil. 23, 4–11; IV Ezra 14.28 ff.	Mark 12.1 ff.; Matt. 23.35 ff.; (Acts 7.2 ff.).

Revelations about the future.

Gen. 49.1; Deut. 31.29; Tob. 14.6 ff.; Jub. 31.2 ff.; 45.14; AEn. 91; TestL. 1.1; AssMos. 2–10; SBar. 78–83; ParalJer. 9.24–28.	Mark 13; John 14.29; 16.4, 12 f. Acts 1.3 ff. (20.22 ff.).

Warnings and final injunctions.

Deut. 30.15; 19; Tob. 14.10 ff.;   Luke 22.24 ff.; Matt. 28.19 f.; John
Jub. 20.21; 36; AEn. 94.1 ff.;   15.22; Acts 1.4 (20.28).
TestR. 1.6; TestS. 7.3; TestL.
19.1; TestA. 1.3; PsPhil. 23.2,
12; 33.1 ff.; IV Ezra 14.13, 34 ff.;
SBar. 77.2 ff.; 84.7; 85.7; SEn.
55.3.

Exhortation to keep his words and instructions.

GEn. 99.10; AEn. 94.5.   John 14.21, 23; cf. Mark 13.31.

Commandment to love.

Jub. 20.2; 36.8; TestG. 6.1; TestN.   John 13.34.
hebr. 1.6.

Woes and controversies.

GEn. 97.7 ff.; 98.9 ff.; 99.1 f., 13 ff.;   Matt. 23.
100.7 ff.; AEn. 94.6 ff.; 95.4 ff.;
96.4 ff.; JosAnt. 4.302 ff.

Comfort and promise.

GEn. 102.4 f.; 103.1 ff.; 104.1 ff.;   Matt. 28, 20b; John 14.1, 18.27;
AEn. 92.2 ff.; 95.3; 96.1 ff.; Test-   16.20 ff., 33.
Jud. 25.4; AssMos. 12.3, 8 ff.;
IV Ezra 14.45; SEn. 50.3.

Problems of intercession.

Negativ: PsPhil. 33.4 f.; SBar. 85;   John 14.13, 16.
SEn. 53.1 f.—Positiv: AssMos.
11.11 ff.; 12.6 f.; SEn. 64.5.

The Departing One prays for those He leaves behind.

Jub. 22.28 ff.; PsPhil. 21.2–6.   Luke 22.32; John 17; (Acts 7.60;
                                                           20.36).

He appoints a 'Successor'.

IV Βασ 2.9 ff.; Num. 20.26; 27.16   Luke 22.31 f.; John 21.15 ff.; cf.
ff.; Deut. 31.14; 34.9; Jub. 19.17;   Matt. 16.18 f.
22.24; AssMos. 1.6 ff.; 10.14 f.;
12.2 f.; PsPhil. 24.4; Melch. 2.4,
13 f.

He blesses those remaining.

Gen. 27.25 ff.; Deut. 33.1; Jub.   John 14.27; 20.21 ff.; (Acts 20.1).
19.23 ff.; 21.25; 22.10 ff.; VitAd-
Ev. 30; PsPhil. 21.10; 24.3 f.;
SEn. 64.4 f.

Those remaining fall down and worship.

AssMos. 11.1; 12.1; SEn. 64.3 f.   Matt. 28.9, 17.

He is transfigured before them.

AEn. 91.1; MartIs. 5.7, 14; PsPhil. John 13.31 f.; 17.1; 20.22 (7.39);
19.16; SEn. 56.2; 64.5.   cf. Mark 9.2 ff.

He rejects earthly food.

SEn. 56.2.   Luke 24.30 f.; John 21.5, 12 f.

He parts from those remaining.

Gen. 24.56; JosAnt. 4.323.   John 20.17.

He utters his last words.

ApMos. 42; MartIs. 5.9, 13; Ber. Mark 15.34; 37; Luke 23.34, 43,
61b; cf. App. I, 43, 45.   46; John 19.26, 28, 30; cf. Matt.
                                  28.20b.

He climbs a solitary hill.

Num. 20.25 ff.; 27.12 f.; Deut. Mark 28.16; Acts 1.12; cf. Mark
32.48 ff.; 34.1 ff.; SBar. 76.3. 9.2.

He enters heaven.
Ascension of body and soul.

GEn. 5.24; Jub. 4.23; AEn. 70.1 Luke 24.50 ff.; Acts 1.9 ff.; Mark
ff.; PsPhil. 1.16; SEn. 67.1 f.; 16.19; Rev. 12.5.
(Heb. 11.5).

Elijah: IV βασ 2.11 f.; Mal. 3.23;
AEn. 89.52; ApEl. 35.

The Servant: Isa. 53.8; cf. 57.1 f.?

The Son of Man: AEn. 71.1, 14;
90.31; IV Ezra 13.3; HEn. 4.2;
48 C 1 (K), 2.

Ezra: IV Ezra 14.9, 13 ff.; 49.

Baruch: SBar. 13.3; 46.7; 76.2 f.

Melchizedek: Melch. 4.

Redeeming the soul.

Moses: (Deut. 34.6); AssMos.
10.12 ff.; 11.5 ff.; PsPhil. 19.12,
16; Jud. 9; ClAlStrom. 6.132,
2 f.; cf. JosAnt. 4.326 (νέφος!).

Adam: VitAdEv. 47; ApMos. 32
f.; 37.

Job: TestJb. 52.6 ff.

Patriarchs: (TestZeb. 10.4 ff.);
TestAbrB. 14; TestAbrA. 20;
TestIss. 17a, E.

Those remaining bewail their loss.

AssMos. 11; PsPhil. 24.6; TestJb. Mark 14.27; Luke 24.20 f.; John
53.3; ParalJer. 9.8 f.   14.18, 27 f.; 16.20 ff.; (Acts
                                  20.38).

Those remaining rejoice in his ascension.

Jub. 21.25); SEn. 67.3.   Luke 24.52 f.; cf. Acts 1.13 f.

APPENDIX VII

Summaries
(Selected Passages)

C: Creed; P: Prayers, Petitions, Intercessions, Prayers for the Dead, Blessings, Vows, Confessions, Thanksgivings; H: Hymns; L: Literary Material in Tractates, etc.; Pa: Parables; S: Sermons, Teaching, Instruction; Co: Controversy-sayings, Improprium; T: Collections of Traditions; *: Abbreviated Forms.

The more instructive examples are underlined.

THE ACTS OF GOD
(1st Person Singular)
(All: Co)

Old Biblical	*Early Christian*
Jer. 2.5–21: Exodus to Prophetic age.	IV Ezra 1.5–40: Exodus to Prophetic age.
Ezek. 20.5–28: Exodus to Canaan.	EvBarthol. 167, v2 (RevBibl., 1922, 21): Exodus/Passion.
	Cyril's Lecture for Good Friday (OrChrist., 1930, 241 ff.): Exodus/Passion.
	MissMozarab (MPL 85, 421 ff.): Exodus/Passion.
	SilvDial. (TSt., III, 2, xxxviii f.): Exodus/Passion.
	IV Ezra 1.33vl (Ibid. xxxix span !) Exodus/Passion.
	Matins for Good Friday (BrevRom, Stadler, 304): Election/Passion.

(2nd Person Singular)
(All: P)

Ex. 15.1–21: Exodus to Canaan.	ApConst. 7.33–38: Creation to the Maccabees; the Way of Christ.
II Ezra 19.1–27: Creation, Abraham to the Exile.	ApConst. 8.5: Abel to Samuel, Christ.
Judth. 9.2–15: Patriarchs, Exodus.	ApConst. 8.12.6–35: Creation to Joshua; the Way of Christ.

PsSol. 17.5–22: David to Roman period.

II Mac. 1.24 f.: Patriarchs, Exodus.

III Mac. 2.2–20: Creation to the building of the temple.

III Mac. 6.2–15: Exodus to Jonah.

IV Ezra 3.4–27: Creation to Exile.

SBar. 21.4–8: Creation and preservation.

ApAn. 9 (TU II 3a, 1899, 151/2): Exodus to Daniel.

Abodah for the Day of Atonement (I. Elbogen, *Stud.z.Gesch.d.jüd. Gottesd.*, 1907, 58 ff.): Creation to Aaron.

The Selichoth of XVIII (REJ XIV, 1887, 245 ff.): Abraham to the monarchy (Maccabean times).

Piut of XVIII, Fragment (J. Elbogen, *D.jüd.Gottesd.*,³ 1931, Suppl. p. 585 f.): Patriarchs, David.

Sachs, *Tef.* 80/2: Creation to Exodus.

Sachs, *Tef.* 664 ff.: Exodus to Exile.

ApConst. 8.12 p. 254: Flood to Palestinian martyrs.

ApConst. 8.41: Patriarchs to Elijah.

PsCyprOrI (Hartel, III, 145): Exile and the Way of Christ.

PsCyprOrII (Ibid. 146 ff.): Exodus to Exile, the Way of Christ.

EvBarthol 167.2 (RevBibl., 1921, 515 f.): Creation to passion.

ActAnanPet. 13 (ActBoll., Feb. 25): Isaac to Daniel.

Martyrs' Prayer (OrChrist., 1915, 303): Jonah to Daniel.

Oratio in Infirmos (A. Vassiliev, Anecdota Graeco-Byzantina, I, 1893): Noah to Daniel, Christ's miracles, Christian martyrs.

Benedictio Chrismatis (H. Lietzmann, *Sacramentarium Gregorianum*, 1921, 45 f.): Creation, Aaron to Christ.

Benedictio Fontis (Ibid. 52 f.): Creation to Christ.

Commendatio Animae (Rituale Romanum, V, 7): Enoch to Daniel, Christian martyrs.

Marriage rites (OrChrist, 1915, 301): Rebeccah to Zipporah, Anna and Elizabeth.

Euchol. Mega (Ibid.): Enoch to Daniel.

LitBas (Brightman 324 ff.): Adam to the prophets. The life of Christ to the last judgement.

(3rd Person Singular)

H: Deut. 32.7–17: Shem to Canaan.

H: Psa. 77.1–72: Exodus to David.

(S: John 1.1–18: Primordial Logos to ascension).

S/L: Jud. 5–11: Fall of the angels to Balaam.

H: Psa. 105.7–46: Exodus to the monarchy.

H*: Psa. 134.8–12: Exodus to Canaan.

H: Psa. 135.1–26: Creation, Exodus to Canaan.

S: Jdth. 5.5–23: Abraham to Exile.

S: Jdth. 8.26: Abraham to Jacob.

S*: II Mac. 8.19 f.: Sennacherib and the Syrians.

S/L: Dam. 1.1–4, 12: Predestination, Abraham to the New Covenant.

H: PsPhil. 32.1–17: Shem to the Judges.

S*: IV Ezra 14.29–33: Exodus to Exile.

P: SBar. 77.21–26: Noah to Soloman.

S: jBer. 13a (K. Michel, Gebet und Bild, 1902, 123): Moses to Daniel.

Pa: Pesikt 22: Creation to Roman period.

S: Gnr. on 40.23: Abraham to Messiah.

S: Exr. on 17.8: Pharaoh to Amalek.

C: Sayings of the Lord: Ch. 63 of this book.

S: I Cl. 31 f.: Abraham to monarchy, Christ and the Church.

C: ApConst. 5.7: Jonah to Daniel, Christ's miracles.

H: SyrEphraem, CarmNiseb, No57 (ed. G. Bickell): Adam to the Syrians, the Baptist.

L: LactDeMortPersec., 2 ff.: Tiberius to Maximus.

L: AugCivD. I–X.

THE MEN OF GOD
Worshippers and Enemies of God

Co*: Jer. 15.1: Moses and Samuel.

Co*: Ezek. 14.14: Noah, Daniel, Job.

H: Psa. 98.6: Moses, Aaron, Samuel.

Pa: Dan. 7: World empires to Son of Man.

S/H: Wisd. 10 f.: Adam to the Wilderness.

Pa/Co: Mark 12.1–9: Moses to Christ.

S: I Cl. 7.5–8.1: Noah to prophets.

S/L: I Cl. 9–12: Enoch to Rahab.

S*: I Cl. 55.3–6: Judith and Esther.

T: I Cl. 42: Christ to the bishops.

S*: II Cl. 6.8: Noah, Job, Daniel.

H: Ecclus. 43–50: Creation, Enoch to Simon.

S: I Mac. 2.50–61: Abraham to Daniel.

Pa: AEn. 85–90: Adam to Messiah.

L: PhilPraemPoen. 7 ff.: Enoch to Moses.

L: PhilVirt 198 ff.: Adam to Jacob.

L: IV Mac. 2 f.: Joseph to Daniel.

S: IV Ezra 7.106–11: Abraham to Hezekiah.

Pa: SBar. 53–74: Creation to Messiah.

S: Asenath 1 (ed. P. Batiffol, 40): Sarah to Rachel.

T: Jub. 7.38 f.: Enoch to Noah.

T: Ab. 1.1: Moses to the Greek Synagogue.

T: AbRN. 1.3 f.: Moses to the Greek Synagogue.

T: HEn. 48.10D: Moses to the men of faith.

T: SEn. 33.9 f.: Adam to Enoch.

T*: Peah 2.6: Moses to Nahum.

S: MEx on 15.11: Pharaoh to the king of Tyre.

S: Pesikt 23: Babylon to Rome.

S: Exr. on 10.1 f.: Babylon to Rome.

S: MidrPs., on Psa. 31.1: Moses to the monarchy.

S: MidrPs., on Psa. 36.1: Moses to David.

Pa/S: MidrPs., on Psa. 36.10: Moses to Roman times.

S: Pesikt 16: Hosea to Malachi.

S: Pesikt 32: Creation to Moses.

L: List of the Prophets (ed. Th. Schermann, 105 f.): Moses to Malachi.

S: JustinDial. 19.3–5: Adam to Moses.

L: ClAlStrom., II, 103 f.: Abraham to Daniel.

S: ClAlStrom., IV, 102 ff.: Enoch to David.

S: ApConst. 2.55: Abel to the prophets, Christ and the apostles.

S: ApConst. 6.12: Enoch to Job.

S/C: ApConst. 7.39: Adam to Phinehas.

P: Marriage rites (TSt., II, 2, 1893, 128): Sarah to Rachel.

S: ActPl. 8.10 ff. (ed. C. Schmidt, 1936): Pharaoh to the apostles.

T: EusHE. 2.1.4: Kurios to Barnabas.

Song of Zicklein (P. Fiebig, *Judentum*, 1916, 64): the succession of
the world empires.

Confessors and Martyrs

S*: IV Mac. 13.9–12: Isaac and
Daniel's time.

S*: IV Mac. 16.20 f.: Isaac and
Daniel's time.

S: IV Mac. 18.11–13: Abel to
Daniel's time.

S: MidrPs., on Psa. 9.13: Simeon to
Akiba.

Further, see App. I.14.

Co*: Luke 11.49–51: Abel to Zechariah.

S: Heb. 11.1–12.2: Creation, Abel
to the Syrians, the Way of Christ.

Co*: Acts 7.1–53: Abraham to the
prophets.

S: I Cl. 4–6: Abel to David, the
Christian martyrs.

S: I Cl. 17 f.: Moses to David.

S: I Cl. 45.2–7: The prophets to
Daniel.

S: Aphraates, De Persecutione (R.
Graffin, *Patrol.Syr.* I, 1894, 932
ff.): Abel to the Exile, the Christian martyrs.

S: Lists of the Apostles (ed. Schermann, 204 f.; cf. 215 f.): Peter to
Philip.

LIST OF ABBREVIATIONS

NB. Some references to the Books of Samuel and Kings are made to the LXX text, and are quoted thus: I, II, III, IV *βας* DaG is the LXX of Daniel; Da*Θ* is the translation of Theodotion. The Psalms throughout are numbered according to the LXX. In the LXX Psalm 9 = Psalms 9 and 10 of the Hebrew and English versions. Hence after Psalm 9 add one to the LXX number to find the Psalm in Hebrew or English Bibles.

AAB	*Abhandlungen der Königliche Preussischen Akademie der Wissenschaften zu Berlin* (philosophische-historische Klasse)
Ab	Pirqe Aboth
AbhdOsloerAkad	*Abhandlungen der Osloer Akademie*
AbRN	Aboth of Rabbi Nathan
Act	Acts
Apoll	,, of Apollonius
AnanPet	,, of Ananias and Peter
Cypr	,, proconsularia Martyrii Cypriani
J	,, of John
Pl	,, of Paul
PlThecl	,, of Paul and Thecla
Thom	,, of Thomas
Verc	,, of Vercellences
AC	*Antike und Christentum*
AeschEum	Aeschylus, *Eumenides*
AGG	*Abhandlungen der Gesellschaft der Wissenschaften zu Göttingen*
AJA	*American Journal of Archeology*
AnBoll	*Analectea Bollandiana*, Ed. de Smedt, v. Hoff & de Backer
AOB	H. Gressmann, *Altorientalische Bilder zum AT²*
AOT	H. Gressmann, *Altorientalische Texte zum AT²*
ap	Apostolic
Ap	Apocalypse
Abr	,, of Abraham, Ed. G. N. Bonwetsch, 1897
An	,, Anonymous (TU, II, 3a, 1899, 151)
El	,, of Elijah, and fragments of a Sophonia Apocalypse, Ed. G. Steindorff in TU, NS, 3a, 1899
P	,, of Peter
Sedr	,, of Sedrach, Ed. M. R. James, in *Texts and Studies*, II, 3, 1893, p. 127 ff.
ApConst	The Apostolic Constitutions
Apul	Apuleius
Met	,, *Metamorphosis*

ArabGild	Gildremeister, Esdrae Lider Quartus Arabic; see IV Ezra (Violet)
Arist	Aristotle
Poet	,, *Poetics*
Pol	,, *Politics*
Rhet	,, *Rhetoric*
ARW	*Archiv für Religionswissenschaften*
AscIs	*The Ascension of Isaiah*, Ed. R. H. Charles, 1900
Asenath	*Le Livre de la Prière d'Aseneth, Studia Patristica*, Ed. P. Batiffol, I, 1889
AssMos	The Assumption of Moses
AugCivD	Augustin, *De Civitate Dei*,
AZ	Abodah Zarah
b	Babylonian Talmud
BBar	Book of Baruch
GBar	Greek-Slav Baruch Apocalypse, Ed. M. R. James, in *Texts and Studies*, V, I, 1897, p. 84 ff.
SBar	Syrian Baruch Apocalypse
Bartholomä	*Die Gathas des Awesta*, Chr. Bartholomä, 1905
BB	Baba Bathra
Bchm	Bachmann, *I Cor.*, 4th ed. with supplement by E. Stauffer
Ber	Berakoth
Bernhardt	M. Bernhardt, *Handbuch zur Münzkunde der Römischen Kaiserzeit*, vol. II, 1926
Bernoulli	J. J. Bernoulli, *Römische Ikonographie*, I, 1882
BM	Baba Mezia
BJb	*Bonner Jahrbücher*
BrevRom	*Breviarum Romanum*, Ed. Stadler
ByzZ	*Byzantinische Zeitschrift*
Cantr	Canticum rabbah (Midrash on the Song of Songs)
CarmNiseb	*Carmina Nisebena*, Ed. G. Bickell, 1866
CGC	*Catalogue of Greek Coins in the British Museum* 1873 ff.
Chrys	Chrysostom
Hom	,, *Homilies*
Sacerdot	,, *De Sacerdotio*
CodVat	Codex Vaticanus
CR	H. Cohen, *Description Historique des Monnaies Frappées sous l'Empire Romain*,[2] 1880 ff.
CRE	H. Mattingly, *Coins of the Roman Empire in the British Museum*, 1923 ff.
Cl	The Epistle of Clement
ClAl	Clement of Alexandria
Paed	*Paedagogus*
QuisDivSal	*Quis dives Salvetur*
Strom	*Stromata*

Dam   *Damaskusschrift* (The Zadokite Fragment), Ed. L.
                Rost, 1933, also, Schecter, 1910, and Zeitlin, 1952.
                ET of Schecter's text in R. H. Charles, *Apocrypha and*
                Pseudepigrapha II, 785 f.
DantePar   Dante, *Paradiso*
Deissmann LAE   A. Deissmann, *Light from the Ancient East*, 1910
Dg   The Epistle of Diognetus
DictAc   *Dictionnaire d'archéologie chrétienne et de liturgie*, 1924 ff.
Did   The Didache
DionChrysOr   Dion, called Chrysostomos, *Orationes*
DittOr   W. Dittenberger, *Orientis Graecae Inscriptiones*, 1902 ff.
DittSyll   W. Dittenberger, *Sylloge Inscriptionum Graecaerom*,[3]
                1915 ff.
DLZ   *Deutsche Literaturzeitung*
Dölger*IXΘYΣ*   F. J. Dölger, *IXΘYΣ*, vol. III, *Der Heilige Fisch in den*
                antiken Religionen und im Christentum, 1922; vol. IV,
                Die Fischdenkmäler in der frühchristlichen Plastik, Malerei
                und Kleinkunst, 1927

ECO   The Egyptian Church Order
EJ   *Encyclopaedia Judaica*
Ekar   Eka rabbati (Midrash on Lamentations)
ELKZ   *Evangelisch-Lutherische Kirchenzeitung*
EMZ   *Evangelische Missionszeitschrift*
En   Enoch
  AEn   *Aethiopian Enoch*, Ed. J. Flemming and Radermacher
  GEn   *Greek Enoch*, Ed. J. Flemming and Radermacher
  HEn   *Hebrew Enoch*, Ed. O. Odeberg, 1928
  SEn   *Slavonic Enoch* (*The Secrets of Enoch*) Ed. G. N.
                    Bonwetsch, 1922, (TU, 44.2). See also R. H. Charles
                    Apocrypha and Pseudepigrapha, II, 163, 281 (AEn)
                    and 425 469 (SEn). (k. Rd. is kürzere Redaktion)
EpAp   *Epistola Apostolorum*, Ed. H. Duensing, in Leitzmann's
                'Kleinen Texten'
  Ar   Epistle of Aristeas
  Jer   „   of Jeremiah (Rahlfs, LXX, 1936)
EphrGr   Ephraem (Greek-Latin section of edn. of J. S. Asse-
                mani, 1732 ff.)
EpiphHaer   Epiphanius Panarion, *Haeresis* . . .
ERE   *Encyclopaedia of Religion and Ethics*, Ed. J. Hastings, 1908 ff.
IV Ezra   The Fourth Book of Ezra (Latin)
  Arm   Armenian translation
  Syr   Syrian translation
  Ath   Aethiopian translation
                (Complete edition, Ed. B. Violet, *Die Esra-Apocalypse*,
                Synoptische Ausgabe, 1910; see also B. Violet, *Die*
                Apokalypsen des Esra und des Baruch in deutscher Gestalt.
                Also R. H. Charles, *Apocalypse and Pseudepigrapha* II,
                542 624

VisEsr	*Visio Esdrae*, Ed. R. L. Bensley, in TSt, 1895, 1–6, 72–82
EurTro	Euripides, *Troades*
Eus	Eusebius
HE	*Ecclesiastical History*
PraepEv	*Praeparatio Evangelica*
Vit Const	*Life of Constantine*
EvBarthol	Gospel of Bartholomew
H	Hebrew Gospel
Nicod	Gospel of Nicodemus, Acta Pilati, Ed. R. A. Lipsius 1886[2]
Pt	Gospel of Peter
Exr	Exodus Rabbah (Midrash on Exodus)
ExT	*Expository Times*
Festschr	Festschrift
ForschFortschr	*Forschungen und Fortschritte*
Fränkel	M. Fränkel, *Die Inschriften von Pergamon* II, 1895
Geldner	*Die Zoroastrische Religion* (Religiongeschichtliches Lesebuch), 1926
Gerke	F. Gerke, *Christus in der spätantiken Plastik*, 1940
GesAufs	*Gesammelte Aufsätze* (Collected Essays)
Gnr	Genesis Rabbah (Midrash on Genesis)
Hag	Hagigah
Hamb	L. Hamburger, *Zeitschrift für Numismatik*, 1892, 241 **ff.**
HambRealEnzJdt	Jakob Hamburger, *Real-Enzyklopädie des Judentums*, 1874 **ff.**
HarvExc	G. A. Reisner, C. St. Fisher, D. G. Lyon, *Harvard Excavations at Samaria*, 1924
Helbig	W. Helbig, *Führer durch die öffentlichen Sammlungen klassischer Altertümer in Rom*,[3] If, 1912 f.
Herm	*Hermes* (Magazine for Classical Philology)
Herm	The Shepherd of Hermas
m	*Mandates*
s	*Similitudes*
v	*Visions*
HebUnColAn	*Hebrew Union College Annual*
HierVir	Hieronymus, *De Viris Illustribus*
HippRef	Hippolytus, *Refutatio Omnium Haeresium*
HipCan	*Hippolytan Canons*, Ed. H. Achelis, 1891
Ign	Ignatius
E	*Letter to the Ephesians*
Mg	,, *to the Magnesians*
Phld	,, *to the Philadelphians*

Pol	*Letter to Polycarp*
R	„ *to the Romans*
Sm	„ *to the Smyrnians*
Tr	„ *to the Trallians*
Inscr	Inscription
IntKZ	*Internationale Kirchliche Zeitschrift*
IrenAdvHaer	Irenaeus, *Adversus Haereses*

j	Jerusalem Talmud
JahreshÖstArchInst	*Jahreshefte des Österreichischen Archäologischen Instituts in Wien*
JbfLtgw	*Jahrbuch für Liturgiewissenschaft*
JBL	*Journal of Biblical Literature*
JeremiasATAO	A. Jeremias, *Das Alte Testament im Lichte des Alten Orients*,[3] 1916
Jos	Flavius Josephus
Ant	*Antiquities*
Ap	*Against Apion*
Bell	*Wars*
Vita	*Life*
JulAfr	Julius Africanus
Justin	Justin Martyr
Apol	*Apology*
Coh	*Cohortatio ad Graecos*
Dial	*Dialogue*

Kennedy	A. B. W. Kennedy, *Petra*, 1925
Ket	Kethuboth
KgP	*Kerygma Petri*, Ed. E. v. Dobschütz, 1893; see also M. R. James, *Apocryphal New Testament*, 1924, 16 ff.
Kohr	Koheleth Rabbah (Midrash on Ecclesiastes)
Kohl-Watzinger	H. Kohl, C. Watzinger, *Antike Synagoge in Galiläa*, 1916
Kollwitz	J. Kollwitz, *Die Lipsanothek von Brescia*, 1933
Kurth	J. Kurth, *Die Mosaiken von Ravenna*,[2] 1912
KW	G. Kittel, *Theologisches Wörterbuch zum NT*

LactDeMortPersec	Lactantius, *De Mortibus Persecutorum*
LidzGinza	M. Lidzbarski, *Ginza*, 1925
r	right part
Lohm	E. Lohmeyer, *Kommentar zur Apokalypse*, 1926
Lommel	H. Lommel, *Die Yäšts des Awesta*, 1927
Ltzm	H. Lietzmann, *Handbuch zum NT*
LutherWA	Luther's works, Weimar edition
Lvr	Leviticus rabbah (Midrash on Leviticus)

MaaseAbr	Maaseh Abraham (Horowitz, *Sammlung kleiner Midrashim*)

MandLit	*Mandaean Liturgy*, Ed. M. Lidzbarski, 1920
Mart	Martyr, Martyrdom
Is	Martyrdom of Isaiah
Pionii	,, of Pionius
Pol	,, of Polycarp
MelSard	Melito of Sardis
Melch	*Melchizedek Legends*, Ed. G. N. Bonwetsch, 1922 (TU 44.2)
MEx	Mekilta Exodus, ancient midrash on Exodus
MidrPr	Midrash on Proverbs
MidrPs	Midrash on Psalms
MidrSS	Midrash on Song of Songs
MissMozarab	Missale et Breviarium Mozarabum
MittderVorderasiatGes	*Mitteilungen der Vorderasiatischen Gesellschaft*
MPL	*Patrologia*, Series Latina, Ed. P. J. Migne
MT	Masoretic Text
Neuss	W. Neuss, *Die Kunst der alten Christen*, 1926
NGG	*Nachrichten der Gesellschaft der Wissenschaften zu Göttingen*
NJBWissJgdb	*Neue Jahrbücher für Wissenschaft und Jugendbildung*
NieuwThTijdschr	*Nieuw Theologisch Tijdschrift*
NS	New Series
NumChron	*The Numismatic Chronicle*
NumismZeitschr	*Numismatische Zeitschrift*
Nur	Numeri Rabbah (Midrash on Numbers)
OdSol	Odes of Solomon
OLZ	*Orientalistische Literatur-Zeitung*
OrChrist	Oriens Christianus
Orig	Origen
inMt	*on Matthew*
inPs	*on the Psalms*
PalMärt	Eusebius, *De Martyribus Palestinae*
Pap	Papyrus
POxy	Oxyrhynchus Papyri
ParalJer	*Paralipomena Jeremiae*, Ed. J. R. Harris, 1889
PassPerpFel	*Passio Perpetuae et Felicitatis*, Ed. R. Knopf, *Ausgewählte Märtyrerakten*,[3] 1929
Past	Pastoral Epistles
PatrolSyr	*Patrologia Syriaca*, Ed. C. Graffin
PaulyW	A. Pauly, *Realencyclopädie der klassischen Altertumswissenschaften*, neue Bearbeitung, begonnen von G. Wissowa, herausgegeben von W. Kroll und K. Mittelhaus
Peah	Peah, tractate of the Talmud
Pes	Pesachim
Pesikt	Pesiktah (of Rabbi Kahana)

Phil	Philo
Cher	*De Cherubim*
ConfLing	*De Confusio Linguarium*
Decal	*De Decalogo*
Exsecr	*De Exsecrationibus*
Fug	*De Fuga et Inventione*
Jos	*De Josepho*
LegAll	*Legum Allegoriae*
Leg(Gai)	*Legatio ad Gaium*
MigrAbr	*De Migratione Abrahami*
Op Mund	*De Opificio Mundi*
PostCain	*De Posteritate Caini*
PraemPoen	*De Praemiis et Poenis*
RerDiv	*Quis Rerum Divinarum Heres sit*
SpecLeg	*De Specialibus Legibus*
Virt	*De Virtutibus*
VitMos	*De Vita Mosis*

PhilSidetes   Philippus Sidetes (in Funk-Bihlmeyer, *Apostolische Väter*, 138)

Philol	Philologus
PirkREl	Pirke Rabbi Eliezer
PJB	*Palästina-Jahrbuch*
PlinEp	Plinius Caecilius Secundus, *Epistulae*
Poim	*Poimandres*, Ed. G. Parthey, 1859
Pol	Epistle of Polycarp

PrBau   E. Preuschen, *Griechisch-deutsches Wörterbuch zu den Schriften des NT und der übrigen urchristlichen Literatur*, bearbeitet von W. Bauer,[2] 1928

ProtevJa	Protevangelium of James
PsClemHom	*Pseudo-Clementine Homilies*, Ed. P. A. de Lagarde, 1865
PsClemRec	*Pseudo-Clementine Recognitions*, Ed. P. A. de Lagarde, 1861 and W. Frankenberg, 1937
PsCyprOrI	*Oratio Cypriani pro martyribus*, Ed. Hartel
PsCyprOrII	*Oratio Cypriani quam sub die passionis sua dixit*, Ed. Hartel
PsPhil	*Pseudo-Philo's Liber Antiquitatum Biblicarum*, Ed. Guido Kisch, Notre Dame, Indiana, 1948. (cf. *The biblical antiquities of Philo* . . . tr. by M. R. James, 1917)
PsPhokyl	Pseudo-Phokylides
PsSol	Psalms of Solomon

Regling   A. v. Sallet und K. Regling, *Die antiken Münzen*[2] (Handbücher der Staatlichen Museen zu Berlin 6), 1922

RevBen	*Revue Bénédictine*
RevBibl	*Revue Biblique*
RGG	*Die Religion in Geschichte und Gegenwart* [2] 1927 ff.
RevHist	*Revue d'Histoire Ecclésiastique*
RevNum	*Revue Numismatique Française*

RH
RHPhR
RHR
Roller
RömMitt

RömQuartalschr
Rostovtzeff

RVV

SAB

SächsAk

SAH

San
Schatzh
SchlJ
SchrdKönigsbGelGes
SDt
SenEp
Sib
Sl
SNu
SocHE
SophAnt
Stefanescu

SB

Strack

Sukenik

Succ

Taan
TacitGerm
Tanch
Tert
    Apol
    Bapt
    Cor
    Marc
    Mart
    Monog
    Or

Rosh Hashanah
Revue d'Histoire et de Philosophie Religieuse
Revue d'Histoire des Religions
Th. Roller, *Les Catacombs de Rome*, I, 1881
Mitteilungen des Deutschen Archäologischen Instituts, Römische Abteilung
Römische Quartalschrift
M. I. Rostovtzeff and others, *The Excavations at Dura-Europos*, Sixth Season (1932–33), 1936
Religionsgeschichtliche Versuche und Vorarbeiten

Sitzungsberichte der Preussischen Akademie der Wissenschaften zu Berlin (philosophische-historische Klasse)
Abhandlungen der Sächsischen Akademie der Wissenschaften
Sitzungsberichte der Heidelberger Akademie der Wissenschaften (philosophische-historische Klasse)
Sanhedrin
Schatzhöhle, tr. by C. Bezold, 1883
A. Schlatter, *Kommentar zum Johannesevangelium*, 1930
Schriften der Königsberger gelehrten Gesellschaft
Sifre Deuteronomium
L. Annaeus Seneca, *Epistulae morales ad Lucilium*
The Sibylline Oracles
Slavonic
Sifre Numeri
Socrates, *Historia Ecclesiastica*
Sophocles, *Antigone*
J. D. Stefanescu, *Annuaire de l'Institut de Philologie et de l'Histoire Or*, 1932, 21 ff; 1933, 403 ff.
H. L. Strack and P. Billerbeck, *Kommentar zum NT aus Talmud und Midrasch*, 1922 ff.
P. L. Strack, *Untersuchungen zur Römischen Reichsprägung des 2 Jahrhunderts*, 1931 ff.
E. L. Sukenik, *Ancient Synagogues in Palestine and Greece*, 1934
Succoth

Taanith
Tacitus, *Germania*
Tanchuma
Tertullian
Apology
De Baptismo
De Corona
Adversus Marcionem
Ad Martyras
De Monogamia
De Oratione

Pat	*De Patientia*
Prax	*Adversus Praxeam*
Pud	*De Pudicitia*
Scap	*Ad Scapulam*
Spect	*De Spectaculis*
Test	Testament
A	., of Asher
B	of Benjamin
D	,, Dan
G	,, of Gad
Iss	,, of Issachar
Jos	,, of Joseph
Jud	,, of Judah
L	,, of Levi
N	,, of Naphtali
R	,, of Reuben
S	,, of Simeon
Zeb	,, of Zebulon

(see R. H. Charles, *Greek Versions of Testaments of the Twelve Patriarchs*, 1908; also ET, *Apocrypha and Pseudepigrapha*, II, 282 367)

Abr	*Testament of Abraham*, Ed. M. R. James, 1892 (TSt, II, 2)
Ad	*Testament of Adam* (=ApAd), Ed. James, Apocrypha anecdota (TSt, II, 3)
40Märt	*Testament of the 40 Martyrs*, Ed. Gebhardt, *Ausgewählte Märtyrerakten* 166 ff.
Jb	*Testament of Job*, Ed. M. R. James, TSt, V, 1, 1899
Sol	*Testament of Solomon*, Ed. Ch. McCown, 1922
Tg	Targum
TgJ	Pseudo Jonathan Targum
ThBl	*Theologische Blätter*
TheophAutol	Theophilus, *Ad Autolycum*
ThLZ	*Theologische Literatur-Zeitung*
ThR	*Theologische Rundschau*
ThStKr	*Theologische Studien und Kritiken*
ThT	*Theologisch Tijdschrift*
Tos	Tosefta
TSt	*Texts and Studies*, Ed. M. R. James
TU	*Texte und Untersuchungen zur Geschichte der altchristlichen Literatur*, 1883 ff.
Vendid	*Vendidat*, tr. by J. Darmesteter und Mills, 1880
VirEcl	Vergil, *Fourth Eclogue*
VitAdEv	Vita Adae et Evae
VitProph	*Prophetarum Vitae Fabulosae*, Ed. Th. Schermann, 1907
VortrBWbg	*Vorträge der Bibliothek Warburg*
WatzingerD	C. Watzinger, *Denkmäler Palästinas*, I, 1933; II, 1935

WilpertK	J. Wilpert, *Die Malereien der Katakomben Roms*, 2 Bände, 1903
WilpertM	J. Wilpert, *Die Römische Mosaiken und Malereien der kirchlichen Bauten vom IV bis XIII Jh.*, 4 Bände, 1916
WilpertZ	J. Wilpert, *Zeitschrift für Katholische Theologie*, 1921, 323 ff.
Wolff	Awesta, *Die heilige Bücher der Parsen*, 1910
WZKM	*Wiener Zeitschrift für die Kunde des Morgenlandes*
XVIII	The 'Eighteen Blessings' (Shemoneh Esreh)
Yeb	Yebamoth
ZAW	*Zeitschrift für die alttestamentliche Wissenschaft*
ZDPV	*Zeitschrift des Deutschen Palästina-Vereins*
ZdZ	*Zwischen den Zeiten*
ZF	Zadokite Fragment
ZKG	*Zeitschrift für Kirchengeschichte*
ZNW	*Zeitschrift für die neutestamentliche Wissenschaft*
ZRGG	*Zeitschrift für Religions- und Geistesgeschichte*
ZRGK	*Zeitschrift für Rechtsgeschichte, Kanonistische Abteilung*
ZSTh	*Zeitschrift für systematische Theologie*
ZThK	*Zeitschrift für Theologie und Kirche*

LIST OF NEW TESTAMENT REFERENCES
IN THE MAIN TEXT